Your complete Aftersales Service
Dedicated to all makes of E

- Specialist service centres in London, Rotherham and Scotland
- Nationwide all makes parts supply
- All makes accident damage and mechanical repairs
- Mobile technicians
- Technical services and training
- Speedline dedicated response: 0800285626

At Optare Product Support our priority is getting and keeping your vehicles on the road….whatever make, whatever model we're here to help you. Whether its servicing, repairs, parts or training, call us today.

Can you please rework the contact details as follows:

London 01708 892440
london.service@optare.com

Scotland - 01236 726738
scotland.service@optare.com

Rotherham - 01709 535101
rotherham.service@optare.com

Parts - 01709 792000

Lower Philips Road Whitebirk Industrial Estate Blackburn BB1 5UD UK
T: + 44 (0) 845 838 9901 F: + 44 (0) 845 838 9902 E: info@optare.com **www.optare.com**

One of First Berkshire's new double-deck Green Line 'coaches', Wright Eclipse Gemini-bodied GL5 (LK58 EDJ), near the Royal Albert Hall on its way west out of London.
Picture RUSSELL YOUNG

THE LITTLE RED BOOK 2008

THE PASSENGER TRANSPORT DIRECTORY FOR THE BRITISH ISLES

Editor Ian Barlex

Riverdene Business Park, Molesey Road, Hersham, Surrey KT12 4RG
Tel: 01932 266600 Fax: 01932 266601

contents

List of Abbreviations 8

Index of Advertisers 8

Foreword 9

Section 1:
Trade Directory 11

Section 2:
Tendering & Regulatory Authorities 63

Section 3:
Organisations and Societies 71

Section 4:
British Isles Operators 79

Section 5:
Index (Trade) 219
Index (British Isles Operators) 225

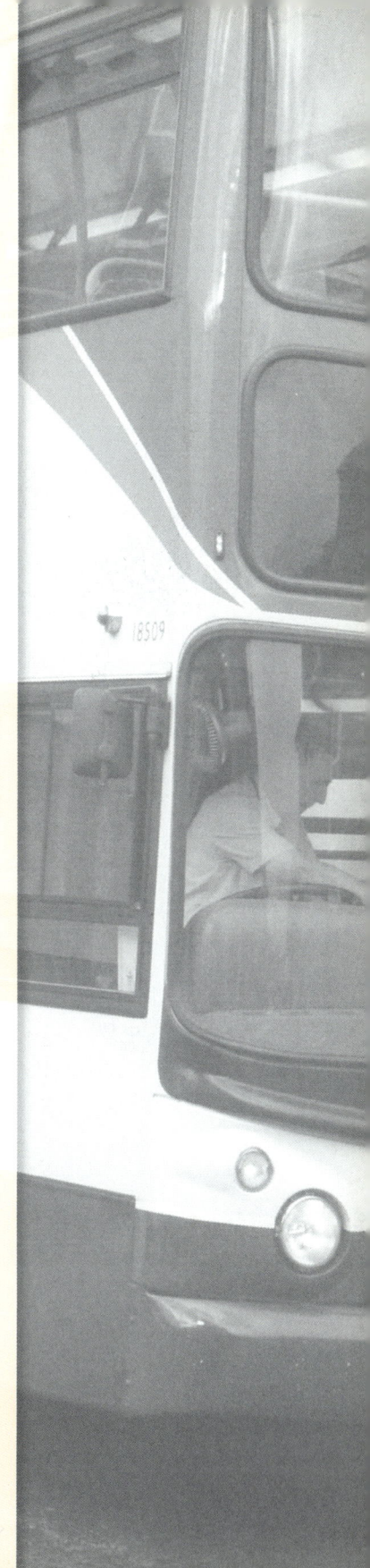

Index to Advertisers

Airconco	19
British Bus Publishing	86
Buses Magazine	85
Chapman Driver Seating	42
Crewe Engines	30
Cummins-Allison	23
Diesel Dye	33
Ian Allan Bookshops	218
Ian Allan Books	62
John Groves Ticket Systems	46
Optare	3
Partline	OBC
Prestolite	28
PSV Glass	6
Scancoin	24
Transport Benevolent Fund	book mark
VIP Group	2
Voith	34 & 48
Walsh's Engineering	31
West End Travel & Rutland Travel	61
Wilkinsons Vehicle Solutions	21

First published 2008

ISBN   978 0711 033 344

All rights reserved. No part of this book may be reproduced or transmitted in any form or by any means, electronic or mechanical, including photocopying, recording or by any information storage and retrieval system, without permission from the publisher in writing.

© Ian Allan Publishing Ltd 2008

Published by Ian Allan Publishing an imprint of Ian Allan Publishing Ltd, Riverdene Business Park, Hersham, Surrey KT12 4RG, and printed by Ian Allan Publishing Ltd, Riverdene Business Park, Hersham, Surrey KT12 4RG.

Visit Ian Allan Publishing web site:
www.ianallanpublishing.com

List of Abbreviations

Acct = Accountant
Admin = Administrative
Asst = Assistant
Ch = Chief
Chmn = Chairman
Co = Company
Comm Man = Commercial Manager
Cont = Controller
Dep = Deputy
Dir = Director
Eng = Engineer
Exec = Executive
Fin = Financial
Gen Man = General Manager
Insp = Inspector
Jnt = Joint
Man = Manager
Man Dir = Managing Director
Mktg = Marketing
Off = Officer
Op = Operating
Ops = Operations
Plan = Planning
Pres = President
Prin = Principal
Prop = Proprietor(s)
Ptnrs = Partner(s)
Reg Off = Registered Office
Sd = Single-deck bus
Sec = Secretary
Supt = Superintendent
Svce = Service
Traf Man = Traffic Manager
Traf Supt = Traffic Superintendent
Tran Man = Transport Manager

Foreword

Welcome to the 2009 edition of the Little Red Book. I feel privileged to have been asked to assume the role of Editor in its 71st year as the leading industry directory.

The usefulness of any directory can be measured by the currency of its entries; with this in mind we have concentrated this year on improving the accuracy of the listings. This has been reflected in over 500 additions, deletions and amendments to the destinations of the questionnaires sent out to operators and suppliers prior to publication, and a huge overhaul of the entries in the book. We are not quite where we would like to be yet, and we will be making further improvements next year, but we feel sure you will notice the difference now. We are very grateful to all those who have taken the trouble, amidst all the other pressures, to update and return their entries. A brief reminder – if there is no change to your entry, please don't worry about re-writing it all. A simple statement to the effect that there is no change will be fine, but please remember to make sure to tell us who you are!

2008 has been an eventful year for the industry and 2009 promises more of the same. The passage of the Local Transport Bill continues, and in several areas authorities and operators are considering their future relationships under the new structures likely to be available when it becomes an Act. The national concessionary fare scheme has been introduced; its effects are still working their way through the system. Likewise the London low emission zone. The latest major development is the onset of the driver CPC with effect from 10 September 2008.

The industry is responding actively and positively to the environmental agenda and the growing realisation that the private car is not the panacea for future mobility. The manufacturers listed in this directory continue to introduce new models and are making great strides with new technology. It is to be hoped that the next edition will be able to illustrate the fast moving developments in hybrid technology. Meanwhile, authorities and operators are co-operating to provide further examples of Bus Rapid Transit schemes to follow in the successful footsteps of Fastrack in Kent and Fastway in West Sussex, which emphasise how the bus can be a realistic and attractive alternative to the car.

Consolidation, restructuring and changes of ownership are part and parcel of industry evolution; they have continued apace during 2008. Our job is to ensure that these changes are all accurately reflected in the directory. Recognising their key place in the industry, we have incorporated some initial expansion of the introductory entries for the major operating groups; we plan to further enhance this section next year. Other well known names have disappeared, some of which have featured in very many past editions of this book.

For the first time, we have introduced a few photographs to illustrate the operations of constituent businesses. We will be happy to receive feedback on whether this is a welcome addition; however our main focus will remain on the provision of a comprehensive and up to date directory.

Finally, readers may note that we have a full page advertisement for Optare Product Support on page 3. The individual listings in the trade sections are still shown as Unitec, as details of Optare's restructuring only came through after these sections had gone to press. This will be rectified next time, and we will publish the updated details again in Buses.

Ian Barlex, Editor

Acknowledgements

I would like to acknowledge the help and support of Paul Appleton and his team at Ian Allan for their hard work and support in producing this edition. And a particular mention for Irena Cornwell, who works very hard to liaise with the advertisers.

I must also thank Tony Pattison, who did such a sterling job as Editor and has been generous in giving his time and support to enable a smooth handover.

Thanks too to Keith Shayshutt, James Lewis and Tony Walmsley, who have kindly allowed us to use some of their photographs, and to operators who have helped with logos and illustrations.

And many thanks to all of our advertisers for their support, without which this directory would be difficult to sustain. Please give them your support and tell them you saw their advertisement in LRB.

How LRB entries are compiled

As always, our principal source of data has been the thousands of questionnaires we send out to operators, manufacturers, suppliers and other organisations. As indicated above, we gave the circulation list a major overhaul this year to try to reflect the many changes that have been happening, to omit ceased businesses, etc.

Where we have not received responses, we have tried to use other publicly available sources to ensure the entries are as accurate as possible.

New entrants to the bus and coach market need not wait for LRB to make contact. If you are active in the industry, and would like to appear in the next edition of LRB (free of charge), please write to the editor of LRB at Ian Allan Publishing Ltd, Foundry Road, Stamford, Lincolnshire PE9 2PP, requesting to receive a form for the next edition.

LRB is used by a substantial number of bus and coach operators, as well as by national and local government, trade organisations, tendering authorities, group travel organisers, hotels and leisure attractions.

Advertising in LRB For information regarding advertising contact: **Irena Cornwell**
Tel: 01780 484635 **Fax:** 01780 763388 **E-mail:** irena.cornwell@ianallanpublishing.co.uk

Gain an advantage...
with AdBlue Storage Solutions

TITAN Environmental, setting the European standards for **AdBlue** Storage

- More cost effective than IBC's or drums and offers an estimated 2 years payback
- Market leading range of AdBlue storage and dispensing in the UK
- Avoid costly emission fines and ensure long term quality of stored AdBlue
- Protect the environment by preventing pollution spillage incidents and avoid expensive fines

TITAN ENVIRONMENTAL
PART OF KINGSPAN ENVIRONMENTAL

Kingspan Environmental

Titan Environmental Limited
Seapatrick Road, Seapatrick, Banbridge,
County Down, Northern Ireland BT32 4PH

www.titanenv.com or visit our group website www.kingspanenv.com

For further information please call 0800 0234 3 or email sales@titanenv.com

Titan provide a range of easy to handle above ground **BlueMaster** tanks which provide highly professional solutions for **AdBlue** storage to all customer groups such as road haulage contractors and bus or coach depots.

Other product ranges include:

Fuel Storage & Security
- Secure Fuel Storage & Dispensing
- Bunded Oil Tanks
- Biofuel Storage & Dispensing
- Fuel Management Systems
- Security Options

Rainwater Harvesting
- Retrofitable Above Ground Systems
- Below Ground Storage Systems
- Waterbutts

Spill Containment & Prevention
- Bunded Pallets & Workfloors
- Spill Kits & Absorbents
- Waste Oil Wells
- IBC Bund

Section 1

Trade Directory

- Vehicle suppliers and dealers
- A-Z listing of suppliers and manufacturers
- Bus & Coach industry service providers

Trade Directory

Vehicle Suppliers & Dealers

Manufacturers of full-size bus and coach chassis and integrals, bus rapid transit vehicles and light rail vehicles

ALEXANDER DENNIS LTD
91 Glasgow Road, Falkirk FK1 4JB
Tel: 01324 621672
Fax: 01324 632469
E-mail: enquiries@alexander-dennis.co.uk
Web sites: www.alexander-dennis.com
Range: hybrid single-deck bus, rear-engined low-floor single-deck bus, chassis for rear-engined low-floor midibus, rear-engined low-floor single-deck bus, mid-engined coach, rear-engined coach, rear-engined low-floor double-deck bus, two- or three-axle, low-floor schoolbus.

AUTOSAN UK
UK Supplier: **Autoholdings**
Bedworth Road, Coventry CV6 6BP
Tel: 024 7636 0011
Web site: www.autosanuk.com
Range: High-floor school bus, single-deck bus, coach

AYATS
UK Supplier: **AYATS (GB) LTD**
Meadow Drive, Earith,
Cambridge PE28 3SA
Tel: 01487 843333
Fax: 01487 843285
E-mail: david@sunfunholidays.co.uk
Web site: www.carroceriasayats.es
Ireland supplier: **Bartons Transport**
Straffan Road, Maynooth, Co Kildare
Tel: 00 353 1 628 6026
Fax: 00 353 1 628 6722
E-mail: info@bartons-transport.ie
Models: Rear-engined integral coach range - up to 15m

BMC UK LTD
Ibstock Road, Coventry CV6 6JR
Tel: 024 7636 3003
Fax: 024 7636 5835
Website: www.bmcukltd.com
Models: integral front-engined schoolbus, integral front-engined midicoach, integral rear-engined 11m low-floor single-deck bus

IRISBUS (UK) LTD
Iveco House, Station Road,
Watford WD17 1SR
Tel: 01923 259660
Fax: 01923 259623
E-mail: info@irisbus.co.uk
Models: midibus, low-floor midibus, minibuses, guided bus system, low-floor rear-engined single-deck bus, low-floor single-deck coach.

KING LONG PLC
UK Supplier: **Autoholdings**
Bedworth Road, Coventry CV6 6BP
Tel: 024 7636 3004
Models: single-deck coach

MAN
UK Supplier: **Neoman Bus UK**
Frankland Road, Blagrove,
Swindon SN5 8YU
Tel: 01793 448355
Fax: 01793 448359
Web site: www.neoman.co.uk

Ireland supplier: **BRIAN NOONE**
Straffan Road, Maynooth, Co Kildare
Tel: 00 353 1 628 6311
Fax: 00 353 1 628 5404
Web site: www.briannooneltd.ie
Models: single-deck low-floor bus, rear-engined coach

MERCEDES-BENZ
UK Supplier:

EVOBUS (UK) LTD
Cross Point Business Park,
Ashcroft Way, Coventry CV2 2TU
Tel: 024 7662 6000
Website: www.evobus.com
Models: rear-engine coach, rear-engine integral low-floor single-deck bus, rear-engine integral low-floor single-deck articulated bus

NEOPLAN
UK Supplier: **Neoman Bus UK**
Frankland Road, Blagrove,
Swindon
SN5 8YU
Tel: 01793 448355
Fax: -1793 448 359
Web site: www.neoman.co.uk
Models: single-deck and double-deck rear-engine integral coaches

OPTARE PLC
Manston Lane, Leeds LS15 8SU
Tel: 0113 264 5182
Fax: 0113 260 6635
E-mail: info@optare.com
Web site: www.optare.com
Models: low-floor minibus, rear-engined integral low-floor single-deck midibus, rear-engined integral low-floor single-deck bus
UK supplier:

OPTARE COACH SALES
Denby Way, Hellaby Industrial Estate,
Hellaby, Rotherham S66 8HR
Tel: 01709 535120
Fax: 01709 535102
E-mail: coachsales@optare.com
Web site: www.optare.com

PLAXTON
Plaxton Park, Cayton Low Road,
Eastfield, Scarborough YO11 3BY
Tel: 01723 581500
Fax: 01723 5813238
E-mail: sales@plaxtonlimited.co.uk
Web site: www.plaxtonlimited.co.uk
Range: coaches, buses, midicoach and midibus bodies
(Part of Alexander Dennis)

SCANIA (GB) LTD
Tongwell, Milton Keynes MK15 8HB
Tel: 01908 210210
Fax: 01908 215040
Web site: www.scania.com
Range: rear-engined low-floor single-deck and double-deck bus chassis, integral low-floor single-deck bus, integral low-floor double-deck bus, rear-engined coach.

SETRA
UK Supplier:

EVOBUS (UK) LTD
Cross Point Business Park, Ashcroft Way,
Coventry CV2 2TU
Tel: 024 7662 6000
Website: www.evobus.com, www.setra.de
Models: rear-engined integral coaches

VAN HOOL
Bernard Van Hoolstraat 58,
B-2500 Lier-Koningshooikt, Belgium
Tel: 00 32 3 420 20 20
Fax: 00 32 3 482 33 60
Website: www.vanhool.be
E-mail: info@vanhool.be
Models: integral coaches

VDL BOVA
Web site: www.vdlbova.nl
UK Suppliers: **MOSELEY (PCV) LTD**
Elmsall Way, Dale Lane, South Elmsall,
Pontefract WF9 2XS
Tel: 01977 609000
Fax: 01977 609900
Web site: www.moseleycoachsales.co.uk

MOSELEY IN THE SOUTH LTD
Summerfield Avenue, Chelston Business Park, Wellington TA21 9JF
Tel: 01823 653000
Fax: 01823 663502
E-mail: enquiries@moseleysouth.co.uk
Web: www.moselesouth.co.uk
Models: Lexio, Magiq, Futura single-deck luxury coach; Synergy double-deck coach

VDL BUS INTERNATIONAL
UK Supplier: **ARRIVA BUS AND COACH**
Lodge Garage, Whitehall Road West,
Cleckheaton BD19 4BJ
Tel: 01274 681144
Fax: 01274 651198
Web site: www.arrivabusandcoach.co.uk
E-mail: busandcoachsales@arriva.co.uk
Models: rear-engined low-floor single-deck bus, rear-engined low-floor double-deck bus, rear-engined coach, rear-engined three-axle single- or double-deck coach.

VOLVO BUS LTD
Wedgnock Lane, Warwick CV34 5YA
Tel: 01926 401777
Fax: 01926 407407
Website: www.volvobuses.volvo.co.uk,
www.volvo.com
Models: rear-engined low-floor single-deck bus, rear-engined low-floor articulated single-deck bus, mid-engined coach, rear-engined integral coach, rear-engined low-floor double-deck bus.

Bus Rapid Transit Vehicles

IRISBUS (UK) LTD
Iveco House, Station Road,
Watford WD17 1SR
Tel: 01923 259660
Fax: 01923 259623

E-mail: info@irisbus.co.uk
Web site: www.irisbus.co.uk
Models: guided bus system

MINITRAM SYSTEMS LTD
12 Waterloo Park Estate,
Bidford on Avon B50 4JH
Tel: 07770 931274
E-mail: martinp@tdi.uk.com
Website: www.minitram.com
Models: Rubber tyre-guided/unguided/rail 7.8m vehicle

VOLVO BUS LTD
Wedgnock Lane, Warwick CV34 5YA
Tel: 01926 401777
Fax: 01926 407407
Website: www.volvobuses.volvo.co.uk,
www.volvo.com
Models: rear-engined low-floor single-deck bus, rear-engined low-floor articulated single-deck bus, rear-engined low-floor double-deck bus *(chassis can be equipped with guidewheels for operation on guideways).*

WRIGHT GROUP
Galgorm, Ballymena,
Northern Ireland BT42 1PY
Tel: 028 2564 1212
Fax: 028 2564 9703
E-mail: info@wright-bus.com
Web site: www.wright-bus.com
Models: StreetCar rapid transit vehicle
(further models - see bodybuilders section).

Light Rail Vehicles

ALSTOM TRANSPORT
Worldwide headquarters: 48 rue Albert Dhalenne, F-93482 Saint-Ouen Cedex, France
Tel: 00 33 1 41 66 90 00
Fax: 00 33 1 41 66 96 66
Web site: www.transport.alstom.com
Models: rail vehicles including light rail vehicles, traction equipment, infrastructure and maintenance services.

BOMBARDIER TRANSPORTATION
Management Office: 1101 Parent Street, Saint-Bruno, Quebec J3V 6E6, Canada
Tel: 00 1 450 441 20 20
Fax: 00 1 450 441 15 15
Web site:
www.transportation.bombardier.com

BOMBARDIER TRANSPORTATION METROS
Litchurch Lane, Derby DE24 8AD
Tel: 01332 344666
Fax: 01332 266271
Models: light rail vehicles, trams, guided or unguided bi-mode rubber tyred electric vehicle.

MINITRAM SYSTEMS LTD
12 Waterloo Park Estate,
Bidford on Avon B50 4JH
Tel: 07770 931274
E-mail: martyinp@tdi.uk.com
Website: www.minitram.com
Models: Rubber tyre-guided/unguided/rail 7.8m vehicle

PARRY PEOPLE MOVERS LTD
Overend Road, Cradley Heath,
Dudley B64 7DD

Tel: 01384 569553
Fax: 01384 637753
E-mail: jpmparry@aol.com
Website: www.parrypeoplemovers.com
Models: Ultra light rail vehicles and trams

TRAM POWER LTD
99 Stanley Raod, Bootle L20 7DA
Website:
www.trampower.co.uk/CityClass.html
Models: Articulated lightweight low-cost tram

Bodybuilders (large vehicles)

BEULAS
UK Suppliers: Base Ltd
57 Clydesdale Place, Moss Side Industrial Estate, Leyland PR26 7QS
Tel: 01772 425355
Fax: 01772 425748
Web site: www.basecoachsales.co.uk

SALVADOR CAETANO (UK) LTD
Mill Lane, Heather, Coalville LE67 2QA
Web site: www.caetano.co.uk
Tel: 01530 263333
Fax: 01530 263379
E-mail: enquiries@caetano.co.uk

SC COACHBUILDERS LTD
Hambledon Road, Waterlooville PO7 7UA
Tel: 023 9225 8211
Fax: 023 9225 5611
E-mail: sccaetano.co.uk
Web site: www.caetano.co.uk
Models: single-deck coach, single-deck low-floor midibus.

EAST LANCASHIRE COACHBUILDERS LTD (OPTARE PLC)
Lower Philips Road, Whitebirk Industrial Estate, Blackburn BB1 5UD
Tel: 01254 504150
Fax: 01254 504197
E-mail: john.horn@elcb.co.uk
Web site: www.elcb.co.uk
Models: double-deck low-floor bus, single-deck low floor bus,
single-deck low-floor midibus

ESKER BUS & COACH SALES LTD
Comagh Business Park, Kilbeggan,
Co Westmeath, Ireland
Tel: 00 353 506 33070
Fax: 00 353 506 33070
E-mail: info@eskerbusandcoach.com
Web site: www.eskerbusandcoach.com
Models: single-deck coach, single-deck low-floor midibus.

IRIZAR
UK spares supplier: Tramontana
Chapelknowe Road, Carfin, Motherwell ML1 5LE
Tel: 01698 861790
Fax: 01698 860778
E-mail: wdt90@tiscali.co.uk
Web site: tramontanacoach.co.uk

ALEXANDER DENNIS LTD
91 Glasgow Road, Falkirk FK1 4JB
Tel: 01324 621 672
Fax: 01324 632 269

E-mail: enquiries@alexander-dennis.com
Web: www.alexander-dennis.com

EXPRESS COACH REPAIRS LTD
Outgang Lane, Pickering, North Yorkshire YO18 7EL
Tel: 01751 475 218
E-mail: simonsheoder@info.co.uk
Web: www.expresscoachrepairs.co.uk

JONCKHEERE
Importer: *Volvo Bus & Coach Centre
Belton Road West,
Loughborough LE11 5HP
Tel: 01509 217777
Fax: 01509 239362
Web site: www.volvo.com
UK Service: Tramontana
Chapelknowe Road, Carfin,
Motherwell ML1 5LE
Tel: 01698 861790
Fax: 01698 860778
E-mail: wdt90@tiscali.co.uk
Web site: tramontanacoach.co.uk

LEICESTER CARRIAGE BUILDERS
Marlow Road, Leicester LE3 2BQ
Tel: 01162 824 270
Fax: 01162 630 554
E-mail: lcbo116@yahoo.co.uk
Web: www.leicestercarriagebuilders.co.uk

MARCOPOLO
UK Suppliers: Base Ltd
57 Clydesdale Place, Moss Side Industrial Estate, Leyland PR26 7QS
Tel: 01772 425355
Fax: 01772 425748
Web site: www.basecoachsales.co.uk

MCV BUS AND COACH LTD
Sterling Place, Elean Business Park,
Sutton, Ely CB6 2QE
Tel: 01353 773000
Fax: 01353 773001
E-mail: vernon.edwards@mcv-uk.com

MOSELEY DISTRIBUTORS LTD
Elmsall Way, Dale Lane,
South Elmsall, Pontefract WF9 2XS
Tel: 01977 609000
Fax: 01977 609900
Web site: www.moseleycoachsales.co.uk

NEOPLAN
UK Supplier: Neoman Bus UK
Frankland Road, Blagrove,
Swindon SN5 8YU
Tel: 01793 448355
Fax: 01793 448359
Web site: www.neoman.co.uk
Models: single-deck coach, also integral coach.

NOGE
UK Supplier: Neoman Bus UK
Frankland Road, Blagrove Swindon SN5 8YU
Tel: 01793 448355
Fax: 01793 448359
Web site: www.neoman.co.uk
Ireland supplier: Brian Noone
Straffan Road, Maynooth, Co Kildare
Tel: 00 353 1 628 6311
Fax: 00 353 1 628 5404
Models: two-axle and three-axle integral coach bodies.

Trade Directory

13

Trade Directory

OPTARE PLC
Manston Lane, Leeds LS15 8SU
Tel: 0113 264 5182
Fax: 0113 260 6635
E-mail: info@optare.com
Web site: www.optare.com
Models: double-deck and single-deck buses, also integral
UK supplier:

OPTARE COACH SALES
Denby Way, Hellaby Industrial Estate,
Hellaby, Rotherham S66 8HR
Tel: 01709 535120
Fax: 01709 535102
E-mail: coachsales@optare.com
Web site: www.optare.com

PLAXTON
Plaxton Park, Cayton Low Road, Eastfield,
Scarborough YO11 3BY
Tel: 01723 581500
Fax: 01723 5813238
E-mail: sales@plaxtonlimited.co.uk
Web site: www.plaxtonlimited.co.uk
Range: coaches, buses, midicoach and midibus bodies
(Part of Alexander Dennis)

VAN HOOL
Bernard Van Hoolstraat 58, B-2500
Lier-Koningshooikt, Belgium
Tel: 00 32 3 420 20 20
Fax: 00 32 3 482 33 60
E-mail: info@vanhool.be
Web site: www.vanhool.be
Models: coach bodies

VDL BERKHOF
UK Supplier: *Arriva Bus & Coach
Lodge Garage, Whitehall Road West,
Gomersal, Cleckheaton BD19 4BJ
Tel: 01274 681144
Models: rear-engined three-axle or two-axle single-deck coach.

WRIGHT GROUP
Galgorm, Ballymena,
Northern Ireland BT42 1PY
Tel: 028 2564 1212
Fax: 028 2564 9703
E-mail: info@wright-bus.com
Web site: www.wright-bus.com
Models: double-deck low-floor bus body, single-deck low-floor articulated bus body, FTR advanced bus rapid transit vehicle, single-deck low-floor bus, single-deck low-entry coach, single-deck low-floor midibus.

Chassis and integral vehicles (small vehicles - under 9m)

ALEXANDER DENNIS LTD
91 Glasgow Road, Falkirk FK1 4JB
Tel: 01324 621 672
Fax: 01324 632 269
E-mail: enquiries@alexander-dennis.com
Web: www.alexander-dennis.com

AVID VEHICLES LTD
Unit 8, Arcot Court, Nelson Road,
Nelson Park, Cramlington NE23 1BB
Tel: 01670 707 040
Fax: 01670 715 230
E-mail: sales@avidvehicles.com
Web: www.avidvehicles.com

FORD MOTOR COMPANY
Ford Motor Co Ltd, Eagle Way,
Brentwood CM13 3BW
Tel: 0845 7111 888
Web site: www.fordvans.co.uk/peoplemovers
Models: Transit, complete minibus or chassis-cowl.

IRISBUS (UK) LTD
Iveco House, Station Road,
Watford WD17 1SR
Tel: 01923 259660
Fax: 01923 259623
E-mail: info@irisbus.co.uk
Web site: www.irisbus.co.uk

JOHN BRADSHAW LTD
New Lane, Stibbington, Peterborough PE8 6LW
Tel: 01780 781801
Web site: www.john-bradshaw.co.uk
Models: Electric minibus/taxi

KVC MANUFACTURING LTD
Cornagh Business Park, Kilbeggan,
Co Westmeath, Ireland
Tel: 00 353 506 32699
Fax: 00 353 506 32691
E-mail: info@kvc.ie
Web site: www.kvc.ie

LDV LTD
Bromford House, Drews Lane,
Birmingham B8 2QG
Tel: 0121 322 2000
Fax: 0121 327 4487
Web site: www.ldv.co.uk
Models: Complete minibus or chassis-cowl

LEICESTER CARRIAGE BUILDERS
Marlow Raod, Leicester LE3 2BQ
Tel: 01162 824 270
Fax: 01162 630 554
E-mail: icbo116@yahoo.co.uk
Web: www.leicestercarriagebuilders.co.uk

MERCEDES-BENZ
UK Supplier: Evobus (UK) Ltd
Cross Point Business Park,
Ashcroft Way, Coventry CV2 2TU
Tel: 024 7662 6000
Website: www.evobus.com
Models: Complete low-floor minibus or chassis cowl

MINITRAM SYSTEMS LTD
12 Waterloo Park Estate,
Bidford on Avon B50 4JH
Tel: 07770 931274
E-mail: martinp@tdi.uk.com
Web site: www.minitram.com
Models: Rubber tyre-guided/unguided/rail 7.8m vehicle

MISTRAL GROUP (UK) PLC
PO Box 130, Chelford Road,
Knutsford, Cheshire WA16 6WX
Tel: 01565 621 881
Fax: 01565 621 882
E-mail: sales@mistral-group.com
Web: www.mistral-group.com

NU-TRACK LTD
Steeple Industrial Estate,
Antrim BT41 1AB
Tel: 028 94 469 550
Fax: 028 94 465 430
E-mail: enquiries@nu-track.co.uk

OPTARE PLC
Manston Lane, Leeds LS15 8SU
Tel: 0113 264 5182
Fax: 0113 260 6635
Web site: www.optare.com
Models: front-engined integral low-floor minibus, rear-engined integral low-floor midibus. UK supplier:

OPTARE COACH SALES
Denby Way, Hellaby Industrial Estate,
Hellaby, Rotherham S66 8HR
Tel: 01709 535120
Fax: 01709 535102
E-mail: coachsales@optare.com
Web site: www.optare.com

RENAULT UK LTD
Rivers Office Park, Denham Way, Maple
Cross, Rickmansworth WD3 9YS
Tel: 01923 855500
Web site: www.renault.co.uk
Models: Complete minibus or chassis-cowl; electric vehicle.

TESLA VEHICLES LIMITED
22 Larbre Crescent, Whickham, Newxastle
Upon Tyne NE16 5YG
Tel: 01914 886 258
Fax: 01914 889 158
E-mail: info@teslavehicles.com
Web: www.teslavehicles.com

TOYOTA (GB) PLC
Great Burgh, Burgh Heath,
Epsom KT18 5UX
Tel: 01737 363633
Mobile: 07785 238798
E-mail: steve.prime@tgb.toyota.co.uk
Web site: www.toyota.com
UK suppliers: ADD Coach Sales
Tel: 01884 860767
Holloway Commercials
Tel: 01902 636661
Salvador Caetano
Tel: 01530 26333
Models: Optimo midicoach, chassis cowl

VAUXHALL MOTORS LTD
Luton LU1 3YT
Tel: 020 7439 0303
Vauxhall Mobility: 0800 731 5267
Web site: www.vauxhall.co.uk
Models: Complete minibus or chassis-cowl.

VOLKSWAGEN COMMERCIAL VEHICLES
Yeomans Drive, Blakelands,
Milton Keynes MK14 5AN
Web site: www.volkswagen-vans.co.uk
Models: Complete minibus or chassis-cowl.

Bodybuilders (small vehicles) inibus conversions

ADVANCED VEHICLE BUILDERS
Upper Mantle Close, Clay Cross S45 9NU
Tel: 01246 250022
Fax: 01246 250016
E-mail: info@minibus.co.uk

ALEXANDER DENNIS LTD
91 Glasgow Road, Falkirk FK1 4JB
Tel: 01324 621 672

14

Trade Directory

Fax: 01324 632 269
E-mail: enquiries@alexander-dennis.com
Web: www.alexander-dennis.com

AVID VEHICLES LTD
Unit 8, Arcot Court, Nelson Road,
Nelson Park, Cramlington NE23 1BB
Tel: 01670 707 040
Fax: 01670 715 230
E-mail: sales@avidvehicles.com
Web: www.avidvehicles.com

BLUE BIRD VEHICLES LTD
Unit 7, Plaxton Park, Cayton Low Road,
Eastfield, Scarborough YO11 3BY
Tel: 01723 860800
Fax: 01723 585235
E-mail: info@bluebirdvehicles.com
Web site: www.bluebirdvehicles.com

BURNT TREE VEHICLE SOLUTIONS
Burnt Tree House, Knights Way, Battlefield Enterprise Park, Harlescott Lane,
Shrewsbury SY1 3JE
Tel: 01743 457650
Web site: www.burnt-tree.co.uk

CHASSIS DEVELOPMENTS
Grovebury Road,
Leighton Buzzard LU7 8SL
Tel: 01525 374151
Web site: www.chassisdevelopments.co.uk

CONCEPT COACHCRAFT
Far Cromwell Road, Bredbury,
Stockport SK6 2SE
Tel: 0161 406 9322
Fax: 0161 406 9588
E-mail: sales@conceptcoachcraft.com
Web site: www.conceptcoachcraft.com

COURTSIDE CONVERSIONS LTD
1 Woodward Road, Howden Industrial Estate, Tiverton EX16 5HS
Tel: 01884 256048
Fax: 01884 256087
E-mail: courtsidesales@aol.com

CROWN COACHBUILDERS LTD
32 Flemington Industrial Park, Flemington,
Motherwell ML1 1SN
Tel: 01698 276087
Fax: 01698 276144
E-mail: davidgreer@hotmail.com
Web site: www.crowncoachbuilders.co.uk

CVI (COMMERCIAL VEHICLE INNOVATION)
Moorfoot View, Bilston, Edinburgh
EH25 9SL
Tel: 0131 473 9300
Web site: www.c-v-i.co.uk

ESKER BUS & COACH SALES LTD
Comagh Business Park, Kilbeggan, Co Westmeath, Ireland
Tel: 00 353 506 33070
Fax: 00 353 506 33070
E-mail: info@eskerbusandcoach.com
Web site: www.eskerbusandcoach.com

ESKER BUS & COACH (UK) LTD
Unit 3, Haigh Moor Drive, Brooklands Park,
Church Lane, Dinnington, Sheffield S25 2JY

Tel: 01909 552244
Fax: 01909 569242
E-mail: info@eskerbusandcoach.co.uk
Web site: www.eskerbusandcoach.co.uk

EXPRESS COACH REPAIRS LTD
Outgang Lane, Pickering,
North Yorkshire YO18 7EL
Tel: 01751 475 218
E-mail: simonsheoder@info.co.uk
Web: www.expresscoachrepairs.co.uk

EURO COACH BUILDERS LTD
Deerybeg Industrial Estate,
Gweedore, Co Donegal, Ireland
Tel: 00 353 75 31528
Fax: 00 353 75 31930
Web site: www.eurocoachbuilders.ie

EXCEL CONVERSIONS LTD
Excel House, Durham Lane,
Armthorpe, Doncaster DN3 3FE
Tel: 01302 835388
Fax: 01302 835389
E-mail: admin@excelconversions.co.uk
Web site: www.excelconversions.co.uk

GM COACHWORK LTD
Trusham, Newton Abbot TQ13 0NX
Tel: 01626 853050
Fax: 01626 855066
Web site: www.gmcoachwork.co.uk

INDCAR SA
Poligono Industrial Torres Pujals, E-17401
Arbucies (Girona), Spain
Web site: www.indcar.com
UK Supplier: Base Ltd

JDC - JOHN DENNIS COACHBUILDERS
25 Westfield Road, Guildford GU1 1RR
Tel: 01483 501457
Web site: www.jdcbus.co.uk

JUBILEE AUTOMOTIVE GROUP
Woden Road South,
Wednesbury WS10 0NQ
Tel: 0121 502 2252
Fax: 0121 502 2558
E-mail: sales@jubileeauto.co.uk

LEICESTER CARRIAGE BUILDERS
Marlow Road, Leicester LE3 2BQ
Tel: 0116 282 4270
Fax: 0116 263 0554
E-mail: lcb0116@yahoo.co.uk
Web site: www.leicestercarriagebuilders.co.uk

MCV BUS AND COACH LTD
Sterling Place, Elean Business Park,
Sutton, Ely CB6 2QE
Tel: 01353 773000
Fax: 01353 773001
E-mail: vernon.edwards@mcv-uk.com

MELLOR COACHCRAFT
Miall Street, Rochdale OL11 1HY
Tel: 01706 860610
Fax: 01706 860042
E-mail: mcsales@woodhall-nicholson.co.uk
Web site: www.woodhall-nicholson.co.uk

MINIBUS OPTIONS LTD
Bingswood Industrial Estate,
Whaley Bridge, High Peak SK23 7LY

Tel: 01663 735355
Fax: 01663 735352
E-mail: info@minibusoptions.co.uk
Web site: www.minibusoptions.co.uk

NU-TRACK LTD
Steeple Industrial Estate, Antrim
BT41 1AB
Tel: 028 9446 9550
Fax: 028 9446 5430
E-mail: enquiries@nu-track.co.uk

OLYMPUS COACHCRAFT LTD
7 Temperance Street,
Manchester M12 6DX
Tel/Fax: 0161 273 4259
E-mail: geoffolympus@aol.com
Web site: www.olympuscoaches.co.uk

OPTARE PLC
Manston Lane, Leeds, LS15 8SU
Tel: 0113 264 5182
Fax: 0113 260 6635
Web site: www.optare.com

PLAXTON LIMITED
Plaxton Park, Cayton Low Road, Eastfield,
Scarborough YO11 3BY
Tel: 01723 581500
Fax: 01723 5813238
Web site: www.plaxtonlimited.co.uk
Range: coaches; midicoach and midibus bodies.

PVS MANUFACTURING LTD
8 Ardboe Business Park, Kilmascally Road,
Ardboe, Dungannon BT71 5BP
Tel: 028 8673 6969
Fax: 028 8673 7178
E-mail: mail@pvsltd.com
Web site: www.conversionspecialists.com

STANFORD COACH WORKS
Mobility House, Stanhope Industrial Park,
Wharf Road, Stanford-le-Hope SS17 0EH
Tel: 01375 676088
Fax: 01375 677999
E-mail: sales@stanfordcoachworks.co.uk
Web site: www.stanfordcoachworks.co.uk
Range: mini- and midibuses, mini- and midicoaches

JOHN STEWART & CO (WISHAW) LTD
Smith Avenue, Garrion Business Park,
Wishaw ML2 0RY
Tel: 01698 373483
Fax: 01698 357185

TAWE COACHBUILDERS LTD
Tawe House, Alloy Industrial Estate,
Pontardawe SA8 4EN
Tel: 01792 832040
Fax: 01792 832041
Web site: www.tawecoachbuildersltd.co.uk

TESLA VEHICLES LIMITED
22 Larbre Crescent, Whickham,
Newxastle Upon Tyne NE16 5YG
Tel: 01914 886 258
Fax: 01914 889 158
E-mail: info@teslavehicles.com
Web: www.teslavehicles.com

TVAC (THE VEHICLE APPLICATION CENTRE)
Centurion Way, Leyland PR26 6TZ
Tel: 01772 457116

15

Web site: www.tvac.com
Range: low-floor mini- and midibuses, mini- and midicoaches

UVMODULAR
Locksley Road, Armytage Road Industrial Estate, Brighouse HD6 1QF
Tel: 01484 400200
Fax: 01484 401125
E-mail: sales@uvmodular.co.uk

WILKER GROUP
Frederick Street, Clara, Co Offaly, Ireland
Tel: 00 353 506 31010
E-mail: info@wilkergroup.com
UK subsidiary
Sandy lane, Ettiley Heath, Sandbach CW11 3NG
Tel: 01270 705999
E-mail: info.uk@wilkergroup.com
Range: low-floor mini- and midibuses, mini- and midicoaches

Dealers

AD COACH SALES
Newbridge Coach Depot, Witheridge EX16 8PY
Tel: 01884 860767
E-mail: enquiries@adcoachsales.co.uk
Web site: www.adcoachsales.co.uk

AJP COMMERCIALS
305-317 Wednesbury Road, Walsall WS2 9QJ
Tel: 01922 639652
Fax: 01922 611700

ALEXANDER DENNIS LTD
91 Glasgow Road, Falkirk FK1 4JB
Tel: 01324 621 672
Fax: 01324 632 269
E-mail: enquiries@alexander-dennis.com
Web: www.alexander-dennis.com

ALLIED VEHICLES LTD
230 Balmore Road, Glasgow G22 6LJ
Tel: 0800 916 3046
Web site: www.alliedvechicles.co.uk/bus
E-mail: info@alliedvechicles.co.uk

ARRIVA BUS AND COACH
Lodge Garage, Whitehall Road West, Cleckheaton BD19 4BJ
Tel: 01274 681144
Fax: 01274 651198
E-mail: busandcoachsales@arriva.co.uk
Web site: www.arrivabusandcoach.co.uk

AVONDALE INTERNATIONAL LTD
451 Clifton Drive North, Lytham St Annes FY8 2PS
Tel: 01253 727211
Fax: 01253 714210

B.A.S.E. LTD
57 Clydesdale Place, Moss Side Industrial Estate, Leyland PR26 7QS
Tel: 01772 425355
Fax: 01772 425748
Web site: www.basecoachsales.co.uk

BLYTHSWOOD MOTORS LTD
1175 Argyle Street, Glasgow G3 8TQ
Tel: 0141 221 3165
Fax: 0141 221 3172
E-mail: blythswoodmotors@aol.com
Web site: www.blythswoodmotors.co.uk

BOB VALE COACH SALES LTD
Kingshill House, Spurlands End Road, Great Kingshill, High Wycombe HP15 6PE
Tel: 01494 716996
Fax: 01494 716331
E-mail: bobvalecoachsale@btconnect.com
Web site: www.bobvalecoachsales.com

BRIAN NOONE
Straffan Road, Maynooth, Co Kildare, Ireland
Tel: 00 353 1 628 6311
Fax: 00 353 1 628 5404
Web site: www.briannoneltd.ie

BRISTOL BUS & COACH SALES
6/7 Freestone Road, St Philips, Bristol BS2 0QN
Tel: 0117 971 0251
Fax: 0117 972 3121
E-mail: simon.munden@bristolbusandcoach.co.uk
Web site: www.bristolbusandcoach.co.uk

BRITISH BUS SALES
Mike Nash, PO Box 534, Dorking RH5 5XB
Tel: 07836 656 692
E-mail: nashionalbus1@btconnect.com
Web: www,bristishbussales.co.uk

SALVADOR CAETANO (UK) LTD
Mill Lane, Heather, Coalville LE67 2QA
Tel: 01530 263333
Fax: 01530 263379
E-mail: enquiries@caetano.co.uk
Web site: www.caetano.co.uk
Models: single-deck coach, single-deck low-floor midibus.

DAWSONRENTALS BUS AND COACH LTD
Delaware Drive, Tongwell, Milton Keynes MK15 8JH
Tel: 01908 218111
Fax: 01908 610156
E-mail: info@dawsongroup.co.uk
Web site: www.dawsongroup.co.uk

EAST LANCASHIRE COACHBUILDERS LTD (OPTARE PLC)
Lower Philips Road, Whitebirk Industrial Estate, Blackburn BB1 5UD
Tel: 01254 504150
Fax: 01254 504197
E-mail: john.horn@elcb.co.uk
Web site: www.elcb.co.uk

ENSIGN BUS CO LTD
Juliette Close, Purfleet Industrial Park, Purfleet RM15 4YF
Tel: 01708 865656
Fax: 01708 864340
E-mail: sales@ensignbus.com
Web site: www.ensignbus.com

ERRINGTONS OF EVINGTON LTD
Glenrise Garage, London Road (A6), Oadby LE2 4RG
Tel: 0116 259 2131
Fax: 0116 259 2313

EVOBUS (UK) LTD
Cross Point Business Park, Ashcroft Way, Coventry CV2 2TU
Tel: 024 7662 6000
Website: www.evobus.com

DAVID FISHWICK VEHICLE SALES
North Valley, Colne BB8 0RF
Tel: 01282 615138/867772

FLEET AUCTION GROUP
Brindley Road, Stephenson Industrial park, Coalville LE67 3HG
Tel: 01530 833535
E-mail: fleet.master@btinternet.com
Web site: www.fleetauctiongroup.com

FURROWS COMMERCIAL VEHICLES
Kemberton Road, Halesfield, Telford TF7 4QS
Tel: 01952 684433

GM COACHWORK LTD
Teign Valley, Trusham, Newton Abbot TQ13 0NX
Tel: 01626 853050
Fax: 01626 855066
Web site: www.gmcoachwork.co.uk
E-mail: david.vadght@gmcoachwork.co.uk

THOMAS HARDIE - WIGAN
Lockett Road, Ashton-in-Makerfield WN4 8DE
Tel: 01942 505124
Fax: 01942 505119

IAN GORDON COMMERCIALS
Schawkark Garage, Stair KA5 5JA
Tel: 01292 591764

HOLLOWAY COMMERCIALS
60 Walsall Road, Willenhall WV13 2EF
Tel: 01902 636661
Fax: 01902 609652
E-mail: sales@hollowaycommercials.co.uk
Web site: www.hollowaycommercials.co.uk

B & D HOLT LTD
Cuthbert Street, Bolton BL3 3SD
Tel: 01204 650999
Fax: 01204 665300
E-mail: bevholt@bdholt.co.uk
Web site: www.bdholt.co.uk

IRISH COMMERCIALS (SALES)
Naas, Co Kildare, Ireland

JAYCAS MINIBUS SALES & CONVERSIONS
Pear Tree Street, Bambas Bridge, Preston PR5 6EZ
Tel: 01772 321491

LVD
Leinster Vehicle Distributors Ltd, Urlingford, Co Kilkenny, Ireland
Tel: 00 353 56 31189/88 3 1899
Web site: www.lvd.ie

THE LONDON BUS EXPORT CO
PO Box 12, Chapstow NP16 5UZ
Tel: 01291 689 741
Fax: 01291 689 361
E-mail: lonbusco@globalnet.co.uk
Web site: www.london-bus.co.uk

LOUGHSHORE AUTOS LTD
26 Killycanavan Road, Ardboe, Dungannon BT71 5BP

Tel: 028 8673 7325
Fax: 028 8673 5882
E-mail: michael@loughshoreautosltd.com
Web site: www.loughshoreautosltd.com

MASS SPECIAL ENGINEERING LTD
Anston, Sheffield S25 4SD
Tel: 01909 550480
Fax: 01909 550486

MID WEST CHELTENHAM LTD
The Coach Centre, Golden Valley, Staverton, Cheltenham GL51 0TE
Tel: 01452 859111
Fax: 01452 859222
Web site: www.bussales.co.uk

MISTRAL GROUP (UK) PLC
PO Box 130, Knutsford WA16 6AG
Tel: 01565 621881
Fax: 01565 621882
E-mail: sales@mistral-group.com
Web site: www.mistral-group.com

MOSELEY (PCV) LTD
Elmsall Way, Dale Lane, South Elmsall, Pontefract WF9 2XS
Tel: 01977 609000
Fax: 01977 609900
Web site: www.moseleycoachsales.co.uk

MOSELEY IN THE SOUTH LTD
Summerfield Avenue, Chelston Business Park, Wellington TA21 9JF
Tel: 01823 653000
Fax: 01823 663502
E-mail: enquiries@moseleysouth.co.uk
Web site: www.moseleysouth.co.uk

MOSELEY DISTRIBUTORS
Rydenmains, Condoratt Road, Glenmavis, Airdrie ML6 0PP
Tel: 01236 750501
Fax: 01236 750503
E-mail: enquiries@moseleydistributors.co.uk
Web site: www.moseleydistributors.co.uk

NEXT BUS LTD
Vincents Road, Bumpers Farm Industrial Estate, Chippenham SN14 6QA
Tel: 01249 462462
Fax: 01249 448844
E-mail: sales@next-bus.co.uk
Web site: www.next-bus.co.uk

OPTARE COACH SALES
Denby Way, Hellaby Industrial Estate, Hellaby, Rotherham S66 8HR
Tel: 01709 535120
Fax: 01709 535102
E-mail: coachsales@optare.com
Web site: www.optare.com

OWENS OF OSWESTRY BMC
Unit 3, Foxen Monor Industrial Park, Four Crosses, Llanymynech SY22 6ST
Tel: 01691 652126
Fax: 01691 831142
E-mail: sales@owens-bmc.co.uk
Web site: www.owens-bmc.co.uk

H W PICKRELL
Gardiners Lane North, Crays Hill, Billericay CM11 2XE
Tel: 01268 521033
Fax: 01268 284951
Web site: www.hwpickrell.co.uk

PLAXTON COACH SALES CENTRE
Ryton Road, Anston, Sheffield S25 4DL
Tel: 01909 551155
Fax: 01909 567994
E-mail: coaches@plaxtonlimited.co.uk
Web site: www.plaxtonlimited.co.uk

SCANIA (GB) LTD
Tongwell, Milton Keynes MK15 8HB
Tel: 01908 210210
Fax: 01908 215040
Web site: www.scania.com

SOUTHDOWN PSV LTD
Silverwood, Snow Hill, Copthorne RH10 3EN
Tel: 01342 715222
Fax: 01342 719619
E-mail: bussales@southdownpsv.co.uk
Web site: www.southdownpsv.co.uk

STAFFORD BUS CENTRE
Unit 27, Moorfields Industrial Estate, Cotes Heath ST21 6QY
Tel: 01782 791774
Fax: 01782 791721
E-mail: mail@staffordbuscentre.com
Web site: www.staffordbuscentre.com

STEPHENSONS OF ESSEX
Riverside Industrial Estate, South Street, Rochford SS4 1BS
Tel: 01702 541511
Fax: 01702 549461
E-mail: sales@stephensonsofessex.com
Web site: www.stephensonsofessex.com

STOKE TRUCK & BUS CENTRE
Bute Street, Fenton, Stoke-on-Trent ST4 3PS
Tel: 01782 598310
Fax: 01782 598674
Web site: www.bmcstoke.co.uk

TAYLOR COACH SALES
102 Beck Road, Isleham, Ely CB7 5QP
Tel (mobile): 07850 241848
Tel: 01638 780010
Tel: 01638 780011
E-mail: taylorscoach@live.co.uk
Web site: www.taylorscoachsales.co.uk

TOYOTA (GB) PLC
Great Burgh, Burgh Heath, Epsom KT18 5UX
Tel: 01737 363633
Fax: 01737 367713
E-mail: steve.miner@tgb.toyota.co.uk
Web site: www.toyota.com
UK suppliers:
ADD Coach Sales
Tel: 01884 860767
Holloway Commercials
Tel: 01902 636661
Salvador Caetano
Tel: 01530 263333

TRAMONTANA COACH DISTRIBUTORS
Chapelknowe Road, Carfin, Motherwell ML1 5LE
Tel: 01698 861790
Fax: 01698 860778
E-mail: wdt90@tiscali.co.uk

UK BUS DISMANTLERS LTD
Streamhall Garage Estate, Linton Trading Estate, Bromyard, Hertforshire HR7 4QT
Tel: 01885 488 448
Fax: 01885 482 127
E-mail: wactonbus@yahoo.co.uk
Web: www.uk-bus.co.uk

USED COACH SALES
PO Box 166, Warrington WA4 5FG
Tel: 0870 062 0616
Fax: 0870 062 4499
Web site: www.usedcoachsales.co.uk

VENTURA BUS + COACH SALES
Unit 39, Hobbs Industrial Estate, Newchapel, Lingfield RH7 6HN
Tel: 01342 835206
Fax: 01342 835813
E-mail: info@venturasales.co.uk
Web site: www.venturasales.co.uk

VOLVO BUS AND COACH CENTRE
Belton Road West, Loughborough LE11 5HP
Tel: 01509 217777
Fax: 01509 239362
Web site: www.volvo.com

WACTON COACH SALES & SERVICES
Linton Trading Estate, Bromyard HR7 4QL
Tel: 01885 482782
Fax: 01885 482127

WEALDEN PSV LTD
The Bus Garage, 64 Whetsted Road, Five Oak Green, Tonbridge TN12 6RT
Tel: 01892 833830
Fax: 01892 836977
E-mail: sales@wealdenpsv.co.uk
Web site: www.wealdenpsv.co.uk

WINCHESTER MARINE LTD (MAJORLINE ENGINEERING)
Baybridge Industrial Units, Baybridge Lane, Owslebury, Winchester SO21 1JN
Tel: 01962 777077
Fax: 01962 777661, 777667
E-mail: winchestermarine@btconnect.com

ALAN WHITE COACH SALES
135 Nutwell Lane, Doncaster DN3 3JR
Tel: 01302 833203
Fax: 01302 831756
E-mail: sales@alanwhitecoachsales.com
Web site: www.alanwhitecoachsales.com

TREVOR WIGLEY & SONS BUS LTD
Baulder Bridge Road, Carlton, Barnsley S71 3HJ
Tel: 01226 713636/716479
Tel: 01226 700199
E-mail: wigleys@btconnect.com
Web site: www.twigley.com

YORKSHIRE BUS & COACH SALES
254A West Ella Road, West Ella, Hull HU10 7SF
Tel: 01482 653503
Fax: 01482 653302
E-mail: craig.porteous@virgin.net

A-Z Listing of Bus, Coach & Tram Suppliers

LIST OF CATEGORIES

Air Conditioning/Ventilation
Audio/Video Systems
Badges - Drivers/Conductors
Batteries
Bicycle Carriers
Body/Electrical Repairs & Refurbishing
Brakes & Brake Linings
Bus Stops/Shelters - see Shelters/Street Furniture
Cash Handling Equipment
Chassis Lubricating Systems
Clutches
Cooling Systems
Destination Indicator Equipment
Door Operating Gear
Drinks Dispensing Equipment
Driving Axles and Gears
Electrical Equipment
Electronic Control
Emission Control Devices
Engineering
Engines
Engine Oil Drain Valves
Exhaust Systems
Fans & Drive Belts
Fare Boxes
Fire Extinguishers
First Aid Equipment
Floor Covering
Fuel, Fuel Management & Lubricants
Garage Equipment
Gearboxes
Hand Driers (Coach Mounted)
Handrails
Headrest Covers/Curtains
Heating & Ventilation Systems
Hub Odometers
In-Coach Catering Equipment
Information Displays - see Passenger Information Systems
Labels, Nameplates & Decals
Lifting Equipment
Lifts/Ramps (Passenger)
Lighting/Lighting Systems
Mirrors/Mirror Arms
Model Buses
Oil Management Systems
Painting/Signwriting
Parts Suppliers
Passenger Information Systems
Pneumatic Valves/Cylinders
Rapid Transit/Priority Equipment
Repairs/refurbishment - see Body/Electrical Repairs
Retarders & Speed Control Systems
Reversing Safety Systems
Roller Blinds - Passenger/Driver
Roof Lining Fabrics
Seat Belts
Seats, Seat Cushions & Seat Frames
Shelters/Street Furniture
Shock Absorbers/Suspension
Steering
Surveillance Systems
Tachograph Calibrators
Tachograph Chart Analysis Service
Tachographs
Tickets, Ticket machines and Ticket Systems
Timetable Display Frames
Toilet Equipment
Transmission Overhaul
Tree Guards
Tyres
Uniforms
Upholstery
Vacuum Systems
Vehicle Washing and Washers
Wheels, Wheeltrims & Covers
Windows & Windscreens

INDUSTRY SERVICE PROVIDERS

Accident Investigation
Accountancy & Audit
Advertising Contractors
Advisory Services
Artwork
Auctioneers & Valuators
Breakdown & Recovery Services
Cleaning Services
Coach Driver Agency
Coach Hire Broker/Rental
Coach Interchange & Parking Facilities
Computer Systems/Software
Consultants
Driver Supply
Driver Training
Exhibition/Event Organisers
Ferry Operators
Finance & Leasing
Graphic Design
Hotels & Hotel Agents
Insurance
Legal & Operations Advisors
Life Insurance & Pensions
Livery Design
Maps for the Bus industry
Marketing Services
Mechanical Investigation
On-Bus Advertising
Printing
Promotional Material
Publications - Magazines & Books
Quality Management Systems
Recruitment
Refreshment Facilities - *see Tourist Venues/Refreshment Facilities*
Timetable Production
Tour Wholesalers
Tourist Venues/Refreshment Facilities
Training & Marketing Services
Vehicle Certification
Vehicle Rental - *see:* Coach Hire Broker/Rental

Trade Directory

Air Conditioning/Ventilation

AIRCONCO
Units 10 (Head Office), 6 (Part Centre),
Middleton Trade Park, Oldham Road,
Middleton, Manchester M24 1QZ
Tel: 0845 402 4014
Fax: 0845 402 4041
E-mail: mail@airconco.carriersutrak.co.uk
Web site: www.airconco.ltd.uk

AMA LTD
Unit 17, Springmill Industrial Estate,
Avening Road, Nailsworth GL6 0BH
Tel: 01453 832884
Fax: 01453 832040
E-mail: ama@ftech.co.uk

ARRIVA BUS AND COACH
Lodge Garage, Whitehall Road West,
Cleckheaton BD19 4BJ
Tel: 01274 681 144
Fax: 01274 651 198
E-mail: busandcoachsales@arriva.co.uk
Web: www.arrivabusandcoach.co.uk

BRT BEARINGS LTD
21-24 Regal Road, Wisbech,
Cambridgeshire PE13 2RQ
Tel: 01945 464 097
Fax: 01945 464 523
E-mail: info@brt-group.com

CARRIER SUTRAK
Unit 6, I O Centre, Barn Way, Lodge Farm
Industrial Estate, Northampton NN5 7UW
Tel: 01604 581468
Fax: 01604 758132
E-mail: kim.neale@carrier.utc.com

CLAYTON HEATERS LTD
Hunter Terrace, Fletchworth Gate,
Burnsall Road, Coventry CV5 6SP
Tel: 02476 691 916
Fax: 02476 691 969
E-mail: admin@claytoncc.co.uk
Web Site: www.claytoncc.co.uk

CONSERVE (UK) LTD
Suite 7, Logistics House, Kingsthorpe Road,
Northampton NN2 6LJ
Tel: 01604 710055
Fax: 01604 710065
E-mail: information@conserveuk.co.uk
Web site: www.conserveuk.co.uk

DIRECT PARTS LTD
Unit 1, Churnet Court, Churnetside Business
Park, Harrison Way, Cheddleton ST13 7EF
Tel: 01538 361777
Fax: 01538 369100
E-mail: sales@direct-group.co.uk
Web site: www.direct-group.co.uk

EBERSPACHER (UK) LTD
Headlands Business Park,
Salisbury Road, Ringwood BH24 3PB
Tel: 01425 480151
Fax: 01425 480152
E-mail: enquiries@eberspacher.com
Web site: www.eberspacher.com

HISPACOLD
See: Clayton Heaters above
Web Site: www.hispacold.es

THE LAWTON MOTOR BODY BUILDING CO LTD
Knutsford Road, Church Lawton, Stoke-on-Trent ST7 3DN
Tel: 01270 882056
Fax: 01270 883014
E-mail: enquiries@lawtonmotorbody.co.uk
Web site: www.lawtonmotorbody.co.uk

M A C LTD
Unit 8, Oldends Lane Industrial Estate,
Oldends Lane, Stonehouse GL10 3RQ
Tel: 01453 828781
Fax: 01453 828167
E-mail: sales@macair.uk.com
Web site: www.macair.uk.com

PLAXTON COACH SALES CENTRE
Ryton Road, Anston, Sheffield S25 4DL
Tel: 01909 551155
Fax: 01909 567994
E-mail: coaches@plaxtonlimited.co.uk
Web site: www.plaxtonlimited.co.uk

SCANIA
Scania Bus & Coach (UK) Ltd, Claylands
Avenue, Worksop S81 7DJ.
Tel: 01909 500822.
Fax: 01909 500165
Web Site: www.scania.co.uk

UNITEC
Parts Division, Denby Way, Hellaby,
Rotherham S66 8HR
Tel: 01709 792000
Fax: 01709 792009
E-mail: parts@optare.com

UNITEC LONDON
Unit Unit 9 , Eurocourt, Olivers Close,
West Thurrock RM20 3EE
Tel: 08444 123222
Fax: 01708 869920
E-mail: london.service@optare.com

UNITEC ROTHERHAM
Denby Way, Hellaby, Rotherham S66 8HR
Tel: 01709 535101
Fax: 01709 535103
E-mail: rotherham.service@optare.com

UNITEC SCOTLAND
Unit 7, Cumbernauld Business Park,
Ward Park Road, Cumbernauld G67 3JZ
Tel: 01236 726738
Fax: 01236 795651
E-mail: scotland.service@optare.com

WEBASTO PRODUCT UK LTD
Webasto House, White Rose Way,
Doncaster DN4 5JH
Tel: 01302 322232
Fax: 01302 322231
E-mail: info@webastouk.com
Web site: www.webasto.co.uk

Audio/Video Systems

AFTERMARKET COACH SUPPLIES (UK) LTD
Unit A, The Etate Office, Arthingworth,
Market Harborough. LE16 8JT
Tel: 0858 525344
Web site: www.acsuk2.abelalways.co.uk

AUTOSOUND LTD
4 Lister Street, Dudley Hill,
Bradford BD4 9PQ
Tel: 01274 688990
Fax: 01274 651318
Web site: www.autosound.co.uk
E-mail: sales@autosound.co.uk

AVT SYSTEMS LTD
Unit 3 & 4, Tything Road, Arden Forest
Trading Estate, Alcester B49 6ES
Tel: 01789 400357
Fax: 01789 400359
E-mail: enquiries@avtsystems.co.uk
Web site: www.avtsystems.co.uk

EXPRESS COACH REPAIRS LTD
Outgang Lane, Pickering YO18 7EL
Tel: 01751 475215.
Fax: 01751475215
Web Site: www.expresscoachrepairs.co.uk

FCAV & CO
Brooklyn House, Coleford Road,
Bream GL15 6EU
Tel: 01594 564552
Fax: 01594 564556
E-mail: info@fcav.co.uk
Web site: www.fcav.co.uk

PSV PRODUCTS
PO Box 166, Warrington WA4 5FG
Tel: 0844 686 4488
Fax: 01925 601534
E-mail: info@psvproducts.com
Web site: www.psvproducts.com

Trade Directory

UNITEC
Parts Division, Denby Way, Hellaby, Rotherham S66 8HR
Tel: 01709 792000
Fax: 01709 792009
E-mail: parts@optare.com

Badges - Drivers/Conductors

GSM-ABBOT BROWN
Castlegarth Works, Thirsk, YO7 1PS
Tel: 01845 522184
Fax: 01845 522206
E-mail: gsmgraphicarts@gsmgroup.co.uk
Web Site: www.gsmabbotbrown.co.uk

MARK TERRILL PSV BADGES
5 De Grey Close, Lewes BN7 2JR
Tel: 01273 474816
Fax: 01273 474816
Mobile: 07770 666159

TRANSPORTATION MANAGEMENT SOLUTIONS
PO Box 15174, Glasgow G3 6WB
Tel: 0141 332 4733
Fax: 0141 354 0076
E-mail: tramsol@aol.com

Batteries

ARRIVA BUS AND COACH
Lodge Garage, Whitehall Road West, Cleckheaton BD19 4BJ
Tel: 01274 681 144
Fax: 01274 651 198
E-mail: busandcoachsales@arriva.co.uk
Web: www.arrivabusandcoach.co.uk

BETA RESEARCH & DEVELOPMENT/ZEBRA BATTERIES
50 Goodsmoor Road, Sinfin, Derby DE24 9GN
Tel: 01332 770500
Fax: 01332 771591
Web site: www.betard.co.uk

CUMMINS UK
Rutherford Drive, Park Farm South, Wellingborough NN8 6AN
Tel: 01933 334200
Fax: 01933 334198
E-mail: cduksales@cummins.com
Web site: www.cummins-uk.com

ENECO LTD
Unit 6, Spring Copse Business Park, Slinfold RH13 0SZ
Tel: 01403 790114
Web site: www.eneco.co.uk

THOMAS HARDIE – WIGAN
Lockett Road, Ashton-in-Makerfield WN4 8DE.
Tel: 01942 505124
Fax: 01942 505119

LEXCEL POWER SYSTEMS PLC
35 Manor Road, Henley on Thames RG9 1LU.
Tel: 01491 874414
E-mail: sales@lexcelpower.com
Web site: www.lexcelpower.com

MASS SPECIAL ENGINEERING LTD
Houghton Road, North Anston S25 4JJ
Tel: 01909 550480
Fax: 01909 550486

PARTLINE LTD
Dockfield Road, Shipley BD17 7AZ
Tel: 01274 531531
Fax: 01274 531088
E-mail: sales@partline.co.uk
Web site: www.partline.co.uk

PLAXTON COACH SALES CENTRE
Ryton Road, Anston, Sheffield S25 4DL
Tel: 01909 551155
Fax: 01909 567994
E-mail: coaches@plaxtonlimited.co.uk
Web site: www.plaxtonlimited.co.uk

POWER BATTERIES (GB) LTD
Units 5-8, Canal View Business Park, Wheelhouse Road, Rugeley WS15 1UY
Tel: 01889 571100
Fax: 01889 577342
Web site: www.bannerbatteriescom

UNITEC
Parts Division, Denby Way, Hellaby, Rotherham S66 8HR
Tel: 01709 792000
Fax: 01709 792009
E-mail: parts@optare.com

UNITEC LONDON
Unit 9, Eurocourt, Olivers Close, West Thurrock RM20 3EE
Tel: 08444 123222
Fax: 01708 869920
E-mail: london.service@optare.com

UNITEC ROTHERHAM
Denby Way, Hellaby, Rotherham S66 8HR
Tel: 01709 535101
Fax: 01709 535103
E-mail: rotherham.service@optare.com

UNITEC SCOTLAND
Unit 7, Cumbernauld Business Park, Ward Park Road, Cumbernauld G67 3JZ
Tel: 01236 726738
Fax: 01236 795651
E-mail: scotland.service@optare.com

VARTA AUTOMOTIVE BATTERIES LTD
Broadwater Park, North Orbital Road, Denham UB9 5AG
Tel: 01895 838999
Fax: 01895 838981
Web site: www.varta-automotive.com

Body/Electrical Repairs & Refurbishing

AD COACH SALES
Newbridge Coach Depot, Witheridge EX16 8PY
Tel: 01884 860787
Fax: 01884 860711
E-mail: enquiries@adcoachsales.co.uk
Web site: www.adcoachsales.co.uk

ARRIVA BUS AND COACH
Lodge Garage, Whitehall Road West, Cleckheaton BD19 4BJ
Tel: 01274 681 144
Fax: 01274 651 198
E-mail: busandcoachsales@arriva.co.uk
Web Site: www.arrivabusandcoach.co.uk

AVS STEPS LTD
Alders Farmhouse, Alders Lane, Whixall SY13 2BR
Tel: 01948 880010
Fax: 01948 880020
E-mail: sales@avssteps.co.uk
Web site: www.avssteps.co.uk

BLACKPOOL COACH SERVICES
Moss Hey Garage, Chapel Road, Blackpool FY4 5HU.
Tel/Fax: 01253 698686

BRISTOL BUS & COACH SALES
6/7 Freestone Road, St Philips, Bristol BS2 0QN
Tel: 0117 971 0251
Fax: 0117 972 3121
E-mail: andrew.munden@bristolbusandcoach.co.uk
Web site: www.bristolbusandcoach.co.uk

BULWARK BUS & COACH ENGINEERING LTD
Gate 3, Bulwark Industrial Estate, Chepstow NP16 5QZ
Tel: 01291 622326
Fax: 01291 622726.

CARLYLE BUS & COACH LTD
Carlyle Business Park, Great Bridge Street, Swan Village, West Bromwich B70 0X4
Tel: 0121 524 1200
Fax: 0121 524 1201
E-mail: admin@carlyleplc.co.uk
Web Site: www.carlyleplc.co.uk

CHANNEL COMMERCIALS PLC
Unit 6, Cobbs Wood Industrial Estate, Brunswick Road, Ashford TN23 1EH
Tel: 01233 629272.
Fax: 01233 636322.
E-mail: info@ccplc.co.uk

CONCEPT COACHCRAFT LTD
Far Cromwell Road. Bredbury, Stockport SK6 2SE
Tel: 0161 406 9322
Fax: 0161 406 9588
E-mail: sales@conceptcoachcraft.com
Web site: www.conceptcoachcraft.com.

CREST COACH CONVERSIONS
Unit 5, Holmeroyd Road, Bentley Moor Lane, Carcroft, Doncaster DN6 7BH
Tel: 01302 723723
Fax: 01302 724724

CROWN COACHBUILDERS LTD
32 Flemington Industrial Park, Flemington, Motherwell ML1 1SN
Tel: 01698 276087
Fax: 01698 262676
E-mail: davidgreer@hotmail.com
Web site: www.crowncoachbuilders.co.uk

EAST LANCASHIRE COACHBUILDERS LTD (ELC) (OPTARE PLC)
Lower Philips Road, Whitebirk Industrial Estate, Blackburn BB1 5UD
Tel: 01254 504150
Fax: 01254 504197
E-mail: john.horn@elcb.co.uk
Web site: www.elcb.co.uk

EASTGATE COACH TRIMMERS
3 Thornton Road Industrial Estate, Pickering YO18 7HZ
Tel/Fax: 01751 472229
E-mail: info@eastgate-coachtrimmers.co.uk
Web Site: eastgate-coachtrimmers.co.uk

EXPRESS COACH REPAIRS LTD
Outgang Lane, Pickering YO18 7EL.
Tel: 01751 475215.
Fax; 01751 475215
Web Site: www.expresscoachrepairs.co.uk

GHE
Unit 30, Fort Industrial Park, Fort Parkway, Castle Bromwich B35 7AR.
Tel: 0121 747 4400.
Fax: 0121 747 4977.
Web: www.ghegroup.com

HANTS & DORSET TRIM LTD
Canada Road, West Wellow SO51 6DE.
Tel: 023 8033 4335

THOMAS HARDIE – WIGAN
Lockett Road, Ashton-in-Makerfield, Wigan WN4 8DE.
Tel: 01942 505124.
Fax: 01942 505119

INVERTEC LTD
Whelford Road, Fairford GL7 4DT
Tel: 01285 713550
Fax: 01285 713548
Mobile: 07802 793828
E-mail: ian@invertec.co.uk
Web site: www.invertec.co.uk

THE LAWTON MOTOR BODY BUILDING CO LTD
Knutsford Road, Church Lawton, Stoke-on-Trent ST7 3DN
Tel: 01270 882056
Fax: 01270 883014
E-mail: enquiries@lawtonmotorbody.co.uk
Web site: www.lawtonmotorbody.co.uk

LEICESTER CARRIAGE BUILDERS
Marlow Road, Leicester LE3 2BQ
Tel: 0116 282 4270
Fax: 0116 263 0554
E-mail: rick.johnson@midlandsco-op.com
Web site: www.leicestercarriagebuilders.co.uk

MARTYN INDUSTRIALS LTD
5 Brunel Way, Durranhill Industrial Esate, Carlisle CA1 3NQ
Tel: 01228 544000
Fax: 01228 544001
E-mail: enquiries@martyn-industrials.co.uk
Web site: www.martyn-industrials.com

MASS SPECIAL ENGINEERING LTD
Houghton Road, North Anston. S25 4JJ.
Tel: 01909 550480.
Fax: 01909 550486

Coach Repairs & Refurbishment Specialists

All jobs of any size undertaken, full written estimates given including on-site inspections if required

Work carried out to the highest standard by experienced coachbuilders

Insurance Approved and pick-up and delivery service available

• Accident Repairs & Resprays • Conversions • Flooring
• Internal Fitting (Audio, Serveries, Toilets, Video Etc)
• Re-panelling Inc Stretch Panels • Seat Conversions Inc Up seating
• Vintage Restorations • Vinyl Lettering

LANCASTER ROAD, CARNABY INDUSTRIAL ESTATE, BRIDLINGTON, EAST YORKSHIRE YO15 3QY
Tel: 01262 603307 Mobile: 07787 576603 Fax: 01262 608208
Email: info@wilkinsonsvehiclesolutions.co.uk
www.wilkinsonsvehiclesolutions.co.uk

MCV BUS & COACH LTD
Sterling Place, Elean Business Park, Sutton CB6 2QE
Tel: 01353 773000
Fax: 01353 773001
E-mail: vernon.edwards@mcv-uk.com

MELLOR COACHCRAFT
Miall Street, Rochdale OL11 1HY
Tel: 01706 860610
Fax: 01706 860042
E-mail: mcsales@woodhall-nicholson.co.uk
Web site: www.woodhall-nicholson.co.uk

MOSELEY (PCV) LTD
Elmsall Way, Dale Lane, South Elmsall WF9 2XS
Tel: 01977 609000
Fax: 01977 609900
Web Site: www.moseleycoachsales.co.uk

NEXT BUS LTD
The Coach Yard, Vincients Road, Bumpers Farm Industrial Estate, Chippenham SN14 6QA
Tel: 01249 462462
Fax: 01249 448844
E-mail: sales@next-bus.co.uk
Web site: www.next-bus.co.uk

OLYMPUS COACHCRAFT LTD
7 Temperance Street, Manchester M12 6HR
Tel/Fax: 0161 273 4259
E-mail: geofolympus@aol.com
Web site: www.olympuscoaches.co.uk

PARTLINE LTD
Dockfield Road, Shipley BD17 7AZ
Tel: 01274 531531
Fax: 01274 531088
E-mail: sales@partline.co.uk
Web site: www.partline.co.uk

PLAXTON
Plaxton Park, Cayton Low Road, Eastfield, Scarborough YO11 3BY
Tel: 01723 581500
Fax: 01723 5813238
E-mail: sales@plaxtonlimited.co.uk
Web site: www.plaxtonlimited.co.uk

PLAXTON COACH SALES CENTRE
Ryton Road, Anston, Sheffield S25 4DL
Tel: 01909 551155
Fax: 01909 567994
E-mail: coaches@plaxtonlimited.co.uk
Web site: www.plaxtonlimited.co.uk

RH BODYWORKS
A140 Ipswich Road, Brome, Eye IP23 8AW
Tel: 01379 870666
Fax: 01379 872106
E-mail: mike.ball@rhbodyworks.co.uk
Web site: www.rhbodyworks.co.uk

TRAMONTANA COACH DISTRIBUTORS
Chapelknowe Road, Carfin, Motherwell ML1 5LE
Tel: 01698 861790
Fax: 01698 860778
E-mail: wdt90@tiscali.co.uk
Web: www.tramontanacoach.co.uk

TRUCKALIGN CO LTD
VIP Trading Estate, Anchor & Hope Lane, London SE7 7RY
Tel: 020 8858 3781
Fax: 020 8858 3781
E-mail: tony.rodwell@dsl.pipex.com

Trade Directory

UNITEC
Parts Division, Denby Way, Hellaby,
Rotherham S66 8HR
Tel: 01709 792000
Fax: 01709 792009
E-mail: parts@optare.com

UNITEC LONDON
Unit 9, Eurocourt, Olivers Close,
West Thurrock RM20 3EE
Tel: 08444 123222
Fax: 01708 869920
E-mail: london.service@optare.com

UNITEC ROTHERHAM
Denby Way, Hellaby, Rotherham S66 8HR
Tel: 01709 535101
Fax: 01709 535103
E-mail: rotherham.service@optare.com

UNITEC SCOTLAND
Unit 7, Cumbernauld Business Park, Ward Park Road, Cumbernauld G67 3JZ
Tel: 01236 726738
Fax: 01236 795651
E-mail: scotland.service@optare.com

VOLVO BUS AND COACH CENTRE
Belton Road West,
Loughborough LE11 5HP
Tel: 01509 217777
Fax: 01509 239362
Web site: www.volvo.com

WILKINSONS VEHICLE SOLUTIONS
62 Scalby Avenue,
Scarborough YO12 6HP
Tel: 01262 603307
Fax: 01262 608208

Bicycle Carriers

JES BUSCYCLE
27-33 High Street, Totton SO40 9HL
Tel: 023 8066 3535

Brakes and Brake Linings

ARRIVA BUS AND COACH
Lodge Garage, Whitehall Road West,
Cleckheaton BD19 4BJ
Tel: 01274 681 144
Fax: 01274 651 198
E-mail: busandcoachsales@arriva.co.uk
Web: www.arrivabusandcoach.co.uk

ARVIN MERITOR
Unit 21, Suttons Park Avenue,
Reading RG6 1LA.
Tel: 0118 935 9126
Web site: www.arvinmeritor.com

BBA FRICTION LTD
PO Box 18, Hunsworth Lane,
Cleckheaton BD19 3UJ.
Tel: 01274 854000.
Fax: 01274 854001.

CAPARO AP BRAKING LTD
Tachbrook Road,
Leamington Spa CV31 3SF.
Tel: 01926 473737.
Fax: 01926 473836
E-Mail:
sales.enquiries@caparoapbraking.com
Web Site: www.caparobraking.co.ltd

DIRECT PARTS LTD
Unit 1, Churnet Court, Churnetside Business Park, Harrison Way, Cheddleton ST13 7EF
Tel: 01538 361777
Fax: 01538 369100
E-mail: sales@direct-group.co.uk
Web site: www.direct-group.co.uk

ERENTEK LTD
Malt Kiln Lane, Waddington,
Lincoln LN5 9RT
Tel: 01522 720065
Fax: 01522 729155
E-mail: sales@erentek.co.uk
Web site: www.erentek.co.uk

HART BROTHERS (ENGINEERING) LTD
Albion Works, Cobden Street,
Salford M6 6LY
Tel: 0161 737 6791

IMEXPART LTD
Links 31, Willowbridge Way,
Whitwood, Castleford WF10 5NP
Tel: 01977 553936
Fax: 01977 604684
E-mail: parts@imexpart.com
Web site: www.imexpart.com

IMPERIAL ENGINEERING
Delamare Road, Cheshunt EN8 9UD
Tel: 01992 6342555
Fax: 01992 630506
E-mail: sales@imperialengineering.co.uk
Web site: www.imperialengineering.co.uk

KELLETT (UK) LTD
8 Stevenson Way, Sheffield S9 3WZ.
Tel: 0114 261 1122
Fax: 0114 261 1199
E-mail: sales@kellett.co.uk

KNORR-BREMSE SYSTEMS FOR COMMERCIAL VEHICLES LTD
Douglas Road, Kingswood, Bristol BS15 8NL.
Tel: 0117 984 6100
Fax: 0117 984 6101
Web site: www.knorr-bremse.com

PARTLINE LTD
Dockfield Road, Shipley BD17 7AZ
Tel: 01274 531531
Fax: 01274 531088
E-mail: sales@partline.co.uk
Web site: www.partline.co.uk

P & P SERGEANT (B & A) LTD
PO Box 11, New Hall Lane, Hoylake, Wirral CH47 4DH
Tel: 01516 325 903
Fax: 01516 325 908
E-mail: enq@sergeant.co.uk
Web Site: www.sergeant.co.uk

ROADLINK INTERNATIONAL LTD
Strawberry Lane, Willenhall WV13 3RL
Tel: 01902 636210
Fax: 01902 606604
E-mail: sales@roadlink-international.co.uk
Web site: www.roadlink-international.co.uk

UNITEC
Parts Division, Denby Way, Hellaby,
Rotherham S66 8HR
Tel: 01709 792000
Fax: 01709 792009
E-mail: parts@optare.com

UNITEC LONDON
Unit 9, Eurocourt, Olivers Close, West Thurrock RM20 3EE
Tel: 018444 123222
Fax: 01708 869920
E-mail: london.service@optare.com

UNITEC ROTHERHAM
Denby Way, Hellaby, Rotherham S66 8HR
Tel: 01709 535101
Fax: 01709 535103
E-mail: rotherham.service@optare.com

UNITEC SCOTLAND
Unit 7, Cumbernauld Business Park, Ward Park Road, Cumbernauld G67 3JZ
Tel: 01236 726738
Fax: 01236 795651
E-mail: scotland.service@optare.com

WABCO AUTOMOTIVE UK
Texas Street, Leeds LS27 0HQ
Tel: 0113 251 2510
Fax: 0113 251 2844
Web; www.wabco-auto.com

WINCHESTER MARINE LTD (MAJORLINE ENGINEERING)
Baybridge Industrial Units, Baybridge Lane, Owslebury, Winchester SO21 1JN.
Tel: 01962 777077
Fax: 01962 777661, 777667
E-mail: winchestermarine@btconnect.com

Cash Handling Equipment

CUMMINS-ALLISON LTD
William H Klotz House, Colonnade Point, Central Boulevard, Progolis Park, Coventry CV6 4BU
Tel: 0800 0186484
Fax: 024 7633 9811
E-mail: sales@cumminsallison.co.uk
Web site: www.cumminsallison.co.uk

CASH PROCESSING SOLUTIONS LTD
Unit 26-27, Portland Court, Kingsway, Luton LU4 8HA
Tel: 01582 402318
Fax: 01582 402318
E-mail: info@cashprocessing.co.uk
Web site: www.cashprocessing.co.uk

ETMSS LTD
C/O Dorset House, 9 Dorset Avenue, Ferndown, Dorset BH22 8HJ
Tel: 0844 800 9299
E-mail: info@etmss.com
Web Site: www.etmss.com

JOHN GROVES TICKET SYSTEMS
12 Magnet Road, EAst Lane Business Park, Wembley HA9 7RG
Tel: 0208 908 9088
Fax: 0208 908 9099
E-Mail: sales@jgts.co.uk
Web site: www.jgts.co.uk

MARK TERRILL TICKET MACHINERY
5 De Grey Close, Lewes BN7 2JR.
Tel: 01273 474816
Fax: 01273 474816
E-mail: mark.terrill@ukonline.co.uk

Trade Directory

QUICK CHANGE (UK) LTD
Yew Tree Cottage, Newcastle,
Monmouthshire
Tel: 01600 750 650
Fax: 01600 750 650
E-mail: info@qchange,org
Web Site: www.qchange.org

SCAN COIN LTD
110 Broadway, Salford Quays M50 2UW
Tel: 0161 873 0505
Fax: 0161 873 0501
E-mail: sales@scancoin.co.uk
Web site: www.scancoin.co.uk

THOMAS AUTOMATICS CO LTD
Bishop Meadow Road,
Loughborough LE11 5RE
Tel: 01509 267611
Fax: 01509 266836
E-mail: sales@thomasa.co.uk
Web site: www.thomasa.co.uk

TRANSPORT TICKET SERVICES LTD
Yew Tree Cottage, Newcastle,
Monmouth NP25 5NT
Tel/Fax: 01600 750650
E-mail: ttsservices@tiscali.com
Web site: www.ticket-machines.co.uk

Chassis Lubricating Systems

PARTLINE LTD
Dockfield Road, Shipley BD17 7AZ
Tel: 01274 531531
Fax: 01274 531088
E-mail: sales@partline.co.uk
Web site: www.partline.co.uk

Clutches

ARRIVA BUS AND COACH
Lodge Garage, Whitehall Road West,
Cleckheaton BD19 4BJ
Tel: 01274 681 144
Fax: 01274 651 198
E-mail: busandcoachsales@arriva.co.uk
Web Site: www.arrivabusandcoach.co.uk

ASHLEY BANKS LTD
5 King Street Estate, Langtoft, Peterborough
PE6 9NF
Tel: 01778 560651
Fax: 01778 560721
E-mail: user@ashleybanks.fsnet.co.uk

BBA FRICTION LTD
PO Box 18, Hunsworth Lane, Cleckheaton
BD19 3UJ.
Tel: 01274 854000.
Fax: 01274 854001.

BUSS BIZZ
Goughs Transport Depot, Morestead,
Winchester SO21 1JD.
Tel: 01962 715555/66.
Fax: 01962 714868.

CAPARO AP BRAKING LTD
Tachbrook Road, Leamington Spa CV31
3ER.
Tel: 01926 473737
Fax: 01926 473836
Email: -
sales.enquiries@caparoapbraking.com
Web Site: www.caproapbraking.com

COACH-AID
Unit 2, Brindley Close, Tollgate Industrial
Estate, Stafford ST16 3SU
Tel: 01785 222666
E-mail: workshop@coach-aid.com
Web site: www.coach-aid.com

EATON LTD
Truck Components Marketing,
PO Box 11, Worsley Road North,
Worsley M28 5GJ.
Tel: 01204 797219.
Fax: 01204 797204.

IMEXPART LTD
Links 31, Willowbridge Way,
Whitwood, Castleford WF10 5NP
Tel: 01977 553936
Fax: 01977 604684
E-mail: parts@imexpart.com
Web site: www.imexpart.com

KELLETT (UK) LTD
8 Stevenson Way, Sheffield S9 3WZ.
Tel: 0114 261 1122.
Fax: 0114 261 1199.
E-mail: sales@kellett.co.uk

PARTLINE LTD
Dockfield Road, Shipley BD17 7AZ
Tel: 01274 531531
Fax: 01274 531088
E-mail: sales@partline.co.uk
Web site: www.partline.co.uk

---

transport **counts on it**

CUMMINS COUNTS EURO

The Advanced Model 1000 from Cummins

- Counts, sorts and batches mixed coins fast
- Flashcard technology for quick and easy software upgrades
- Prints audit trail
- **We also provide a range of note counters and mixed note scanners**

CUMMINS
CUMMINS-ALLISON LTD.

0800 0186484
www.cumminsallison.co.uk

23

⚡ SCAN COIN

AUTOMATED CASH DEPOSITING SYSTEM

Fast and accurate processing of bank notes, coins and transport tokens plus dropsafe for depositing of non-cash items.

Safe, secure and easy to use.

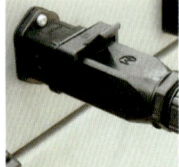
Network capability

Fast coin deposit

High capacity printer

Envelope dropsafe

Note acceptance

- Easy to install, through-the-wall or free-standing
- Front or rear access for changing vaults and for servicing
- Fully customisable user interface
- All totals displayed on-screen
- Multiple coin acceptance and value counting
- Bank notes accepted in any direction
- Vehicle defect reporting
- Exchange rates can be programmed into the system
- Wide range of additional software available

SCAN COIN Ltd
Dutch House, 110 Broadway Salford Quays
Salford M50 2UW

CALL 0161 873 0505
VISIT www.scancoin.co.uk
EMAIL sales@scancoin.co.uk

P & P SERGEANT (B&A) LTD
PO Box 11, New Hall Lane,
Hoylake CH47 4DH
Tel: 0151 632 5903
Fax: 0151 632 5908
E-mail: enq@sergeant.co.uk
Web site: www.sergeant.co.uk

SHAWSON SUPPLY LTD
12 Station Road, Saintfield, County Down,
Northern Ireland BT24 7DU
Tel: 028 9751 0994
Fax: 028 9751 0816
E-mail: info@shawsonsupply.com
Web site: www.shawsonsupply.com

UNITEC
Parts Division, Denby Way,
Hellaby, Rotherham S66 8HR
Tel: 01709 792000
Fax: 01709 792009
E-mail: parts@optare.com

UNITEC LONDON
Unit 9, Eurocourt, Olivers Close,
West Thurrock RM20 3EE
Tel: 018444 123222
Fax: 01708 869920
E-mail: london.service@optare.com

UNITEC ROTHERHAM
Denby Way, Hellaby, Rotherham S66 8HR
Tel: 01709 535101
Fax: 01709 535103
E-mail: rotherham.service@optare.com

UNITEC SCOTLAND
Unit 7, Cumbernauld Business Park,
Ward Park Road, Cumbernauld G67 3JZ
Tel: 01236 726738
Fax: 01236 795651
E-mail: scotland.service@optare.com

WINCHESTER MARINE LTD (MAJORLINE ENGINEERING)
Baybridge Industrial Units, Baybridge Lane,
Owslebury, Winchester SO21 1JN.
Tel: 01962 777077.
Fax: 01962 777661, 777667
E-mail: winchester@bt.connect.com

Cooling Systems

ARRIVA BUS AND COACH
Lodge Garage, Whitehall Road West,
Cleckheaton BD19 4BJ
Tel: 01274 681 144
Fax: 01274 651 198
E-mail: busandcoachsales@arriva.co.uk
Web Site: www.arrivabusandcoach.co.uk

CLAYTON HEATERS LTD
Hunter Terrace, Fletchworth Gate,
Burnsall Road, Coventry CV5 6SP
Tel: 02476 691 916
Fax: 02476 691 969
E-mail: admin@claytoncc.co.uk
Web Site: www.claytoncc.co.uk

DIRECT PARTS LTD
Unit 1, Churnet Court, Churnetside Business
Park, Harrison Way, Cheddleton ST13 7EF
Tel: 01538 361777
Fax: 01538 369100
E-mail: sales@direct-group.co.uk
Web site: www.direct-group.co.uk

IMEXPART LTD
Links 31, Willowbridge Way,
Whitwood, Castleford WF10 5NP
Tel: 01977 553936
Fax: 01977 604684
E-mail: parts@imexpart.com
Web site: www.imexpart.com

PACET MANUFACTURING LTD
Wyebridge House, Cores End Road,
Bourne End SL8 5HH
Tel: 01628 526754
Fax: 01628 810080
E-mail: sales@pacet.co.uk
Web site: www.pacet.co.uk

PARTLINE LTD
Dockfield Road, Shipley BD17 7AZ
Tel: 01274 531531
Fax: 01274 531088
E-mail: sales@partline.co.uk
Web site: www.partline.co.uk

SILFLEX LTD
Coed Cae Lane Industrial Estate,
Pontyclun CF72 9HJ
Tel: 01443 238464
Fax: 01443 237781
E-mail: silflex@silflex.com
Web site: www.silflex.com

UNITEC LONDON
Unit 9, Eurocourt, Olivers Close,
West Thurrock RM20 3EE
Tel: 018444 123222
Fax: 01708 869920
E-mail: london.service@optare.com

UNITEC ROTHERHAM
Denby Way, Hellaby, Rotherham S66 8HR
Tel: 01709 535101
Fax: 01709 535103
E-mail: rotherham.service@optare.com

UNITEC SCOTLAND
Unit 7, Cumbernauld Business Park,
Ward Park Road, Cumbernauld G67 3JZ
Tel: 01236 726738
Fax: 01236 795651
E-mail: scotland.service@optare.com

WINCHESTER MARINE LTD (MAJORLINE ENGINEERING)
Baybridge Industrial Units, Baybridge Lane,
Owslebury, Winchester SO21 1JN.
Tel: 01962 777077.
Fax: 01962 777661, 777667
E-mail: winchester@bt.connect

Destination Indicator Equipment

BRIGHT-TECH DEVELOPMENTS LTD
Fleets Point House, Willis Way,
Poole BH15 3SS
Tel: 01202 679627
Fax: 01202 684579
E-mail: kpoultney@bright-tech.co.uk
Web site: www.bright-tech.co.uk

HANOVER DISPLAYS LTD
Unit 24, Cliffe Industrial Estate,
Lewes BN8 6JL
Tel: 01273 477528
Fax: 01273 407766
E-mail: sales@hanoverdisplays.com
Web site: www.hanoverdisplays.com

INDICATORS INTERNATIONAL LTD
41 Aughrim Road, Magherafelt,
Northern Ireland BT45 6JX.
Tel: 028 7963 2591.
Fax: 028 7963 3927.
E-mail: sales@indicators-int.com
Web site: www.indicators-int.com

INVERTEC LTD
Whelford Road, Fairford GL7 4DT
Tel: 01285 713550
Fax: 01285 713548
Mobile: 07802 793828
E-mail: sales@invertec.co.uk
Web site: www.invertec.co.uk

McKENNA BROTHERS LTD
McKenna House, Jubilee Road, Middleton,
Manchester M24 2LX
Tel: 0161 655 3244
Fax: 0161 655 3059
E-mail: info@mckennabrothers.co.uk
Web site: www.mckennabrothers.co.uk

NORBURY BLINDS LTD
41-45 Hanley Street, Newtown, Birmingham
B19 3SP
Tel: 0121 359 4311
Fax: 0121 359 6388
E-mail: info@norbury-blinds.com
Web site: www.norbury-blinds.com

PARTLINE LTD
Dockfield Road, Shipley BD17 7AZ
Tel: 01274 531531
Fax: 01274 531088
E-mail: sales@partline.co.uk
Web site: www.partline.co.uk

PERCY LANE PRODUCTS LTD
Lichfield Road, Tamworth B79 7TL
Tel: 01827 63821
Fax: 01827 310159
E-mail: sales@percy-lane.co.uk
Web site: www.percy-lane.co.uk

PLAXTON COACH SALES CENTRE
Ryton Road, Anston, Sheffield S25 4DL
Tel: 01909 551155
Fax: 01909 567994
E-mail: coaches@plaxtonlimited.co.uk
Web site: www.plaxtonlimited.co.uk

TOP GEARS DESTINATIONS
46 Fulwood Hall Lane, Fulwood,
Preston PR2 8DD
Tel/Fax: 01772 700536
E-mail: steve@pitlane-2000.com
Web site: www.pitlane-2000.com

VULTRON INTERNATIONAL LTD
Unit 2 Stadium Way, Elland Road,
Leeds LS11 0EW
Tel: 01133 877 310
Fax: 01133 877 317
E-mail: sales@vultron.co.uk
Web Site: www.vultron.co.uk

WEBASTO PRODUCT UK LTD
Webasto House, White Rose Way,
Doncaster Carr DN4 5JH
Tel: 01302 322232
Fax: 01302 322231
E-mail: info@webastouk.com
Web site: www.webasto.co.uk

Trade Directory

Door Operating Gear

AIR DOOR SERVICES
The Pavilions, Holly Lane Industrial Estate, Atherstone CV9 2QZ
Tel: 01827 11660
Fax: 01827 713577
E-mail: airdoorservices@aol.com

CARLYLE BUS & COACH LTD
Carlyle Business Park, Great Bridge Street, Swan Village, West Bromwich B70 0X4
Tel: 0121 524 1200
Fax: 0121 524 1201
E-mail: admin@carlyleplc.com
Web Site: www.carlyleplc.co.uk

CRESCENT FACILITIES LTD
72 Willow Crescent, Chapeltown, Sheffield S35 1QS
Tel/fax: 0114 2451050
E-mail: cfl.chris@btinternet.com
Web site: www.cflparts.com

DEANS SYSTEMS (UK) LTD
PO Box 8, Borwick Drive, Grovehill, Beverley HU17 0HQ
Tel: 01482 868111
Fax: 01482 881890
E-mail: customerservice@deanssystems.com
Web Site: www.deanssystems.com

ERENTEK LTD
Malt Kiln Lane, Waddington, Lincoln LN5 9RT
Tel: 01522 720065
Fax: 01522 729155
E-mail: sales@erentek.co.uk
Web site: www.erentek.co.uk

KELLETT (UK) LTD
8 Stevenson Way, Sheffield S9 3WZ.
Tel: 0114 261 1122.
Fax: 0114 261 1199.
E-mail: sales@kellett.co.uk

KARIVE LIMITED
PO Box 205, Southam CV47 0ZL
Tel: 01926 813938
Fax: 01926 814898
E-mail: karive.ltd@btinternet.com
Web site: www.karive.co.uk

KNORR-BREMSE SYSTEMS FOR COMMERCIAL VEHICLES LTD
Douglas Road, Kingswood, Bristol BS15 8NL.
Tel: 0117 984 6100.
Fax: 0117 984 6101.
Web site: www.knorr-bremse.com

THE LAWTON MOTOR BODY BUILDING CO LTD
Knutsford Road, Church Lawton, Stoke-on-Trent ST7 3DN
Tel: 01270 882056
Fax: 01270 883014
E-mail: enquiries@lawtonmotorbody.co.uk
Web site: www.lawtonmotorbody.co.uk

NEXT BUS LTD
The Coach Yard, Vincents Road, Bumpers Farm Industrial Estate, Chippenham SN14 6QA
Tel: 01249 462462
Fax: 01249 448 844
E-mail: sales@next-bus.co.uk
Web site: www.next-bus.co.uk

PARTLINE LTD
Dockfield Road, Shipley BD17 7AZ
Tel: 01274 531531
Fax: 01274 531088
E-mail: sales@partline.co.uk
Web site: www.partline.co.uk

PETERS DOOR SYSTEMS (UK) LTD
Bradbury Drive, Springwood Industrial Estate, Braintree CM7 2ET
Tel: 01376 555255
Fax: 01376 555292
E-mail: sales@petersdoors.co.uk

PLAXTON
Plaxton Park, Cayton Low Road, Eastfield, Scarborough YO11 3BY
Tel: 01723 581500
Fax: 01723 5813238
E-mail: sales@plaxtonlimited.co.uk
Web site: www.plaxtonlimited.co.uk

PLAXTON COACH SALES CENTRE
Ryton Road, Anston, Sheffield S25 4DL
Tel: 01909 551155
Fax: 01909 567994
E-mail: coaches@plaxtonlimited.co.uk
Web site: www.plaxtonlimited.co.uk

PNEUMAX LTD
Unit 8, Venture Industrial Park, Fareham Road, Gosport PO13 0BA
Tel: 01329 823999
Fax: 01329 822345
E-mail: sales@pneumax.co.uk
Web site: www.pneumax.co.uk

UNITEC
Parts Division, Denby Way, Hellaby, Rotherham S66 8HR
Tel: 01709 792000
Fax: 01709 792009
E-mail: parts@optare.com

UNITEC LONDON
Unit 9, Eurocourt, Olivers Close, West Thurrock RM20 3EE
Tel: 018444 123222
Fax: 01708 869920
E-mail: london.service@optare.com

UNITEC ROTHERHAM
Denby Way, Hellaby, Rotherham S66 8HR
Tel: 01709 535101
Fax: 01709 535103
E-mail: rotherham.service@optare.com

UNITEC SCOTLAND
Unit 7, Cumbernauld Business Park, Ward Park Road, Cumbernauld G67 3JZ
Tel: 01236 726738
Fax: 01236 795651
E-mail: scotland.service@optare.com

VAPOR-STONE UK LTD
2nd Avenue, Centrum 100, Burton-on-Trent DE14 3WF
Tel: 01283 743300
Fax: 01283 743333
Web site: www.wabtec.com

WABCO AUTOMOTIVE UK LTD
Texas Street, Morley LS27 0HQ.
Tel: 0113 251 2510
Fax: 0113 251 2844
Web Site: www.wabco-auto.com

Drinks Dispensing Equipment

BRADTECH LTD
Unit 3, Ladford Covert, Seighford, Stafford ST18 9QL
Tel: 01785 282800
Fax: 01785 282558
E-mail: sales@bradtech.ltd.uk
Web site: www.bradtech.ltd.uk

DRINKMASTER LTD
Drinkpac House, Plymouth Road, Liskeard PL14 3PG
Tel: 01579 342082
Fax: 01579 342591
E-mail: info@drinkmaster.co.uk
Web site: www.drinkmaster.co.uk

ELSAN LTD
Bellbrook Park, Uckfield TN22 1QF
Tel: 01825 748200
Fax: 01825 761212
E-mail: sales@elsan.co.uk
Web site: www.elsan.co.uk

THE LAWTON MOTOR BODY BUILDING CO LTD
Knutsford Road, Church Lawton, Stoke-on-Trent ST7 3DN
Tel: 01270 882056
Fax: 01270 883014
E-mail: enquiries@lawtonmotorbody.co.uk
Web site: www.lawtonmotorbody.co.uk

PLAXTON
Plaxton Park, Cayton Low Road, Eastfield, Scarborough YO11 3BY
Tel: 01723 581500
Fax: 01723 5813238
E-mail: sales@plaxtonlimited.co.uk
Web site: www.plaxtonlimited.co.uk

PSV PRODUCTS
PO Box 166, Warrington WA4 5FG
Tel: 0844 686 4488
Fax: 01925 601534
E-mail: info@psvproducts.com
Web site: www.psvproducts.com

SHADES TECHNICS LTD
Units E3 & E4, Rd Park, Stephenson Close, Hoddesdon, Hetrtfordshire EN11 0BW
Tel: 01992 501683
Fax: 01992 501669
E-mail: sales@shades-technics.com
Web site: www.shades-technics.com

Driving Axles & Gears

ALBION AUTOMOTIVE LTD
South Street, Scotstoun, Glasgow G14 0DT.
Tel: 0141 434 2400
Fax: 0141 959 6362
E-mail: sales@albion_auto.co.uk
Web site: www.albion_auto.co.uk

ARRIVA BUS AND COACH
Lodge Garage, Whitehall Road West, Cleckheaton BD19 4BJ
Tel: 01274 681 144
Fax: 01274 651 198
E-mail: busandcoachsales@arriva.co.uk
Web Site: www.arrivabusandcoach.co.uk

Trade Directory

ARVIN MERITOR
Unit 21, Suttons Park Avenue,
Reading RG6 1LA.
Tel: 0118 935 9126
Fax: 0118 935 9138
E-mail: james.randall@arvinmeritor.com
Web site: www.arvinmeritor.com

BUSS BIZZ
Goughs Transport Depot, Morestead,
Winchester SO21 1JD.
Tel: 01962 715555/66.
Fax: 01962 714868.

CRESCENT FACILITIES LTD
72 Willow Crescent, Chapeltown, Sheffield
S35 1QS
Tel/fax: 0114 2451050
E-mail: cfl.chris@btinternet.com
Web site: www.cflparts.com

DIRECT PARTS LTD
Unit 1, Churnet Court, Churnetside Business
Park, Harrison Way, Cheddleton ST13 7EF
Tel: 01538 361777
Fax: 01538 369100
E-mail: sales@direct-group.co.uk
Web site: www.direct-group.co.uk

EATON LTD
Truck Components Marketing, PO Box 11,
Worsley Road North,
Worsley M28 5GJ
Tel: 01204 797219.
Fax: 01204 797204.

HART BROTHERS (ENGINEERING) LTD
Albion Works, Cobden Streeet, Salford,
Manchester M6 6LY
Tel: 0161 737 6791

HL SMITH TRANSMISSIONS LTD
Enterprise Business Park, Cross Road,
Albrighton, Wolverhampton WV7 3BJ
Tel: 01902 373011
Fax: 01902 373608
Web Site: www.hlsmith.co.uk

IMPERIAL ENGINEERING
Delamare Road, Cheshunt EN8 9UD
Tel: 01992 6342555
Fax: 01992 630506
E-mail: sales@imperialengineering.co.uk
Web site: www.imperialengineering.co.uk

LH GROUP SERVICES LTD
Graycar Business Park, Barton Under
Needwood, Burton-on-Trent DE13 8EN
Tel: 01283 722600
Fax: 01283 722622
E-mail: lh@lh-group.com
Web site: www.lh-group.com

NEXT BUS LTD
The Coach Yard, Vincents Road, Bumpers
Farm Industrial Estate, Chippenham SN14 6QA
Tel: 01249 462462
Fax: 01249 448 844
E-mail: sales@next-bus.co.uk
Web site: www.next-bus.co.uk

PARTLINE LTD
Dockfield Road, Shipley BD17 7AZ
Tel: 01274 531531
Fax: 01274 531088
E-mail: sales@partline.co.uk
Web site: www.partline.co.uk

UNITEC
Parts Division, Denby Way, Hellaby,
Rotherham S66 8HR
Tel: 01709 792000
Fax: 01709 792009
E-mail: parts@optare.com

WINCHESTER MARINE LTD (MAJORLINE ENGINEERING)
Baybridge Industrial Units, Baybridge Lane,
Owslebury, Winchester SO21 1JN.
Tel: 01962 777077.
Fax: 01962 777661, 777667
E-mail: winchestermarine@btconnect

ZF POWERTRAIN
Stringes Close, Willenhall WV13 1LE
Tel: 01902 366000
Fax: 01902 366504
E-mail: sales@powertrain.org.uk
Web site: www.powertrain.org.uk

Electrical Equipment

AVT SYSTEMS LTD
Units 3 & 4 Tything Road, Arden Forest
Industrial Estate, Alcester B49 6ES
Tel: 01789 400357
Fax: 01789 400359
E-mail: enquires@avtsystems.co.uk
Web site: www.avtsystems.co.u

BRADTECH LTD
Unit 3, Ladford Covert, Seighford,
Stafford ST18 9QL
Tel: 01785 282800
Fax: 01785 282558
E-mail: sales@bradtech.ltd.uk
Web site: www.bradtech.ltd.uk

BRITAX PMG LTD
Bressingby Industrial Estate,
Bridlington YO16 4SJ
Tel: 01262 670161
Fax: 01262 605666
E-mail: info@britax-pmg.com
Web site: www.britax-pmg.com

CARLYLE BUS & COACH LTD
Carlyle Business Park, Great Bridge Street,
Swan Village, West Bromwich B70 0X4
Tel: 0121 524 1200
Fax: 0121 524 1201
E-mail: admin@carlyleplc.co.uk
Web Site: www.carlyleplc.co.uk

CRESCENT FACILITIES LTD
72 Willow Crescent, Chapeltown,
Sheffield S35 1QS
Tel/fax: 0114 2451050
E-mail: cfl.chris@btinternet.com
Web site: www.cflparts.com

DIRECT PARTS LTD
Unit 1, Churnet Court, Churnetside Business
Park, Harrison Way, Cheddleton ST13 7EF
Tel: 01538 361777
Fax: 01538 369100
E-mail: sales@direct-group.co.uk
Web site: www.direct-group.co.uk

IMEXPART LTD
Links 31, Willowbridge Way,
Whitwood, Castleford WF10 5NP
Tel: 01977 553936
Fax: 01977 604684
E-mail: parts@imexpart.com
Web site: www.imexpart.com

INTELLITEC LTD
VIP Trading Estate, Anchor & Hope Lane
Charlton, London SE7 7RY
Tel/Fax: 020 8858 3781
E-mail: sales@intellitec.co.uk
Web Site: www.intellitec.co.uk

INVERTEC LTD
Whelford Road, Fairford GL7 4DT
Tel: 01285 713550
Fax: 01285 713548
Mobile: 07802 793828
E-mail: ian@invertec.co.uk
Web site: www.invertec.co.uk

KARIVE LIMITED
PO Box 205, Southam CV47 0ZL
Tel: 01926 813938
Fax: 01926 814898
E-mail: karive.ltd@btinternet.com
Web site: www.karive.co.uk

LEXCEL POWER SYSTEMS PLC
35 Manor Road,
Henley on Thames RG9 1LU.
Tel: 01491 874414.
E-mail: sales@lexcelpower.com
Web site: lexcelpower.com

NEALINE WINDSCREEN WIPER PRODUCTS
Unit 1, The Sidings Industrial Estate,
Birdingbury Road, Marton CV23 9RX
Tel: 01926 633256
Fax: 01926 632600

PACEL ELECTRONICS
Fleets Point House, Willis Way,
Poole BH15 3SS
Tel: 01202 676616
Fax: 01202 681357
E-mail: sales@pacel.co.uk
Web site: www.pacel.co.uk

PACET MANUFACTURING LTD
Wyebridge House, Cores End Road,
Bourne End SL8 5HH
Tel: 01628 526754
Fax: 01628 810080
E-mail: sales@pacet.co.uk
Web site: www.pacet.co.uk

PARTLINE LTD
Dockfield Road, Shipley BD17 7AZ
Tel: 01274 531531
Fax: 01274 531088
E-mail: sales@partline.co.uk
Web site: www.partline.co.uk

PLAXTON
Plaxton Park, Cayton Low Road,
Eastfield, Scarborough YO11 3BY
Tel: 01723 581500
Fax: 01723 5813238
E-mail: sales@plaxtonlimited.co.uk
Web site: www.plaxtonlimited.co.uk

PLAXTON COACH SALES CENTRE
Ryton Road, Anston, Sheffield S25 4DL
Tel: 01909 551155
Fax: 01909 567994
E-mail: coaches@plaxtonlimited.co.uk
Web site: www.plaxtonlimited.co.uk

Trade Directory

PNEUMAX LTD
Unit 8, Venture Industrial Park,
Fareham Road, Gosport PO13 0BA
Tel: 01329 823999
Fax: 01329 822345
E-mail: sales@pneumax.co.uk
Web site: www.pneumax.co.uk

PRESTOLITE ELECTRIC
Unit 48, The Metropolitan Park, 12-16
Bristol Road, Greenford UB6 8UP
Tel: 020 8231 1137
Fax: 020 8575 9575
E-mail: eu_info@prestolite.com
Web site: www.prestolite.com

UNITEC
Parts Division, Denby Way,
Hellaby, Rotherham S66 8HR
Tel: 01709 792000
Fax: 01709 792009
E-mail: parts@optare.com

WINCHETER MARINE LTD (MAJORLINE ENGINEERING)
Baybridge Industrial Units, Baybridge Lane,
Owslebury, Winchester SO21 1JN.
Tel: 01962 777077.
Fax: 01962 777661, 777667
E-mail: wonchestermarine@btconnect.com

Electronic Control

ACTIA UK LTD
Unit 81, Mochdre Industrial Estate,
Newtown SY16 4LE
Tel: 01686 611150
Fax: 01686 621068
E-mail: mail@actia.co.uk
Web site: www.actia.co.uk

AVT SYSTEMS LTD
Unit 3, Tything Road, Arden Forest Trading
Estate, Alcester B49 6ES
Tel: 01789 400357
Fax: 01789 400359
E-mail: enquiries@avtsystems.co.uk
Web site: www.avtsystems.co.uk

CRESCENT FACILITIES LTD
72 Willow Crescent, Chapeltown, Sheffield
S35 1QS
Tel/fax: 0114 2451050
E-mail: cfl.chris@btinternet.com
Web site: www.cflparts.com

INTELLITEC LTD
14a Church Street, Rothersthorpe,
Northampton NN7 3JD
Tel/Fax: 01604 830 690
E-mail: sales@intellitec.co.uk
Web Site: www.intellitec.co.uk

KNORR-BREMSE SYSTEMS FOR COMMERCIAL VEHICLES LTD
Douglas Road, Kingswood,
Bristol BS15 8NL.
Tel: 0117 984 6100.
Fax: 0117 984 6101.
Web site: www.knorr-bremse.com

PARTLINE LTD
Dockfield Road, Shipley BD17 7AZ
Tel: 01274 531531
Fax: 01274 531088
E-mail: sales@partline.co.uk
Web site: www.partline.co.uk

UNITEC
Parts Division, Denby Way,
Hellaby, Rotherham S66 8HR
Tel: 01709 792000
Fax: 01709 792009
E-mail: parts@optare.com

VDO KIENZLE UK LTD
36 Gravelly Industrial Park,
Birmingham B24 8TA.
Tel: 0121 326 1234.
Fax: 0121 326 1299

WABCO AUTOMOTIVE UK
Texas Street, Morley LS27 0HQ.
Tel: 0113 251 2510.
Fax: 0113 251 2844.
Web Site: www.wabco-auto.com

Emission Control Devices

CUMMINS UK
Rutherford Drive, Park Farm South,
Wellingborough NN8 6AN
Tel: 01933 334200
Fax: 01933 334198
E-mail: cduksales@cummins.com
Web site: www.cummins-uk.com

DINEX EXHAUSTS LTD
14 Chesford Grange, Woolston,
Warrington WA1 4RE
Tel: 01925 849849
Fax: 01925 849850
E-mail: dinex@dinex.co.uk
Web site: www.dinex.dk

Suppliers of rotating electrics to the Bus & Coach Industry

THE POWER OF EXCELLENCE

www.prestolite.com   Sales Tel: + 44 20 8231 1137   Email: eu_info@prestolite.com

PARTLINE LTD
Dockfield Road, Shipley BD17 7AZ
Tel: 01274 531531
Fax: 01274 531088
E-mail: sales@partline.co.uk
Web site: www.partline.co.uk

PLAXTON
Plaxton Park, Cayton Low Road,
Eastfield, Scarborough YO11 3BY
Tel: 01723 581500
Fax: 01723 5813238
E-mail: sales@plaxtonlimited.co.uk
Web site: www.plaxtonlimited.co.uk

UNITEC
Parts Division, Denby Way, Hellaby,
Rotherham S66 8HR
Tel: 01709 792000
Fax: 01709 792009
E-mail: parts@optare.com

Engineering

ARRIVA BUS AND COACH
Lodge Garage, Whitehall Road West,
Cleckheaton BD19 4BJ
Tel: 01274 681 144
Fax: 01274 651 198
E-mail: busandcoachsales@arriva.co.uk
Web Site: www.arrivabusandcoach.co.uk

BUSS BIZZ
Goughs Transport Depot, Morestead,
Winchester SO21 1JD.
Tel: 01962 715555/66.
Fax: 01962 714868.

COACH-AID
Unit 2, Brindley Close, Tollgate Industrial
Estate, Stafford ST16 3SU
Tel: 01785 222666
E-mail: workshop@coach-aid.com
Web site: www.coach-aid.com

CUMMINS UK
Rutherford Drive, Park Farm South,
Wellingborough NN8 6AN
Tel: 01933 334200
Fax: 01933 334198
E-mail: cduksales@cummins.com
Web site: www.cummins-uk.com

DIRECT PARTS LTD
Unit 1, Churnet Court, Churnetside Business
Park, Harrison Way, Cheddleton ST13 7EF
Tel: 01538 361777
Fax: 01538 369100
E-mail: sales@direct-group.co.uk
Web site: www.direct-group.co.uk

ERENTEK LTD
Malt Kiln Lane, Waddington, Lincoln LN5 9RT
Tel: 01522 720065
Fax: 01522 729155
E-mail: sales@erentek.co.uk
Web site: www.erentek.co.uk

FTA VEHICLE INSPECTION SERVICE
Hermes House, St John's Road, Tunbridge Wells TN4 9UZ.
Tel: 01892 526171
Fax: 01892 534989
E-mail: enquiries@fta.co.uk
Web site: www.fta.co.uk

THOMAS HARDIE – WIGAN
Lockett Road, Ashton-in-Makerfield,
Wigan WN4 8DE.
Tel: 01942 505124.
Fax: 01942 505119.

HART BROTHERS (ENGINEERING) LTD
Albion Works, Cobden Street,
Salford, Manchester M6 6LY
Tel: 0161 737 6791

HILTECH DEVELOPMENTS
22 Larbre Crescent, Whickham,
Newcastle upon Tyne NE16 5YG
Tel: 0191 488 6258
Fax: 0191 488 9158
E-mail: executive@hiltechdevelopments.com
Web site: www.hiltechdevelopments.com

IMEXPART LTD
Links 31, Willowbridge Way,
Whitwood, Castleford WF10 5NP
Tel: 01977 553936
Fax: 01977 604684
E-mail: parts@imexpart.com
Web site: www.imexpart.com

IMPERIAL ENGINEERING
Delamare Road, Cheshunt EN8 9UD
Tel: 01992 6342555
Fax: 01992 630506
E-mail: sales@imperialengineering.co.uk
Web site: www.imperialengineering.co.uk

JBF SERVICES LTD
Southedge Works, Hipperholme,
Halifax HX3 8EF
Tel: 01422 202840
Fax: 01422 206070
E-mail: jbfservices@aol.com

LEYLAND PRODUCT DEVELOPMENTS LTD
Aston Way, Leyland, Preston PR26 7TZ
Tel: 01772 435834
E-mail: sales@lpdl.co.uk
Web site: www.lpdl.co.uk

LH GROUP SERVICES LTD
Graycar Business Park, Barton Under
Needwood, Burton-on-Trent DE13 8EN
Tel: 01283 722600
Fax: 01283 722622
E-mail: lh@lh-group.com
Web site: www.lh-group.com

MARSHALLS COMMERCIAL ENGINEERING LTD
Firbank Way, Leighton Buzzard LU7 4YP
Tel: 01525 375301
Fax: 01525 850967
Web site: www.mce-ltd.com

MASS SPECIAL ENGINEERING LTD
Houghton Road, North Anston,
Sheffield S25 4JJ
Tel: 01909 550480.
Fax: 01909 550486.

PLAXTON
Plaxton Park, Cayton Low Road,
Eastfield, Scarborough YO11 3BY
Tel: 01723 581500
Fax: 01723 5813238
E-mail: sales@plaxtonlimited.co.uk
Web site: www.plaxtonlimited.co.uk

PNEUMAX LTD
Unit 8, Venture Industrial Park, Fareham
Road, Gosport PO13 0BA
Tel: 01329 823999
Fax: 01329 822345
E-mail: sales@pneumax.co.uk
Web site: www.pneumax.co.uk

QUEENSBRIDGE (PSV) LTD
Milner Way, Longlands Industrial Estate,
Ossett WF5 9JE
Tel: 01924 281871
Fax: 01924 281807
E-mail: enquiries@queensbridgeltd.co.uk
Web site: www.queensbridgeltd.co.uk

TESLA VEHICLES LIMITED
22 Larbre Crescent, Whickham, Newxastle
Upon Tyne NE16 5YG
Tel: 01914 886 258
Fax: 01914 889 158
E-mail: info@telsavehicles.com
Web Site: www.teslavehicles.com

TRANSPORT DESIGN INTERNATIONAL
12 Waterloo Road Estate, Bidford on Avon
B50 4JH
Tel: 01789 490370
Fax: 01789 490592
E-mail: enquiries@tdi.uk.com
Web site: www.tdi.uk.com

UNITEC
Parts Division, Denby Way, Hellaby,
Rotherham S66 8HR
Tel: 01709 792000
Fax: 01709 792009
E-mail: parts@optare.com

UNITEC LONDON
Unit 9 Eurocourt, Olivers Close, West
Thurrock RM20 3EE
Tel: 08444123222
Fax: 01708 869920
E-mail: london.service@optare.com

UNITEC ROTHERHAM
Denby Way, Hellaby, Rotherham S66 8HR
Tel: 01709 535101
Fax: 01709 535103
E-mail: rotherham.service@optare.com

UNITEC SCOTLAND
Unit 7, Cumbernauld Business Park, Ward
Park Road, Cumbernauld G67 3JZ
Tel: 01236 726738
Fax: 01236 795651
E-mail: scotland.service@optare.com

WINCHESTER MARINE LTD (MAJORLINE ENGINEERING)
Baybridge Industrial Units, Baybridge Lane,
Owslebury, Winchester SO21 1JN.
Tel: 01962 777077.
Fax: 01962 777661, 777667
E-mail: winchestermarine@btconnect.com

Engines

ARRIVA BUS AND COACH
Lodge Garage, Whitehall Road West,
Cleckheaton BD19 4BJ
Tel: 01274 681 144
Fax: 01274 651 198
E-mail: busandcoachsales@arriva.co.uk
Web site: www.arrivabusandcoach.co.uk

Trade Directory

BUSS BIZZ
Goughs Transport Depot, Morestead, Winchester SO21 1JD.
Tel: 01962 715555/66.
Fax: 01962 714868.

CRAIG TILSEY & SON LTD
Unit 7, Moorfield Industrial Estate, Cotes Heath, Stoke-on-Trent ST21 6QY
Tel: 01782 791524
Fax: 01782 791316

CREWE ENGINES
Warmingham Road, Crewe CW1 4PQ
Tel: 01270 526333
Fax: 01270 526433
E-mail: sales@creweengines.co.uk
Web site: www.creweengines.co.uk

CUMMINS UK
Rutherford Drive, Park Farm South, Wellingborough NN8 6AN
Tel: 01933 334200
Fax: 01933 334198
E-mail: cduksales@cummins.com
Web site: www.cummins-uk.com

DAF COMPONENTS LTD
Eastern Bypass, Thame OX9 3FB
Tel: 01844 261111
Fax: 01844 217111
Web site: www.daftrucks.com.

DAYCO – TRANSPORT & TRADE DISTRIBUTION LTD
Davis House, Lodge Causeway Trading Estate, Fishponds, Bristol BS16 3JB.
Tel: 0117 965 9999.
Fax: 0117 965 4724.

DIESEL POWER ENGINEERING
Goughs Transport Depot, Morestead, Winchester SO21 1JD.
Tel/Fax: 01962 711314

HART BROTHERS (ENGINEERING) LTD
Albion Works, Cobden Street, Salford, Manchester M6 6LY
Tel: 0161 737 6791

IVECO
Iveco Ford Truck Ltd, Iveco Ford House, Station Road, Watford WD1 1SR.
Tel: 01923 246400.
Fax: 01923 240574.

LH GROUP SERVICES LTD
Graycar Business Park, Barton Under Needwood, Burton-on-Trent DE13 8EN
Tel: 01283 722600
Fax: 01283 722622
E-mail: lh@lh-group.com
Web site: www.lh-group.com

MAN TRUCK & BUS UK LTD
Frankland Road, Blagrove, Swindon SN5 8YU.
Tel: 01793 448000.
Fax: 01793 448262.

NEXT BUS LTD
The Coach Yard, Vincents Road, Bumpers Farm Industrial Estate, Chippenham SN14 6QA
Tel: 01249 462462
Fax: 01249 448844
E-mail: sales@next-bus.co.uk
Web site: www.next-bus.co.uk

PARTLINE LTD
Dockfield Road, Shipley BD17 7AZ
Tel: 01274 531531
Fax: 01274 531088
E-mail: sales@partline.co.uk
Web site: www.partline.co.uk

PERKINS GROUP LTD
Peterborough PE1 5NA.
Tel: 01733 567474.
Fax: 01733 582240.
Web site: www.perkins.com

QUEENSBRIDGE (PSV) LTD
Longlands Industrial Estate, Milner Way, Ossett WF5 9JE
Tel: 01924 281871
Fax: 01924 281807
E-mail: craig@queensbridgeltd.co.uk
Web site: www.queensbridgeltd.co.uk

SHAWSON SUPPLY LTD
12 Station Road, Saintfield, County Down, Northern Ireland BT24 7DU
Tel: 028 9751 0994
Fax: 028 9751 0816
E-mail: info@shawsonsupply.com
Web site: www.shawsonsupply.com

UNITEC
Parts Division, Denby Way, Hellaby, Rotherham S66 8HR
Tel: 01709 792000
Fax: 01709 792009
E-mail: parts@optare.com

UNITEC LONDON
Unit 9 Eurocourt, Olivers Close, West Thurrock RM20 3EE
Tel: 08444123222
Fax: 01708 869920
E-mail: london.service@optare.com

Mercedes engines

Highest quality, Lowest price.
Direct from the Uk's No.1 for 25 years.

also..

Join the UK's major bus & coach groups and choose Crewe Engines for Mercedes-Benz engines. From fast delivery of an exchange engine to collection of your vehicle and fitting of the engine, we have the expertise and resources to provide great service at very competitive prices.

ENGINES
- UK's No.1 for remanufactured Mercedes engines
- Also MAN, Cummins, Iveco, Volvo, DAF, etc
- Petrol & diesel, 1950's to present day, 4 cyl to V12
- Fast, friendly & efficient - excellent reputation

ENGINE PARTS
- Full range of highest quality original equipment parts
- Pistons, crankshaft bearings, gasket sets, etc
- Cylinder heads, camshafts, crankshafts, etc

Call now for a quote or free info-pack
☎ **01270 526333**

www.creweengines.co.uk
e-mail: sales@creweengines.co.uk

Crewe Engines Ltd

Trade Directory

UNITEC ROTHERHAM
Denby Way, Hellaby, Rotherham S66 8HR
Tel: 01709 535101
Fax: 01709 535103
E-mail: rotherham.service@optare.com

UNITEC SCOTLAND
Unit 7, Cumbernauld Business Park, Ward Park Road, Cumbernauld G67 3JZ
Tel: 01236 726738
Fax: 01236 795651
E-mail: scotland.service@optare.com

WALSH'S ENGINEERING LTD
Barton Moss Road, Eccles, Manchester M30 7RL
Tel: 0161 787 7017
Fax: 0161 787 7038
E-mail: walshs@gardnerdiesel.co.uk
Website: www.gardnerdiesel.co.uk

WEALDSTONE ENGINEERING
Sanders Lodge Industrial Estate, Rushden NN10 6AZ.
Tel: 01933 354600
Fax: 01933 354601
Web site: www.wealdstone.co.uk

WINCHESTER MARINE LTD (MAJORLINE ENGINEERING)
Baybridge Industrial Units, Baybridge Lane, Owslebury, Winchester SO21 1JN.
Tel: 01962 777077.
Fax: 01962 777661, 777667
E-mail: winchestermarine@btconnect.com

Engine Oil Drain Valves

FUMOTO ENGINEERING OF EUROPE
Normandy House, 35 Glategny Esplanade, St Peter Port, Guernsey GY1 2BP
Tel: 01481 716987
Fax: 01481 700374
E-mail: info@fumoto-valve.com

MARTYN INDUSTRIALS LTD
5 Brunel Way, Durranhill Industrial Esate, Carlisle CA1 3NQ
Tel: 01228 544000
Fax: 01228 544001
E-mail: enquiries@martyn-industrials.co.uk
Web site: www.martyn-industrials.com

PARTLINE LTD
Dockfield Road, Shipley BD17 7AZ
Tel: 01274 531531
Fax: 01274 531088
E-mail: sales@partline.co.uk
Web site: www.partline.co.uk

WALLMINSTER LTD
Unit 22, Chelsea Wharf, 15 Lots Road, London SW10 0QJ
Tel: 020 7352 2727
Fax: 020 7352 3990
E-mail: info@tankcontainers.co.uk

Exhaust Systems

ARRIVA BUS AND COACH
Lodge Garage, Whitehall Road West, Cleckheaton BD19 4BJ
Tel: 01274 681 144
Fax: 01274 651 198
E-mail: busandcoachsales@arriva.co.uk
Web site: www.arrivabusandcoach.co.uk

ARVIN MERITOR
Unit 21, Suttons Park Avenue, Reading RG6 1LA.
Tel: 0118 935 9126
Fax: 0118 935 9138
E-mail: james.randall@arvinmeritor.com
Web site: www.arvinmeritor.com

ASHLEY BANKS LTD
5 King Street Estate, Langtoft, Peterborough PE6 9NF
Tel: 01778 560651
Fax: 01778 560721
E-mail: user@ashleybanks.fsnet.co.uk

BUSS BIZZ
Goughs Transport Depot, Morestead, Winchester SO21 1JD.
Tel: 01962 715555/66.
Fax: 01962 714868.

CARLYLE BUS & COACH LTD
Carlyle Business Park, Great Bridge Street, Swan Village, West Bromwich B70 0X4
Tel: 0121 524 1200
Fax: 0121 524 1201
E-mail: admin@carlyleplc.co.uk
Web site: www.carlyleplc.co.uk

CRESCENT FACILITIES LTD
72 Willow Crescent, Chapeltown, Sheffield S35 1QS
Tel/fax: 0114 2451050
E-mail: cfl.chris@btinternet.com
Web site: www.cflparts.com

DINEX EXHAUSTS LTD
14 Chesford Grange, Woolston, Warrington WA1 4RE
Tel: 01925 849849
Fax: 01925 849850
E-mail: dinex@dinex.co.uk
Web site: www.dinex.dk

WALSH'S ENGINEERING LTD

COMMERCIAL DIESEL ENGINE SPECIALISTS

Barton Moss Road. Eccles. Manchester. M30 7RL

SUPPLIERS OF ALL TYPES OF RECONDITIONED ENGINE UNITS, PARTS AND SERVICE TO THE TRANSPORT INDUSTRY

FOR DETAILS CONTACT
CHARLIE HUGHES
OR
STEVE BRADLEY

TEL:- 0161 787 7017   FAX:- 0161 787 7038
E-MAIL:-walshs@gardnerdiesel.co.uk

Trade Directory

EMINOX LTD
North Warren Road,
Gainsborough DN21 2TU
Tel: 01427 810088
Fax: 01427 810061
E-mail: marketing@eminox.com
Web site: www.eminox.com

IMEXPART LTD
Links 31, Willowbridge Way,
Whitwood, Castleford WF10 5NP
Tel: 01977 553936
Fax: 01977 604684
E-mail: parts@imexpart.com
Web site: www.imexpart.com

PARTLINE LTD
Dockfield Road, Shipley BD17 7AZ
Tel: 01274 531531
Fax: 01274 531088
E-mail: sales@partline.co.uk
Web site: www.partline.co.uk

UNITEC
Parts Division, Denby Way,
Hellaby, Rotherham S66 8HR
Tel: 01709 792000
Fax: 01709 792009
E-mail: parts@optare.com

UNITEC LONDON
Unit 9 Eurocourt, Olivers Close,
West Thurrock RM20 3EE
Tel: 08444123222
Fax: 01708 869920
E-mail: london.service@optare.com

UNITEC ROTHERHAM
Denby Way, Hellaby, Rotherham S66 8HR
Tel: 01709 535101
Fax: 01709 535103
E-mail: rotherham.service@optare.com

UNITEC SCOTLAND
Unit 7, Cumbernauld Business Park,
Ward Park Road, Cumbernauld G67 3JZ
Tel: 01236 726738
Fax: 01236 795651
E-mail: scotland.service@optare.com

**WINCHESTER MARINE LTD
(MAJORLINE ENGINEERING)**
Baybridge Industrial Units, Baybridge Lane,
Owslebury, Winchester SO21 1JN.
Tel: 01962 777077.
Fax: 01962 777661, 777667
E-mail: winchestermarine@btconnect.com

Fans & Drive Belts

ARRIVA BUS AND COACH
Lodge Garage, Whitehall Road West,
Cleckheaton BD19 4BJ
Tel: 01274 681 144
Fax: 01274 651 198
E-mail: busandcoachsales@arriva.co.uk
Web: www.arrivabusandcoach.co.uk

BRT BEARINGS LTD
21-24 Regal Road, Wisbech,
Cambridgeshire PE13 2RQ
Tel: 01945 464 097
Fax: 01945 464 523
E-mail: info@brt-group.com

CARLYLE BUS & COACH LTD
Carlyle Business Park, Great Bridge Street,
Swan Village, West Bromwich B70 0X4
Tel: 0121 524 1200
Fax: 0121 524 1201
E-mail: admin@carlyleplc.co.uk
Web site: www.carlyleplc.co.uk

CLAYTON HEATERS LTD
Hunter Terrace, Fletchworth Gate,
Burnsall Road, Coventry CV5 6SP
Tel: 02476 691 916
Fax: 02476 691 969
E-mail: admin@claytoncc.co.uk
Web site: www.claytoncc.co.uk

CUMMINS UK
Rutherford Drive, Park Farm South,
Wellingborough NN8 6AN
Tel: 01933 334200
Fax: 01933 334198
E-mail: cduksales@cummins.com
Web site: www.cummins-uk.com

DIRECT PARTS LTD
Unit 1, Churnet Court, Churnetside Business
Park, Harrison Way, Cheddleton ST13 7EF
Tel: 01538 361777
Fax: 01538 369100
E-mail: sales@direct-group.co.uk
Web site: www.direct-group.co.uk

IMEXPART LTD
Links 31, Willowbridge Way,
Whitwood, Castleford WF10 5NP
Tel: 01977 553936
Fax: 01977 604684
E-mail: parts@imexpart.com
Web site: www.imexpart.com

PACET MANUFACTURING LTD
Wyebridge House, Cores End Road,
Bourne End SL8 5HH
Tel: 01628 526754
Fax: 01628 810080
E-mail: sales@pacet.co.uk
Web site: www.pacet.co.uk

PARTLINE LTD
Dockfield Road, Shipley BD17 7AZ
Tel: 01274 531531
Fax: 01274 531088
E-mail: sales@partline.co.uk
Web site: www.partline.co.uk

QUEENSBRIDGE (PSV) LTD
Longlands Industrial Estate, Milner Way,
Ossett WF5 9JE
Tel: 01924 281871
Fax: 01924 281807
E-mail: craig@queensbridgeltd.co.uk
Web site: www.queensbridgeltd.co.uk

UNITEC
Parts Division, Denby Way,
Hellaby, Rotherham S66 8HR
Tel: 01709 792000
Fax: 01709 792009
E-mail: parts@optare.com

**WINCHESTER MARINE LTD
(MAJORLINE ENGINEERING)**
Baybridge Industrial Units, Baybridge Lane,
Owslebury, Winchester SO21 1JN.
Tel: 01962 777077.
Fax: 01962 777661, 777667
E-mail: westministermarine@btconnect.com

Fare Boxes

M BISSELL DISPLAY LTD
Unit 15, Beechwood Business Park,
Burdock Close, Cannock WS11 7GB
Tel: 01543 502115
Fax: 01543 502118
E-mail: sales@bisselldisplay.com
Web site: www.bisselldisplay.com

**CUBIC TRANSPORTATION
SYSTEMS LTD**
AFC House, Honeycrock Lane,
Salfords RH1 5LA
Tel: 01737 782200
Fax: 01737 789759
Web site: www.cubic.com

ETMSS LTD
C/O Dorset House, 9 Dorset Avenue,
Ferndown, Dorset BH22 8HJ
Tel: 0844 800 9299
E-mail: info@etmss.com
Web: www.etmss.com

**JOHN GROVES
TICKET SYSTEMS**
12 Magnet Road, East Lane Business
Park Wembley HA9 7RG
Tel: 0208 908 9088
Fax: 0208 908 9099
E-mail: sales@jgts.co.uk
Web site: www.jgts.co.uk

**MARK TERRILL
TICKET MACHINERY**
5 De Grey Close, Lewes BN7 2JR.
Tel: 01273 474816
Fax: 01273 474816
E-mail: mark.terrill@ukonline.co.uk

Fire Extinguishers

ASHLEY BANKS LTD
5 King Street Estate, Langtoft,
Peterborough PE6 9NF
Tel: 01778 560651
Fax: 01778 560721
E-mail: user@ashleybanks.fsnet.co.uk

CARLYLE BUS & COACH LTD
Carlyle Business Park, Great Bridge Street,
Swan Village, West Bromwich B70 0X4
Tel: 0121 524 1200
Fax: 0121 524 1201
E-mail: admin@carlyleplc.co.uk
Web: www.carlyleplc.co.uk

CI COACHLINES
Pools Lane, Highwood, Essex CM1 3QL
Tel: 01245 248 669

**FIREMASTER
EXTINGUISHER LTD**
Firex House, 174-176 Hither Green Lane,
London SE13 6QB
Tel: 020 8852 8585
Fax: 020 8297 8020
E-mail: info@firemaster.co.uk
Web site: www.firemaster.co.uk

**HAPPICH V & I
COMPONENTS LTD**
Unit 30/31, Fort Industrial Park, Fort
Parkway, Castle Bromwich B35 7AR.
Tel: 0121 747 4400
Fax: 0121 747 4977
E-mail: sales@happich.co.uk
Web site: www.happich.co.uk

KELLETT (UK) LTD
8 Stevenson Way, Sheffield S9 3WZ.
Tel: 0114 261 1122.
Fax: 0114 261 1199.
E-mail: sales@kellett.co.uk

THE LAWTON MOTOR BODY BUILDING CO LTD
Knutsford Road, Church Lawton, Stoke-on-Trent ST7 3DN
Tel: 01270 882056
Fax: 01270 883014
E-mail: enquiries@lawtonmotorbody.co.uk
Web site: www.lawtonmotorbody.co.uk

PARTLINE LTD
Dockfield Road, Shipley BD17 7AZ
Tel: 01274 531531
Fax: 01274 531088
E-mail: sales@partline.co.uk
Web site: www.partline.co.uk

PLAXTON
Plaxton Park, Cayton Low Road, Eastfield, Scarborough YO11 3BY
Tel: 01723 581500
Fax: 01723 5813238
E-mail: sales@plaxtonlimited.co.uk
Web site: www.plaxtonlimited.co.uk

PLAXTON COACH SALES CENTRE
Ryton Road, Anston, Sheffield S25 4DL
Tel: 01909 551155
Fax: 01909 567994
E-mail: coaches@plaxtonlimited.co.uk
Web site: www.plaxtonlimited.co.uk

PSV PRODUCTS
PO Box 166, Warrington WA4 5FG
Tel: 0844 686 4488
Fax: 01925 601534
E-mail: info@psvproducts.com
Web site: www.psvproducts.com

SAFEGUARD
Kiln Lane, Swindon SN2 2NP
Tel: 01793 512999
Fax: 01793 511345

First Aid Equipment

ASHLEY BANKS LTD
5 King Street Estate, Langtoft, Peterborough PE6 9NF
Tel: 01778 560651
Fax: 01778 560721
E-mail: user@ashleybanks.fsnet.co.uk

BRADTECH LTD
Unit 3, Ladford Covert, Seighford, Stafford ST18 9QL
Tel: 01785 282800
Fax: 01785 282558
E-mail: sales@bradtech.ltd.uk
Web site: www.bradtech.ltd.uk

CARLYLE BUS & COACH LTD
Carlyle Business Park, Great Bridge Street, Swan Village, West Bromwich B70 0X4
Tel: 0121 524 1200
Fax: 0121 524 1201
E-mail: admin@carlyleplc.co.uk
Web site: www.carlyleplc.co.uk

CI COACHLINES
Pools Lane, Highwood, Essex CM1 3QL
Tel: 01245 248 669

FIREMASTER EXTINGUISHER LTD
Firex House, 174-176 Hither Green Lane, London SE13 6QB
Tel: 020 8852 8585
Fax: 020 8297 8020
E-mail: info@firemaster.co.uk
Web site: www.firemaster.co.uk

HAPPICH V & I COMPONENTS LTD
Unit 30/31, Fort Industrial Park, Fort Parkway, Castle Bromwich B35 7AR
Tel: 0121 747 4400
Fax: 0121 747 4977
E-mail: sales@happich.co.uk
Web site: www.happich.co.uk

PARTLINE LTD
Dockfield Road, Shipley BD17 7AZ
Tel: 01274 531531
Fax: 01274 531088
E-mail: sales@partline.co.uk
Web site: www.partline.co.uk

PLAXTON
Plaxton Park, Cayton Low Road, Eastfield, Scarborough YO11 3BY
Tel: 01723 581500
Fax: 01723 5813238
E-mail: sales@plaxtonlimited.co.uk
Web site: www.plaxtonlimited.co.uk

PLAXTON COACH SALES CENTRE
Ryton Road, Anston, Sheffield S25 4DL
Tel: 01909 551155
Fax: 01909 567994
E-mail: coaches@plaxtonlimited.co.uk
Web site: www.plaxtonlimited.co.uk

PSV PRODUCTS
PO Box 166, Warrington WA4 5FG
Tel: 0844 686 4488
Fax: 01925 601534
E-mail: info@psvproducts.com
Web site: www.psvproducts.com

SAFEGUARD
Kiln Lane, Swindon SN2 2NP
Tel: 01793 512999
Fax: 01793 511345

TRAMONTANA
Chapelknowe Road, Carfin, Motherwell ML1 5LE
Tel: 01698 861790
Fax: 01698 860778
E-mail: wdt90@tiscali.co.uk
Web site: www.tramontanacoach.co.uk

Floor Coverings

ALTRO
Works Road, Letchworth SG6 1NW
Tel: 01462 480480
Fax: 01462 480010
E-mail: lkni@altro.co.uk
Web site: www.altrotransfloor.com

AUTOMATE WHEEL COVERS LTD
California Mills, Oxford Road, Gomersal, Cleckheaton BD19 4HQ
Tel: 01274 862700
Fax: 01274 851989
E-mail: sales@wheelcovers.co.uk
Web site: www.wheelcovers.co.uk

AUTOMOTIVE TEXTILE INDUSTRIES
Unit 15 & 16, Priest Court, Springfield Business Park, Grantham NG31 7BG
Tel: 01476 593050
Fax: 01476 593607
E-mail: sales@autotex.com
Web site: www.autotex.com

CARLYLE BUS & COACH LTD
Carlyle Business Park, Great Bridge Street, Swan Village, West Bromwich B70 0X4
Tel: 0121 524 1200
Fax: 0121 524 1201
E-mail: admin@carlyleplc.co.uk
Web site: www.carlyleplc.co.uk

COACH CARPETS
Unit 12, Hamilton Street, Blackburn BB2 4AJ.
Tel: 01254 53549.
Fax: 01254 261873.

FIRTH FURNISHINGS LTD
Unit 6, Grange Road, Batley WF17 6LH.
Tel: 01924 478294
Fax: 01924 423729

THE LAWTON MOTOR BODY BUILDING CO LTD
Knutsford Road, Church Lawton, Stoke-on-Trent ST7 3DN
Tel: 01270 882056
Fax: 01270 883014
E-mail: enquiries@lawtonmotorbody.co.uk
Web site: www.lawtonmotorbody.co.uk

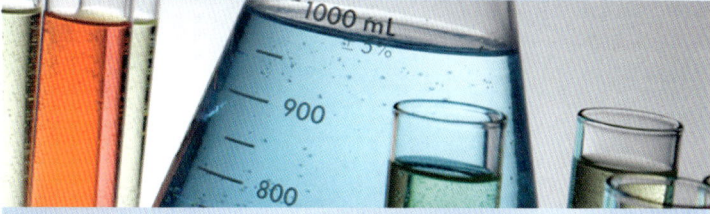

MARTYN INDUSTRIALS LTD
5 Brunel Way, Durranhill Industrial Esate, Carlisle CA1 3NQ
Tel: 01228 544000
Fax: 01228 544001
E-mail: enquiries@martyn-industrials.co.uk
Web site: www.martyn-industrials.com

PARTLINE LTD
Dockfield Road, Shipley BD17 7AZ
Tel: 01274 531531
Fax: 01274 531088
E-mail: sales@partline.co.uk
Web site: www.partline.co.uk

TIFLEX LTD
Tiflex House, Liskeard PL14 4NB
Tel: 01579 320808
Fax: 01579 320802
E-mail: marketing@tiflex.co.uk
Web site: www.tiflex.co.uk

TRIMPLEX SAFETY TREAD LTD
Trident Works, Mulberry Way, Belvedere DA17 6AN
Tel: 020 8311 2101
Fax: 020 8312 1400
E-mail: safetytread@btconnect.com
Web site: www.safetytread.co.uk

Fuel, Fuel Management & Lubricants

CUMMINS UK
Rutherford Drive, Park Farm South, Wellingborough NN8 6AN
Tel: 01933 334200
Fax: 01933 334198
E-mail: cduksales@cummins.com
Web site: www.cummins-uk.com

DIESEL DYE LTD
PO BOX 2094, Stoke on Trent ST7 2WR
Tel: 0845 0773921
E-mail: resh@dieseldye.com
Web site: www.dieseldye.com

INTERLUBE SYSTEMS LTD
St Modwen Road, Plymouth PL6 8LH
Tel: 01752 676000
Fax: 01752 676001
E-mail: info@interlubesystems.com
Web site: www.interlubesystems.com

JMW
Systems House, Pentland Industrial Estate, Loanhead EH20 9QH
Tel: 0131 440 3633
Fax: 0131 440 3637
E-mail: enquiries@jmw-group.co.uk
Web site: www.jmw-group.co.uk

PARTLINE LTD
Dockfield Road, Shipley BD17 7AZ
Tel: 01274 531531
Fax: 01274 531088
E-mail: sales@partline.co.uk
Web site: www.partline.co.uk

TRISCAN SYSTEMS LTD
Phoenix Park, Blackwater Road, Blackburn, Lancashire BB11 5RW
Tel: 08452 253 100
Fax: 08452 253 101
E-mail: info@triscansystems.com
Web: www.triscansystems.com

Garage Equipment

BUTTS OF BAWTRY GARAGE EQUIPMENT
Station Yard, Station Road, Bawtry, Doncaster DN10 6QD
Tel: 01302 710868
Fax: 01302 719481
E-mail: info@buttsequipment.com
Web site www.jhmbuttco.com

TERENCE BARKER TANKS
Phoenix Road, Havershill, Suffolk CB9 7EA
Tel: 01376 330661
Fax: 01440 715460
E-mail: sales.tbtanks.co.uk
Web site: www.terencebarkertanks.co.uk

DIRECT PARTS LTD
Unit 1, Churnet Court, Churnetside Business Park, Harrison Way, Cheddleton ST13 7EF
Tel: 01538 361777
Fax: 01538 369100
E-mail: sales@direct-group.co.uk
Web site: www.direct-group.co.uk

GEMCO EQUUIPMENT LTD
153-156 Bridge Street, Northampton NN1 1QG
Tel: 01604 828500
Fax: 01604 633159
E-mail: sales@gemco.co.uk
Web site: www.gemco.co.uk

MAJORLIFT HYDRAULIC EQUIPMENT LTD
Arnold's Field Industrial Estate, Wickwar, Wotton-under-Edge GL12 8JD
Tel: 01454 299299
Fax: 01454294003
Web site: www.majorlift.com
E-mail: info@majorlift.com

PHIL STOCKFORD GARAGE EQUIPMENT LTD
7 Badger Way, North Cheshire Trading Estate, Prenton CH43 3HQ
Tel: 0151 609 1007
Fax: 0151 609 1008
E-mail: phil@psge.u-net.com
Web site: www.vehicle-lifts.co.uk

SOMERS TOTALKARE LTD
15 Forge Trading Estate, Mucklow Hill, Halesowen B62 8TR
Tel: 0121 585 2700
Fax: 0121 585 2725
E-mail: sales@somerstotalkare.co.uk
Web site: www.somerstotalkare.co.uk

STERTIL UK LTD
Unit A, Brackmills Business Park, Caswell Road, Northampton NN4 7PW
Tel: 0870 770 6607
Fax: 01604 662014
E-mail: info@stertiluk.com
Web site: www.stertiluk.com

VARLEY & GULLIVER LTD
57 Alfred Street, Sparkbrook, Birmingham B12 8JR.
Tel: 0121 773 2441.
Fax: 0121 766 6875.
Web site: www.v-and-g.co.uk

V L TEST SYSTEMS LTD
3-4 Middle Slade, Buckingham Industrial Park, Buckingham MK18 1WA
Tel: 01280 822488
Fax: 01280 822489
E-mail: sales@vltestuk.com
Web site: www.vltest.com

Gearboxes

ALLISON TRANSMISSION
Allison House, 36 Duncan Close, Moulton Park, Northampton NN3 6WL
Tel: 01525 408600
Fax: 01604 495110

ARRIVA BUS AND COACH
Lodge Garage, Whitehall Road West, Cleckheaton BD19 4BJ
Tel: 01274 681 144
Fax: 01274 651 198
E-mail: busandcoachsales@arriva.co.uk
Web site: www.arrivabusandcoach.co.uk

DAVID BROWN VEHICLE TRANSMISSIONS LTD
Park Gear Works, Lockwood, Huddersfield HD4 5DD.
Tel: 01484 465500
Fax: 01484 465518

Driving Down Costs with DIWA Excellence. That moves us.

www.voithturbo.com

5 STAR SERVICE
★ Exchange Transmissions
★ Expert Installation
★ Voith Dedicated Technicians
★ Genuine Spare Parts and Components
★ OEM Assured Quality

Call 020 8667 3032

Voith Turbo

VOITH
Engineered reliability.

BUSS BIZZ
Goughs Transport Depot, Morestead, Winchester SO21 1JD.
Tel: 01962 715555/66.
Fax: 01962 714868.

EATON LTD
Truck Components Marketing, PO Box 11, Worsley Road North, Worsley M28 5GJ
Tel: 01204 797219.
Fax: 01204 797204.

GARDNER PARTS LTD
Barton Hall, Hardy Street, Eccles M30 7WA.
Tel: 0161 786 1900
Fax: 0161 788 8949
E-mail: sales@gardnerparts.co.uk
Web site: www.gardnerparts.co.uk

HART BROTHERS (ENGINEERING) LTD
Albion Works, Cobden Street, Salford, Manchester M6 6LY
Tel: 0161 737 6791

HL SMITH TRANSMISSIONS LTD
Enterprise Business Park, Cross Road, Albrighton, Wolverhampton WV7 3BJ
Tel: 01902 373011
Fax: 01902 373608
Web site: www.hlsmith.co.uk

LH GROUP SERVICES LTD
Graycar Business Park, Barton Under Needwood, Burton-on-Trent DE13 8EN
Tel: 01283 722600
Fax: 01283 722622
E-mail: lh@lh-group.com
Web site: www.lh-group.com

NEXT BUS LTD
The Coach Yard, Vincents Road, Bumpers Farm Industrial Estate, Chippenham SN14 6QA
Tel: 01249 462462
Fax: 01249 448 844
E-mail: sales@next-bus.co.uk
Web site: www.next-bus.co.uk

PARTLINE LTD
Dockfield Road, Shipley BD17 7AZ
Tel: 01274 531531
Fax: 01274 531088
E-mail: sales@partline.co.uk
Web site: www.partline.co.uk

QUEENSBRIDGE (PSV) LTD
Longlands Industrial Estate, Milner Way, Ossett WF5 9JE
Tel: 01924 281871
Fax: 01924 281807
E-mail: craig@queensbridgeltd.co.uk
Web site: www.queensbridgeltd.co.uk

SHAWSON SUPPLY LTD
12 Station Road, Saintfield, County Down, North Ireland BT24 7DU
Tel: 028 9751 0994
Fax: 028 9751 0816
E-mail: info@shawsonsupply.com
Web site: www.shawsonsupply.com

UNITEC
Parts Division, Denby Way, Hellaby, Rotherham S66 8HR
Tel: 01709 792000
Fax: 01709 792009
E-mail: parts@optare.com

UNITEC LONDON
Unit 9 Eurocourt, Olivers Close, West Thurrock RM20 3EE
Tel: 08444123222
Fax: 01708 869920
E-mail: london.service@optare.com

UNITEC ROTHERHAM
Denby Way, Hellaby, Rotherham S66 8HR
Tel: 01709 535101
Fax: 01709 535103
E-mail: rotherham.service@optare.com

UNITEC SCOTLAND
Unit 7, Cumbernauld Business Park, Ward Park Road, Cumbernauld G67 3JZ
Tel: 01236 726738
Fax: 01236 795651
E-mail: scotland.service@optare.com

VOITH TURBO LTD
6 Beddington Farm Road, Croydon CR0 4XB
Tel: 020 8667 3032
Fax: 020 8667 0403
E-mail: john.domigan@voith.com
Web site: www.voithturbo.com

VOR TRANSMISSIONS LTD
Little London House, St Anne's Road, Willenhall WV13 1DT
Tel: 08000 184141
Fax: 01902 603868
E-mail: sales@vor.co.uk
Web site: www.vor.co.uk

TREVOR WIGLEY & SONS BUS LTD
Baulder Bridge Road, Carlton, Barnsley S71 3HJ
Tel: 01226 713636/716479
Fax: 01226 700199
E-mail: wigleys@btconnect.com
Web site: www.twigley.com

WINCHESTER MARINE LTD (MAJORLINE ENGINEERING)
Baybridge Industrial Units, Baybridge Lane, Owslebury, Winchester SO21 1JN.
Tel: 01962 777077
Fax: 01962 777661, 777667
E-mail: winchestermarine@btconnect.com

ZF POWERTRAIN
Stringes Close, Willenhall WV13 1LE
Tel: 01902 366000
Fax: 01902 366504
E-mail: sales@powertrain.org.uk
Web site: www.powertrain.org.uk

Hand Driers (in coaches)

ABACUS TUBULAR PRODUCTS LTD
Abacus House, Highlode Industrial Estate, Ramsey PE26 2RB
Tel: 01487 710700
Fax: 01487 710626
E-mail: f.riole@abacus-+p.com
Web: www.abacus-+p.com

BRADTECH LTD
Unit 3, Ladford Covert, Seighford, Stafford ST18 9QL
Tel: 01785 282800
Fax: 01785 282558
E-mail: sales@bradtech.ltd.uk
Web site: www.bradtech.ltd.uk

CARLYLE BUS & COACH LTD
Carlyle Business Park, Great Bridge Street, Swan Village, West Bromwich B70 0X4
Tel: 0121 524 1200
Fax: 0121 524 1201
E-mail: admin@carlyleplc.co.uk
Web site: www.carlyleplc.co.uk

CROWN COACHBUILDERS LTD
32 Flemington Industrial Park, Flemington, Motherwell ML1 1SN.
Tel: 01698 276087
Fax: 01698 262676
E-mail: davidgreer@hotmail.com
Web site: www.crowncoachbuilders.co.uk

DEANS POWERED DOORS
PO Box 8, Borwick Drive, Grovehill, Beverley HU17 0HQ
Tel: 01482 868111
Fax: 01482 881890
E-mail: info@deans-doors.com

GABRIEL & CO LTD
Abro Works, 10 Hay Hall Road, Tyseley, Birmingham B11 2AU
Tel: 0121 248 3333
Fax: 0121 248 3330
E-mail: contact@gabrielco.com
Web site: www.gabrielco.com

HAPPICH V & I COMPONENTS LTD
Unit 30/31, Fort Industrial Park, Fort Parkway, Castle Bromwich B35 7AR.
Tel: 0121 747 4400
Fax: 0121 747 4977
E-mail: sales@happich.co.uk
Web site: www.happich.co.uk

JBF SERVICES LTD
Southedge Works, Hipperholme, Halifax HX3 8EF
Tel: 01422 202840
Fax: 01422 206070
E-mail: jbfservices@aol.com

PLAXTON
Plaxton Park, Cayton Low Road, Eastfield, Scarborough YO11 3BY
Tel: 01723 581500
Fax: 01723 5813238
E-mail: sales@plaxtonlimited.co.uk
Web site: www.plaxtonlimited.co.uk

PLAXTON COACH SALES CENTRE
Ryton Road, Anston, Sheffield S25 4DL
Tel: 01909 551155
Fax: 01909 567994
E-mail: coaches@plaxtonlimited.co.uk
Web site: www.plaxtonlimited.co.uk

SHADES TECHNICS LTD
Units E3 & E4, Rd Park, Stephenson Close, Hoddesdon, Hetrtfordshire EN11 0BW
Tel: 01992 501683
Fax: 01992 501669
E-mail: sales@shades-technics.com
Web site: www.shades-technics.com

UNWIN SAFETY SYSTEMS
Unwin House, The Horseshoe, Coat Road, Martock TA12 6EY
Tel: 01935 827740
Fax: 01935 827760
E-mail: sales@unwin-safety.co.uk
Web site: wwwunwin-safety.com

Trade Directory

Headrest Covers & Curtains

ABACUS TUBULAR PRODUCTS LTD
Abacus House, Highlode Industrial Estate, Ramsey PE26 2RB
Tel: 01487 710700
Fax: 01487 710626
E-mail: f.riole@abacus-+p.com
Web site: www.abacus-+p.com

ARRIVA BUS AND COACH
Lodge Garage, Whitehall Road West, Cleckheaton BD19 4BJ
Tel: 01274 681 144
Fax: 01274 651 198
E-mail: busandcoachsales@arriva.co.uk
Web site: www.arrivabusandcoach.co.uk

CI COACHLINES
Pools Lane, Highwood, Essex CM1 3QL
Tel: 01245 248 669

DUOFLEX LTD
Trimmingham House, 2 Shires Road, Buckingham Road Industrial Estate, Brackley NN13 7EZ
Tel: 01280 701366
Fax: 01280 704799
E-mail: sales@duoflex.co.uk
Web site: www.duoflex.co.uk

ORVEC INTERNATIONAL LTD
Malmo Road, Hull HU7 0YF.
Tel: 01482 625333
Fax: 01482 625335.
E-mail: service@orvec.co.uk
Web site: www.orvec.co.uk

Heating & Ventilation Systems

AIRCONCO LTD
Unit 10, Middleton Trade Park, Oldham Road, Middleton M24 1QZ
Tel: 0845 402014
Fax: 0845 4024041
E-mail: mail@airconco.carriersutrak.co.uk

ARRIVA BUS AND COACH
Lodge Garage, Whitehall Road West, Cleckheaton BD19 4BJ
Tel: 01274 681 144
Fax: 01274 651 198
E-mail: busandcoachsales@arriva.co.uk
Web site: www.arrivabusandcoach.co.uk

CARLYLE BUS & COACH LTD
Carlyle Business Park, Great Bridge Street, Swan Village, West Bromwich B70 0X4
Tel: 0121 524 1200
Fax: 0121 524 1201
E-mail: admin@carlyleplc.co.uk
Web site: carlyleplc.co.uk

CI COACHLINES
Pools Lane, Highwood, Essex CM1 3QL
Tel: 01245 248 669

CLAYTON HEATERS LTD
Hunter Terrace, Fletchworth Gate, Burnsall Road, Coventry CV5 6SP
Tel: 02476 691 916
Fax: 02476 691 969
E-mail: admin@claytoncc.co.uk
Web site: www.claytoncc.co.uk

CONSERVE (UK) LTD
Suite 7, Logistics House, Kingsthorpe Road, Northampton NN2 6LJ
Tel: 01604 710055
Fax: 01604 710065
E-mail: information@conserveuk.co.uk
Web site: www.conserveuk.co.uk

EBERSPACHER (UK) LTD
Headlands Business Park, Salisbury Road, Ringwood BH24 3PB
Tel: 01425 480151
Fax: 01425 480152
E-mail: enquiries@eberspacher.com
Web site: www.eberspacher.com

HAPPICH V & I COMPONENTS LTD
Unit 30/31, Fort Industrial Park, Fort Parkway, Castle Bromwich B35 7AR.
Tel: 0121 747 4400
Fax: 0121 747 4977
E-mail: sales@happich.co.uk
Web site: www.happich.co.uk

KARIVE LIMITED
PO Box 205, Southam CV47 0ZL
Tel: 01926 813938
Fax: 01926 814898
E-mail: karive.ltd@btinternet.com
Web site: www.karive.co.uk

KELLETT (UK) LTD
8 Stevenson Way, Sheffield S9 3WZ.
Tel: 0114 261 1122
Fax: 0114 261 1199
E-mail: sales@kellett.co.uk

NEALINE WINDSCREEN WIPER PRODUCTS
Unit 1, The Sidings Industrial Estate, Birdingbury Road, Marton CV23 9RX
Tel: 01926 633256
Fax: 01926 632600

PARTLINE LTD
Dockfield Road, Shipley BD17 7AZ
Tel: 01274 531531
Fax: 01274 531088
E-mail: sales@partline.co.uk
Web site: www.partline.co.uk

PIONEER WESTON
206 Cavendish Place, Birchwood Park, Warrington WA3 6WU
Tel: 01925 853000
Fax: 01925 853030
E-mail: info@pwi-ltd.com
Web site: www.pwi-ltd.com

PLAXTON COACH SALES CENTRE
Ryton Road, Anston, Sheffield S25 4DL
Tel: 01909 551155
Fax: 01909 567994
E-mail: coaches@plaxtonlimited.co.uk
Web site: www.plaxtonlimited.co.uk

ROADLINK INTERNATIONAL LTD
Strawberry Lane, Willenhall WV13 3RL
Tel: 01902 636210
Fax: 01902 606604
E-mail: sales@roadlink-international.co.uk
Web site: www.roadlink-international.co.uk

SHADES TECHNICS LTD
Units E3 & E4, Rd Park, Stephenson Close, Hoddesdon, Hetrtfordshire EN11 0BW
Tel: 01992 501683
Fax: 01992 501669
E-mail: sales@shades-technics.com
Web site: www.shades-technics.com

UNITEC
Parts Division, Denby Way, Hellaby, Rotherham S66 8HR
Tel: 01709 792000
Fax: 01709 792009
E-mail: parts@optare.com

WEBASTO PRODUCT UK LTD
Webasto House, White Rose Way, Doncaster DN4 5JH
Tel: 01302 322232
Fax: 01302 322231
E-mail: info@webastouk.com
Web site: www.webasto.co.uk

Hub Odometers

In-coach Catering Equipment

AVT SYSTEMS LTD
Unit 3, Tything Road, Arden Forest Trading Estate, Alcester B49 6ES
Tel: 01789 400357
Fax: 01789 400359
E-mail: enquiries@avtsystems.co.uk
Web site: www.avtsystems.co.uk

BRADTECH LTD
Unit 3, Ladford Covert, Seighford, Stafford ST18 9QL
Tel: 01785 282800
Fax: 01785 282558
E-mail: sales@bradtech.ltd.uk
Web site: www.bradtech.ltd.uk

ELSAN LTD
Bellbrook Park, Uckfield TN22 1QF
Tel: 01825 748200
Fax: 01825 761212
E-mail: sales@elsan.co.uk
Web site: www.elsan.co.uk

EXPRESS COACH REPAIRS LTD
Outgang Lane, Pickering YO18 7EL.
Tel: 01751 475215.
Fax: 01751 475215
Web site: www.expresscoachrepairs.co.uk

PLAXTON COACH SALES CENTRE
Ryton Road, Anston, Sheffield S25 4DL
Tel: 01909 551155
Fax: 01909 567994
E-mail: coaches@plaxtonlimited.co.uk
Web site: www.plaxtonlimited.co.uk

PSV PRODUCTS
PO Box 166, Warrington WA4 5FG
Tel: 0844 636 4488
Fax: 01925 601534
E-mail: info@psvproducts.com
Web site: www.psvproducts.com

SHADES TECHNICS LTD
Units E3 & E4, Rd Park, Stephenson Close, Hoddesdon, Hetrtfordshire EN11 0BW
Tel: 01992 501683
Fax: 01992 501669
E-mail: sales@shades-technics.com
Web site: www.shades-technics.com

Labels, Nameplates & Decals

FIRST CHOICE NAMEPLATES, LABELS & SIGNS
Lynden 2c, Russell Avenue,
Balderton, Newark NG24 3BT
Tel: 01636 678035
Fax: 01636 707066
E-mail: firstchoice@handbag.com

THE LAWTON MOTOR BODY BUILDING CO LTD
Knutsford Road, Church Lawton,
Stoke-on-Trent ST7 3DN
Tel: 01270 882056
Fax: 01270 883014
E-mail: enquiries@lawtonmotorbody.co.uk
Web site: www.lawtonmotorbody.co.uk

McKENNA BROTHERS LTD
McKenna House, Jubilee Road,
Middleton, Manchester M24 2LX
Tel: 0161 655 3244
Fax: 0161 655 3059
E-mail: info@mckennabrothers.co.uk
Web site: www.mckennabrothers.co.uk

Lifting Equipment

AUTOLIFT LTD
Unit 440/41, Alma Works, Sticker Lane,
Bradford BD1 8RL
Tel: 01274 680744
Fax: 01274 680042
E-mail: sales@autoliftuk.co.uk
Web: www.autoliftuk.co.uk

PLAXTON
Plaxton Park, Cayton Low Road, Eastfield,
Scarborough YO11 3BY
Tel: 01723 581500
Fax: 01723 5813238
E-mail: sales@plaxtonlimited.co.uk
Web site: www.plaxtonlimited.co.uk

Lifts/Ramps (Passenger)

COMPAK RAMPS LTD
VIP Trading Estate, Anchor & Hope Lane,
London SE7 7RY
Tel: 020 8858 3781
Fax: 020 8858 3781
E-mail: tony.rodwell@dsl.pipex.com

CROWN COACHBUILDERS LTD
32 Flemington Industrial Park, Flemington,
Motherwell ML1 1SN.
Tel: 01698 276087
Fax: 01698 262676
E-mail: davidgreer@hotmail.com
Web site: www.crowncoachbuilders.co.uk

DIRECT PARTS LTD
Unit 1, Churnet Court, Churnetside Business
Park, Harrison Way, Cheddleton ST13 7EF
Tel: 01538 361777
Fax: 01538 369100
E-mail: sales@direct-group.co.uk
Web site: www.direct-group.co.uk

MARTYN INDUSTRIALS LTD
5 Brunel Way, Durranhill Industrial Esate,
Carlisle CA1 3NQ
Tel: 01228 544000
Fax: 01228 544001
E-mail: enquiries@martyn-industrals.co.uk
Web site: www.martyn-industrials.com

PASSENGER LIFT SERVICES LTD
Unit 10, Crystal Drive, Sandwell Business
Park, Smethwick B66 1QG.
Tel: 0121 552 0600.
Fax: 0121 552 0200.
Web site: www.pls-access.co.uk

PNEUMAX LTD
Unit 8, Venture Industrial Park,
Fareham Road, Gosport PO13 0BA
Tel: 01329 823999
Fax: 01329 822345
E-mail: sales@pneumax.co.uk
Web site: www.pneumax.co.uk

RATCLIFF TAIL LIFTS LTD
Bessemer Road,
Welwyn Garden City AL7 1ET
Tel: 01707 325571
Fax: 01707 327752
Web site: www.ratcliff.co.uk

RICON UK LIMITED
Littlemoss Business Park, Littlemoss Road,
Droylsden, Manchester M43 7EF
Tel: 0800 435677
Fax: 0161 301 6050
E-mail: info@riconuk.com
Web site: www.riconuk.com

TRUCKALIGN CO LTD
VIP Trading Estate, Anchor & Hope Lane,
London SE7 7RY
Tel: 020 8858 3781
Fax: 020 8858 3781
E-mail: tony.rodwell@dsl.pipex.com

Lighting & Lighting Design

ATLAS LIGHTING COMPONENTS
3 King George Close, Eastern Avenue,
West Romford RM7 7PP.
Tel: 01708 776375
Fax: 01708 776376

BRITAX PMG LTD
Bressingby Industrial Estate,
Bridlington YO16 4SJ
Tel: 01262 670161
Fax: 01262 605666
E-mail: info@britax-pmg.com
Web site: www.britax-pmg.com

CARLYLE BUS & COACH LTD
Carlyle Business Park, Great Bridge Street,
Swan Village, West Bromwich B70 0XA
Tel: 0121 524 1200
Fax: 0121 524 1201
E-mail: admin@carlyleplc.com
Web site: www.carlyle.co.uk

CRESCENT FACILITIES LTD
72 Willow Crescent, Chapeltown,
Sheffield S35 1QS
Tel/fax: 0114 2451050
E-mail: cfl.chris@btinternet.com
Web site: www.cflparts.com

CSM LIGHTING
Suite 1b, Cobb House, Oyster Lane,
Byfleet KT14 7DU
Tel: 01932 349661
Fax: 01932 349991
Web site: www.csmauto.com

HAPPICH V & I COMPONENTS LTD
Unit 30/31, Fort Industrial Park, Fort
Parkway, Castle Bromwich B35 7AR.
Tel: 0121 747 4400
Fax: 0121 747 4977
E-mail: sales@happich.co.uk
Web site: www.happich.co.uk

IMEXPART LTD
Links 31, Willowbridge Way, Whitwood,
Castleford WF10 5NP
Tel: 01977 553936
Fax: 01977 604684
E-mail: parts@imexpart.com
Web site: www.imexpart.com

INVERTEC LTD
Whelford Road, Fairford GL7 4DT
Tel: 01285 713550
Fax: 01285 713548
Mobile: 07802 793828
E-mail: ian@invertec.co.uk
Web site: www.invertec.co.uk

KELLETT (UK) LTD
8 Stevenson Way, Sheffield S9 3WZ.
Tel: 0114 261 1122.
Fax: 0114 261 1199.
E-mail: sales@kellett.co.uk

PARTLINE LTD
Dockfield Road, Shipley BD17 7AZ
Tel: 01274 531531
Fax: 01274 531088
E-mail: sales@partline.co.uk
Web site: www.partline.co.uk

UNITEC
Parts Division, Denby Way, Hellaby,
Rotherham S66 8HR
Tel: 01709 792000
Fax: 01709 792009
E-mail: parts@optare.com

Mirrors/Mirror Arms

ASHTREE GLASS LTD
Brownroyd Street, Bradford BD8 9AF
Tel: 01274 546732
Fax: 01274 548525
E-mail: sales@ashtreeglass.co.uk
Web site: www.ashtreeglass.co.uk

Oil Management Systems

IMEXPART LTD
Links 31, Willowbridge Way, Whitwood,
Castleford WF10 5NP
Tel: 01977 553936
Fax: 01977 604684
E-mail: parts@imexpart.com
Web site: www.imexpart.com

INTERLUBE SYSTEMS LTD
St Modwen Road, Plymouth PL6 8LH
Tel: 01752 676000
Fax: 01752 676001
E-mail: info@interlubesystems.co.uk
Web site: www.interlubesystems.co.uk

STERTIL UK LTD
Unit A, Brackmills Business Park, Caswell
Road, Northampton NN4 7PW
Tel: 0870 7706607
Fax: 01604 668014
E-mail: info@stertiluk.com
Web site: www.stertiluk.com

Trade Directory

Painting & Signwriting

BLACKPOOL COACH SERVICES
Burton Road, Blackpool FY4 4NN.
Tel/Fax: 01253 698686

BULWARK BUS & COACH ENGINEERING LTD
Gate 3, Bulwark Industrial Estate, Chepstow NP16 5QZ
Tel: 01291 622326.
Fax: 01291 622726.

CHANNEL COMMERCIALS PLC
Unit 6, Cobbs Wood Industrial Estate, Brunswick Road, Ashford TN23 1EH.
Tel: 01233 629272.
Fax: 01233 636222.
E-mail: info@ccplc.co.uk

EXPRESS COACH REPAIRS LTD
Outgang Lane, Pickering YO18 7EL.
Tel: 01751 475215.
Fax: 01751 475215
Web: www.expresscoachrepairs.co.uk

HANTS & DORSET TRIM LTD
Canada Road, West Wellow SO51 6DE.
Tel: 023 8033 4335

LANCES MOBILE PAINTING
20 Hillham Crescent, Boost Town, Worseley, Manchester M28 1FY
Tel: 07974 862022

THE LAWTON MOTOR BODY BUILDING CO LTD
Knutsford Road, Church Lawton, Stoke-on-Trent ST7 3DN
Tel: 01270 882056
Fax: 01270 883014
E-mail: enquiries@lawtonmotorbody.co.uk
Web site: www.lawtonmotorbody.co.uk

McKENNA BROTHERS LTD
McKenna House, Jubilee Road, Middleton, Manchester M24 2LX
Tel: 0161 655 3244
Fax: 0161 655 3059
E-mail: info@mckennabrothers.co.uk
Web site: www.mckennabrothers.com

NORBURY BLINDS LTD
41-45 Hanley Street, Newtown, Birmingham B19 3SP
Tel: 0121 359 4311
Fax: 0121 359 6388
E-mail: info@norbury-blinds.com
Web site: www.norbury-blinds.com

PLAXTON
Plaxton Park, Cayton Low Road, Eastfield, Scarborough YO11 3BY
Tel: 01723 581500
Fax: 01723 5813238
E-mail: sales@plaxtonlimited.co.uk
Web site: www.plaxtonlimited.co.uk

PLAXTON COACH SALES CENTRE
Ryton Road, Anston, Sheffield S25 4DL
Tel: 01909 551155
Fax: 01909 567994
E-mail: coaches@plaxtonlimited.co.uk
Web site: www.plaxtonlimited.co.uk

RH BODYWORKS
A140 Ipswich Road, Brome, Eye IP23 8AW
Tel: 01379 870666
Fax: 01379 872106
E-mail: mike.ball@rhbodyworks.co.uk
Web site: www.rhbodyworks.co.uk

UNITEC LONDON
Unit 9 Eurocourt, Olivers Close, West Thurrock RM20 3EE
Tel: 08444123222
Fax: 01708 869920
E-mail: london.service@optare.com

UNITEC ROTHERHAM
Denby Way, Hellaby, Rotherham S66 8HR
Tel: 01709 535101
Fax: 01709 535103
E-mail: rotherham.service@optare.com

UNITEC SCOTLAND
Unit 7, Cumbernauld Business Park, Ward Park Road, Cumbernauld G67 3JZ
Tel: 01236 726738
Fax: 01236 795651
E-mail: scotland.service@optare.com

VOLVO BUS AND COACH CENTRE
Belton Road West, Loughborough LE11 5HP
Tel: 01509 217777
Fax: 01509 239362
Web site: www.volvo.com

Parts Suppliers

AIR DOOR SERVICES
Unit D, The Pavillions, Holly Lane Industrial Estate, Atherstone CV9 2QZ.
Tel: 01827 711660
Fax: 01827 713577
Web site: www.airdoorservices.co.uk

ARRIVA BUS AND COACH
Lodge Garage, Whitehall Road West, Cleckheaton BD19 4BJ
Tel: 01274 681 144
Fax: 01274 651 198
E-mail: busandcoachsales@arriva.co.uk
Web: www.arrivabusandcoach.co.uk

ASHLEY BANKS LTD
5 King Street Estate, Langtoft, Peterborough PE6 9NF
Tel: 01778 560651
Fax: 01778 560721
E-mail: user@ashleybanks.fsnet.co.uk

ASHTREE GLASS LTD
Brownroyd Street, Bradford BO8 9AF
Tel: 01274 546 732
Fax: 01274 548 525
E-mail: sales@ashtreeglass.co.uk
Web: www.ashtreeglass.co.uk

M BARNWELL SERVICES LTD
Reginald Road, Smethwick B67 5AS
Tel: 0121 429 8011
Fax: 0121 434 3016
E-mail: sales@barnwell.co.uk
Web site: www.barnwell.co.uk

BRADTECH LTD
Unit 3, Ladford Covert, Seighford, Stafford ST18 9QL
Tel: 01785 282800
Fax: 01785 282558
E-mail: sales@bradtech.ltd.uk
Web site: www.bradtech.ltd.uk

BRITISH BUS SALES
Mike Nash, PO Box 534, Dorking RH5 5XB
Tel: 07836 656 692
E-mail: nationalbus1@btconnect.com
Web: www.britishbussales.co.uk

BRT BEARINGS LTD
21-24 Regal Road, Wisbech, Cambridgeshire PE13 2RQ
Tel: 01945 464 097
Fax: 01945 464 523
E-mail: info@brt-group.com

BUSS BIZZ
Goughs Transport Depot, Morestead, Winchester SO21 1JD.
Tel: 01962 715555/66.
Fax: 01962 714868.

CARLYLE BUS & COACH LTD
Carlyle Business Park, Great Bridge Street, Swan Village, West Bromwich B70 0X4
Tel: 0121 524 1200
Fax: 0121 524 1201
E-mail: admin@carlyleplc.co.uk
Web site: www.carlyleplc.co.uk

CLAYTON HEATERS LTD
Hunter Terrace, Fletchworth Gate, Burnsall Road, Coventry CV5 6SP
Tel: 02476 691 916
Fax: 02476 691 969
E-mail: admin@claytoncc.co.uk
Web: www.claytoncc.co.uk

COACH-AID
Unit 2, Brindley Close, Tollgate Industrial Estate, Stafford ST16 3SU
Tel: 01785 222666
E-mail: workshop@coach-aid.com
Web site: www.coach-aid.com

CONSERVE (UK) LTD
Suite 7, Logistics House, 1 Horsley Road, Kingsthorpe Road, Northampton NN2 6LJ
Tel: 01604 710055
Fax: 01604 710065
E-mail: information@conserveuk.co.uk
Web site: www.conserveuk.co.uk

CRESCENT FACILITIES LTD
72 Willow Crescent, Chapeltown, Sheffield S35 1QS
Tel/fax: 0114 2451050
E-mail: cfl.chris@btinternet.com
Web site: www.cflparts.com

CREST COACH CONVERSIONS
Unit 5, Holmeroyd Road, Bentley Moor Lane, Carcroft, Doncaster DN6 7BH
Tel: 01302 723723
Fax: 01302 724724

CREWE ENGINES
Warmingham Road, Crewe CW1 4PQ
Tel: 01270 526333
Fax: 01270 526433
E-mail: sales@creweengines.co.uk
Web site: www.creweengines.co.uk

CUMMINS UK
Rutherford Drive, Park Farm South, Wellingborough NN8 6AN
Tel: 01933 334200
Fax: 01933 334198
E-mail: cduksales@cummins.com
Web: www.cummins-uk.com

DINEX EXHAUSTS LTD
14 Chesford Grange, Woolston,
Warrington WA1 4RE
Tel: 01925 849849
Fax: 01925 849850
E-mail: dinex@dinex.co.uk
Web site: www.dinex.dk

DIRECT PARTS LTD
Unit 1, Churnet Court, Churnetside Business Park, Harrison Way, Cheddleton ST13 7EF
Tel: 01538 361777
Fax: 01538 369100
E-mail: sales@direct-group.co.uk
Web site: www.direct-group.co.uk

ERENTEK LTD
Malt Kiln Lane, Waddington,
Lincoln LN5 9RT
Tel: 01522 720065
Fax: 01522 729155
E-mail: sales@erentek.co.uk
Web site: www.erentek.co.uk

GARDNER PARTS LTD
Barton Hall, Hardy Street, Eccles,
Manchester M30 7WA.
Tel: 0161 786 1900
Fax: 0161 788 8949
E-mail: sales@gardnerparts.co.uk
Web: www.gardnerparts.co.uk

HAPPICH V & I COMPONENTS LTD
Unit 30/31, Fort Industrial Park, Fort Parkway, Castle Bromwich B35 7AR.
Tel: 0121 747 4400
Fax: 0121 747 4977
E-mail: sales@happich.co.uk
Web site: www.happich.co.uk

HART BROTHERS (ENGINEERING) LTD
Albion Works, Cobden Street,
Salford, Manchester M6 6LY
Tel: 0161 737 6791

THOMAS HARDIE – WIGAN
Lockett Road, Ashton-in-Makerfield WN4 8DE
Tel: 01942 505124.
Fax: 01942 505119.

IMEXPART LTD
Links 31, Willowbridge Way, Whitwood,
Castleford WF10 5NP
Tel: 01977 553936
Fax: 01977 604684
E-mail: parts@imexpart.com
Web site: www.imexpart.com

IMPERIAL ENGINEERING
Delamare Road, Cheshunt EN8 9UD
Tel: 01992 6342555
Fax: 01992 630506
E-mail: sales@imperialengineering.co.uk
Web site: www.imperialengineering.co.uk

KARIVE LIMITED
PO Box 205, Southam CV47 0ZL
Tel: 01926 813938
Fax: 01926 814898
E-mail: karive.ltd@btinternet.com
Web site: www.karive.co.uk

KELLETT (UK) LTD
8 Stevenson Way, Sheffield S9 3WZ
Tel: 0114 261 1122.
Fax: 0114 261 1199.
E-mail: sales@kellett.co.uk

KNORR-BREMSE SYSTEMS FOR COMMERCIAL VEHICLES LTD
Douglas Road, Kingswood,
Bristol BS15 8NL.
Tel: 0117 984 6100
Fax: 0117 984 6101.
Web site: www.knorr-bremse.com

THE LAWTON MOTOR BODY BUILDING CO LTD
Knutsford Road, Church Lawton, Stoke-on-Trent ST7 3DN
Tel: 01270 882056
Fax: 01270 883014
E-mail: enquiries@lawtonmotorbody.co.uk
Web site: www.lawtonmotorbody.co.uk

LH GROUP SERVICES LTD
Graycar Business Park, Barton Under Needwood, Burton-on-Trent DE13 8EN
Tel: 01283 722600
Fax: 01283 722622
E-mail: lh@lh-group.com
Web site: www.lh-group.com

MOCAP LIMITED
Hortonwood 35, Telford TF1 7YW
Tel: 01952 670247
Fax: 01952 670241
Web site: www.mocap.co.uk
E-mail: sales@mocap.co.uk

NEXT BUS LTD
The Coach Yard, Vincents Road, Bumpers Farm Industrial Estate, Chippenham SN14 6QA
Tel: 01249 462462
Fax: 01249 448 844
E-mail: sales@next-bus.co.uk
Web site: www.next-bus.co.uk

PARTLINE LTD
Dockfield Road, Shipley BD17 7AZ
Tel: 01274 531531
Fax: 01274 531088
E-mail: sales@partline.co.uk
Web site: www.partline.co.uk

PLAXTON
Plaxton Park, Cayton Low Road,
Eastfield, Scarborough YO11 3BY
Tel: 01723 581500
Fax: 01723 5813238
E-mail: sales@plaxtonlimited.co.uk
Web site: www.plaxtonlimited.co.uk

PLAXTON COACH SALES CENTRE
Ryton Road, Anston, Sheffield S25 4DL
Tel: 01909 551155
Fax: 01909 567994
E-mail: coaches@plaxtonlimited.co.uk
Web site: www.plaxtonlimited.co.uk

PNEUMAX LTD
Unit 8, Venture Industrial Park,
Fareham Road, Gosport PO13 0BA
Tel: 01329 823999
Fax: 01329 822345
E-mail: sales@pneumax.co.uk
Web site: www.pneumax.co.uk

PSV GLASS
Hillbottom Road,
High Wycombe HP12 4HJ
Tel: 01494 533131
Fax: 01494 462675
E-mail: sales@psvglass.co.uk
Web site: www.psvglass.com

Q'STRAINT
73-76 John Wilson Business Park,
Whitstable. Kent CT5 3QU
Tel: 01227 773 035
Fax: 01227 770 035
E-mail: info@qstraint.co.uk
Web: www.qstraint.com

QUEENSBRIDGE (PSV) LTD
Longlands Industrial Estate,
Milner Way, Ossett WF5 9JE
Tel: 01924 281871
Fax: 01924 281807
E-mail: craig@queensbridgeltd.co.uk
Web site: www.queensbridgeltd.co.uk

ROADLINK INTERNATIONAL LTD
Strawberry Lane, Willenhall WV13 3RL
Tel: 01902 636210
Fax: 01902 606604
E-mail: sales@roadlink-international.co.uk
Web site: www.roadlink-international.co.uk

SHADES TECHNICS LTD
Units E3 & E4, Rd Park, Stephenson Close, Hoddesdon, Hetrtfordshire EN11 0BW
Tel: 01992 501683
Fax: 01992 501669
E-mail: sales@shades-technics.com
Web site: www.shades-technics.com

SHAWSON SUPPLY LTD
12 Station Road, Saintfield, County Down, Northern Ireland BT24 7DU
Tel: 028 9751 0994
Fax: 028 9751 0816
E-mail: info@shawsonsupply.com
Web site: www.shawsonsupply.com

TRAMONTANA COACH DISTRIBUTORS
Chapelknowe Road, Carfin,
Motherwell ML1 5LE
Tel: 01698 861790
Fax: 01698 860778
E-mail: wdt90@tiscali.co.uk
Web: www.tramontanacoach.co.uk

TREVOR WIGLEY & SON BUS LTD
Passenger Vehicle Dismantling/Spares
Works: Boulder Bridge Lane, off Shaw Lane, Barnsley S71 3HJ
Correspondence: 148 Royston Road, Cudworth, Barnsley S72 8BN
Tel: 01226 713636
Fax: 01226 700199
E-mail: wigleys@btintenet.com
Web site: www.twigley.com

UNITEC
Parts Division, Denby Way, Hellaby,
Rotherham S66 8HR
Tel: 01709 792000
Fax: 01709 792009
E-mail: parts@optare.com

VOLVO BUS AND COACH CENTRE
Belton Road West,
Loughborough LE11 5HP
Tel: 01509 217777
Fax: 01509 239362
Web site: www.volvo.com

WABCO AUTOMOTIVE UK LTD
Texas Street, Morley LS27 0HQ.
Tel: 0113 251 2510.
Fax: 0113 251 2844.
Web: www.wabco-auto.com

Trade Directory

WACTON COACH SALES & SERVICES
Linton Trading Estate, Bromyard HR7 4QL.
Tel: 01885 482782.
Fax: 01885 482127

WALSH'S ENGINEERING
Barton Moss Road, Eccles, Manchester M30 7RL
Tel: 0161 787 7017
Fax: 0161 787 7038
E-mail: walshs@gardnerdiesel.co.uk
Website: www.gardnerdiesel.co.uk

WINCHESTER MARINE LTD (MAJORLINE ENGINEERING)
Baybridge Industrial Units, Baybridge Lane, Owslebury, Winchester SO21 1JN.
Tel: 01962 777077.
Fax: 01962 777661, 777667
E-mail: winchestermarine@btconnect.com

ZF POWERTRAIN
Stringes Close, Willenhall WV13 1LE
Tel: 01902 366000
Fax: 01902 366504
E-mail: sales@powertrain.org.uk
Web site: www.powertrain.org.uk

Passenger Information Systems

AVT SYSTEMS LTD
Units 3 & 4, Tything Road, Arden Forest Industrial Estate, Alcester B49 6ES
Tel: 01789 400357
Fax: 01789 400359
E-mail: enquiries@avtsystems.co.uk.co.uk
Web site: www.avtsystems.co.uk

M BISSELL DISPLAY LTD
Unit 15, Beechwood Business Park, Burdock Close, Cannock WS11 7GB
Tel: 01543 502115
Fax: 01543 502118
E-mail: sales@bisselldisplay.com
Web site: www.bisselldisplay.com

BRIGHT-TECH DEVELOPMENTS LTD
Fleets Point House, Willis Way, Poole BH15 3SS
Tel: 01202 679627
Fax: 01202 684579
E-mail: kpoultney@bright-tech.co.uk
Web site: www.bright-tech.co.uk

HANOVER DISPLAYS LTD
Unit 24, Cliffe Industrial Estate, Lewes BN8 6JL
Tel: 01273 477528
Fax: 01273 407766
E-mail: hanover@hanoverdisplays.com
Web site: www.hanoverdisplays.com

JOURNEY PLAN LTD
Dickson Street, Dunfermline KY12 7SL
Tel: 01383 731048
Fax: 01383 731788
Web site: www.journeyplan.co.uk

McKENNA BROTHERS LTD
McKenna House, Jubilee Road, Middleton, Manchester M24 2LX
Tel: 0161 655 3244
Fax: 0161 655 3059
E-mail: info@mckennabrothers.co.uk
Web site: www.mckennabrothers.co.uk

MOTIONAL MEDIA LTD
Unit 4, Waltham Court, Hare Hatch, Milley Lane, Reading RG10 9AA
Tel: 01189 406353
Fax: 01189 406352
E-mail: james@momedia.tv
Web site: www.momedia.tv

SSL SIMULATION SYSTEMS LTD
Unit 12, Market Industrial Estate, Yatton BS49 4RF
Tel: 01934 838803
Fax: 01934 876202
E-mail: ssl@simulation-systems.co.uk
Web site: www.simulation-systems.co.uk

TRAPEZE GROUP (UK) LTD
The Mill, Staverton, Nr Trowbridge, Bath BA14 6PH
Tel: 01225 784200
Fax: 01225 784222
E-Mail: info@trapezegroup.co.uk
Web site: www.trapezegroup.co.uk

VULTRON INTERNATIONAL LTD
Unit 2, Stadium Way, Elland Road, Leeds LS11 0EW
Tel: 0113 387 7310
Fax: 0113 387 7317
E-mail: jmoorhouse@vultron.co.uk

Pneumatic Valves/Cylinders

PNEUMAX LTD
Unit 8, Venture Industrial Park, Fareham Road, Gosport PO13 0BA
Tel: 01329 823999
Fax: 01329 822345
E-mail: sales@pneumax.co.uk
Web site: www.pneumax.co.uk

UNITEC
Parts Division, Denby Way, Hellaby, Rotherham S66 8HR
Tel: 01709 792000
Fax: 01709 792009
E-mail: parts@optare.com

Rapid Transit/Priority Equipment

ALSTOM TRANSPORT SA
48 rue Albert Dhalenne, F-93482 Saint-Ouen Cedex, France
Tel: 00 33 1 41 66 90 00
Fax: 00 33 1 41 66 96 66
Web site: www.transport.alstom.com

BALFOUR BEATTY RAIL PLANT LTD
PO Box 5065, Raynesway, Derby DE21 7QZ
Tel: 07967 669551
Fax: 01332 288222
Web site: www.bbrail.com
E-mail: info.bbrpl@bbrail.com

BRECKNELL WILLIS & CO LTD
PO Box 10, Chard TA20 2DE
Tel: 01460 64941
Fax: 01460 66122
Web site: www.brecknell-willis.co.uk

BRISTOL ELECTRIC RAILBUS LTD
Heron House, Chiswick Mall, London W4 2PR
Tel: 020 8995 3000
Fax: 020 8994 6060
E-mail: james@skinner.demon.co.uk

JMW
Systems House, Pentland Industrial Estate, Loanhead EH20 9QH
Tel: 0131 440 3633
Fax: 0131 440 3637
E-mail: enquiries@jmw-group.co.uk
Web site: www.jmw-group.co.uk

PARRY PEOPLE MOVERS LTD
Overend Road, Cradley Heath, Dudley B64 7DD
Tel: 01384 569553
Fax: 01384 637753
E-mail: jpmparry@aol.com
Website: www.parrypeoplemovers.com

PRE METRO OPERATION LTD
21 Woodglade Croft, Kings Norton, Birmingham B38 8TD
Tel: 0121 243 9906
Fax: 0121 243 9906
E-mail: premetro@aol.com
Web site: www.premetro.co.uk

SIEMENS TRAFFIC CONTROLS LTD
Sopers Lane, Poole BH17 7ER
Tel: 01202 782000
Web site: www.siemenstraffic.com

SUSTRACO LTD
Heron House, Chiswick Mall, London W4 2PR
Tel: 020 8995 3000
Fax: 020 8994 6060
Web site: www.ultralightrail.com

Repairs/Refurbishment - see body repairs above

Retarders & Speed Control Systems

ARRIVA BUS AND COACH
Lodge Garage, Whitehall Road West, Cleckheaton BD19 4BJ
Tel: 01274 681 144
Fax: 01274 651 198
E-mail: busandcoachsales@arriva.co.uk
Web: www.arrivabusandcoach.co.uk

BUSS BIZZ
Goughs Transport Depot, Morestead, Winchester SO21 1JD.
Tel: 01962 715555/66.
Fax: 01962 714868.

CHASSIS DEVELOPMENTS LTD
Grovebury Road, Leighton Buzzard LU7 8SL.
Tel: 01525 374151.
Fax: 01525 370127
Web site: www.chassisdevelopments.co.uk

PARTLINE LTD
Dockfield Road, Shipley BD17 7AZ
Tel: 01274 531531
Fax: 01274 531088
E-mail: sales@partline.co.uk
Web site: www.partline.co.uk

P & P SERGEANT (B & A) LTD
PO Box 11, New Hall Lane,
Hoylake, Wirral CH47 4DH
Tel: 01516 325 903
Fax: 01516 325 908
E-mail: enq@sergeant.co.uk
Web site: www.sergeant.co.uk

TELMA RETARDER LTD
25 Clarke Road, Mount Farm,
Milton Keynes MK1 1LG
Tel: 01908 642822
Fax: 01908 641348
E-mail: telma@telma.co.uk
Web site: www.telma.co.uk

VOITH TURBO LTD
6 Beddington Farm Road,
Croydon CR0 4XB
Tel: 020 8667 3032
Fax: 020 8667 0403
E-mail: john.domigan@voith.com
Web site: www.voithturbo.com

WABCO AUTOMOTIVE UK LTD
Texas Street, Morley LS27 0HQ.
Tel: 0113 251 2510.
Fax: 0113 251 2844
Web site: www.wabco-auto.com

Reversing Safety Systems

AUTOSOUND LTD
4 Lister Street, Dudley Hill,
Bradford BD4 9PQ
Tel: 01274 688990
Fax: 01274 651318
Web site: www.autosound.co.uk
E-mail: sales@autosound.co.uk

ASHTREE GLASS LTD
Brownroyd Street, Bradford BO8 9AF
Tel: 01274 546 732
Fax: 01274 548 525
E-mail: sales@ashtreeglass.co.uk
Web: www.ashtreeglass.co.uk

AVT SYSTEMS LTD
Unit 3 & 4, Tything Road, Arden Forest
Trading Estate, Alcester B49 6ES
Tel: 01789 400 357
Fax: 01789 400 359
E-mail: enquiries@avtsystems.co.uk
Web: www.avtsystems.co.uk

BRIGADE ELECTRONICS plc
Brigade House, The Mills, Station Road,
South Darenth DA4 9BD
Tel: 01322 420 300
Fax: 01322 420 343
E-mail: info@brigade-electronics.co.uk
Web site: www.brigade-electronics.com

CARLYLE BUS & COACH LTD
Carlyle Business Park, Great Bridge Street,
Swan Village, West Bromwich B70 0XA
Tel: 0121 524 1200
Fax: 0121 524 1201
E-mail: admin@carlyleplc.co.uk
Web site: carlyleplc.co.uk

CLAN TOOLS & PLANT LTD
3 Greenhill Avenue, Giffnock,
Glasgow G46 6QX.
Tel: 0141 638 8040.
Fax: 0141 638 8881.
E-mail: clantools@btconnect.com
Web: www.clantools.com

KELLETT (UK) LTD
8 Stevenson Way, Sheffield S9 3WZ.
Tel: 0114 261 1122.
Fax: 0114 261 1199.
E-mail: sales@kellett.co.uk

PLAXTON COACH SALES CENTRE
Ryton Road, Anston, Sheffield S25 4DL
Tel: 01909 551155
Fax: 01909 567994
E-mail: coaches@plaxtonlimited.co.uk
Web site: www.plaxtonlimited.co.uk

Roller Blinds - Passenger & Driver

ABACUS TUBULAR PRODUCTS LTD
Abacus House, Highlode Industrial Estate,
Ramsey PE26 2RB
Tel: 01487 710700
Fax: 01487 710626
E-mail: f.riole@abacus-+p.com
Web: www.abacus-+p.com

CARLYLE BUS & COACH LTD
Carlyle Business Park, Great Bridge Street,
Swan Village, West Bromwich B70 0XA
Tel: 0121 524 1200
Fax: 0121 524 1201
E-mail: admin@carlyleplc.co.uk
Web site: carlyleplc.co.uk

HAPPICH V & I COMPONENTS LTD
Unit 30/31, Fort Industrial Park, Fort
Parkway, Castle Bromwich B35 7AR.
Tel: 0121 747 4400
Fax: 0121 747 4977
E-mail: sales@happich.co.uk
Web site: www.happich.co.uk

TEMPLE MANUFACTURING CO LTD
Unit 2, First Avenue, West Denbigh,
Bletchley, Milton Keynes MK1 1 DX
Tel: 01908 642233
Fax: 01908 373396
E-mail: iantemple@btconnect.com

WIDNEY UK LTD
Plume Street, Aston, Birmingham B6 7SA
Tel: 0121 327 5500
Fax: 0121 328 2466
E-mail: richard@widney.co.uk
Web site: www.widney.co.uk

Roof-Lining Fabrics

ABACUS TUBULAR PRODUCTS LTD
Abacus House, Highlode Industrial Estate,
Ramsey PE26 2RB
Tel: 01487 710700
Fax: 01487 710626
E-mail: f.riole@abacus-+p.com
Web: www.abacus-+p.com

ARDEE COACH TRIM LTD
Artnalivery, Ardll, Louth
Tel: 00 353 41 685 3599
Fax: 00 353 41 685 7016
E-mail: ardeecoachtrim@eircom.net

AUTOMATE WHEEL COVERS LTD
California Mills, Oxford Road,
Gomersal BD19 4HQ
Tel: 01274 862700
Fax: 01274 851989
E-mail: sales@wheelcovers.co.uk
Web site: www.euroliners.com

AUTOMOTIVE TEXTILE INDUSTRIES
Unit 15 & 16, Priest Court, Springfield
Business Park, Grantham NG31 7BG
Tel: 01476 593050
Fax: 01476 593607
E-mail: sales@autotex.com
Web site: www.autotex.com

HAPPICH V & I COMPONENTS LTD
Unit 30/31, Fort Industrial Park, Fort
Parkway, Castle Bromwich B35 7AR.
Tel: 0121 747 4400
Fax: 0121 747 4977
E-mail: sales@happich.co.uk
Web site: www.happich.co.uk

Seat belts/restraint systems

ABACUS TUBULAR PRODUCTS LTD
Abacus House, Highlode Industrial Estate,
Ramsey PE26 2RB
Tel: 01487 710700
Fax: 01487 710626
E-mail: info@abacus-tp.com

ARDEE COACH TRIM LTD
Artnalivery, Ardll, Louth
Tel: 00 353 41 685 3599
Fax: 00 353 41 685 7016
E-mail: ardeecoachtrim@eircom.net

ARRIVA BUS AND COACH
Lodge Garage, Whitehall Road,
West Cleckheaton BD19 4BJ
Tel: 01274 681 144
Fax: 01274 651 198
E-mail: busandcoachsales@arriva.co.uk
Web site: www.arrivabusandcoach.co.uk

CARLYLE BUS & COACH LTD
Carlyle Business Park, Great Bridge Street,
Swan Village, West Bromwich B70 0XA
Tel: 0121 524 1200
Fax: 0121 524 1201
E-mail: admin@carlyleplc.co.uk
Web site: www.carlyleplc.co.uk

CI COACHLINES
Pools Lane, Highwood, Essex CM1 3QL
Tel: 01245 248 669

ELITE SERVICES LTD
Unit 3/6, Adswood Industrial Estate,
Addswood Road, Stockport SK3 8LF
Tel: 0161 480 0617
Fax: 0161 480 3099

THE LAWTON MOTOR BODY BUILDING CO LTD
Knutsford Road, Church Lawton,
Stoke-on-Trent ST7 3DN
Tel: 01270 882056
Fax: 01270 883014
E-mail: enquiries@lawtonmotorbody.co.uk
Web site: www.lawtonmotorbody.co.uk

MTB EQUIPMENT LTD
Sixth Avenue, Zone Two, Deeside
Industrial Park, Deeside CH5 2LB
Tel: 0870 870 1282
Fax: 01244 289 818
E-mail: info@mtb-equipment.com
Web site: www.mtb-equipment.com

Trade Directory

NEXT BUS LTD
The Coach Yard, Vincents Road,
Bumpers Farm Industrial Estate,
Chippenham SN14 6QA
Tel: 01249 462462
Fax: 01249 448 844
E-mail: sales@next-bus.co.uk
Web site: www.next-bus.co.uk

PARTLINE LTD
Dockfield Road, Shipley BD17 7AZ
Tel: 01274 531531
Fax: 01274 531088
E-mail: sales@partline.co.uk
Web site: www.partline.co.uk

PLAXTON
Plaxton Park, Cayton Low Road,
Eastfield, Scarborough YO11 3BY
Tel: 01723 581500
Fax: 01723 5813238
E-mail: sales@plaxtonlimited.co.uk
Web site: www.plaxtonlimited.co.uk

PLAXTON COACH SALES CENTRE
Ryton Road, Anston, Sheffield S25 4DL
Tel: 01909 551155
Fax: 01909 567994
E-mail: coaches@plaxtonlimited.co.uk
Web site: www.plaxtonlimited.co.uk

Q'STRAINT
73-76 John Wilson Business Park,
Whitstable. Kent CT5 3QU
Tel: 01227 773 035
Fax: 01227 770 035
E-mail: info@qstraint.co.uk
Web site: www.qstraint.com

SAFETEX LTD
Unit 16/17, Bookham Industrial Park,
Church Road, Bookham KT23 3EV
Tel: 01372 451272
Fax: 01372 451282
E-mail: sales@safetex.com
Web site: www@safetex.com

SECURON (AMERSHAM) LTD
Winchmore Hill, Amersham HP7 0NZ.
Tel: 01494 434455.
Fax: 01494 726499.
E-mail: enquiries@securon.co.uk
Web site: www.securon.co.uk

TRAMONTANA COACH DISTRIBUTORS
Chapelknowe Road, Carfin,
Motherwell ML1 5LE
Tel: 01698 861790
Fax: 01698 860778
E-mail: wdt90@tiscali.co.uk
Web: www.tramontanacoach.co.uk

UNWIN SAFETY SYSTEMS
Unwin House, The Horseshoe, Coat Road,
Martock TA12 6EY
Tel: 01935 827740
Fax: 01935 827760
E-mail: sales@unwin-safety.co.uk
Web site: wwwunwin-safety.com

Seats/seat cushions & seat frames

ABACUS TUBULAR PRODUCTS LTD
Abacus House, Highlode Industrial Estate,
Ramsey PE26 2RB
Tel: 01487 710700
Fax: 01487 710626
E-mail: f.riole@abacus-+p.com
Web site: www.abacus-+p.com

ARDEE COACH TRIM LTD
Artnalivery, Ardll, Louth
Tel: 00 353 41 685 3599
Fax: 00 353 41 685 7016
E-mail: ardeecoachtrim@eircom.net

ARRIVA BUS AND COACH
Lodge Garage, Whitehall Road West,
Cleckheaton BD19 4BJ
Tel: 01274 681 144
Fax: 01274 651 198
E-mail: busandcoachsales@arriva.co.uk
Web site: www.arrivabusandcoach.co.uk

BERNSTEIN ENGINEERING LTD
Unit 4, East 41 Garside Way, Stocklake,
Aylesbury HP20 1BH
Tel: 01296 395889
Fax: 01296 394939
E-mail: contact@bernsteinengineering.co.uk
Web: www.bernsteinengineering.co.uk

CAMIRA FABRICS LTD
Hopton Mills, Mirfield WF1 8HE
Tel: 01924 490591
Fax: 01924 495605
Web site: www.camirafabrics.com

CARLYLE BUS & COACH LTD
Carlyle Business Park, Great Bridge Street,
Swan Village, West Bromwich B70 0XA
Tel: 0121 524 1200
Fax: 0121 524 1201
E-mail: admin@carlyleplc.co.uk
Web site: www.carlyleplc.co.uk

CHAPMAN DRIVERS SEATING
68 Burners Lane, Kiln Farm, Milton
Keynes MK11 3HD
Tel: 0845 838 2305
Fax: 0845 838 2909
Web site: www.chapmandriverseating.com

COGENT PASSENGER SEATING LTD
Prydwen Road, Swansea West Industrial
Estate, Swansea SA5 4HN
Tel: 01792 585444
Fax: 01792 588191
Web site: www.cogentseating.co.uk
E-mail: enquiries@cogentseating.co.uk

DUOFLEX LTD
Trimmingham House, 2 Shires Road,
Buckingham Road Industrial Estate,
Brackley NN13 7EZ
Tel: 01280 701366
Fax: 01280 704799
E-mail: sales@duoflex.co.uk
Web site: www.duoflex.co.uk

HAPPICH V & I COMPONENTS LTD
Unit 30/31, Fort Industrial Park, Fort
Parkway, Castle Bromwich B35 7AR.
Tel: 0121 747 4400
Fax: 0121 747 4977
E-mail: sales@happich.co.uk
Web site: www.happich.co.uk

JBF SERVICES LTD
Southedge Works, Hipperholme,
Halifax HX3 8EF
Tel: 01422 202840
Fax: 01422 206070
E-mail: jbfservices@aol.com

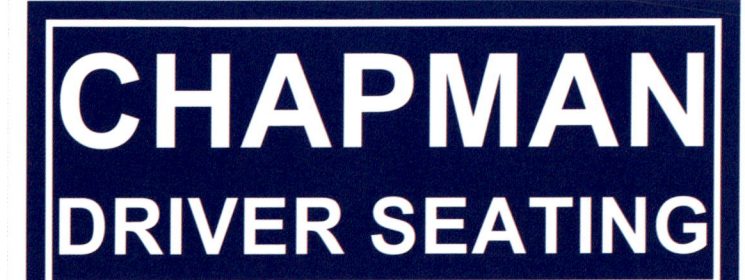

CHAPMAN DRIVER SEATING

www.chapmandriverseating.com

Contact Details
☎ 0845 838 2305   📠 0845 838 2909

42

KAB SEATING LTD
Round Spinney, Northampton NN3 8RS
Tel: 01604 790500
Fax: 01604 790155
E-mail: infouk@cvgrp.com
Web: www.kabseating.com

THE LAWTON MOTOR BODY BUILDING CO LTD
Knutsford Road, Church Lawton, Stoke-on-Trent ST7 3DN
Tel: 01270 882056
Fax: 01270 883014
E-mail: enquiries@lawtonmotorbody.co.uk
Web site: www.lawtonmotorbody.co.uk

LUNAR SEATING LTD
Unit 3, Packhorse Place, Watling Street, Kensworth LU6 3QU
Tel: 01582 841535
Fax: 01582 841749
E-mail: sue@lunar-seating.co.uk

MTB EQUIPMENT LTD
Sixth Avenue, Zone Two, Deeside Industrial Park, Deeside CH5 2LB
Tel: 0870 870 1282
Fax: 01244 289 818
E-mail: info@mtb-equipment.com
Web site: www.mtb-equipment.com

NEXT BUS LTD
The Coach Yard, Vincents Road, Bumpers Farm Industrial Estate, Chippenham SN14 6QA
Tel: 01249 462462
Fax: 01249 448844
E-mail: sales@next-bus.co.uk
Web site: www.next-bus.co.uk

PHOENIX SEATING LTD
Unit 47, Bay 3, Second Avenue, Pensnett Estate, Kingswinford DY6 7UZ
Tel: 01384 296622

PLAXTON COACH SALES CENTRE
Ryton Road, Anston, Sheffield S25 4DL
Tel: 01909 551155
Fax: 01909 567994
E-mail: coaches@plaxtonlimited.co.uk
Web site: www.plaxtonlimited.co.uk

RESCROFT LTD
20 Oxleasow Road, East Moons Moat, Redditch B98 0RE
Tel: 01527 521300
Fax: 01527 521301
Web site: www.rescroft.com
E-mail: enquiries@rescroft.com

SCANDUS UK
Unit 21, Gainsborough Trading Estate, Rufford Road, Stourbridge DY9 7ND
Tel: 01384 443409
Fax: 01384 443 932
Web site: www.scandusuk.co.uk

TUBE PRODUCTS LTD
PO Box 13, Oldbury, Warley B69 4PF.
Tel: 0121 552 1511.
Fax: 0121 544 6026.

WINCHESTER MARINE LTD (MAJORLINE ENGINEERING)
Baybridge Industrial Units, Baybridge Lane, Owslebury, Winchester SO21 1JN.
Tel: 01962 777077.
Fax: 01962 777661, 777667
E-mail: winchestermarine.btconnect.com

WOODBRIDGE FOAM UK LTD
Stakehill Industrial Estate, Manchester M24 2SJ
Tel: 0161 654 2500.
Fax: 0161 653 4433

Shelters/Street Furniture

M BISSELL DISPLAY LTD
Unit 15, Beechwood Business Park, Burdock Close, Cannock WS11 7GB
Tel: 01543 502115
Fax: 01543 502118
E-mail: sales@bisselldisplay.com
Web site: www.bisselldisplay.com

BUS SHELTERS LTD
Dyffryn Business Park, Llantwit Major Road, Llandow CF71 7PY
Tel: 01446 795444
Fax: 01446 793344
E-mail: bus@shelters.co.uk
Web site: www.shelters.co.uk

CARMANAH UK
68 Basepoint Business Centre, Metcalf Way, Crawley RH11 7XX
Tel: 0870 345 9548 0208 323 8028
E-mail: info@carmanah.co.uk
Web site: www.carmanah.co.uk

GABRIEL & COMPANY LTD
Abro Works, 10 Hay Hall Road, Tyseley, Birmingham B11 2AU
Tel: 0121 248 3333
Fax: 0121 248 3330
E-mail: contact@gabrielco.com
Web site: www.gabrielco.com

MACEMAIN + AMSTAD
Boyle Road, Willowbrook Industrial Estate, Corby NN17 5XU
Tel: 01536 401331
Fax: 01536 401298
E-mail: enquiries@macemainamstad.com
Web site: www.macemainamstad.com

QUEENSBURY SHELTERS
Queensbury House, Fitzherbert Road, Farlington, Portsmouth PO6 1SE
Tel: 023 9221 0052
Fax: 023 9221 0059
Web site: www.queensbury.org

TRUEFORM ENGINEERING LTD
Unit 4, Pasadena Trading Estate, Pasadena Close, Hayes UB3 3NQ
Tel: 020 8561 4959
Fax: 020 8848 1397
E-mail: sales@trueform.co.uk
Web site: www..trueform.co.uk

WHITELEY ELECTRONICS
Victoria Street, Mansfield NG18 5RW
Tel: 01623 415600
Fax: 01623 420484
E-mail: sales@whiteleyelectronics.com
Web site: www.whiteleyelectronics.com

Shock Absorbers/Suspension

ASHLEY BANKS LTD
5 King Street Estate, Langtoft, Peterborough PE6 9NF
Tel: 01778 560651
Fax: 01778 560721
E-mail: user@ashleybanks.fsnet.co.uk

CRESCENT FACILITIES LTD
72 Willow Crescent, Chapeltown, Sheffield S35 1QS
Tel/fax: 0114 2451050
E-mail: cfl.chris@btinternet.com
Web site: www.cflparts.com

DIRECT PARTS LTD
Unit 1, Churnet Court, Churnetside Business Park, Harrison Way, Cheddleton ST13 7EF
Tel: 01538 361777
Fax: 01538 369100
E-mail: sales@direct-group.co.uk
Web site: www.direct-group.co.uk

ERENTEK LTD
Malt Kiln Lane, Waddington, Lincoln LN5 9RT
Tel: 01522 720065
Fax: 01522 729155
E-mail: sale@erentek.co.uk
Web site: www.erentek.co.uk

GLIDE RITE
Mill Lane, Passfield, Liphook GU30 7RP
Tel: 01428 751711
Fax: 01428 751677
Web site: www.glide-rite.net

IMEXPART LTD
Links 31, Willowbridge Way, Whitwood, Castleford WF10 5NP
Tel: 01977 553936
Fax: 01977 604684
E-mail: parts@imexpart.com
Web site: www.imexpart.com

KELLETT (UK) LTD
8 Stevenson Way, Sheffield S9 3WZ.
Tel: 0114 261 1122.
Fax: 0114 261 1199.
E-mail: sales@kellett.co.uk

NEXT BUS LTD
The Coach Yard, Vincents Road, Bumpers Farm Industrial Estate, Chippenham SN14 6QA
Tel: 01249 462462
Fax: 01249 448844
E-mail: sales@next-bus.co.uk
Web site: www.next-bus.co.uk

PARTLINE LTD
Dockfield Road, Shipley BD17 7AZ
Tel: 01274 531531
Fax: 01274 531088
E-mail: sales@partline.co.uk
Web site: www.partline.co.uk

POLYBUSH
Clywedog Road South, Wrexham Industrial Estate, Wrexham LL13 9XS
Tel: 01978 664316
Fax: 01978 661190
E-mail: sales@polybush.co.uk
Web site: www.polybush.co.uk

ROADLINK INTERNATIONAL LTD
Strawberry Lane, Willenhall WV13 3RL
Tel: 01902 636210
Fax: 01902 606604
E-mail: sales@roadlink-international.co.uk
Web site: www.roadlink-international.co.uk

SHAWSON SUPPLY LTD
12 Station Road, Saintfield, County Down, Northern Ireland BT24 7DU
Tel: 028 9751 0994
Fax: 028 9751 0816
E-mail: info@shawsonsupply.com
Web site: www.shawsonsupply.com

UNITEC
Parts Division, Denby Way, Hellaby, Rotherham S66 8HR
Tel: 01709 792000
Fax: 01709 792009
E-mail: parts@optare.com

Trade Directory

WINCHESTER MARINE LTD (MAJORLINE ENGINEERING)
Baybridge Industrial Units, Baybridge Lane, Owslebury, Winchester SO21 1JN.
Tel: 01962 777077.
Fax: 01962 777661, 777667
E-mail: winchestermarine@btconnect.com

Steering

ARRIVA BUS AND COACH
Lodge Garage, Whitehall Road West, Cleckheaton BD19 4BJ
Tel: 01274 681 144
Fax: 01274 651 198
E-mail: busandcoachsales@arriva.co.uk
Web site: www.arrivabusandcoach.co.uk

CRESCENT FACILITIES LTD
72 Willow Crescent, Chapeltown, Sheffield S35 1QS
Tel/fax: 0114 2451050
E-mail: cfl.chris@btinternet.com
Web site: www.cflparts.com

DIRECT PARTS LTD
Unit 1, Churnet Court, Churnetside Business Park, Harrison Way, Cheddleton ST13 7EF
Tel: 01538 361777
Fax: 01538 369100
E-mail: sales@direct-group.co.uk
Web site: www.direct-group.co.uk

HL SMITH TRANSMISSIONS LTD
Enterprise Business Park, Cross Road, Albrighton, Wolverhampton WV7 3BJ
Tel: 01902 373011
Fax: 01902 373608
Web: www.hlsmith.co.uk

IMEXPART LTD
Links 31, Willowbridge Way, Whitwood, Castleford WF10 5NP
Tel: 01977 553936
Fax: 01977 604684
E-mail: parts@imexpart.com
Web site: www.imexpart.com

IMPERIAL ENGINEERING
Delamare Road, Cheshunt EN8 9UD
Tel: 01992 6342555
Fax: 01992 630506
E-mail: sales@imperialengineering.co.uk
Web site: www.imperialengineering.co.uk

NEXT BUS LTD
The Coach Yard, Vincents Road, Bumpers Farm Industrial Estate, Chippenham SN14 6QA
Tel: 01249 462462
Fax: 01249 468844
E-mail: sales@next-bus.co.uk
Web site: www.next-bus.co.uk

PARTLINE LTD
Dockfield Road, Shipley BD17 7AZ
Tel: 01274 531531
Fax: 01274 531088
E-mail: sales@partline.co.uk
Web site: www.partline.co.uk

PSS - STEERING & HYDRAULICS DIVISION
Folgate Road, North Walsham NR28 0AJ
Tel: 01692 406017
Fax: 01692 406957
E-mail: sales@pss.co.uk
Web site: www.pss.co.uk

ROADLINK INTERNATIONAL LTD
Strawberry Lane, Willenhall WV13 3RL
Tel: 01902 636210
Fax: 01902 606604
E-mail: sales@roadlink-international.co.uk
Web site: www.roadlink-international.co.uk

SHAWSON SUPPLY LTD
12 Station Road, Saintfield, County Down, Northern Ireland BT24 7DU
Tel: 028 9751 0994
Fax: 028 9751 0816
E-mail: info@shawssonsupply.com
Web site: www.shawssonsupply.com

UNITEC
Parts Division, Denby Way, Hellaby, Rotherham S66 8HR
Tel: 01709 792000
Fax: 01709 792009
E-mail: parts@optare.com

UNITEC LONDON
Unit 9, Euro Court, Olivers Close, West Thurrock RM20 3EE
Tel: 08444 123222
Fax: 01708 869900
E-mail: london.service@optare.com

UNITEC ROTHERHAM
Denby Way, Hellaby, Rotherham S66 8HR
Tel: 01709 535101
Fax: 01709 535103
E-mail: rotherham.service@optare.com

UNITEC SCOTLAND
Unit 7, Cumbernauld Business Park, Ward Park Road, Cumbernauld G67 3JZ
Tel: 01236 726738
Fax: 01236 795651
E-mail: scotland.service@optare.com

WINCHESTER MARINE LTD (MAJORLINE ENGINEERING)
Baybridge Industrial Units, Baybridge Lane, Owslebury, Winchester SO21 1JN.
Tel: 01962 777077.
Fax: 01962 777661, 777667
E-mail: winchestermarine@btconntect.com

ZF POWERTRAIN
Stringes Close, Willenhall WV13 1LE
Tel: 01902 366000
Fax: 01902 366504
E-mail: sales@powertrain.org.uk
Web site: www.powertrain.org.uk

Surveillance Systems

AUTOSOUND LTD
4 Lister Street, Dudley Hill, Bradford BD4 9PQ
Tel: 01274 688990
Fax: 01274 651318
Web site: www.autosound.co.uk
E-mail: sales@autosound.co.uk

AVT SYSTEMS LTD
Unit 3 & 4, Tything Road, Arden Forest Trading Estate, Alcester B49 6ES
Tel: 01789 400 357
Fax: 01789 400 359
E-mail: enquiries@avtsystems.co.uk
Web: www.avtsystems.co.uk

BRIGADE ELECTRONICS plc
Brigade House, The Mills, Station Road, South Darenth DA4 9BD
Tel: 01322 420 300
Fax: 01322 420 343
E-mail: info@brigade-electronics.co.uk
Web site: www.brigade-electronics.com

CLAN TOOLS & PLANT LTD
3 Greenhill Avenue, Giffnock, Glasgow G46 6QX.
Tel: 0141 638 8040.
Fax: 0141 638 8881.
E-mail: clantools@btconnect.com
Web site: www.clantools.co.uk

CYBERLYNE COMMUNICATIONS LTD
Unit 5, Hatfield Way, South Church Enterprise Park, Bishop Auckland DL14 6XB
Tel: 01388 773761
Fax: 01388 773778
E-mail: k.brockelhurst@cyberlyne.co.uk
Web site: www.cyberlyne.co.uk

DIRECT PARTS LTD
Unit 1, Churnet Court, Churnetside Business Park, Harrison Way, Cheddleton ST13 7EF
Tel: 01538 361777
Fax: 01538 369100
E-mail: sales@direct-group.co.uk
Web site: www.direct-group.co.uk

KELLETT (UK) LTD
8 Stevenson Way, Sheffield S9 3WZ.
Tel: 0114 261 1122.
Fax: 0114 261 1199.
E-mail: sales@kellett.co.uk

KNORR-BREMSE SYSTEMS FOR COMMERCIAL VEHICLES LTD
Douglas Road, Kingswood, Bristol BS15 8NL.
Tel: 0117 984 6100.
Fax: 0117 984 6101.
Web site: www.knorr-bremse.com

LOOK CCTV LTD
Unit 4, Wyrefields, Poulton-le-Fylde FY6 8JX
Tel: 01253 891222
Fax: 01253 891221
Web site: www.lookcctv.com
E-mail: enquiries@lookcctv.com

PARTLINE LTD
Dockfield Road, Shipley BD17 7AZ
Tel: 01274 531531
Fax: 01274 531088
E-mail: sales@partline.co.uk
Web site: www.partline.co.uk

PSV PRODUCTS
PO Box 166, Warrington WA4 5FG
Tel: 0844 686 4488
Fax: 01925 601534
E-mail: info@psvproducts.com
Web site: www.psvproducts.com

WABCO AUTOMOTIVE UK LTD
Texas Street, Morley LS27 0HQ.
Tel: 0113 251 2510
Fax: 0113 251 2844
Web: www.wabco-auto.com

WEBASTO PRODUCT UK LTD
Webasto House, White Rose Way, Doncaster Carr DN4 5JH
Tel: 01302 322232
Fax: 01302 322231
E-mail: info@webastouk.com
Web site: www.webasto.co.uk

WINCHESTER MARINE LTD (MAJORLINE ENGINEERING)
Baybridge Industrial Units, Baybridge Lane, Owslebury, Winchester SO21 1JN.
Tel: 01962 777077.
Fax: 01962 777661, 777667
E-mail: winchestermarine@btconnect.com

Tachographs

ARRIVA BUS AND COACH
Lodge Garage, Whitehall Road West,
Cleckheaton BD19 4BJ
Tel: 01274 681 144
Fax: 01274 651 198
E-mail: busandcoachsales@arriva.co.uk
Web site: www.arrivabusandcoach.co.uk

CHASSIS DEVELOPMENTS LTD
Grovebury Road,
Leighton Buzzard LU7 8SL.
Tel: 01525 374151
Fax: 01525 370127
E-mail: Sales@chassisdevelopments.com
Web site: www.chassisdevelopment.co.uk

ERF MEDWAY LTD
Sir Thomas Longley Road, Medway City
Estate, Rochester ME2 4QW.
Tel: 01634 711144.
Fax: 01634 711188.

THOMAS HARDIE – WIGAN
Lockett Road,
Ashton-in-Makerfield WN4 8DE.
Tel: 01942 505124.
Fax: 01942 505119.

PARTLINE LTD
Dockfield Road, Shipley BD17 7AZ
Tel: 01274 531531
Fax: 01274 531088
E-mail: sales@partline.co.uk
Web site: www.partline.co.uk

PLAXTON
Plaxton Park, Cayton Low Road,
Eastfield, Scarborough YO11 3BY
Tel: 01723 581500
Fax: 01723 5813238
E-mail: sales@plaxtonlimited.co.uk
Web site: www.plaxtonlimited.co.uk

PLAXTON COACH SALES CENTRE
Ryton Road, Anston, Sheffield S25 4DL
Tel: 01909 551155
Fax: 01909 567994
E-mail: coaches@plaxtonlimited.co.uk
Web site: www.plaxtonlimited.co.uk

SIEMENS VDO TRADING LTD
36 Gravelly Industrial Park,
Birmingham B24 8TA.
Tel: 0121 326 1234
Fax: 0121 326 1299
Web site: www.siemens-datatrack.com

UNITEC LONDON
Unit 9, Eurocourt, Olivers Close,
West Thurrock RM20 3EE
Tel: 01844 123222
Fax: 01708 869920
E-mail: london.service@optare.com

UNITEC ROTHERHAM
Denby Way, Hellaby, Rotherham S66 8HR
Tel: 01709 535101
Fax: 01709 535103
E-mail: rotherham.service@optare.com

UNITEC SCOTLAND
Unit 7, Cumbernauld Business Park,
Ward Park Road, Cumbernauld G67 3JZ
Tel: 01236 726738
Fax: 01236 795651
E-mail: scotland.service@optare.com

WARD INTERNATIONAL CONSULTING LTD
Funtley Court, 19 Funtley Hill, Fareham
PO16 7UY
Tel: 01329 280280
Fax: 01329 221010
E-mail: info@wardint.co.uk
Web site: www.wardint.com

WINCHESTER MARINE LTD (MAJORLINE ENGINEERING)
Baybridge Industrial Units, Baybridge Lane,
Owslebury, Winchester SO21 1JN.
Tel: 01962 777077.
Fax: 01962 777661, 777667
E-mail: winchestermarine@btconnect.com

Tachograph Calibrators

ARRIVA BUS AND COACH
Lodge Garage, Whitehall Road West,
Cleckheaton BD19 4BJ
Tel: 01274 681 144
Fax: 01274 651 198
E-mail: busandcoachsales@arriva.co.uk
Web site: www.arrivabusandcoach.co.uk

MARSHALLS COMMERCIAL ENGINEERING LTD
Firbank Way, Leighton Buzzard LU7 4YP
Tel: 01525 375301
Fax: 01525 850967
Web site: www.mce-ltd.com

PLAXTON
Plaxton Park, Cayton Low Road, Eastfield,
Scarborough YO11 3BY
Tel: 01723 581500
Fax: 01723 5813238
E-mail: sales@plaxtonlimited.co.uk
Web site: www.plaxtonlimited.co.uk

PLAXTON COACH SALES CENTRE
Ryton Road, Anston, Sheffield S25 4DL
Tel: 01909 551155
Fax: 01909 567994
E-mail: coaches@plaxtonlimited.co.uk
Web site: www.plaxtonlimited.co.uk

SIEMENS VDO TRADING LTD
36 Gravelly Industrial Park, Birmingham B24 8TA
Tel: 0121 326 1234
Fax: 0121 326 1299
Web site: www.siemens-datatrack.com

UNITEC LONDON
Unit 9, Eurocourt, Olivers Close, West
Thurrock RM20 3EE
Tel: 01844 123222
Fax: 01708 869920
E-mail: london.service@optare.com

UNITEC ROTHERHAM
Denby Way, Hellaby, Rotherham S66 8HR
Tel: 01709 535101
Fax: 01709 535103
E-mail: rotherham.service@optare.com

UNITEC SCOTLAND
Unit 7, Cumbernauld Business Park, Ward
Park Road, Cumbernauld G67 3JZ
Tel: 01236 726738
Fax: 01236 795651
E-mail: scotland.service@optare.com

WINCHESTER MARINE LTD (MAJORLINE ENGINEERING)
Baybridge Industrial Units, Baybridge Lane,
Owslebury, Winchester SO21 1JN.
Tel: 01962 777077.
Fax: 01962 777661, 777667
E-mail: winchestermarine@btconnect.com

Tachograph Chart Analysis Service

CI COACHLINES
Pools Lane, Highwood, Essex CM1 3QL
Tel: 01245 248 669

IBPTS
43 Cage Lane, Felixstowe,
Suffolk OP11 9BJ
Tel: 01394 672 344
Fax: 01394 672 344
E-mail: info@ibpts.co.uk
Web: www.ibpts.co.uk

CHASSIS DEVELOPMENTS LTD
Grovebury Road, Leighton Buzzard LU7 8SL.
Tel: 01525 374151.
Fax: 01525 370127.
E-mail: sales@chassisdevelopments.com
Web site:
www.chassissdevelopments.co.uk

TRANSPORT & TRAINING SERVICES LTD
Warrington Business Park, Long Lane,
Warrington WA2 8TX
Tel: 01925 243 500
Fax: 01925 243 000
E-mail: tachographsuk@aol.com
Web site: www.transporttrainingservices.com

SIEMENS VDO TRADING LTD
36 Gravelly Industrial Park, Birmingham B24 8TA
Tel: 0121 326 1234
Fax: 0121 326 1299
Web site: www.siemens-datatrack.com

Tickets, Ticket Machines and Ticket Systems

ACT - APPLIED CARD TECHNOLOGIES
Langley Gate, Kington Langley, Chippenham
SN15 5SE
Tel: 01249 751 200
Fax: 01249 751 201
Email: info@card.co.uk
Web site: www.card.co.uk

ALMEX INFORMATION SYSTEMS
Metric House, Westmead Industrial Estate
Westlea, Swindon SN5 7AD
Tel: 01793 647931
Fax: 01793 647802
E-mail: info@almex.co.uk
Web site: www.almex.co.uk

ATOS ORIGIN
4 Triton Square, Regents Place,
London NW1 3HG
Tel: 020 7830 4444
Fax: 020 7830 4445
Web site: www.atosorigin.co.uk

Trade Directory

45

John Groves

TICKET SYSTEMS

your one stop shop for fare collection

www.jgts.co.uk

Tel: 0208 908 9088
Fax: 0208 908 9099
email: sales@jgts.co.uk

authorised UK agent for
PARKEON

PayCell®

CAMBIST

PENDAMATIC

Trade Directory

BEMROSEBOOTH LTD
Stockholm Road, Sutton Fields Industrial Estate, Hull HU7 0XY
Tel: 01482 826343
Fax: 01482 371386
E-mail: lprecious@bemrosebooth.com
Web site: www.bemrosebooth.com

CANN PRINT
Block C, Unit 2, Crookedholm Commercial Centre, Mainroad, Crookedholm, Kilmarnock KA3 6JT
Tel: 01563 572440
Fax: 01563 544933
E-mail: info@cannprint.com
Web site: www.cannprint.com

CUBIC TRANSPORTATION SYSTEMS LTD
AFC House, Honeycrock Lane, Salfords, Redhill RH1 5LA
Tel: 01737 782200
Fax: 01737 789759
Web site: www.cubic.com

DE LA RUE
De La Rue House, Jays Close, Viables, Basingstoke RG22 4BS
Tel: 01256 605000
Fax: 01256 605004
Web site: www.delarue.com

KEITH EDMONDSON TICKET ROLLS
Garden House, Tittensor, Stoke-on-Trent ST12 9HQ
Tel: 01782 372305
Fax: 01782 351136
E-mail: keith@ticketrolls.co.uk
Web site: www.ticketrolls.co.uk

ETMSS LTD
C/O Dorset House, 9 Dorset Avenue, Ferndown, Dorset BH22 8HJ
Tel: 0844 800 9299
E-mail: info@etmss.com
Web: www.etmss.com

JOHN GROVES TICKET SYSTEMS
12 Magnet Road, East Lane Business Park, Wembley HA9 7RG
Tel: 0208 908 9088
Fax: 0208 908 9099
Web site: www.jgts.co.uk
E-Mail: sales@jgts.co.uk

INIT
Broadway Business Centre, 32a Stoney Street, The Lace Market, Nottingham NG1 1LL
Tel: 0115 988 6916
Web site: www.init-ka.de

MARK TERRILL TICKET MACHINERY
5 De Grey Close, Lewes BN7 2JR.
Tel: 01273 474816
Fax: 01273 474816
E-mail: mark.terrill@ukonline.co.uk

PAYPOINT PLC
1 The Boulevard, Shire Park, Welwyn Garden City AL7 1EL
Tel: 01707 60300
Email: grahambloye@paypoint.co.uk
Web site: www.paypoint.co.uk

SCAN COIN LTD
110 Broadway, Salford Quays M50 2UW
Tel: 0161 873 0505
Fax: 0161 873 0501
E-mail: sales@scancoin.co.uk
Web site: www.scancoin.co.uk

SCHADES LTD
Brittain Drive, Codnor Gate Business Park, Ripley DE5 3RZ
Tel: 01773 748721
Fax: 01773 745601
Web site: www.schades.com
E-mail: sales@schades.co.uk

STUART MANUFACTURING CO LTD
Craft Avenue, 135 Hayes Lane, Kenley CR8 5JR
Tel: 020 8668 8107
Fax: 020 8668 8277
E-mail: sales@smco.co.uk
Web site: www.smco.co.uk

THOMAS AUTOMATICS CO LTD
Bishop Meadow Road, Loughborough LE11 5RE
Tel: 01509 267611
Fax: 01509 266836
E-mail: sales@thomasa.co.uk
Web site: www.thomasa.co.uk

TRANSPORT TICKET SERVICES LTD
Yew Tree Cottage, Newcastle, Monmouth NP25 5NT
Tel/Fax: 01600 750650
E-mail: ttsservices@tiscali.com

WAYFARER TRANSIT SYSTEMS LTD
10 Willis Way, Fleets Industrial Estate, Poole BH15 3SS
Tel: 01202 339339
Fax: 01202 339369
E-mail: sales@wayfarer.co.uk
Web site: www.wayfarer.co.uk

Timetable Display Frames

M BISSELL DISPLAY LTD
Unit 15, Beechwood Business Park, Burdock Close, Cannock WS11 7GB
Tel: 01543 502115
Fax: 01543 502118
E-mail: sales@bisselldisplay.com
Web site: www.bisselldisplay.com

BROADWATER MOULDINGS LTD
Horham, Eye IP21 5JL.
Tel: 01379 384145.
Fax: 01379 384150
Web site: www.broadwater.co.uk

GABRIEL & CO LTD
Abro Works, 10 Hay Hall Road, Tyseley, Birmingham B11 2AU
Tel: 0121 248 3333
Fax: 0121 248 3330
E-mail: contact@gabrielco.com
Web site: www.gabrielco.com

Toilet Equipment

ARRIVA BUS AND COACH
Lodge Garage, Whitehall Road West, Cleckheaton BD19 4BJ
Tel: 01274 681 144
Fax: 01274 651 198
E-mail: busandcoachsales@arriva.co.uk
Web site: www.arrivabusandcoach.co.uk

BRADTECH LTD
Unit 3, Ladford Covert, Seighford, Stafford ST18 9QL
Tel: 01785 282800
Fax: 01785 282558
E-mail: sales@bradtech.ltd.uk
Web site: www.bradtech.ltd.uk

CARLYLE BUS & COACH LTD
Carlyle Business Park, Great Bridge Street, Swan Village, West Bromwich B70 0XA
Tel: 0121 524 1200
Fax: 0121 524 1201
E-mail: admin@carlyleplc.co.uk
Web site: www.carlyleplc.co.uk

ELSAN LTD
Bellbrook Park, Uckfield TN22 1QF
Tel: 01825 748200
Fax: 01825 761212
E-mail: sales@elsan.co.uk
Web site: www.elsan.co.uk

EXPRESS COACH REPAIRS LTD
Outgang Lane, Pickering YO18 7EL.
Tel: 01751 475215.
Fax: 01751 475215
Web site: www.expresscoachrepairs.co.uk

THE LAWTON MOTOR BODY BUILDING CO LTD
Knutsford Road, Church Lawton, Stoke-on-Trent ST7 3DN
Tel: 01270 882056
Fax: 01270 883014
E-mail: enquiries@lawtonmotorbody.co.uk
Web site: www.lawtonmotorbody.co.uk

PSV PRODUCTS
PO Box 166, Warrington WA4 5FG
Tel: 0844 686 4488
Fax: 01925 601534
E-mail: info@psvproducts.com
Web site: www.psvproducts.com

SHADES TECHNICS LTD
Units E3 & E4, Rd Park, Stephenson Close, Hoddesdon, Hetrtfordshire EN11 0BW
Tel: 01992 501683
Fax: 01992 501669
E-mail: sales@shades-technics.com
Web site: www.shades-technics.com

TRAMONTANA COACH DISTRIBUTORS
Chapelknowe Road, Carfin, Motherwell ML1 5LE
Tel: 01698 861790
Fax: 01698 860778
E-mail: wdt90@tiscali.co.uk
Web site: www.tramontanacoach.co.uk

Transmission Overhaul

BUSS BIZZ
Goughs Transport Depot, Morestead, Winchester SO21 1JD.
Tel: 01962 715555/66.
Fax: 01962 714868.

GARDNER PARTS LTD
Barton Hall, Hardy Street, Eccles, Manchester M30 7WA.
Tel: 0161 786 1900
Fax: 0161 788 8949
E-mail: sales@gardnerpars.co.uk
Web site: www.gardnerparts.co.uk

47

HL SMITH TRANSMISSIONS LTD
Enterprise Business Park, Cross Road, Albrighton, Wolverhampton WV7 3BJ
Tel: 01902 373011
Fax: 01902 373608
Web site: www.hlsmith.co.uk

LH GROUP SERVICES LTD
Graycar Business Park, Barton Under Needwood, Burton-on-Trent DE13 8EN
Tel: 01283 722600
Fax: 01283 722622
E-mail: lh@lh-group.com
Web site: www.lh-group.com

PARTLINE LTD
Dockfield Road, Shipley BD17 7AZ
Tel: 01274 531531
Fax: 01274 531088
E-mail: sales@partline.co.uk
Web site: www.partline.co.uk

SHAWSON SUPPLY LTD
12 Station Road, Saintfield, County Down, Northern Ireland BT24 7DU
Tel: 028 9751 0994
Fax: 028 9751 0816
E-mail: info@shawsonsupply.com
Web site: www.shawsonsupply.com

UNITEC
Parts Division, Denby Way, Hellaby, Rotherham S66 8HR
Tel: 01709 792000
Fax: 01709 792009
E-mail: parts@optare.com

UNITEC LONDON
Unit 9, Eurocourt, Olivers Close, West Thurrock RM20 3EE
Tel: 018444 123222
Fax: 01708 869920
E-mail: london.service@optare.com

UNITEC ROTHERHAM
Denby Way, Hellaby, Rotherham S66 8HR
Tel: 01709 535101
Fax: 01709 535103
E-mail: rotherham.service@optare.com

UNITEC SCOTLAND
Unit 7, Cumbernauld Business Park, Ward Park Road, Cumbernauld G67 3JZ
Tel: 01236 726738
Fax: 01236 795651
E-mail: scotland.service@optare.com

VOITH TURBO LTD
6 Beddington Farm Road, Croydon CR0 4XB
Tel: 020 8667 3032
Fax: 020 8667 0403
E-mail: john.domigan@voith.com
Web site: www.voithturbo.co.uk

VOR TRANSMISSIONS LTD
Little London House, St Anne's Road, Willenhall WV13 1DT
Tel: 08000 184141
Fax: 01902 603868
E-mail: sales@vor.co.uk
Web site: www.vor.co.uk

ZF POWERTRAIN
Stringes Close, Willenhall WV13 1LE
Tel: 01902 366000
Fax: 01902 366504
E-mail: sales@powertrain.org.uk
Web site: www.powertrain.org.uk

Tree Guards

GABRIEL & COMPANY LTD
APRO Works, 10 Ham Hall Road, Birmingham B11 2AU
Tel: 0121 248 3333
Fax: 0121 248 3330
Web site: www.gabrielco.com

Tyres

DUNLOP TYRES LTD
TyreFort, 88-98 Wingfoot Way, Birmingham B24 9HY
Tel: 0121 306 6000
Fax: 0121 306 6437
Web site: www.dunloptyres.co.uk

SNOWCHAINS EUROPRODUCTS
Borough Green TN15 8DG
Tel: 01732 884408
Fax: 01732 884564
Web site: www.snowchains.co.uk

UNITEC LONDON
Unit 9, Eurocourt, Olivers Close, West Thurrock RM20 3EE
Tel: 08444 123222
Fax: 01708 869920
E-mail: london.service@optare.com

UNITEC ROTHERHAM
Denby Way, Hellaby, Rotherham S66 8HR
Tel: 01709 535101
Fax: 01709 535103
E-mail: rotherham.service@optare.com

Uniforms

ALLEN & DOUGLAS CORPORATE CLOTHING LTD
Unit 8, Lombard Way, Banbury OX16 3EZ
Tel: 01295 228452
Fax: 01295 257937
E-mail: sales@aandd.co.uk
Web site: www.aandd.co.uk

IMAGE FIRST CORPORATE CLOTHING LTD
Exhibition House, Grape Street, Leeds LS10 1BX
Tel: 0113 243 3855
Fax: 0113 242 1040
E-Mail: reception@image-first.co.uk
Web site: www.image-first.co.uk

HANDLEY BUS & COACH UNIFORMS
Unit 3, 18 Croydon Street, Leeds LS11 9RT
Tel: 0113 245 7008
Fax: 0113 245 9643
E-mail: tor@tordesigns.com
Web-Site: www.tordesigns.com

LEISUREWEAR DIRECT LTD
4A South Street North, New Whittington, Chesterfield S43 2AB
Tel: 01246 454447
Fax: 0870 755 9842
E-mail: jane@leisureweardirect.com
Web site: www.leisureweardirect.com

RAINBOW CORPORATEWEAR
Gosforth Road, Derby DE24 8HU
Tel: 01332 342616
Fax: 01332 362328
Web site: www.rainbow-corporatewear.co.uk

TALISMAN
26 North Road, Yate BS37 7DA
Tel: 01454 335177
Fax: 01454 335133
E-mail: sales@talisman.ms.com
Web site: www.talisman.ms.com

Driving Down Costs with DIWA Excellence. That moves us.

www.voithturbo.com

5 STAR SERVICE
- ★ Exchange Transmissions
- ★ Expert Installation
- ★ Voith Dedicated Technicians
- ★ Genuine Spare Parts and Components
- ★ OEM Assured Quality

Voith Turbo

Call 020 8667 3032

VOITH Engineered reliability.

Upholstery

ABACUS TUBULAR PRODUCTS LTD
Abacus House, Highlode Industrial Estate, Ramsey PE26 2RB
Tel: 01487 710700
Fax: 01487 710626
E-mail: f.riole@abacus-+p.com
Web site: www.abacus-+p.com

ARDEE COACH TRIM LTD
Artnalivery, Ardll, Louth
Tel: 00 353 41 685 3599
Fax: 00 353 41 685 7016
E-mail: ardeecoachtrim@eircom.net

AUTOMOTIVE TEXTILE INDUSTRIES
Unit 15 & 16, Priest Court, Springfield Business Park, Grantham NG31 7BG
Tel: 01476 593050
Fax: 01476 593607
E-mail: sales@autotex.com
Web site: www.autotex.com

BLACKPOOL TRIM SHOPS LTD
Brun Grove, Blackpool FY1 6PG
Tel: 01253 766762
Fax: 01253 798443
E-mail: sales@blackpooltrimshops.co.uk
Web site: www.blackpooltrimshops.co.uk

BRIDGE OF WEIR LEATHER CO LTD
Baltic Works, Bridge of Weir PA11 33RH.
Tel: 01505 612132.
Fax: 01505 614964.
E-mail: mail@bowleather.co.uk
Web site: www.bowleather.co.uk

CAMIRA FABRICS LTD
Hopton Mills, Mirfield WF1 8HE
Tel: 01924 490591
Fax: 01924 495605
E-mail: info@camirafabrics.co.uk
Web site: www.camirafabrics.com

DUOFLEX LTD
Trimmingham House, 2 Shires Road, Buckingham Road Industrial Estate, Brackley NN13 7EZ
Tel: 01280 701366
Fax: 01280 704799
E-mail: sales@duoflex.co.uk
Web site: www.duoflex.co.uk

EXPRESS COACH REPAIRS LTD
Outgang Lane, Pickering YO18 7EL.
Tel: 01751 475215.
Fax: 01924 495605.
Web: www.expresscoachrepairs.co.uk

FIRTH FURNISHINGS LTD
Unit 6, Grange Road, Batley WF17 6LH
Tel: 01924 478294.
Fax: 01924 423729.

JOHN HOLDSWORTH & CO LTD
Shaw Lodge Mills, Halifax HX3 9ET
Tel: 01422 433000
Fax: 01422 433300
E-mail: sales@holdsworth.co.uk
Web site: www.holdsworth.co.uk

THE LAWTON MOTOR BODY BUILDING CO LTD
Knutsford Road, Church Lawton, Stoke-on-Trent ST7 3DN
Tel: 01270 882056
Fax: 01270 883014
E-mail: enquiries@lawtonmotorbody.co.uk
Web site: www.lawtonmotorbody.co.uk

MARTYN INDUSTRIALS LTD
5 Brunel Way, Durranhill Industrial Esate, Carlisle CA1 3NQ
Tel: 01228 544000
Fax: 01228 544001
E-mail: enquiries@martyn-industrials.co.uk
Web site: www.martyn-industrials.com

WIDNEY UK LTD
Plume Street, Aston, Birmingham B6 7SA.
Tel: 0121 327 5500.
Fax: 0121 328 2466.
E-mail: richard@widney.co.uk

Vacuum Systems

SMART CENTRAL COACH SYSTEMS
5 Kings Acre House, 329 Kings Acre Road, Hereford HR6 8LB
Tel: 01432 276380
Fax: 01432 351800
E-mail: info@smartcoachsystems.co.uk
Web site: www.smartcoachsystems.co.uk

Vehicle Washing & Washers

ATLANTIS INTERNATIONAL LTD
18 Weldon Road, Loughborough LE11 5RA
Tel: 01509 233770
Fax: 01509 210542
E-mail: sales@atlantisint.co.uk
Web: www.atlantisinternational.co.uk

BRADTECH LTD
Unit 3, Ladford Covert, Seighford, Stafford ST18 9QL
Tel: 01785 282800
Fax: 01785 282558
E-mail: sales@bradtech.ltd.uk
Web site: www.bradtech.ltd.uk

CI COACHLINES
Pools Lane, Highwood, Essex CM1 3QL
Tel: 01245 248 669

MONOWASH (BRUSH REPLACEMENT SERVICE)
8 Contessa Close, Farnborough BR6 7ER.
Tel: 01689 860061.
Fax: 01689 861469

NATIONWIDE CLEANING & SUPPORT SERVICES LTD
Airport House, Purley Way, Croydon CR0 0XZ
Tel: 020 8288 3580
Fax: 020 8288 3581
Web site: www.nationwidefm.com

SMITH BROS & WEBB LTD
Britannia House, Arden Forest Industrial Estate, Alcester B49 6EX
Tel: 01789 400096
Fax: 01789 400231
E-mail: info@vehicle-washing-systems.co.uk
Web site: www.vehicle-washing-systems.co.uk

SOMERS TOTALKARE LTD
15 Forge Trading Estate, Mucklow Hill, Halesowen B62 8TR
Tel: 0121 585 2700
Fax: 0121 585 2725
E-mail: sales@somerstotalkare.co.uk
Web site: www.somerstotalkare.co.uk

WINDOW CLEAN SERVICES
309 Cow Gate, Edinburgh EH1 1NA
Tel: 0131 556 5720
Fax: 0131 558 7377

Wheels, Wheeltrims & Covers

ABACUS TUBULAR PRODUCTS LTD
Abacus House, Highlode Industrial Estate, Ramsey PE26 2RB
Tel: 01487 710700
Fax: 01487 710626
E-mail: f.riole@abacus-+p.com
Web site: www.abacus-+p.com

ALCOA WHEEL PRODUCTS EUROPE
Industrieweg 135, 3583 PAAL, Belgium
Tel: 00 32 11 458464
Fax: 00 21 11 455630
E-mail: info.wheels@alcoa.com
Web site: www.alcoawheels.com

AUTOMATE WHEEL COVERS LTD
California Mills, Oxford Road, Gomersal BD19 4HQ
Tel: 01274 862700
Fax: 01274 851989
E-mail: sales@wheelcovers.co.uk
Web site: www.euroliners.com

HATCHER COMPONENTS LTD
Broadwater Road, Framlingham IP13 9LL.
Tel: 01728 723675.
Fax: 01728 724475.
E-mail: info@hatchercomp.co.uk

J. HIPWELL & SON
427 Warwick Road, Greet, Birmingham B20 1JE.
Tel: 0121 706 5471.
Fax: 0121 706 0502

THE LAWTON MOTOR BODY BUILDING CO LTD
Knutsford Road, Church Lawton, Stoke-on-Trent ST7 3DN
Tel: 01270 882056
Fax: 01270 883014
E-mail: enquiries@lawtonmotorbody.co.uk
Web site: www.lawtonmotorbody.co.uk

UNITEC
Parts Division, Denby Way, Hellaby, Rotherham S66 8HR
Tel: 01709 792000
Fax: 01709 792009
E-mail: parts@optare.com

Windows and Windscreens

ARRIVA BUS AND COACH
Lodge Garage, Whitehall Road West, Cleckheaton BD19 4BJ
Tel: 01274 681 144
Fax: 01274 651 198
E-mail: busandcoachsales@arriva.co.uk
Web site: www.arrivabusandcoach.co.uk

Trade Directory

49

Trade Directory

AUTOGLASS COACH & BUS SERVICES
PO Box 343, Goldington Road,
Bedford MK40 3BX
Tel: 01234 279572
Fax: 01234 279460
Tel: 01234 279559

BRITAX PMG LTD
Bressingby Industrial Estate,
Bridlington YO16 4SJ
Tel: 01262 670161
Fax: 01262 605666
E-mail: info@britax-pmg.com
Web site: www.britax-pmg.com

CARLYLE BUS & COACH LTD
Carlyle Business Park, Great Bridge Street,
Swan Village, West Bromwich B70 0XA
Tel: 0121 524 1200
Fax: 0121 524 1201
E-mail: admin@carlyleplc.co.uk
Web site: www.carlyleplc.co.uk

CRESCENT FACILITIES LTD
72 Willow Crescent, Chapeltown,
Sheffield S35 1QS
Tel/fax: 0114 2451050
E-mail: cfl.chris@btinternet.com
Web site: www.cflparts.com

EXPRESS COACH REPAIRS LTD
Outgang Lane, Pickering YO18 7EL
Tel: 01751 475215.
Fax: 01751 475215
Web site: www.expresscoachrepairs.co.uk

B HEPWORTH & CO LTD
4 Merse Roadt, Redditch B98 9HL
Tel: 01527 61243
Fax: 01527 66836
Web site: www.b-hepworth.com
E-mail: bhepworth@b-hepworth.com

INDUSTRIAL & COMMERCIAL WINDOW CO LTD
Unit 2, Caldervale Industrial Estate,
Horbury Junction, Wakefield WF4 5ER.
Tel: 01924 260106.
Fax: 01924 260152.

J W GLASS LTD
Units 6 & 7, Scropton Road,
Hatton DE65 5DT
Tel: 01283 520202
Fax: 01283 520022
E-mail: info@jwglass.co.uk
Web site: www.jwglass.co.uk

THE LAWTON MOTOR BODY BUILDING CO LTD
Knutsford Road, Church Lawton,
Stoke-on-Trent ST7 3DN
Tel: 01270 882056
Fax: 01270 883014
E-mail: enquiries@lawtonmotorbody.co.uk
Web site: www.lawtonmotorbody.co.uk

NEALINE WINDSCREEN WIPER PRODUCTS
Unit 1, The Sidings Industrial Estate,
Birdingbury Road, Marton CV23 9RX
Tel: 01926 633256
Fax: 01926 632600

PARTLINE LTD
Dockfield Road, Shipley BD17 7AZ
Tel: 01274 531531
Fax: 01274 531088
E-mail: sales@partline.co.uk
Web site: www.partline.co.uk

PERCY LANE PRODUCTS LTD
Lichfield Road, Tamworth B79 7TL
Tel: 01827 63821
Fax: 01827 310159
E-mail: sales@percy-lane.co.uk
Web site: www.percy-lane.co.uk

P & P SERGEANT (B & A) LTD
PO Box 11, New Hall Lane,
Hoylake, Wirral CH47 4DH
Tel: 01516 325 903
Fax: 01516 325 908
E-mail: enq@sergeant.co.uk
Web: www.sergeant.co.uk

PLAXTON COACH SALES CENTRE
Ryton Road, Anston, Sheffield S25 4DL
Tel: 01909 551155
Fax: 01909 567994
E-mail: coaches@plaxtonlimited.co.uk
Web site: www.plaxtonlimited.co.uk

PSV GLASS
Hillbottom Road,
High Wycombe HP12 4HJ
Tel: 01494 533131
Fax: 01494 462675
E-mail: sales@psvglass.co.uk
Web site: www.psvglass.com

TRAMONTANA COACH DISTRIBUTORS
Chapelknowe Road, Carfin,
Motherwell ML1 5LE
Tel: 01698 861790
Fax: 01698 860778
E-mail: wdt90@tiscali.co.uk
Web: www.tramontanacoach.co.uk

UNITEC
Parts Division, Denby Way,
Hellaby, Rotherham S66 8HR
Tel: 01709 792000
Fax: 01709 792009
E-mail: parts@optare.com

UNITEC LONDON
Unit 9, Eurocourt, Olivers Close,
West Thurrock RM20 3EE
Tel: 01844 123222
Fax: 01708 869920
E-mail: london.service@optare.com

UNITEC ROTHERHAM
Denby Way, Hellaby, Rotherham S66 8HR
Tel: 01709 535101
Fax: 01709 535103
E-mail: rotherham.service@optare.com

UNITEC SCOTLAND
Unit 7, Cumbernauld Business Park,
Ward Park Road, Cumbernauld G67 3JZ
Tel: 01236 726738
Fax: 01236 795651
E-mail: scotland.service@optare.com

VOLVO BUS AND COACH CENTRE
Belton Road West,
Loughborough LE11 5HP
Tel: 01509 217777
Fax: 01509 239362
Web site: www.volvo.com

WIDNEY UK LTD
Plume Street, Aston, Birmingham B6 7SA.
Tel: 0121 327 5500.
Fax: 0121 328 2466.
E-mail: richard@widney.co.uk

INDUSTRY SERVICE PROVIDERS

Accident Investigation

KERNOW ASSOCIATES
18 Tresawla Court,
Tolvaddon, Camborne TR14 0HF.
Tel/Fax: 01209 711870.
E-mail: 106472.3264@compuserve.com

Accountancy & Audit

BARRONS CHARTERED ACCOUNTANTS
Monometer House, Rectory Grove,
Leigh on Sea SS9 2HN
Tel: 01702 481910
Fax: 01702 481911
E-mail: mail@barrons-bds.com
Web site: www.barrons-bds.com

BORLAND NINDER DIXON LLP
Axe Sien, Axe Road, Drimpton,
Beamnster, Dorset DT8 3RJ
Tel: 01460 272 769/07460271680
Fax: 01460 271680
E-mail: borlandnd@btinternet.com

Advertising Contractors

DECKER MEDIA LTD
Decker House, Lowater Street,
Carlton, Nottingham NG4 1JJ
Tel: 0115 940 2406.
Fax: 0115 940 2407.
E-mail: sales@deckermedia.co.uk,
Web site: www.deckermedia.co.uk

Advisory Services

ADGROUP LTD
Ad House, East Parade, Harrogate HG1 5LT
Tel: 01423 706690
Fax: 01423 502522
E-mail: info@adbus.info
Web site: www.adbus.info

AD COACH SALES
Newbridge Coach Depot,
Witheridge EX16 8PY
Tel: 01884 860787
Fax: 01884 860711
E-mail: enquiries@adcoachsales.co.uk
Web site: www.adcoachsales.co.uk

ADG TRANSPORT CONSULTANCY
Oak Cottage, Royal Oak,
Machen CF83 8SN
Tel: 01633 441491
Fax: 01633 440591
E-mail: a.dgettins@btinternet.com

ANDY IZATT
10 Briton Court, St Thomas's Road,
Spalding PE11 2TS
Tel: 01775 712542
E-mail: andy.izatt@btinternet.com
Web site: andy.izatt.btinternet.co.uk

AUSTIN ANALYTICS
Crown House, 183 High Street,
Bottisham, Cambridge CB25 9BB
Tel: 07730 943 415
Fax: 07005 946 854
E-mail: john@analytics.co.uk
Web site: www.analytics.co.uk

Trade Directory

BRITISH BUS SALES
Mike Nash, PO Box 534, Dorking RH5 5XB
Tel: 07836 656 692
E-mail: nashionalbus1@btconnect.com
Web site: www.bristishbussales.co.uk

CAREYBROOK LTD
PO Box 205, Southam CV47 0ZL
Tel: 01926 813938
Fax: 01926 814898
E-mail: info@careybrook.com
Web site: www.careybrook.com

CAPOCO DESIGN
Stone Cross House, Chickgrove,
Salisbury SP3 6NA
Tel: 01722 716722
Fax: 01722 716226
E-mail: design@capoco.co.uk

CHADWELL ASSOCIATES LTD
3 Caledonian Close, Ilford, IG3 9QF
Tel: 0208 590 5697
E-mail: lb@chadwellassociates.co.uk

COLIN BUCHANAN
Newcombe House, 45 Notting Hill Gate,
London W11 3PB
Tel: 020 7309 7000
Fax: 020 7309 0906
E-mail: london@cbuchanan.co.uk
Web site: www.cbuchanan.co.uk

COACH DIRECT
The Coach House, 22 South Street,
Rochford SS4 1BQ
Tel: 0870 550 2069
Fax: 0870 070 2069
E-mail: info@coachdirect.co.uk
Web site: www.coachdirect.co.uk

ETMSS LTD
9 Dorset Avenue, Ferndown BH22 8HJ
Tel: 0844 800 9299
E-mail: info@etmss.com
Web site: www.etmss.com

FCAV & CO
Brooklyn House, Coleford Road,
Bream GL15 6EU
Tel: 01594 564552
Fax: 01594 564556
E-mail: info@fcav.co.uk
Web site: www.fcav.co.uk

IBPTS
43 Cage Lane, Felixstowe,
Suffolk OP11 9BJ
Tel: 01394 672 344
Fax: 01394 672 344
E-mail: info@ibpts.co.uk
Web site: www.ibpts.co.uk

LEYLAND PRODUCT DEVELOPMENTS LTD
Aston Way, Leyland, Preston PR26 7TZ
Tel: 01772 435834
E-mail: sales@lpdl.co.uk
Web site: www.lpdl.co.uk

MINIMISE YOUR RISK
11 Chatsworth Park,
Telscombe Cliffs BN10 7DZ
Tel: 01273 580189
Fax: 01273 580189
E-mail: minimise@btconnect.com
Web site: www.minimiseyourrisk.co.uk

MVA
Duke Street, Woking GU21 5DH
Tel: 01483 728051
Fax: 01483 755207
Web site: www.mvaconsultancy.com

MYSTERY TRAVELLERS
6A Mays Yard, Down Raod, Horndean,
Wateriooville, Hampshire PO8 0YP
Tel: 02392 797 707
Fax: 02392 591 700
E-mail: info@mystery-travellers.com
Web site: www.bestchart.co.uk

PRE METRO OPERATIONS LTD
21 Woodglade Croft, Kings Norton,
Birmingham B38 8TD
Tel: 01212 439 906
Fax: 01212 439 906
E-mail: premetro@aol.com
Web site: www.premetro co.uk

PROFESSIONAL TRANSPORT SERVICES
12 Silverdale, Stanford-le-Hope SS17 8BG
Tel: 01375 675262
Web site: www.proftranserv.co.uk
E-mail: enquiries@proftranserv.com

STEPHEN C MORRIS
PO Box 119, Shepperton TW17 8UX
Tel: 01932 232574
E-mail: buswriter@btinternet.com

SALTIRE COMMUNICATIONS
39 Lilyhill Terrace, Edinburgh EH8 7DR
Tel: 0131 652 0205
E-mail: gavin.booth@btconnect.com

TRANSPORTATION MANAGEMENT SOLUTIONS
6 Woodlands Terrace, Glasgow G3 6DD.
Tel: 0141 332 4733.
Fax: 0141 354 0076.
E-mail: tramsol@aol.com

TRANSPORT & TRAINING SERVICES LTD
Warrington Business Park,
Long Lane, Warrington WA2 8TX
Tel: 01925 243 500
Fax: 01925 243 000
E-mail: tachographsuk@aol.com
Web site: www.transporttrainingservices.com

WARD INTERNATIONAL CONSULTING LTD
Funtley Court, 19 Funtley Hill,
Fareham PO16 7UY
Tel: 01329 280280
Fax: 01329 221010
E-mail: info@wardint.co.uk
Web site: www.wardint.com

Artwork

ADGROUP LTD
Ad House, East Parade, Harrogate HG1 5LT
Tel: 01423 706690
Fax: 01423 502522
E-mail: info@adbus.info
Web site: www.adbus.info

BEST IMPRESSIONS
15 Starfield Road, London W12 9SN
Tel: 020 8740 6443
Fax: 020 8740 9134
E-mail: talk2us@best-impressions.co.uk
Web site: www.best-impressions.co.uk

FWT
Aztec House, 397-405 Archway Road,
London N6 4EY
Tel: 020 7347 3700
Fax: 020 7347 3701
E-mail: sales@fwt.co.uk
Web site: www.fwt.co.uk

PLUM DIGITAL PRINT
Suite 1, Cornerstone House, Stafford Park
13, Telford, Shropshire TF3 3AZ
Tel: 01952 204 920
E-mail: nigel.greenaway@busandcoach.com
Web site: www.plumdigitalprint.co.uk

TITAN BUS UK LTD
52 East Parade, Harrogate HG1 5LT
Tel: 01423 526253
Fax: 01423 502522
E-mail: info@titanbus.co.uk
Web site: www.titanbus.co.uk

TONY GREAVES GRAPHICS
19 Perth Mount, Horsforth, Leeds LS18 5SH
Tel/Fax: 0113 258 4795
E-mail: tony@greavesgraphics.fsnet.co.uk

MCKENNA BROTHERS
Jubilee Road, Middleton,
Manchester, M24 2LX
Tel: 0161 655 3244
Fax: 0161655 3059
E-mail: info@mckennabrothers.co.uk
Web site: www.mckennabrothers.co.uk

MCV BUS & COACH LTD
Sterling Place, Elean Business Park,
Sutton CB6 2QE
Tel: 01353 773000
Fax: 01353 773001
E-mail: vernon.edwards@mcv-uk.com

NEERMAN & PARTNERS
c/o 22 Larbre Crescent, Whickham,
Newcastle-upon-Tyne NE16 5YG
Tel: 0191 488 6258
Fax: 0191 488 9158
Web site: www.neerman.net
E-mail: info@neerman.net

TIME TRAVEL UK
247 Bradford Road, Stanningley,
Pudsey, Leeds LS28 6QB
Tel: 0113 255 1188
E-mail: nick.baldwin@tinyworld.co.uk

VETRO DESIGN
247 Bradford Road, Pudsey,
Leeds LS28 6QB
Tel: 01132 551188
E-mail: nick@vetrodesign.co.uk

Auctioneers & Valuators Breakdown & Recovery Services

NB - Operator lists also indicate bus and coach operators able to provide breakdown and recovery services.

AD COACH SALES
Newbridge Coach Depot, Witheridge EX16 8PY
Tel: 01884 860767
Fax: 01884 860711
E-mail: enquiries@adcoachsales.co.uk
Web site: www.adcoachsales.co.uk

BRITISH BUS SALES
Mike Nash, PO Box 534, Dorking RH5 5XB
Tel: 07836 656692
E-mail: nashionalbus1@btconnect.com
Web site: www.britishbussales.co.uk

51

Trade Directory

BUZZLINES LTD
Unit G1, Lympne Industrial Park,
Hythe CT21 4LR
Tel: 01303 261870
Fax: 01303 230093
E-mail: sales@buzzlines.co.uk
Web site: www.buzzlines.co.uk

CHANNEL COMMERCIALS PLC
Unit 6, Cobbs Wood Industrial Estate,
Brunswick Road, Ashford TN23 1EH.
Tel: 01233 629272.
Fax: 01233 636322.
E-mail: info@ccplc.co.uk

COACH-AID
Unit 2, Brindley Close, Tollgate Industrial Estate, Stafford ST16 3SU
Tel: 01785 222666
E-mail: workshop@coach-aid.com
Web site: www.coach-aid.com

LANTERN RECOVERY SPECIALISTS PLC
Lantern House, 39/41 High Street,
Potters Bar EN6 5AJ
Tel: 0870 6090333
Fax: 01707 640450
Web site: www.lanternrecovery.org

THOMAS HARDIE – WIGAN
Lockett Road,
Ashton-in-Makerfield WN4 8DE.
Tel: 01942 505124
Fax: 01942 505119

MASS SPECIAL ENGINEERING LTD
Houghton Road, North Anston S25 4JJ.
Tel: 01909 550480.
Fax: 01909 550486.

TRUCKALIGN CO LTD
VIP Trading Estate, Anchor & Hope Lane,
London SE7 7RY
Tel: 020 8858 3781
Fax: 020 8858 3781

UNITEC LONDON
Unit 9, Eurocourt, Olivers Close,
West Thurrock RM20 3EE
Tel: 08444 123222
Fax: 01708 869920
E-mail: london.service@optare.com

UNITEC ROTHERHAM
Denby Way, Hellaby, Rotherham S66 8HR
Tel: 01709 535101
Fax: 01709 535103
E-mail: rotherham.service@optare.com

UNITEC SCOTLAND
Unit 7, Cumbernauld Business Park,
Ward Park Road, Cumbernauld G67 3JZ
Tel: 01236 726738
Fax: 01236 795251
E-mail: scotland.service@optare.com

Coach Driver Agencies

ANTAL INTERNATIONAL NETWORK
Kestrel House, 111 Heath Road,
Twickenham TW1 1AF
Tel: 0870 770 1604
E-mail: bcoyne@antal.com
Web site: www.antal.com

CI COACHLINES
Pools Lane, Highwood, Essex CM1 3QL
Tel: 01245 248 669

DRIVER HIRE CANTERBURY
East Suite, Parsonage Office, Nackington,
Canterbury CT4 7AD
Tel: 01227 479529
Fax: 01227 479531
E-mail: canterbury@driver-hire.co.uk

FRASER EAGLE MANAGEMENT SERVICES
4 Mead Way, Shuttleworth Mead Business Park, Padiham BB12 9NG
Tel: 08700 842713
Fax: 08700 842726
E-mail: info@frasereagle.com
Web site: www.frasereagle.com

THE PENINSULA GROUP
Trematon Drive, St Peter's Way, Ivybridge PL21 0HT
Tel (office hrs): 01752 896471
Mobile/Direct: 07909 695438
Owner: Mike Yedermann **Touring Man**: Brian Madge
Associated companies: Peninsula Cars & Eastward Coaches (see operators section - Devon)

Cleaning services

TARA SUPPORT SERVICES LTD
32 Derby Road, Enfield EN3 4AW
Tel: 0845 450 0607
Fax: 0845 450 0608
E-mail: info@tarasupport.co.uk
Web site: www.tarasupport.co.uk

Coach Hire Brokers/ Vehicle Rental

CI COACHLINES
Pools Lane, Highwood, Essex CM1 3QL
Tel: 01245 248 669

COACH DIRECT
The Coach House, 22 South Street,
Rochford SS4 1BQ
Tel: 0870 550 2069
Fax: 0870 070 2069
E-mail: info@coachdirect.co.uk
Web site: www.coachdirect.co.uk

COACHFINDER LTD
Woodbank House, 24 Matley Close,
Newton, Hyde SK14 4UE
Tel: 0161 368 7877
E-mail: enquiries@coachfinder.uk.com
Web site: www.coachfinder.uk.com

DAWSONRENTALS BUS AND COACH LTD
Delaware Drive, Tongwell, Milton Keynes MK15 8JH
Tel: 01908 218111
Fax: 01908 610156
E-mail: info@dawsongroup.co.uk
Web site: www.dawsongroup.co.uk

FRASER EAGLE MANAGEMENT SERVICES
4 Mead Way, Shuttleworth Mead Business Park, Padiham BB12 9NG
Tel: 08700 842713
Fax: 08700 842726
E-mail: info@frasereagle.com
Web site: www.frasereagle.com

HAYWARD TRAVEL (CARDIFF)
2 Murch Crescent, Dinas Powys CF64 4RF
Tel: 029 2051 5551
Fax: 029 2051 5113
E-mail: haytvl@aol.com
Web site: haywardtravel.co.uk

NEXT BUS LTD
The Coach Yard, Vincents Road,
Bumpers Farm Industrial Estate,
Chippenham SN14 6QA
Tel: 01249 462462
Fax: 01249 448844
E-mail: sales@next-bus.co.uk
Web site: www.next-bus.co.uk

TRAMONTANA COACH DISTRIBUTORS
Chapelknowe Road, Carfin,
Motherwell ML1 5LE
Tel: 01698 861790
Fax: 01698 860778
E-mail: wdt90@tiscali.co.uk
Web site: www.tramontanacoach.co.uk

YORKSHIRE BUS & COACH SALES
254A West Ella Road,
West Ella, Hull HU10 7SF
Tel: 01482 653302
Fax: 01482 653302
E-mail: craig.porteous@virgin.net

Coach Interchange & Parking Utilities

T & E DOCHERTY
40 Bank Street, Irvine KA12 0LP
Tel: 01294 278440
Fax: 01294 272510
Web site: www.coach-hires.co.uk

SAMMYS GARAGE
Victoria Coach Station, Arrivals Hall, 3 Eccleston Place, London SW1W 9NF
Tel: 020 7793 7533/7730/8867

TRAVELGREEN COACHES
Canda Lodge, Hampole Bank Lane,
Skellow, Doncaster DN6 8LF
Tel: 01302 722227
Fax: 01302 727999
(also B&B accommodation)

VICTORIA COACH STATION LTD
164 Buckingham Palace Road, London SW1W 9TP
Tel: 020 7824 0015
Fax: 020 7824 0008
Web site: www.tfl.co.uk

Computer Systems/Software

ACIS
ACIS House, Knaves Beech Business Centre, Loudwater HP10 9QR
Tel: 01628 524900
Fax: 01628 523222
E-mail: enquiries@acis.uk.com
Web site: www.acis.uk.com

AUTOPRO SOFTWARE
1 Kingsmeadow, Norton Cross, Runcorn WA7 6PB
Tel: 01928 715962
Fax: 01928 714538
E-mail: sales@autoprouk.com
Web site: www.autoprosoftware.co.uk

DISTINCTIVE SYSTEMS LTD
Amy Johnson Way, York YO30 4XT
Tel: 01904 692269
Fax: 01904 690810
E-mail: sales@distinctive-systems.com
Web site: www.distinctive-systems.com

ETMSS LTD
C/O Dorset House, 9 Dorset Avenue, Ferndown, Dorset BH22 8HJ
Tel: 0844 800 9299
E-mail: info@etmss.com
Web: www.etmss.com

OMNIBUS
Hollinwood Business Centre, Albert Street, Hollinwood, Oldham, Lancashire OL8 3QL
Tel: 0161 683 3100
Fax: 0161 683 3102
Web site: www.omnibus.uk.com

PROFESSIONAL TRANSPORT SERVICES
12 Silverdale, Stanford-le-Hope SS17 8BG
Tel: 01375 675262
Web site: www.proftranserv.co.uk
E-mail: enquiries@proftranserv.com

ROEVILLE COMPUTER SYSTEMS
Station House, East Lane, Stainforth, Doncaster DN7 5HF
Tel: 01302 841333
Fax: 01302 843966
E-mail: sales@roeville.com
Web site: www.roeville.com

TAGTRONICS LTD
Suite 408, Daisyfield Business Centre, Appleby Street, Blackburn BB1 3BL
Tel: 01254 297730
Fax: 01254 698484
E-mail: info@tagtronics.co.uk
Web site: www.tagtronics.co.uk

TRANMAN SOLUTIONS
Thornbury Office Park, Midland Way, Thornbury BS35 2BS.
Tel: 01454 874000.
Fax: 01454 874001.
E-mail: tranman@civica.co.uk

TRAPEZE GROUP (UK) LTD
The Mill, Staverton, Trowbridge, Bath BA14 6PH
Tel: 01225 784200
Fax: 01225 784222
E-mail: info@trapezegroup.co.uk
Website: www.trapezegroup.co.uk

TRAVEL INFORMATION SYSTEMS
Grand Union House, 20 Kentish Town Road, London NW1 9NX
Tel: 020 7428 1288
Fax: 020 7267 2745
E-mail: enquiries@travelinfosystems.com
Web site: www.tranman@civica.co.uk

Consultants

ADG TRANSPORT CONSULTANCY
Oak Cottage, Royal Oak, Machen CF83 8SN
Tel: 01633 441491
Fax: 01633 440591
E-mail: a.dgettins@btinternet.com

AUSTIN ANALYTICS
Crown House, 183 High Street, Bottisham, Cambridge CB25 9BB
Tel: 07730 943 415
Fax: 07005 946 854
E-mail: john@analytics.co.uk
Web site: www.analytics.co.uk

AUTOPRO SOFTWARE
1 Kingsmeadow, Norton Cross, Runcorn WA7 6PB
Tel: 01928 715962
Fax: 01928 714538
E-mail: sales@autoprouk.com
Web site: www.autoprosoftware.co.uk

BESTCHART LTD
6A Mims Yard, Down Road, Horndean, Waterlooville PO8 0YP
Tel: 023 9259 7707
Fax: 023 9259 1700
E-mail: info@bestchart.co.uk
Web site: www.bestchart.co.uk

BORLAND NINDER DIXON LLP
Axe Sien, Axe Road, Drimpton, Beamnster, Dorset DT8 3RJ
Tel: 01460 272 769
Fax: 01460 271680
E-mail: borlandnd@btinternet.com

BRITISH BUS SALES
Mike Nash, PO Box 534, Dorking RH5 5XB
Tel: 07836 656 692
E-mail: nashionalbus1@btconnect.com
Web site: www,britishbussales.co.uk

CAREYBROOK LTD
PO Box 205, Southam CV47 0ZL
Tel: 01926 813938
Fax: 01926 814898
E-mail: info@careybrook.com
Web site: www.careybrook.com

CHADWELL ASSOCIATES LTD
3 Caledonian Close, Ilford IG3 9QF
Tel: 0208 590 5697
E-mail: lb@chadwellassociates.co.uk

CI COACHLINES
Pools Lane, Highwood, Essex CM1 3QL
Tel: 01245 248 669

COACH DIRECT
The Coach House, 22 South Street, Rochford SS4 1BQ
Tel: 0870 550 2069
Fax: 0870 070 2069
E-mail: info@coachdirect.co.uk
Web site: www.coachdirect.co.uk

COLIN BUCHANAN
Newcombe House, 45 Notting Hill Gate, London W11 3PB
Tel: 020 7309 7000
Fax: 020 7309 0906
E-mail: london@cbuchanan.co.uk
Web site: www.cbuchanan.co.uk

CRONER CCH GROUP LTD
145 London Road, Kingston upon Thames KT2 6SR.
Tel: 020 8247 1261.
Fax: 020 8547 2638.
E-mail: info@croner.cch.co.uk

DCA DESIGN INTERNATIONAL
19 Church Street, Warwick CV34 4AB
Tel: 01926 499461
Fax: 01926 401134
Web site: www.dca-design.com/transport

ELLIS TRANSPORT SERVICES
61 Bodycoats Road, Chandlers Ford SO53 2HA
Tel: 023 8027 0447
Fax: 023 8027 6736
E-mail: info@ellistransportservices.co.uk
Web: www.ellistransportservices.co.uk

ETMSS LTD
C/O Dorset House, 9 Dorset Avenue, Ferndown, Dorset BH22 8HJ
Tel: 0844 800 9299
E-mail: info@etmss.com
Web: www.etmss.com

R W FAULKS FCIT
Penthouse J, Ross Court, Putney Hill, London SW15 3NY
Tel: 020 8785 1584
E-mail: rexfaulks@aol.com

FINANCIAL INSPECTION SERVICES LTD
PO Box 1075, Beaminster DT8 3YA.
Tel: 01460 74337.
Fax: 01460 72154.
E-mail: fininspect@aol.com

4 FARTHINGS INTERNATIONAL RECRUITMENT
128 Percy Road, Hampton, Middlesex TW12 2JW
Tel: 0870 770 1604, 020 8941 3147
E-mail: info@4farthings.co.uk
E-mail: www.4farthings.co.uk

IBPTS
43 Cage Lane, Felixstowe, Suffolk OP11 9BJ
Tel: 01394 672 344
Fax: 01394 672 344
E-mail: info@ibpts.co.uk
Web: www.ibpts.co.uk

LEYLAND PRODUCT DEVELOPMENTS LTD
Aston Way, Leyland, Preston PR26 7TZ
Tel: 01772 435834
E-mail: sales@lpdl.co.uk
Web site: www.lpdl.co.uk

LEONARD GREEN ASSOCIATES
2 Short Clough Close, Reedsholme, Rawtenstall BB4 8PT
Tel: 01706 218539
Fax: 01706 601485
E-mail: lgreen@dsl-pipex.com

JACOBS BABTIE GROUP LTD
School Green, Shinfield, Reading RG2 9HL.
Tel: 0118 988 1555.
Fax: 0118 988 1653.

Trade Directory

KERNOW ASSOCIATES
18 Tresawla Court, Tolvaddon,
Camborne TR14 0HF.
Tel/Fax: 01209 711870.
E-mail: 106472.3264@compuserve.com

MASS SPECIAL ENGINEERING LTD
Houghton Road North Anston,
Sheffield S25 4SJ.
Tel: 01909 550480.
Fax: 01909 550486.

MAUN INTERNATIONAL
New Cross House, 8-10 Mansfield Road,
Sutton in Ashfield NG17 4GR.
Tel: 01623 555621.
Fax: 01623 555671.

MINIMISE YOUR RISK
11 Chatsworth Park,
Telscombe Cliffs BN10 7DZ
Tel: 01273 580189
Fax: 01273 580189
E-mail: minimise@btconnect.com
Web site: www.minimiseyourrisk.co.uk

MOTT MACDONALD
St Anne House, Wellesley House,
Croydon CR9 2UL
Tel: 020 8774 2000
Fax: 020 8681 5706
E-mail: marketing@mottmac.com
Web site: www.mottmac.com

MYSTERY TRAVELLERS
6A Mays Yard, Down Raod, Horndean,
Wateriooville, Hampshire PO8 0YP
Tel: 02392 797 707
Fax: 02392 591 700
E-mail: info@mystery-travellers.com
Web: www.bestchart.co.uk

NEERMAN & PARTNERS
c/o 22 Larbre Crescent, Whickam,
Newcastle-upon-Tyne NE16 5YG
Tel: 0191 488 6258
Fax: 0191 488 9158
Web site: www.neerman.net
E-mail: info@neerman.net

OMNIBUS
Hollinwood Business Centre, Albert Street,
Hollinwood, Oldham OL8 3QL
Tel: 0161 683 3100
Fax: 0161 683 3102
Web site: www.omnibus.uk.com

PARRY PEOPLE MOVERS LTD
Overend Road, Cradley Heath,
Dudley B64 7DD
Tel: 01384 569553
Fax: 01384 637753
E-mail: jpmparry@aol.com
Website: www.parrypeoplemovers.com

PJA LTD
Locks House, Locks Lane,
Wantage, Oxon OX12 9EH
Tel: 01235 771 791
E-mail: info@pj-associates.co.uk
Web site: www.pj-associates.co.uk

PRE METRO OPERATIONS LTD
21 Woodglade Croft, Kings Norton,
Birmingham B38 8TD
Tel: 01212 439 906
Fax: 01212 439 906
E-mail: premetro@aol.com
Web site: www.premetro co.uk

PROFESSIONAL TRANSPORT SERVICES
12 Silverdale, Stanford-le-Hope SS17 8BG
Tel: 01375 675262
Web site: www.proftranserv.co.uk
E-mail: enquiries@proftranserv.com

ROBERTSON TRANSPORT CONSULTING LTD
Field House, Braceby, Sleaford NG34 0SZ
Tel: 01529 497354
E-mail: robertson@rtclincs.co.uk

SALTIRE COMMUNICATIONS
39 Lilyhill Terrace, Edinburgh EH8 7DR
Tel: 0131 652 0205
E-mail: gavin.booth@btconnect.com

SPECIALIST TRAINING & CONSULTANCY SERVICES LTD
6 Venture Court, Metcalfe Drive, Altham
Industrial Estate, Accrington BB5 5TU
Tel: 01282 687090
Fax: 01282 687091
E-mail: enquiries@specialisttraining.co.uk
Web site: www.specialisttraining.co.uk

TAS PARTNERSHIP LTD
Guildhall House, Guildhall Street,
Preston PR1 3NU
Tel: 01772 204988
Fax: 01722 562070
Web site: www.tas.uk.net

THOMAS KNOWLES - TRANSPORT CONSULTANT
41 Redhills, Eccleshall ST21 6JW
Tel: 01785 859414
Fax: 01785 859414
E-mail: thmsknw@aol.com

TRANSPORT & TRAINING SERVICES LTD
Warrington Business Park,
Long Lane, Warrington WA2 8TX
Tel: 01925 243 500
Fax: 01925 243 000
E-mail: tachographsuk@aol.com
Web site: www.transporttrainingservices.com

TRANSPORTATION MANAGEMENT SOLUTIONS
6 Woodlands Terrace, Glasgow G3 6DD.
Tel: 0141 332 4733.
Fax: 0141 354 0076.
E-mail: tramsol@aol.com

TRANSPORT DESIGN INTERNATIONAL
12 Waterloo Road Estate,
Bidford on Avon B50 4JH
Tel: 01789 490370
Fax: 01789 490592
E-mail: enquiries@tdi.uk.com
Web site: www.tdi.uk.com

VCA
No1, The Eastgate Office Centre,
Eastgate Road, Bristol BS5 6XX
Tel: 0117 951 5151
Fax: 0117 952 4103
E-mail: paul.cooke@vca.gov.uk
Web site: www.vca.gov.uk

WARD INTERNATIONAL CONSULTING LTD
Funtley Court, 19 Funtley Hill,
Fareham PO16 7UY
Tel: 01329 280280
Fax: 01329 221010
E-mail: info@wardint.co.uk
Web site: www.wardint.com

WEST END TRAVEL & RUTLAND TRAVEL
The Lakeside Bus & Coach Centre,
Dixon Drive, Off Leicester Road,
Melton Mowbray, Leicestershire
LE13 0DA
Tel: 01664 563 498
Fax: 01664 568 568
Email: john.penniston@btconnect.com

Driver Supply

WEBB'S
St Peters Farm, Middle Drove,
Peterborough PE14 8JJ
Tel: 01945 430123
E-mail: webb-s-cant@fsbdial.co.uk

Driver Training

ADG TRANSPORT CONSULTANCY
Oak Cottage, Royal Oak,
Machen CF83 8SN
Tel: 01633 441491
Fax: 01633 440591
E-mail: a.dgettins@btinternet.com

BUZZLINES LTD
Unit G1, Lympne Industrial Park,
Hythe CT21 4LR
Tel: 01303 261870
Fax: 01303 230093
Web site: www.buzzlines.co.uk

COACH DIRECT
The Coach House, 22 South Street,
Rochford SS4 1BQ
Tel: 0870 550 2069
Fax: 0870 070 2069
E-mail: info@coachdirect.co.uk
Web site: www.coachdirect.co.uk

DATS (DAVE'S ACCIDENT & TRAINING SERVICES)
13 Kingfisher Close, The Willows,
Torquay TQ2 7TF
Tel: 07747 686789
E-Mail: davepboulter@btinternet.com
Web site: www.datservices.org

IBPTS
43 Cage Lane, Felixstowe,
Suffolk OP11 9BJ
Tel: 01394 672 344
Fax: 01394 672 344
E-mail: info@ibpts.co.uk
Web: www.ibpts.co.uk

MINIMISE YOUR RISK
11 Chatsworth Park,
Telscombe Cliffs BN10 7DZ
Tel: 01273 580189
Fax: 01273 580189
E-mail: minimise@btconnect.com
Web site: www.minimiseyourrisk.co.uk

Trade Directory

OMNIBUS TRAINING LTD
2 Purley, Croydon CR0 3JT
Tel: 020 8006 7259
Fax: 020 8009 7001
E-mail: enquiries@omnibusltd.com

SKILLPLACE TRAINING
Acacia Avenue, Sandfields Estate,
Port Talbot SA12 7DW.
Tel: 01639 899849

SPECIALIST TRAINING & CONSULTANCY SERVICES LTD
6 Venture Court, Metcalfe Drive, Altham Industrial Estate, Accrington BB5 5TU
Tel: 01282 687090
Fax: 01282 687091
E-mail: enquiries@specialisttraining.co.uk
Web site: www.specialisttraining.co.uk

TRANSPORT & TRAINING SERVICES LTD
Warrington Business Park,
Long Lane, Warrington WA2 8TX
Tel: 01925 243 500
Fax: 01925 243 000
E-mail: tachographsuk@aol.com
Web site: www.transporttrainingservices.com

VOSA
Vehicle & Operator Services Agency, Commercial Projects Unit, Berkeley House, Croydon Road, Bristol BS5 0DA
Tel: 0117 954 3359
Fax: 0117 954 3212
E-mail: commercial.training@vosa.gov.uk

Exhibition/Event Organisers

COACH & BUS
PO Box 1359, Leamington Spa CV32 5GT.
Tel: 020 7240 5800.
Fax: 020 7240 5805.
E-mail: info@expom.co.uk
Web site: www.cpt-uk.org

COACH DISPLAYS LTD
21 The Poynings, Richings Park,
Iver SL0 9DS
Tel: 01753 631170
Fax: 01753 655980
E-mail: info@coachdisplays.co.uk
Web site: www.coachdisplays.co.uk

EXPO MANAGEMENT LTD
Olympus Avenue,
Leamington Spa CV34 6BF
Tel: 01926 888123
Fax: 01926 888004
E-mail: info@expom.co.uk
Web site: www.expom.co.uk

MCI EXHIBITIONS LTD
1 Rye Hill Office Park, Birmingham Road, Allesley, Coventry CV5 9AB.
Tel: 02476 408020
Fax: 02476 408019
E-mail: gina@motorcycleshow.co.uk
Web site: www.motorcycleshow.co.uk

THE LONDON BUS EXPORT CO
PO Box 12, Chepstow NP16 5UZ
Tel: 01291 689 741
Fax: 01291 689 361
E-mail: lonbusco@globalnet.co.uk
Web site: www.london-bus.co.uk

Ferry Operators

BRITTANY FERRIES GROUP TRAVEL
The Brittany Centre, Wharf Road,
Portsmouth PO2 8RU
Tel: 0870 901 2100
Fax: 0870 901 3100
E-mail: grouptravel@brittany-ferries.co.uk
Web site: www.brittany-ferries.co.uk/grouptravel

CALEDONIAN MACBRAYNE LTD
Head Office, The Ferry Terminal,
Gourock PA19 1QP
Tel: 01475 650100
Web site: www.calmac.co.uk

CONDOR FERRIES LTD
Condor House, New Harbour Road South, Hamworthy, Poole BH15 4AJ
Tel: 01202 207 207
Fax: 01202 685 184
E-mail: reservations@condorferries.co.uk
Web site: www.condorferries.co.uk

DFDS SEAWAYS
Scandinavia House, Refinery Road, Parkeston CO12 4QG
Tel: 08771 882 0881
Web site: www.dfdsseaways.co.uk

EUROTUNNEL
PO Box 2000, Folkestone CT18 8XY
Tel: 08702 430401
Fax: 01303 288909
Web site: www.eurotunnel.com

IRISH FERRIES LTD
Groups Department, Salt Island,
Holyhead LL65 1DR
Tel: 08705 329129
Fax: 01407 760340
Web site: www.irishferries.ie
www.irishferries.com

ISLE OF MAN STEAM PACKET COMPANY
Imperial Buildings, Douglas IM1 2BY
Tel: 01624 661661
Tel: 01624 645618
E-mail: resesteam-packet.com
Web site: www.steam-packet.com

NORFOLKLINE
Norfolk House, Eastern Dock,
Dover CT16 1JA
Tel: 0870 870 1020
Web site: www.norfolkline.com

P&O FERRIES
Channel House, Channel View Road,
Dover CT17 9TJ
Tel: 08716 641641
Fax: 08707 625325
E-mail: groups@poferries.com
Web site: www.poferries.com

RED FUNNEL
Red Funnel Travel Centre,
12 Bugle Street, Southampton SO14 2JY
Tel: 0844 844 9988
Fax: 0844 844 2698
E-mail: post@redfunnel.co.uk
Web site: www.redfunnel.co.uk

SEAFRANCE
Whitfield Court, Honeywood Close,
Whitfield CT16 3PX
Tel: 087012 222 800
Fax: 08700 644 775
E-mail: groups@seafrance.fr
Web site: www.seafrance.com

STENA LINE
Station Approach, Holyhead LL65 1DQ
Tel: 08705 20 44 02
E-mail: groups@stenaline.com
Web site: www.stenaline.co.uk/groups

SUPERFAST FERRIES
The Terminal Building,
Port of Rosyth KY11 2XP
Tel: 0870 234 221
Web site: www.superfast.com

TRANSMANCHE FERRIES
Newhaven Ferry Port, Railway Approach, Newhaven BN9 0DF
Tel: 0800 917 1201
Web site: www.transmancheferries.co.uk, www.ldlines.com

WIGHTLINK ISLE OF WIGHT FERRIES
70 Broad Street, Portsmouth PO1 2LB
Tel: 0870 582 7744
Fax: 023 9285 5257
E-mail: sales@wightlink.co.uk
Web site: www.wightlink.co.uk

Finance/Leasing

AD COACH SALES
Newbridge Coach Depot,
Witheridge EX16 8PY
Tel: 01884 860767
Fax: 01884 860711
E-mail: enquiries@adcoachsales.co.uk
Web site: www.adcoachsales.co.uk

ARRIVA BUS AND COACH LTD
Lodge Garage, Whitehall Road West, Cleckheaton BD19 4BJ.
Tel: 01274 681144.
Fax: 01274 651198.
Web site: www.arrivabusandcoach.co.uk
E-mail: busandcoachsales@arriva.co.uk

DAWSONRENTALS BUS AND COACH LTD
Delaware Drive, Tongwell, Milton Keynes MK15 8JH
Tel: 01908 218111
Fax: 01908 218 444
E-mail: contactus@dawsongroup.co.uk
Web site: www.dawsongroup.co.uk

HANSAR FINANCE LTD
Bridgeway House, Mellor Road, Cheadle Hulme SK8 5AU
Tel: 0161 488 4000
Fax: 0161 488 4567
E-mail: sales@hanser.co.uk
Web site: www.hansar.co.uk

LHE FINANCE LTD
21 Headlands Business Park, Salisbury Road, Ringwood BH24 3PB
Tel: 01425 474070
Fax: 01425 474090
Web site: www.lhefinance.co.uk

MCV BUS & COACH LTD
Sterling Place, Elean Business Park,
Sutton CB6 2QE
Tel: 01353 773000
Fax: 01353 773001
E-mail: vernon.edwards@mcv-uk.com

55

MISTRAL GROUP (UK)PLC
Booths Hall, Chelford Road, Knutsford WA16 6QZ
Tel: 01565 621881
Fax: 01565 621882
E-mail: sales@mistral-group.com
Web site: www.mistral-group.com

NEXT BUS LTD
The Coach Yard, Vincents Road, Bumpers Farm Industrial Estate, Chippenham SN14 6QA
Tel: 01249 462462
Tel: 01249 448844
E-mail: sales@next-bus.co.uk
Web site: www.next-bus.co.uk

NORTON FOLGATE FG PLC
50A St Andrew Street, Hertford SG14 1JA.
Tel: 01992 537735
Fax: 01992 537733
E-mail: help@nortonfolgate.co.uk
Fax: www.nortonfolgate.co.uk

ROADLEASE
Crossroads, Anston, Sheffield S25 7ES.
Tel: 01909 551177.
Fax: 01909 567994.
E-mail: roadlease@kirkbycoachandbus.com
Web site: www.roadlease.com

VOLVO FINANCIAL SERVICES
Wedgnock Lane, Warwick CV34 5YA
Tel: 01926 498888
Fax: 01926 410278

Graphic Design

ADGROUP LTD
Ad House, East Parade, Harrogate HG1 5LT
Tel: 01423 706690
Fax: 01423 502522
E-mail: info@adbus.info
Web site: www.adbus.info

BEST IMPRESSIONS
15 Starfield Road, London W12 9SN
Tel: 020 8740 6443
Fax: 020 8740 9134
E-mail: talk2us@best-impressions.co.uk
Web site: www.best-impressions.co.uk

FWT
Aztec House 397-405 Archway Road, London N6 4EY
Tel: 020 7347 3700
Fax: 020 7347 3701
E-mail: sales@fwt.co.uk
Web site: www.fwt.co.uk

HATTS GARAGE & SERVICES
Foxham, Chippenham SN15 4NB
Tel: 01249 742000
Fax: 01249 740447
E-mail: mike@hattstravel.co.uk
Web site: www.hattsgarage.co.uk

IMAGE & PRINT GROUP
Unit 9, Oakbank Industrial Estate, Garscube Road, Glasgow G20 7LU
Tel: 0141 353 1900
Fax: 0141 353 8611

McKENNA BROTHERS LTD
McKenna House, Jubilee Road, Middleton, Manchester M24 2LX
Tel: 0161 655 3244
Fax: 0161 655 3059
E-mail: info@mckennabrothers.co.uk
Web site: www.mckennabrothers.co.uk

NEERMAN & PARTNERS
c/o 22 Larbre Crescent, Whickham, Newcastle-upon-Tyne NE16 5YG
Tel: 0191 488 6258
Fax: 0191 488 9158
Web site: www.neerman.net
E-mail: info@neerman.net

PLUM DIGITAL PRINT
Suite 1, Cornerstone House, Stafford Park 13, Telford, Shropshire TF3 3AZ
Tel: 01952 204 920
E-mail: nigel.greenaway@busandcoach.com
Web: www.plumdigitalprint.co.uk

RH BODYWORKS
A140 Ipswich Road, Brome, Eye IP23 8AW
Tel: 01379 870666
Fax: 01379 872138
E-mail: mike.ball@rhbodyworks.co.uk
Web site: www.rhbodyworks.co.uk

TIME TRAVEL UK
247 Bradford Road, Stanningley, Pudsey, Leeds LS28 6QB
Tel: 0113 255 1188
E-mail: nick.baldwin@tinyworld.co.uk

TITAN BUS UK LTD
52 East Parade, Harrogate HG1 5LT
Tel: 01423 526253
Fax: 01423 502522
E-mail: info@titanbus.co.uk
Web site: www.titanbus.co.uk

VETRO DESIGN
247 Bradford Road, Pudsey, Leeds LS28 6QB
Tel: 01132 551188
E-mail: nick@vetrodesign.co.uk

Hotels

CALOTELS HOTELS
88 Jordan Avenue, Stretton, Burton-on-Trent DE13 0JD
Tel: 01283 542455
Fax: 01283 542455

CIE TOURS INTERNATIONAL
Loveitts Farm, Brinklow CV23 0LG
Tel: 01788 833388
Fax: 01788 833710
E-mail: anne@ciegroups.freeserve.co.uk
Web site: www.cietours.co.uk

GRASSHOPPER INN
Moorhouse, Westerham TN16 2EU
Tel: 01959 563136
Fax: 01959 564823
E-mail: info@grasshopperinn.co.uk
Web site: www.grasshopperinn.co.uk

STAGE HOTEL – LEICESTER
299 Leicester Road, (A5199) Wigston Fields, Leicester LE18 1JW
Tel: 0116 288 6161
Fax: 0116 257 3900
Web: www.stagehotel.co.uk

Insurance

BELMONT INTERNATIONAL LTD
Becket House, Vestry Road, Otford, Sevenoaks TN14 5EL
Tel: 01732 744700
Fax: 01732 745499
Web: www.belmontint.com
E-mail: phil.white@belmontint.com

BRITISH BUS SALES
Mike Nash, PO Box 534, Dorking RH5 5XB
Tel: 07836 656 692
E-mail: nashionalbus1@btconnect.com
Web: www.britishbussales.co.uk

R. L. DAVISON & CO LTD
Bury House, 31 Bury Street, London EC3A 5AH.
Tel: 020 7816 9876
Fax: 020 7816 9880
Web: www.rlddavison.co.uk

P J HAYMAN & CO LTD
Stansted House, Rowlands Castle PO9 6BR
Tel: 08452 393 526
Web site: www.pjhayman.com

OMNI WHITTINGTONS
Arthur Castle House, 33 Creechurch Lane, London EC3A 5EB
Tel: 020 7709 9991
Fax: 020 7456 1225.
Web: whittingtoninsurance.com

RIGTON INSURANCE SERVICES LTD
Chevin House, Otley Road, Guiseley, Leeds LS20 8BH
Tel: 01943 879539
Fax: 01943 875529
E-mail: enquiries@rigtoninsurance.co.uk
Web site: www.rigtoninsurance.co.uk

TOWERGATE CHAPMAN STEVENS
Towergate House, 22 Wintersells Road, Wintersells Business Park, Byfleet KT14 7LF
Tel: 01932 334140
Fax: 01932 351238
E-mail: tcs@towergate.co.uk
Web site: www.towergate.co.uk

VOLVO INSURANCE SERVICES
Wedgnock Lane, Warwick CV34 5YA
Tel: 01926 401777.
Fax: 01926 407407.
Web site: www.volvo.com

WILLIS LTD
10 Trinity Square, London EC3P 3AX
Tel: 020 7488 8111
Fax: 020 7975 2884
E-mail: warren.dann@willis.com
Web site: www.willis.com

WILSURE INSURANCE BROKERS
9 Crusader Business Park, Stephenson Road West, Clacton on Sea CO15 4TN.
Tel: 01255 420564.
Fax: 01255 222764.
E-mail: info@wilsure.co.uk
Web site: www.wilsure.co.uk

WRIGHTSURE GROUP
799 London Road, West Thurrock RM20 3LH.
Tel: 01708 865553.
Fax: 01708 865100.
E-mail: info@wrightsure.com
Web site: www.wrightsure.com

Legal & Operations Advisers

BORLAND NINDER DIXON LLP
Axe Sien, Axe Road, Drimpton, Beaminster, Dorset DT8 3RJ
Tel: 01460 272 769
Fax: 01460 271680
E-mail: borlandnd@btinternet.com

COACH DIRECT
The Coach House,
22 South Street, Rochford SS4 1BQ
Tel: 0870 550 2069
Fax: 0870 070 2069
E-mail: info@coachdirect.co.uk
Web site: www.coachdirect.co.uk

ELLIS INTERNATIONAL TRANSPORT CONSULTING LTD
61 Bodycoats Road,
Chandlers Ford SO53 2HA
Tel: 023 8027 0447
Fax: 023 8027 6736
E-mail: info@ellistransportservices.co.uk
Web site: www.ellistransportservices.co.uk

FREIGHT TRANSPORT ASSOCIATION
Hermes House, St John's Road,
Tunbridge Wells TN4 9UZ.
Tel: 01892 526171
Fax: 01892 534989
E-mail: enquiries@fta.co.uk
Web site: www.fta.co.uk

IBPTS
43 Cage Lane, Felixstowe,
Suffolk OP11 9BJ
Tel: 01394 672 344
Fax: 01394 672 344
E-mail: info@ibpts.co.uk
Web: www.ibpts.co.uk

KERNOW ASSOCIATES
18 Tresawla Court, Tolvaddon,
Camborne TR14 0HF.
Tel/Fax: 01209 711870.
E-mail: 106472.3264@compuserve.com

MINIMISE YOUR RISK
11 Chatsworth Park,
Telscombe Cliffs BN10 7DZ
Tel: 01273 580189
Fax: 01273 580189
E-mail: minimise@btconnect.com
Web site: www.minimiseyourrisk.co.uk

PELLYS LLP SOLICITORS
The Old Monastary, Windmill, Bishops,
Stortford, Hertfordhire CM23 2ND
Tel: 01279 758 080
Fax: 01279 467 565
E-mail: office@pellys.co.uk
Web site: www.pellys.co.uk

PROFESSIONAL TRANSPORT SERVICES
12 Silverdale, Stanford-le-Hope SS17 8BG
Tel: 01375 675262
Web site: www.proftranserv.co.uk
E-mail: enquiries@proftranserv.com

WARD INTERNATIONAL CONSULTING LTD
Funtley Court, 19 Funtley Hill,
Fareham PO16 7UY
Tel: 01329 280280
Fax: 01329 221010
E-mail: info@wardint.co.uk
Web site: www.wardint.com

WEDLAKE SAINT
91-93 Farringdon Road, London EC1M 3LN.
Tel: 020 7400 4100.
Fax: 020 7242 3100.
Web site: www.wedlakesaint.co.uk

Life Insurance & Pensions

WILSURE INSURANCE BROKERS
9 Crusader Business Park, Stephenson
Road West, Clacton on Sea CO15 4TN.
Tel: 01255 420564.
Fax: 01255 222764.
E-mail: info@wilsure.co.uk
Web site: www.wilsure.co.uk

Livery Design

ADGROUP LTD
Ad House, East Parade, Harrogate HG1 5LT
Tel: 01423 706690
Fax: 01423 502522
E-mail: info@adbus.info
Web site: www.adbus.info

BEST IMPRESSIONS
15 Starfield Road, London W12 9SN
Tel: 020 8740 6443
Fax: 020 8740 9134
E-mail: talk2us@best-impressions.co.uk
Web site: www.best-impressions.co.uk

CHANNEL COMMERCIAL PLC
Unit 6, Cobbs Wood Industrial Estate,
Brunswick Road, Ashford TN23 1EH.
Tel: 01233 629272.
Fax: 01233 636322.
E-mail: info@ccplc.co.uk

THE LONDON BUS EXPORT CO
PO Box 12, Chepstow NP16 5UZ
Tel: 01291 689 741
Fax: 01291 689 361
E-mail: lonbusco@globalnet.co.uk

TONY GREAVES GRAPHICS
19 Perth Mount, Horsforth, Leeds LS18 5SH
Tel/Fax: 0113 258 4795
E-mail: tony@greavesgraphics.fsnet.co.uk

HATTS GARAGE & SERVICES
Foxham, Chippenham SN15 4NB
Tel: 01249 742000
Fax: 01249 740447
E-mail: MIKE@hattstravel.co.uk
Web site: www.hattsgarage.co.uk

McKENNA BROTHERS LTD
McKenna House, Jubilee Road,
Middleton, Manchester M24 2LX
Tel: 0161 655 3244
Fax: 0161 655 3059
E-mail: info@mckennabrothers.co.uk
Web site: www.mckennabrothers.co.uk

NEERMAN & PARTNERS
c/o 22 Larbre Crescent, Whickham,
Newcastle-upon-Tyne NE16 5YG
Tel: 0191 488 6258
Fax: 0191 488 9158
Web site: www.neerman.net
E-mail: info@neerman.net

PLUM DIGITAL PRINT
Suite 1, Cornerstone House, Stafford Park
13, Telford, Shropshire TF3 3AZ
Tel: 01952 204 920
E-mail:
nigel.greenaway@busandcoach.com
Web site: www.plumdigitalprint.co.uk

TIME TRAVEL UK
247 Bradford Road, Stanningley,
Pudsey, Leeds LS28 6QB
Tel: 0113 255 1188
E-mail: nick.baldwin@tinyworld.co.uk

TITAN BUS UK LTD
52 East Parade, Harrogate HG1 5LT
Tel: 01423 526253
Fax: 01423 502522
E-mail: info@titanbus.co.uk
Web site: www.titanbus.co.uk

VETRO DESIGN
247 Bradford Road, Pudsey,
Leeds LS28 6QB
Tel: 01132 551188
E-mail: nick@vetrodesign.co.uk

Maps for the Bus Industry

BEST IMPRESSIONS
15 Starfield Road, London W12 9SN
Tel: 020 8740 6443
Fax: 020 8740 9134
E-mail: talk2us@best-impressions.co.uk
Web site: www.best-impressions.co.uk

FWT
Aztec House, 397-405 Archway Road,
London N6 4EY
Tel: 020 7347 3700
Fax: 020 7347 3701
E-mail: sales@fwt.co.uk
Web site: www.fwt.co.uk

TONY GREAVES GRAPHICS
19 Perth Mount, Horsforth, Leeds LS18 5SH
Tel/Fax: 0113 258 4795
E-mail: tony@greavesgraphics.fsnet.co.uk

IMAGE & PRINT GROUP
Unit 9, Oakbank Industrial Estate,
Garscube Road, Glasgow G20 7LU.
Tel: 0141 353 1900.
Fax: 0141 353 8611.
E-mail: alan@imageandprint.co.uk
Web site: www.imageandprint.co.uk

OMNIBUS
Hollinwood Business Centre, Albert Street,
Hollinwood, Oldham OL8 3QL
Tel: 0161 683 3100
Fax: 0161 683 3102
Web site: www.omnibus.uk.com

PINDAR PLC
31 Edison Road, Aylesbury HP19 8TE
Tel: 01296 390100
Fax: 01296 381233
Web site: www.pindar.com

TIME TRAVEL UK
247 Bradford Road, Stanningley,
Pudsey, Leeds LS28 6QB
Tel: 0113 255 1188
E-mail: nick.baldwin@tinyworld.co.uk

VETRO DESIGN
247 Bradford Road,
Pudsey, Leeds LS28 6QB
Tel: 01132 551188
E-mail: nick@vetrodesign.co.uk

Marketing Services

ADG TRANSPORT CONSULTANCY
Oak Cottage, Royal Oak,
Machen CF83 8SN
Tel: 01633 441491
Fax: 01633 440591
E-mail: a.dgettins@btinternet.com

COACH DIRECT
The Coach House, 22 South Street,
Rochford SS4 1BQ
Tel: 0870 550 2069
Fax: 0870 070 2069
E-mail: info@coachdirect.co.uk
Web site: www.coachdirect.co.uk

CREATIVE MANAGEMENT DEVELOPMENT LTD
52 Okebourne Park, Liden,
Swindon SN3 6AJ
Tel: 07771 732185
Fax: 01793 491786
E-mail: jowencmd@aol.com
Web site: www.cmd-training.co.uk

GOSKILLS LTD
Concorde House, Trinity Park,
Solihull B37 7UQ
Tel: 01216 355 520
Fax: 01216 355 521
E-mail: info@goskills.org
Web: www.goskills.org

KERNOW ASSOCIATES
18 Tresawla Court, Tolvaddon,
Camborne TR14 0HF.
Tel/Fax: 01209 711870.
E-mail: 106472.3264@compuserve.com

Mechanical Investigation

KERNOW ASSOCIATES
18 Tresawla Court, Tolvaddon,
Camborne TR14 0HF.
Tel/Fax: 01209 711870.
E-mail: 106472.3264@compuserve.com

UNITEC LONDON
Unit 9, Eurocourt, Olivers Close,
West Thurrock RM20 3EE
Tel: 08444 123222
Fax: 01708 869920
E-mail: london.service@optare.com

UNITEC ROTHERHAM
Denby Way, Hellaby, Rotherham S66 8HR
Tel: 01709 535101
Fax: 01709 535103
E-mail: rotherham.service@optare.com

UNITEC SCOTLAND
Unit 7, Cumbernauld Business Park,
Ward Park Road, Cumbernauld G67 3JZ
Tel: 01236 726738
Fax: 01236 795651
E-mail: scotland.service@optare.com

On-Bus Advertising

ADGROUP LTD
Ad House, East Parade, Harrogate HG1 5LT
Tel: 01423 526253
Fax: 01423 502522
E-mail: info@adbus.info
Web site: www.adbus.info

BEST IMPRESSIONS
15 Starfield Road, London W12 9SN
Tel: 020 8740 6443
Fax: 020 8740 9134
E-mail: talk2us@best-impressions.co.uk
Web site: www.best-impressions.co.uk

DECKER MEDIA LTD
Decker House, Lowater Street,
Carlton, Nottingham NG4 1JJ
Tel: 0115 940 2406
Fax: 0115 940 2407
E-mail: sales@deckermedia.co.uk
Web site: www.deckermedia.co.uk

TIME TRAVEL UK
247 Bradford Road, Stanningley,
Pudsey, Leeds LS28 6QB
Tel: 0113 255 1188
E-mail: nick.baldwin@tinyworld.co.uk

TITAN BUS UK LTD
52 East Parade, Harrogate HG1 5LT
Tel: 01423 526253
Fax: 01423 502522
E-mail: info@titanbus.co.uk
Web site: www.titanbus.co.uk

Printing/Publishing

BEMROSEBOOTH LTD
Stockholm Road, Sutton Fields Industrial
Estate, Hull HU7 0XY
Tel: 01482 826343
Fax: 01482 371386
E-mail: lprecious@bemrosebooth.com
Web site: www.bemrosebooth.com

BEST IMPRESSIONS
15 Starfield Road, London W12 9SN
Tel: 020 8740 6443
Fax: 020 8740 9134
E-mail: talk2us@best-impressions.co.uk
Web site: www.best-impressions.co.ukl

THE HENRY BOOTH GROUP
Stockholm Road, Sutton Fields Industrial
Estate, Hull HU7 0XY
Tel: 01482 826343.
Fax: 01482 839767.
E-mail: mshanley@henrybooth.co.uk
Web site: www.henrybooth.co.uk

FWT
Aztec House, 397-405 Archway Road,
London N6 4EY
Tel: 020 7347 3700
Fax: 020 7347 3701
E-mail: sales@fwt.co.uk
Web site: www.fwt.co.uk

TONY GREAVES GRAPHICS
19 Perth Mount, Horsforth, Leeds LS18 5SH
Tel/Fax: 0113 258 4795
E-mail: tony@greavesgraphics.fsnet.co.uk

IAN ALLAN PRINTING LTD
Riverdene Business Park,
Molesey Road, Hersham KT12 4RG.
Tel: 01932 266600
Fax: 01932 266601
E-mail:
jonathan.bingham@ianallanprinting.co.uk
Web site: www.ianallanprinting.co.uk

IMAGE & PRINT GROUP
Unit 9, Oakbank Industrial Estate,
Garscube Road, Glasgow G20 7LU
Tel: 0141 353 1900
Fax: 0141 353 8611
E-mail: alan@imageandprint.co.uk
Web site: www.imageandprint.co.uk

MIDLAND COUNTIES PUBLICATIONS
4 Watling Drive, Hinckley LE10 3EY
E-mail:midlandbooks@compuserve.com

PINDAR PLC
31 Edison Road, Aylesbury HP19 8TE
Tel: 01296 390100
Fax: 01296 381233
Web site: www.pindar.com

PLUM DIGITAL PRINT
Suite 1, Cornerstone House, Stafford Park
13, Telford, Shropshire TF3 3AZ
Tel: 01952 204 920
E-mail: nigel.greenaway@buscoach.com
Web: www.plumdigitalprint.co.uk

TIME TRAVEL UK
247 Bradford Road,
Stanningley, Pudsey LS28 6QB
Tel: 0113 255 1188
E-mail: nick.baldwin@tinyworld.co.uk

TRANSPORT STATIONERY SERVICES
61 Bodycoats Road,
Chandlers Ford SO53 2HA
Tel: 07041 471008
Fax: 07041 471009
E-mail:
info@transportstationeryservices.co.uk

VETRO DESIGN
247 Bradford Road,
Pudsey, Leeds LS28 6QB
Tel: 01132 551188
E-mail: nick@vetrodesign.co.uk

Promotional Material

BEST IMPRESSIONS
15 Starfield Road, London W12 9SN
Tel: 020 8740 6443
Fax: 020 8740 9134
E-mail: talk2us@best-impressions.co.uk
Web site: www.best-impressions.co.uk

BRITISH BUS PUBLISHING LTD
16 St Margarets Drive, Telford TF1 3PH
Tel: 01952 255 669
E-mail: bill@britishbuspublishing.co.uk
Web site: www.britishbuspublishing.co.uk

FWT
Aztec House, 397-405 Archway Road,
London N6 4EY
Tel: 020 7347 3700
Fax: 020 7347 3701
E-mail: sales@fwt.co.uk
Web site: www.fwt.co.uk

IBPTS
43 Cage Lane, Felixstowe,
Suffolk OP11 9BJ
Tel: 01394 672 344
Fax: 01394 672 344
E-mail: info@ibpts.co.uk
Web site: www.ibpts.co.uk

MARKET ENGINEERING
43-44 North Bar, Banbury OX16 0TH
Tel: 01295 277050
Fax: 01295 297030
E-mail: contact@m-eng.com
Web site: www.marketengineering.co.uk

PINDAR PLC
31 Edison Road, Aylesbury HP19 8TE
Tel: 01296 390100
Fax: 01296 381233
Web site: www.pindar.com

PLUM DIGITAL PRINT
Suite 1, Cornerstone House, Stafford Park
13, Telford, Shropshire TF3 3AZ
Tel: 01952 204 920
E-mail:
nigel.greenaway@busandcoach.com
Web site: www.plumdigitalprint.co.uk

SALTIRE COMMUNICATIONS
39 Lilyhill Terrace, Edinburgh EH8 7DR
Tel: 0131 652 0205
E-mail: gavin.booth@btconnect.com

STEPHEN C MORRIS
PO Box 119, Shepperton TW17 8UX
Tel: 01932 232574
E-mail: buswriter@btinternet.com

TIME TRAVEL UK
247 Bradford Road, Stanningley,
Pudsey, Leeds LS28 6QB
Tel: 0113 255 1188
E-mail: nick.baldwin@tinyworld.co.uk

TONY GREAVES GRAPHICS
19 Perth Mount, Horsforth, Leeds LS18 5SH
Tel/Fax: 0113 258 4795
E-mail: tony@greavesgraphics.fsnet.co.uk

VETRO DESIGN
247 Bradford Road,
Pudsey, Leeds LS28 6QB
Tel: 01132 551188
E-mail: nick@vetrodesign.co.uk

Publications - Magazines & Books

BRITISH BUS PUBLISHING LTD
16 St Margarets Drive, Telford TF1 3PH
Tel: 01952 255 669
E-mail: bill@britishbuspublishing.co.uk
Web site: www.britishbuspublishing.co.uk

BUSES
Ian Allan Publishing Ltd, Riverdene Business Park, Molesey Road, Hersham KT12 4RG.
Tel: 01932 266600
Fax: 01932 266601
Web site: www.busesmag.com

BUS & COACH BUYER
The Publishing Centre, 1 Woolram Wygate,
Spalding PE11 1NU
Tel: 01775 711777
Fax: 01775 711777
E-mail: bcbsales@busandcoachbuyer.com

BUS & COACH PROFESSIONAL
Suite 1, Cornerstone House,
Stafford Park 13, Telford TF3 3AZ
Tel: 01952 204 920
E-mail: jo.taylor@busnadcoach.com
Web site: www.busandcoach.com

BUS USER
Bus Users UK, PO Box 320,
Portsmouth PO5 3SD
Tel: 023 9281 4493
Fax: 023 9285 3080
Web site: www.bususers.org

BUSES WORLDWIDE
37 Oyster Lane, Byfleet, Surrey KT14 7HS
Tel: 01932 352 351
E-mail: membership@busesworldwide.org
Web site: www.busesworldwide.org

COACH & BUS WEEK
3 The Office Village, Cygnet Park,
Hampton, Peterborough PE7 8FD
Tel: 01733 293240
Fax: 0845 2802927
E-mail: jacqui.grobler@rouncymedia.co.uk
Web site: www.cbwnet.co.uk

CRONER CCH GROUP LTD
145 London Road,
Kingston upon Thames KT2 6SR
Tel: 020 8247 1261
Fax: 020 8547 2638
E-mail: info@croner.cch.co.uk

HB PUBLICATIONS LTD
3 Ingham Grove, Hartlepool. TS25 2H
Tel: 01429 293611
E-mail: sales@hbpub.co.uk
Web site: www.hppub.co.uk

JANES URBAN TRANSPORT SYSTEMS
163 Brighton Road, Coulsdon CR5 2YH
Tel: 020 8700 3700
Web site: www.janes.com/www.juts.janes.com

PLUM DIGITAL PRINT
Suite 1, Cornerstone House, Stafford Park 13, Telford, Shropshire TF3 3AZ
Tel: 01952 204 920
E-mail: nigel.greenaway@busandcoach.com
Web site: www.plumdigitalprint.co.uk

ROUTE ONE
Expo Publishing, Suite 4, Century House, Towermead Business Park, Fletton,
Peterborough PE2 9DY
Tel: 0870 241 8745
Fax: 0870 241 8891
E-mail: mike.morgan@route-one.net
Web site: www.route.one.net

SALTIRE COMMUNICATIONS
39 Lilyhill Terrace, Edinburgh EH8 7DR
Tel: 0131 652 0205
E-mail: gavin.booth@btconnect.com

SOE
22 Greencoat Place, London SW1 1PR
Tel: 02076 301 111
Fax: 02076 306 667
E-mail: soe@soe.org.uk
Web site: www.soe.org.uk

STEPHEN C MORRIS
PO Box 119, Shepperton TW17 8UX
Tel: 01932 232574
E-mail: buswriter@btinternet.com

TIME TRAVEL UK
247 Bradford Road, Stanningley,
Pudsey, Leeds LS28 6QB
Tel: 0113 255 1188
E-mail: nick.baldwin@tinyworld.co.uk

TRAMWAYS & URBAN TRANSIT/LRTA PUBLICATIONS
13A The Precinct, Broxbourne EN10 7HY
Web site: www.lrta.org

TRANSIT MAGAZINE
Quadrant House, 250 Kennington Lane,
London SE11 5RD
Tel: 0845 270 7954
Fax: 0845 270 7961
E-mail: ed.transit@landor.co.uk
Web site: www.transitmagazine.co.uk

VETRO DESIGN
247 Bradford Road,
Pudsey, Leeds LS28 6QB
Tel: 01132 551188
E-mail: nick@vetrodesign.co.uk

Quality Management Systems

FTA VEHICLE INSPECTION SERVICE
Hermes House, St John's Road,
Tunbridge Wells TN4 9UZ.
Tel: 01892 526171
Fax: 01892 534989
E-mail: enquiries@fta.co.uk
Web site: www.fta.co.uk

IBPTS
43 Cage Lane, Felixstowe,
Suffolk OP11 9BJ
Tel: 01394 672 344
Fax: 01394 672 344
E-mail: info@ibpts.co.uk
Web site: www.ibpts.co.uk

PROFESSIONAL TRANSPORT SERVICES
12 Silverdale, Stanford-le-Hope SS17 8BG
Tel: 01375 675262
Web site: www.proftranserv.co.uk
E-mail: enquiries@proftranserv.com

TRANSPORT STATIONERY SERVICES
61 Bodycoats Road, Chandlers Ford,
Hampshire SO53 2HA
Tel: 07041 471 008
Fax: 07041 471 009
E-mail: info@transportstationeryservices.co.uk

VCA
No1, The Estate Office Centre,
Eastgate Road, Bristol BS5 6XX
Tel: 0117 952 4126
Fax: 0117 952 4104
E-mail: paul.cooke@vca.gov.uk
Web site: www.vca.gov.uk

VOSA COMMERCIAL PROJECTS UNIT
Berkeley House, Croydon Street,
Bristol BS5 0DA
Tel: 0117 954 3359
Fax: 0117 954 3496
E-mail: commercial.training@vosa.gov.uk

Recruitment

4 FARTHINGS INTERNATIONAL RECRUITMENT
128 Percy Road, Hampton,
Middlesex TW12 2JW
Tel: 0870 770 1604, 020 8941 3147
E-mail: info@4farthings.co.uk
Web site: www.4farthings.co.uk

Timetable Production

BEMROSEBOOTH LTD
Stockholm Road, Sutton Fields Industrial Estate, Hull HU7 0XY
Tel: 01482 826343
Fax: 01482 371386
E-mail: lprecious@bemrosebooth.com
Web site: www.bemrosebooth.com

Trade Directory

BEST IMPRESSIONS
15 Starfield Road, London W12 9SN
Tel: 020 8740 6443
Fax: 020 8740 9134
E-mail: talk2us@best-impressions.co.uk
Web site: www.best-impressions.co.uk

FWT
Aztec House, 397-405 Archway Road,
London N6 4EY
Tel: 020 7347 3700
Fax: 020 7347 3701
E-mail: sales@fwt.co.uk
Web site: www.fwt.co.uk

TONY GREAVES GRAPHICS
19 Perth Mount, Horsforth, Leeds LS18 5SH
Tel/Fax: 0113 258 4795
E-mail: tony@greavesgraphics.fsnet.co.uk

IBPTS
43 Cage Lane, Felixstowe,
Suffolk OP11 9BJ
Tel: 01394 672 344
Fax: 01394 672 344
E-mail: info@ibpts.co.uk
Web site: www.ibpts.co.uk

IMAGE & PRINT GROUP
Unit 9, Oakbank Industrial Estate,
Garscube Road, Glasgow G20 7LU.
Tel: 0141 353 1900.
Fax: 0141 353 8611.
E-mail: alan@imageandprint.co.uk
Web site: www.imageandprint.co.uk

OMNIBUS
Hollinwood Business Centre, Albert Street,
Hollinwood, Oldham OL8 3QL
Tel: 0161 683 3100
Fax: 0161 683 3102
Web site: www.omnibus.uk.com

PINDAR PLC
31 Edison Road, Aylesbury HP19 8TE
Tel: 01296 390100
Fax: 01296 381233
Web site: www.pindar.com

PLUM DIGITAL PRINT
Suite 1, Cornerstone House, Stafford Park
13, Telford, Shropshire TF3 3AZ
Tel: 01952 204 920
E-mail:
nigel.greenaway@busandcoach.com
Web site: www.plumdigitalprint.co.uk

PROFESSIONAL TRANSPORT SERVICES
12 Silverdale, Stanford-le-Hope SS17 8BG
Tel: 01375 675262
Web site: www.proftranserv.co.uk
E-mail: enquiries@proftranserv.com

TIME TRAVEL UK
247 Bradford Road, Stanningley,
Pudsey, Leeds LS28 6QB
Tel: 0113 255 1188
E-mail: nick.baldwin@tinyworld.co.uk

TRAVEL INFORMATION SYSTEMS
Grand Union House, 20 Kentish Town Road,
London NW1 9NX
Tel: 020 7428 1288
Fax: 020 7267 2745
E-mail: enquiries@travelinfosystems.com
Web site: www.travelinfosystems.com

VETRO DESIGN
247 Bradford Road,
Pudsey, Leeds LS28 6QB
Tel: 01132 551188
E-mail: nick@vetrodesign.co.uk

Tour Wholesalers

ACTION TOURS LTD
5 Aston Street, Shifnal,
Shropshire TR11 8DW
Tel: 01952 462 462
Fax: 01952 462 555
E-mail: info@actiontours.co.uk
Web: www.actionoturs.co.uk

ALBATROSS TRAVEL GROUP LTD
Albatross House, 14 New Hythe Lane,
Larkfield ME20 6AB
Tel: 01732 879191
Fax: 01732 522968
E-mail: sales@albatross-tours.com
Web site: www.albatross-tours.com

BOTEL LTD
Botel House, 50 Northern Road,
Wickersley, Rotherham S66 1EN
Tel: 01709 703535
Fax: 01709 703555
E-mail: sales@botel.co.uk
Web site: www.botel.co.uk

CI COACHLINES
Pools Lane, Highwood,
Chelmsford CM1 3QL
Tel: 01245 248669
Fax: 01245 603534
E-mail: cicoachlines@btinternet.com

CIE TOURS INTERNATIONAL
Loveitts Farm, Brinklow CV23 0LG
Tel: 01788 833388
Fax: 01788 833710
E-mail: anne@ciegroups.freeserve.co.uk
Web site: www.cietours.co.uk

FJORD LINE
Norway House, Royal Quays,
North Shields NE29 6EG
Tel: 0191 296 1313
Fax: 0191 296 1540
E-mail: fjordline.uk@fjordline.com
Web site: www.fjordline.com

GREATDAYS TRAVEL GROUP
2 Stamford Park Road,
Altrincham WA15 9EN
Tel: 0161 928 9966
Fax: 0161 928 1332
E-mail: sales@greatdays.co.uk
Web site: www.greatdays.co.uk

GREATDAYS TRAVEL GROUP
10A Thurloe Place, London SW7 2RZ
Tel: 020 7584 0748
Fax: 020 7591 0375
E-mail: travel@london.greatday.co.uk
Web site: www.greatdays.co.uk

INDEPENDENT COACH TRAVEL (WHOLESALING) LTD
South Quay Travel and Leisure Ltd, Studios
20/21, Colman's Wharf, 45 Morris Road,
London E14 6PA
Tel: 020 7538 4627
Fax: 020 7538 8239
E-mail: aheaton@ictsqt.co.uk
Web site: www.ictsqt.co.uk

TRAVELPATH 3000
PO Box 32 Grantham NG31 7JA
Tel: 01476 570187
Fax: 01476 572718
E-mail: info@travelpath3000.com
Web site: www.travelpath3000.com

Tourist Venues Refreshment Facilities

■ In this section we include brief directions and facilities, where available.
■ Entries listed in county order.

KENT
GRASSHOPPER INN
Moorhouse, Westerham TN16 2EU
Tel: 01959 563136
Fax: 01959 564823
E-mail: info@grasshopperinn.co.uk
Web site: www.grasshopperinn.co.uk
on A25 near Westerham, Kent, close to M25 (jct 5 and 6); coffee, drinks, lunch dinner; large car park with coach bays

LEICESTERSHIRE
BELVOIR CASTLE
Grantham NG32 1PE
Tel: 01476 871004
Fax: 01476 871018
E-mail: mary@belvoircastle.com
Web site: www.belvoircastle.com
West of Grantham between A52 and A607, follow signposts. Castle tours. Group luncheon/light menus.

SURREY
GRASSHOPPER INN
Moorhouse, Westerham TN16 2EU
Tel: 01959 563136
Fax: 01959 564823
E-mail: info@grasshopperinn.co.uk
Web site: www.grasshopperinn.co.uk
on A25 near Westerham, Kent, close to M25 (jct 5 and 6); coffee, drinks, lunch dinner; large car park with coach bays

SOMERSET
THE JANE AUSTEN CENTRE
40 Gay Street, Bath BA1 2NT
Tel: 01225 443000
Fax: 01225 443018
Web site: www.janeausten.co.uk

Training Services

BUZZLINES LTD
Unit G1, Lympne Industrial Park,
Hythe CT21 4LR
Tel: 01303 261870
Fax: 01303 230093
Web site: www.buzzlines.co.uk

COACH DIRECT
The Coach House, 22 South Street,
Rochford SS4 1BQ
Tel: 0870 550 2069
Fax: 0870 070 2069
E-mail: info@coachdirect.co.uk
Web site: www.coachdirect.co.uk

CREATIVE MANAGEMENT DEVELOPMENT LTD
52 Okebourne Park, Liden,
Swindon SN3 6AJ
Tel: 07771 732185
Fax: 01793 491786
E-mail: jowencmd@aol.com
Web site: www.cmd-training.co.uk

DATS (DAVE'S ACCIDENT & TRAINING SERVICES)
13 Kingfisher Close, The Willows, Torquay
TQ2 7TF
Tel: 07747 686789
E-Mail: davepboulter@btinternet.com
Web site: www.datservices.org

Trade Directory

GOSKILLS
Concorde House, Trinity Park,
Solihull B37 7UQ
Tel: 0121 635 5520
Fax: 0121 635 5521
E-mail: info@goskills.org
Web site: www.goskills.org

IBPTS
43 Cage Lane, Felixstowe, Suffolk OP11 9BJ
Tel: 01394 672 344
Fax: 01394 672 344
E-mail: info@ibpts.co.uk
Web site: www.ibpts.co.uk

MARKET ENGINEERING
23a Parsons Street, Banbury OX16 5LY
Tel: 01295 277050
Fax: 01295 297030
E-mail: contact@m-eng.com
Web site: www.marketengineering.com

MINIMISE YOUR RISK
11 Chatsworth Park, Telscombe Cliffs BN10 7DZ
Tel: 01273 580189
Fax: 01273 580189
E-mail: minimise@btconnect.com
Web site: www.minimiseyourrisk.co.uk

OMNIBUS TRAINING LTD
2 Purley Way, Croydon CR0 3JP
Tel: 020 8006 7259
Fax: 020 8090 7001
E-mail: enquiries@omnibusltd.com

PROFESSIONAL TRANSPORT SERVICES
12 Silverdale, Stanford-le-Hope SS17 8BG
Tel: 01375 675262
Web site: www.proftranserv.co.uk
E-mail: enquiries@proftranserv.com

SOE
22 Greencoat Place, London SW1 1PR
Tel: 02076 301 111
Fax: 02076 306 667
E-mail: soe@soe.org.uk
Web site: www.soe.org.uk

SPECIALIST TRAINING & CONSULTANCY SERVICES LTD
6 Venture Court, Metcalfe Drive, Altham Industrial Estate, Accrington BB5 5TU
Tel: 01282 687 090
Fax: 01282 687091
E-mail: enquiries@specialisttraining.co.uk
Web site: www.specialisttraining.co.uk

TRANSPORT & TRAINING SERVICES LTD
Warrington Business Park, Long Lane, Warrington WA2 8TX
Tel: 01925 243 500
Fax: 01925 243 000
E-mail: tachographsuk@aol.com
Web site: www.transporttrainingservices.com

WEST END TRAVEL & RUTLAND TRAVEL
The Lakeside Bus & Coach Centre, Dixon Drive, Off Leicester Road, Melton Mowbray, Leicestershire LE13 0DA
Tel: 01664 563 498
Fax: 01664 568 568
Email: john.penniston@btconnect.com

Vehicle Certification

VCA
No1, The Estate Office Centre, Eastgate Road, Bristol BS5 6XX
Tel: 0117 952 4126
Fax: 0117 952 4104
E-mail: paul.cooke@vca.gov.uk
Web site: www.vca.gov.uk

Expert Advice, Training and Support for all your transport needs

TRAINING
- PCV
- LCV
- Disabled Passenger Transport
- NVQ Level 2 Road Passenger Transport
- Tachograph (including digital)
- CPC Road Passenger
- Driver Hours 561 Training
- Passenger Evacuation Fire
- Drivers CPC

CONSULTANCY
- Operator Licence
- Bus Service Procurement
- Service Scheduling
- Legal Requirements
- Drivers Daily Walk Round Checks
- Driver Assessment

FUTURE OFFERINGS
- Passenger (PSV) PCV
- Haulage (HGV) LCV
- Driver CPC Training

WEST END TRAVEL & RUTLAND TRAVEL

West End Travel and Rutland Travel,
The Lakeside Bus & Coach Centre,
Dixon Drive, Off Leicester Road,
Melton Mowbray, Leicestershire LE13 0DA
Telephone: 01664 563 498 Fax: 01664 568 568
Email: john.penniston@btconnect.com

NEW BOOKS for Autumn

Ian Allan PUBLISHING

NEW IN OCTOBER

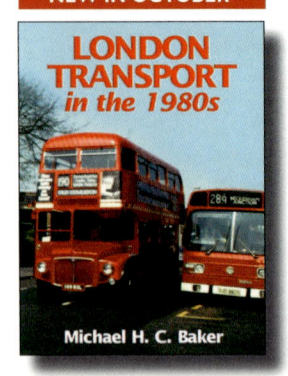

LONDON TRANSPORT in the 1980s
Michael H.C. Baker

The 1980s were a decade of significant change for London Transport. The last of the RFs and RTs left service, closely followed by the first large scale withdrawal of the Routemaster.

Michael Baker details the history of public transport during the 1980s, to provide a concise overview of this period of dramatic and turbulent change for London Transport accompanied by some fine contemporary photographs.

Hardback • 235 x 172mm • 96pp •
c150 mono photographs •
ISBN: 978 0 7110 3283 5 • £16.99

NEW IN OCTOBER

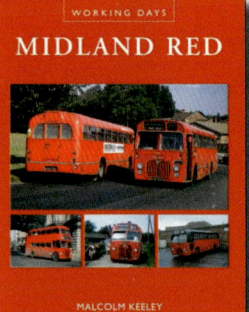

WORKING DAYS: MIDLAND RED
Malcom Keeley

This new book concentrates on the day-to-day operations of one of the greatest names in the British bus industry. Individual chapters examine vehicle maintenance and construction, the role of the depot manager and bus crews to provide an overview of how a major bus company operated in the years between the end of World War 2 and the incorporation of Midland Red into the National Bus Company in 1969. Fascinating first hand material and rare photographs make this a volume for Midland Red enthusiasts to treasure.

Hardback • 280 x 215mm • 112pp •
c175 colour & mono photographs •
ISBN: 978 0 7110 3316 0 • £16.99

RECENTLY PUBLISHED TITLES...

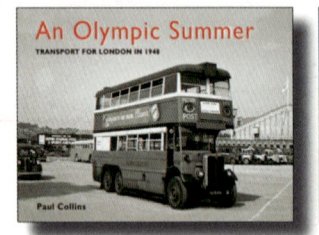

OLYMPIC SUMMER: TRANSPORT FOR LONDON IN 1948
Paul Collins
ISBN: 978 0 7110 3309 2
Hardback • £19.99

LOST LONDON IN COLOUR
Kevin McCormack
ISBN: 978 0 7110 3335 1
Hardback • £14.99

THE HEYDAY OF THE BRISTOL RE
Kevin Lane
ISBN: 978 0 7110 3276 7
Hardback • £14.99

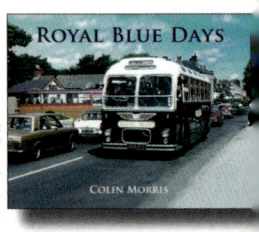

ROYAL BLUE DAYS
Colin Morris
ISBN: 978 0 7110 3234 7
Hardback • £16.99

NEW CATALOGUE OUT NOW!

For a FREE copy of our latest full colour catalogue please write to:
Marketing Dept, Molesey Road, Hersham, Surrey KT12 4RG
Tel: 01932 266600 or e-mail marketing@ianallanpublishing.co.uk

Visit our new and improved website **www.ianallanpublishing.com**

AVAILABLE FROM ALL GOOD BOOKSHOPS, including **IAN ALLAN BOOK & MODEL SHOPS**

BIRMINGHAM
Tel: 0121 643 2496
47 Stephenson Street, B2 4DH

LONDON
Tel: 020 7401 2100
45/46 Lower Marsh, Waterloo SE1 7RG

CARDIFF
Tel: 029 2039 0615
31 Royal Arcade, CF10 1AE

MANCHESTER
Tel: 0161 237 9840
5 Piccadilly Station Approach M1 2GH

NEW! GIFT CARDS now available
Ask in-store for further details

Also available from our mail order department:
Ian Allan Publishing Mail Order Dept • 4 Watling Drive • Hinckley • Leics • LE10 3EY Tel: 01455 254450 • Fax: 01455 233737
e-mail: orders@midlandbooks.com • P&P UK - please add 10%, min £4.25 • Overseas - please add 15%, min £6.00/Highlands & Islands £2.50 extra
Mastercard/Visa/Maestro cards accepted • Please make cheques payable to Ian Allan Publishing Ltd

REMEMBER! SUBS CLUB CARD HOLDERS GET 10% OFF ALL IAN ALLAN BOOK

Section 2

Tendering & Regulatory Authorities

- Tendering & Regulatory Authorities etc
- PTAs
- PTEs
- Passenger Transport Regional Authorities
- Transport Coordinating Offiicers
- Traffic Commissioners
- Office of Fair Trading
- Department for transport

Tendering & Regulatory Authorities

Passenger Transport Authorities

Greater Manchester PTA
PO Box 532, Town Hall,
Manchester M60 2LA
Tel: 0161 234 3335
Fax: 0161 236 6459
Chmn: Cllr M. Colledge
Vice-Chmn: Cllr K Whitmore
Clerk: Sir Howard Bernstein.
Web: www.gmpta.gov.uk

Merseyside PTA
24 Hatton Garden, Liverpool L3 2AN
Tel: 0151 227 5181
Fax: 0151 236 2457
Chmn: Cllr Mark Dowd
Vice-Chmn: Cllr Hugh G. Lloyd
Clerk: Steve Maddox
Gen Man Mersey Tunnels: John Gillard.
Operates with Merseyside PTE (qv) as Merseytravel.

South Yorkshire PTA
PO Box 37, Regent Street,
Barnsley S70 2PQ.
Tel: 01226 772848.
Web site: www.southyorks.org.uk
Chmn: Cllr Ms. A. Milner
Vice-Chmn: Cllr Ms. J. Wilson
Clerk/Treasurer: W J Wilkinson.

Tyne & Wear PTA
Civic Centre, Newcastle upon Tyne
NE99 2BN.
Tel: 0191 203 3209.
Fax: 0191 203 3180.
Web site: www.twpta.gov.uk
Chmn: Cllr D. Wood
Vice-Chairman & Monitoring Officer: T. Hanson
Clerk: K. G. Lavery
Deputy Clerk & Treasurer: D. Johnson
Engineer: J. Millar
Legal advisor: V. A. Dodds.

West Midlands PTA
Room 120, Centro House,
16 Summer Lane, Birmingham B19 3SD.
Tel: 0121 214 7507
Fax: 0121 233 1841
Web site: www.wmpta.org.uk
E-mail for Councillors: tateam@centro.org.uk
E-mail for Committee Team: ptateam@centro.org.uk
Chair: Cllr G Clarke
Vice-Chair: Cllr L. Clark
Clerk: Ms S Manzie
Deputy Clerk/Solicitor: C Hinde
Treasurer: Ms A Ridgewell
Head of Communications: Conrad Jones

West Yorkshire PTA
Wellington House, 40-50 Wellington Street,
Leeds LS1 2DE.
Tel: 0113 251 7272.
Fax: 0113 251 7373.
Web site: www.wypta.gov.uk
Chmn: Cllr C. Greaves
Vice-Chmn: Cllr R. Downes
Clerk to the Authority: K T Preston, OBE.

Passenger Transport Executives

Centro (West Midlands PTE)
Centro House, 16 Summer Lane,
Birmingham B19 3SD
Tel: 0121 200 2787
Fax: 0121 214 7010
Web site: www.centro.org.uk
The Executive is responsible to the West Midlands Passenger Transport Authority
Director General: Geoff Inskip
Services Director: Stephen Rhodes
Projects Director: Tom Magrath
Resources Director: Trevor Robinson
Member of Executive/Treasurer to PTA: Angie Rigwell
PTA Committee: Dan Essex, Marion Cheatham

GMPTE
2 Piccadilly Place, Manchester M1 3BG
Tel: 0161 244 1000
Web site: www.gmpte.com
GMPTE is responsible to the Greater Manchester Passenger Transport Authority. The PTE is responsible for contracting socially necessary bus services and supporting the local rail service. It also owns the Metrolink light rail system on behalf of the Authority and is responsible for planning for the future of the Metrolink network.
   GMPTE and the Authority are also committed to developing accessible transport, funding Ring and Ride, a fully accessible door to door transport service for people with mobility difficulties.
   The PTE administers the concessionary fares scheme, which allows participants (pensioners, children and people with disabilities) either free or reduced rate travel. GMPTE owns and is responsible for the upkeep of bus stations and on-street infrastructure. It also provides information about public transport through telephone information lines, timetables, general publicity and Travelshops.
Interim Chief Executive: David Leather
Finance & Corprate Services Director: Steve Warrener
Interim Strategy Director: Adam Goulcher
Organisational Development Director: Urvashi Bramwell
Service Delivery Director: Michael Renshaw
Interim Projects Director: Paul Griffiths

Merseyside Passenger Transport Authority and Executive (Merseytravel)
24 Hatton Garden, Liverpool L3 2AN
Tel: 0151 227 5181
Fax: 0151 236 2457
Web site: www.merseytravel.gov.uk
Merseytravel ensures the availability of public transport in Merseyside, including financial support for the Merseyrail rail network and those bus services not provided for by the private sector.
   It also promotes public transport by providing bus stations and infrastructure, comprehensive travel tickets and free travel with minimum restrictions for the elderly and those with mobility difficulties.
   Merseytravel also owns and operates the Mersey ferries and Mersey tunnels.
Chair to PTA: Cllr M Dowd
Vice-Chair to PTA: Cllr H. Lloyd
Chief Executive PTA & Director General PTE: Neil Scales OBE
Clerk to PTA: Steve Maddox
Director of Resources: John Wilkinson
Director of Resources: Jim Barclay
Director of Operations: Alan Stilwell

Nexus (Tyne & Wear PTE)
Nexus House, St James Boulevard,
Newcastle upon Tyne NE1 4AX
Tel: 0191 203 3333 **Fax**: 0191 203 3180
Director General: Bernard Garner
Director, Metro: Mick Carbro
Web site: www.nexus.org.uk
Metro: www.tyneandwearmetro.co.uk
Nexus operates within the policies of the Tyne & Wear Passenger Transport Authority. Nexus owns and operates both the Tyne & Wear Metro system and the Shields Ferry (between North Shields and South Shields). Nexus ensures that bus services not operated commercially are provided where there is evidence of social need; operates a demand-responsive transport system, U-call; and organises the provision of special transport for those who can only use ordinary public transport with difficulty if at all. Nexus adminsters the Concessionary Travel scheme and provides comprehensive travel information and sales outlets for countywide season tickets, as well as related administrative support for the scheme.
Rolling Stock: 90 light rail cars
Ferries: MFs 'Pride of the Tyne' and 'Shieldsman'

South Yorkshire Passenger Transport Executive
PO Box 801, Exchange Street,
Sheffield S2 5YT
Director General: David Brown
Tel: 0114 276 7575
Fax: 0114 275 9908
Web site: www.sypte.co.uk
The Executive is responsible to the South Yorkshire Passenger Transport Authority.

West Yorkshire Passenger Transport Executive (Metro)
Wellington House, 40-50 Wellington Street,
Leeds LS1 2DE
Tel: 0113 251 7272
Fax: 0113 251 7333
Web site: www.wymetro.com
WYPTE activities are conducted under the corporate name Metro.
   Metro is financed and supported by the West Yorkshire Passenger Transport Authority.
Director General: Kieran Preston, OBE

Passenger Transport Regional Authorities

Strathclyde Partnership for Transport (SPT)
Consort House, 12 West George Street,
Glasgow G2 1HN
Tel: 0141 332 6811
Fax: 0141 332 3076
Web site: www.spt.co.uk
Dir of bus ops: Eric Stewart

Transport *for* London
Windsor House, 42-50 Victoria Street,
London SW1H 0TL
Tel: 020 7941 4500
Web Site: www.tfl.gov.uk
Transport *for* London (T*f*L) took over most of the functions of London Transport from July 2000. It is under the control of the Mayor of London and Greater London Authority. TfL assumed control of London Underground Ltd in 2003.
Commissioner for Transport: Peter Hendy, CBE
Managing Director Surface Transport: David Brown
Director of Operations: Mike Weston
Coach Manager: Darek Podwiazka

Director of Road Safety Unit: Chris Lines
Director of the Congestion Charge: Malcolm Murray-Clark
Traffic Manager: Nick Morris
Managing Director for London Rail: Ian Brown
Head of London Trams: Phil Hewitt

TfL subsidiary companies:

London Buses Ltd
172 Buckingham Palace Road, London SW1W 9TN.
Tel: 020 7222 5600.
Director of Performance: Clare Kavanagh

Victoria Coach Station Ltd
164 Buckingham Palace Road, London SW1W 9TP.
Tel: 020 7730 3466.
Fax: 020 7730 2589

London River Services Ltd
172 Buckingham Palace Road, London SW1W 9TN.
Tel: 020 7222 5600.

London Underground Ltd
55 Broadway, London SW1H 0BD.
Tel: 020 7222 5600
Managing Director: Tim O'Toole

Transport Co-ordinating Officers

Under the Transport Act 1978 the non-Metropolitan Counties were given power to co-ordinate public transport facilities in their areas. From 1 April 1996 Welsh Counties and Scottish Regions were replaced by new single-tier authorities. At the same time certain English Counties were replaced by new single-tier authorities. The major role is now to secure socially necessary services which are not provided commercially. The names of most of the responsible officers are set out below.

ENGLAND

Bedfordshire County Council
Chris Pettifer, Integrated Passenger Transport Manager, Integrated Passenger Transport Unit, Bedfordshire County Council, County Hall, Cauldwell Street, Bedford MK42 9AP
Tel: 01234 228881

Bracknell Forest Borough Council
R. Cook, Time Square, Bracknell RG12 1JD
Tel: 01344 424642

Buckinghamshire
R. Slevin, County Passenger Transport Officer, County Hall, Aylesbury HP20 1YZ.
Tel: 01296 383751
Fax: 01296 383749

Cambridgeshire
B. E. Jackson, Head of Passenger Transport, Department of Environment & Transport, Mailbox ET1015, Shire Hall, Castle Hill, Cambridge CB3 0AP.
Tel: 01223 717744
Fax: 01223 717789

Cheshire
G. Goddard, County Transport Co-ordinator, Rivacre Business Centre, Mill Lane, Ellesmere Port CH66 3TL.
Tel: 01244 603218
Fax: 01244 603200

Cornwall County Councill
Passenger Transport UNit, County Hall, Truro TR1 3AY
Tel: 01872 322003
Fax: 01872 323844
E-mail: snicholson@cornwall.gov.uk
Web site: www.cornwall.gov.uk

Cumbria County Council
Lonsdale Building, The Courts, Carlisle CA3 8NA
Tel: 01228 606720
Fax: 01228 606755
E-mail: graham.whiteley@cumbriacc.gov.uk
Web site: www.cumbriacc.gov.uk

Derbyshire
T. M. Hardy, Public Transport Manager, County Hall, Matlock DE4 3AG
Tel: 01629 580000
Fax: 01629 585740

Devon
Bruce Thompson, Transport Co-ordination Service Manager, Matford Offices, County Hall, Exeter EX2 4QW
Tel: 01392 383244
Fax: 01392 382904
E-mail: bruce.thompson@devon.gov.uk
Web site: www.devon.gov.uk

Dorset
David Dawkins, Integrated Transport Unit Manager, County Hall, Dorchester DT1 1XJ
Tel: 01305 224554
Fax: 01305 225166
E-mail: d.dawkins@dorsetcc.gov.uk
Web site: www.dorsetcc.gov.uk

Durham
County Hall, Durham DH1 5UQ.
Tel: 0191 383 3435
Fax: 0191 383 4096
Web: www.durham.gov.uk

East Riding of Yorkshire Council
Passenger Services, The Offices, Beverley Depot, Annie Reed Road, Beverley HU17 0LF
Tel: 01482 395529
Fax: 01482 395090

East Sussex
N Smith, Group Manager (Passenger Transport), Transport & Environment, East Sussex County Council, County Hall, St Anne's Crescent, Lewes BN7 1UE.
Tel: 01273 482326
Fax: 01273 474361
E-mail: nick.smith@eastsussexcc.gov.uk

Essex
J Pope, Group Manager, Passenger Transport, Highways & Transportation, County Hall, Chelmsford CM1 1QH
Tel: 01245 437506
Fax: 01245 496764
Web site: www.essexcc.gov.uk

Gloucestershire
Operations & Procurement Manager, Shire Hall, Bearland, Gloucester GL1 2TH
Tel: 01452 425968

Hampshire
K Wilcox, Head of Passenger Transport, Hampshire County Council, Environment Department, The Castle, Winchester SO23 8UD.
Tel: 01962 846997
Fax: 01962 845855
E-mail: keith.wilcox@hants.gov.uk

Hartlepool Borough Council
Ian Jopling, Transport Team Leader, Department of Neighbourhood Services, Bryan Hanson House, Hanson Square, Hartlepool TS24 7BT
Tel: 01429 284140
Fax: 01429 860830
E-mail: ian.jopling@hartlepool.gov.uk
Web site: www.hartlepool.gov.uk

Hertfordshire County Council
Passenger Transport Unit, PO Box 99, Hertford SG13 8TJ
Tel: 01992 556725
Web site: www.intalink.org.uk

Hull City Council
Web site: www.hullcc.gov

Isle of Wight Council
A A Morris, Transport Manager, Jubilee Stores, The Quay, Newport PO30 2EH
Tel: 01983 823710
Fax: 01983 823707

Kent County Council
Julia Seaward, Head of Transport, Commercial Services, Kent County Council, Gibson Drive, Kings Hill, West Malling ME19 4QG
Tel: 01622 605091
Fax: 01622 605084
E-mail: passenger.transport@kent.gov.uk
Web site: www.kentpublictransport.info

Lancashire
Stuart Wrigley, Head of Transport Policy, PO Box 9, Guild House, Cross Street, Preston PR1 8RD
Tel: 01772 534660
Fax: 01772 533833

Leicestershire
Tony Kirk, Group Manager (Public Transport), Department of Highways, Transportation & Waste Management, County Hall, Glenfield, Leicester LE3 8RJ
Tel: 0116 265 6270
Fax: 0116 265 7181
E-mail: tkirk@leics.gov.uk
Web site: www.leics.gov.uk

Lincolnshire
A R Cross, Head of Transport Services, 4th Floor, City Hall, Beaumont Fee, Lincoln LN1 1DN
Tel: 01522 553132
Fax: 01522 568735

Norfolk
Tracey Jessop, Head of Passenger Transport, Department of Planning & Transportation, County Hall, Martineau Lane, Norwich NR1 2SG
Tel: 01603 224368
Fax: 01603 222144

Northamptonshire
Sustainable Transport Manager, Northamptonshire County Council, Riverside House, Riverside Way, Bedford Road, Northampton NN1 5NX
Tel: 01604 236711

Northumberland
John Hodgson, Network Development Officer, Integrated Transport Unit, Community and Environmental Services

Tendering & Regulatory Authorities

Tendering & Regulatory Authorities

Directorate, Northumberland County Council, County Hall, Morpeth NE61 2EF
Tel: 01670 534837
Fax: 01670 533086
E-mail: jhodgson@northumberland.gov.uk

North Yorkshire
R Owens, Passenger Transport Officer, County Hall, Northallerton DL7 8AH
Tel: 01609 780780, Ext 2870
Fax: 01609 779838

Nottinghamshire County Council
County Hall, West Bridgford, Nottingham NG2 7QP
Tel: 0115 982 3823
E-mail: enquiries@nottscc.gov.uk
Web site: www.nottinghamshire.gov.uk

Oxfordshire
R Helling, Public Transport Officer, Environmental Services, Speedwell House, Speedwell Street, Oxford OX1 1NE
Tel: 01865 815859
Fax: 01865 815085

Reading Borough Council
Mrs P Baxter, Civic Centre, Reading RG1 7TD
Tel: 0118 939 0813

Shropshire
K R Gallop, Principal Passenger Transport Officer, Environment Department, The Shirehall, Abbey Foregate, Shrewsbury SY2 6ND
Tel: 01743 253031
Fax: 01743 254382

Slough Borough Council
R Fraser, PO Box 570, Slough SL1 1FA

Somerset County Council
County Hall, The Crescent, Taunton TA20 1JS
Tel: 01823 356700
Fax: 01823 351356
E-mail: transport@somerset.gov.uk
Web site: www.somerset.gov.uk

Staffordshire
Charles Soutar, Head of Passenger Transport, Development Services Department, Riverway, Stafford ST16 3TJ
Tel: 01785 276735
Fax: 01785 276621

Suffolk
M Bradshaw, Public Transport Manager, Environment & Transport Department, Endeavour House, 8 Russell Road, Ipswich IP1 2BX
Tel: 01473 265050
Fax: 01473 216884
E-mail: mitchell.bradshaw@et.suffolkcc.gov.uk

Surrey County Council
A Teer, Group Manager Passenger Transport, Room 306, County Hall, Penrhyn Road, Kingston-on-Thames KT1 2DY
Tel: 020 8541 9371
Fax: 020 8541 9389
E-mail: alan.teer@surreycc.gov.uk
Web site: surreycc.gov.uk/passenger_transport

Warwickshire
K McGovern, Passenger Tranport Operations Manager, Warwickshire County Council, Environment & Economy Directorate, PO Box 43, Shire Hall, Warwick CV34 4SX
Tel: 01926 412930
Fax: 01926 418041
E-mail: passengertransport@warwickshire.gov.uk
Web site: www.warwickshire.gov.uk

West Berkshire Council
J Sherry, Market Street, Newbury
Tel: 01635 42400

West Sussex County Council
Mark Miller, Group Manager, Transport Co-ordination, Highways and Transport, The Grange, Tower Street, Chichester PO19 1RH
Tel: 01243 777811
Web site: www.westsussex.gov.uk

Wiltshire
I White, Passenger Transport Co-ordinator, Environmental Services Dept, County Hall, Trowbridge BA14 8JD
Tel: 01225 713317
Fax: 01225 713565
E-mail: ianwhite@wiltshire.gov.uk

Royal Borough of Windsor & Maidenhead
E Mouser, Yorkstream House, St Ives Road, Maidenhead SL6 1RF
Tel: 01628 796732
Fax: 01628 796774

Wokingham
Roland Clausen-Thue, Transport, Environment Service, Shute End, Wokingham RG40 1WL
Tel: 0118 974 6468
Fax: 0118 974 6486

Worcestershire County Council
Passenger Transport Group, PO Box 82, Pershore Lane, Worcester WR4 0AA
Tel: 01905 768411
Fax: 01905 768438
Web site: www.worcestershire.gov.uk

WALES

Anglesey
Isle of Anglesey County Council, Highways & Transportation Service, Council Offices, Llangefni LL65 2UY
Tel: 01248 752457
Fax: 01248 724839
E-mail: dwrpl@anglesey.gov.uk
Web site: www.anglesey.gov.uk

Blaenau Gwent
Blaenau Gwent County Borough Council, Municipal Offices, Civic Centre, Ebbw Vale NP3 6XB
Tel: 01495 350555
Fax: 01495 301255

Bridgend County Borough Council
D H Beynon, Transport Co-ordinating Manager, Transport & Engineering, Morien House, Bennet Street, Bridgend CF31 3SH
Tel: 01656 643643
Fax: 01656 668126
Web site: www.bridgend.gov.uk

Caerphilly County Borough Council
Huw Morgan, Principal Passenger Transport Officer, Council Offices, Pontllanfraith, Blackwood NP12 2YW.
Tel: 01495 235089
Fax: 01495 235045
E-mail: morgash@caerphilly.gov.uk
Web site: www.caerphilly.gov.uk

Cardiff
Cardiff County Council, Traffic & Transportation Service, County Hall, Atlantic Wharf, Cardiff CF10 4UW

Carmarthenshire
Dir of Economic Development: Gerald Campbell Phillips. Carmarthenshire Council Council, County Hall, Carmarthen SA31 1JP.
Tel: 01267 234567
Fax: 01267 230848

Ceredigion
Cyngor Sir Ceredigion, County Council, County Hall, Market Street, Aberaeron SA46 0AT.
Tel: 01545 572501
Fax: 01545 571089

Conwy
Conwy County Borough Council, Bodlondeb, Conwy LL32 8DU.
Tel: 01492 574000, 592114
Fax: 01492 592114

Denbighshire
Denbighshire County Council, Transport & Infrastructure Department, Caledfryn, Smithfield Road, Denbigh LL15 2NJ
Tel: 01824 706847
Fax: 01824 706970
Web site: www.denbighshire.gov.uk

Flintshire County Council
Directorate of Environment & Regeneration, County Hall, Mold CH7 6NG
Tel: 01352 704530
Fax: 01352 704540
Web site: www.flintshire.gov.uk

Gwynedd Council
M Cowban, Public Transport Officer, Council Offices, Shirehall 56, Caernarfon LL55 1SH.
Tel: 01286 679541
Fax: 01286 673324
E-mail: malcolmwaltercowban@gwynnedd.gov.uk

Isle of Anglesey County Council
Highways & Transportation Service, Council Offices, Llangefni, Anglesey LL77 7TW
Tel: 01248 752300
Fax: 01248 757332
E-mail: pen@anglesey.gov.uk
Web: www.anglesey.gov.uk

Merthyr Tydfil
Martin Haworth, Senior Transport Officer, Merthyr Tydfil County Borough Council, Civic Centre, Castle Street, Merthyr Tydfil CF47 8AN
Tel: 01685 726288
Fax: 01685 387982
E-mail: martin.howarth@merthyr.gov.uk

Monmouthshire
Monmouthshire Passenger Transport Unit, County Hall, Cwmbran NP44 2XH
Tel: 01633 644644
Fax: 01633 644777
E-mail: passengertransportunit@monmouthshire.gov.uk

Neath Port Talbot
Neath Port Talbot County Borough Council, Civic Centre, Port Talbot SA13 1PJ
Tel: 01639 763333
Fax: 01639 763444

Newport
Dir. of Development/Transport: Brian Adcock, Newport County Borough Council, Civic Centre, Newport NP9 4UR.
Tel: 01633 244491
Fax: 01633 244721

Pembrokeshire County Council
M Hubert, Transport and Fleet Manager, County Hall, Haverfordwest SA61 1TP
Tel: 01437 764551
Fax: 01437 775008
E-mail: hubert.mathias@pembrokeshire.gov.uk

Powys
Transport Co-ordination Unit, County Hall, Llandrindod Wells LD1 5LG.
Tel: 01597 826260 **Fax:** 01597 826260

Rhondda Cynon Taf
Rhondda Cynon Taf County Borough Council, Integrated Transport Unit, Sardis House, Sardis Road, Pontypridd CF37 1DU
Tel: 01443 494700 **Fax:** 01443 494875
Web site: www.rhonddacynontaff.gov.uk

City & County of Swansea
Civic Centre, Oystermouth Road, Swansea SA1 3SN
Tel: 01792 636000
Fax: 01792 635270
E-mail: transportation.engineering@swansea.gov.uk
Web site: www.swansea.gov.uk

Torfaen
Torfaen County Borough Council, Civic Centre, Pontypool NP4 6YB.
Tel: 01495 762200
Fax: 01495 755513

Vale of Glamorgan Council
Dock Offices, Barry Docks, Barry CF63 4RT
Tel: 01446 704687
Fax: 01446 704891
E-mail: cedwards@valeofglamorgan.gov.uk
Web site: www.valeofglamorgan.gov.uk

Wrexham
Wrexham County Borough Council, Crown Buildings, Chester Street, Wrexham LL13 8BG
Tel: 01978 292000
Fax: 01978 292106

SCOTLAND

Aberdeen City
The Director, Environment & Infrastructure Services, Aberdeen City Council, St Nicholas House, Broad Street, Aberdeen AB10 1WL
Tel: 01224 523762
Fax: 01224 523764.
E-mail: rwaters@roads.aberdeen.net.uk.
Web site: www.aberdeencity.gov.uk

Aberdeenshire
R McKenzie, Public Transport Manager, Aberdeenshire Council, Woodhill House, Westburn Road, Aberdeen AB16 5GB.
Tel: 01224 664585
Fax: 01224 662005
E-mail: richard.mckenzie@aberdeenshire.gov.uk
Web site: www.aberdeenshire.gov.uk

Angus Council
L Millar, Transport Manager, Angus Council, St James House, St James Road, Forfar DD8 2ZD
Tel: 01307 461774

Fax: 01307 473711
E-mail: millarle@angus.gov.uk
Web site: www.angus.gov.uk/transport

Argyll and Bute Council
B D Blades, Public Transport Officer, Kilmory, Lochgilphead PA31 8RT
Tel: 01546 604360
Fax: 01546 604291 **Web site:** www.argyll-bute.gov.uk

Clackmannanshire
Public Transport Officer, Development & Environment Services, Clackmannanshire Council, Kilncraigs, Greenside Street, Alloa FK10 1EB
Tel: 01259 450000

Dundee City
Mark Devine, Transport Officer, Dundee City Council, Planning & Transportation Department, Floor 16, Tayside House, Crichton Street, Dundee DD1 3RB.
Tel: 01382 433831
Fax: 01382 433313
E-mail: mark.devine@dundeecity.gov.uk.
Web site: www.dundeecity.gov.uk

Dumfries & Galloway
D Kirkpatrick, Team leader (Passenger Transport), Dumfries & Galloway Council, Militia House, English Street, Dumfries DG1 2HR.
Tel: 01387 260133
Fax: 01387 260383

East Ayrshire
East Ayrshire Council, London Road, Kilmarnock KA3 7BU

East Dunbartonshire
East Dunbartonshire Council, PO Box 4, Civic Way, Kirkintilloch G66 4TJ

East Lothian
Transport Planning Manager, Department of Planning, East Lothian Council, 25 Court Street, Haddington EH41 3HA

East Renfrewshire
East Renfrewshire Council, Eastwood Park, Rouken Glen Road, Giffnock G46 6UG

City of Edinburgh Council
Max Thomson, Public Transport Manager, City Development, 1 Cockburn Street, Edinburgh EH1 1BJ
Tel: 0131 469 3631
Fax: 0131 469 3635.
E-mail: max.thomson@edinburgh.gov.uk

Falkirk
Stephen Bloomfield, Public Transport Co-ordinator, Development Services, Falkirk Council, Abbotsfold House, David's Loan, Falkirk FK2 7YZ.
Tel: 01324 504723
Fax: 01324 504914

Fife
Trond Haugen, Transportation Manager - Transportation Services, Fife Council, Fife House, North Street, Glenrothes KY7 5LT
Tel: 01592 413106
Fax: 01592 413061
E-mail: trond.haugen@fife.gov.uk

Highland
Transport Officer, Highland Council, Glenurquhart Road, Inverness IV3 5NX.
Tel: 01463 702457

Fax: 01463 702606.
E-mail: public.transport@highland.gov.uk

Inverclyde
Inverclyde Council, Municipal Buildings, Greenock PA15 1LY

Midlothian
Travel Team - Room 9, Dundas Buildings, 62A Polton Street, Bonnyrigg, Midlothan EH19 3YD.
Tel: 01315 615 443
Fax: 01316 542 797.
Web: midlothian.gov.uk
E-mail: karl.vanters@midlothian.gov.uk

Moray
Peter Findlay, Public Transport Manager, Moray Council, Council Office, Academy Street, Elgin IV30 1LL
Tel: 01343 562541
Fax: 01343 545628.
E-mail: peter.findlay@moray.gov.uk

North Ayrshire
North Ayrshire Council, Cunningham House, Irvine KA12 8EE

North Lanarkshire
North Lanarkshire Council, Po Box 14, Civic Centre, Motherwell ML1 1TW
Tel: 01224 664580
Fax: 01224 662005

Orkney
Orkney Islands Council, Council Offices, School Place, Kirkwall KW15 1NY

Perth & Kinross
Andrew J Warrington, Public Transport Manager; The Environment Service, Pullar House, 35 Kinnoull Street, Perth PH1 5GD.
Tel: 01738 476530
Fax: 01738 476510
E-mail: awarrington@pkc.gov.uk

Renfrewshire
Renfrewshire Council, North Building, Cotton Street, Paisley PA1 1WB

Scottish Borders
B Young, Transport Policy Manager, Scottish Borders Council, Council Headquarters, Newtown St Boswells, Melrose TD6 0SA.
Tel: 01835 824000
Fax: 01835 823008

Shetland Islands
Ian Bruce, Service Manager - Transport Operations, Infrastructure Service Dept., Shetland Islands Council, Grantfield, Lerwick ZE1 0NT.
Tel: 01595 744872
Fax: 01595 744869
E-mail: ian.bruce@sic.shetland.gov.uk

South Ayrshire
South Ayrshire Council, County Buildings, Wellington Square, Ayr KA7 1DR

South Lanarkshire
South Lanarkshire Council, Council Offices, Almada Street, Hamilton ML3 0AA. *(No Public Transport responsibilities - see SPT)*

Stirling
Stirling Council, Council Headquarters, Viewforth, Stirling FK8 2ET

West Dunbartonshire
West Dunbartonshire Council, Council Offices, Garshake Road, Dunbarton,

Tendering & Regulatory Authorities

G82 3PU. (No Public Transport responsibilities - see SPT)

Western Isles
Western Isles Council, Council Offices, Balivanich, Benbecula HS7 5LA

West Lothian
Roy Mitchell, Public Transport Manager, West Lothian Council, County Buildings, Linlithgow EH49 7EZ
Tel: 01506 775282
Fax: 01506 775265
E-mail: roy.mitchell@westlothian.gov.uk
Web site: www.westlothian.gov.uk

Traffic Commissioners

Web site: www.vosa.gov.uk

EASTERN TRAFFIC AREA
City House, 126-130 Hills Road, Cambridge CB2 1NP
Tel: 01223 531060
Fax: 01223 309681
Traffic Commissioner: Richard Turfitt
Deputy Traffic Commissioners: D. N. Stevens, R. C. Lockwood, M. J. Guy, Marcia Davis, Gillian Ekins
Area covered: Leicestershire, Lincolnshire, Cambridgeshire, Norfolk, Suffolk, Essex, Bedfordshire, Northamptonshire, Hertfordshire, Buckinghamshire.

NORTH EASTERN TRAFFIC AREA
Hillcrest House, 386 Harehills Lane, Leeds LS9 6NF
Tel: 0870 606 0440
Fax: 0113 248 9607
Traffic Commissioner: Tom Macartney
Deputy Traffic Commissioners: M. Hinchcliffe, Ms L Perrett, P J Mulvenna
Area covered: Northumberland, Tyne & Wear, Co Durham, Yorkshire, Nottinghamshire
Web site: www.vosa.gov.uk

NORTH WESTERN TRAFFIC AREA
Hillcrest House, 386 Harehills Lane, Leeds LS9 6NF
Tel: 0870 606 0440 **Fax**: 0113 248 9607
Traffic Commissioner: Beverley Bell.
Deputy Traffic Commissioners: M Hinchcliffe, Ms L Perrett, P J Mulvenna, S Evans.
Area covered: Cumbria, Lancashire, Greater Manchester, Merseyside, Cheshire, Derbyshire.
Web site: www.vosa.gov.uk

SCOTTISH TRAFFIC AREA
J Floor, 3 Lady Lawson Street, Edinburgh EH3 9SE
Tel: 0131 200 4955 **Fax**: 0131 229 0682
Traffic Commissioner: Miss Joan Aitken
Deputy Traffic Commissioner: R H McFarlane
Area covered: Scotland

SOUTH EASTERN & METROPOLITAN TRAFFIC AREA
Ivy House, 3 Ivy Terrace, Eastbourne BN21 4QT.
Tel: 01323 452421
Fax: 01323 721057
Traffic Commissioner: Philip Brown

Area covered: Greater London, Kent, Surrey, Sussex

WELSH TRAFFIC AREA
38 George Road, Birmingham B15 1PL
Tel: 0121 609 6832
 Fax: 0121 456 4241
Traffic Commissioner: Nick Jones
Deputy Traffic Commissioners: A Jenkins, A L Maddrell, C R Seymour, J Astle, M Dorrington, S Evans, T Seculer.
Area covered: Wales.

WEST MIDLAND TRAFFIC AREA
38 George Road, Birmingham B15 1PL
Tel: 0121 609 6832
Fax: 0121 456 4241
Traffic Commissioner: Nick Jones
Deputy Traffic Commissioners: A Jenkins, A L Maddrell, C R Seymour. J Astle, M Dorrington, S Evans, T Seculer.
Area covered: Shropshire, Staffordshire, West Midlands, Warwickshire, Worcestershire, Herefordshire.

WESTERN TRAFFIC AREA
2 Rivergate, Bristol BS1 6EH
Tel: 0870 606 0440
Traffic Commissioner: Sarah Bell
Deputy Traffic Commissioners: Brig M. H. Turner, Mrs F. R. Burton, A. L. Maddrell.
Administrative Director: Tim Hughes.
Area covered: Cornwall, Devon, Somerset, Dorset, Hampshire, Wiltshire, Gloucestershire, Oxfordshire, Berkshire.

Office of Fair Trading

The Office of Fair Trading (OFT) plays a leading role in promoting and protecting consumer interests throughout the UK, while ensuring that businesses are fair and competitive. The tools to carry out this work are the powers granted to the OFT under consumer and competition legislation.
Address: Fleetbank House, 2-6 Salisbury Square, London EC4Y 8JX
Tel: 020 7211 8000
Fax: 020 7211 8800
Web site: www.oft.gov.uk
E-mail: enquiries@oft.gsi.gov.uk
Enquiries: 08457 22 44 99

Department for Transport

4/24 Great Minster House, 76 Marsham Street, London SW1P 4DR
Tel: 020 7944 3000
Web site: www.dft.gov.uk

Permanent Secretary: Robert Devereux
Director General, Railways & National Works: Dr Mike Mitchell

Executive Agencies: (includes:)
Driving Standards Agency (DSA)
Driver and Vehicle Licensing Agency (DVLA)

Highways Agency (HA)
Chief Executive: Archie Robertson
Tel: 08457 50 40 30
Web Site: www.highways.gov.uk

Vehicle Certification
VCA
No1, The Estate Office Centre, Eastgate Road, Bristol BS5 6XX

Tel: 0117 952 4126
Fax: 0117 952 4104
E-mail: paul.cooke@vca.gov.uk
Web site: www.vca.gov.uk

Vehicle and Operator Services Agency (VOSA) (see also Driver Training A-Z Manufacturers section)
Web site: www.transportoffice.gov.uk

Advisory Non-Departmental Bodies: (includes:)

Commission for Integrated Transport
Chmn: Peter Hendy
Tel: 020 7944 8300
E-mail: cfit@dft.gsi.gov.uk

Disabled Persons Transport Advisory Committee
E-mail: dptac@dft.gsi.gov.uk

Executive Non-departmental Bodies: (includes:)

Health and Safety Commission

Health and Safety Executive

Tribunals

Traffic Areas

Public Corporations

Civil Aviation Authority

Transport for London

The Disabled Persons Transport Advisory Committee
Department for Transport
Great Minster House, 76 Marsham Street, London SW1P 4DR
Tel: 020 7944 8011
Minicom: 020 7944 3277
Fax: 020 7944 6998
E-mail: dptac@dft.gov.uk
Web site: www.dptac.gov.uk
Chair: Neil Betteridge
The Disabled Persons Transport Advisory Committee (DPTAC) is a statutory body established under Section 125 of the Transport Act 1985 to advise the Secretary of State for Transport on matters affecting the transport needs of disabled people. Membership is limited to a Chairman plus twenty members, at least half of whom must be disabled.

Mobility and Inclusion Unit
(address as above)
Tel: 020 7944 8021
Minicom: 020 7944 3277
Fax: 020 7944 6102
E-mail: miu@dft.gsi.gov.uk
Web site: www.dptac.gov.uk
Disability Rights Commission
Web site: www.drc-gb.org.uk

Rail Accident Investigation Branch
The Wharf, Stores Road, Derby DE21 4BA
Chief Inspector: Carolyn Griffiths
Tel: 01332 253300
Fax: 01332 253301
E-mail: enquiries@raib.gov.uk
Web site: www.raib.gov.uk
RAIB is the independent railway accident investigation organisation for the UK and is listed in LRB because its remit covers street tramways.

Section 3

Organisations and Societies

- British Operators Organisations
- Institutions
- International Associations
- Other Organisations
- First Aid and Sports Associations
- Trade Organisations
- Societies
- Passenger Transport Museums

British Operators' Organisations

ALBUM - ASSOCIATION OF LOCAL BUS COMPANY MANAGERS

The Association represents the professional views of the Executive Directors of those bus companies owned by district council and major independent operators on matters specifically affecting locally-owned bus company management and operations.
Chairperson: M Robson, Ipswich Buses Ltd, 7 Constantine Road, Ipswich IP1 2DL
Tel: 01473 232600
Secretary: S Burd, Blackpool Transport Services Ltd, Rigby Road, Blackpool FY1 5DD **Tel**: 01253 473041

COACH OPERATORS FEDERATION

Oakwood, Radway, Sidmouth EX10 8TW
Tel: 07768 846138 **Fax**: 01395 513508
E-mail: ejreece@btinternet.com
Web: www.cofed.net

THE COACH TOURISM COUNCIL

10 Bermondsey Exchange, 179-181 Bermondsey St, London SE1 3UW
Tel: 0870 850 2839 **Fax**: 020 7407 6880
E-mail: admin@coachtourismcouncil.co.uk
Web site: www.coachtourismcouncil.co.uk
The CTC's mission is to promote tourism and travel by coach.

COMMUNITY TRANSPORT ASSOCIATION

Highbank, Halton Street, Hyde SK14 2NY
Tel: 0161 351 1475 **Fax**: 0161 351 7221
Advice Service Tel: 0845 130 6195
E-mail: infi@ctauk.org
Web site: www.ctauk.org
The community transport sector is vast. There are over 100,000 minibuses serving over 10 million passengers every year being operated for use by voluntary and community groups, schools, colleges and Local Authorities, or to provide door-to-door transport for people who are unable to use other public transport. This door-to-door transport is not limited to minibuses though; there are very many voluntary car schemes throughout the UK where volunteers will use their own cars to provide transport for individuals. Overcoming social exclusion is at the heart of what community transport has always been about. The CTA is committed to helping its members achieve this objective in their area both in terms of the direct support it can offer such as training, developmental support etc. but also by lobbying on behalf of the movement with government and other important agencies.

CONFEDERATION OF PASSENGER TRANSPORT UK

34-43 Russell Street, London WC2B 5HA
Tel: 020 7240 3131
Fax: 020 7240 6565
E-mail: cpt@cpt-uk.org
Web site: www.cpt-uk.org
The Confederation of Passenger Transport UK (CPT) is the trade association representing the UK's bus and coach operators and the light rail sector. CPT has wide responsibilities ranging from representation on government working parties (national, local, EU); establishing operating codes of practice; advising on legal, technical and mechanical standards; management of the Bonded Coach Holiday Scheme, a government recognised consumer travel protection scheme and Coachmarque, an industry quality standard; 24-hour Crisis Control service for members; organisation of industry events and the first point of contact for the media on transport and other related issues.

OFFICERS AND COUNCIL
President: Giles Fearnley
Immediate Past President: Alan Scoles
Chief Executive: Simon Posner
Manager, Chief Executive's Office: Miss L Tang
Finance Director: W Wright
Communications Director: J Major
Public Affairs Officer: C Nice
Director of Membership: Peter Gomersall
Director of Policy Development: S Salmon
Director of Coaching: S Barber
Technical Executive: C Copelin
Operations Executives: J Burch, S Smith
Fixed Track Executive: D Walmsley
Director, Government Relations, Northern Ireland: Karen Magill
The Ecos Centre, Broughshane Road, Ballymena, Co Antrim BT43 7QA
Tel: 0282 563 8938
Chair, CPT Northern Ireland: William Wright
Director of Government Relations, Scotland: Mrs M Rodger, 29 Drumsheugh Gardens, Edinburgh EH3 7RN
Tel: 0131 272 2150
Fax: 0131 272 2152
Director of Government Relations, Wales: J Pockett, 70 Hillside View, Craigwen, Pontypridd CF37 2LG
Tel: 01443 485814
Fax: 01443 485816
Regional Managers
East Midlands: Andrew Norman, 12 Cumberhills Grange, Duffield Derby DE22 2TA
Tel: 01332 840586
London & Home Counties: Miss L Tang, 34-43 Russell Street, London WC2B 5HA
Tel: 020 7240 3131
Fax: 020 7240 6565
Northern: David Holding, Foxwood House, 6 The Dene, Chester Moor, Chester-le-Street DH2 3TB
Tel: 0191 388 7694
Fax: 0191 388 7694

North Western: Leonard Green, 2 Short Clough Close, Reedsholme, Rawtenstall BB4 8PT
Tel: 01706 218539
Fax: 01706 601485
Scotland: Jeremy Tinsley, 29 Drumsheugh Gardens, Edinburgh EH3 7RN
Tel: 0131 272 2150
Fax: 0131 272 2152
Wales: John Pocket, 70 Hillside View, Craigwer, Pontyprydd CF27 2LG
Tel/Fax: 01443 485814
West Midlands: P Bateman, Drury House, 34-43 Russell St, London WC2B 5HA
Tel: 020 7240 3131
Fax: 020 7240 6565
South West: R Anderson, Heather Cottage, Smokey Cross, Haytor, Newton Abbot TQ13 9QU
Tel: 01364 661365
Fax: 01752 777931
Yorkshire: G Peach, Green Acres, 332 Barnsley Road, Flockton WF4 4AT
Tel: 01924 840767
Fax: 01924 849685

PASSENGER TRANSPORT EXECUTIVE GROUP

Wellington House, 40-50 Wellington Street, Leeds LS1 2DE
Tel: 0113 251 7204
Fax: 0113 251 7333
Web site: www.pteg.net
Chair: Neil Scales
PTEG brings together and promotes the interests of the six Passenger Transport Executives (PTEs) in England. Transport for London is an associate member.

Institutions

THE CHARTERED INSTITUTE OF LOGISTICS & TRANSPORT

Logistics & Transport Centre, Earlstrees Court, Earlstrees Road, Corby NN17 4AX
Tel: 01536 740100 **Fax**: 01536 740101
E-mail: enquiry@ciltuk.org.uk.
Web site: www.ciltuk.org.uk
The Chartered Institute of Logistics and Transport (UK) is the professional body for individuals and organisations involved in all disciplines, modes and aspects of logistics and transport.
The Institute's 22,000 members have privileged access to a range of benefits and services, which support them, professionally and personally, throughout their careers and help connect them with world-wide expertise.
For further information and to join please contact Membership Services, Tel: 01536 740104 or visit the CILT(UK) web site above

THE INSTITUTE OF THE MOTOR INDUSTRY

Fanshaws, Brickendon, Hertford SG13 8PQ
Tel: 01992 511521
Fax: 01992 511548

E-mail: imi@motor.org.uk
Web site: www.motor.org.uk

The Institute of the Motor Industry (IMI) is the professional association for individuals working in the retail motor industry and is the leading awarding body of vocational qualifications in the automotive sector. With some 25,000 members and 45,000 registered students at 350 assessment centres, the IMI is focused on improving professional standards through the recognition, qualification and development of individuals.

Qualifications offered by the Institute include NVQs/SVQs, technical certificates, vehicle sales awards, Quality Assured Awards and Certificate/Diploma in automotive retail management (ARMS).

The IMI governs the industry's Automotive Technician Accreditation (ATA) initiative, which has more than 4500 nationally-accredited technicians since launching in 2005.

OFFICERS AND VICE PRESIDENTS
Patron: HRH Prince Michael of Kent KCVO FIMI.
President: Garel Rhys CBE FIMI
Honorary Treasurer: Edward Clark FIMI.
Chairman of the council: Steve Nash FIMI
Chief Executive: Sarah Sillars FIMI
Company Secretary: Alan Tyrer FIMI

THE INSTITUTE OF TRANSPORT ADMINISTRATION

The Old Studio, 25 Greenfield Road, Westoning MK45 5JD
Tel: 01525 634940
Fax: 01525 750016
E-mail: director@iota.org.uk
Web site: www.iota.org.uk
Registered Friendly Society: No 53 SA
OFFICERS
President: Dr Michael Asteris
Trustees: Gideon Fiegel FInstTA, John D Bailey FInstTA, Malcolm Braid FInstTA, Ian Marshall FInstTA,
National Chairman:
Rev Terry Dobson FInstTA
National Chairman Elect:
Ian Franklin MInstTA
Immediate Past Chairman:
Adrian Gettins FInstTA
National Treasurer: Ray Rowsell FInstTA
Finance & General Purposes Chairman: Ray Rowsell FInstTA
Chairman Education, Membership & Training Committee:
Stan Heagren FInstTA
Chairman External Affairs Committee:
Mike Walker FInstTA

THE INSTITUTION OF MECHANICAL ENGINEERS

1 Birdcage Walk, London SW1H 9JJ
Tel: 020 7222 7899
Fax: 020 7222 4557
Web site: www.imeche.org.uk
Founded in 1847
Chief Executive: William Edgar
President: Willaim M Banks

Engineering Director:
Dr Colin Brown C Eng FIMechE
Incorporates as the Automobile Division the former Institution of Automobile Engineers and as the Railway Division the former Institution of Locomotive Engineers.

SOE

22 Greencoat Place, London SW1P 1PR
Tel: 020 7630 1111
Fax: 020 7630 6677
E-mail: soe@soe.org.uk
Web site: www.soe.org.uk
Web: www.soe.org.uk
The SOE is the umbrella professional body for those working in road transport and plant engineering. The IRTE is a professional sector within the SOE.

TRL LTD (TRANSPORT RESEARCH LABORATORY)

Address: Crowthorne House, Nine Mile Ride, Wokingham RG40 3GA
Tel: 01344 773131
Fax: 01344 770356
E-mail: enquiries@trl.co.uk
Web site: www.trl.co.uk

International Associations

INTERNATIONAL ROAD TRANSPORT UNION (IRU)

Founded in 1948 in Geneva, the IRU is an international association of national road transport federations which has consultative status in the United Nations. One of its two Transport Councils is concerned with road passenger transport.
General Secretariat: IRU, Centre International, 3 Rue de Varembe, B.P.44, 1211 Geneva 20, Switzerland
Tel: 00 41 22 918 2700
Fax: 00 41 22 918 2741
E-mail: info@iru.org
Web site: www.iru.org

UITP, THE INTERNATIONAL ASSOCIATION OF PUBLIC TRANSPORT

President: Roberto Cavalieri (Italy)
Secretary General: Hans Rat
Offices: Rue Sainte Marie 6, B-1080 Bruxelles, Belgium
Tel: 00 32 2 673 6100
Fax: 00 32 2 660 1072
Web site: www.uitp.org

WORLD ROAD ASSOCIATION (PIARC)

Hon Sec/Hon Treas: John Smart, IHT, 6 Endsleigh Street, London WC1H 0DZ
Tel: 0207 391 9927
E-mail:john.smart@iht.org
Web site: www.piarc.org
The Association is an international body with headquarters in Paris, administered by an elected President and other office bearers. Members are recruited from governments, local authorities, technical and industrial groups and private individuals whose interests are centred on roads and road traffic. The association is maintained by subscriptions from its members. International congresses are held every four years.

OFFICE BEARERS
President: O Michaud (Switzerland)
International Vice-Presidents: P Anguitas Salas (Chile), C Jordan (Australia), K Ghellab (Morocco)
Secretary General: J F Corte, PIARC, La Grande Arche, Paroi Nord, Niveau 8, 92055 La Defense Cedex, France
Tel: 00 33 1 47 96 81 21
Fax: 00 33 1 49 00 02 02

The British National Committee's role is to ensure adequate representation of British methods and experience on PIARC's international committees and Congresses, to disseminate the findings of those committees and generally look after British interests. The present officers of this committee are:
Patron: Minister for Transport.
UK President: Steve Lee
UK Chairman: W J McCoubrey
Vice-Chairman: S Clarke
Hon Treasurer: C B Goodwillie
Hon Secretary/Hon Treasurer: J Smart

Other Organisations

ASSOCIATION OF TRANSPORT CO-ORDINATING OFFICERS (ATCO)

Web site: www.atco.org.uk
Chairman: John Hodgkins
Chairman, Bus Sub-Committee:
David Neilson
The Association of Transport Coordinating Officers was formed in 1974 to bring together local authority officers whose work involved what were then new county council responsibilities for passenger transport. ATCO members include senior staff directly concerned with strategic policy development and implementation for securing of passenger transport services for a wide range of public authorities. These include shire counties and unitary councils in England, Wales and Scotland, Passenger Transport Executives, TfL, the Isle of Man, the States of Jersey and Northern Ireland. Through exchanging information and views the Association helps formulate policies and standards and promotes transport initiatives aimed at achieving better passenger transport services for all.
Members give advice to the Local Government Association and the Convention of Scottish Local Authorities. ATCO cooperates with the Community Transport Association and Passenger Transport Executive Group.

BUS USERS UK

PO Box 2950, Stoke-on-Trent ST4 9EW
Tel: 01782 442855
Fax: 01782 442886

E-mail: enquiries@bususers.org
Web site: www.bususers.org
Bus Users UK was formed in 1985 to bring together national and local organisations with an interest in bus services and concerned individual bus users to seek to give an effective voice to the consumer. It is actively involved in developing constructive dialogue between the users and providers of bus services. It publishes a quarterly newsletter – *Bus User*.
Life President: Caroline Cahm
Chairman: Gavin Booth
Secretary: Susan Dawson
Treasurer: Stephen Le Bras
Activity Officer in Wales: Barclay Davies, Bus Users UK Wales, c/o PTI Cymru, Leckwith Offices, Sloper Road, Cardiff CF11 8TB
Tel: 029 2022 1370
E-mail: wales@bususers.org
Bus User **Editor**: Stephen Morris, PO Box 119, Shepperton TW17 8UX
Tel: 01932 232574
Fax: 01932 246394
E-mail: editor@bususers.org
Operations Officer: Phil Tonks

BUSK
18 Windsor Road, Newport NP19 8NS
Tel: 01633 274944
E-mail: buskuk@aol.com
Formerly known for its Belt Up School Kids campaign, BUSK is now known through the European Union as an authority on vehicular safety for children and young people.

COACH DRIVERS CLUB
37 Tyndall Court, Commerce Road, Lynch Wood, Peterborough PE2 6LR
Tel: 01733 405738 **Fax**: 01733 405745
E-mail: barbara@expom.co.uk
Web site: www.coachdriversclub.com
Membership club for coach drivers, coaching and tourism. Offers accident cover, magazine, yearbook, members' website, legal advice.

GOSKILLS
Concorde House, Trinity Park,
Solihull B37 7UQ
Tel: 0121 635 5520
Fax: 0121 635 5521
Web site: goskills.org
GoSkills is the Sector Skills Council for passenger transport.

LIGHT RAIL TRANSIT ASSOCIATION
c/o 8 Berwick Place,
Welwyn Garden City, AL7 4TU
Tel/Fax: 01179 517785
Web site: www.lrta.org
E.mail: office@lrta.org
Founded in 1937 to advocate and encourage interest in light rail and modern tramways. Monthly magazine is Tramways & Urban Transit. Membership enquiries to:
Membership Secretary: Roger Morris
E-mail: membership@lrta.org

President: Michael Parker
Chairman: David F Russell
Deputy Chairman: Geoff Lusher
Editor in Chief, TAUT: Howard Johnston

LOCAL GOVERNMENT ASSOCIATION
Local Government House,
Smith Square, London SW1P 3HZ
Tel: 020 7664 3131
Fax: 020 7664 3030
Web Site: www.lga.gov.uk
The Local Government Association was formed by the merger of the Association of County Councils, the Association of District Councils and the Association of Metropolitan Authorities in 1997. The LGA has just under 500 members, including all 238 shire district councils; 36 metropolitan district councils; 34 county councils; 46 new unitary authorities; 33 London authorities; and 22 Welsh authorities. In addition, the LGA represents police authorities, fire authorities and passenger transport authorities. The LGA provides the national voice for local communities in England and Wales; its members represent over 50 million people, employ more than 2 million staff and spend over £65 billion on local services. Amongst the LGA's policy priorities is integrated transport; local authorities lead the way in encouraging the use of public transport and thereby reducing congestion, ill-health and environmental damage through a programme of partnerships between local authorities and other agencies.

President: Lord Richard Best
Chair: Sir Andy Bruce-Lockhart OBE (Conservative, Kent CC)
Vice-Chairs: Sir Jeremy Beecham (Labour, Newcastle), Peter Chalke (Conservative, Wiltshire)
Deputy Chairs:
Ian Swithenbank CBE (Labour, Northumberland) Chris Clarke OBE (Liberal Democrat, Somerset) Chloe Lambert (Independent, Aylesbury Vale) Margaret Eaton OBE (Conservative, Bradford)
Chief Executive: Paul Coen
Director of Economic & Environmental Policy: Sarah Wood
Director of Communications & Public Affairs: Oona Muirhead
Programme Manager, Planning: Lee Searles

LONDON TRAVELWATCH
6 Middle Street, London EC1A 7JA
Tel: 020 7505 9000
Fax: 020 7505 9003
Web site: www.londontravelwatch.org.uk
E-mail: info@londontravelwatch.org.uk
Formerly the London Transport Users Committee, London TravelWatch is the independent statutory body set up to represent the interests of the users of all transport for which the Greater London Authority and Transport for London is responsible for operating, providing, procuring and licensing. London TravelWatch is also the Rail Passengers Committee for London.
Interim Chair: David Leibling
Chief Executive: Janet Cooke

ROAD OPERATORS' SAFETY COUNCIL (ROSCO)
Cowley House, Watlington Road,
Oxford OX4 6GA
Tel: 01865 775552
Fax: 01865 775552
E-mail: rosco-oxford@supanet.com
Web site: www.rosco.org.uk
Chairman: Peter Shipp
Secretary: Tony Beetham

THE ROYAL SOCIETY FOR THE PREVENTION OF ACCIDENTS
Edgbaston Park, 353 Bristol Road,
Birmingham B5 7ST
Tel: 0121 248 2000
Fax: 0121 248 2001
RoSPA promotes safety at work and in the home, at leisure and in schools, on (or near water) and on the roads, through providing information, publicity, training and consultancy.
The Society works with central and local government, the caring services, the police and public and private sector organisations large and small. Some work is funded by grant and sponsorship, but most relies on the support of the Society's membership. The Society also produces and supplies a comprehensive selection of publications ranging from reference books to low-cost booklets for mass distribution.
Training Offered: Training courses cover practical skills and management training through to professional qualifications in Health and Safety.
Chief Executive: Tom Mullarkey

STATUS
c/o Michael Hughes, Manchester Metropolitan University, Chester Street, Manchester M1 5GD
Tel: 0161 247 2640
Fax: 0161 247 6779
Web site: www.status.org.uk
E-mail: m.p.hughes@mmu.ac.uk
STATUS others members, from all areas of the specialist road transport industry, with engineering development and test services, technical legislative consultancy and a range of general technical information.
It is involved on behalf of its members in contributing to consultation documents, influencing transport related legislation and lobbying government departments and agencies.
The organisation can call on a diverse range of personnel to help deal with more difficult problems. A primary benefit is the availability of telephone consultancy on technical or legislative matters.
STATUS plays a prominent role in representing its members' interests on

TRANSPORT 2000

Transport 2000, 1st Floor,
The Impact Centre, 12-18 Hoxton Street,
London N1 6NG
Tel: 020 7613 0743
Fax: 020 7613 5280.
Web site: www.bettertransport.org.uk
E-mail: info@bettertransport.org.uk
Transport 2000 is a campaign and research group that seeks greener, cleaner transport patterns through greater use of public transport, walking and cycling.
President: Michael Palin
Executive Director: Stephen Joseph

TRANSPORT BENEVOLENT FUND

87A Leonard Street, London EC2A 4QS
Tel: 08450 100 500 **Fax**: 0870 831 2882
Web site: www.tbf.org.uk
E-mail: help@tbf.org.uk
TBF is a Registered Charity (No 1058032) and was founded in 1923. Membership is open to most staff engaged in the public transport industry. Members pay £1 a week and in return are granted, at the discretion of the Trustees, cash help, convalescence, recuperation, a wide range of complementary medical treatments, legal advice, and medical equipment in times of need. Membership covers the employee and their partner and dependent children. Subject to age and length of membership, free membership may be awarded on leaving the industry. There are payroll deduction facilities in many companies.
Director: Chris Godbold
Senior Trustee: Ray Jordan (President)
Patrons: Sir Wilfrid Newton, CBE (Past Chairman, London Transport), Brian Souter (Stagecoach Group), Lew Adams OBE (BT Police Authority), Sir Moir Lockhead OBE (FirstGroup), Peter Hendy CBE (Transport for London), Robert Crow (RMT), Graham Stevenson (Unite), Gerry Doherty (TSSA), Keith Norman (ASLEF), David Martin (Arriva), Keith Ludeman (Go-Ahead Group), Roger Bowker CBE (East London Bus Group), Bob Rixham (Amicus),Richard Bowker CBE (National Express), Charlie Beaumont (Transdev), John O'Brien (Veolia), Ian Coucher (Network Rail) Simon Posner (CPT).

First Aid & Sports Associations

NATIONAL PASSENGER TRANSPORT SPORTS ASSOCIATION

President: Ian Davies
Secretary: V Hills, 2 St Aidans Avenue, Grangetown, Sunderland SR2 9SF
Tel: 0191 567 2504
 Fax: 0191 203 3177
E-mail: nptsasec@btinternet.com
Web site: www.nptsa.co.uk
The association organises inter-company sporting activities for the bus, coach, light rail and heavy rail industries. Currently 16 different sports are covered, each with competitions through the year, with trophies provided often by bus sponsors. A regular magazine is published. Corporate membership is provided to large transport undertakings. Furher information is available from the Secretary, address above.

Trade Organisations and Associations

BEAMA LTD

Offices: Westminster Tower, 3 Albert Embankment, London SE1 7SL.
Tel: 020 7793 3000
Fax: 020 7793 3003
E-mail: info@beama.org.uk
The British Electrotechnical & Allied Manufacturers' Association.
Founded 1902. Incorporated 1905.
Objects: By co-operative action to promote the interests of the industrial, electrical and electronic manufacturing industries of Great Britain.
Director-General: A. A. Bullen

FEDERATION OF ENGINE REMANUFACTURERS

Director: Brian Ludford
Address: 49 Mewstone Avenue, Wembury, Plymouth PL9 0JT
Tel: 01752 863681
Web Site: www.fer.co.uk.

FREIGHT TRANSPORT ASSOCIATION VEHICLE INSPECTION SERVICE

Address: Hermes House, St John's Road, Tunbridge Wells TN4 9UZ.
Tel: 01892 526171
Web Site: www.fta.co.uk.
The Freight Transport Association represents the interests of over 11,000 companies throughout the UK. FTA carries out over 100,000 vehicle inspections each year including many PSVs. The FTA Vehicle Inspection Service supports operators in maintaining their vehicles in a roadworthy condition - both mechanically and legally.
Further details from Alan Osborne, Head of Vehicle Inspection Services, FTA, Tunbridge Wells (01892 526171).
Publications: *Freight* (monthly journal), FTA Yearbook.
Chief Executive: Richard Turner.

LOW CARBON VEHICLE PARTNERSHIP

Address: 83 Victoria Street,
London SW1H 0HW
Tel: 020 3178 7859
E-mail: secretariat@lowcvp.org.uk
Web site: www.lowcvp.org.uk
The LowCVP is an action and advisory group providing a forum through which partners can work together towards shared goals and take the lead in the transition to a low-carbon future for road transport in the UK.
Bus Working Group Chmn: Bob Bryson (Alexander Dennis)

MIRA LTD

Registered Office: MIRA Ltd, Watling Street, Nuneaton CV10 0TU
Tel: 024 7635 5000.
Fax: 024 7635 5355.
MIRA an independent product engineering and technology centre and offers skills in innovation, problem-solving and consultancy.
Chairman: M Beasley
Executive Directors:
Managing Director: J. R. Wood.
Director of Finance & Company Secretary: C J N Phillipson.
Director of Engineering: G. Townsend

SOCIETY OF MOTOR MANUFACTURERS & TRADERS (SMMT)

Forbes House, Halkin Street, London SW1X 7DS.
Tel: 020 7235 7000
Web site: www.smmt.co.uk
E-mail: buscoachweb@smmt.co.uk

THE VEHICLE BUILDERS & REPAIRERS ASSOCIATION LTD

Offices: Belmont House,
Gildersome, Leeds LS27 7TW.
Tel: 0113 253 8333 **Fax:** 0113 238 0496
E-mail: vbra@vbra.co.uk
Web site: www.vbra.co.uk
Director General: M Tagg
Journal Editor: Judi Barton

Societies

THE ASSOCIATION OF FRIENDS OF THE BRITISH COMMERCIAL VEHICLE MUSEUM TRUST

The Association was formed when The British Commercial Vehicle Museum was opened in 1983. Its aims are to support the full-time staff in matters of publicity, fund raising, maintenance and documentation of exhibits, work in the archives, organising rallies, etc. Facilities for members include a newsletter, free admission to the museum to undertake museum work and socialise with colleagues. New members are always welcome and special rates exist for families, students and senior citizens.

legislative matters and lobbies government agencies on behalf of members.
A monthly newsletter is published, featuring industry related stories.

Hon Chairman: H Hatcher
Hon Secretary: A Pritchard
Hon Treasurer: A Pritchard
Members of the Committee: E Simister, D Lewis, J Gardner
Museum Manager: A Buchan
Address: The British Commercial Vehicle Museum, King Street, Leyland, Preston PR25 2LE **Tel**: 01772 451011

ASTON MANOR ROAD TRANSPORT MUSEUM

Contact address: The Old Tram Depot, 208-216 Witton Lane, Aston, Birmingham B6 6QE
Phone: 0121 322 2298
Web site: www.amrtm.org.uk
Company limited by guarantee. Registered as a charity.
The museum is uniquely housed in a former depot of Birmingham's first-generation tramways. The display of commercial and passenger vehicles reflects the history of construction and operation in the West Midlands, and there are numerous displays of transport artefacts, tickets, notices and photographs. Joining as a Friend of the Museum gives entitlement to free entry and a quarterly newsletter. The museum is open on Saturdays, Sundays and Bank Holidays throughout the year, with a range of special events featuring a free heritage bus service to and from the city centre. Situated on Travel West Midland's bus services 7 and 11 and close to Aston railway station.
Further information from:
Chairman: Geoff Lusher, 86 Heritage Court, Warstone Lane, Jewellery Quarter, Birmingham B18 6HU

BRITISH BUS PRESERVATION GROUP

25 Oldfield Road,
Bexleyheath DA7 4DX
Membership enquiries: 51 Market Close, Shirebrook, Mansfield NG20 8AE
Tel: 07940 771439
Web site: www.bbpg.co.uk
E-mail: info@bbpg.co.uk
The BBPG was formed in 1990 and has been responsible for securing the future of more than 250 historic buses and coaches, many of which were saved at extremely short notice from being broken up. The society has more than 600 members, both individuals and preservation groups. The BBPG caters for all bus enthusiasts, whether or not they own a bus.
Chairman: Glyn Matthews.
General Secretary: Mike Lloyd.
Membership Secretary: Harry Glover.

BRITISH TROLLEYBUS SOCIETY

Formed as the Reading Transport Society in 1961, the present title was adopted in 1971, having acquired a number of trolleybuses for preservation from all over Britain. In 1969 it founded the Trolleybus Museum at Sandtoft, near Doncaster, where its vehicles are housed and regularly operate on mains power from the overhead wiring. West Yorkshire Transport Circle merged into the Society in January 1991. Currently membership stands at about 320. Members receive a monthly journal *Trolleybus* containing news and articles from home and abroad. Additionally members can subscribe to *Bus Fare* and *Wheels*, monthly magazines for motorbus operation in the Thames Valley and West Yorkshire areas respectively. Monthly meetings are also held in Reading, London. and Bradford.
Chairman: G P Bilbe, 12 Belle Avenue, Reading RG6 7BL
Secretary: A. J. Barton, 2 Josephine Court, Southcote Road, Reading RG30 2DG.
Treasurer: R. V. Fawcett, 57 Sutcliffe Avenue, Earley RG6 7JN
Web site: www.sandtoft.org

BUSES WORLDWIDE (BWW)

Web site: www.busesworldwide.org
E-mail: membership@busesworldwide.org
Established in 1982 to associate those particularly interested in bus operation in countries other than their own. Meetings are held, a bi-monthly magazine is published and visits abroad are organised.
Chairman: R Stedall
Membership Secretary: S. Guess, 37 Oyster Lane, Byfleet KT14 7HS
News Editor: N. R. Bartlett, 1 Hopping Jacks Lane, Danbury, Chelmsford CM3 4PN.
Features Editor: D. Corke, 8 Priestland Gardens, Berkhamsted HP4 2GT

CLASSIC BUS HERITAGE TRUST (INCORPORATING THE ROUTEMASTER HERITAGE TRUST)

The Classic Bus Heritage Trust aims to advance preservation of buses and coaches by fostering the interests of the general public. It is a Registered Charity.
Treasurer & Hon Sec: W. Ackroyd, 8 Twining Road, Ventnor, Isle of Wight PO38 1TX

ESSEX BUS ENTHUSIASTS' GROUP

Web site: www.essexbus.org.uk
This group was formed in 1962, under its previous title, Eastern National Enthusiasts' Group. The present title was adopted in 1987 to reflect more fully the activities of the group. A monthly magazine is circulated to all members giving information on all aspects of First Essex Buses, Thamesway, Colchester and Southend and all other operators in Essex. Meetings are arranged on a regular basis whilst tours are also organised. A range of publications and photographs is also available. Membership is open to all over the age of 12.

Membership Secretary: Derek Stebbing, Conifers, Thorpe Road, Weeley, Clacton-on-Sea CO16 9JJ
Tel: 01255 830732
E-mail: derekstebbing@hotmail.com

GB BUS GROUP

Membership Enquiries: 192 Alvechurch Road, West Heath, Birmingham B31 3PW
Tel: 0121 624 8641
Chairman: G Nichols
Secretery: M Brown
Treasurer: F Gold
The GB Bus Grpoup was formed in 2006 to help attractb new enthusiasts to the hobby. It provides a monthly magazine as well as a full range of bus and coach fleetbooks covering UK and Ireland. The GB Bus Group is a member of the UK Transport Group.

HISTORIC COMMERCIAL VEHICLE SOCIETY

The Society was founded in 1958 and four years later absorbed the Vintage Passenger Vehicle Society and the London Vintage Taxi Club. Its membership of over 4,000 owns more than 6,000 preserved vehicles. Activities include the organisation of rallies, among them the well known London to Brighton and Trans-Pennine runs. The club caters for all commercial vehicles over 20 years old.
OFFICERS
President: Lord Montagu of Beaulieu
Senior Exec Officer and
Vice-President: M. Banfield, Iden Grange, Cranbrook Road, Staplehurst TN12 0ET
Tel: 01580 892929. **Fax**: 01580 893227.
E-mail: hcvs@btinternet.com
Web site: www.hcvs.co.uk

LEYLAND NATIONAL GROUP

Web site: www.leylandnationalgroup.org
E-mail: enquiries@leylandnationalgroup.org
Address: 27 Dukeshill Road, Bracknell RG42 2DU
Tel: 01344 640095
The Leyland National Group was formed in 1997 and has members throughout Great Britain and abroad. Although the group does not own any vehicles itself, some of its members are bus owners. There are more than 100 Leyland Nationals from a variety of operators preserved by group members. However, one does not need to own a bus to join the group, as membership is open to anyone with an interest in Leyland Nationals. The group also caters for those interested in the derivatives of the Leyland National; the Leyland-DAB, Leyland B21 and Leyland National bodied rail vehicles. Members receive a colour illustrated quarterly magazine, exclusive access to the members' only area on the group's website as well as other benefits. Please contact the Membership Secretary for more information

about the group, the benefits of membership and to receive a membership application form.
Chairman: Mick Berg
Secretary: David Layton
Address: 24 Patterson Court, Farnol Road, Dartford DA1 5DT
Tel: 01322 278050
E-mail: secretary@leylandnationalgroup.org
Treasurer: Mike Bellinger
Magazine Editor: Claire Barrett
Membership Secretary: Tim Wild
Address: 27 Dukeshill Road, Bracknell, RG42 2DU
Tel: 01344 640095
E-mail: membership@leylandnationalgroup.org

LINCOLNSHIRE VINTAGE VEHICLE SOCIETY

Road Transport Museum, Whisby Road, North Hykeham LN6 5TR Tel: 01522 500566/689497
The LVVS was founded in 1959 by local businessmen with the aim of forming a road transport museum. Charitable status was obtained some time ago, and with a capital grant from its local district council, it has now completed the first stage of its new museum project. Over 60 vehicles dating from the 1920s to the 1980s can be seen in the new exhibition hall with many more in the workshop. Opening times November–April Sundays 13.00-16.00. May–October Mon-Fri 12.00-16.00, Sun 10.00-16.00.
Chairman: S Milner
Hon Treasurer: J Child
Secretary: Mrs J Jefford
Web site: www.lvvs.org.uk

LONDON OMNIBUS TRACTION SOCIETY (LOTS)

Unit N305, Westminster Business Square, 1-45 Durham Street
London SE11 5JH
Web site: www.lots.org.uk
Formed in 1964, LOTS has some 2,500 members and is the largest bus enthusiast society in the United Kingdom.
A colour Illustrated monthly newsletter is sent to all members. This covers all the current operators in the former London Transport central and country areas,and includes General and Industry News, Route Developments, Vehicle News, Publicity News, as well as subsequent disposal information for vehicles and Service Vehicle information. Monthly meetings as normally held in central London featuring guest speakers, slide and film presentations during the year as well as the annual free bus rides from central London using vehicles of London interest.
Regular LOTS publications include fleet allocations and route working publications, an annual review of the routes, vehicles and operations of London buses, as well as the popular annual London Bus and Tram Fleetbook. A quarterly 64-page glossy magazine the London Bus Magazine (LBM) has been produced for over 35 years. Regular sales lists are produced and sent out to all members through the year. An information service is also available to all members to help with those historical queries.
The Autumn Transport Spectacular (ATS) is held in London every autumn and is one of London's biggest transport sales.
All enquiries should be directed to the above address.

THE M & D AND EAST KENT BUS CLUB

42 St Albans Hill,
Hemel Hempstead HP3 9NG
Web site: www.mdekbusclub.org.uk
E-mail: n.king112@btinternet.com
This club was formed in 1952 with the object of bringing together all those interested in road passenger transport in an area covering Kent and East Sussex. Facilities for members include a monthly news booklet (illustrated), information service, tours, meetings, vehicle photograph sales and vehicle preservation. A series of publications is also produced, including illustrated fleet histories.
Hon Chairman: J. V. Spillett
Hon Sec: P J Evans
Hon Editor: N D King
Hon Treasurer: N D King
Membership Officer: J. A. Fairley
Photographic Officer: B.Weeden
Sales Officer: to be appointed
Tours Officer: D. R. Cobb
Management Committee: N. D. King, R. A. Lewis, J. V. Spillett, P. J. Evans, D M Jones.
Area Organisers in Ashford, Dover, Folkestone, Hastings, North-East Kent, Maidstone and the Medway Towns.

NATIONAL TROLLEYBUS ASSOCIATION

15 Cambrian Crescent,
Oulton Broad NR32 3HW
Web site: www.trolleybus.co.uk/nta
Formed in 1963, and incorporated in 1968 as The Trolleybus Museum Co Ltd. The vehicles and ancillary equipment collected by the NTA since its inception are now owned by the company, which is limited by guarantee and is a registered charity. Members receive *Trolleybus Magazine*, a printed and illustrated bi-monthly journal documenting all aspects of trolleybus operation past and present throughout the world.
Chairman: R. D. Helliar-Symons
Secretary: J. H. Ward
Treasurer: I Martin
Membership Secretary: I Martin
Enquiries: TMCMembSec@hotmail.com

THE OMNIBUS SOCIETY

Website: www.omnibussoc.org.
The Omnibus Society was founded in 1929. Today it is a nationwide organisation with a network of provincial branches, offering a comprehensive range of facilities for those interested in the bus and coach industry. The Society has accumulated a wealth of information on public road transport. Members have the opportunity to receive and exchange data on every aspect of the industry including route developments, operational/traffic matters and fleet changes. Each branch has a full programme of activities and publishes its own Branch Bulletin to give local news of route changes, etc. A scheme exists whereby members subscribe to receive bulletins from branches other than that of which they are a member. A programme of indoor meetings is customary during winter, including film shows, invited speakers and discussions. In the summer months visits to manufacturers and tours to operators are featured.
OFFICERS
100 Sandwell Street, Walsall W51 3EB
President: Gavin Booth
Vice-Presidents: F P Groves, A W Mills, G Wedlake, T. F. McLachlan, K. W. Swallow, R. G. Westgate, Professor John Hibbs.
Chairman: B. Le Jeune.
Secretary: A. J. Francis, 185 Southlands Road, Bromley BR2 9QZ.
Treasurer: H. L. Barker, 31 High Street, Tarporley CW6 0DP.
Editor, Society's Publications:
Cyril McIntyre
Members of the Council: I. D. Barlex, J. Hart, D. M. Persson, D. Roy, J Howie and nominations from each branch
Branch Officers:
Midland Branch: C R Warn, 11 The Meadows, Shawbury, Shrewsbury SY4 4HS
South Wales and West Branch:
A J Armstrong, 16 Stanley Grove, Weston-super-Mare BS23 3EB
Northern Branch: Philip Battersby, 12 Crescent Lodge, Tile Crescent, Middlesbrough TS5 6SF.
North Western & Yorkshire Branch:
P. Wilkinson, 10 Bradley Close, Timperley, Altrincham WA15 6SH
Scottish Branch: I. Allan, 10 Miller Avenue, Crossford, Dunfermline KY12 8PY
Essex & South Suffolk Group: J. L. Rugg, 86 Worthing Road, Laindon SS15 6JU
East Midland Group: A. Oxley, 4 Gordon Close, Attenborough, Nottingham NN4 9UF
Herts & Beds Group: R. C. Barton, 5 Viscount Court, Knights Field, Luton LU2 7LD
London Historical Research Group:
D A Ruddom, 57 Bluebridge Road, Brookmans Park, Hatfield AL9 7UW
Provincial Historical Research Group:
A E Jones, 8 Poplar Drive, Church Stretton S76 7BW

THE PSV CIRCLE

15 Port Close, Lordswood,
Chatham ME5 8DU
Tel: 01634 867519
E-mail: circlepostoffice.aol.com
Web site: www.psv-circle.org.uk

The Circle is an association of over 2000 members, interested in various ways in the vehicles used by the passenger transport industry on the roads of the United Kingdom and abroad. Membership is open to all over the age of 16, and in certain exceptional cases to those under this age. News Sheets, comprising nine regional sections, are published each month, together with numerous supplements and fleet histories which fully record information relating to operators, chassis builders and body constructors. There is no entrance fee. Annual subscriptions vary with the number of regional news sheets required, with a minimum for one area and graded additional payments according to members' requirements. Frequent meetings, mainly of a social nature, are held in London and several provincial towns.

HONORARY OFFICERS
Chairman: C. R. Costella
Secretary: J E Skilling
Treasurer: M D Bissex
Managing Editor: S Curl
The above with another eight members constitute the Committee of Management, and for convenience all mail other than editorial matters is handled at the above address.

RIBBLE ENTHUSIASTS' CLUB
23 Richmond Road, Hindley Green, Wigan WN2 4ND
Tel: 01942 253497
E-mail: mjyat@msn.com
Website: http://homepage.manx.net/JHL/REC/index.htm
Founded in 1954 by the late T. B. Collinge for the study of road transport past and present and in particular Ribble Motor Services and associated companies. Meetings are held and a monthly news sheet produced.
Life President: A E Chapman
Life Vice President: M. Shires
Vice President: C Bowles
Committee Chairman: D Bailey MBE
Secretary/Tours: M J Yates, 23 Richmond Road, Hindley Green, Wigan WN2 4ND
Treasurer: R A Harpum, 22 Woodside Road, Ferndown BH22 9LD
Records: S Blake, 23 Fairfield Road, North Shore, Blackpool FY1 2RA
Sales Dept: Mr & Mrs B Ashcroft, 11 Regent Road, Walton le Dale, Preston PR5 4QA
Sales Dept: Assistant: Mrs J Yates, 23 Richmond Road, Hindley Green, Wigan WN2 4ND
Archive: B Ashcroft, 11 Regent Road, Walton Le Dale, Preston PR5 4QA
Editor: R Kenyon, 18 Hatfield Road, Accrington BB5 6DF
Membership Sec: B Downham, 203 Brindle Road, Bamber Bridge, Preston PR5 6YL

ROADS AND ROAD TRANSPORT HISTORY ASSOCIATION
Web site: www.rrtha.org.uk
Founded in 1992, the association promotes, encourages and co-ordinates the study of the history of roads and road transport, both passenger and freight. It aims to encourage those interested in a particular aspect of transport to understand their chosen subject in the context of developments in other areas and at other periods. It publishes a newsletter four times a year and holds an annual conference each autumn. Membership is open to professional bodies/transport societies, museums and individuals.
President: Professor John Hibbs, OBE
Chairman: Garry Turvey, CBE
Hon. Secretary: Christopher Hogan, 124 Shenstone Avenue, Stourbridge DY8 3EJ
E-mail: roadsandRTHA@aol.com

ROUTEMASTER ASSOCIATION
23 Oakhurst Drive, Crewe, Cheshire CW2 6UE **Tel**: 0870 720 2920 **E-mail**: grahamsteph1011@hotmail.co.uk **Web Site**: www.routemaster.org.uk
The Routemaster Operators & Owners Association provides assistance, advice and news for operators, owners and enthusiasts of these vehicles. From the specification of a screw to a complete bus, the Association provides authoritative technical information. Bus rallies and events are organised and other selected events are supported each year. Members receive a quarterly news magazine and discounts on parts and accessories including a maintenance manual, owners handbook technical bulletins, suppliers handbook, badges and transfers, window sealing rubber and many other unique products. Large batches of Routemaster spares have been acquired from the London bus operators including mechanical units, electrical items and bodywork spares.
President: Colin Curtis OBE
Secretary: Mike Fuller
Chairman: Andrew Morgan, 45 Princess Diana Drive, St Albans, Herts AL4 0DZ **E-mail**: andrewmorgan1368@tiscali.co.uk

THE SAMUEL LEDGARD SOCIETY
C/O 58 Kirklees Drive, Farsley, Pudsey LS28 5TE
Tel: 0113 236 3695 **Fax**: 0113 259 1125
E-mail: rennison@mailcc.co.uk
Website: wwwsamuelledgardsociety.org.uk
The Samuel Ledgard Society was formed in 1998 at the Rose & Crown Inn, Otley, during the second annual reunion of the devotees of this well-known bus company. Reunions are held twice yearly at Armley during April and Otley on or about October 14. A Christmas dinner is also part of the established calendar of events. The quarterly journal of the Society, *The Chat*, is published in March, June, September and December each year. Founding officers were Barry Rennison, Tony Greaves and Don Bate, all of whom have a wealth of knowledge about the Samuel Ledgard company. Membership is open to all with a subscription of £5 - contact any member of the Committee for details.

Hon President: Samuel Ledgard Mather AMIRTE (Retd)
COMMITTEE
Chairman: Barry Rennison, 58 Kirklees Drive, Farsley, Pudsey LS28 5TE
Vice-Chairman, Magazine Editor & Publicity Officer: Tony Greaves, 19 Perth Mount, Horsforth LS18 5SH
Treasurer: Bryan Whitham, 4 Airedale Drive, Horsforth LS18 4ER
Secretary & Membership: Margaret Rennison, 58 Kirklees Drive, Farsley, Pudsey LS28 5TE

SCOTTISH TRAMWAY & TRANSPORT SOCIETY
PO Box 7342, Glasgow G51 4YQ
Founded in 1951 as the Scottish Tramway Museum Society, the Society claims to be 'Scotland's foremost tramway enthusiast organisation', publishing books and videos on tramways and other transport subjects and supporting the National Tramway Museum. Monthly meetings and newsletter.
Hon President: B M Longworth
Gen Secretary: H. McAulay
E-mail: stts-glasgow@virgin.net
Hon Treasurer: A. Ramsay
Members of Committee: A Murray, N Bates, A Muir, B Quinn, F W B Mitchell, I Stewart

SOUTH YORKSHIRE TRANSPORT MUSEUM
UNIT 9, Waddington Way, Aldwarke, Rotherham S65 3SH
Tel: 0114 255 3010
The Sheffield Bus Museum Trust was formed in 1987 with the purpose of co-ordinating the bus preservation movement in Sheffield and to establish a permanent museum. This was initially achieved at the former Sheffield Tramways Company's Tinsley Tram Depot but in 2007 the Trust moved its collection to new premises at Aldwarke, Rotherham. At the same time the museum was re-branded to the name above. The majority of the Trust's collection is local and extremely varied, ranging from a 1926 Sheffield tramcar to a 1985 Dennis Domino. In recent years the Museum Trust has benefitted from Heritage Fund Lottery grants. The museum is an educational charity and promotes an ever-expanding schools visits programme. The museum is open to the public on a monthly basis from March to December.
Chairman: M W Greenwood
Membership Secretary: Dr. John Willis, 2 Pwll-Y-Waen, Ty'n-Y-Groes, Conwy LL32 8TQ.

SOUTHDOWN ENTHUSIASTS' CLUB
Web site: www.southdownenthusiastsclub.org.uk
This club was founded in 1954 to bring together people interested in the vehicles, routes and history of Southdown Motor Services Ltd and now includes Stagecoach

Tendering & Regulatory Authorities

76

South (Hastings & District, South Coast Buses, Southdown, Hampshire Bus, Hants & Surrey, East Kent), Brighton & Hove, Eastbourne Buses and First Hampshire and Dorset. There is a monthly news publication and winter meetings. Membership is open to persons aged 14 years and over and details may be had from the Hon Secretary.

Hon Chairman: J Allpress, 9 Phoenix Way, Southwick, Brighton BN42 4HQ
Hon Secretary: N Simes, 11 High Cross Fields, Crowborough TN6 2SN
Hon Treasurer: D E Still, 12 Westway Close, Mile Oak, Portslade BN42 2RT
Hon Sales Officer: D Chalkley, 6 Valebridge Drive, Burgess Hill RH15 0RW
Hon News Sheet Editor: P Gainsbury, Park Cottage, Guestling TN35 4LT
Hon Publications Officer: J Smith, 1 Sackville Way, Worthing BN14 8BJ
Committee Member: J Barley, 84 Kipling Avenue, Brighton BN2 6UE.
Hon Photographic Officer: C Churchill, 53 Monks Close, Lancing BN15 9DB

SWINDON VINTAGE OMNIBUS SOCIETY

10 Fraser Close, Nythe, Swindon SN3 3RP
Tel: 01793 526001
E-mail: davenicol@supanet.com
Preserved Daimler Weymann double deck, ex Swindon corporation society vehicle. Also Bristol RESL ECW ex-Thamesdown Transport.
Chairman: M. Naughton
Secretary: D. Nicol
Treasurer: D. Mundy

THE TRANSPORT MUSEUM, WYTHALL
Birmingham & Midland Motor Omnibus Trust

The Transport Museum, Chapel Lane, Wythall B47 6JX
Tel: 01217 337432
Web site: www.bammot.org.uk
E-mail: enquiries@bammot.org.uk
The Trust dates back to 1973, taking its present title in 1977, when it became a registered educational charity to establish and develop a regional transport museum.

Three large halls, the most recent built with the assistance of the Heritage Lottery Fund and opening in 2007, house a broad collection of around 100 buses, coaches, fire engines and battery-electric vehicles from all parts of the Midlands and beyond. Birmingham and the Black Country especially are featured, and the museum has a unique collection of buses and coaches designed, built and operated by Midland Red, a company which pioneered many technical innovations over a 50 year manufacturing period.

A museum archive to record the development of the bus and coach industry in the Midlands is also being established, with collections of photographs, uniforms, tickets, ticket equipment and street furniture.

Members receive the bi-monthly museum journal *Omnibus* containing details of museum developments. The museum is open to the public every weekend between March and the end of November. Special event days are held on some Sundays and holiday Mondays when vehicles are on display and historic bus services operate, including a link with Birmingham city centre. Also buses for hire - see West Midlands in Operators section.

TRAMWAY & LIGHT RAILWAY SOCIETY

Web site: www.tramwayinfo.co.uk
Founded in 1938, the Tramway & Light Railway Society caters for those interested in all aspects of tramways. Members receive *Tramfare*, a bi-monthly illustrated magazine. There are regular meetings throughout the country. The Society promotes tramway modelling, drawings, castings, and technical details are available to modellers. There are also comprehensive library facilities. For fuller details of the Society and of membership please write to the Membership Secretary.

HONORARY OFFICERS
President: P J Davis.
Vice-Presidents: E R Oakley, G. B. Claydon, C.B
Chairman: J R Prentice, 216 Brentwood Road, Romford RM1 2RP.
Secretary: G R Tribe, 47 Soulbury Road, Linslade, Leighton Buzzard LU7 7RW.
Membership Secretary: H J Leach, 6 The Woodlands, Brightlingsea CO7 0RY.

THE TRANSPORT TICKET SOCIETY

An association of students and collectors of passenger tickets and fare collection methods. Founded in 1946, the TTS now has some 500 members worldwide. An illustrated monthly Journal, and regular distributions of tickets, keep members up to date with both historical and recent developments in ticketing in all modes of transport. The TTS welcomes offers of obsolete tickets for distribution to members. Full details of membership together with a sample Journal will be sent on request to the TTS publicity officer, or visit the TTS website: www.transport-ticket.com.
Publicity Officer: Martin Rickitt, Bromes House, Isle Abbots, Taunton TA3 6RW.
Tel: 01460 281228
E-mail: mrickitt@hotmail.com
Chairman: John Tolson
Membership Secretary: David Randall
General Secretary: Patrick Geall
Treasurer: Graham Wootton.
Managing Editor: David Harman

THE TRANSPORT TRUST

202 Lambeth Road, London SE1 7JW
Tel: 020 7928 6464
Fax: 020 7928 6565
E-mail: hq@thetransporttrust.org.uk
Web Site: www.thetransporttrust.org.uk
The national charity for the preservation and restoration of Britain's transport heritage.

Passenger Transport Museums

This list is in addition to those shown in the main Society section above

ABBEY PUMPING STATION
Contact address: Corporation Road, Leicester LE4 5PX
Phone: 0116 299 5111
Fax: 0116 299 5125
Web site: www.leicester.gov.uk/museums, www.leicestermuseums.ac.uk

AMBERLEY WORKING MUSEUM
Contact address: Amberley, Arundel BN18 9LT
Phone: 01798 831370
Fax: 01798 831831
E-mail: office@amberleymuseum.co.uk
Web site: www.amberleymuseum.co.uk

ASTON MANOR ROAD TRANSPORT MUSEUM
(*See Societies section*)

BLACK COUNTRY LIVING MUSEUM TRANSPORT GROUP
Contact address: Tipton Road, Dudley DY1 4SQ
Phone: 0121 557 9643
Web site: wwww.bclm.co.uk

BRISTOL ROAD TRANSPORT COLLECTION
Contact address: William Staniforth, 37 Corbett Road, Birmingham B47 5LP (SAE please)
E-mail: william.staniforth@virgin.net

BRITISH COMMERCIAL VEHICLE MUSEUM
Contact address: King Street Leyland PR25 2LE
Phone: 01772 451011
Fax: 01772 451015

CASTLE POINT TRANSPORT MUSEUM
Contact address: 105 Point Road, Canvey Island SS8 7TP
Phone: 01268 684272

CAVAN & LEITRIM RAILWAY
Contact address: Narrow Gauge Station, Station Road, Dromod, Co Leitrim, Ireland

Tendering & Regulatory Authorities

77

Phone/fax: 00353 71 9638599
Web site: www.irish-railway.com
E-mail: info@irish-railway.com

COBHAM BUS MUSEUM - THE LONDON BUS PRESERVATION TRUST LTD
Contact address: Redhill Road, Cobham, Surrey, KT11 1EF
Phone/Fax: 01932 868665
Web site: www.lbpt.org
E-mail: cobhambusmuseum@aol.com

COVENTRY TRANSPORT MUSEUM
Contact address: Millennium Place, Hales Street, Coventry CV1 1PN
Phone: 024 7623 4270
Fax: 024 7623 4284
E-mail: enquiries@transport-museum.com

DOVER TRANSPORT MUSEUM
Contact address: Willingdon Road, Port Zone White Cliffs Business Park, Whitfield, Dover CT16 2HJ
Phone: 01304 822409

EAST ANGLIA TRANSPORT MUSEUM
Contact address: Chapel Road, Carlton Colville, Lowestoft NR33 8BL
Phone: 01502 518459
Fax: 01502 584658
E-mail: enquiries@eatm.org.uk
Web site: www.eatm.org.uk

GRAMPIAN TRANSPORT MUSEUM
Contact address: Alford AB33 8AE
Phone: 01975 562292
Fax: 01975 562180
E-mail: info@g-t-m.freeserve.co.uk
Web site: www.gtm.org.uk

IPSWICH TRANSPORT MUSEUM
Contact address: Old Trolleybus Depot, Cobham Road, Ipswich IP3 9JD
Phone: 01473 715666
E-mail: www.ipswichtransportmuseum.co.uk.html

ISLE OF WIGHT BUS MUSEUM
Contact address: 28 Westmill Road, Newport PO30 5RG
Phone: 01983 526422
E-mail: nharris.westmill@tiscali.co.uk

KEIGHLEY BUS MUSEUM TRUST
Contact address: 47 Brantfell Drive, Burnley BB12 8AW
Phone: 01282 413179
E-Mail: shmdboard@aol.com
Web site: www.kbmt.org.uk

LONDON TRANSPORT MUSEUM
Contact address: 39 Wellington Street, London WC2E 7BB.

Phone: 020 7379 6344; recorded information 020 7565 7299
E-mail: resourcedesk@ltmuseum.co.uk
Web site: www.ltmuseum.co.uk

MANCHESTER MUSEUM OF TRANSPORT
Contact address: Boyle Street, Cheetham, Manchester M8 8UW
Phone: 0161 205 2122
Fax: 0161 202 1110
E-mail: busmuseum@btconnect.com
Web site: www.gmts.co.uk or www.manchester.bus.museum

MIDLAND ROAD TRANSPORT GROUP — BUTTERLEY
Contact address: 21 Ash Grove, Mastin Moor, Chesterfield S43 3AW
Phone: Midland Road Transport Group — 01246 473619
Midland Railway 01773 747674, Visitor Information Line (01773) 570140.

MUSEUM OF TRANSPORT
Contact address: Kelvin Hall, 1 Bunhouse Road, Glasgow G3 8DP
Phone: 0141 287 2720 (school bookings on 0141 565 4112/3)
Fax: 0141 287 2692

NATIONAL MUSEUM OF SCIENCE AND INDUSTRY
Contact address: Exhibition Road, London SW7 2DD
Phone: 0207 942 4105 or 01793 814466
E-mail: s.evans@nmsi.ac.uk

THE NORTH OF ENGLAND OPEN AIR MUSEUM
Contact address: Beamish DH9 0RG
Phone: 0191 370 4000
Fax: 0191 370 4001
E-mail: museum@beamish.org.uk
Web site: www.beamish.org.uk

THE NATIONAL TRAMWAY MUSEUM
Crich, Matlock DE4 5DP
Tel: 01773 854321
Fax: 01773 854320
The Society was founded in 1955 to establish and operate a working tramway museum. The Museum is at Crich Tramway Village, Crich, near Matlock, in Derbyshire, and owns over 70 English, Irish, Scottish, Welsh and overseas tramcars. Members receive a copy of the Society's quarterly journal and can participate in the running of the museum.
Patron: HRH The Duke of Gloucester GCVO
Vice-Presidents: G. S. Hearse, W. G. S. Hyde, G. B. Claydon, D. J. H. Senior, A W Bond
Chairman: C. Heaton
Vice-Chairman: R T Pennyfather
Hon Secretary: I. M. Dougill

Hon Treasurer: P R Moore
Operations Superintendent: K. B. Hulme

NORTH WEST MUSEUM OF ROAD TRANSPORT
Contact address: The Old Bus Depot, 51 Hall Street, St Helens WA10 1DU
E-mail: general@hallstreetdepot.info
Web site: www.hallstreetdepot.info
Due to open late 2006

NOTTINGHAM TRANSPORT HERITAGE CENTRE
Contact address: Mere Way, Ruddington, Nottingham NG11 6NX
Phone: 0115 940 5705
E-mail: geoffrey.clark3@ntworld.com
Web site: http://www.nthc.co.uk

OXFORD BUS MUSEUM
Contact address: Station Yard, Long Hanborough OX29 8LA
Phone: 01993 883617 (Answerphone) or 01993 881662

SCOTTISH VINTAGE BUS MUSEUM
Contact address: M90 Commerce Park, Lathalmond, Dumfermline, Fife KY12 OSJ
Phone: 01383 623380
Website: www.busweb.co.uk/svbm

THE TRANSPORT MUSEUM, WYTHALL
Birmingham & Midland Motor Omnibus Trust

(*See Societies section*)

TRANSPORT MUSEUM SOCIETY OF IRELAND
Contact address: Howth Castle Demesne, Howth, Dublin 13, Ireland
Phone/Fax: 00 353 1 848 0831
E-mail: info@nationaltransportmuseum.org
Web site: www.nationaltransportmuseum.org

TROLLEYBUS MUSEUM AT SANDTOFT
Contact address: Belton Road, Sandtoft, Doncaster DN8 5SX
Phone: 01724 711391
E-mail: enquiries@sandtoft.org
Web site: www.sandtoft.org

ULSTER FOLK & TRANSPORT MUSEUM
Contact address: Cultra, Holywood BT18 0EU
Phone: 028 9042 8428

WIRRAL TRANSPORT MUSEUM
Contact address: Pacific Road, Birkenhead L41 5HN
Phone: 0151 666 2756

Tendering & Regulatory Authorities

Section 4
British Isles Operators

Major Groups	80

English Operators
Bedfordshire	87
Berkshire (including Bracknell Forest, Reading, Slough, West Berkshire, Windsor & Maidenhead, Wokingham)	88
Bristol	90
Buckinghamshire, Milton Keynes	92
Cambridgeshire, Peterborough City	93
Cheshire, Halton and Stockport	96
Cornwall	98
Cumbria	100
Derbyshire	102
Devon	105
Dorset, Bournemouth, Poole	109
Durham	111
East Sussex, Brighton & Hove	113
East Riding of Yorkshire, City of Kingston upon Hull	115
Essex	116
Gloucestershire	120
Greater Manchester,	123
Hampshire	126
Herefordshire	129
Hertfordshire	130
Isle of Wight	132
Kent	133
Lancashire	136
Leicestershire, City of Leicester, Rutland	139
Lincolnshire	141
London	142
Merseyside area	148
Middlesex	149
Norfolk	151
North Lincolnshire, North East Lincolnshire	153
North Yorkshire, York	154
Northamptonshire	157
Northumberland	158
Nottinghamshire, Nottingham	159
Oxfordshire	161
Shropshire	162
Somerset	164
South Yorkshire	166
Staffordshire	169
Suffolk	171
Surrey	173
Tyne & Wear	175
Warwickshire	177
West Midlands	177
West Sussex	181
West Yorkshire	182
Wiltshire	185
Worcestershire	187

Channel Islands Operators
Alderney	188
Guernsey	188
Jersey	188

Isle of Man Operators
Isle of Man	188

Isles of Scilly Operators
Isles of Scilly	188

Scottish Operators
Aberdeen, City of	189
Aberdeenshire	189
Angus	190
Argyll & Bute	190
Borders	191
Clackmannanshire	191
Dumfries & Galloway	191
Dundee, City of	192
East Ayrshire	193
East Lothian	193
East Ayrshire	193
Edinburgh, City of	193
Falkirk	194
Fife	194
Glasgow, City of	194
Highland	195
Inverclyde	196
Midlothian	196
Moray	196
North Ayrshire	196
North Lanarkshire	197
Orkney	198
Perth & Kinross	198
Renfrewshire	199
Shetland	199
South Ayrshire	199
South Lanarkshire	199
Stirling	200
West Dunbartonshire	201
West Lothian	201
Western Isles	201

Welsh Operators
Anglesey	202
Blaenau Gwent	202
Bridgend	202
Caerphilly	203
Cardiff	203
Carmarthenshire	203
Ceredigion	204
Conwy	205
Denbighshire	205
Flintshire	206
Gwynedd	206
Merthyr Tydfil	207
Monmouthshire	207
Neath & Port Talbot	207
Newport	208
Pembrokeshire	208
Powys	208
Rhondda Cynon Taf	209
Swansea, City and County of	210
Torfaen	210
Vale of Glamorgan	210
Wrexham	211

Northern Ireland Operators
Northern Ireland	212

Republic of Ireland Operators
Republic of Ireland	213

MAJOR GROUPS

ARRIVA

ARRIVA PLC
1 Admiral Way, Doxford International Business Park, Sunderland SR3 3XP
Tel: 0191 520 4000
Fax: 0191 520 4001
E-mail: enquiries@arriva.co.uk
Web site: www.arriva.co.uk
Chairman:
Sir Richard Broadbent KCB
Chief Executive:
David Martin
Directors:
Steve Lonsdale, Steve Clayton
Non-Executive Directors:
Veronica Palmer OBE, Simon Batey, Nick Buckles, Steve Williams

Arriva Passenger Services
487 Dunstable Road, Luton, LU4 8DS
Tel: 01582 587000

Managing Director (UK Regions):
Mike Cooper
Commercial Director:
Chris Hopkins
Engineering Director:
Mark Bowd

Operating Regions, Group Companies, Principal Depots (UK Bus):

• **Arriva Scotland West**
(see Renfrewshire)
Depots at Inchinnan, Johnstone

• **Arriva Yorkshire**
(see West Yorkshire)
Depots at Castleford, Dewsbury, Heckmondwike, Selby, Wakefield

• **Arriva North East**
(see Tyne & Wear)
Depots at Alnwick, Ashington, Bishop Auckland, Blyth, Darlington, Durham, Hexham, Loftus, Newcastle, Peterlee, Redcar, Stockton

• **Arriva North West & Wales**
(see Merseyside, Conwy)
Depots (North West): Birkenhead, Bolton, Bootle, Chester, Liverpool, Manchester, Runcorn, St Helens, Skelmersdale, Southport, Winsford, Wythenshawe
Depots (Wales): Aberystwyth, Bangor, Llandudno, Rhyl, Wrexham

• **Arriva Midlands**
(see Derbyshire, Leicestershire, Staffordshire)
Depots at Burton on Trent, Cannock, Coalville, Derby, Leicester, Oswestry, Shrewsbury, Stafford, Swadlincote, Tamworth, Telford, Wigston

• **Arriva Shires & Essex**
(see Bedfordshire, Buckinghamshire)
Depots at Aylesbury, Harlow, Hemel Hempstead, High Wycombe, Luton, Milton Keynes (MK Metro), Stevenage, Ware, Watford

• **Arriva London**
(see London)
Depots at Barking, Battersea, Brixton, Croydon, Edmonton, Enfield, Hackney, Norwood, Palmers Green, Stamford Hill, Thornton Heath, Tottenham, Wood Green

• **Arriva Southern Counties**
(see Essex, Kent, Surrey)
Depots at Cranleigh, Dartford, Gillingham, Grays, Guildford, Horsham, Maidstone, Northfleet, Southend, Tonbridge (New Enterprise), Tunbridge Wells

• **The Original Tour**
(see London)

• **Tellings Golden Miller Group**
(see Durham, Essex, Kent, London, Surrey)
Includes Burtons Coaches, Classic Coaches, Excel Passenger Logistics, Flight Delay Services, Linkline Coaches, Network Colchester, OFJ Connections, Tellings Golden Miller Coaches

Overseas Interests:
Arriva has extensive overseas interests in the Czech Republic (bus), Denmark (bus and rail), Germany (bus and rail), Hungary (bus), Italy (bus), Netherlands (bus and rail), Poland (rail), Portugal (bus), Slovakia (bus), Spain (bus), Sweden (bus and rail)

UK Rail Franchises:
Arriva Trains Wales, Cross Country

Other Interests:
Arriva Bus & Coach
(see Trade Directory)

80

FIRSTGROUP PLC

395 King Street, Aberdeen AB24 5RP
Tel: 01224 650000
Fax: 01224 650099
Web Site: www.firstgroup.com

Chairman:
Martin Gilbert
Deputy Chairman and Chief Executive:
Sir Moir Lockhead
Directors:
Dean Finch
(Chief Operating Officer, USA),
Nicholas Chevis
(Acting Finance Director),
Sidney Barrie
(Commercial Director & Company Secretary)
Non-Executive Directors:
Audrey Baxter, David Begg, David Dunn, James Forbes, John Sievwright, Martyn Williams

Managing Director (UK Bus):
Nicola Shaw
Chief Operating Officer:
David Kaye
Business Efficiency & Engineering Director:
David Liston
Customer Service & Communications Director:
Leon Daniels
Finance Director:
John Hoskin
Projects Director:
Douglas Downie
Safety Director:
Janet Ault

Operating Regions, Group Companies, Principal Depots (UK Bus):

• First Aberdeen
Grampian Coaches Mairs Coaches
(see City of Aberdeen)

• First Edinburgh
(see Stirling)
Depots at Balfron, Bannockburn, Dalkeith, Galashiels, Larbert, Linlithgow, Livingston, Musselburgh

• First Glasgow
(see City of Glasgow)
Depots at Blantyre, Cumbernauld, Dumbarton, Overtown

• First West Yorkshire
(includes First Bradford, First Calderdale & Huddersfield, First Leeds)
(see West Yorkshire)
Depots at Bradford, Halifax, Huddersfield, Leeds

• First York
(see North Yorkshire)

• First South Yorkshire
(see South Yorkshire)
Depots at Doncaster, Rotherham, Sheffield

• First Manchester
(see Greater Manchester)
Depots at Bolton, Bury, Ince, Manchester, Oldham, Tameside, Wigan

• First in North Staffordshire, Chester & The Wirral
(see Cheshire, Staffordshire)
Depots at Chester, Crewe, Newcastle, Stoke, Wirral

• First Leicester
(see Leicestershire)

• First Northampton
(see Northamptonshire)

• First Eastern Counties
(see Norfolk)
Depots at Great Yarmouth, Ipswich, Kings Lynn, Lowestoft, Norwich

• First Essex
(see Essex)
Depots at Basildon, Braintree, Chelmsford, Clacton, Colchester, Hadleigh, Harwich

• First London
(see London)
Depots at Alperton, Dagenham, Greenford, Hayes, Leyton, Northumberland Park, Uxbridge, Westbourne Park, Willesden Junction

• First Berkshire
(see Berkshire)
Depots at Bracknell, Slough

• First Wyvern
(see Worcestershire)
Depots at Hereford, Kidderminster, Redditch, Worcester

• First Cymru
(see City & County of Swansea)
Depots at Bridgend, Carmarthen, Haverfordwest, Llanelli, Pontardawe, Port Talbot, Swansea

• First Bristol
(see Bristol)

• First Hampshire & Dorset
(see Hampshire)
Depots at Bridport, Fareham, Portsmouth, Southampton, Weymouth

• First Somerset & Avon
(see Somerset)
Depots at Bath, Bridgwater, Bristol, Taunton, Weston super Mare, Yeovil

• First Devon & Cornwall
(see Cornwall, Devon)
Depots at Barnstaple, Camborne, Plymouth, Truro (Truronian)

Overseas Interests:
First has bus operations in the Republic of Ireland - Aircoach (See Republic of Ireland) and in Germany and the USA

UK Rail Operations:
First Capital Connect, First Great Western, First Trans Pennine Express, First ScotRail, GB Railfreight, Hull Trains

Major Groups

81

Major Groups

Go-Ahead

GO-AHEAD GROUP PLC
41-51 Grey Street, Newcastle upon Tyne
NE1 6EE
Tel: 0191 232 3123
Fax: 0191 221 0315
E-mail: admin@go-ahead.com
Web Site: www.go-ahead.com

Non-Executive Chairman:
Sir Patrick Brown
Group Chief Executive:
Keith Ludeman
Group Finance Director:
Nicholas Swift
Group Company Secretary:
Carolyn Sephton
Non-Executive Directors:
Andrew Allner, Rupert Pennant-Rea

Operating Regions
Group Companies
Principal Depots
(UK Bus):

• **Go North East**
(see Tyne & Wear)
Depots at Ashington, Chester le Street, Gateshead, Newcastle, Stanley, Sunderland, Washington, Winlaton

• **Oxford Bus Company**
(see Oxfordshire)

• **Go-Ahead London**
(includes Blue Triangle, Docklands Buses, London Central, London General)
(see Essex, London)
Depots at Bexleyheath, Camberwell, Merton, New Cross, Peckham, Putney, Rainham, Silvertown, Stockwell, Sutton, Waterloo

• **Metrobus**
(see West Sussex)
Depots at Crawley, Croydon, Orpington

• **Brighton & Hove Bus & Coach Company** *(see East Sussex)*

• **Go South Coast**
(includes Bells Coaches, Bluestar, Damory Coaches, Kingston Coaches, Levers Coaches, Marchwood Motorways, Southern Vectis, Tourist Coaches, Wilts & Dorset)
(see Dorset, Hampshire, Isle of Wight, Wiltshire)
Depots at Blandford, Eastleigh, Figheldean, Lymington, Newport IOW, Poole, Ringwood, Salisbury, Swanage, Totton

Other interests:
Aviance (airport servicing), Meteor Parking

UK Rail Franchises:
London Midland, South Eastern, Southern

national express

NATIONAL EXPRESS GROUP PLC
75 Davies Street, London W1K 5HT
Tel: 020 7529 2000
Fax: 020 7529 2100
E-mail: info@natex.co.uk
Web Site:
www.nationalexpressgroup.com

Chairman:
David Ross
Chief Executive:
Richard Bowker CBE
Deputy Chairman:
Jorge Cosmen
Non-Executive Directors:
Miranda Curtis, Roger Devlin,
Sir Andrew Foster, Tim Score
Company Secretary:
Tony McDonald
Chief Executive, UK Division:
Ray O'Toole
Chief Executive, ALSA Group:
Javier Carbajo
Chief Executive Officer, North America:
Brian Stock

Operating Regions
Group Companies
Principal Depots
(UK Bus):

• **Kings Ferry Travel Group**
(see Kent)

• **National Express**
(See West Midlands)

• **Travel Dundee**
(see Dundee City)

• **Travel London**
(Includes Travel London, Travel Surrey)
(see London, Surrey)
Depots at Battersea, Byfleet, Croydon, Hayes, Twickenham, Walworth

• **Travel Midland Metro**
(see West Midlands)

• **Travel West Midlands**
(See West Midlands)
Depots at Birmingham, Coventry, Dudley, Walsall, West Bromwich, Wolverhampton

Overseas interests:
National Express has extensive interests in Spain (ALSA, Continental Auto), Canada (Stock Transportation) and the USA (Durham School Services)

UK Rail Franchises:
c2c, National Express East Coast, National Express East Anglia

TRANSDEV
Developing mobility

TRANSDEV PLC
Garrick House, Stamford Brook Garage,
74 Chiswick High Road, London W4 1SY
Tel: 020 8400 6052
Fax: 020 8400 6053
E-mail: information@transdevplc.co.uk
Web Site: www.transdevplc.co.uk

Chief Executive:
Francois Xavier Perin
Chief Operating Officer:
Charlie Beaumont
Finance Director:
Peter Gillespie

Operating Regions
Group Companies
Principal Depots
(UK Bus):

• **Blazefield Lancashire**
(includes Burnley & Pendle, Lancashire United, Northern Blue)
(see Lancashire)
Depots at Blackburn, Burnley

• **Blazefield Yorkshire**
(includes Harrogate & District, Keighley & District, Transdev York, Yorkshire Coastliner)
(see North Yorkshire, West Yorkshire)
Depots at: Harrogate, Keighley, Malton, York

• **Bournemouth Transport**
(see Dorset)

• **Edinburgh Tram**
(Transdev will be the operator)

• **London United Busways**
(see Middlesex)
Depots at Fulwell, Hounslow, Hounslow Heath, Shepherd's Bush, Stamford Brook, Tolworth

• **London Sovereign**
(see Middlesex)
Depots at Edgware, Harrow

• **Nottingham City Transport** (part owned) *(see Nottinghamshire)*

• **Nottingham Express Transit**
(part of operating group)

Overseas interests:
Transdev has bus and rail interests in Australia Canada, France, Germany, Italy and Portugal

Parent Group:
Transdev's Parent Group is Transdev SA, part of the French Group
Caisse des Depots

82

Stagecoach

STAGECOACH GROUP PLC
10 Dunkeld Road, Perth PH1 5TW
Tel: 01738 442111
Fax: 01738 643648
Web Site: www.stagecoachgroup.com

Non-Executive Chairman:
Robert Spiers
Chief Executive:
Brian Souter
Finance Director:
Martin Griffiths
Non-Executive Directors:
Ewan Brown CBE, Iain Duffin OBE,
Ann Gloag OBE, Sir George Mathewson,
Dr Janet Morgan CBE, Garry Watts

Managing Director UK Bus:
Les Warneford
Regional Director North:
Robert Andrew
Regional Director Scotland:
Tom Wileman

Operating Regions
Group Companies
Principal Depots
(UK Bus):

• Stagecoach East Scotland
(Includes Bluebird Buses, JW Coaches, Rennies of Dunfermline, Fife Scottish Omnibuses, Stagecoach Highland, Stagecoach in Orkney, Stagecoach in Perth, Strathtay Scottish Omnibuses)
(see City of Aberdeen, Aberdeenshire, City of Dundee, Fife, Highland, Orkney, Perth & Kinross)
Depots at Aberdeen, Arbroath, Banchory, Blairgowrie, Cowdenbeath, Dundee, Dunfermline, Elgin, Forfar, Fort William, Glenrothes, Inverness, Kirkwall, Kirriemuir, Methil, Montrose, Perth, Peterhead, St Andrews, Tain, Thurso, Wick

• Stagecoach West Scotland
(Includes Stagecoach Glasgow, Western Buses)
(see South Ayrshire)
Depots at Ardrossan, Arran, Ayr, Cumnock, Dumfries, Glasgow, Kilmarnock, Stranraer

• Scottish Citylink Coaches (part owned) *(see City of Glasgow)*

• Stagecoach North East
(Includes Stagecoach Hartlepool, Newcastle, South Shields, Sunderland, Teesside, Transit)
(see Durham, Tyne & Wear)
Depots at Hartlepool, Newcastle, South Shields, Stockton, Sunderland

• Stagecoach North West
(Includes Stagecoach in Cumbria, Lancashire, Lancaster)
(see Cumbria)
Depots at Barrow, Carlisle, Chorley, Kendal, Lancaster, Preston, Whitehaven

• Stagecoach Merseyside
(see Merseyside)
Depot at Liverpool

• Stagecoach Manchester
(see Greater Manchester)
Depots at Glossop, Manchester, Stockport, Tameside

• Manchester Metrolink
(see Greater Manchester)

• Stagecoach Yorkshire
(Includes Stagecoach Sheffield, Stagecoach Supertram, Stagecoach Yorkshire)
(see South Yorkshire)
Depots at Barnsley, Doncaster, Rawmarsh, Shafton, Sheffield

• Stagecoach East Midlands
(Includes Stagecoach East Midlands, Hull, Lincolnshire)
(see Derbyshire, East Riding, Lincolnshire)
Depots at Chesterfield, Gainsborough, Grimsby, Hull, Lincoln, Mansfield, Newark, Scunthorpe, Skegness, Worksop

• Stagecoach East
(Includes Stagecoach in Bedford, Northamptonshire)
(see Northamptonshire)
Depots at Bedford, Corby, Kettering, Northampton

• Stagecoach Cambridgeshire
(Includes Stagecoach in Cambridge, Peterborough)
(see Cambridgeshire)
Depots at Cambridge, Ely, Peterborough

• Stagecoach Oxfordshire
(see Oxfordshire)
Depots at Banbury, Oxford, Witney

• Stagecoach in Warwickshire
(see Warwickshire)
Depots at Leamington Spa, Nuneaton, Rugby, Stratford upon Avon

• Stagecoach West
(Includes Stagecoach Cheltenham, Cotswolds, Gloucester, Swindon, Wye & Dean)
(see Gloucestershire)
Depots at Cheltenham, Coleford, Gloucester, Stroud, Swindon

• Stagecoach South East
(Includes Stagecoach in East Kent & Hastings, Hampshire, Hants & Surrey, Stagecoach South)
(see Hampshire, Kent, West Sussex)
Depots at Aldershot, Andover, Ashford, Basingstoke, Chichester, Dover, Folkestone, Hastings, Herne Bay, Portsmouth, Thanet, Winchester, Worthing

• Stagecoach South West
(Includes Stagecoach Devon, Stagecoach Cooks Coaches)
(see Devon, Somerset)
Depots at Barnstaple, Chard, Exeter, Exmouth, Honiton, Paignton, Torquay, Wellington

• Stagecoach in South Wales
(see Torfaen)
Depots at Aberdare, Blackwood, Brynmawr, Caerphilly, Cwmbran, Merthyr, Porth

Overseas Interests:
The group has significant bus and coach operations in North America

UK Rail Franchises:
East Midlands Trains, Island Line, South West Trains, Virgin West Coast (joint venture)

83

VEOLIA TRANSPORT (UK) LTD
37-41 Old Queen Street, London SW1H 9JA
Tel: 020 7393 2700
Fax: 020 7393 2859
Web Site: www.veolia-transport.co.uk

Chairman:
John O'Brien
Chief Operating Officer:
Steve McAleavy
Managing Director, Veolia Transport Cymru:
Charles Lewis
Managing Director, Veolia Transport England:
Steve Campbell
Human Resources Director:
David Goldstraw

Group Companies (UK Bus):
• Alpha Bus & Coach
(see East Riding)
• Astons Coaches Ltd
(see Worcestershire)
• Paul James Coaches
(see Leicestershire)
• Veolia Cymru
(Includes Bebb Travel, Pullman Coaches, Thomas of Barry)
(see Rhondda Cynon Taf, City & County of Swansea, Vale of Glamorgan)
• Veolia Midlands
(Dunn Line Holdings)
(See Nottinghamshire)

Parent Company:
Veolia Environnement

Overseas interests:
Veolia has substantial worldwide transport interests

WELLGLADE LTD
Mansfield Road, Heanor, Derbyshire DE75 7BG
Tel: 01773 536309
Fax: 01773 536310

Chairman:
B R King
Commercial Director:
R F Morgan
Finance Director:
G Sutton

Group Companies:
• Derby Community Transport
(see Derbyshire)
• Kinchbus
(see Derbyshire)
• Notts & Derby
(see Derbyshire)
• Trent Barton
(see Derbyshire)

EYMS GROUP LTD
252 Anlaby Road, Hull HU3 2RS
Tel: 01482 327142
Fax: 01482 212040
Web Site: www.eymsgroup.co.uk
Chairman:
Peter Shipp

Finance Director:
Peter Harrison

Group Companies:
• East Yorkshire Motor Services
(including Scarborough & District Motor Services)
(see East Riding, North Yorkshire)
Depots at Beverley, Bridlington, Driffield, Elloughton, Hornsea, Hull, Pocklington, Scarborough, Withernsea
• Finglands Coachways
(see Greater Manchester)
• Whittle Coach & Bus
(see Shropshire)

ROTALA PLC
80 Cannon Street, London EC4N 6HL
Tel: 020 7621 6770
Fax: 020 7621 5771
E-Mail: info@rotalaplc.co.uk
Web Site: www.rotalaplc.co.uk

Chairman:
John Gunn
Chief Executive & Finance Director:
Kim Taylor
Managing Director:
Simon Dunn
Non-Executive Directors:
Nick Kennedy, Geoffrey Flight

Group Companies:
• Central Connect
(see West Midlands)
• Diamond Bus
(See West Midlands)
• Flights Hallmark
(See West Midlands)
• Ludlows of Halesowen
(See West Midlands)
• Surrey Connect
(See Surrey)
• Wessex Connect
(see Bristol)

COMFORT DELGRO
Hygeia House, 66-68 College Road, Harrow, HA1 1BE
Tel: 020 8218 8888
Fax: 020 8218 8899
Web Site: www.comfortdelgro.com.sg
Group Companies (UK Bus):

• Metroline Travel
(see Middlesex)
Depots at Brentford, Cricklewood, Edgware, Harrow Weald, Holloway, Kings Cross, North Wembley, Perivale, Potters Bar, Watford, West Perivale, Willesden
• Scottish Citylink Coaches (part owned) (see City of Glasgow)
• Westbus Coach Services
(see London)

Other Interests (UK):
Computer Cab and other taxi interests

Parent Company:
Comfort DelGro Corporation

Overseas Interests:
The group has major bus and taxi operations in Australia, China, Malaysia, Singapore and Vietnam

EAST LONDON BUS GROUP
2 Clements Road, Ilford, IG1 1BA
Tel: 020 8477 7200
Fax: 020 8477 7222
Web Site: www.elbg.com

Chief Executive:
Nigel Barrett
Chief Financial Officer:
Paul Cox
Engineering Director:
Peter Sumner

Group Trading Names:
East London, Selkent

Depots at Barking, Bow, Bromley, Catford, Leyton, Plumstead, Rainham, Romford, Upton Park, West Ham

PRIORITY SUBSCRIPTION FORM

SAVE 15%
off a subscription to *Buses* Magazine

THE WORLD'S BIGGEST SELLING BUS MAGAZINE SINCE 1949

Buses Magazine	Normal Price	15% Discount
12 issues UK	£44.40	£37.74
12 issues EUROPE	£53.20	£45.22
12 issues ROW	£58.20	£49.47

CALL:
+44 (0)1932 266 622

FAX:
+44 (0)1932 266 633

ONLINE:
www.busesmag.com

Or send coupon (or photocopy) below to:
Buses Magazine Subscriptions, Ian Allan Publishing Ltd,
Riverdene Business Park, Molesey Road,
Hersham, Surrey, KT12 4RG.

Offer ends 1 December 2009. QUOTE CODE LRBBU

SUBSCRIBER INFORMATION

Please start subscription with _____ issue

Mr/Mrs/Miss/Ms: _____ Forename: _____

Surname: _____

Address: _____

Post Code: _____

Daytime Tel No: _____

Email: _____

Debit / Credit Card   LRBBU

Please debit my card for the amount of £ _____

☐ Mastercard   ☐ Visa   ☐ Switch/Maestro

Card Number: _____

Exp Date: _____   Start Date: _____

Issue No: _____   Sec No: _____

Signature: _____   Date: _____

Cheque - Please make payable to Ian Allan Publishing

I enclose a cheque to the value of £ _____

AUTUMN READING FOR THE REAL ENTHUSIAST

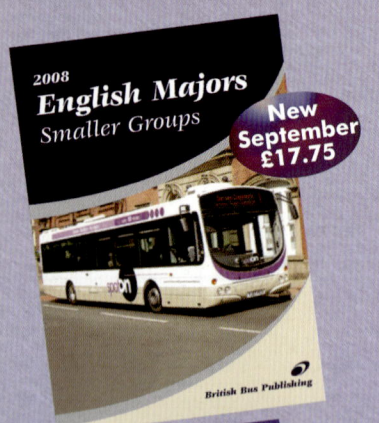

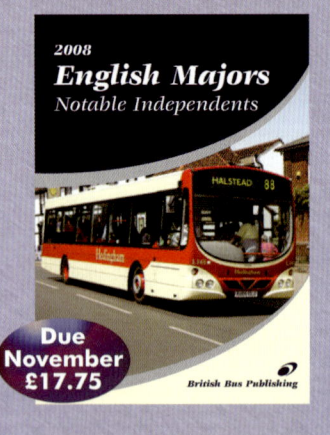

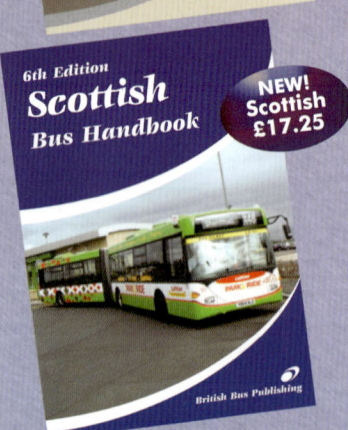

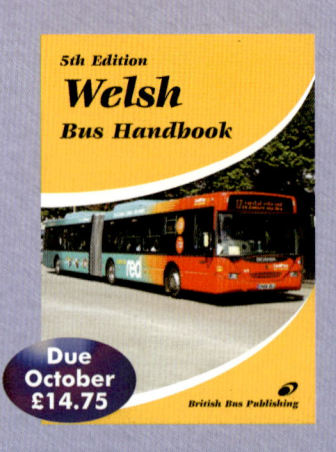

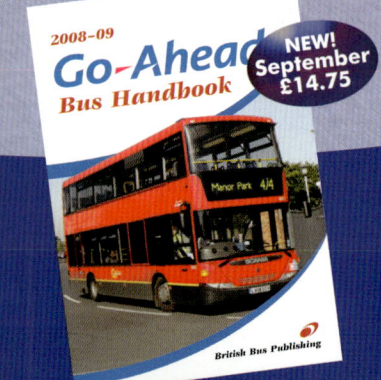

2008
English Majors
Smaller Groups

New September £17.75

2008
English Majors
Notable Independents

Due November £17.75

2008
First
Bus Handbook

2008 First £17.75

6th Edition
Scottish
Bus Handbook

NEW! Scottish £17.25

5th Edition
Welsh
Bus Handbook

Due October £14.75

2008
Stagecoach
Bus Handbook

2008 Stagecoach £17.25

2008-09
Go-Ahead
Bus Handbook

NEW! September £14.75

British Bus Publishing

Orders for all your Bus Handbooks and other Transport Books may be placed with our mail order department. To order, simply telephone the order line. Payment may be made by Visa, Mastercard, Switch, Maestro, Cheque or Postal Order. We also specialise in Hong-Kong sourced die-cast models and Rietze models. For latest models please call the order line.
9am–9pm Monday–Thursday

01952 255669

www.britishbuspublishing.co.uk

British Bus Publishing, 16 St Margaret's Drive, Telford TF1 3PH

BEDFORDSHIRE

AtoB TRAVEL (LUTON) LTD
UNIT 54, BILTON WAY, LUTON LU1 1UU
Tel: 01582 733333
Fax: 01582 733331
Web site: www.atobexec.com
Fleet: 50 - coach, minicoach, midicoach
Chassis: incl: Ford. Mercedes.
Bodies: incl: Ford. Mercedes.
Ops incl: school contracts, private hire
Livery: Silver

ARRIVA THE SHIRES & ESSEX LTD
487 DUNSTABLE ROAD, LUTON
LU4 8DS
Tel: 01582 587000/08701 201088
Web site: www.arrivabus.co.uk
Fleetname: Arriva the Shires & Essex.
Man Dir: Paul Woolmore
Fleet: 550 - double-deck bus, single-deck bus, coach, minibus.
Ops incl: local bus services, school contracts, excursions & tours, private hire, express.
Livery: Aquamarine and Cream.
Ticket System: Wayfarer 3, Prestige.

BARFORDIAN COACHES LTD
500 GOLDINGTON ROAD, BEDFORD
MK41 0DX
Tel: 01234 355440
Fax: 01234 355310
E-mail: info@barfordiancoaches.co.uk
Web site: www.barfordiancoaches.co.uk
Man Dir: P Bullard **Dir**: K Bullard **Ops Man**: K Hargreaves
Fleet: 24 - 5 double-deck bus, 1 single-deck bus, 12 coach, 2 double-deck coach, 1 midicoach, 1 minibus, 2 minicoach.
Chassis: 1 Bedford. 11 Bova. 4 Leyland. 1 MCW. 3 Mercedes. 2 Neoplan. 1 Toyota. 1 Volvo.
Bodies: 2 Alexander. 11 Bova. 1 Caetano. 1 Duple. 2 ECW. 1 Jonckheere. 1 MCW. 1 Mellor. 2 Neoplan. 1 Plaxton. 1 other.
Ops incl: local bus services, school contracts, excursions & tours, private hire, continental tours.
Livery: Orange/Yellow/White
Ticket System: Almex

CEDAR COACHES
ARKWRIGHT ROAD, BEDFORD
MK42 0LE.
Tel: 01234 354054
Fax: 01234 219210
E-mail: nikki@cedarcoaches.co.uk
Web site: www.cedarcoaches.co.uk
Man Dir: Eric Reid **Co Sec**: Nichola Graham **Dirs**: Donna Reid, Kevin Reid
Fleet: 30 - 17 double-deck bus, 4 single-deck bus, 6 coach, 1 double-deck coach, 2 minicoach.
Chassis: Ayats. Bova. Irisbus. Iveco. Leyland. Scania. Volvo.
Bodies: Ayats. Beulas. Bova
Ops incl: local bus services, school contracts, excursions & tours, private hire.
Livery: Red/Yellow

PREMIER CONNECTIONS LTD
AVIATION HOUSE, BUILDING 123, PERGUAL WAY, LUTON AIRPORT, LU2 9PA
Tel: 01582 424140
Fax: 01582 727093
E-mail: sales@premier.gb.com
Web site: www.premier.gb.com
Ops inc: school contracts, private hire
Livery: White

CENTREBUS LTD
14 SEDGWICK ROAD, LUTON LU4 9DT
Tel: 08707 444746
Web site: www.centrebus.co.uk
Man Dir: Peter Harvey **Ops Di**: Neil Harris
Fleet: 60 single-deck bus
Ops incl: local bus services
Livery: Blue/Orange
Ticket system: Wayfarer 3

CHILTERN TRAVEL
THE COACH HOUSE, BARFORD ROAD, BLUNHAM MK44 3NA
Tel: 01767 641400
Fax: 01767 641358
E-mail: chilterntravel@hotmail.com
Fleet: 17 - 3 single-deck bus, 12 coach, 2 minibus.
Chassis: 2 Bova. 2 Iveco. 3 Mercedes. 1 Neoplan. 3 Optare. 1 Renault. 3 Volvo.
Bodies: 2 Beulas. 2 Bova. 3 Mercedes. 1 Neoplan. 3 Optare. 2 other.
Ops incl: local bus services, private hire, continental tours, school contracts, excursions & tours.

CORPORATE COACHING
EAGLE HOUSE, EAGLE CENTRE WAY, LUTON LU4 9US
Tel: 01525 715872
Fax: 01525 713020
E-mail: sales@corp-coach.co.uk
Web site: www.corp-coach.co.uk
Man Dir: Doreen Collins **Ops Dir**: Peter Collins
Fleet: 8 - 4 midicoach, 4 minicoach.
Chassis: 8 Mercedes-Benz.
Ops incl: private hire, express.
Livery: Blue/Silver

DUNN-LINE GROUP
See Nottinghamshire

EXPRESSLINES LTD
FENLAKE ROAD INDUSTRIAL ESTATE, BEDFORD MK42 0HB
E-mail: info@expresslinesltd.co.uk
Web site: www.expresslinesltd.co.uk
Tel: 01234 268704
Fax: 01234 272212
Dirs: Chris Spriggs, Richard Harris
Fleet: 15 - 4 midibus, 3 midicoach, 8 minicoach.
Chassis: 6 Ford Transit. 5 Mercedes-Benz. 4 Optare.
Bodies: 8 Optare. 7 other.

Ops incl: local bus services, school contracts, private hire.
Livery: Red/White/Silver
Ticket System: Wayfarer & Almex

FLIGHTS HALLMARK
See West Midlands

GRANT PALMER PASSENGER SERVICES
UNIT 2, LAWRENCE WAY, DUNSTABLE
LU6 1BD
E-mail: email@grantpalmer.com
Web site: www.grantpalmer.com
Tel: 01582 600844
Ops incl: local bus services
Livery: Red/White

HERBERTS TRAVEL
UNIT 5, OLD ROWNEY FARM, SHEFFORD SG17 5QH
Tel: 01234 382000
Fax: 01234 381117
Ops Dir: D S Dougall **Man Dir**: D M Dougall **Fleet Eng**: S Myers
E-mail: booking@herberts-travel.co.uk
Web site: www.herberts-travel.co.uk
Fleet: 21 - 6 double-deck bus, 5 midibus, 4 midicoach, 1 minibus, 5 minicoach.
Chassis: 5 Ford Transit. 5 Leyland. 3 MCW. 4 Mercedes. 2 Optare. 1 Toyota. 1 Volvo.
Bodies: 4 Alexander. 1 Caetano. 2 ECW. 1 Leyland. 1 MCW. 4 Optare. 1 Plaxton. 6 other.
Ops incl: private hire, school contracts, local bus services.
Livery: White.
Ticket system: Wayfarer

MARSHALLS COACHES
FIRBANK WAY, LEIGHTON BUZZARD
LU7 4YP
Tel: 01525 376077
Fax: 01525 850967
Recovery: 01525 375301
E-mail: info@marshalls-coaches.co.uk
Web site: www.marshalls-coaches.co.uk
Fleetname: MCE Ltd
Prop: G Marshall **Ops Man**: I White
Wkshp Man: R Winters
Fleet: 28 - 3 double-deck bus, 22 coach, 2 double-deck coach, 1 midicoach.
Chassis: 3 Ayats. 4 Dennis. 3 Iveco. 2 Leyland. 1 Mercedes. 15 Volvo.
Bodies: 3 Ayats. 3 Beulas. 1 Caetano. 3 East Lancs. 5 Jonckheere. 1 Mercedes. 10 Plaxton.
Ops incl: private hire, school contracts, continental tours.
Livery: Blue/Multicoloured.

ON A MISSION COACHES
UNIT 5, HOLLINGDON DEPOT, STEWKLEY ROAD, SOULBURY, LEIGHTON BUZZARD, LU7 ODH.
Tel: 01525 270911
Fax: 01525 270908
E-mail: info@onamissioncoaches.co.uk
Web site: www.luxury-coaches.co.uk
Dirs: J Ellaway, M Bjeloboba
Fleet: 20
Ops inc: School contracts, excursion & tours private hire.
Livery: White

87

RED KITE COMMERCIAL SERVICES
UNIT 2, LEYS YARD, DUNSTABLE ROAD, TILSWORTH, LEIGHTON BUZZARD LU7 9PU
Tel: 01525 211441
Props: D. Hoar, R. H. Savage
Fleet: 18 - 15 double-deck bus, 3 coach.
Ops incl: local bus services, school contracts, excursions and tours, private hire, school contracts.
Livery: Red/Blue

SAFFORD COACHES LTD
See Cambridgeshire

SHOREYS TRAVEL
119 CLOPHILL ROAD, MAULDEN MK45 2AE.
Tel: 01525 860694
Fax: 01525 861850.

E-mail: shoreystravel@talk21.com
Prop: E C J Shorey **Ptnrs**: D Shorey, G Shorey **Ch Eng**: D Bunker
Fleet: 8 - 7 double deck bus, 1 coach.
Chassis: 3 Leyland. 7 MCW.
Bodies: 7 MCW. 3 Leyland.
Ops incl: school contracts, private hire.
Livery: White/Green
Ticket System: Wayfarer.

TATES COACHES
See Hertfordshire

THREE STAR COACHES (LUTON)
Unit Guardian Business Park, Dallow Road, Luton LU4 9GF
Tel: 01582 722626
Fax: 01582 484034
E-mail: sales@threestarcoaches.com
Ops Man: Kevin Green
Fleet: 11 - 5 coach, 3 midicoach, 2 minicoach, 1 double-deck coach .
Chassis: Dennis 3. Ayats 1. 1 MAN. 2 Volvo. Mercedes 4. Scania 2. Volvo 2.
Bodies: incl: 2 Mercedes. Ayats 1. Berkhof 6. Hispano 2. Mercedes-Benz 2. Flaxton 2.
Ops incl: School contracts, excursions & tours, private hire. express. continental tours.
Livery: Blue

VILLAGER MINIBUS (SHARNBROOK) LTD
SHARNBROOK UPPER SCHOOL, ODELL ROAD, SHARNBROOK MK44 1JL
Tel: 01234 781920
Fleet: 1 minibus
Chassis: 1 Ford
Ops incl: local bus services, private hire
Ticket system: printed book

BERKSHIRE (WEST BERKSHIRE, BRACKNELL FOREST, READING, SLOUGH, WINDSOR & MAIDENHEAD, WOKINGHAM)

1ST CHOICE SCORPIO TRAVEL
67 WEST END COURT, WEST END LANE, STOKE POGES SL2 4NB
Tel: 01753 648435
Fax: 01753 644878
E-mail: admin@scorpiotravel.net
Web site: www.scorpiotravel.net
Ptnrs: Don Hughes, Gill Hughes.
Fleet: 1 coach
Chassis: Iveco
Body: Beulas
Ops incl: excursions & tours, private hire, continental tours.
Livery: Silver/Cerise/Teal

ALDERMASTON COACHES
GRANGE LANE, BEENHAM, READING RG7 5PP
Tel: 0118 971 3257
Fax: 0118 971 2722
Ptnrs: D. Arlott, T. Arlott, P. Arlott
Ops incl: private hire, school contracts.
Livery: White

BURGHFIELD MINI COACHES LTD
BURGHFIELD FARM, MILL ROAD, BURGHFIELD BRIDGE RG30 3SS
Tel/Fax: 0118 959 0719
E-mail: burghfield.coaches@virgin.net
Dir: Susan McCouid
Fleet: 38 - 30 minibus, 8 minicoach.
Chassis: Citroen. Dennis. Leyland. Mercedes-Benz. Optare. Renault.
Ops incl: local bus services, school contracts, private hire.

COURTNEY COACHES LTD
BERKSHIRE BUSINESS CENTRE, DOWNMILL ROAD, BRACKNELL RG12 1QFS
Tel: 01344 412302

Fax: 01344 868980/422278
E-mail: enquiries@courtneycoaches.com
Web site: www.courtneycoaches.com
Man Dir: Bill Courtney-Smith
Fleet: 37 - 5 double-deck bus, 11 coach, 3 double-deck, 4 single-deck bus, 14 minibus.
Chassis: 1 Ayats. 1 Iveco. 7 Leyland. 1 Marshall. 14 Mercedes. 1 Neoplan. 3 Optare. 2 Scania. 7 Volvo.
Ops incl: local bus services. School contracts, Private Hire
Livery: Orange/White.

FERNHILL TRAVEL LTD
LONGSHOT LANE, BRACKNELL RG12 1RL
Tel: 01344 621413
Fax: 01344 488669
E-mail: office@fernhill.co.uk
Web site: www.fernhill.co.uk
Ops incl: School Contracts, Private Hire
Livery: Red/White

FIRST IN BERKSHIRE
COLDBOROUGH HOUSE, MARKET STREET, BRACKNELL RG12 1JA
Tel: 01344 868688
Fax: 01344 868332
Web site: www.firstgroup.com
Man Dir: Adrian Jones
Comm Dir: Andrew Taylor
Chief Operating Officer: Chris Dexter.
Fleet: 115 - 6 double-deck bus, 68 single-deck bus, 24 midibus, 17 coach.
Chassis: 6 Bluebird. 55 Dennis. 8 Mercedes. 33 Scania. 13 Volvo.
Bodies: 19 Alexander. 8 Berkhof. 6 Bluebird. 1 Irizar. 8 Mercedes. 10 Northern Counties. 43 Plaxton. 20 Wright.
Ops incl: local bus services, school contracts, express.
Livery: FirstGroup/Green Line
Ticket System: Wayfarer

HAYWARDS COACHES
169 NEW GREENHAM PARK, THATCHAM RG19 6HN
Tel: 0118 547 4561
Fax: 01635 821128
Dir: Simon Weaver
Fleet: 33 - 4 single-deck bus, 22 coach, 6 double-deck coach, 1 mini
Chassis: 8 Bova. 7 Scania. 9 Volvo.
Bodies: 8 Bova. 6 East Lancs. 7 Irizar. 3 Plaxton.
Ops incl: local bus services, school contracts
Livery: Electric Blue
Subsidiary of Weavaway Travel

HODGE'S COACHES (SANDHURST) LTD
100 YORKTOWN ROAD, SANDHURST GU47 9BH.
Tel: 01252 873131
Fax: 01252 874884.
E-mail: enquiries@hodges-coaches.co.uk
Web site: www.hodges-coaches.co.uk
Man Dir: P Hodge **Dir**: M Hodge, M Hodge
Fleet: 21 - 18 single-deck coach, 1 midicoach, 2 minicoach.
Chassis: 4 Bedford. 2 DAF, 1 MAN, 2 Toyota, 12 Volvo
Bodies: 10 Berkhof. 7 Caetano. 1 Duple. 3 Plaxton.
Ops incl: excursions & tours, private hire, continental tours, school contracts.
Livery: Blue/Gold

HORSEMAN COACHES LTD
WHITLEY WOOD ROAD, READING RG2 8GG
Tel: 0118 975 3811
Fax: 0118 975 3515
Recovery: 0118 9753811

E-mail:
privatehire@horsemancoaches.myzen.co.uk
Man Dir: Keith Horseman **Ops Dir**: James Horseman **Ch Eng**: Derrick Holton **personnel**: Anne Fletcher **Ser Man**: Trevor Underwood
Fleet: 59 - 50 coach, 9 midicoach.
Chassis: 1 Dennis. 4 Iveco. 9 Toyota. 45 Volvo.
Bodies: 4 Beulas. 3 Berkhof. 9 Caetano. 42 Plaxton. 1 UVG.
Ops incl: local bus services, school contracts, excursions & tours, private hire, continental tours.
Livery: multi-coloured

KINGFISHER MINI COACHES

357 BASINGSTOKE ROAD, READING RG2 0JA
Tel: 0118 931 3454
Prop: Kevin Pope
Fleet: 13 - 5 minibus, 8 minicoach.
Chassis: incl. 6 Leyland. 4 Mercedes.
Ops incl: private hire. school contracts
Livery: White/Orange

MEMORY LANE VINTAGE OMNIBUS SERVICES

78 LILLIBROOKE CRESCENT, MAIDENHEAD SL6 3XQ
Tel: 01628 825050
Fax: 01628 825851
E-mail: admin@memorylane.co.uk
Web site: www.memorylane.co.uk
Prop: M J Clarke
Fleet: 6 - 4 double-deck bus, 2 single-deck bus
Chassis: 5 AEC. 1 Bristol
Bodies: 1 ECW. 1 MCW. 4 Park Royal.
Ops incl: private hire
Livery: Original operators

NEWBURY & DISTRICT

169 NEW GREENHAM PARK, NEWBURY RG19 6HN
Tel: 01635 33855
Fax: 01635 821128
Dir: Simon Weaver
Ops incl: local bus services
Livery: White
Ticket System: Wayfarer 3
Subsidiary of Weavaway travel.

READING & WOKINGHAM COACHES

33 MURRAY ROAD, WOKINGHAM RG41 2TA
Tel: 0118 979 3983
Fax: 0118 979 4330
Props: Mark Way, Sharon Way.

Fleet: 10 - 8 coach, 2 minibus
Chassis: 1 Dennis. 1 Iveco. 1 Mercedes. 1 Setra. 1 Toyota. 5 Volvo.
Bodies: 1 Beulas. 2 Berkhof. 1 Caetano. 1 Ikarus. 1 Jonckheere. 1 Mercedes. 1 Setra. 2 Van Hool.
Ops incl: excursions & tours, private hire, school contracts, continental tours.
Livery: White

READING HERITAGE TRAVEL

PO BOX 147, READING RG1 6PP
Tel: 07850 220151
Tran Man: M J Russell
Fleet: 1 double-deck bus.
Chassis: 1 AEC
Bodies: 1 Park Royal
Ops incl: private hire
Livery: Red/Cream
Ticket System: Almex

READING TRANSPORT LTD

GREAT KNOLLYS STREET, READING RG1 7HH
Tel: 0118 959 4000
Fax: 0118 957 5379
Recovery: 0118 958 7625
E-mail: info@reading-buses.co.uk
Web site: www.reading-buses.co.uk
Fleetname: Reading Buses, Newbury Buses, Goldline
Chmn: Tony Jones **Ch Exec Off**: James Freeman **Ops Dir**: Sam Simpson
Goldline Man: Norman Fryer-Saxby
Newbury Buses Man: Paul Lightowler **Reading Buses Man**: Glynne Davies **Eng Man**: vacant **Personnel Man**: Caroline Anscombe
Fleet: 191 - 83 double-deck bus, 73 single-deck bus, 9 single-deck coach, 26 midibus.
Chassis: 27 DAF. 7 Dennis. 1 MAN. 41 Optare. 115 Scania.
Bodies: 1 Alexander. 62 East Lancs. 6 Irizar. 12 Omni. 58 Optare. 6 Plaxton. 3 Van Hool. 36 Wright.
Ops incl: local bus services, school contracts, excursions & tours, private hire, continental tours.
Livery: various brand liveries
Ticket System: Wayfarer TGX150

STEWARTS OF MORTIMER (PRIVATE HIRE) LTD

JAMES LANE, GRAZELEY GREEN, READING, RG7 1NE
Tel: 0118 983 1231
Fax: 0118 983 1232
E-mail: quotes@somph.co.uk
Web site: www.somph.co.uk
Ops incl: private hire
Livery: Silver

TOP TRAVEL COACHES
See Hampshire

VINCE COACHES

AYRES HOUSE, AYRES LANE, BURGHCLERE RG20 9HG
Tel: 01635 278308
Prop: D L. Vince
Fleet: 5 coaches
Chassis/Bodies: 2 Berkhof. 3 Dennis.
Ops incl: private hire, school contracts.

WEAVAWAY TRAVEL

169 NEW GREENHAM PARK, NEWBURY RG19 6HN
Tel: 01635 820028
Fax: 01635 821128
Dir: Simon Weaver
Fleet: 33 - 4 single-deck bus, 22 coach, 6 double-deck coach, 1 minicoach.
Chassis: 8 Bova. 4 DAF. 4 Dennis. 1 Mercedes. 10 Scania. 6 Volvo.
Bodies: 3 Berkhof. 8 Bova. 9 East Lancs. 7 Irizar. 1 MCW. 1 Plaxton. 4 Van Hool.
Ops incl: school contracts, private hire.
Livery: Electric Blue

WHITE BUS SERVICES

NORTH STREET GARAGE, WINKFIELD SL4 4TP
Tel: 01344 88262
Fax: 01344 886403
E-mail: reception@whitebus.co.uk
Dir: D. E. Jeatt
Fleet: 12 - 3 single-deck bus, 9 coach.
Chassis: include DAF, Bedford. Dennis, Man
Bodies: Duple. Optare. Plaxton. Van Hool.
Ops incl: local bus services, school contracts, private hire.
Livery: White/grey skirt.
Ticket System: Wayfarer Saver, Setright

WINDSORIAN COACHES

373 HATTON ROAD, BEDFONT, FELTHAM TW14 9QS
Tel: 01753 860131
Fax: 020 8751 5054
Web site: www.windsoriancoaches.co.uk
Man Dir: Martin Cornell **Gen Man**: Gilbert Parsons
Fleet: 10 - 8 single-deck coach, 2 midicoach.
Chassis: 7 Dennis. 2 Mercedes. 1 Volvo.
Bodies: 2 Mellor. 8 Plaxton.
Ops incl: school contracts, excursions & tours, private hire, continental tours.
Livery: White/Blue

♿	Vehicle suitable for disabled	🛇	Seat belt-fitted Vehicle
T	Toilet-drop facilities available	🍴	Coach(es) with galley facilities
R	Recovery service available	❄	Air-conditioned vehicle(s)
	Open top vehicle(s)v	👥	Coaches with toilet facilities
R24	24 hour recovery service		Replacement vehicle available
	Vintage Coach(s) available		

BERKSHIRE (WEST BERKSHIRE, BRACKNELL FOREST, READING, SLOUGH, WINDSOR & MAIDENHEAD,

BRISTOL

ABUS
104 WINCHESTER ROAD, BRISLINGTON BS4 3NL
Tel: 0117 977 6126
E-mail: alan@abus.co.uk
Web site: www.abus.co.uk
Chmn/Man Dir: Alan Peters
Fleet: 20 - 17 double-deck bus, 3 midibus,
Chassis: 2 Bristol. 6 DAF. 10 Leyland. 1 Mercedes Benz. 2 Optare. 2 Scania.
Bodies: 9 Alexander. 2 ECW. 3 East Lancs. 1 Northern Counties. 7 Optare. 1 Paxton
Ops incl: local bus services
Livery: Cream/White/Maroon or Orange
Ticket System: Wayfarer 3

AZTEC COACH TRAVEL
6/8 EMERY ROAD, BRISLINGTON BS4 5PF
Tel: 0117 977 0314.
Fax: 0117 977 4431.
Man Dir: I. Fortune. **Fleet Eng**: D. Harvey.
Ops Man: P. Rixon.
Fleet: 15 - 13 midicoach, 2 minibus.
Chassis: 1 Freight Rover. 14 Mercedes.
Bodies: 2 Optare. 7 Reeve Burgess. 4 Autobus Classique.
Ops incl: excursions & tours, private hire, continental tours, school contracts.
Livery: White with diagonal red/orange stripes.

BERKELEY COACH & TRAVEL
HAM LANE, PAULTON BS39 7PL
Tel: 01761 413196
Fax: 01761 416469
Proprietor: Mr T. Pow
Fleet: 6 6 single-deck coach
Chassis: 6 Volvo
Ops incl: school contracts, private hire.

BLAGDON LIONESS COACHES LTD
See Somerset

BLUE IRIS COACHES
25 CLEVEDON ROAD, NAILSEA BS48 1EH
Tel: 01275 851121
Fax: 01275 856522
E-mail: enquiry@blueiris.co.uk
Web site: www.blueiris.co.uk
Dirs: Philip Hatherall, Tony Spiller
Fleet: 15 - 2 single-deck bus, 7 single-deck coach, 6 minicoach.
Chassis: 2 Mercedes. 6 Scania. 6 Toyota. 1 Volvo.
Bodies: 1 Alexander. 6 Caetano. 1 Carlyle. 6 Irizar. 1 Plaxton.
Ops incl: private hire, local bus services, school contracts.
Livery: 2-tone Blue/White.
Ticket System: Setright

PETER CAROL PRESTIGE COACHING
BAMFIELD HOUSE, WHITCHURCH BS14 0XD
Tel: 01275 839839
Fax: 01275 835604
E-mail: charter@petercarol.co.uk
Web site: www.luxurycoach.co.uk
Gen Man: Peter Collis
Fleet: 9 - 9 single-deck coach.
Chassis: 2 Bova. 1 BMC. 1 MAN. 5 Mercedes-Benz.
Bodies: 1 BMC. 2 Bova. 5 Mercedes Benz, 1 other body parts.
Ops incl: excursions & tours, private hire.

EAGLE COACHES
FIRECLAY HOUSE, NETHAM ROAD, ST GEORGE BS5 9PJ
Tel: 0117 955 7130
Fax: 0117 941 1107
E-mail: office@eagle-coaches.co.uk
Web site: www.eagle-coaches.co.uk
Fleet: 15 - 2 double-deck bus, 11 coach, 1 midicoach,1 minicoach
Chassis: 11 DAF. 1 Iveco. 1 Leyland. 1 Mercedes. 1 Scania.
Bodies: 2 Alexander. 1 Autobus. 1 Optare. 11 Van Hool.
Ops incl: school contracts, excursions & tours, private hire
Livery: Yellow

EASTVILLE COACHES LTD
15 ASHGROVE ROAD, REDLAND BS6 6NA
Tel: 0117 971 0657
Fax: 0117 971 5824.
Man Dir: T. Reece.
Fleet: 14 - 6 double-deck bus, 8 coach.
Chassis: 6 Bristol. 1 DAF. 7 Volvo.
Bodies: 6 ECW. 2 Plaxton. 6 Van Hool.
Ops incl: local bus services, school contracts, private hire, continental tours.
Livery: Myosotis Blue/White.

EUROTAXIS
JORROKS EST, WESTERLEIGH BS37 8QH
Tel: 0871 250 5555
Fax: 0871 250 4444
Recovery: 0871 250 3333
E-mail: juan@eurotaxis.com
Web site: www.eurotaxis.com
Co Sec: Juan Sanzo, **Dir**: Keith Sanzo, William Sanzo
Fleet: 84 - 10 double-deck bus, 4 single-deck bus, 10 single-deck coach, 40 midibus, 10 midicoach, 5 minibus, 5 minicoach.
Chassis: 8 Dennis. 2 Leyland. 60 Mercedes. 2 Optare. 2 Renault. 10 Volvo.

Ops incl: local bus services, school contracts, private hire, excursions & tours, continental tours
Livery: All White
Ticket system: Wayfarer 2

FIRST BRISTOL
ENTERPRISE HOUSE, EASTON ROAD, BRISTOL BS5 0DZ
Tel: 0117 955 8211
Fax: 0117 955 1248
Web site: www.firstgroup.com
Man Dir: Justin Davies **Eng Dir**: Richard Noble **Fin Dir**: Mike Gahan **Ops Dir**: Jenny McLeod
Fleet: 314 - 133 double-deck bus, 44 single-deck bus, 124 midibus, 13 minibus.
Chassis: 115 Dennis. 91 Leyland. 19 Mercedes. 89 Volvo.
Bodies: 29 Alexander. 8 East Lancs. 35 Leyland. 70 Northern Counties.102 Plaxton. 30 Roe. 40 Wright.
Ops incl: local bus services, school contracts.
Livery: First Bus Barbie 1+2
Ticket System: Wayfarer

GLENVIC OF BRISTOL LTD
THE OLD COLLIERY, STANTON WICK, PENSFORD BS39 4BZ
Tel: 01761 490116
Fax: 0117 907 7032
Dirs: Paul Holvey, Philip Holvey **Ops Man/Comp Sec**: Paul Holvey **Eng**: Nick Reed
Fleet: 13 - 4 double-deck bus, 5 coach, 4 minicoach
Chassis: 2 LDV. 7 Leyland. 2 Mercedes-Benz. 2 Volvo.

GRAHAM'S COACHES
7 WYCK BECK ROAD, BRENTRY BS10 7JD
Tel/Fax: 0117 950 9398
Prop: Graham P Smith
Fleet: 8 - 5 double-deck bus, 3 midicoaches.
Chassis: 1 DAF. 2 Dennis. 2 Leyland. 1 Optare. 2 Volvo.
Bodies: 2 Alexander. 2 Jonckheere. 1 Optare. 1 Van Hool.
Ops incl: private hire, school contracts.
Livery: White/Red/Maroon

ARNOLD LIDDELL COACHES
89 JERSEY AVENUE, BRISLINGTON BS4 4QX.
Tel: 0117 977 2011.
Prop: Michael. Liddell. **Gen Man**: Arnold. Liddell. **Fleet Eng**: Robert Liddell
Fleet: 2 - 1 coach, 1 midicoach.
Chassis: 1 Leyland. 1 Mercedes.
Ops incl: excursions & tours, school contracts.
Livery: Blue/White.

MARTINS SELF DRIVE MINICOACH HIRE

GRINDELL ROAD GARAGE,
1 GRINDELL ROAD, REDFIELD
BS5 9PG.
Tel: 0117 955 1042.
Fax: 0117 939 3383.
Fleet: 12 - 12 minibus.
Chassis: 12 Ford Transit.
Ops incl: Self Drive Minicoach Hire.

NORTH SOMERSET COACHES

COATES ESTATE, SOUTHFIELD ROAD,
NAILSEA BS48 1JN
Tel/Fax: 01275 859123
Prop: David Fricker
Web: www.northsomersetcoaches.co.uk
Fleet: 5 2 single-deck bus.
3 single-deck coach.
Chassis: 3 Alexander Dennis. 2 Volvo.
Bodies: 1 Alexander Dennis. 1 Berkhof. 1 Optare. 1 Plaxton. 1 VAn Hool
Ops incl: local bus sevice. school contracts,excursions & tours, private hire.
Livery: white/crimson/cream **Ticket System:** Wayfarer saver

PREMIER TRAVEL LTD

ALBERT CRESCENT, ST PHILIPS
BS2 0SU
Tel: 0117 9300 5550
Fax: 0117 9300 5551
Man Dir: Glenn Bond
Fleet: 5 - 1 double-deck bus, 2 coach, 1 double-deck coach, 1 minicoach.
Chassis: 9 Bova. 1 DAF. 1 Freight Rover. 1 Leyland. 1 Volvo
Bodies: 1 Bova. 1 ECW. 2 Van Hool.
Ops incl: school contracts, continental tours, private hire.
Livery: White/Red with blue lettering.

SOUTH GLOUCESTERSHIRE BUS & COACH COMPANY

PEGASUS PARK, GYPSY PATCH LANE, PATCHWAY BS34 6QD
Tel: 0117 931 4340
Fax: 0117 979 9400
Man Dir: Roger Durbin **Gen Man:** Mike Owen **Wkshp Man:** Mark Wood **Sales Man:** Tony Lavoie **Route Man:** Martyn Edney
Fleet: 49 - 9 double-deck bus. 2 single-deck bus. 1 coach. 1 double-deck coach. 3 minibus.
Chassis: 10 Dennis. 35 Leyland. 15 Mercedes. 1 Toyota. 38 Volvo.
Bodies: 20 Alexander. 1 Caetano. 16 Northern Counties. 38 Plaxton. 6 Reeve Burgess. 12 Van Hool. 2 Wadham Stringer. 4 Wright.
Ops incl: local bus service, school contracts, excursions & tours, private hire, continental tours, express.
Livery: Blue/White.
Ticket system: Wayfarer 2

SOMERBUS LTD
See Somerset

TURNERS COACHWAYS (BRISTOL) LTD

59 DAYS ROAD, ST PHILIPS BS2 0QS
Tel: 0117 955 9086
Fax: 0117 955 6948
E-mail: admin@turnerscoachways.co.uk
Web site: www.turners-coachways.co.uk
Man Dir: Tony Turner. **Private Hire Man:** Liz Venn **Traf Man:** Tony Harvey
Fleet: 31 - 30 coach, 1 minicoach.
Chassis: 7 Scania. 2 Setra. 1 Toyota. 20 Volvo.
Bodies: 2 Berkhof. 7 Irizar. 14 Jonckheere. 1 Optare. 2 Plaxton. 2 Setra. 2 Van Hool.
Ops incl: school contracts, private hire
Livery: Silver/Blue

WESSEX CONNECT

PEGASUS PARK, GYPSY PATCH LANE, PATCHWAY BS34 6QD
Tel: 0117 969 8661
Fax: 0117 969 8662
E-mail: info@connectbuses.com
Web site: www.wessexconnect.net
Part of Flights Hallmark,subsidiary of Rotala (see Major Groups).

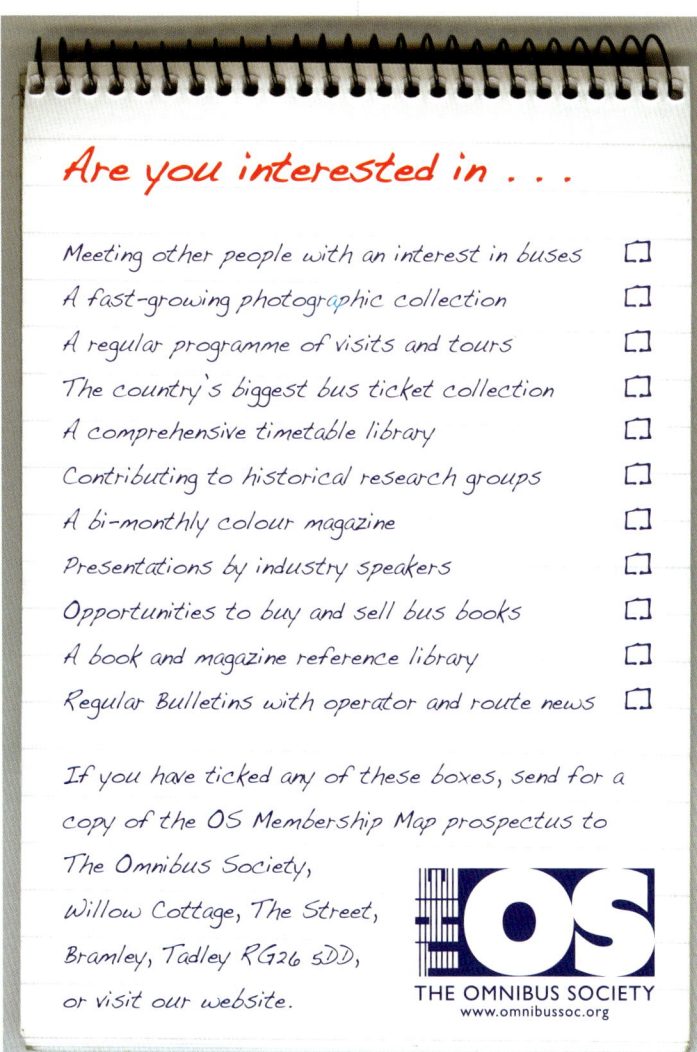

Are you interested in . . .

- Meeting other people with an interest in buses ☐
- A fast-growing photographic collection ☐
- A regular programme of visits and tours ☐
- The country's biggest bus ticket collection ☐
- A comprehensive timetable library ☐
- Contributing to historical research groups ☐
- A bi-monthly colour magazine ☐
- Presentations by industry speakers ☐
- Opportunities to buy and sell bus books ☐
- A book and magazine reference library ☐
- Regular Bulletins with operator and route news ☐

If you have ticked any of these boxes, send for a copy of the OS Membership Map prospectus to The Omnibus Society, Willow Cottage, The Street, Bramley, Tadley RG26 5DD, or visit our website.

OS — THE OMNIBUS SOCIETY
www.omnibussoc.org

BUCKINGHAMSHIRE, MILTON KEYNES

AUTODOUBLE LTD
90 HAINAULT AVENUE, GIFFARD PARK, MILTON KEYNES MK14 5PE.
Tel: 01908 281350.
Fleetname: Starlight.
Fin Dir/Sec: N. A Gibbard.
Traf Man/Dir: K. G. Gibbard.
Fleet: 5 - 1 coach, 1 midibus, 3 minicoach.
Chassis: 2 Bedford. 1 Bristol. 2 Ford Transit.
Bodies: 1 ECW. 1 Plaxton. 2 Dormobile. 1 Tricentrol.
Ops incl: private hire, school contracts.
Livery: White/Burgundy.

BRAZIERS MINI COACHES
17 VICARAGE ROAD, WINSLOW MK18 3BE
Tel: 01296 712201
E-mail: pbrazier@btconnect.com
Web site: www.brazierscoaches.co.uk
Fleet: 3 minibus
Chassis: 3 LDV
Ops incl: private hire, school contracts

CAROUSEL BUSES LTD
1 HAYDEN HOUSE, BAKER STREET, HIGH WYCOMBE HP11 2RX
Tel: 01494 533436
E-mail: enquiries@carouselbuses.com
Web site: www.carouselbuses.com
Man Dir/Co Sec: S Burns **Fin Dir:** J Robinson
Fleet: 41 - 22 double-deck bus, 19 single-deck bus
Chassis: 1 AEC. 6 DAF. 10 Dennis.3 Irisbus. 6 Leyland. 12 MCW. 3 Mercedes
Bodies: 3 East Lancs. 4 Leyland. 12 MCW. 3 Mercedes. 3 Northern Counties. 3 Optare. 1 Park Royal. 11 Plaxton. 1 Wright.
Ops incl: Local bus services, school contracts, private hire.
Livery: Red/Dark Red
Ticket system: Wayfarer 3

DRP TRAVEL
1 THE MEADWAY, LOUGHTON, MILTON KEYNES MK5 8AN
Tel: 01908 394141
Web site: www.drptravel.co.uk
E-mail: drptravel@talktalk.net
Man: D R Pinnock
Fleet: 3 minibus
Chassis/Bodies: 1 Iveco. 1 Optare. 1 Renault
Ops incl: school contracts, private hire.

HOWLETTS COACHES
UNIT 2, STATION ROAD INDUSTRIAL ESTATE, WINSLOW MK18 3DZ
Tel: 01296 713201
Fax: 01296 715879
Prop: R. S. Durham
Fleet: 8 - 2 double-deck bus, 6 coach.
Chassis: 1 Bedford. 4 DAF. 2 MCW. 1 Setra.
Ops incl: private hire, continental tours, school contracts.
Livery: Brown/White.

LANGSTON & TASKER
23 QUEEN CATHERINE ROAD, STEEPLE CLAYDON MK18 2PZ
Tel/Fax: 01296 730347

Ptnrs: Mrs J Langston, Mrs M A Fenner
Man: J Langston **Ops Man:** A P Price
Fleet: 19 - 13 single-deck coach, 6 minibus.
Chassis: 1 Bedford. 4 Dennis. 1 Iveco. 2 Leyland. 4 Mercedes. 1 Toyota. 6 Volvo.
Bodies: 1 Autobus. 2 Caetano. 3 Duple. 2 Jonckheere. 3 Mercedes. 6 Plaxton. 1 Transbus. 1 Wadham Stringer.
Ops incl: local bus services, school contracts, private hire
Livery: White/Red
Ticket system: Wayfarer

MAGPIE TRAVEL LTD
BINDERS INDUSTRIAL ESTATE, CRYERS HILL, HIGH WYCOMBE HP15 6LJ
Tel: 01494 715381
Dir: David Harris **Co sec:** Amanda Ash
Fleet: 14-1Double-deck bus, 2 Single-deck bus 7 coach, 4 midibus.
Chassis: 1 Dennis. 1 Leyland. 1 MCW 6 Mercedes. 5 Volvo.
Bodies: 1 Alexander Dennis. 1 Jonckheere. 1 Leyland. 1 MCV. 1 Mellor 1 Optare. 2 Plaxton. 2 Reeve Burgess. 2 Van Hool. 2 other.
Ops incl: local bus services, school contracts, private hire.
Livery: White/Black
Ticket System: Almex

MK METRO LTD
UNIT 3, ARDEN PARK, OLD WOLVERTON, MILTON KEYNES MK12 5RN
Tel: 01908 225100
Fax: 01908 313553
Gen Man: M Heywood
Fleet: 101 - double-deck bus, single-deck bus, midibus.
Chassis: DAF.Dennis. Mercedes. Optare.Scania. Volvo.
Bodies: Alexander. Caetano. Optare. Plaxton. Wright.
Ops incl: local bus services, school contracts
Livery: Blue/Yellow.
Ticket System: Wayfarer 3
Part of Arriva plc

MOTTS COACHES AYLESBURY LTD
GARSIDE WAY, STOCKLAKE, AYLESBURY HP20 1BH
Tel: 01296 398300
Fax: 01296 398386
E-mail: info@mottstravel.com
Web site: www.mottstravel.com
Fleetname: Motts Travel
Man Dir: M R Mott **Ops Dir:** C J Mott

Eng Dir: I Scutt **Tours Dir:** C Joel
Traf Man: H Shanks
Fleet: 45 - 5 double-deck bus, 4 single-deck bus, 28 coach, 2 double-deck coach, 2 midibus, 4 midicoach
Chassis: 6 Leyland. 3 MCW. 4 Mercedes. 2 Neoplan. 2 Optare. 3 Scania. 25 Volvo.
Bodies: 1 Esker. 3 Irizar. 16 Jonckheere. 3 MCW. 4 Neoplan. 8 Plaxton. 1 Van Hool. 2 Sitcar.
Ops incl: local bus services, school contracts, excursions & tours, private hire, continental tours.
Livery: White/Yellow/Green.
Ticket System: Wayfarer.

PAYNES COACHES & CAR HIRE LTD
6 BALMER CUT, BUCKINGHAM INDUSTRIAL ESTATE, BUCKINGHAM MK18 1UL.
Tel: 01280 813108, 817761.
Dirs: J. V. & K. R. Jeffs.
Fleet: 14 - 12 coach, 2 minicoach.
Chassis: Bedford. Ford. Leyland.
Bodies: 4 Caetano. 1 Duple. 2 Jonckheere. 3 Leyland. 1 Mercedes. 2 Optare. 1 Plaxton.
Ops incl: local bus services, excursions & tours, private hire, express, continental tours.
Livery: Green/Cream.
Ticket System: Almex/Wayfarer.
Subsidiary of Jeffs Coaches, Helmdon
Part of the Bowen Group

REDLINE BUSES
8 GATEHOUSE WAY, AYLESBURY HP19 8DE
Tel/Fax: 01296 426786
E-mail: kwk@redlinebuses.com
Web site: www.redlinebuses.com
Prop: Khan Wali
Fleet: 24-7 Double-deck bus 6 Single-deck bus 4 coach 7 Minibus
Chassis: 1 Alexander Dennis 2 Dennis 1 Enterprise 1 Ford 3 Leyland 3 Mercedes 3 Optare 10 Volvo
Bodies: 5 Alexander Dennis 2 Jonckheere 3 Northern Counties 3 Optare 6 Plaxton 1 Van Hool 3 Wright 1 Other
Ops incl: local bus services, school contracts, private hire.
Livery: Red
Ticket System: Wayfarer TGX.

RED ROSE TRAVEL LTD
BLINKING OWL GARAGE, OXFORD ROAD, AYLESBURY HP17 8TT
Tel: 01296 747926
Fax: 01296 612196
Web site: www.redrosetravel.com
Dirs: Chris Day, Taj Khan
Fleet: 25 single-deck bus.
Chassis: 10 Dennis. 1 Leyland. 5 Mercedes. 7 Optare 2 Volvo.
Ops incl: local bus services, school contracts, private hire.
Livery: Red/Yellow
Ticket System: Wayfarer.

SOULS COACHES LTD
2 STILEBROOK ROAD, OLNEY
MK46 5EA
Tel: 01234 711242
Fax: 01234 240130
Recovery: 07739 097775
E-mail: sales@souls-coaches.co.uk
Web site: www.souls-coaches.co.uk
Man Dir: David Soul **Sales Man**: Wendy Cheshire **Traf Man**: Neil McCormick
Ops man: Steve Neale **Wkshp Man**: Drew Blunt
Fleet: 41 - 4 Double-deck bus 2 Single-deck bus 31 Coach 1 Double-deck coach 3 minicoach
Chassis: 5 Dennis 2 Leyland 1 Man 2 Mercedes 5 Setra 3 Toyota 14 Volvo. **Bodies**: 5 Jonckheere 2 Leyland 2 mercedes 1 Neoplan 3 Optare 15 Plaxton 5 Setra.
Ops incl: local bus services, school contracts, excursions & tours, private hire, continental tours.
Livery: Red/Gold
Ticket System: Wayfarer.

VALE TRAVEL
61 FLEET STREET, AYLESBURY
HP20 2PA
Tel: 01296 484348
Fax: 01296 435309
E-mail: vale_travel@yahoo.co.uk
Web site: www.valetravel.co.uk
Prop: Wazir Zaman
Fleet: 10
Ops Inc: School contracts excursions and tours private hire.
Livery: Multi

WOOTTENS
THE COACH YARD, LYCROME ROAD, LYE GREEN, CHESHAM HP5 3LG
Tel: 01494 774411
Fax: 01494 784597
E-mail: info@woottens.co.uk
Web site: www.woottens.co.uk
Dirs: N H Wooten **Ops Man**: M J Wootten
Ops Man: P Williams **Chief Eng**: R A Gomm
Fleet Name: Wooltens, Tiger Line
Fleet: 25 - 2 double-deck bus, 6 single-deck bus, 17 coach.
Chassis: 8 Leyland 17 Volvo.
Bodies: 1 Alexander. 1 Berkhof. 2 ECW. 1 East Lancs. 2 Jonckheere. 2 Leyland. 15 Plaxton.
Ops incl: local bus services, excursions and tours, continental tours, private hire, school contracts.
Livery: White with coloured swirls.
Ticket System: Wayfarer.

CAMBRIDGESHIRE, CITY OF PETERBOROUGH

ANDREWS COACHES
20 CAMBRIDGE ROAD, FOXTON
CB2 6SH
Tel: 01223 873002
Fax: 01223 873036
E-mail: andrewscoaches@aol.com
Web site: www.andrewscoaches.co.uk
Dirs: F Miller, J Miller **Ops Sup**: A Miller
Fleet: 5 coach
Chassis: 1 DAF. 4 Volvo.
Bodies: 1 Duple. 1 Irizar. 3 Plaxton.
Ops incl: private hire, school contracts

C & G COACHES
HONEYSOME LODGE, HONEYSOME ROAD, CHATTERIS PE16 6SB
Tel: 01354 692200
Fax: 01354 694433
Recovery: 07771 962 105
E-mail: info@candgcoaches.co.uk
Web site: www.candgcoaches.co.uk
Prtnrs: Mrs C Day, G Ellwood, R Day
Ops Man: C Smith
Fleet: 24 - 1 double-deck bus, 23 coach
Chassis: 3 Bedford. 1 Bova. 2 Leyland. 1 MCW. 1 Neoplan. 11 Scania. 5 Volvo.
Bodies: 2 Berkhof. 1 Bova. 2 Duple. 1 ECW. 8 Irizar. 1 MCW. 1 Neoplan. 8 Plaxton. 1 Van Hool.
Ops incl: school contracts, excursions & tours, private hire, continental tours
Livery: White/Red/Yellow

COLLINS COACHES
UNIT 4, CAMBRIDGE ROAD INDUSTRIAL ESTATE, CAMBRIDGE CB4 6AZ
Tel: 01223 420462
Fax: 01223 424739
E-mail: collinscoaches@sagehost.co.uk, office@collinscoaches.net
Ptnrs: C. R. Collins, R. T. Collins **Off Man**: Jacky Liptrot **Garage Man**: R D Curtis
Fleet: 19 - 3 coach, 3 midicoach, 13 minibus.
Chassis: 1 Bedford. 2 Dennis. 5 Ford Transit. 2 Freight Rover. 4 Iveco. 2 LDV.
Ops incl: excursions & tours, school contracts, private hire.
Livery: White/Orange

RON W DEW & SONS LTD
CHATTERIS ROAD, SOMERSHAM PE17 3DN.
Tel: 01487 740241.
Fax: 01487 740341.
E-mail: sales@dews-coaches.com
Web site: www.dews-coaches.com
Chmn: David Dew. **Ops Man**: Simon Dew.
Fleet: 10 - 3 single-deck bus, 7 single-deck coach.
Chassis: 2 Bedford, 1 DAF, 5 Scania, 2 Volvo.
Bodies: 2 Berkhof, 3 Irizar, 2 Van Hool.
Ops incl: local bus sevrices, excursions & tours, private hire, continental tours, school contracts.
Livery: Green/Grey.

EMBLINGS COACHES
BRIDGE GARAGE, GUYHIRN, WISBECH PE13 4ED.
Tel: 01945 450253.
Fax: 01945 450770
Man Dir: John Embling

FENN HOLIDAYS
WHITTLESEY ROAD, MARCH PE15 0AG
Tel: 01354 653329
Fax: 01354 650647
E-mail: info@fennholidays.co.uk
Web site: www.fennholidays.co.uk
Man Dir: Peter Fenn **Dir**: Margaret Fenn
Off Man: Catherine Cross
Fleet: 4 coach
Chassis: 2 Bova. 2 Van Hool.
Bodies: 2 Bova. 2 Van Hool.
Ops incl: excursions & tours, private hire, continental tours
Livery: multicolour
Ticket System: Setright.

GRETTON'S COACHES
ARNWOOD CENTRE, NEWARK ROAD, PETERBOROUGH PE1 5YH
Tel: 01733 311008
Fax: 01733 319859
Prop: Roger Gretton
Fleet: 15 - 12 coach, 2 midicoach, 1 minicoach.
Chassis: 2 Bedford. 1 Mercedes. 12 Scania.
Ops incl: school contracts, excursions & tours, private hire.
Livery: Silver/Red/Maroon

GREYS OF ELY
41 COMMON ROAD, WITCHFORD ELY CB6 2HY
Tel: 01353 662300
Fax: 01353 662412
E-mail: sales@greysofely.co.uk
Web site: www.greysofely.co.uk
Prop: D Grey **Co Sec**: R Grey **Ops Man**: C Covill
Fleet: 15 - 11 double-deck coach, 1 midibus, 3 minicoach.
Chassis: 11 Dennis. 3 Mercedes. 1 Fiat.
Bodies: 2 Berkhof. 1 Caetano. 13 Plaxton. 2 Euro
Ops incl: school contracts, private hire
Livery: Cream/Green

DEREK HIRCOCKS COACHES
THE OLD BARN, SCHOOL ROAD, UPWELL PE14 9EW
Tel: 01945 773461.
Fleetname: Upwell & District.
Prop: D. Hircock. **Eng**: W. Hircock.
Sec: Ms. C. Hircock.
Fleet: 7 coach.
Chassis: 4 AEC. 3 Leyland.
Ops incl: excursions & tours, private hire, school contracts.
Livery: Red/White/Blue.

93

JANS COACHES
23 TOWNSEND, SOHAM CB7 5DD
Tel: 01353 721344
Fax: 01353 721341
E-mail: janscoaches@aol.com
Dirs: Roland Edwards, Janet Edwards, Stuart Edwards
Fleet: 8 - 3 double-deck bus, 3 coach, 1 double-deck coach, 1 minicoach.
Chassis: 1 Dennis. 1 Iveco. 1 Leyland. 2 MAN. 2 MCW. 1 Neoplan.
Bodies: 1 Berkhof. 2 MCW. 3 Neoplan. 1 Northern Counties. 1 Indcar.
Ops incl: excursions & tours, private hire, continental tours, school contracts.
Livery: White.

MIL-KEN TRAVEL LTD
11 LYNN ROAD, LITTLEPORT, ELY CB6 1QG
Tel: 01353 860705
Fax: 01353 863222
E-mail: milken@btconnect.com
Web-site: www.milkentravel.com
Man Dir: Jason Miller **Fleet Eng:** Ian Martin **Gen Man:** Mark Rogers
Fleet: 39 - 37 coach, 2 minibus.
Chassis: 2 DAF. 5 Dennis. 2 LDV. 30 Volvo.
Bodies: 1 Berkhof. 3 Duple. 3 Jonckheere. 25 Plaxton. 4 Van Hool. 3 other.
Ops incl: private hire, continental tours, excursions & tours, school contracts.

NEAL'S TRAVEL LTD
102 BECK ROAD, ISLEHAM CB7 5QP
Tel: 01638 780066
Fax: 01638 780011
E-mail: sales@nealstravel.com
Web site: www.nealstravel.com
Dirs: Bridget Paterson, Graham Neal, Lionel Neal, Nancy Neal
Fleet: 19 - 9 coach, 1 midibus, 7 midicoach, 2 minibus.
Chassis: 1 Iveco. 1 MAN. 11 Mercedes. 6 Volvo.
Bodies: 1 Indcar. 3 Jonckheere. 2 Mercedes. 1 Neoplan. 3 Optare. 4 Plaxton. 2 Sunsundegui. 3 other.
Ops incl: local bus services, school contracts, private hire, excursions & tours, continental tours.
Livery: White/Blue, Silver/Blue
Ticket system: Wayfarer

D A PAYNE COACH HIRE
UNIT 2, FOUNDRY WAY, LITTLE END ROAD INDUSTRIAL ESTATE, EATON SOCON PE19 8JH.
Tel: 01480 473272.
Fax: 01480 211252
E-mail: david@dapaynecoachehire.co.uk
Web site: www.dapaynecoachire.co.uk
Prop: D A Payne **Sec:** Mrs Carole Allen
Ops Man: R Wood
Fleet: 10 - 3 coach, 1 midibus, 1 midicoach, 2 minibus, 3 minicoach.
Chassis: include 3 Setra. 1 Toyota. 1 Volvo.
Bodies: include 1 Caetano. 1 Plaxton. 3 Setra..
Ops incl: school contracts, excursions & tours, private hire.

PETERBOROUGH TRAVEL CONSULTANTS
12 BUCKLAND CLOSE, NETHERTON, PETERBOROUGH PE3 9UQ
Tel: 01733 267025
Fax: 01733 267025
E-mail: petertravelcon@aol.com
Props: Mrs P C Greeves
Fleet: 3 - 2 coach, 1 midicoach.
Chassis: 1 DAF. 2 Setra.
Ops incl: excursions & tours, school contracts, private hire, continental tours.
Livery: Blue/White/Red

PLANET TRAVEL
PLANET HOUSE, MEADOW DROVE, EARITH PE17 3QE.
Tel: 01487 843333.
Fax: 01487 843285.
Prop: D. J. Collier. **Ch Eng:** B. Turnock.
Co Acct: M. Sloman. **Traf Man:** R. Birchenough. **Ops Man:** Mrs C. Stafford.
Fleet: 9 - 7 coach, 1 double-deck coach, 1 midicoach.
Chassis: 5 Bova. 1 Mercedes. 1 Scania. 2 Seddon.
Bodies: 1 Berkhof. 5 Bova. 2 Setra. 1 RH2000.
Ops incl: private hire, continental tours.

ROBINSON KIMBOLTON
19 THRAPSTON ROAD, KIMBOLTON PE28 0HW
Tel: 01480 860581
E-mail: robinsoncharles@btconnect.com
Web site: www.robinsonkimbolton.co.uk
Man Dir: Charles Robinson
Fleet: 9 - 8 coach, 1 minibus
Chassis: 7 Dennis. 1 Scania. 1 Toyota.
Bodies: 3 Berkhof. 1 Caetano. 1 Duple. 3 Plaxton. 1 Van Hool.
Ops incl: private hire, school contracts.
Livery: Cream/Brown/Red

SAFFORD COACHES LTD
THE DRIFT, LITTLE GRANSDEN, SANDY SG19 3DW
Tel: 01767 677395
Fax: 01767 677742
E-mail: saffordscoaches@btconnect.com
Web site: www.saffordscoaches.co.uk
Dirs: Miss Tracey Gillett, Mrs Shirley Gillett.
Fleet: 12 - 1 single-deck bus, 11 coach.
Chassis: 1 Bova. 1 Mercedes. 10 Volvo.
Bodies: 1 Bova. 1 Caetano. 2 Jonckheere. 1 Mercedes. 7 Plaxton.
Ops incl: school contracts, excursions & tours, private hire, continental tours.
Livery: White with Blue/Yellow

SHAWS OF MAXEY
49 HIGH STREET, MAXEY PE6 9EF
Tel: 01778 342224

Fax: 01778 380378
Ptnrs: Jane Duffelen Richard Shaw, Christopher Shaw
Fleet: 25 - 1 single-deck bus, 20 coach, 3 midicoach, 1 minicoach.
Chassis: 3 Bedford. 1 Bova. 2 DAF. 1 Dennis. 2 Mercedes. 1 Optare. 1 Toyota. 14 Volvo.
Bodies: 1 Autobus. 1 Berkhof. 1 Bova. 1 Caetano. 5 Jonckheere. 13 Plaxton. 1 Optare. 2 other.
Ops incl: local bus services, school contracts, excursions & tours, private hire, continental tours.
Livery: Blue/White

STAGECOACH IN CAMBRIDGESHIRE
100 COWLEY ROAD, CAMBRIDGE CB4 0DN
Tel: 01223 420544
Fax: 01223 420065
E-mail: cambridge.enquiries@stagecoachbus.com
Web site: www.stagecoachbus.com
Man Dir: Andy Campbell **Com Dir:** Philip Norwell
Fleet: 242 - 119 double-deck bus, 54 single-deck bus, 8 coach, 48 midibus, 7 minibus, 6 open-top bus.
Chassis: 61 Dennis, 2 Ford Transit. 53 MAN. 7 Optare. 50 Transbus. 69 Volvo.
Bodies: 148 Alexander. 28 Northern Counties. 7 Optare. 9 Plaxton. 50 Transbus
Ops incl: local bus services.
Livery: Stagecoach
Ticket system: Wayfarer 3

STAGECOACH IN PETERBOROUGH
351 LINCOLN ROAD, PETERBOROUGH, PE1 2PF
Tel: 01733 554575
E-mail: peterborough.enquiries@stagecoach.com
Web site: www.stagecoachbus.com
Man Dir: Andy Cambell
Ops incl: Local bus services
Livery: Stagecoach
Ticket System: Wayferer

TOWLERS COACHES LTD
CHURCH ROAD, EMNETH PE14 8AA
Tel: 01945 583645
Fax: 01945 583645
E-mail: joanne@towlerscoaches.fsnet.co.uk
Dirs: Mark Towler, Wendy Shepherd, Anton Towler, Joanne Walton
Fleet: 7 - 3 double-deck bus, 3 coach, 1 double-deck coach
Chassis: 1 Bova. 1 Bristol. 3 Leyland. 1 Scania. 1 LAG-EOS.
Bodies: 1 Bova. 1 Duple. 1 ECW. 1 East Lancs. 1 Jonckheere. 1 Plaxton. 1 LAG EOS.
Ops incl: school contracts, excursions & tours, private hire.
Livery: Green/Cream/Orange

VICEROY OF ESSEX LTD
See Essex

WEBB'S
ST PETERS FARM, MIDDLE DROVE
PE14 8JJ
Tel: 01945 430123
E-mail: webb-s-cant@fsbdial.co.uk
Prop: Barry Webb
Fleet: 3 - 1 midicoach,1 minicoach, 1 minibus.
Ops incl: local bus services

WHIPPET COACHES LTD
CAMBRIDGE ROAD, FENSTANTON
PE18 9JB
Tel: 01480 463792
Fax: 01480 495264
Web site: www.go-whippet.co.uk
Dirs: J. T. Lee, P. H. Lee, M. H. Lee.
Fleet: 49 - 20 double-deck bus, 6 single-deck bus, 20 coach, 3 minibus.
Chassis: Bedford, Leyland, Scania, Volvo.
Bodies: Duple, East Lancs, Leyland, Northern Counties, Park Royal, Plaxton, Van Hool, Alexander.
Ops incl: local bus service, school contracts, excursions & tours, private hire, express.
Livery: Blue/Cream with logo.
Ticket System: Almex Eurofare.

W & M TRAVEL
10 MAIN ROAD, PARSON DROVE, WISBECH PE13 4LF
Tel: 01945 700492
Fax: 01945 700964
Recovery: 01945 700942
Dir: W Norman
Fleet: 6 - 3 single-deck bus, 3 coach
Chassis: Bedford. DAF. Dennis. Scania.
Bodies: Berkhof. Duple. Plaxton. Marcopolo
Ops incl: local bus services, school contracts, excursions & tours, private hire

---

CHESHIRE, HALTON & STOCKPORT

ANGEL TRAVEL
108 GORSEY LANE, WARRINGTON WA2 7RY
Tel: 07090 741550
Fax: 01925 445591
E-mail: angeltravelwarrington@yahoo.co.uk
Dir: Richard Keane
Fleet: 3 minibus.
Chassis: LDV. Mercedes.
Ops incl: school contracts, private hire, excursions & tours.
Livery: Blue/White

ANTHONYS TRAVEL
8 CORMORANT DRIVE, RUNCORN WA7 4UD
Tel: 01928 561460
Fax: 01928 561460
Emergency: 01928 576050
E-mail: anthonys@fsbdial.co.uk
Recovery: 07920 154240
E-mail: anthonys@fsbdial.co.uk
Web site: www.anthonys-travel.co.uk
Partners: Richard Bamber, Anne Bamber, Tony Bamber **Gen Man**: Jodie Waring
Eng: Stephen Knight
Fleet: 17 - 9 single-deck coach, 1 minibus, 7 minicoach.
Chassis: 3 LDV. 1 MAN. 5 Mercedes. 5 Neoplan. 1 Optare. 2 Scania. 1 Setra.
Bodies: 1 Berkhof. 1 Irizar. 5 Mercedes. 5 Neoplan. 1 Optare. 1 Setra.
Ops incl: local bus services, school contracts, private hire, excursion & tours.
Livery: multi coloured
Ticket system: Setright/Wayfarer

ARROWEBROOK COACHES
THE OLD COACH YARD, WERVIN ROAD, CROUGHTON CH2 4DA
Tel: 01244 382444
Fax: 01244 379777
Prop: A. G. Parsons
Ops Incl: local bus services
Livery: White/Green.

BARRATT'S COACHES LTD
UNIT 15, MILLBANK WAY, SPRINGVALE INDUSTRIAL ESTATE, SANDBACH CW11 3GQ
Tel: 08450 625096
Fax: 08450 627728
E-mail: gilbarratt@tiscali.co.uk
Web site: www.barrattscoaches.co.uk
Dir: Gillian Barratt, D Bate
Fleet: 18 - coaches, double-deck coach, midibus, midicoach
Chassis: 1 Leyland. 1 Mercedes. 2 Neoplan. 14 Volvo.
Bodies: 1 Jonckheere. 1 Mercedes. 2 Neoplan. 8 Plaxton. 6 Van Hool.
Ops incl: local bus services, school contracts, private hire.
Livery: White.

BENNETT'S TRAVEL
ATHLONE ROAD, LONGFORD, WARRINGTON WA2 8JJ
Tel/Fax: 01925 415299.
Fleetname: Warrington Coachways
Prop.: B. A. Bennett, D. B. Bennett.
Ops incl: local bus services
Livery: White/Blue.

A. & H. BOOTH LTD
See Greater Manchester

BOSTOCK'S COACHES
SPRAGG STREET GARAGE, CONGLETON CW12 1QH
Tel: 01260 273108
Fax: 01260 276338
E-mail: sales@holmeswood.uk.com
Web site: www.holmeswood.uk.com
Dirs: J F Aspinall, M Aspinall, C H Aspinall, D E Aspinall, M F Aspinall, M J Forshaw **Ops Man**: M E Bostock
Tours Man: J. Bostock-Gibson **Ch Eng**: M Boniface
Fleet: 40 - 3 double-deck bus, 33 coach, 1 double-deck coach, 2 midicoach, 1 minicoach.
Chassis: 1 Ayats. 1 Bova. 7 DAF. 6 Dennis. 2 Iveco. 4 Leyland. 4 MAN. 9 Scania. 6 Volvo.
Bodies: 1 Ayats. 1 Beulas. 2 Berkhof. 1 Bova. 3 Caetano. 2 ECW. 1 East Lancs. 4 Ikarus. 1 Indcar.1 Irizar. 6 Marcopolo. 8 Plaxton. 9 Van Hool.
Ops incl: local bus services, excursions & tours, private hire, continental tours, school contracts.
Livery: Green
(Subsidiary of Holmeswood Coaches, Lancashire)

H E BROWN & SONS
8 GREENFIELD ROAD, GREENFIELD FARM INDUSTRIAL ESTATE, CONGLETON CW12 4TR
Tel: 01260 275281
Fax: 01260 280955
Fleetname: Browns Coaches.
Prop: Dennis Brown
Fleet: 5 - 3 coach, 1 double deck coach, 1 midibus.
Chassis: 1 Leyland. 1 Neoplan. 1 Optare. 1 Volvo. 1 Van Hool
Bodies: 2 Duple. 1 Neoplan.1 Optare. 1 Van Hool.
Ops incl: local bus services, school contract, private hire.
Livery: White/Red.
Ticket System: Setright.

DOBSON'S BUSES LTD
WINCHAM PARK, CHAPEL STREET, WINCHAM, NORTHWICH CW9 6DA
Tel/Fax: 01606 350200
Man Dir: I P Dobson **Ch Eng**: P J Dobson
Ops Man: R P Dobson **Co Sec**: R E Dobson
Fleet: 15 - 8 double-deck bus, 2 coach, 5 midibus
Chassis: 2 Daimler. 2 Dennis. 1 Iveco. 6 Leyland. 2 Mercedes. 2 Peugeot.
Bodies: include: 1 Duple. 1 Marshall. 1 Mellor. 2 Plaxton. 2 Peugeot.
Ops Include: local bus services, school contracts, private hire
Ticket system: Datafare

FIRST IN CHESTER & THE WIRRAL
669 NEW CHESTER ROAD, ROCK FERRY CH42 1PZ
Tel: 0151 645 8661
See Merseyside includes Former Chester City Transport

JOHN FLANAGAN COACH TRAVEL
2 REDDISH HALL COTTAGES, BROAD LANE, GRAPPENHALL, WARRINGTON WA4 3HS
Tel: 01925 266115
Fax: 01925 261100
Recovery: 01925 266115
E-mail: admin@flanagancoaches.co.uk
Web site: www.flanagancoaches.co.uk
Fleet: 7 - 3 coach, 1 midicoach, 3 minicoach.
Chassis: 1 Dennis. 1 Ford. 3 Mercedes. 2 Volvo.
Bodies: 1 Berkhof. 1 Esker. 2 Mercedes. 1 UVG. 1 Van Hool. 1 other.
Ops incl: private hire, school contracts, excursions and tours.
Livery: Red/Black/White
(Subsidiary of Holmeswood Coaches, Lancashire)

CAMBRIDGESHIRE, CITY OF PETERBOROUGH

HALTON BOROUGH TRANSPORT LTD

MOOR LANE, WIDNES WA8 7AF
Tel: 0151 423 3333
Fax: 0151 424 2362
E-mail: enquiries@haltontransport.co.uk
Web site: www.haltontransport.co.uk
Fleetname: Halton Transport
Man Dir: Chris Adams **Eng Man:** Phil Matthews **Traf Man:** David Steadman **Fin Man:** Adele Cookson
Fleet: 61 - 61 single-deck bus,
Chassis: 8 Alexander Dennis, 47 Dennis, 6 Leyland
Bodies: 6 Leyland. 55 Marshall/MCV.
Ops incl: local bus services.
Livery: Red/Cream.
Ticket System: Wayfarer III

HULME HALL COACHES LTD

1 STANLEY ROAD, CHEADLE HULME SK8 6PL
Tel: 0161 486 1187
Fax: 0161 482 8125
E-mail: hulmehallcoaches@talk21.com
Web site: www.hulmehallcoaches.co.uk
Man Dir: D. Herald **Tran Man:** C. J. O'Neill **Traf Man:** I Johnson **Fl Eng:** P Henshall

Fleet: 12 - 7 double-deck bus, 1 single-deck bus, 3 coach, 1 midibus.
Chassis: 6 Bristol. 1 Iveco. 1 Leyland. 1 Leyland National. 3 Volvo.
Bodies: 7 ECW. 1 East Lancs. 1 Mellor. 3 Plaxton.
Ops incl: local bus services, school contracts, private hire.
Livery: Red/Cream
Ticket System: Wayfarer

LE-RAD COACHES & LIMOUSINES

328 HYDE ROAD, WOODLEY SK6 1PF
Tel: 0161 430 2032
Recovery: 0770 314 5500
Prop: Derek & Jean Mycock
Fleet: 3 - 2 coach, 1 minicoach.
Chassis: 1 DAF. 1 Ford. 1 LDV.
Ops incl: private hire, excursions & tours

ROY McCARTHY COACHES

THE COACH DEPOT, SNAPE ROAD, MACCLESFIELD SK10 2NZ
Tel: 01625 425060
Fax: 01625 619853
Email: sales@roymccarthycoaches.co.uk
Web Site: www.roymccarthycoaches.co.uk
Senr Ptnr: A McCarthy **Ptnr:** M Lomas

Fleet: 10 coach.
Chassis: 1 Bedford. 2 Dennis. 1 MAN. 6 Volvo.
Bodies: 1 Berkhof. 1 Caetano. 8 Plaxton
Ops incl: school contracts, excursions & tours, private hire, continental tours.
Livery: Blue/Cream

MARPLE MINI COACHES

5 GROSVENOR ROAD, MARPLE SK6 6PR.
Tel: 0161 881 9111
Owner: G. W. Cross
Fleet: 2 minicoach
Chassis: Ford Transit, LDV.
Ops incl: school contracts, private hire.
Livery: White/Gold.

MAYNE COACHES LTD

MARSH HOUSE LANE, WARRINGTON WA1 3AU
Tel: 01925 445588
Fax: 01925 232300
E-mail: warrington@mayne.co.uk
Web site: www.mayne.co.uk
Chmn/Man Dir: S B Mayne **Co Sec:** D Mayne **Gen Man:** R W Vernon **Asst Gen Man:** A Dykes **Traf Man:** J Drake **Ch Eng:** E Sutcliffe

Fleet: 31 - 5 double-deck bus, 26 coach.
Chassis: 2 Bova. 6 Leyland. 16 Scania. 7 Volvo.
Bodies: 2 Bova. 1 Duple. 5 East Lancs. 11 Irizar. 12 Plaxton.
Ops incl: local bus services, school contracts, private hire.
Livery: Red/Cream

MEREDITHS COACHES LTD
LYDGATE, WELL STREET, MALPAS SY14 8DE
Tel: 01948 860405
Fax: 01948 860162
E-mail: info@meredithscoaches.co.uk
Web site: www.meredithscoaches.co.uk
Dirs: J K Meredith, Mrs M E Meredith, D J Meredith **Co Sec**: Mrs Kirin Meredith **Ch Eng**: C Bellis
Fleet: 16
Chassis: 1 Ford. 4 Leyland. 11 Volvo.
Bodies: 12 Plaxton. 2 Van Hool. 2 Wadham Stringer.
Ops incl: local bus services, school contracts, private hire.

MILLMANS COACHES
STATION YARD, GREEN LANE, PADGATE, WARRINGTON WA1 4JR
Tel: 01925 813181
Fax: 01925 813181
Prop: Eric Millman
Fleet: 6 coach
Chassis: 2 DAF. 3 Leyland, 1 Volvo
Bodies: 1 Duple. 5 Plaxton.
Ops incl: local bus services, school contracts, private hire.
Livery: Blue/White

MOORE'S COACHES LTD
53 REES CRESCENT, HOLMES CHAPEL CW4 7NL.
Tel/Fax: 01477 537004
Dirs: D. M. Moore, J. C. Moore.
Fleet: 4 coach.
Chassis: 1 Dennis. 1 Scania. 1 Volvo. 1 Van Hool.
Bodies: 1 Jonckheere. 1 Plaxton. 2 Van Hool.
Ops incl: excursions & tours, private hire, express, continental tours, school contracts.
Livery: Moore's Coaches/Nat. Express.

NIDDRIE COACHES
LEVIN STREET, MIDDLEWICH CW10 9AS
Tel: 01606 832343
Fax: 01606 833449
(Subsidiary of Baker's Coaches, Staffordshire)

SELWYNS TRAVEL SERVICES
CAVENDISH FARM ROAD, WESTON, RUNCORN WA7 4LU
Tel: 01928 564515
Fax: 01928 591872
Recovery: 01928 572108
E-mail: sales@selwyns.co.uk
Web site: www.selwyns.co.uk
Man Dir: Selwyn A Jones **Gen Man**: Alan P Williamson **Co Sec/Acct**: Richard E Williams **Fleet Eng**: Cledwyn Owen
Fleet: 44 - 9 single-deck bus, 33 coach, 1 midibus, 1 minicoach.
Chassis: 31 DAF. 1 Caetano. 1 Dennis. 2 Mercedes. 1 Optare. 2 Volvo. 6 Tecnobus.
Bodies: 1 Caetano. 3 Ikarus. 2 Mercedes. 1 Optare. 6 Pantheon. 2 Plaxton. 27 Van Hool.
Ops incl: local bus services, school contracts, excursions & tours, private hire, express, continental tours.
Livery: White/Blue/Orange/Green
Ticket System: Wayfarer
See also Greater Manchester

W A SHEARINGS LTD
BARLEYCASTLE LANE, APPLETON, WARRINGTON WA4 4FR.
Tel: 01925 214600
Fax: 01925 262606
Ops Man: Chris Brown
See also W A Shearings Ltd, Greater Manchester.

JIM STONES COACHES
THE JAYS, LIGHT OAKS LANE, GLAZEBURY, WARRINGTON WA3 5LH
Tel/Fax: 01925 766465
E-mail: jimstones@ic24.net
Web site: www.jimstonescoaching.com
Ptnrs: J B Stones, Mrs J P Stones, **Gen Man**: R Dyson
Fleet: 16 - single-deck bus.
Chassis: 12 Dennis. 4 Leyland.
Bodies: 1 DAB. 2 East Lancs. 13 Plaxton.

Ops incl: local bus services, school contracts
Livery: Blue/White
Ticket System: Almex, Wayfarer 3, Setright

WARRINGTON BOROUGH TRANSPORT LTD
WILDERSPOOL CAUSEWAY, WARRINGTON WA4 6PT
Tel: 01925 634296
Fax: 01925 418382
Web site: www.warringtonboroughtransport.co.uk
Fleetname: Network Warrington
Man Dir: Nigel Featham **Fin Dir**: John Bannister **Ops Man**: Charlie Shannon **Eng Man**: Damian Graham
Fleet: 115 - 34 double-deck bus, 69 midibus, 12 minibus.
Chassis: 47 Daf, 41 Dennis, Optare, 28 Volvo
Bodies: 18 Alexander Dennis, 41 Marshall/mcv, 10 Northern Counties, 12 Optare, 47 Wright
Ops incl: local bus services, school contracts, private hire.
Livery: Red/Cream
Ticket System: Wayfarer 3

WHITEGATE TRAVEL LTD
15 BEAUTY BANK, WHITEGATE, NORTHWICH CW8 2BP
Tel: 01606 882760
Fax: 01606 883356
Owner: K. Prince
Fleet: 12 minibus
Chassis: 1 Ford Transit. 2 Freight Rover. 2 Iveco. 2 Mercedes. 5 Leyland DAF.
Ops incl: local bus services, school contracts, private hire.
Livery: Yellow/White

	Vehicle suitable for disabled		Seat belt-fitted Vehicle
T	Toilet-drop facilities available		Coach(es) with galley facilities
R	Recovery service available		Air-conditioned vehicle(s)
	Open top vehicle(s)v		Coaches with toilet facilities
R24	24 hour recovery service		c Replacement vehicle available
			Vintage Coach(es) available

CORNWALL

CARADON RIVIERA TOURS
THE GARAGE, UPTON CROSS, LISKEARD PL14 5AX
Tel: 01579 362226.
Fax: 01579 362220
Prop: John K. Deeble.
Fleet: 39 - 6 single-deck bus, 28 coach, 1 midibus, 3 minicoach, 1 mincoach.
Chassis: 1 Bedford. 2 Bristol. 4 Dennis. 1 Freight Rover. 3 LDV. 26 Leyland. 2 MCW.
Bodies: 4 Alexander. 4 Duple. 4 East Lancs. 2 MCW. 4 Optare. 17 Plaxton. 1 UVG. 3 Wadham Stringer.
Ops incl: local bus services, school contracts, excursions & tours, private hire.
Livery: Cream/Blue.
Ticket System: Setright.

DAC COACHES LTD
RYLANDS GARAGE, ST ANNE'S CHAPEL, GUNNISLAKE PL18 9HW
Tel: 01822 834571
Fax: 01822 833881
Recovery: 01822 833378
E-mail: dac.coaches@btconnect.com
Web site: www.daccoaches.co.uk
Dirs: Bernard Harding, Nick Smith
Fleet: 10 - 4 coach, 1 double-deck bus, 2 midibus, 3 minicoach.
Chassis: 1 Bedford. 1 Bristol. 1 Ford. 3 Mercedes. 1 Peugeot. 3 Volvo.
Bodies: Duple. ECW. 9 Plaxton. Van Hool.
Ops incl: local bus services, school contracts, excursions & tours, private hire, continental tours.
Livery: Blue/White/Red/Yellow.
Ticket System: Almex.

DARLEY FORD TRAVEL
DARLEY FORD, LISKEARD PL14 5AS
Tel: 01579 362272
Fax: 01579 363425
Owner: Albert J Deeble
Fleet: 8
Chassis: 2 Scania. 6 Volvo.
Bodies: include 1 Berkhof.
Ops incl: private hire, excursions & tours, continental tours.
Livery: White

FIRST IN DEVON & CORNWALL
See Devon

GROUP TRAVEL
DUNMERE ROAD GARAGE, BODMIN PL31 2QN
Tel: 01208 77989
Fax: 01208 77989
E-mail: grouptravel@btinternet.com
Web site: grouptravelcoachhire.com
Dirs: Dawn Moon, David Benny
Fleet: 21 - 7 coach, 13 midibus, 1 minicoach.
Chassis: 1 Autosan. 1 Leyland. 1 MAN. 2 Marshall. 10 Mercedes. 1 Optare. 4 Volvo.
Bodies: 1 Caetano. 1 Jonckheere. 2 Marshall/MCV. 5 Mellor. 1 Optare. 3 Plaxton. 4 Reeve Burgess. 2 Van Hool. 2 other.
Ops incl: local bus services, school contracts, excursions & tours, private hire
Livery: Silver/Turquoise + blue logo
Ticket system: Almex A90

HOOKWAYS JENNINGS
LANSDOWNE ROAD, BUDE EX23 8BN.
Tel: 01288 352359
Fax: 01288 352140
Recovery: 07850 038707
E-mail: barry@hookways.com
Web site: www.hookways.com
Man Dir: Alistair Gray **Dirs:** Kym Hookway, Sue Hookway, Jason Hookway, Martin Hookway **(Eng)**, Julie Hookway **(Sec)**
Fleet: See Devon
Chassis: 1 Leyland. 1 MAN. 3 Mercedes. 1 Scania. 4 VW. 43 Volvo
Bodies: 1 Irizar. 6 Jonckheere. 41 Plaxton. 1 Wright.
Ops incl: school contracts, excursions & tours, private hire, express, continental tours.
Livery: Yellow
Part of Hookways Pleasureways (Devon)

HOPLEYS COACHES LTD
GOVER FARM, GOVER HILL, MOUNT HAWKE, TRURO TR4 8BH.
Tel: 01872 553786
E-mail: hopleyscoaches@tiscali.co.uk
Web site: www.hopleyscoaches.com
Ptnrs: B. Hopley, D. R. Hopley, N. A. Hopley.
Fleet: 16 - 1 double-deck bus, 4 single-

deck bus, 11 coach.
Chassis: 1 Bedford. 1 Bristol. 3 Volvo.
Bodies: 1 Duple. 1 ECW. 1 Jonckheere. 1 Plaxton. 1 Wright.
Ops incl: local bus services, school contracts, excursions & tours, private hire.
Livery: Red/White/Grey.
Ticket System: Wayfarer 3.

MOUNTS BAY COACHES
4 ALEXANDRA ROAD, PENZANCE TR18 4LY
Tel: 01736 363320
Fax: 01736 366985
E-mail: enquires@mountsbaycoaches.co.uk
Web site: www.mountsbaycoaches.co.uk
Dir: J M Oxenham
Fleet: 10 - 8 single-deck coach, 1 midicoach, 1 minibus.
Chassis: 1 Dennis. 1 LDV. 1 Toyota. 7 Volvo.
Bodies: 1 Caetano.1 Duple. 8 Van Hool.
Ops incl: school contracts, excursions & tours, private hire.

OTS MINIBUS & COACH HIRE
48 FORE STREET, CONSTANTINE, FALMOUTH TR11 5AB
Tel: 01326 340703
Fax: 01326 340404
E-mail: salots@hotmail.com
Web site: www.otsfalmouth.co.uk
Prop: Stephen Moore
Fleet: 5 - 1 single-deck coach, 1 midicoach, 2 minibus, 1 minicoach.
Chassis: 4 Mercedes. 1 Volvo.
Ops incl: local bus services, school contracts, excursions & tours.
Livery: blue/brown
Ticket system: manual

PENMERE MINIBUS SERVICES
28 BOSMOOR ROAD, FALMOUTH TR11 4PU
Tel/Fax: 01326 314165
E-mail: enquiries@penmereminibus.co.uk
Web site: www.penmereminibus.co.uk
Man: Ben Moore
Fleet: 2 - 1 minibus, 1 minicoach.
Chassis: 2 Mercedes.
Ops incl: local bus services, school contracts, private hire.
Livery: Blue/Brown stripes.
Ticket system: Manual

ROSELYN COACHES LTD
R24
MIDDLEWAY GARAGE, ST BLAZEY ROAD, PAR PL24 2JA
Tel: 01726 813737
Fax: 01726 813739
Recovery: 01726 813737
Web site: www.roselyncoaches.co.uk
Dirs: Jonathan Ede, Karen Paramor **Ch Eng:** Graham Paramor **Ops Man:** John

Stoneman **Gen Man:** Mike Heppell
Fleet: 38 - 10 double-deck bus, 28 coach
Chassis: 2 Bova. 2 Bristol. 1 DAF. 1 Iveco. 8 Leyland. 25 Volvo.
Bodies: 2 Bova. 1 Caetano. 5 ECW. 2 East Lancs. 1 Jonckheere. 3 Northern Counties. 15 Plaxton. 9 Van Hool.
Ops incl: school contracts, excursions & tours, private hire, continental tours.
Livery: Green/Gold

SUMMERCOURT TRAVEL
THE OLD COACH GARAGE, SUMMERCOURT TR8 5DR
Tel: 01726 861108
Fax: 01726 860093
Web site: www.summercourttravel.com
Ops incl: local bus services, private hire.
Livery: White

TAVISTOCK COMMUNITY TRANSPORT
GREENLANDS, ST ANN'S CHAPEL, GUNNISLAKE PL18 9HW
Tel: 01822 833574
E-mail: keithp44@btinternet.com
Fleetname: Tavistock Country Bus
Chmn: K W Potter **Sec:** A Everitt
Fleet: 1 minibus
Chassis: Iveco
Body: G M Coachwork.
Ops incl: local bus services, private hire.
Livery: Red/White
Ticket System: Wayfarer

TILLEY'S COACHES
THE COACH STATION, WAINHOUSE CORNER, BUDE EX23 0AZ.
Tel: 01840 230244.
Man Dir: Paul Tilley
Fleet: 12 coaches
Chassis: incl: 1 Irisbus
Bodies: incl: 1 Indcar
Livery: White/Cream/Maroon.

TRELEY MOTORS
ST BURYAN, PENZANCE TR19 6DZ
Tel: 01736 810322
Chmn: J Ley **Chied Eng:** A J Ley **Co Sec:** A D Ley
Fleet: 4 - 3 single-deck coach, 1 minicoach
Chassis/Body: 3 Dennis. 1 Mercedes.
Ops incl: school contracts, excursions & tours, private hire
Livery: White

TRURONIAN LTD
24 LEMON STREET, TRURO TR1 2LS
Tel: 01872 273453
Fax: 01872 222522
E-mail: enquiries@truronian.co.uk
Web site: www.truronian.co.uk
Fleet: 60 - 4 double-deck bus, 35 single-deck bus, 13 coach, 3 articulated bus, 2

midibus, 2 minibus, 1 midicoach.
Ops incl: local bus services, school contracts, excursions & tours, private hire, express, continental tours.
Livery: Red/Silver.
Ticket System: Almex
Subsidiary of First Devon & Cornwall (See Devon)

WESTERN GREYHOUND LTD
R24
WESTERN HOUSE, ST AUSTELL STREET, SUMMERCOURT, NEWQUAY TR8 5DR
Tel: 01637 871871
Fax: 01872 510151 extn: 25
E-mail: enquiries@westerngreyhound.com
Web site: www.westerngreyhound.com
Man Dir: Mark Howarth **Co Sec:** Mari Howarth **Dir:** Robin Orbell **Ops Man:** Brian James
Fleet: 86 - 10 double-deck bus, 5 single-deck bus, 2 open-top bus, 61 midibus, 4 minibus, 4 heritage.
Chassis: 1 AEC Routemaster. 2 Bristol. 70 Mercedes. 10 Volvo. 3 Routemaster.
Bodies: 2 ECW. 8 East Lancs. 2 Leyland. 5 Mercedes-Benz. 4 Park Royal. 62 Plaxton. 3 Other.
Ops incl: local bus services, school contracts, excursions & tours, private hire.
Livery: Green/White
Ticket System: ERG & Wayfarer

WHEAL BRITON TRAVEL
R24
MOOR COTTAGE, BLACKWATER, TRURO TR4 8ET
Tel: 01872 560281
Fax: 01872 560691
Prop: Stephen J Palmer
Fleet: 22- 20 single-deck coach, 1 midicoach,1 minibus.
Chassis: 1 LDV. 1 Toyota. 20 Volvo.
Bodies: 1 Caetano. 5 Jonckheere. 14 Plaxton. 2 Van Hool.
Ops incl: school contracts, excursions & tours, private hire, continental tours
Livery: Cream

F. T. WILLIAMS TRAVEL
DOLCOATH INDUSTRIAL PARK, DOLCOATH ROAD, CAMBORNE TR14 8RU
Tel: 01209 717152.
Fax: 01209 612511.
Prop: F. T. Williams.
Livery: White/Gold/Black.
THE COACH STATION, WAINHOUSE CORNER, BUDE EX23 0AZ.
Tel: 01840 230244.
Man Dir: Paul Tilley
Fleet: 12 coaches
Chassis: incl: 1 Irisbus
Bodies: incl: 1 Indcar
Livery: White/Cream/Maroon.

CORNWALL

	Vehicle suitable for disabled	R24	24 hour recovery service
T	Toilet-drop facilities available		Replacement vehicle available
R	Recovery service available		Vintage Coach(es) available
	Open top vehicle(s)v		
	Coach(es) with galley facilities		
	Air-conditioned vehicle(s)		
	Coaches with toilet facilities		

CUMBRIA

D K & N BOWMAN
R24
BURTHWAITE HILL, BURTHWAITE, WREAY, CARLISLE CA4 0RT
Tel: 01697 473262
Fax: 01697 473262
E-mail: enquiries@bowmans-coaches.co.uk
Web site: www.bowmans-coaches.co.uk
Ptnrs: David K Bowman, Nora Bowman
Fleet: 8 coach.
Chassis: 4 AEC. 2 Dennis. 2 Scania.
Bodies: 1 Irizar. 1 Jonckheere. 3 Plaxton. 1 Berkhof. 2 Duple. 1 Van Hool.
Ops incl: school contracts, excursions and tours, private hire.
Livery: Ivory/Red

S H BROWNRIGG
ENNERDALE MILL, EGREMONT CA22 2PN
Tel: 01946 820205
Fax: 01946 821919
Web site: www.shbrownrigg.co.uk
Chmn: R J Cook **Dirs**: Mr & Mrs D L Marshall, Mrs L Holliday
Fleet: 28 - 15 coach, 3 midibus, 10 minibus.
Chassis: 3 Ford. 4 Leyland. 9 Mercedes. 1 Scania. 1 Volkswagen. 10 Volvo.
Bodies: 1 Alexander. 17 Plaxton. 1 Van Hool. 2 Wright. 7 other.
Ops incl: local bus services, school contracts, private hire.
Livery: Purple/White

CALDEW COACHES LTD
6 CALDEW DRIVE, DALSTON, CARLISLE CA5 7NS
Tel/Fax: 01228 711690
E-mail: caldewcoachesltd@aol.com
Web site: www.caldewcoaches.co.uk
Dirs: Hugh McKerrell, Ann McKerrell, Bill Rogers **Co Sec**: Mandy Rogers
Fleet: 11 - 2 single-deck bus, 1 midicoach, 4 minibus, 4 minicoach.
Chassis: 10 Mercedes. 1 Volvo.
Bodies: 10 Mercedes. 1 Van Hool.
Ops incl: school contracts, excursions & tours, private hire.
Livery: White/Red

CARR'S COACHES
CONTROL TOWER, THE AIRFIELD, SILLOTH CA7 4NS
Tel: 01697 331276
Fax: 01697 333826
Web site: www.carrs-coaches.co.uk
Prop: A J Markley **Ch Eng**: Fred Gill
Fleet: 9 - 4 coach, 2 midibus, 1 midicoach, 2 minibus.
Chassis: 1 Dennis. 3 Ford Transit. 1 Leyland. 2 Mercedes. 2 Scania.
Bodies: 2 Duple. 1 Optare. 2 Van Hool.
Ops incl: local bus services, school contracts, private hire.
Livery: Blue/White.

CLARKSON COACHWAYS LTD
UNIT 2B, ASHBURNER WAY, WALNEY ROAD INDUSTRIAL ESTATE, BARROW IN FURNESS LA14 5UZ
Tel: 01229 828022
Fax: 01229 828022
E-mail: info@clarksoncoachways.co.uk
Web site: www.clarksoncoachways.co.uk
Dirs: Susan Clarkson, Neil Clarkson
Fleet: 13 - 8 single-deck bus, 1 open-top bus, 3 midicoach, 1 minicoach. **Chassis**: 5 Dennis. 1 Ford. 1 Leyland. 3 MAN. 1 Mercedes-Benz.
Bodies: 1 Alexander. 4 Berkhof. 3 Caetano. 1 Crest. 1 Marcopolo. 1 Optare.
Ops incl: school contracts, excursions & tours, private hire.
Livery: two-tone Green

COAST TO COAST PACKHORSE LTD
CHESTNUT HOUSE, CROSBY GARRETT, KIRKBY STEPHEN CA17 4PR
Tel: 01768 371777
Fax: 01768 371777
E-mail: packhorse@cumbria.com
Web site: www.cumbria.com/packhorse
Operator: J. Bowman.
Fleet: 3 minibus.
Chassis: 2 Ford Transit. 1 Freight Rover.
Ops incl: local bus services, school contracts, private hire.

CUMBRIA COACHES LTD
ALGA HOUSE, BRUNEL WAY, DURRANHILL INDUSTRIAL ESTATE, CARLISLE CA1 3NQ.
Tel: 01228 404300.
Fax: 01228 404309.
Dir: Dennis Smith, H. Humble
Ops Man: S. Hall.
Fleet: 12 - 8 coach, 4 double-deck coach.
Chassis: 2 Neoplan. 2 Setra. 8 Volvo.
Bodies: 4 Duple. 2 Jonckheere. 2 Neoplan. 2 Plaxton. 2 Setra.
Ops incl: excursions & tours, private hire, express, continental tours, school contracts.

D & H TRAVEL LTD
66 STRAMONGATE, KENDAL LA9 4BD
Tel: 01539 730555
Fax: 01539 723181
Recovery: 07971 205314
Web site: www.dhtravel.co.uk
Dir: Derek Henderson **Ops Man**: John Robinson
Fleet: 15 - 2 single-deck bus, 3 single-deck coach, 6 midibus, 2 midicoach, 2 minicoach
Chassis: 5 Ford. 9 Mercedes. 1 Scania.
Bodies: 2 Ikarus. 1 Jonckheere. 6 Plaxton.
Ops incl: excursions & tours, private hire, continental tours, school contracts, local bus services.
Livery: White

DAGLISH COACHES
R T
BECK LEA, PASTURE ROAD, ROWRAH, FRIZINGTON CA26 3XN
Tel/Fax: 01946 861940
E-mail: daglish.coaches@bobertd.demon.co.uk
Web site: www.daglishcoaches.co.uk
Dir: R. Daglish
Fleet: 13 - 10 coach, 1 double-deck coach, 2 minibus.
Chassis: 3 DAF. 1 Ford Transit. 1 LDV. 4 Leyland. 1 Leyland National. 1 MAN. 1 MCW. 1 Scania.
Ops incl: excursions & tours, private hire, school contracts.
Livery: Yellow/Blue/Red

GRAND PRIX COACHES
R
MAIN STREET, BROUGH CA17 4AY
Tel: 01768 341328
Web site: www.grand-prix-services.com
E-mail: allison@fsbdial.co.uk
Fax: 01768 341517
Fleet: 28 -11 single-deck bus, 10 coach, 1 midicoach, 5 minibus, 1 minicoach.
Chassis: 3 Ford Transit. 2 LDV. 1 Mercedes. 11 Volvo.
Bodies: 1 Alexander Dennis. 1 Caetano. 1 Duple. 2 MCW. 2 Mercedes. 5 Plaxton. 1 Van Hool.
Ops incl: local bus services, school contracts, excursions & tours, private hire.
Livery: White
Ticket System: Wayfarer TGX150

JOHN HOBAN TRAVEL LTD
22 KING STREET, WORKINGTON CA14 4DJ
Tel: 01900 603579
Fax: 01900 605528
E-mail: johnahoban@aol.com
Ptnrs: John Hoban, Allison Hoban
Fleet: 6 minicoach, 4 midicoach.
Chassis/Bodies: 10 Mercedes
Ops incl: local bus services, private hire

IRVINGS COACH HIRE LTD
JESMOND STREET, CARLISLE CA1 2DE
Tel: 01228 521666
Fax: 01228 515792
E-mail: office@irvings-coaches.co.uk
Web site: www.irvings-coaches.co.uk
Man Dir: R Irving **Dir**: Miss A Irving **Tran Man**: J Treasurer
Fleet: 10 - 10 single-deck coach.
Chassis: 2 DAF. 8 Volvo.
Bodies: 2 Bova. 1 Duple. 2 Plaxton. 1 Sunsundegui. 4 Van Hool.
Ops incl: excursions & tours, private hire, school contracts.
Livery: Orange/Black/White.

K & B TRAVEL LTD
33 KING STREET, PENRITH CA11 7AY
Tel: 01768 868600
Fax: 01768 862715
E-mail: mail@kbtravel.co.uk
Web site: www.kbtravel.co.uk
Man Dir: G Lund **Dirs**: B Bainbridge (**Co Sec**), T Lund
Fleet: 15 - 10 coach, 1 minibus, 4 midibus.
Chassis: 5 MAN. 5 Mercedes. 4 Volvo.
Bodies: 1 Berkhof. 4 Mercedes. 5 Neoplan. 1 Optare. 4 Van Hool.
Ops incl: local bus services, excursions & tours, private hire, school contracts, continental tours.
Livery: Blue with Green lettering

LADYBIRD TRAVEL
22 CLIFTON COURT, WORKINGTON CA14 3HR
Tel: 01900 61155
Fax: 01900 61155
E-mail: grahame.ladybird@virgin.net
Web site: www.ladybird-travel.com
Fleet: 14-11 coach, 1 midicoach, 2 minicoach.
Chassis: 4 DAF. 1 Dennis. 4 Iveco. 2 Optare. 1 Volvo.
Bodies: 4 Beulas. 2 Ikarus. 1 Marcopolo. 2 Optare. 1 Plaxton. 2 Van Hool.
Ops incl: excursions & tours, private hire, school contracts.
Livery: White with red/black stripes

LAKES SUPERTOURS
1 HIGH STREET, WINDERMERE LA23 1AF.
Tel: 01539 442751.
Fax: 01539 446026.
Dir: R. Minford, A. Dobson
Fleet: 9 minibus.
Chassis: 8 Renault. 1 Fiat.
Ops incl: excursions & tours.
Livery: White/Purple/Gold.

MESSENGERS COACHES LTD
MEALSGATE STATION, MEALSGATE, WIGTON CA7 1JP
Tel: 01697 371111
Fax: 01697 371112
E-mail: angie@messengerscoaches.co.uk
Web site: www.messengerscoaches.co.uk
Dirs: Liam Walker, Angie Walker
Fleet: 8 7 single-deck coach 1 midicoach
Chassis: 1 Mercedes-Benz. 7 Volvo.
Bodies: 3 Plaxton. 5 Van Hool.
Ops incl: school contracts, excursions & tours, private hire, continental tours.

MOUNTAIN GOAT LTD (incl PARK TOURS AND TRAVEL)
VICTORIA STREET, WINDERMERE LA23 1AD
Tel: 015394 45161
Fax: 015394 45164
E-mail: enquiries@mountain-goat.com
Web site: www.mountain-goat.com
Dirs: Peter Nattrass, Stephen Broughton
Office Man: Sue Todd
Fleet: 16 minicoach
Chassis: 1 Ford Tourneo. 1 LDV. 14 Renault.
Ops incl: local bus services, excursions & tours, private hire, continental tours, school contracts.
Livery: Green/Red on White
Ticket system: Wayfarer

NBM HIRE LTD
CROMWELL ROAD, PENRITH CA11 7JW
Tel: 01768 890030
Fleet: coach, bus, minibus
Ops incl: excursions & tours, private hire, school contracts

REAYS COACHES LTD
R24
STRAWBERRY FIELDS, SYKE PARK, WIGTON CA7 9NE
Tel: 016973 49999
Fax: 016973 49900
E-mail: info@reays.co.uk
Web site: www.reays.co.uk
Dirs: C W Reay, N Reay **Ch Eng**: J M McGill **Ops Man**: C W Reay **Co Sec**: N Reay
Fleet: 33 - 5 single-deck bus, 17 coach, 1 double-deck coach, 5 midicoach, 4 minicoach.
Chassis: 10 DAF. 15 Mercedes. 2 Neoplan. 4 Scania. 2 Volvo.
Bodies: 6 Alexander. 10 Bova. 4 Irizar. 3 Mercedes. 2 Neoplan. 4 Optare. 4 Plaxton.
Ops incl: local bus services, school contracts, excursions & tours, private hire, continental tours.
Livery: White/Blue/Gold.

ROBINSONS COACHES
STATION ROAD GARAGE, APPLEBY CA16 6TX
Tel: 01768 351424
Fax: 01768 352199
Prop: S E Graham
Fleet: 9 - 5 coach, 4 minibus.
Chassis: 1 DAF. 2 Dennis. 3 LDV. 1 Mercedes. 2 Volvo.
Bodies: include: 1 Mercedes. 1 Plaxton. 1 UVG. 2 Van Hool. 1 Wadham Stringer.
Ops incl: local bus services, school contracts, excursions & tours, private hire.
Livery: White/Green

SIMS TRAVEL
HUNHOLME GARAGE, BOOT, HOLMROOK CA19 1TF
Tel: 019467 23277
Fax: 019467 23158
E-mail: simstravel@hotmail.com
Ptnrs: J Andrew Sim, D Peter Sim
Fleet: 9 - 6 coach, 2 midicoach, 1 minicoach.
Chassis: 3 Mercedes. 1 Neoplan. 5 Volvo.
Bodies: 1 Autobus. 1 Berkhof. 1 Mercedes. 1 Neoplan. 2 Plaxton. 2 Van Hool, 1 Other.
Ops incl: excursions & tours, private hire, school contracts.

STAGECOACH NORTH WEST
BROADACRE HOUSE, 16-20 LOWTHER STREET, CARLISLE CA3 8DA
Tel: 01228 597222
Fax: 01228 597888
E-mail: northwest.enquiries@stagecoachbus.com
Web site: www.stagecoachbus.com
Fleetname: Stagecoach Cumbria/Lancaster/Lancashire
Man Dir: Chris Bowles **Eng Dir**: Paul W Lee **Ops Dir**: Phil Smith **Com Dir**: James Mellor
Fleet: 519 - 164 double-deck bus, 121 single-deck bus, 15 single-deck coach, 6 open-top bus, 74 midibus, 139 minibus.
Chassis:19 Alexander Dennis. 31 Dennis. 40 Leyland. 30 Man. 49 Mercedes-Benz. 103 Optare. 94 Transbus. 153 Volvo.
Bodies: 230 Alexander Dennis. 5 East Lancs. 8 Jockheere. 6 Leyland. 12 Marshall/MCV. 7 Northern Counties. 103 Optar 10 Pl;axton. 143 Transbus. 1 Van Hool. 1 Wright.
Ops incl: local bus services, school contracts, excursions & tours, express.
Livery: Stagecoach -UK bus
Ticket System: Wayfarer TGX150

F W STAINTON & SON LTD
39 BURTON ROAD, KENDAL LA9 7LJ
Tel: 01539 720156.
Fax: 01539 740287.
Web site: www.staintons coaches.co.uk
Fleetname: Staintons Olympic Holidays.
Man Dir: R. S. Stainton. **Ops Man**: C. J. Stainton. **Ch Eng**: I. M Stainton.
Fleet: 21 coach. 2 midicoach. 1 minicoach.
Chassis: 2 Bova 8 DAF 4 Mercedes, 5 Setra, 5 Volvo.
Ops incl: excursions & tours, private hire, continental tours.
Livery: Blue/Green/Silver.

STEVE'S OF AMBLESIDE LTD
GALAVA GATE, BORRANS ROAD, AMBLESIDE LA22 0EN
Tel: 01539 433544.
Fax: 01539 432018.
Dir: S. A. Wise. **Sec**: Mrs E. Wise.
Fleet: 2 minibus.
Chassis: 1 Freight Rover. 1 Renault.
Ops incl: excursions & tours, private hire, school contracts. **Livery**: White.

TITTERINGTON COACHES LTD
THE GARAGE, BLENCOW, PENRITH CA11 0DG
Tel: 01768 483228
Fax: 01768 483680
E-mail: enquiries@titteringtoncoaches.co.uk
Web site: www.titteringtonholidays.co.uk
Dirs: Ian Titterington, Paul Titterington, Colin Titterington
Fleet: 15 coach
Chassis: 1 Iveco. 1 Leyland. 1 MAN. 1 Mercedes. 11 Volvo.
Bodies: 1 Beulas. 1 Duple. 5 Jonckheere. 2 Neoplan. 4 Plaxton. 2 Van Hool.
Ops incl: excursions & tours, private hire, continental tours, school contracts
Livery: Mustard/White

CUMBRIA

TOWER COACHES
THE GARAGE, BURNFOOT, WIGTON CA7 9HL
Tel: 01697 349600
Props: M D Sellars, Mrs T Sellars
Fleet: 5 - 2 coach, 2 midibus, 1 minibus.
Chassis: 1 DAF. 1 Leyland. 2 Mercedes. 1 Renault.
Bodies: 1 Alexander. 1 Holdsworth. 2 Plaxton. 1 Reeve Burgess.
Ops incl: local bus services, school contracts, private hire.
Livery: Dark Blue/Grey
Ticket System: Almex A

THE TRAVELLERS CHOICE
See Lancashire

TUERS MOTORS LTD
R24
BRIDGE HOUSE, MORLAND, PENRITH CA10 3AY
Tel: 01931 714224
Fax: 01931 714236
Fleet: 7 - 4 coach, 1 midicoach, 2 minicoach
Chassis: 1 AEC. 1 DAF. 1 Ford Transit. 1 Mercedes. 1 Toyota. 2 Volvo.
Bodies: 1 Caetano. 3 Plaxton. 2 Reeve Burgess. 1 Van Hool.
Ops incl: excursions & tours, private hire, school contracts, continental tours.
Livery: Cream/Red

WRIGHT BROS (COACHES) LTD
R24 T
CENTRAL GARAGE, NENTHEAD, ALSTON CA9 3NP.
Tel: 01434 381200.
Fax: 01434 382089.
E-mail: wrightbros@btinternet.com
Web Site: www.wrightscoaches.co.uk
Chmn/Man Dir: J. G. Wright.
Dir: C. I. Wright.
Fleet: 12 - 10 coach, 2 double-deck coach.
Chassis: 5 Bedford. 2 Scania. 5 Volvo.
Bodies: 2 Jonckheere. 7 Plaxton. 2 Van Hool. 1 Ikarus.
Ops incl: local bus services, school contracts, private hire, continental tours.
Livery: Cream/Black/Gold.
Ticket System: Almex.

DERBYSHIRE

ANDREW'S OF TIDESWELL LTD
R24 T
ANCHOR GARAGE, TIDESWELL SK17 8RB
Tel: 01298 871222
Fax: 01298 872412
E-mail: info@andrews-of-tideswell.co.uk
Web site: www.andrews-of-tideswell.co.uk
Dirs: R. B. Andrew, P. D. Andrew
Fleet: 18 - 2 double-deck bus, 11 coach, 2 double-deck coach, 2 midicoach, 1 minicoach.
Chassis: 2 Ford. 2 Leyland. 3 Mercedes. 1 Scania. 2 Setra. 8 Volvo.
Bodies: 2 Alexander. 3 Mercedes. 5 Plaxton. 2 Setra. 6 Van Hool.
Ops incl: excursions & tours, private hire, continental tours, school contracts
Livery: Cream/Ivory/Red flash.

ARRIVA DERBY LTD
R
ASCOT DRIVE, OFF LONDON ROAD, DERBY DE24 8ND
Tel: 01332 861500
Fax: 01332 861501
Fleetname: Arriva Serving Derby.
Man Dir: R A Hind. **Fin Dip**: J C Barlow
Ops Dir: A Lloyd. **Eng Dip**: M Evans
Fleet: See Arriva Midlands
Ops incl: local bus services, school contracts, private hire.
Livery: Aquamarine/Cotswold Stone
Ticket System: Wayfarer II.

BAGNALLS COACHES
T
THE COACH STOP, GEORGE HOLMES WAY, SWADLINCOTE DE11 9DF
Tel: 01283 551964
Fax: 01283 552287
Dir/Ops Man: John Bagnall **Dir/Clerk**: Pat Bagnall **Dir/Ch Eng**: Karl Bagnall
Dir/Clerk: Gavin Bagnall
Fleet: 12 - single-deck bus, coach
Chassis: 12 Volvo
Bodies: 1 East Lancs. 1 Jonckheere. 1 Plaxton. 10 Van Hool.
Ops incl: local bus services, excursions & tours, private hire, school contracts.
Livery: various

BAKEWELL COACHES
24 MOORHALL, BAKEWELL DE45 1FP
Tel: 01629 813995

BOWERS COACHES
ASPINCROFT GARAGE, CHAPEL-EN-LE-FRITH SK23 0NU
Tel: 01298 812204
Fax: 01298 816103
E-mail: enquiries@bowerscoaches.co.uk
Web site: www.bowersbuses.com
Fleet: 34 - 7 single-deck bus, 6 coach, 19 midibus, 1 minibus. 1 van.
Chassis: 2 Dennis. 5 Leyland National. 1 MAN. 9 Mercedes. 10 Optare. 4 Scania. 1 Setra.
Bodies: 4 Alexander. 2 Irizar. 5 Leyland National. 10 Optare. 5 Reeve Burgess. 1 Setra. 3 Van Hool.
Ops incl: local bus services, school contracts, excursions & tours, private hire, continental tours.
Subsidiary of Centrebus - See Leicershire

CLOWES COACHES
T
BARROWMOOR, LONGNOR NEAR BUXTON SK17 0QP
Tel: 01298 83292
Fax: 01298 83838
E-mail: clowescoaches@btconnect.com
Dirs: George A Clowes, Kathleen M Clowes
Fleet: 12 - 7single-deck coach, 4 midibus, 1 minicoach
Chassis: 3 Alexander Dennis. 4 Mercedes. 2 Neoplan. 2 Scania.1 Toyota.
Bodies: 3 Alexander. 2 Irizar. 2 Neoplan. 1 Van Hool. 3 Other
Ops incl: local bus services, school contracts, excursions & tours, private hire.
Livery: Cream/Green/Red
Ticket system: Manual

COX'S OF BELPER
GOODS ROAD, BELPER DE56 1UU
Tel: 01773 822395
Fax: 01773 821157
E-mail: coxsofbelper@lineone.net
Prop: Bernard Bembridge
Fleet: 6 - 2 coach, 1 midicoach, 1 minibus, 1 minicoach, 1 midibus.
Chassis: 1 LDV. 3 Mercedes. 2 Volvo
Bodies: 1 Carlyle. 1 Jonckheere. 1 Mercedes. 1 VanHool. 2 conversions
Ops incl: excursions & tours, private hire, school contracts.
Livery: White/Blue

CRESSWELL'S COACHES (GRESLEY) LTD
3 SHORTHEATH ROAD, MOIRA, SWADLINCOTE DE12 6AL
Tel: 01283 217215
Fax: 01283 550043
Recovery: 01283 217215
E-mail: info@cresswellscoaches.com
Web site: www.cresswellscoaches.com
Man Dir: David Cresswell **Dir**: Jean Raynor **Ch Eng**: Steve Lloyd **Tran Man**: John Collins
Fleet: 19 - 13 coach, 6 minicoach
Chassis: 4 Iveco. 6 Mercedes. 1 Optare. 9 Volvo.
Bodies: 4 Beulas. 2 Johckheere. 2 Marshall/MCV. 3 Mercedes. 1 Optare. 6 Plaxton. 1 Reeve Burgess.1 Van Hool.
Ops incl: local bus services, school contracts, excursions & tours, private hire, continental tours.
Ticket System: Wayfarer

CRISTAL HIRE COACHES OF SWANWICK
19 CROMWELL DRIVE, SWANWICK DE55 1DB.
Tel: 01773 604932.
Prop: A. Hunt. **Co Sec**: Mrs Christine Hunt.
Fleet: 2 coach.
Chassis: 1 Bova. 1 Leyland.
Ops incl: excursions & tours, private hire, school contract.

102

DAWSON'S MINICOACHES
10 HOLLAND CLOSE, MORTON
DE55 6HE
Tel: 01773 873149.
Prop: S. R. Dawson
Fleet: 4 - 2 minibus, 2 minicoach.
Chassis: 2 Ford Transit. 2 Freight Rover.
Ops incl: private hire, school contracts.
Livery: Grey/White/Blue stripe.

DERBY COMMUNITY TRANSPORT
R24
MEADOW ROAD GARAGE, MEADOW ROAD, DERBY DE1 2BH
Tel: 01332 380738
E-mail: derbyct@btinternet.com
Fleet: 28 minibus
Chassis: LDV. Mercedes.
Ops incl: local bus services, school contracts
Part of the Wellglade Group

K&H DOYLE
LYDFORD ROAD, ALFRETON DE55 7RQ
Tel: 01773 546546
Fax: 01773 546547
Prop. K Doyle.
Ops Incl: local bus services
Livery: Beige.

TIM DRAPER'S GOLDEN HOLIDAYS
SEVERN SQUARE, ALFRETON
DE55 7BQ
Tel: 01773 590808
Fax: 01773 590034
E-mail: tim.draper@btconnect.com
Dirs: Tim Draper, Pam Draper, Clair Draper
Fleet: 10 - 1 double-deck bus, 6 coach, 1 midibus, 2 minibus.
Chassis: 1 DAF. 1 Iveco. 1 LDV. 1 MAN. 1 MCW. 2 Mercedes. 3 Volvo.
Bodies: 1 Beulas. 1 MCW. 2 Mercedes. 1 Noge. 2 Plaxton. 2 Van Hool.
Ops incl: excursions & tours, school contracts, private hire
Livery: White/Red/Yellow
Ticket System: Almex, Wayfarer 3, Setright

DUNN-LINE GROUP
See Nottinghamshire

'E' COACHES OF ALFRETON
1 MANOR COURT, RIDDINGS DE55 4DG
Tel: 01773 541222
Fax: 01629 825522
Owner: K. Bacon
Fleet: 5 - 2 midicoach, 3 minicoach.
Chassis: 3 Mercedes. 2 LDV.
Bodies: 2 Autobus. 3 Crest.
Ops incl: local bus service, school contract, excursions & tours, private hire.
Livery: Blue/White.

FELIX BUS SERVICES LTD
157 STATION ROAD, STANLEY DE7 6FJ
Tel: 0115 932 5332
Fax: 0115 932 6096
Web site: www.felixbuxandcoach.co.uk
Ops Man: Ian Middup
Fleet: 13 - 8 single-deck bus, 3 single-deck coach, 2 midibus.
Chassis: 2 Iveco. 1 Leyland. 2 Optare. 3 Scania. 2 VDL. 3 Volvo.
Bodies: 2 Alexander Dennis. 1 Leyland. 2 Optare. 5 Plaxton. 3 Wright.
Ops incl: local bus services, school contracts, excursions & tours, private hire.
Livery: Red/White
Ticket system: Wayfarer TGX150

FLIGHTS HALLMARK
See West Midlands

GLOVERS COACHES LTD
MOOR FARM ROAD EAST, ASHBOURNE DE6 1HD
Tel/Fax: 01335 300043
E-mail: gloverscoaches@btconnect.com
Web site: www.gloverscoaches.com
Dirs: Stephen Mason, Heather Mason
Fleet: single-deck bus, single-deck coach, midicoach.
Chassis: Alexander Dennis. Leyland. Volvo.
Bodies: Alexander Dennis. Jonkheere. Plaxton.
Ops incl: local bus services, school contracts, excursions & tours, private hire, continental tours.
Livery: Blue/Cream.
Ticket System: Wayfarer

GOLDEN GREEN LUXURY TRAVEL
GOLDEN GREEN GARAGE, LONGNOR SK17 0QP
Tel: 01298 83583.
Fax: 01298 83584
Props: John and Gill Worth
Fleet: 5 midicoach.
Chassis: 5 Mercedes.
Ops incl: school contracts, excursions & tours, private hire.

HARPUR'S COACHES
WINCANTON CLOSE, DERBY
DE24 8NB
Tel: 01332 757677
Fax: 01332 757259
E-mail: harpurscoaches@tiscali.co.uk
Web site: www.harpurscoaches.co.uk
Man Dir: Nick Harpur
Fleet: 27 - 10 double-deck bus, 4 single-deck bus, 13 coach.
Chassis: 1 AEC. 2 Leyland. 9 MCW. 11 Volvo.
Bodies: 7 MCW. 1 Park Royal. 15 Plaxton.
Ops incl: school contracts, excursions & tours, private hire.
Livery: Cream/Brown

HARRISON'S TRAVEL
154 SOMERCOTES HILL,
SOMERCOTES, ALFRETON DE55 4HU
Tel: 01773 833337

G & J HOLMES (COACHES) LTD
124A MARKET STREET, CLAY CROSS S45 9LY
Tel/Fax: 01246 863232.
Ops incl: local bus services

HENRY HULLEY & SONS LTD
DERWENT GARAGE, BASLOW
DE45 1RP
Tel: 01246 582246
Fax: 01246 583161
E-mail: www.hulleys-of-baslow.co.uk
Web site: info@hulleys-of-baslow.co.uk
Fleetname: Hulleys of Baslow
Dirs: P Eades, R W Eades
Fleet: 19 - 13 single-deck bus, 3 single-deck coach, 2 midibus, 1 minibus.
Chassis: 1 DAF. 8 Dennis. 5 MAN. 1 Mercedes. 3 Optare. 1 Volvo.
Bodies: 2 Marshall/MCV. 8 Optare. 8 Plaxton. 1 Wright.
Ops incl: local bus services, school contracts, private hire.
Livery: Buses: Cream/Blue; Coaches: White/Blue
Ticket System: Wayfarer 3

JOHNSON'S TOURS
See Nottinghamshire

KINCHBUS LTD
MANSFIELD ROAD, HEANOR DE75 7BG
Tel: 01775 536309
Web site: www.kinchbus.co.uk
Fleet: 35 - 8 double-deck bus, 9 single-deck bus, 18 minibus.
Chassis: 2 Dennis. 8 Leyland. 11 Mercedes. 11 Optare. 3 Volvo.
Ops incl: local bus services
Livery: Blue/Yellow
Ticket System: Wayfarer
Part of the Wellglade Group

LEANDER TRAVEL
7 WORDSWORTH AVENUE,
SWADLINCOTE DE11 0DZ
Tel/fax: 01283 213780
E-mail: pat@leandercoaches.co.uk
Web site: www.leandercoaches.co.uk
Fleetname: Leander Coaches
Prop: M. W. Bugden
Fleet: 4 coach, 1 minicoach.
Chassis: 3 DAF. 1 LDV. 1 Volvo.
Ops incl: excursions & tours, private hire, school contracts, continental tours.

DERBYSHIRE

103

LITTLE TRANSPORT LTD

HALLAM FIELDS ROAD, ILKESTON DE7 4AZ
Tel: 0115 932 8581
Fax: 0115 932 5163
Recovery: 07919 020835
E-mail: enqiries@littlestravel.co.uk
Web site: www.littlestravel.co.uk
Fleetname: Little's Travel

Dirs: Steve Wells, Paul Wright
Fleet: 20 - 11 double-deck bus, 9 coach
Chassis: 3 Bova. 4 DAF. 5 Leyland. 2 Leyland National. 1 MCW. 4 Scania. 1 Volvo.
Bodies: 3 Bova. 5 East Lancs. 1 Ikarus. 6 Leyland. 2 Leyland National. 3 Van Hool.
Ops incl: excursions & tours, private hire, school contracts, local bus services, continental tours.
Livery: White
Ticket system: Almex

MACPHERSON COACHES LTD

THE GARAGE, HILL STREET, DONISTHORPE DE12 7PL
Tel: 01530 270226
Fax: 01530 273669
E-mail: travel@macphersoncoaches.co.uk
Web site: www.macphersoncoaches.co.uk
Man Dir: D MacPherson. **Sales Man**: P. Krawse.**Fleet Eng**: C.Underwood
Fleet: 16 - 1 single-deck bus, 10 single-deck coach, 3 midibus, 2 midicoach,
Chassis: 1 Dennis. 3 Mercedes-Benz.1 Optare. 8 Setra. 1 Volvo
Bodies: 3 Mercedes-Benz. 1 Optare. 3 Plaxton. 8 Setra. 1 other.
Ops incl: local bus services, school contracts, excursions & tours, private hire, continental tours.
Livery: Cream/Red
Ticket System: Wayfarer.

MYKANN COACH HIRE

29 WARREN DRIVE, LINTON, SWADLINCOTE DE12 6QP
Tel: 01283 762673
E-mail: mykanncoachhire@hotmail.com
Fleet: 2 coach
Chassis/bodies: 1 MAN. 1 Setra.
Bodies: 1 Jonckheere. 1 Setra.
Ops incl: private hire, school contracts.
Livery: Multi

NOTTS & DERBY TRACTION CO LTD
MANSFIELD ROAD, HEANOR DE75 7BG
Fleet: 49 - 5 double-deck bus, 32 single-deck bus, 12 minibus. **Chassis**: 18 Dennis. 5 Leyland. 12 Mercedes. 3 Optare. 11 Volvo. **Livery**: Blue/Green**Ticket System**: Almex (Part of the Wellglade Group)

PROTOURS LTD

UNIT 2, RYDER CLOSE, SWADLINCOTE DE11 9EU
Tel: 01283 217012
Fax: 01283 550685.
E-mail: kramsdall@protours.co.uk
Web Site: www.protours.co.uk
Dept Man: Kevin Ramsdal.
Fleet: 18 - 17 single-deck coach, 1 midicoach.
Chassis: 1 BMC, 1 Scania, 16 Volvo.
Bodies: 10 Berkhof. 1 BMC. 1 Irzar. 1 Plaxton. 5 Van Hool.
Ops incl: excursions & tours, private hire, express, continental tours, school contracts
Livery: Blue & White

RINGWOOD LUXURY COACHES

SPEEDWELL GARAGE, CROMPTON ROAD, SPEEDWELL INDUSTRIAL ESTATE, STAVELEY S43 3PG
Tel/Fax: 01246 476366
Prop: David T Brockbank
Fleet: 6 - 2 midicoach, 4 minicoach
Chassis: 5 Mercedes
Bodies: 1 Caetano. 4 Mercedes. 1 Sitcar
Ops incl: school contracts, private hire

SLACKS TRAVEL
(K V & G L SLACK LTD)

THE TRAVEL CENTRE, LUMSDALE, MATLOCK DE4 5LB
Tel: 01629 582826
Fax: 01629 580519
E-mail: enquiries@slackscoaches.co.uk
Web site: www.slackscoaches.co.uk
Man Dir: G L Slack **Ch Eng**: R M Slack
Co Sec: D R Slack **Tran Man**: J Gough
Fleet: 19 - 15 coach, 2 midicoach, 2 minibus.
Chassis: 5 DAF. 3 Dennis. 2 Ford. 2 Ford Transit. 3 Iveco. 2 Mercedes. 1 Neoplan. 1 Scania. 1 Volvo.
Bodies: 1 Autobus. 3 Beulas. 1 Jonckheere. 1 Mercedes. 1 Neoplan. 5 Plaxton. 5 Van Hool.
Ops incl: excursions & tours, private hire, continental tours, school contracts

STAGECOACH EAST MIDLANDS

NEW STREET, CHESTERFIELD S40 2LQ
Tel: 01246 222018
Fax: 01246 232205
Web site: www.stagecoachbus.com
Fleetname: Stagecoach East Midlands
Man Dir: Paul Lynch **Ops Dir**: Richard Kay **Eng Dir**: John Taylor **Com Dir**: John Pope **Service Quality Man**: John Curtis
Fleet: 502 - 193 double-deck bus, 76 single-deck bus, 33 single-deck coach, 126 midibus, 3 articulated coach, 71 minibus.
Chassis: 148 Dennis, 1 Ford, 117 Leyland, 71 Mercedes, 16 Optare, 2 Scania, 147 Volvo.
Bodies: 324 Alexander, 2 Duple, 15 ECW, 33 East Lancs, 13 Jonckheere, 33 Northern Counties, 17 Optare, 2 Park Royal, 58 Plaxton, 4 Van Hool, 1 Wadham Stringer.
Ops incl: local bus services, school contracts, private hire, express.
Livery: Stagecoach new.
Ticket System: ERG.

TM TRAVEL LTD
See South Yorkshire

TRENT BARTON

MANSFIELD ROAD, HEANOR DE75 7BG
Tel: 01773 712265
Tel: 01773 536333
E-mail: enquiries@trentbarton.co.uk
Web site: www.trentbarton.co.uk
Chmn/Man Dir: B R King **Com Dir**: R F Morgan **Fin Dir**: G Sutton
Fleet: 303 - 287 single-deck bus, 16 coach.
Chassis: 36 Dennis. 132 Optare. 100 Scania. 35 Volvo.
Bodies: 8 Irizar. 132 Optare. 44 Plaxton. 119 Wright.
Ops incl: local bus services.
Livery: Red/Brands

WARRINGTON COACHES LTD

ILAM MOOR LANE, ILAM, ASHBOURNE DE6 2AZ
Tel: 01335 350204
Fax: 01335 350204
E-mail: info@warringtoncoaches.co.uk
Web site: www.warringtoncoaches.co.uk
Dirs: K Warrington, M A Boydon, L Boyton
Fleet: 8 - 3 single-deck coaches, 3 mincoach, 2 midicoach
Chassis: 1 BMC. 3 Dennis. 3 LDV. 1 Mercedes.
Bodies: 1 BMC. 1 Marcopolo. 3 Plaxton. 3 other.
Ops incl: local bus services, school contracts, excursons & tours, private hire
Livery: White with Red/Gold/Black

P J WILDE & D A WARD

T/A ALBERT WILDE COACHES, 121 PARKSIDE, HEAGE, BELPER DE56 2AG
Tel/fax: 01773 856655
Dirs: Philip J Wilde, David Ward
Fleet: 5 coach.
Chassis: 4 DAF. 1 Leyland.
Ops incl: excursions & tours, school contracts.

WOODWARD'S COACHES LTD

100 HIGH STREET EAST, GLOSSOP SK13 8QF
See Courtesy Coaches, Greater Manchester

YESTERYEAR MOTOR SERVICES

10 LADY GATE, DISEWORTH, DERBY DE74 2QF
Tel/fax: 01332 810774
E-mail: yesteryear10@hotmail.com
Prop: D. J. Moores
Fleet: 2 - 1 single-deck bus, 1 coach.
Chassis: Bedford, Leyland.
Bodies: Duple, ECW.
Ops incl: private hire.
Livery: Green/Cream.
Ticket System: Bell Punch.

DEVON

A B COACHES LTD
WILLS ROAD, TOTNES INDUSTRIAL ESTATE, TOTNES TQ9 5XN
Tel: 01803 864161
Fax: 01803 864008
E-mail: abcoaches@btconnect.com
Web site: www.abcoaches.co.uk
Dirs: B T Smith, L Smith, M Chalk, R Chalk
Fleet: 15 - 1 single-deck bus, 12 single-deck coaches, 1 midicoach.
Ops incl: school contracts, excursions & tours, private hire.
Livery: Cream/Red

AXE VALLEY MINI TRAVEL
BUS DEPOT, 26 HARBOUR ROAD, SEATON EX12 2NA
Tel/Fax: 01297 625959
Fleetname: AVMT
Prop: Mrs F. M. Searle **Traf Man**: J. R. Paddon.
Fleet: 9 - 5 double-deck bus, 4 midibus.
Chassis: 1 Dodge. 2 Iveco. 1 Leyland. 4 MCW. 1 Optare.
Bodies: 1 Leyland. 1 Reeve Burgess. 4 MCW. 2 Dormobile. 1 Optare.
Ops incl: local bus services.
Livery: Maroon/White.
Ticket System: Wayfarer.

AYREVILLE COACHES
202 NORTH PROSPECT ROAD, PLYMOUTH PL2 2PR
Tel: 01752 605450.
Fax: 01752 219366.
E-mail: ayrevillecoaches@tinyonline.co.uk
Owner: M. J. Buley.
Fleet: 6 - 3 midicoach, 3 minibus.
Chassis: 1 Ford, 1 Iveco, 4 Mercedes.
Bodies: 2 Carlyle, 1 Reeve Burgess, 1 Devon Conversion, 2 Pilcher Green.
Ops incl: private hire, school contracts.
Livery: White.

BLAKES COACHES LTD
EAST ANSTEY, TIVERTON EX16 9JJ
Tel: 01398 341160
Fax: 01398 341594
Recovery: 01398 341160
E-mail: info@blakescoaches.co.uk
Web: www.blakescoaches.co.uk
Man Dir: David Blake **Dir**: Janet Blake
Fleet: 9 - 7 single-deck coach, 2 midicoach
Chassis: 1 Mercedes-Benz. 6 Scania. 1 Toyota. 1 Volvo.
Bodies: 1 Cantaeno. 2 Irizar. 5 Van Hool. 1 Other
Ops incl: school contracts, excursions & tours, private hire, continental tours
Livery: Silver/Blue/Green

CARMEL COACHES
STATION ROAD, NORTHLEW, OKEHAMPTON EX20 3BN
Tel: 01409 221237
Fax: 01409 221226
E-mail: carmelcoaches@hotmail.com
Web: www.carmelcoaches.co.uk
Dirs: Tony Hazell
Fleet: 26 - 7 single-deck bus, 18 single-deck coach, 1 midicoach.
Chassis: 3 Alexander Dennis. 8 Bova. 1 DAF. 8 Mercedes. 1 Optare. 5 Scania. 1 Toyota. 1 Albion.
Bodies: 8 Bova. 1 Caetano. 1 Duple. 3 Irizar. 1 Marshall/MCV. 1 Optare. 4 Plaxton. 2 Van Hool. 1 other.
Ops incl: local bus services, school contracts, excursions & tours, private hire
Livery: White
Ticket System: Almex

COUNTRY BUS
KING CHARLES BUSINESS PARK, OLD NEWTON ROAD, HEATHFIELD, NEWTON ABBOT TQ12 6UT
Tel: 01626 833664
Fax: 01626 835648
Web site: www.countrybusdevon.co.uk
Man Dir: Ms A Ellison
Fleet: 18 minibus.
Chassis: 14 Ford Transit. 4 Iveco.
Ops incl: local bus services, school contracts, private hire.
Livery: Orange/White.
Ticket System: Setright.

DAISH'S TRAVEL
PARKHILL ROAD, TORQUAY TQ1 2DY
Tel: 0870 902 1412
Web site: www.daishs.com
Fleet: 9 coach
Ops incl: excursions & tours, private hire, continental tours

DARTLINE COACHES
LANGDONS BUSINESS PARK, CLYST ST MARY, EXETER EX5 1AF
Tel: 01392 872900
Fax: 01392 872909
E-mail: info@dartline-coaches.co.uk
Web site: www.dartline-coaches.co.uk
Dir: David Dart, Dave Hounslow. **Ops**: Kevin Busby
Fleet: 34 - 6 single-deck bus, 19 single-deck coach, 3 midicoach, 6 minibus
Chassis: 3 Bova. 5 Dennis. 6 Optare. 1 Scania. 10 Volvo.
Bodies: 1 Berkhof. 3 Bova. 1 Caetano. 1 Irizar. 14 Plaxton. 1 Sunsundegui. 1 Van Hool
Ops incl: local bus services, school contracts, excursions & tours, private hire.
Livery: White/Green
Ticket System: Almex.

DART PLEASURE CRAFT LTD
5 LOWER STREET, DARTMOUTH TQ6 9AJ
Tel/FAX: 01803 834488
E-mail: sales@riverlink.co.uk
Web site: www.riverlink.co.uk
Fleet: 7 - 4 double-deck bus, 2 single-deck bus, 1 open-top
Ops incl: local bus services, private hire.
Livery: Blue/White
Ticket System: Almex.

DAWLISH COACHES LTD
SHUTTERTON INDUSTRIAL ESTATE, DAWLISH EX7 0NH
Tel: 01626 862525
Fax: 01626 867167
Web site: www.dawlishcoaches.com
Dir: John Weaver
Fleet: 34 - 28 coach, 2 midibus, 4 midicoach.
Chassis: 13 Bova. 2 Iveco. 5 Mercedes. 10 Volvo. 2 other.
Bodies: 2 Beulas. 2 Berkhof. 13 Bova. 1 Caetano. 2 Duple. 1 Plaxton. 9 Van Hool.
Ops incl: local bus services, school contracts, private hire.
Livery: Red/Blue/White
Ticket System: Setright

DOWN MOTORS & OTTER COACHES
1 MILL STREET, OTTERY ST MARY EX11 1AB
Tel: 01404 812002
Tel: 01404 811128
Ptnrs: W M Down, A G Down, C P Down
Fleet: 10 - 9 single-deck coach, 1 midicoach.
Chassis: 2 Bedford. 1 Bova. 4 Dennis. 1 Iveco. 1 MAN. 1 Toyota.
Bodies: 1 Beulas. 1 Bova. 4 Caetano. 2 Duple. 2 Plaxton.
Ops incl: school contracts, excursions & tours, private hire.
Livery: Ivory/red

C.J. DOWN
THE GARAGE, MARY TAVY, TAVISTOCK PL19 9PA
Tel: 01822 810242
Tel: 01822 810242
E-mail: downscoaches@aol.com
Proprietors: Mr & Mrs. C.J Down. **Ops Man**: W.J.Wakem. **Chief Eng**: W.J.Lashbrook
Fleet: 15 - 15 single-deck coach
Chassis: 15 Volvo.
Bodies: 1 Duple. 8 Jockheere. 6 Plaxton.
Ops incl: school contracts, excursions & tours, private hire.
Livery: Cream

105

AST TEIGNBRIDGE COMMUNITY TRANSPORT
THE MANOR HOUSE, OLD TOWN STREET, DAWLISH EX7 9AP
Tel: 01626 888890
Fax: 01626 889253
E-mail: etcta@lineone.net
Man: Jenny Connor **Coordinator**: Jan Green
Fleet: 3 minibus, 3 car.
Chassis: 1 Ford. 1 Ford Transit. 1 LDV. 1 Renault. 1 Fiat. 1 Volkswagen
Ops incl: school contracts, excursions and tours, private hire.

EASTWARD COACHES
1 BARLANDS WAY, DOLTON, WINKLEIGH EX19 8QB
Tel: 01805 804659
Fax: 01805 804659
E-mail: eastwardcoaches@btopenworld.com
Props: Karen Wonnacott, Nick Woolacott
Tran Man: Mike Yedermann
Fleet: 6 - 5 coach, 1 minibus.
Chassis: 1 AEC. 2 Bedford. 1 DAF. 1 Ford. 1 Freight Rover.
Bodies: 1 Carlyle. 4 Plaxton. 1 Van Hool.
Ops incl: school contracts, excursions & tours, private hire.
Livery: White with Green/Red stripes

FILERS TRAVEL LTD
SLADE LODGE, SLADE ROAD, ILFRACOMBE EX34 8LB
Tel: 01271 863819
Fax: 01271 867281
E-mail: info@filers.co.uk
Web site: www.filers.co.uk
Dirs: Roy Filer
Fleet: 20 - 10 single-deck coach, 7 midibus, 1 midicoach, 2 minibus.
Chassis: 2 Bova. 1 LDV. 3 MAN. 1 Marshall. 4 Mercedes. 1 Scania. 1 Volkswagen. 4 Volvo.
Bodies: 2 Plaxton.
Ops incl: local bus services, excursions & tours, private hire, school contracts, continental tours.
Livery: White/Blue/Yellow
Ticket system: Almex

FIRST DEVON & CORNWALL LTD
THE RIDE, CHELSON MEADOW, PLYMOUTH PL9 7JT
Tel: 01752 495150
E-mail: firstdevonandcornwall@firstgroup.com
Web site: www.firstgroup.com
Fleetname: First
Man Dir: Marc Reddy **Fin Dir**: Chris Hayter **Eng Dir**: Phil Pannell **Comm Dir**: Simon Newport **Gen Man (Devon)**: Steve Grigg **Gen Man (Cornwall)**: Chris Casson
Fleet: 322 - double-deck bus, single-deck bus, coach, open-top bus, midibus,

minibus.
Chassis: 4 Bristol. 157 Dennis. 28 Leyland. 29 Mercedes. 19 Optare. 85 Volvo.
Bodies: 56 Alexander. 20 ECW. 18 East Lancs. 6 Marshall. 4 Northern Counties. 21 Optare. 1 Park Royal. 142 Plaxton. 9 Transbus. 5 Van Hool. 23 Wright. 17 other.
Ops incl: local bus services, school contracts, private hire, express.
Livery: First Group
Ticket System: Almex Optima.

GARRETT COACHES LTD
3 STOKES CLOSE, NEWTON ABBOT TQ12 3YY
Tel: 01626 366580
Fax: 01626 353733
E-mail: garrettcoach@tesco.net
Dir: P Garrett.
Fleet: 3 - 2 coach, 1 minibus.
Chassis/Bodies: 2 Bova. 1 Mercedes.
Ops incl: private hire, school contracts.
Livery: White

GOLD STAR COACHES
18 WOODVILLE ROAD, TORQUAY TQ1 1LP
Tel/Fax: 01803 200080
Prop: E Stirk
Fleet: 9 minicoach
Chassis: 2 Ford Transit. 5 LDV. 2 Mercedes.
Ops incl: private hire, school contracts
Livery: Green/Cream

GREY CARS OF TORBAY
6/7 DANEHEATH BUSINESS PARK, HEATHFIELD, NEWTON ABBOTT TQ12 6TL
Tel: 01626 833038
Fax: 01626 835920
E-mail: office@greycars.com
Web site: www.greycars.com
Man Dir: Duncan Millman, **Dir**: Bruce Millman, **Ops Manager**: Colin Holt, **Workshop Man**: Mark Hacking, **Co Sec**: Diane Millman
Fleet: 13 - 12 single-deck coach, 1 Minicoach
Chassis: 1 Dennis. 1 Toyota. 11 Volvo
Bodies: 3 Berkhof. 1 Caetano. 5 Plaxton. 4 Van Hool
Ops incl: school contracts, excursions & tours. private hire.
Livery: Grey & yellow/turqoise

GUSCOTT'S COACHES LTD
THE GARAGE, CROFT GATE, HALWILL EX21 5TL
Tel: 01409 221661
Fax: 01409 221435
Dirs: T Guscott, C D Guscott.
Fleet: 5 - 4 coach, 1 double-deck coach.
Chassis: 1 DAF. 1 Neoplan. 3 Volvo.
Bodies: 1 Duple. 1 Neoplan. 2 Plaxton.
Ops incl: local bus services, school contracts, private hire.
Livery: Cream/Blue/Red

HEARDS COACHES
FORE STREET, HARTLAND, BIDEFORD EX39 6BD
Tel: 01237 441233
Fax: 01237 441789
E-mail: info@heardscoaches.co.uk
Web Site: www.heardscoaches.co.uk
Fleet name: Heards Coaches
Dirs: G Heard, B Heard.
Fleet: 14 coach
Chassis: 2 Dennis. 1 MAN. 2 Scania. 9 Volvo.
Bodies: 2 Berkhof. 1 Caetano. 2 Irizar. 1 Noge. 2 Plaxton. 6 Van Hool.
Ops incl: school contracts, private hire.

HEMMINGS COACHES LTD
POWLERS PIECE GARAGE, PUTFORD, HOLSWORTHY EX22 7XW
Tel: 01237 451282
Fax: 01237 451920
E-mail: hemmingscoaches@aol.com
Dirs: Ken & Linda Hemmings
Fleet: 6 - 6 single-deck coach
Chassis: 1 Bova. 3 Mercedes. 1 Neoplan. 1 Scania.
Bodies: 1 Berkhof. 1 Bova. 3 Mercedes. 1 Neoplan..
Ops incl: excursions & tours, private hire, continental tours, school contracts
Livery: Ruby

HILLS SERVICES LTD
THE GARAGE, STIBB CROSS, LANGTREE, TORRINGTON EX38 8LH
Tel: 01805 601203
Fax: 01805 601476
Recovery: 01805 601102
E-mail: hills.servicesltd@btinternet.com
Dirs: David J Hearn, Mrs M E Hearn
Fleet: 27 - 14 coach, 3 midibus, 10 minibus.
Chassis: 4 DAF. 2 Ford Transit. 10 LDV. 3 Mercedes. 9 Volvo.
Bodies: 1 Bova. 5 Jonckheere. 1 Mellor. 2 Plaxton. 2 Reeve Burgess. 6 Van Hool.
Ops incl: excursions & tours, private hire, school contracts.

HOOKWAYS CLASSIC TOURS
16 WINNER STREET, PAIGNTON TQ3 3BJ
Tel: 01803 527959
Fax: 01803 522069
Tel: 07850 038707
E-mail: linn@hookways.com
Web site: www.hookways.com
Man Dir: Alistair Gray **Dirs**: Kym Hookway, Sue Hookway, Jason Hookway, Martin Hookway **(Eng)**, Julie Hookway **(Sec)**
Fleet: See Hookways Pleasureways
Ops incl: school contracts, excursions & tours, private hire, express, continental tours.
Livery: Yellow

DEVON

106

HOOKWAYS GREENSLADES
PEEK HOUSE, PINHOE TRADING ESTATE, VENNY BRIDGE, EXETER EX4 8JN
Tel: 01392 469210
Fax: 01392 466036
Recovery: 07850 038707
E-mail: alistair@hookways.com
Web site: www.hookways.com
Man Dir: Alistair Gray **Dirs**: Kym Hookway, Sue Hookway, Jason Hookway, Martin Hookway **(Eng)**, Julie Hookway **(Sec)**
Fleet: 45 - 40 coach, 2 midicoach, 1 minibus, 2 minicoach,
Chassis: 1 Leyland. 5 Mercedes. 1 Scania. 2 VW. 36 Volvo
Bodies: 1 Irizar. 12 Jonckheere. 17 Plaxton. 1 Wright 4 Berkhof, 6 Van Hool, 4 other.
Ops incl: local bus services, school contracts, excursions & tours, private hire, express, continental tours.
Livery: Yellow
Ticket System: Wayfarer

HOOKWAYS PLEASUREWAYS COACHES
THE GARAGE, MEETH EX20 3EP
Tel: 01837 810257
Fax: 01837 810066.
Recovery: 07850 038707
E-mail: lesley@hookways.com
Web site: www.hookways.com
Man Dir: Alistair Gray **Dirs**: Kym Hookway, Sue Hookway, Jason Hookway, Martin Hookway **(Eng)**, Julie Hookway **(Sec)**
Fleet: 45 - 40 coach, 2 midicoach, 1 minibus, 2 minicoach,
Chassis: 1 Leyland. 5 Mercedes. 1 Scania. 2 VW. 36 Volvo
Bodies: 1 Irizar. 12 Jonckheere. 17 Plaxton. 1 Wright 4 Berkhof, 6 Van Hool, 4 other.
Ops incl: school contracts, excursions & tours, private hire, express, continental tours.
Livery: Yellow

IVYBRIDGE & DISTRICT COMMUNITY TRANSPORT
DOURO COURT, BROOK ROAD, IVYBRIDGE PL21 0LS.
Tel: 01752 690444.
Fleetname: Ivybridge Ring & Ride.
Co-ordinator: Mrs S. Jenkins.
Chmn: I. Martin.
Fleet: 1 minibus. **Chassis/Body**: LDV.
Ops incl: local bus services, private hire.

KINGDOM'S TOURS LTD
WESTFIELD GARAGE, EXETER ROAD, TIVERTON EX16 5NZ
Tel: 01884 252373
Fax: 01884 252 646
Web site: www.kingdoms-tours.co.uk
Dirs: Ronald Kingdom, Stephen Kingdom, Russell Kingdom
Fleet: 24 - 12 coach, 4 midicoach, 5 minibus, 3 minicoach.
Chassis: 1 Ford. 3 Iveco. 1 MAN. 10 Mercedes. 6 Scania. 3 Volvo.
Bodies: 1 Beulas. 6 Irizar. 3 Mellor. 7 Mercedes. 1 Neoplan. 3 Van Hool. 3 other.
Ops incl: school contracts, excursions & tours, private hire, continental tours.

MID DEVON COACHES
STATION ROAD, BOW, CREDITON EX17 6JD
Tel/Fax: 01363 82200
E-mail: enquiries@middevoncoaches.co.uk
Web site: www.middevoncoaches.co.uk
Prop: Mrs L. A. Hamilton
Fleet: 22 - 18 single-deck coach, 2 minicoach, 2 minibus.
Chassis: 2 DAF. 3 Ford. 3 Ford Transit. 5 Leyland. 4 Scania. 2 Toyota. 2 Volvo.
Bodies: 2 Bova.. 2 Caetano. 1 Irizar. 2 Jonckheere. 10 Plaxton.
Ops incl: school contracts, excursions & tours, private hire, continental tours.
Livery: Green/Cream.

MOOR TO SEA
1 SOPHIA WAY, TOTNES ROAD, NEWTON ABBOT TQ12 1YW.
Tel/Fax: 01626 362002.
E-mail: moortosea@eurobell.co.uk
Owner/Operator: Robert Clifford.
Fleet: 1 midicoach.
Chassis: Volvo. **Body**: Plaxton.
Ops incl: private hire. **Livery**: White.

PARAMOUNT MINI-COACHES
6 VENN CRESCENT, HARTLEY, PLYMOUTH PL3 5PJ.
Tel: 01752 767255
Fax: 01752 767255
Prop: B. M. Couch
Fleet: 5 - 1 midicoach, 2 minibus, 2 minicoach.
Chassis: 2 Ford Transit. 1 Leyland. 2 Mercedes.
Ops incl: excursions & tours, private hire, school contracts.
Touring Man: Brian Madge
Associated companies: Peninsula Drivers (see A-Z Driver Hire) Eastward Coaches (see above)

PLYMOUTH CITYBUS LTD
1 MILEHOUSE ROAD, PLYMOUTH PL3 4AA
Tel: 01752 662271
Fax: 01752 567209
E-mail: md@plymouthbus.co.uk
Man Dir/Co Sec: Mr Jackford **Ops Dir**: Mr Piggott **Fin Controller**: Mr Perring
Fleet: 169 - 19 double-deck bus, 100 single-deck bus, 12 coach, 1 open-top bus, 23 midibus, 15 minibus.
Chassis: 1 Leyland. 30 Mercedes.
Bodies: 100 Alexander. 30 Mercedes. 25 Plaxton.
Ops incl: local bus services, excursions & tours, private hire. continental tours, school contracts.
Livery: Red/White
Ticket system: Wayfarer TGX

POWELLS COACHES
2 BARRIS, LAPFORD, CREDITON EX17 6PT
Tel/Fax: 01363 83468
Prop: James P Powell, Mrs D.M.Powell, W R Powell
Fleet: 5 single-deck coach
Chassis: 1 DAF. 1 Leyland. 1 Mercedes. 2 Volvo.
Bodies: 1 Jonckheere. 1 Mercedes. 1 Plaxton. 2 Van Hool.
Ops incl: school contracts, excursions & tours, private hire.

RADMORES TRAVEL
4 WOODFORD CRESCENT, PLYMPTON PL7 4QY
Tel/Fax: 01752 335391
Owner: John Williams **Man**: Sarah Hale
Fleetname: Radmores Coaches
Fleet: 5 - 1 double-deck bus, 2 midibus, 2 midicoach.
Chassis: 1 DAF. 1 Ford Transit. 1 Iveco. 1 Toyota.
Bodies: 1 Caetano. 1 Mellor. 1 Reeve Burgess.
Ops incl: local bus services, school contracts, excursions & tours, private hire.
Livery: Red/Gold

RAYS COACHES
88 KINGS TAMERTON ROAD, ST BUDEAUX PL5 2BW
Tel: 01752 369000

REDWOODS TRAVEL
UNIT 3, STATION ROAD, HEMYOCK, CULLOMPTON EX15 3SE
Tel: 01823 680288
Fax: 01823 681096
E-mail: info@redwoodstravel.com
Web site: www.redwoodstravel.com
Dir: Paul Redwood **Comp Sec**: Jacquie Redwood **Ch Eng**: Garry Morrisey
Fleet: 22 - 18 single-deck coach, 3 minibus, 1 midicoach.
Chassis: 3 LDV. 5 Scania. 10 Volvo.
Bodies: 3 Noge. 9 Plaxton. 1 Van Hool.
Ops incl: local bus services, school contracts, excursions & tours, private hire, continental tours
Livery: White/Red/Turquoise

SEWARD COACHES
GLENDALE, DALWOOD, AXMINSTER EX13 7EJ
Tel/Fax: 01404 881343.
Proprietor: Richard Seward **Joint Ptnr**: Ivy Seward **Office Manager**: Catherine Seward **Chief Mech**: Keith Mitchell
Fleet: 20 - 3 single-deck bus, 11 single-deckbcoach, 3 midicoach, 3 minicoach
Chassis: 2 Bova. 1 BMC. 2 DAF. 3 Dennis. 1 Irisbus. 3 Leyland. 1 Toyota. 2 MAN. 3 Mercedes. 1 Renault. 1 Temsa.
Bodies: 1 Berkhof. 2 Bova. 3 Caetano. 1 Hispano. 2 Leyland.1 Marcopolo. 1 Optare. 2 Plaxton. 1 BMC. 1 Wadham Stringer. 5 Other
Ops incl: local bus services, school contracts, private hire.
Livery: Cream/Orange/Green

STAGECOACH SOUTH WEST
BELGRAVE ROAD, EXETER EX1 2LB d
Tel: 01392 439439
Tel: 01392 889727
Web site: www.stagecoachbus.com
Man Dir: ms m Hargreaves **Eng Dir**: M Horide **Ops Dir**: R Stevens **Ops Man (Exeter)**: B George **Ops Man (Torbay)**: R MaAllister **Eng Man (Exeter)**: A Noel **Eng Man (Torbay)**: M Rundle **Customer Ser Man**: M Whittle **Resource Man**: G Bailey
Fleet: 304 - 108 double-deck bus, 13 single-deck bus, 6 coach, 3 open-top bus, 115 midibus, 59 minibus.
Chassis: 159 Dennis/Transbus. 14 Leyland. 22 Mercedes. 37 Optare. 16 Scania. 56 Volvo.
Bodies: 239 Alexander. 1 ECW. 3 Marshall. 11 Northern Counties. 37 Optare. 6 Plaxton. 2 Roe. 5 Wright.
Ops incl: local bus services, school contracts
Livery: Stagecoach UK bus livery - Blue/Red/Orange/White
Ticket System: Wayfarer 3.

STREETS COACHWAYS LTD
THE OLD AERODROME, CHIVENOR, BARNSTAPLE EX31 4AY
Tel: 01271 815069
Fax: 01271 817233
E-mail: sandra@streetscoachways.co.uk
Dirs: M Street. **Fleet Eng**: S.M. Street.
Company Sec: S. Popham
Fleet: 14 - 7 single-deck coach, 7 minibus.
Chassis: 1 Bova. 1 Damlier. 1 DAF. 2 Dennis. 7 LDV. 1 MAN. 2 Mercedes-Benz. 1 Neoplan.
Bodies: 1 Berkof. 1 Bova. 1Neoplan. 1 Wadham Stringer
Ops incl: private hire, school contracts.

TALLY HO! COACHES LTD
STATION YARD INDUSTRIAL ESTATE, KINGSBRIDGE TQ7 1ES
Tel: 01548 853081
Fax: 01548 853602
E-mail: info@tallyhocoaches.com
Web site: www.tallyhocoaches.com
Man Dir: Don McIntosh
Dir: Richard Pullan
Fleet: approx. 50
Chassis: 5 Alexander Dennis. 1 DAF. 2 Dennis. 3 Ford Transit. 1 LDV. 12 Leyland. 13 Mercedes. 11 Renault. 4 Scania. 1 Toyota. 5 Volvo.

Bodies: 8 Alexander dennis. 1 Caetano. 3 Duple. 3 East Lancs. 4 Irizar. 3 Marshall. 1 Mercedes. 2 Optare. 10 Plaxton. 1 Reeve Burgess. 4 Van Hool. 4 Wright. 1 Wadham Stringer. 1 other.
Ops incl: local bus services, school contracts, excursions & tours, private hire. continental tours
Livery: Blue/White
Ticket system: Almex Optima

TAVISTOCK COMMUNITY TRANSPORT
See Cornwall

TAW & TORRIDGE COACHES LTD
GRANGE LANE, MERTON, OKEHAMPTON EX20 3ED
Tel: 01805 603400
Fax: 01805 603559
Recovery: 01805 603400
E-mail: enquiries@tawandtorridge.co.uk
Web site: www.tawandtorridge.co.uk
Man Dir: Tony Hunt **Dir/Ops Man**: Mark Hunt **Dir/Co Sec**: Linda Hunt **Dir**: Tracey Laughton **Fleet Eng/Dir**: Chris Laughton
Fleet: 39 - 30 single-deck coach, 7 minibus, 2 midicoach
Chassis: 6 Dennis. 1 Ford Transit. 4 LDV. 2 Mercedes-Benz. 2 Toyota. 1 Van Hool. 23 Volvo.
Bodies: 1 Autobus. 1 Berkhof. 2 Caetano. 9 Jonckheere. 12 Plaxton. 3 Van Hool. 5 Wadham Stringer. 6 Other.
Ops incl: school contracts, excursions & tours, private hire, continental tours.
Livery: Miami Blue/Silver

TOTNES & DARTMOUTH RING & RIDE
C/O RED CROSS CENTRE, BABBAGE ROAD, TOTNES TQ9 5JA.
Tel: 01803 867878.
Co-ordinator: L. Clark.
Fleet: 3 minibus.
Chassis: 2 Ford Transit. 1 Peugeot.
Ops incl: local bus services, school contracts, excursions & tours, private hire.

TOWN & COUNTRY COACHES
UNIT 8B, SILVERLANDS ROAD, DECOY INDUSTRIAL ESTATE, NEWTON ABBOT TQ12 5ND
Tel: 01626 201052
Tran Man: Geoff Wilkins

TRATHENS TRAVEL SERVICES
BURRINGTON WAY, PLYMOUTH PL5 3LS
Tel: 01752 794545/790565
Fax: 01752 777931
Chmn: D I Park **Dir**: John Bettinson
Fleet: 50 - 49/70/83-seat coach, double-deck coach, sleeper coach.
Ops incl: express, continental tours.
Livery: White with Red and Yellow lining;
National Express: White.
(Subsidiary of Parks of Hamilton)

TURNERS TOURS
BACK LANE INDUSTRIAL ESTATE, CHULMLEIGH EX18 7AA
Tel: 01769 580242
Fax: 01769 581281
E-mail: coaches@turnerstours.co.uk
Web site: www.turnerstours.co.uk
Dir: S.L. Gilson, P.C.Gilson
Fleet: 28 - 16 single-decker coach, 7 single-deck bus, 2 midibus, 2 midicoach, 1 minibus.
Chassis: Alexander Dennis. 1 LDV. 1 Mercedes- Benz. Volvo.
Bodies: Alexander Dennis. Caetano. Jonckheere. Marshall/MC. Mercedes. Plaxton. Reeve Burgess. Other
Ops incl: local bus services, school contracts, excursions & tours, private hire, express, continental tours.
Livery: Cream.
Ticket System: ALMEX

T. W. COACHES LTD
HACHE LANE, SOUTH MOLTON EX36 3EH
Tel: 01769 572139
Fax: 01769 574182
E-mail: twcoaches@ukf.net
Dirs: C Tearall, N Williams **Eng**: R Bradshaw
Fleet: 16 coaches - 7 coach, 2 midibus, 6 midicoach, 1 minibus
Chassis: 3 Dennis, 13 Mercedes
Bodies: 1 Jonckheere. 1 Mellor, 6 Mercedes, 4 Optare, 3 Plaxton. 1 Setra.
Ops incl: local bus services, school contracts, excursions & tours, private hire, continental tours.
Livery: Blue
Ticket system: Almex

W A SHEARINGS
BARTON HILL WAY, TORQUAY TQ2 8JG
Tel: 01803 326016.
Fax: 01803 316059.
Depot Man: David Braund.
See also W A Shearings Ltd, Greater Manchester

WILLS MINI COACHES
2 LOWER UNION ROAD, KINGSBRIDGE TQ7 1EF
Tel/Fax: 01548 852140.
Man Dir: E. G. Wills. **Dir/Co Sec**: Mrs G. M. Wills.
Fleet: 5 minibus.
Chassis: 4 LDV. 1 Mercedes.
Ops incl: school contracts, private hire.

WOOD BROTHERS TRAVEL LTD
HAREWOOD GARAGE, BOSSELL ROAD, BUCKFASTLEIGH TQ11 0AL.
Tel: 01364 642666
Fax: 01364 643870.
E-mail: woodbrotherstravel@hotmail.co.uk
Man Dir: R.C.Wood **Comp Sec**: S. Wood
Dirs: R.D. Wood, R. Wood, A.S. Carter
Fleet: 14 - 9 single-deck coach, 1 midicoach, 3 minibus, 1 minicoach
Chassis: 4 Dennis, 2 Layland, 4 Mercedes-Benz, 1 Volkswagen, 3 Volvo.
Ops incl: local bus service, school contracts, private hire.
Livery: Yellow/White.

DORSET, BOURNEMOUTH, POOLE

BARRY'S COACHES LTD
9 CAMBRIDGE ROAD, GRANBY INDUSTRIAL ESTATE, WEYMOUTH DT4 9TJ
Tel: 01305 784850
Fax: 01305 782252
E-mail: barryscoaches@hotmail.co.uk
Fleet: 25 - 20 coach, 3 midicoach, 2 minicoach.
Man Dir: Mrs M Newsam **Fleet Eng**: Mr G Newsam **Co Sec**: Mrs M Hills
Chassis: 4 Dennis. 2 Iveco. 1 MAN. 9 Scania. 9 Volvo.
Bodies: 4 Berkhof. 2 Caetano. 1 Duple. 9 Irizar. 3 Jonckheere. 2 Neoplan. 2 Plaxton. 2 Van Hool.
Ops incl: school contracts, excursions & tours, private hire, continental tours.
Livery: White/Blue/Yellow

BLUEBIRD COACHES (WEYMOUTH) LTD
450 CHICKERELL ROAD, WEYMOUTH DT3 4DH
Tel: 01305 786262
Fax: 01305 766223
Recovery: 01305 786262/07771 561060
E-mail: martyn@bluebirdcoaches.com
Web site: www.bluebirdcoaches.com
Dirs: Martyn Hoare, Stephen Hoare
Fleet: 22 - 20 coach, 1 midicoach, 1 minibus.
Chassis: 7 DAF. 1 Mercedes. 2 Neoplan. 1 Volkswagen. 11 Volvo.
Bodies: 7 Bova. 1 Caetano. 3 Jonckheere. 2 Neoplan. 4 Plaxton. 5 Van Hool.
Ops incl: school contracts, excursions & tours, private hire, continental tours.
Livery: White/Blue/Orange

BOURNEMOUTH TRANSPORT LTD
YEOMANS WAY, BOURNEMOUTH BH8 0BQ
Tel: 01202 636000
Fax: 01202 636001
E-mail: mail@yellowbuses.co.uk
Web site: www.yellowbuses.co.uk
Fleetname: Yellow Buses
Service Delivery Dir: D T Lott **Eng Dir**: G Corrie **Fin Dir**: Mrs C Partridge.
Fleet: 118 - 65 double-deck bus, 36 single-deck bus, 14 coach, 3 open-top bus.
Chassis: 4 DAF. 55 Dennis. 4 Scania. 55 Volvo.
Bodies: 10 Alexander. 5 Caetano. 84 East Lancs. 5 Plaxton. 4 Van Hool. 10 Wright.
Ops incl: local bus services, school contracts, express.
Livery: bright Yellow
Ticket System: Wayfarer 3
Subsidiary of the Transdev Group

COACH HOUSE TRAVEL
16 POUNDBURY WEST INDUSTRIAL ESTATE, DORCHESTER DT1 2PG
Tel: 01305 267644
Fax: 01305 260608
Prop: Les Watts. **Ops Man**: John Woollen. **Co Sec**: Sarah Fursy Taylor **Ch Eng**: Phillip Watts
Fleet: 17 - 8 coach, 3 single-deck bus, 2 midicoach, 4 minibus.
Chassis: 4 DAF. 3 Dennis. 2 Iveco. 4 Mercedes. 4 Volvo.
Bodies: 1 Berkhof, 1 Bova. 3 LDV. 4 Marshall. 4 Plaxton. 1 Van Hool.
Ops incl: local bus services, school contracts, excursions & tours, private hire, continental tours.
Livery: Red/White with red/blue stripes.

DAMORY COACHES
UNIT 1, CLUMP FARM, SHAFTESBURY LANE, BLANDFORD FORUM DT11 7TD
Tel: 01258 452545
Fax: 01258 451930
E-mail: igray@damorycoach.co.uk
Local Man: I Gray **Man Dir**: Alex Carter **Eng Dir**: Geoff Parsons
Ops Dir: Andrew Wickham **Fin Dir**: Matt Dolphin
Fleet: 44 - 8 double-deck bus, 8 single-deck bus, 13 coach, 9 midibus, 1 double-deck coach 6 minicoach.
Chassis: 8 Bristol. 10 DAF. 6 LDV. 9 Optare. 11 Volvo.
Bodies: 8 ECW. 3 Ikarus. 2 Northern Counties. 9 Optare. 11 Plaxton. 5 Van Hool. 6 other.
Ops incl: local bus services, school contracts, excursions & tours, private hire, continental tours.
Livery: Turquoise/Maroon/White
Ticket system: Wayfarer
(Part of the Go-Ahead Group)

DORSET COUNTY COUNCIL PASSENGER TRANSPORT SECTION
EDUCATION TRANSPORT GARAGE, GROVE TRADING ESTATE, DORCHESTER DT1 1ST
Tel: 01305 224540
Fax: 01305 225166
E-mail: kevinrclarke@dorsetcc.gov.uk
Fleet Sup: K Clarke **Pass Tran Man**: B Thirlwall
Fleet: 10 - six 70-seat, four 53-seat
Chassis: 2 Dennis. 2 Cummins. 6 Scania.
Bodies: 6 Irizar. 4 Plaxton
Ops incl: school contracts, affiliated school and youth organisation day excursions

EXCELSIOR COACHES LTD
CENTRAL BUSINESS PARK, BOURNEMOUTH BH1 3SJ
Tel: 01202 652222
Fax: 01202 652223
E-mail: krobins@excelsior-coaches.com
Web site: www.excelsior-coaches.com
Man Dir: Kathy Tilbury
Fleet: 25 - 19 coach, 2 midicoach, 4 minibus
Chassis: 6 Mercedes. 19 Volvo
Bodies: 5 Caetano. 2 Esker. 2 Jonckheere. 4 Mercedes. 9 Plaxton. 3 Sunsundegui.
Ops incl: excursions & tours, private hire, express, continental tours.
Livery: Cream

MIKE HALFORD COACHES
KISEM, NORTH MILLS, BRIDPORT DT6 3AH
Tel/Fax: 01308 421106
Prop: M G Halford
Fleet: 7 - 3 midicoach, 4 minibus
Chassis: 7 Mercedes
Ops incl: local bus services, private hire, school contracts

HOMEWARD BOUND TRAVEL
137 LYNWOOD DRIVE, WIMBORNE BH21 1UU
Tel: 01202 884491
Fax: 01202 885664
E-mail: enquiries@homewardboundtravel.co.uk
Web site: www.homewardboundtravel.co.uk
Prop: Louisa Fairhead
Fleet: 3 minicoach
Chassis: 3 Renault
Bodies: 3 other.
Ops incl: excursions & tours, private hire, continental tours.
Livery: Silver/Purple/Green

POWELLS COACHES
THORNFORD GARAGE, THORNFORD DT9 6QN
Tel: 01935 872390
Fleet: 3 coach
Ops incl: local bus services, excursions & tours, private hire.
Livery: Red/White.

109

RAMON TRAVEL
7 HARCOURT ROAD, BOSCOMBE BH5 2JG.
Tel: 01202 432690.
Fax: 01202 432690.
Owner/Ops: C. Rochester.
Fleet: 6 - 1 coach, 1 midicoach, 4 minibus.
Chassis: 1 Bedford. 4 Freight Rover.
Ops incl: excursions & tours, private hire, school contracts.

ROADLINER PASSENGER TRANSPORT LTD
BANBURY ROAD, POOLE BH17 0GA
Tel: 01202 385055
Fax: 01202 690370
Recovery: 01202 385055
E-mail: mark@roadliner.biz
Web site: www.roadliner.biz
Fleetname: Roadliner
Man Dir: M Self **Dir:** Mrs J Self **Gen Man:** M Towers **Ch Eng:** B Ling
Fleet: 13 - 1 single-deck bus, 7 coach, 2 double-deck coach, 2 midicoach, 1 minicoach
Chassis: 1 Ford Transit, 1 LDV. 1 Leyland. 2 Mercedes. 1 Optare. 6 Scania. 2 Volvo.
Bodies: 1 Beulas. 1 Concept. 2 East Lancs. 6 Irizar. 1 Leyland. 2 Optare.
Ops incl: local bus services, school contracts, excursions & tours, private hire, express, continental tours
Livery: Green/Black/Silver
Ticket system: Wayfarer

SEA VIEW COACHES (POOLE) LTD
10 FANCY ROAD, POOLE BH12 4QZ
Tel: 01202 741439
Fax: 01202 740241
E-mail: info@seaviewcoaches.com
Web site: www.seaviewcoaches.com
Man Dir: D K Tarr **Dir:** D E Tarr **Co Sec:** Mrs D Wigmore
Fleet: 26 - 18 coach, 4 minibus, 2 midicoach. 2 minicoach.
Chassis: Man, Iveco, Mercedes
Bodies: 4 Beulas 3 Mercedes 16 Noge.
Ops incl: school contracts, excursions & tours, private hire, continental tours.
Livery: Silver

SHAFTESBURY & DISTRICT MOTOR SERVICES LTD
UNIT 2, MELBURY WORKSHOPS, CANN COMMON, SHAFTESBURY SP7 0EB
Tel/Fax: 01747 854359
E-mail: info@sdbuses.co.uk

Web site: www.sdbuses.co.uk
Dir: Roger Brown **Co Sec:** Liam Stacey
Fleet: 16 - 4 double-deck bus, 3 single-deck bus, 8 coach, 1 minicoach.
Chassis: 5 AEC. 1 Bristol. 1 DAF. 5 Leyland. 1 Optare. 1 Toyota. 2 Volvo.
Bodies: 1 Alexander. 1 Berkhof. 1 Caetano. 1 Duple. 1 Ikarus. 1 Jonckheere. 1 Leyland. 2 MCW. 1 Optare. 3 Park Royal. 3 Plaxton.
Ops incl: local bus services, school contracts, private hire.
Livery: Red
Ticket System: Wayfarer II

SOVEREIGN COACHES
PINE LODGE, ROUSDON, LYME REGIS DT7 3RD
Tel: 01297 23000
Fax: 01297 22466
E-mail: sov_coaches@btinternet.com
Ptnrs: R A Keech, C M Keech, R C Keech
Fleet: 9 - 5 midicoach, 4 minicoach.
Chassis: 1 Irisbus. 1 Iveco. 5 Mercedes. 2 Toyota.
Bodies: 1 Autobus. 3 Mercedes. 1 Plaxton. 4 other.
Ops incl: school contracts, excursions & tours, private hire.
Livery: White

SHAMROCK BUSES LTD
50A HOLTON ROAD, HOLTON HEATH TRADING PARK, POOLE BH16 6LJ
Tel: 01202 621581
Fax: 01202 623657
E-mail: office@shamrockbuses.co.uk
Web site: www.shamrockbuses.co.uk
Man Dir Ops: K H Baynton **Man Dir Finance:** M A Judge **Eng Dir:** S J Bracher
Fleet: 30-3 Alexander Dennis 24 Leyland 3 Volvo.
Bodies: 8 Alexander Dennis 10 ECW 3 East Lancs 2 Marshall/MCV 1 Northern Counties 6 Optare
Ops Inc: Local bus services, school contracts, private hire
Livery: Orange/Green
Ticket Systems: Wayfarer

SURELINE
UNIT 17, TRADECROFT INDUSTRIAL ESTATE, PORTLAND DT5 2LN
Tel: 01305 823039
Fax: 01305 822936
Web site: www.surelinebuses.co.uk
Dir: David Beaman **Ops Dir:** Bill Landucci
Ops incl: local bus services

VICTORY TOURS
BANBURY ROAD, POOLE BH17 0GA
Tel: 01202 681003
Fax: 01202 681003
E-mail: victorytours@btconnect.com
Web site: www.victorytours.biz
Man Dir: Mark Self **Dir:** Joan Self
Ops Dir: Sue Mitchell **Com Sec:** Nigel Hargreeves
Fleet: 5-4 single deck coach 1 midicoach
Chassis: 1 Bristol. 3 irisbus 1 Mercedes. 156 Optare. 51 Volvo.
Bodies: 3 beulas 1 Duple 1 Optare
Ops incl: School contracts, excursions & tours, private hire, express continaental tours.
Livery: Blue/Black/Silver

WILTS & DORSET BUS COMPANY LTD
TOWNGATE HOUSE, 2-8 PARKSTONE ROAD, POOLE BH15 2PR
Tel: 01202 680888/673555
Fax: 01202 670244
E-mail: enquiries-poole@wdbus.co.uk
Web site: www.wdbus.co.uk
Man Dir: A Carter **Ops Dir:** A Wickham **Eng Dir:** G Parsons
Fleet: 344 - 132 double-deck bus (incl. convertible open-top), 64 single-deck bus, 7 coach, 141 minibus.
Chassis: 25 Bristol. 96 DAF. 16 Leyland. 30 Mercedes. 156 Optare. 51 Volvo.
Bodies: 2 Duple. 35 ECW. 13 East Lancs. 30 Mercedes. 7 Northern Counties. 237 Optare. 11 Plaxton. 2 Roe. 3 Van Hool. 34 Wright.
Ops incl: local bus services, school contracts, private hire, express.
Livery: Red/White/Black Red/Blue
Ticket System: Wayfarer TGX
(Part of the Go-Ahead Group)

2 & 4th LIMITED
5 HEATHFIELD WAY, WEST MOORS, FERNDOWN BH22 0DA
Tel/Fax: 01202 870724
E-mail: nwiain@aol.com
Web site: www.2and4th.com
Man Dir: Lian Newman **Dir:** Gillian Newman
Fleet: 3-1 single deck coach, 1 midicoach, 1 minicoach
Chassis: 1 LDV, 1 mercedes-Benz, 1 Scania
Bodies: 1 Plaxton, 2 Other
Ops inc: Schoolcontracts, excurison & tour, private hire, express
Livery: White

DURHAM

ALFA COACHES LTD
17 RAMSGATE, STOCKTON-ON-TEES TS18 1BS.
Tel: 01642 678066
Fax: 01642 673462
Fleetname: Gladwin Tours
Man Dir: P. Sawbridge. **Man:** M. Gladwin.
Co Sec: P. Sawbridge. **Ops Man:** D. Squire
Fleet: 8 coach
Chassis: DAF
Bodies: 5 Ikarus. 3 Van Hool
Ops incl: excursions & tours, private hire, continental tours
Livery: Beige with Blue lettering
See also Alfa Travel Lancashire

BROWNS OF DURHAM
1 LEESFIELD DRIVE, MEADOWFIELD, DURHAM DH7 8NG
Tel: 0191 3780398
Recovery: 0191 378 0393
E-mail: info@brownscoachesltd.com
Dir: Ralph Brown
Fleet: 6 coach
Chassis: 1 Bova. 5 DAF.
Bodies: include LAG. EOS
Ops incl: excursions & tours, private hire, continental tours.

CLASSIC COACHES LTD
CLASSIC HOUSE, MORRISON ROAD, ANNFIELD PLAIN DH9 7RX
Tel: 01207 282288
Fax: 01207 282333
Recovery: 07736 178599
E-mail: sales@classic-coaches.co.uk
Web site: www.classic-coaches.co.uk
Man Dir: Ian Shipley
Fleet: 66 - 4 double-deck bus, 10 single-deck bus, 50 coach, 2 double-deck coach.
Chassis: 2 DAF. 1 Dennis. 4 MCW. 9 Mercedes. 12 Scania. 36 Volvo.
Bodies: 3 Berkhof. 7 Caetano. 12 Irizar. 4 MCW. 2 Neoplan. 26 Plaxton.
Ops incl: local bus services, school contracts, excursions & tours, private hire, continental tours
Livery: Red/Gold
Part of Tellings Golden Miller
Subsidiary of Arriva

COCHRANE'S
4 FARADAY ROAD, NORTH EAST INDUSTRIAL ESTATE, PETERLEE SR8 5AP.
Tel: 0191 586 2136.
Fax: 0191 586 5566.
Fleetname: Cochrane's Kelvin Travel.
Owner: I. P. Cochrane.
Fleet: 7 - 5 single-deck bus, 2 minicoach.
Chassis: 4 Bedford. 1 DAF. 1 Ford. 1 Freight Rover.
Bodies: 5 Plaxton. 2 others.
Ops incl: school contracts.
Livery: Orange/Black.
Ticket System: Setright.

COMPASS ROYSTON TRAVEL LTD
BOWESFIELD LANE INDUSTRIAL ESTATE, STOCKTON-ON-TEES TS18 3EG
Tel: 01642 606644
Fax: 01642 608617
Man Dir: G Walton **Trans Man:** M. Metcalfe
Fleet: 55 - double-deck bus, coach, midicoach.
Chassis: Bristol. Daimler. Ford. Leyland. Mercedes. Volvo.
Bodies: ECW. Jonckheere. Mercedes. Plaxton. Sunsundegui. Van Hool.
Ops incl: excursions & tours, private hire, express, continental tours, school contracts.
Livery: White with Red/Maroon stripe.
Associated with Procters Coaches, North Yorkshire

DUNN-LINE (HOLDINGS) LTD
See Nottinghamshire

DURHAM CITY COACHES LTD
BRANDON LANE, BRANDON, DURHAM DH7 8PG
Tel: 0191 378 0540
Fax: 0191 378 1985
E-mail: sales@durhamcitycoaches.co.uk
Web site: www.durhamcitycoaches.co.uk
Man Dir: Michael Lightfoot. **Co Sec:** Christine Lightfoot **Ops Man:** Malcolm Burnip
Fleet: 14 - 10 coach, 4 midicoach.
Chassis: 2 Bova. 4 Mercedes. 8 Volvo.
Bodies: 2 Bova. 3 Jonckheere. 4 Mercedes. 1 Optare. 3 Plaxton. 1 Van Hool
Ops incl: excursions & tours, private hire, continental tours, school contracts.
Livery: Black/Red/Gold

DURHAM TRAVEL SERVICES (DTS)
SEAHAM GARAGE INDUSTRIAL ESTATE, SEAHAM SR7 0PW
Tel: 0191 521 0202
Fax: 0191 521 0202
Subsidiary of Dunn-Line Holdings, part of Veolia Transport UK

ENTERPRISE TRAVEL
19 PINE GROVE, DARLINGTON DL3 8JF
Tel/Fax: 01325 286924
E-mail: coachhire@aol.com
Web site: www.enterprisecoachhire.co.uk
Dirs: B R Brown, Mrs B M Brown
Fleet: 6 - 5 single-deck coach, 1 minicoach.
Chassis: 2 Bova. 1 MAN. 2 Mercedes. 1 Setra.
Bodies: 2 Bova. 1 Mercedes. 1 Setra. 1 Van Hool. 1Wadham Stringer
Ops incl: private hire, school contracts, excursions & tours.
Livery: White with red/green reliefs.

GARDINERS TRAVEL
COULSON STREET, SPENNYMOOR DL16 7RS
Tel: 01388 814417
Fax: 01388 811466
E-mail: gardiners.travel@virgin.net
Man Dir: John Gardiner **Tran Man:** Harry Revel
Fleet: 8 - 6 coach, 2 midibus.
Chassis: 1 Iveco. 1 Leyland. 2 Optare. 4 Volvo.
Bodies: 1 Beulas. 1 Jonckheere. 2 Optare. 3 Plaxton. 1 Van Hool.
Ops incl: local bus services, school contracts, excursions & tours, private hire, continental tours.
Livery: Cream/Maroon
Ticket system: AES

GARNETT'S COACHES
UNIT E1, ROMAN WAY INDUSTRIAL ESTATE, TINDALE CRESCENT, BISHOP AUCKLAND DL14 9AW.
Tel: 01388 604419.
Fax: 01388 609549.
Fleet Ops Man: Paul Garnett
Fleet: incl: coach
Chassis: incl: 4 Volvo.
Bodies: incl: 1 Sunsundegui.
Ops incl: excursions & tours, private hire, continental tours.
Livery: Yellow/Red/Black.

GRIERSONS COACHES
SEDGEFIELD ROAD GARAGE, FISHBURN, STOCKTON-ON-TEES TS21 4DD.
Tel: 01740 620209.
Fax: 01740 621243.
Prop: C. & D. Grierson.
Fleet: 20 - 5 double-deck bus, 6 single-deck bus, 4 coach, 1 midicoach, 4 minibus.
Chassis: 1 DAF. 1 Ford. 1 Ford Transit. 2 Freight Rover. 2 Mercedes. 1 Scania. 13 Volvo.
Bodies: 1 Carlyle. 3 Jonckheere. 2 Mercedes. 13 Plaxton. 1 Reeve Burgess. 1 Van Hool.
Ops incl: excursions & tours, private hire, express, continental tours.
Livery: Blue/Red.

HODGSONS COACHES
20 GALGATE, BARNARD CASTLE DL12 8BG.
Tel: 01833 630730.
Fax: 01833 630830.
Props: J. K. Hodgson, G. A. Hodgson.
Fleet: 6 - 2 coach, 1 midicoach, 3 minicoach.
Chassis: 1 Bedford. 1 Bova. 1 Leyland. 1 Mercedes.
Bodies: 1 Bova. 1 Plaxton. 1 Elme. 3 Concept Coach Craft.
Ops incl: local bus services, school contracts, excursions & tours, private hire, continental tours.

HUMBLES COACHES
UP YONDER, ROBSON STREET, SHILDON DL4 1EB
Tel: 01388 772772
Fax: 01388 772211
Dirs: Mr M Humble, Mrs P West **Ops Man**: Mrs K Towler
Fleet: 8 - 2 single-deck coach, 2 midicoach, 4 minicoach
Chassis: incl. 3 LDV. 2 Mercedes-Benz
Bodies: incl 2 Neoplan
Ops incl: school contracts, excursions & tours, private hire.

J & C COACHES
COACH DEPOT, GROAT DRIVE, AYCLIFFE INDUSTRIAL PARK, NEWTON AYCLIFFE DL5 6HY.
Tel: 01325 312728.
Fax: 01325 320385.
Snr Ptnr: J. N. Jones.
Ptnrs: A. Jones, N. Jones, D. Jones.
Fleet: 10 - 6 coach, 1 midicoach, 3 minicoach.
Chassis: 4 DAF. 1 Dennis. 1 Ford Transit. 1 Freight Rover. 2 Mercedes. 1 Setra.
Bodies: 4 Bova. 1 Duple. 1 Leyland. 2 Mercedes. 1 Setra.
Ops incl: school contracts, excursions & tours, private hire, continental tours.
Livery: various

JAYLINE BAND SERVICES LTD
UNIT 8A, KILBURN DRIVE, SEAVIEW INDUSTRIAL ESTATE, HORDEN SR8 4TQ
Tel: 0191 586 5787
Fax: 0191 586 5836
E-mail: jaylinetravel@hotmail.com
Web site: jaylinetravel.com
Prop: Jason Rogers **Dir**: Neil Tait
Fleet: 7 - 3 single-deck coach, 4 double-deck coach.
Chassis: 1 DAF. 5 Scania. 1 Volvo.
Bodies: 3 Berkhof. 1 Jonckheere. 3 Van Hool
Ops incl: private hire
Livery: Blue

KINGSLEY COACHES LTD
See Tyne & Wear

LEE'S COACHES LTD
MILL ROAD GARAGE, LITTLEBURN INDUSTRIAL ESTATE, LANGLEY MOOR DH7 8HE
Tel: 0191 378 0653
Fax: 0191 378 9086
E-mail: info@leescoaches.co.uk
Web site: www.leescoaches.co.uk
Man Dor: Malcolm Lee **Dirs**: Colin Lee
Comp Sec: Jean Lee
Fleet: 12 - 11 singe-deck coach, 1 minicoach
Chassis: 1Bova. 1 Mercedes. 10 Volvo.
Bodies: 3 Berkhof. 1 Bova. 3 Caetano. 1 Jonckheere. 1 Mercedes. 2 Plaxton. 1 Van Hool.
Ops incl: school contracts, excursions & tours, private hire, continental tours
Livery: Blue/Silver

MAUDES COACHES
REDWELL GARAGE, HARMIRE ROAD, BARNARD CASTLE DL12 8QJ
Tel: 01833 637341
Fax: 01833 631888
Prop: Stephen Maude
Fleet: 6 - 4 coach, 1 midicoach, 1 minicoach.
Chassis: 2 Mercedes. 4 Volvo.
Bodies: 1 Jonckheere. 2 Mercedes. 1 Plaxton. 2 Van Hool.
Ops incl: local bus services, school contracts, excursions & tours, private hire.
Livery: Red/White.

NORTON MINI TRAVEL
5 PLUMER DRIVE, NORTON TS20 1HF.
Tel: 01642 555832.
Owner: R. Spears.
Fleet: 2 minicoach.
Chassis: 1 Iveco, 1 Freight Rover.
Ops incl: private hire, school contracts.
Livery: White/Purple.

RICHARDSON COACHES
3 OXFORD ROAD, HARTLEPOOL TS25 5SS.
Tel/Fax: 01429 272235.
Man Dir/Ch Eng: T. Richardson.
Dir/Co Sec/Traf Man: D. Richardson.
Fleet: 8 coach.
Chassis: 1 DAF. 4 Leyland. 1 Mercedes. 1 Toyota. 1 Volvo.
Bodies: 1 Caetano. 1 Leyland. 1 Mercedes. 4 Plaxton. 1 Van Hool.
Ops incl: excursions & tours, private hire.
Livery: Green/Red/White.

ROBERTS TOURS
36 NORTH ROAD WEST, WINGATE TS28 5AP.
Tel: 01429 838268.
Fax: 01429 838228.
E-mail: robertstours@aol.com
Web site: www.robertstours.com
Dirs: T. G. Roberts, D Roberts, C. A. Harper.
Fleet: 14 coach, 1 midibus.
Chassis: 5 Bova. 5 DAF. 2 Leyland 2 Volvo.
Bodies: 5 Bova. 8 Plaxton. 1 Wadham Stringer.
Ops incl: excursions & tours, private hire, express, school contracts.
Livery: Cream/Green.

SCARLET BAND BUS & COACH LTD
WELFARE GARAGE, STATION ROAD, WEST CORNFORTH, FERRYHILL DL17 9LA
Tel: 01740 654247
Fax: 01740 656068
E-mail: sband@freeuk.com
Dirs: G Torrrance **Tran Man**: A Dolan
Fleet: 29 - 2 double-deck bus, 3 single-deck bus, 5 single-deck coach, 12 midibus, 7 minibus.
Chassis: 2 Dennis. 7 Leyland. 2 MCW, 7 Mercedes. 10 Optare. 1 Volvo.
Bodies: 1 Alexander Dennis. 5 Leyland. 2 MCW. 7 Mercedes-Benz. 1 Optare. 3 Wadham Stringer
Ops incl: local bus services, school contracts, private hire.
Livery: Red/Cream/Scarlet
Ticket System: Wayfarer 3

SHERBURN VILLAGE COACHES
FRONT STREET, SHERBURN VILLAGE DH6 1QY
Tel: 0191 372 1531
Fax: 0191 372 1531
Prop: John Cousins.
Fleet: 7 - 2 coach, 3 midibus, 2 midicoach.
Chassis: 1 MAN. 4 Mercedes. 2 Volvo.
Bodies: 1 Autobus. 1 Berkhof. 1 Caetano. 3 Plaxton. 1 Wadham Stringer.
Ops incl: local bus services, excursions & tours, private hire.
Livery: Red/White
Ticket System: AES.

SNOWDON COACHES
SEASIDE LANE, EASINGTON SR8 3TW.
Tel: 0191 527 0535.
Fax: 0191 527 3280.
Prop: A. Snowdon. **Man**: G. Parkin.
Ch Eng: J. R. Main. **Sec**: V. Dowson.
Fleet: 16 coach.
Chassis: 1 Bova. 1 MAN. 14 Volvo.
Bodies: 1 Bova. 14 Plaxton. 1 Van Hool.
Ops incl: private hire, school contracts.
Livery: White with Pink reliefs.

STAGECOACH TRANSIT
CHIRCH ROAD, STOCKTON TS18 2HW
Tel: 01642 602112
Web site: www.stagecoachbus.com
Man Dir: John Conroy
Fleet: 207
Chassis: incl: Dennis. MAN. Mercedes. Scania. Volvo.
Bodies: Alexander. Leyland. Plaxton.
Ops incl: local bus services
Livery: Stagecoach

STANLEY BUSES & MINICOACHES
THE BUS STATION, STANLEY DH9 OTD
Tel: 01207 237424.
Fax: 01207 233233.
Web site: www.minicoachhire.co.uk
Dir: Robert Scott
Fleet: 36 - 2 single-deck bus, 10 minibus, 14 minicoach, 7 taxi-bus
Ops incl: local bus services, private hire
Livery: White/Orange

TOWN & COUNTRY MOTOR SERVICES LTD
UNIT 2, HENSON ROAD, YARM ROAD BUSINESS PARK, DARLINGTON DL1 4QD.
Tel: 01325 489966.
E-mail: sales@townandcountrycoaches.co.uk
Web site: www.townandcountrycoaches.co.uk
Fleetname: Town & Country.
Man Dir: Philip Notman
Fleet: 3 - 1 single-deck bus, 1 midibus, 1 midicoach.

Chassis: 2 Leyland. 2 Mercedes.
Bodies: 1 Duple. 1 Marshall, 1 Plaxton.
Ops incl: local bus services, school contracts, private hire.
Livery: White/Blue.
Ticket System: Almex.

PAUL WATSON TRAVEL
BRIDGE HOUSE, MOOR ROAD, STAINDROP DL2 3LF
Tel/Fax: 01833 660471
E-mail: paul@pwatsontravel.fslife.co.uk
Web site: www.paulwatsontravel.co.uk
Prop: Paul Watson

Fleet: 4 - 2 coach, 1 midicoach, 1 minibus
Chassis: 1 Ford Transit. 1 Mercedes. 2 Volvo.
Ops incl: excursions & tours, private hire, continental tours, school contracts
Livery: White

WEARDALE MOTOR SERVICES LTD
STANHOPE DL13 2YQ
Tel: 01388 528235
Fax: 01388 526080
Dirs: Messrs Gibson

Fleet: 30 - 11 double-deck bus, 4 single-deck bus, 10 coach, 3 minibus, 1 minicoach, 1 midibus.
Chassis: Bova. DAF. Iveco. Leyland. MAN. MCW. Mercedes. Neoplan. Optare. Scania. Volvo.
Bodies: Alexander. Berkhof. Bova. ECW. Ikarus. MCW. Mercedes. Neoplan. Optare. Plaxton. Roe.
Ops incl: local bus services, excursions & tours, school contracts, private hire, express, continental tours.
Livery: Red/White
Ticket System: Wayfarer

EAST SUSSEX, BRIGHTON & HOVE

BARCROFT TOURS & EVENTS
60 QUEENS ROAD, HASTINGS TN34 1RE
Tel: 01424 200201
Fax: 01424 200206
Recovery: 07977 004371
E-mail: info@barcrofttours.co.uk
Web site: www.barcrofttours.co.uk
Fleet: 2 - 2 single-deck coach.
Chassis: 1 Mercedes-Benz. 1 Volvo
Bodies: 1 Caetano. 1 Setra.
Ops incl: excursions & tours, private hire, continental tours.

BRIGHTON & HOVE BUS & COACH CO
43 CONWAY STREET, HOVE BN3 3LT
Tel: 01273 886200
Fax: 01273 822073
E-mail: info@buses.co.uk
Web site: www.buses.co.uk
Fleetname: Brighton & Hove
Chmn: Keith Ludeman **Man Dir:** Roger French **Dirs:** Phil Woodgate, Mike Best, Roger Freit., Nick Swift
Fleet: 290 - 213 double-deck bus, 67 single-deck bus, 10 single-deck coach.
Chassis: 1 Bristol. 128 Dennis. 1 Optare. 133 Scania. 27 Volvo.
Bodies: 7 Alexander. 1 ECW. 169 East Lancs. 4 Irizar. 8 Marshall. 8 Optare. 72 Plaxton. 21 Wright.
Ops incl: local bus services, school contracts, excursions & tours, private hire, continental tours.
Livery: Red/Black/Cream
Ticket System: Wayfarer TGX
Subsidiary of Go Ahead Group

BRIGHTONIAN COACHES
3 THE AVENUE, BRIGHTON BN2 4GF
Tel: 01273 696195
Props: Laurence R Walker, Susan M Walker
Fleet: 2 coach
Chassis: 2 Volvo.
Bodies: 1 Duple 1 Plaxton.
Ops incl: school contracts, private hire.
Livery: White

C & S COACHES
STATION ROAD, HEATHFIELD TN21 8DF
Tel: 01435 866600
Fax: 01435 868264
E-mail: info@candscoaches.co.uk
Ptnrs: Chris Hicks, Geoff Shaw **Ch Eng:** Paul Matthews
Fleet: 37 - incl 1 double-deck coach, 1 midicoach.
Chassis: 20 DAF. 2 Leyland. 6 Scania. 9 Volvo.
Bodies: 2 Jonckheere. 6 Plaxton. 1 Reeve Burgess. 28 Van Hool.
Ops incl: school contracts, private hire.
Livery: White with red/black/grey graphics

COASTAL COACHES
18 WEST POINT, NEWICK BN8 4NU
Tel: 01825 723024
E-mail: enquires@wwwcoastalcoaches.com
Web-site: www.coastalcoaches.com
Fleetname: Coastal
Prop: Peter Jenkins **Ops Man:** Robert Morgan
Fleet: 10 - 10 single-deck bus.
Chassis: 3 Alexander Dennis. 6 Dennis. 1 Transbus.
Bodies: 9 Alexander Dennis. 1 Transbus.
Ops incl: local bus services
Livery: Green/white/blue
Ticket System: Wayfarer 3

CUCKMERE COMMUNITY BUS LTD
THE OLD RECTORY, LITLINGTON, POLEGATE BN26 5RB
Tel: 01323 870920
Web site: www.cuckmerebus.freeuk.com
Chmn: Beryl Smith **Organiser:** Philip Ayers **Deputy Organiser:** John Bunce
Hire Orgniser: Jeff Innes **Sec:** Susan de Angeli **Treasurer:** Andrew Cottingham
Fleet: 8 - 8 minibus
Chassis: 8 Mercedes.
Bodies: 2 Alexander. 4 Mercedes. 2 Constable
Ops incl: local bus services, excursions, private hire.
Livery: Green/Cream
Ticket system: Wayfarer TGX

EASTBOURNE BUSES LTD
BIRCH ROAD, EASTBOURNE BN26 6PD
Tel: 01323 416416
Fax: 01323 643034
E-mail: mailbox@eastbournebuses.co.uk
Web site: www.eastbournebuses.co.uk
Man Dir: Steve Barnett
Fleet: 47 - 13 double-deck bus, 34 single-deck bus
Chassis: 28 DAF. 7 Dennis. 2 Leyland. 10 MAN.
Ops incl: local bus services, school contracts
Livery: base Blue with branding.
Ticket System: Wayfarer

L J EDWARDS COACH HIRE
BELLBANKS CORNER, MILL ROAD, HAILSHAM BN27 2AH
Tel: 01323 440622
Fax: 01323 442555
E-mail: info@ljedwards.co.uk
Web site: www.ljedwards.co.uk
Prop: L J Edwards **Gen Man:** Anthony Burkill **Comp Acct:** David Maynard
Fleet: 13 - 7 single-deck coach, 2 midicoach, 2 minibus, 2 minicoach
Chassis: 6 Bova. 2 Irisbus. 1 Mercedes. 2 Toyota. 2 Voltwagen.
Bodies: 1 Beulas. 6 Bova. 2 Caetano. 1 Indcar. 1 Mercedes. 2 Other
Ops incl: excursions & tours, private hire, continental tours, school contracts.
Livery: White/Red

EMPRESS COACHES LTD
10/11 ST MARGARETS ROAD, ST LEONARDS-ON-SEA TN37 6EH
Tel/Fax: 01424 430621
E-mail: info@empresscoaches.com
Web site: www.empresscoaches.com
Dir: Stephen Dine **Ch Eng:** Kelvin Bowen
Fleet: 10 - 1 coach, 2 midibus, 1 midicoach, 6 minibus.
Chassis: 1 Dennis. 2 Ford Transit. 2 Iveco. 1 Mercedes. 1 Optare. 1 Toyota. 1 CVE Omni.
Bodies: 1 Caetano. 1 Chassis Developments. 1 Devco. 1 Mellor. 2 Optare. 2 UVG. 1 Wadham Stringer.
Ops incl: school contracts, private hire.
Livery: Burgundy/Ivory

HAMS TRAVEL
THE WHITE HOUSE, LONDON ROAD, FLIMWELL TN5 7PL
Tel: 01580 879537
FAX: 01580 879629
E-mail: info@hamstravel.co.uk
Web site: www.hamstravel.co.uk
Ops incl: School contracts private hire, .
Livery: Red/Orange/Brown.

OCEAN COACHES
19 STONERY CLOSE, PORTSLADE BN41 2TD.
Tel/Fax: 01273 278385.
Web site: www.oceancoaches.net
E-mail: info@oceancoaches.net
Prop: Peter Woodcock.
Fleet: 1 coach.
Chassis: Volvo. **Body:** Ikarus.
Ops incl: private hire, school contracts.
Livery: Cream/Red.

PAVILION COACHES
144 NEVILL AVENUE, HOVE BN3 7NH
Tel: 01273 732405
E-mail: nicky2168@hotmail.com
Web-site: www.pavilioncoaches.co.uk
Joint owners: Peter Hammer, Nicky Hammer
Fleet: 2 - double-deck bus, coach

Chassis: 1 Leyland. 1 Volvo.
Bodies: 1 Park Royal. 1 Plaxton
Ops incl: excursions & tours, private hire, continental tours

RAMBLER COACHES
WESTRIDGE MANOR, WHITWORTH ROAD, HASTINGS TN37 7PZ
Tel: 01424 752505
Fax: 01424 751815
Ptnrs: Colin Rowland, J. Goodwin.
Fleet: 38 - 5 single-deck bus, 26 coach, 1 midibus, 3 midicoach. 1 minicoach.
Chassis: 8 Bedford. 4 Dennis. 2 Leyland National. 5 Mercedes. 1 Scania. 18 Volvo.
Bodies: 5 Berkhof. 1 Duple. 2 Leyland National. 2 Optare. 17 Plaxton. 7 Van Hool. 1 Reeve Burgess. 1 Wadham Stringer. 1 Wright. 1 Hispano.
Ops incl: local bus services, school contracts, excursions & tours, private hire, continental tours.
Livery: White, Green/Black.
Ticket System: Wayfarer.

RENOWN COACHES LTD
1A BEECHING ROAD, BEXHILL-ON-SEA TN39 3LG
Tel: 01424 210744

Fax: 01424 212651
E-mail; renowncoaches@yahoo.co.uk
Web Site: www.renowncoaches.co.uk
Fleet Names: Renown, Cavendish Motor Services
Man Dir: Christian Harmer
Fleet: 70 - 17 double-deck bus, 49 single-deck bus, 4 coach
Chassis: 1 AEG, 38 Dennis, 16 Leyland, 11 Optare, 4 Volvo
Ops incl: local bus services, school contracts, excursions & tours, private hire, continental tours.

STAGECOACH IN HASTINGS
BEAUFORT ROAD, SILVERHILL, ST LEONARDS ON SEA TN37 6PL
Tel: 01424 445600
Fax: 01424 435340
E-mail: enquiries.southeast@stagecoachbus.com
Web site: www.stagecoachbus.com/hastings
Man Dir: Paul Southgate **Ops Dir:** Neil Install **Eng Dir:** Keith Dyball
Fleet: 63 - 23 double-deck bus, 40 single-deck bus.
Chassis: 27 Dennis. 4 Leyland. 6 Scania. 26 Volvo
Bodies: 45 Alexander. 18 Northern Counties.
Ops incl: local bus services.
Livery: Stagecoach

SUSSEX COUNTRY COACH HIRE
TERMINAL BUILDING, SHOREHAM AIRPORT. BN43 5FF
Tel: 01273 465500
Fax: 01273 453040
Web: www..sussex-country.co.uk
E-mail: sxcountry@tiscalli.co.uk
Ptnrs: A Wright, Mrs m Keates
Fleet: 4 - 2 single-deck coach, 1 midicoach, 1 minibus
Chassis: 1 LDV. 1 Mercedes-Benz. 2 Volvo.
Bodies: 1 Plaxton. 1 Van Hool. 1 Other.
Ops incl: school contracts, excurions & tours, private tours, continental tours
Livery: Blue/Yellow/Green on White

WISE COACHES LTD
74 HIGH STREET, HAILSHAM BN27 1AU
Tel: 01323 844321
E-mail: info@wisecoaches.co.uk
Web site: www.wisecoaches.co.uk
Fleet: 4 coach.
Chassis: 3 DAF. 1 Iveco.
Bodies: 1 Beulas. 1 Berkhof. 1 Ikarus. 1 Ovi.
Ops incl: excursions & tours, private hire, school contracts.
Livery: Red/Silver

EAST RIDING OF YORKSHIRE, CITY OF KINGSTON UPON HULL

ABBEY COACHWAYS LTD
MEADOWCROFT GARAGE, LOW STREET, CARLTON DN14 9PH
Tel: 01405 860337
Fax: 01405 869433
Dirs: Mrs L E Baker, S J Stockdale.
Fleet: 5 coaches.
Chassis: 1 Scania. 4 Volvo.
Bodies: 1 Jonckheere. 4 Plaxton.
Ops incl: school contracts, private hire

ACKLAMS OF BEVERLEY
39 LADYGATE, BEVERLEY HU17 8BX
Tel: 01482 887666
Fax: 01482 874949
Web site: www.acklams-coaches-beverley.co.uk
Prop: Paul Acklam
Fleet: 10 - 5 coach, 2 midicoach, 3 minicoach.
Chassis: 2 DAF. 3 Dennis. 2 LDV. 2 Mercedes.
Bodies: 1 Optare. 6 Plaxton.
Ops incl: local bus services, school contracts, private hire.
Livery: Red/Grey

ALPHA BUS & COACH CO
DAIRYCOATES INDUSTRIAL ESTATE, WILTSHIRE ROAD, HULL HU4 6PA
Tel: 01482 353941
Fax: 01482 353771
Web site: www.veolia-transport.co.uk
Fleet: 37 - 13 double-deck bus, 9 single-deck bus, 12 coach, 1 midibus, 2 minibus.
Chassis: 8 Dennis. 1 Ford Transit. 10 MAN. 9 Mercedes. 9 Volvo.
Bodies: 4 East Lancs. 10 MCW. 9 Mercedes. 1 Optare. 8 Plaxton. 5 other.
Ops incl: local bus services, school contracts, private hire, continental tours.
Livery: Purple/Silver
Ticket system: Almex
(Subsidiary of Dunn Line Holdings, part of the Veolia Group)

R DRURY COACHES
6 BLENHEIM DRIVE, GOOLE DN14 6SL
Tel/Fax: 01405 763440
Web site: rdrurycoaches.tripod.com
Dirs: Roland Drury, Richard Drury
Fleet: 5 coach, 1 midicoach
Chassis: 1 Toyota. 5 Volvo.
Bodies: 1 Caetano. 5 Plaxton.
Ops incl: local bus services, school contracts, private hire.
Livery: White/Green/Yellow

EAST YORKSHIRE MOTOR SERVICES LTD
252 ANLABY ROAD, HULL HU3 2RS
Tel: 01482 327142
Fax: 01482 212040
E-mail: enquiries@eyms.co.uk
Web site: www.eyms.co.uk
Chmn: Peter Shipp **Fin Dir**: Peter Harrison **Com Man**: Bob Rackley **Ch Eng**: David Heptinstall **Co Sec**: Paul Leeman **Ops Man**: Ray Hilll
Fleet: 320 - 153 double-deck bus, 90 single-deck bus, 27 single-deck coach, 8 open-top bus, 42 midibus, 42 minibus.
Chassis: 12 Aleaxander Dennis. 2 AEC. 1 Bedford. 1 Bristol. 41 Dennis. 6 Entrprise. 25 Leyland. 11 MAN. 20 Mercedes. 15 Optare. 1 Transbus. 185 Volvo.
Bodies: 59 Alexander Dennis. 7 Berkhof. 10 Caetano. 1 Duple. 1 ECW. 1 East Lancs. 2 Mercedes-Benz. 60 Northern Counties. 30 Optare. 1 Park Royal. 77 Plaxton. 13 Transbus. 1 Willowbrook. 57 Wright
Ops incl: local bus services, school contracts, excursion & tours, private hire, express, continental tours.
Livery: buses - Burgundy/Cream.
Ticket System: Wayfarer TGX150

MANOR TRAVEL
2 MANOR DRIVE, MAIN STREET, BEEFORD YO25 8BB.
Tel: 01262 488431.
E-mail: alan@manor-travel.co.uk
Web site: www.manor-travel.co.uk
Man Dir: Alan Hammond

NATIONAL HOLIDAYS
THE TRAVEL CENTRE, SPRINGFIELD WAY, ANLABY, HULL HU10 6RJ
Tel: 01482 569006
Fax: 01482 569003
E-mail: info@national-holidays.co.uk
Web site: www.national-holidays.co.uk
Ch Exec: Dennis Wormwell **Dir**: Graham Rogers **Ops Man**: Adrian Hutchinson
Fleet: 81 coach
Chassis: 81 Volvo.
Bodies: 29 Jonckheere. 40 Plaxton. 12 Van Hool.
Ops incl: excursions & tours, private hire, continental tours.
Livery: White
(Subsidiary company of of WA Shearings)

PEARSON COACHES LTD
9 HEADLANDS ROAD, ALDBROUGH HU11 4RR
Tel: 01964 527260 **Fax**: 01964 527774
E-mail: enquiries@pearsonscoaches.co.uk
Web site: www.pearsonscoaches.co.uk

Dirs: Mrs V Pearson, S Colley
Fleet: 10 - 5 single-deck coach, 5 midicoach.
Bodies: 4 Mercedes-Benz. 1 UVG. 5 Van Hool
Chassis: 5 Mercedes. 5 Volvo
Ops incl: local bus services, school contracts, excursions & tours, private hire.
Livery: Light Grey with Red stripes.
Ticket system: Wayfarer

COLLIN PHILLIPSON MINI-COACHES
1 HILLCREST, OUSEFLEET, GOOLE DN14 8HP
Tel: 01405 704394
Prop: Collin Phillipson **Tran Man**: Tracey Phillipson
Fleet: 1 minicoach
Chassis: 1 Mercedes
Bodies: 1 Excell
Ops incl: school contracts, private hire

ELLIE ROSE TRAVEL LTD
BANKSIDE INDUSTRIAL ESTATE, VALLETTA STREET, HEDON ROAD, HULL HU9 5NP
Tel: 01482 890616
Fax: 01482 899359:
E-mail: info@ellierosetravel.karoo.co.uk
Man Dirs: Mr J Houghton **Co Dir**: Mrs S. Houghton **Co Sec**: Mrs Houghton
Fleet: 51 - 20 double-deck bus, 10 single-deck bus, 10 single-deck coach,1 open top bus, 2 midibus, 4 midicoach, 4 minibus,
Chassis: 6 DAF. 6 Dennis. 4 Frieght Rover. 4 LDV. 10 Leyland. 15 MCW. 10 Volvo.
Bodies: 1 Caetano. 3 ECW. 14 Leyland. 15 MCW. 1 Mercedes-Benz. 2 Optare. 4 Plaxton. 1 Setra.
Ops incl: local bus services, school contract, excursions & tours, private hire.
Livery: White
Ticket system: Wayfarer.

STAGECOACH IN HULL
FOSTER STREET, HULL HU8 8BT
Tel: 01482 222333
Fax: 01482 217623
Web site: www.stagecoachbus.com
Dirs: as Stagecoach East Midland
Fleet: 132 - double-deck bus, single-deck bus, coach, midibus
Chassis: incl: 85 Dennis. 22 Volvo.
Bodies: incl: 22 Alexander. 28 Northern Counties. 14 Plaxton.
Ops incl: local bus services, express.
Livery: Stagecoach
Ticket system: Wayfarer 3.

SWEYNE COACHES
LONGSHORES, REEDNESS ROAD, SWINEFLEET DN14 8ER.
Tel: 01405 704263

♿	Vehicle suitable for disabled	Seat belt-fitted Vehicle	R24	24 hour recovery service
T	Toilet-drop facilities available	Coach(es) with galley facilities		Replacement vehicle available
R	Recovery service available	Air-conditioned vehicle(s)		Vintage Coach(es) available
	Open top vehicle(s)v	Coaches with toilet facilities		

115

ESSEX

ANITA'S COACHES
ROOMS 4-5, AIRWAYS HOUSE, FIRST AVENUE, STANSTED AIRPORT CM24 1RY
Tel: 01279 661551
E-mail: anitas.coaches@virgin.net
Web site: www.anitascoaches.com
Dirs: E A S Wheeler, Mrs V A Wyatt
Fleet: 7 - 5 coach, 1 midicoach, 1 minicoach
Chassis: 2 DAF. 1 MAN. 1 Mercedes. 3 Volvo.
Bodies: 2 Bova. 4 Caetano. 1 Plaxton
Ops incl: local bus services, school contracts, private hire, continental tours.

APT COACHES LTD
UNIT 27, RAWRETH INDUSTRIAL ESTATE, RAWRETH LANE, RAYLEIGH SS6 9RL
Tel: 01268 783878
Fax: 01268 782656
E-mail: admin@aptcoaches.co.uk
Web site: www.aptcoaches.co.uk
Man Dir: Peter Thorn
Fleet: 13 - 12 coach, 1 minicoach.
Chassis: 3 Alexander Dennis. 1 Bova. 1 Mercedes. 8 Scania.
Bodies: 1 Bova. 4 Irizar.1 Mercedes-Benz. 2 Neoplan. 4 Van Hool. 1 Wadham Stringer..
Ops incl: school contracts, private hire, continental tours
Livery: White/Pink

ARRIVA SOUTHEND LTD
20 SHORT STREET, SOUTHEND ON SEA, SS2 5BY
Tel: 01622 697000
Fax: 01702 697001
Web site: www.arrivabus.co.uk
Man Dir: Heath Williams
A division of Arriva Southern Counties
See Kent

B J S TRAVEL
61A HIGH STREET, GREAT WAKERING SS3 0EF
Tel: 01702 219403
Fax: 01702 216472
Prop: Brian Snow
Fleet: 2 - 1 single-deck coach, 1 midicoach.
Chassis: 1 Mercedes-Benz. 1 Scania.
Bodies: 1 Irizar. 1 Reeve Burgess.
Ops incl: private hire.
Livery: White.

BLUE DIAMOND COACHES
37 HOLMES MEADOW, HARLOW CM19 5SG.
Tel:/Fax: 01279 427524.
FE-mail: beau.aukett@ntlworld.com
Prop: J. Robilliard. **Sec**: A. Aukett.
Fleet: 4 - 1 single-deck BUS, 2 midibus, 1 midicoach.
Chassis: 1 Alexander Dennis. 3 Mercedes-Benz.
Bodies: 4 Plaxton.
Ops incl: school contracts, private hire.
Livery: Blue/White.

BLUE TRIANGLE BUSES LTD
UNIT 3C, DENVER INDUSTRIAL ESTATE, RAINHAM RM13 9DD
Tel: 01708 631001/550743
Fax: 01708 522227
Web site: www.btbuses.com
Fleet: 101 - 78 double-deck bus, 23 single-deck bus
Chassis: 8 AEC. 51 Dennis. 15 Leyland. 11 Leyland National. 23 MCW. 5 Volvo.
Bodies: 5 Alexander. 8 Caetano. 34 East Lancs. 6 Leyland. 23 MCW. 13 Park Royal. 20 Plaxton. 1 Saunders. 3 Weymann.
Ops incl: local bus services, excursions & tours
Livery: Red/Cream
(Part of the Go-Ahead group)

BORDACOACH
25B ULFA COURT, EASTWOOD ROAD, RAYLEIGH SS6 7JD
Tel: 01268 747608
Prop: David Stubbington
Fleet: 1 single-deck coach.
Chassis: 1 Volvo
Body: 1 Van Hool
Ops incl: school contracts, private hire.
Livery: White

BRENTWOOD COACHES
79 WASH ROAD, HUTTON, BRENTWOOD CM13 1DL.
Tel: 01277 233144.
Fax: 01277 201386.
Prop: A. J. Brenson. **Ch Eng**: K. Wright.
Sec: Mrs P. Alexander. **Traf Man**: B. Pierce.
Fleet: 11 Coaches
Chassis: MAN, Volvo.
Bodies: Caetano, Jonckheere, Plaxton, Van Hool
Ops incl: excursions & tours, private hire, school contracts, continental tours.
Livery: White/Brown/Orange/Yellow.
Ticket System: Almex.

C I CLUB CLASS TRAVEL
POOLS LANE, HIGHWOOD, CHELMSFORD CM1 3QL
Tel: 01245 24866
E-mail: cicoachlines@btopenworld.com
Props: S Lodge, I Lodge.
Fleet: 8 - 6 single-deck coach, 1 midicoach, 1 minibus
Chassis: 4 Iveco. 1 Optare. 1 Temsa
Body: 4 Beulas
Ops incl: local bus service, private hire, school contracts, continental tours
Livery: Silver

C N ENTERPRISES LTD
9 BARTHOLOMEW DRIVE, HAROLD WOOD RM3 0WB
Tel/Fax: 01708 379700
E-mail: cnenterprise1@aol.com
ManDir: Colin Nossek **Dir**: Vena Nossek
Fleet: 1 coach.
Chassis: 1 Volvo.
Bodies: 1 Jonckheere.
Ops incl: excursions & tours, private hire.

CEDRIC COACHES
1 THE AVENUE, WIVENHOE CO7 9AH
Tel: 01206 824363
Fax: 01206 822253
E-mail: info@cedriccoaches.com
Web site: www.cedriccoaches.com
Dirs: Stephen Peck, Alan Short, Derek Hambling, Simon Osborne
Fleet: 23 - 10 double-deck bus, 1 single-deck bus, 10 coach, 1 double-deck coach. 1 minibus
Chassis: 3 Bova. 1 Bristol. 9 Leyland. 1 Mercedes. 2 Setra. 5 Volvo.
Bodies: 3 Bova. 10 ECW. 3 Jonckheere. 1 Plaxton. 2 Setra. 1 Van Hool.
Ops incl: local bus services, school contracts, private hire.
Livery: Orange/Red/Yellow/White
Ticket system: Wayfarer

CHADWELL HEATH COACHES
30 REYNOLDS AVENUE, CHADWELL HEATH RM6 4NT
Tel: 020 8590 7505
Fax: 020 8597 8883
Props: John Thompson, Lynn Thompson.
Fleet: 5 coach.
Chassis: 2 Leyland. 3 Volvo.
Bodies: 3 Berkhof. 1 Duple. 1 Plaxton.
Ops incl: excursions & tours, private hire, school contracts.
Livery: Country cream

CHARIOTS OF ESSEX LTD
THE COACH HOUSE, 1 ONE TREE HILL, STANFORD-LE-HOPE SS17 9NH
Tel: 01268 581444
Fax: 01268 581555
Man Dir: K T Flavin **Dir**: W J Collier
Fleet: 18 - 3 double-deck bus, 2 single-deck bus, 4 single-deck coach, 1 midicoach, 7 minibus, 1 minicoach.
Chassis: Bova. DAF. Freight Rover. Iveco. Mercedes. Toyota.
Bodies: Bova. Caetano. Marshall/MCV. MCW.
Ops incl: local bus services, school contracts, private hire, express.
Livery: Orange/Yellow
Ticket system: Wayfarer

CLINTONA MINICOACHES
LITTLE WARLEY HALL LANE, BRENTWOOD CM13 3HA
Tel: 01277 215526
Fax: 01277 200038
E-mail: enquiries@clintona.co.uk
Web site: www.clintona.co.uk
Fleet name: Clintona
Ptnrs: Robin Staines, Barbara Staines.
Fleet: 21 - 8 midibus, 6 midicoach, 1 minibus, 6 minicoach.
Chassis: 1 Ford Transit. 1 Iveco. 3 LDV. 16 Mercedes.
Ops incl: local bus services, school contracts, private hire.
Livery: White/Blue.
Ticket System: Wayfarer 3

COOKS COACHES
607 LONDON ROAD, WESTCLIFF-ON-SEA SS0 9PE
Tel: 01702 344702
Fax: 01702 436887
E-mail: info@cookscoaches.co.uk
Web site: www.cookscoaches.co.uk
Prop: W E Cook
Fleet: 12 - 12 single-deck coach
Chassis: 11 Bova. 1 Scania.
Bodies: 11 Bova. 1 Irizar
Ops incl: excursions & tours, private hire, continental tours.
Livery: Red/White
Ticket System: Distinctive

COUNTY COACHES
2 CRESCENT ROAD, BRENTWOOD CM14 5JR
Tel: 01277 201505
Fax: 01277 225918
E-mail: enquiries@countycoaches.com
Web site: www.countycoaches.com
Off Man: C A Jee **Tran Man**: R J Pratt
Fleet: 11 - 8 single-deck coach, 1 minicoach, 2 midibus.
Chassis: 2 Ayats. 2 Mercedes. 1 Toyota. 6 Volvo.
Bodies: 2 Ayats. 1 Berkhof. 3 Caetano. 1 Jonckheere. 2 Mercedes.1 Van Hool. 1 other
Ops incl: excursions & tours, private hire, school contracts.
Livery: Green/White

STAINES CRUSADER COACHES
CRUSADER BUSINESS PARK, STEPHENSON ROAD WEST, CLACTON-ON-SEA CO15 4HP
Tel: 01255 425453
Fax: 01255 222683
Recovery: 01255 431777
E-mail: info@crusader-holidays.co.uk
Web site: www.crusader-holidays.co.uk
Man Dir: Michael Holden **Chairman**: Neil Popham **Comm Dir**: Michael Drinkwater
Finance Dir: Martyn Burke **Dir**: Lisa Childs **Gen Man**: Terry Blanchflower **Ch Eng**: Mark Brooke
Fleet: 26 - 26 single-deck coach
Chassis/Bodies: 26 Setra
Ops incl: excursions & tours, continental tours, private hire
Livery: White/Blue/Red

CUNNINGHAM CARRIAGE COMPANY
THE CARRIAGE HOUSE, FOBBING ROAD, CORRINGHAM SS17 9BG
Tel: 01375 676578.
Fax: 01375 679719.
Prop: Pat Cunningham **Junior Ptnr**: Sarah Cunningham
Fleet: 1 coach.
Chassis: 1 Scania.
Bodies: 1 Irizar.
Ops incl: private hire, express.
Livery: White
Ticket System: Setright.

DOCKLANDS MINIBUSES LTD
See London

DONS COACHES DUNMOW LTD
PARSONAGE DOWNS, GREAT DUNMOW CM6 2AT
Tel: 01371 872644
Fax: 01371 876055
E-mail: jamie@donscoaches.fsnet.co.uk
Web: www.donscoaches.fsnet.co.uk
Dirs: S D Harvey
Fleet: 16 - 3 double-deck bus, 10 coach, 2 midicoach, 1 minicoach.
Chassis: 1 Ayats. 1 Caetana. 1 Dennis. 1 Jonckheere. 1 Mercedes. 3 Neoplan. 2 Plaxton.
Bodies: 2 Alexander. 1 Ayats. 2 Caetano. 2 Duple. 1 Marcopolo. 3 Neoplan. 3 Plaxton.
Ops incl: private hire, school contracts.
Livery: Red/Yellow/Blue

EAST LONDON BUS GROUP
See London

EDS MINIBUS & COACH HIRE
257 PRINCESS MARGARET ROAD, EAST TILBURY RM18 8SB
Tel/Fax: 01375 858049
Props: E Sammons, Mrs S Sammons
Fleet: 2 - 1 coach, 1 minibus.
Chassis/Body: MAN/Algarve
Ops incl: Private hire, excursions & tours

ENSIGN BUS CO LTD
JULIETTE CLOSE, PURFLEET INDUSTRIAL PARK, PURFLEET RM15 4YF
Tel: 01708 865656
Fax: 01708 864340
E-mail: sales@ensignbus.com
Web-site: www.ensignbus.com
Chmn: Peter Newman **Dirs**: Ross Newman(**Sales**), Brian Longley (**Eng**), Steve Newman (**City Sightseeing**) **Com Dir**: Gary Nicholass **Eng Man**: Roger Jackson
Fleet (Purfleet): 36 - 24 double-deck bus, 8 single-deck bus, 1 coach, 4 open-top bus.
Chassis: 14 AEC. 1 Bristol. 2 Daimler. 6 Dennis. 12 MCW. 2 Volvo.
Bodies: 1 Ayats. 12 MCW. 1 Northern Counties. 11 Park Royal. 6 UVG. 2 Craven. 1 Weymann.
Ops incl: local bus services, private hire.
Livery: Blue/Silver
Ticket System: Almex A90

EXCALIBUR COACH TRAVEL
44 MOUNTVIEW CRESCENT, ST LAWRENCE BAY, SOUTHMINSTER CM0 7NR
Tel: 01621 779980
Fax: 01621 778928
E-mail: info@excaliburcoach.co.uk
Web site: www.excaliburcoach.co.uk
Prop: Trevor Wynn
Fleet: 3 minibus.
Chassis: 1 Ford Transit. 1 LDV.
Ops incl: private hire, school contracts.

EXCEL PASSENGER LOGISTICS LTD
R24
AIRWAYS HOUSE, FIRST AVENUE, STANSTED AIRPORT CM24 1RY
Tel: 01279 681800
Fax: 01279 682268
Recovery: 07770 873614
E-mail: mail@excelpl.co.uk
Web site: www.excelcoaches.co.uk
Man Dir: Graham Hayden **Eng**: Carl Johnson
Fleet: 54
Chassis: 2 Ayats. 10 Dennis. 12 Leyland. 4 MAN. 8 Mercedes. 11 Scania. 1 Scania. 6 Volvo.
Bodies: include: 2 Ayats. 5 Irizar. 1 Setra
Ops incl: local bus services, school contracts
Subsidiary of Arriva

FARGO COACHLINES
ALLVIEWS, SCHOOL ROAD, RAYNE, BRAINTREE CM7 6SS
Tel : 01376 321817
Fax: 01376 551236
E-mail: enquiries@fargocoachlines.co.uk
Web site: www.fargocoachlines.co.uk
Prop: L J Smith
Fleet: 8 Minibus
Ops incl: private hire
Livery: White

FERRERS COACHES LTD
117B HULLBRIDGE ROAD, SOUTH WOODHAM FERRERS CM3 5LL
Tel: 01245 320456.
Dir: A. Read, G. Read.
Fleet: 4 - 2 coach, 2 minibus.
Chassis: 2 Dennis. 1 Ford Transit. 1 Freight Rover.
Ops incl: excursions & tours, private hire, school contracts.

FIRST ESSEX BUSES
WESTWAY, CHELMSFORD CM1 3AR
Tel: 01245 243400
Web site: www.firstgroup.com
Man Dir: R Dorr **Ops Dir**: Duncan Cameron **Eng Dir**: S Little **Fin Dir**: M Dolphin **Div Man N Essex**: L Berry **Div Man S Essex**: C McCormick
Fleet: 341 - 42 double-deck bus, 272 single-deck bus, 1 open-top double-deck bus, 17 midibus, 9 midicoach.
Chassis: 1 Bristol. 204 Dennis. 17 Leyland. 54 Mercedes-Benz. 38 Scania. 27 Volvo.
Bodies: 36 Alexander. 12 ECW. 21 East Lancs. 16 Marshall/MCV. 37 Northern Counties. 28 Optare. 136 Plaxton. 17 Transbus. 38 Wright.
Ops incl: local bus service, school contracts.
Livery: First Group - White/Blue/Magenta
Ticket System: Wayfarer

FORDS COACHES
THE GARAGE, FAMBRIDGE ROAD, ALTHORNE CM3 6BZ
Tel: 01621 740326
Fax: 01621 742781
Web site: www.fordscoaches.co.uk
Prop: A A W Ford **Ch Eng**: A W Ford
Fleet: 22 - 8 double-deck bus, 1 single-deck bus, 8 single-deck coach. 3 double-deck coach, 2 midicoach
Chassis: 6 Alexander Dennis 1 AEC. 1 Bedford. 8 Leyland. 3 Scania.
Bodies: 2 Alexander. 1 Ayats. 1 Beulas. 2 Berkhof. 1 Caetano. 6 ECW. 1 Indcar. 1 Mellor. 1 Optare. 2 Plaxton. 4 Van Hool.
Ops incl: local bus services, school contracts, excursions & tours, private hire.
Livery: White/Multi-colour stripe
Ticket system: Wayfarer

GALLEON TRAVEL LTD
ENTERPRISE HOUSE, 17 PERRY ROAD, HARLOW CM18 7PN
TEL: 01279 432048
Fleet Name: Galleon Travel, Shire Coaches, Trustline Buses
E-mail: galleontravel@btopenworld.com
Web site: www.galleontravel.co.uk
Man Dir: Helen Bowden **Ops Dir**: Mark Bowden **Priv Hire Dir**: Megan Baker **Gen Man**: Steve Stapleton **Eng Man**: Derek Collier **Business Man**: James Doherty
Fleet: 37 - 7 double-deck bus, 20 single-deck bus, 5 coach, 2 double-deck coach, 2 minibus
Chassis: 1 Ayats. 28 Dennis. 1 MAN. 3 Optare. 4 Scania.
Bodies: 2 Alexnder. 1 Ayats. 1 Berkhof. 1 Carlyle. 6 East Lancs. 3 Irizar. 2 Leyland. 4 Marshall. 14 Plaxton. 2 Transbus. 1 UVG.
Ops incl: Local Bus Service, School Contracts, Excursions & Tours, Private Hire
Livery: Maroon (coach) Yellow/Red/Blue (bus)
Ticket System: Almex A90

GATWICK FLYER LTD
DANES ROAD, ROMFORD RM7 OHL
Tel: 01708 730555
Fax: 01708 751231
Web site: www.gatwickflyer.co.uk
Fleetnames: Gatwick Flyer, Avon Coaches
Fleet: 15 - 6 coach, 9 minicoach.
Ops incl: private hire, express.

GENIAL TRAVEL
43 PEACE ROAD, STANWAY, COLCHESTER CO3 OHL.
Tel/Fax: 01206 571513
Prop: Trevor Brookes
Fleet: 1 coach.
Chassis: 1 DAF
Body: 1 Van Hool
Ops incl: excursions & tours, private hire.
Livery: White/Blue/Yellow.

PETER GODWARD COACHES
UNITS 3&4 MLLS COURT, SWINBOURNE ROAD, BURNT MILLS INDUSTIAL ESTATE, BALSILDON SS13 1EH
Tel: 01268 591834
Fax: 01268 591835
E-mail: peter.godward@virgin.net
Prop: P R Godward, A M Godward
Fleet: 12 - 8 single-deck coach, 3 double-deck bus, 1 minicoach.
Chassis: 4 Iveco. 4 Scania. 3 Volvo. 1 LDV.
Body: 4 Beulas. 3 ECW. 4 Irizar.
Ops incl: school contracts, excursions & tours, private hire, express, continental tours.
Livery: White

GOLDEN BOY COACHES
See Hertfordshire

GOODWIN'S COACHES
ALWYNN, LONDON ROAD, BLACK NOTLEY, BRAINTREE CM7 8QQ
Tel: 01376 321096
Prop: A. M. Goodwin. **Sec**: I. B. Goodwin.
Fleet: 6 - 5 coach, 1 minibus.
Chassis: 3 Bedford. 2 Volvo.
Bodies: 1 Berkhof. 4 Plaxton. 1 Crystal.
Ops incl: excursions & tours, private hire.
Livery: White/Blue/Grey stripes.

GRAHAM'S
19 CHURCH ROAD, KELVEDON CO5 9JH
Tel: 01376 570150.
Fax: 01376 570657
Prop: G. Ellis.
Livery: White/Blue.

HAILSTONE TRAVEL LTD
82 BRACKLEY CRESCENT, BASILDON SS13 1RA
Tel: 0845 388 3848
Fax: 01268 543066
E-mail: info@hailstonetravel.co.uk
Web site: www.hailstonetravel.co.uk
Dirs: Mrs Tina Hailstone, Lawrence Hailstone
Fleet: 7 single-deck coach.
Chassis: 7Mercedes.
Ops incl: school contracts, excursions & tours, private hire
Livery: White

HARDY MILES COACHES LTD
259 HAMSTEL ROAD, SOUTHEND ON SEA SS2 4LB
Tel: 01701 612222
Fax: 01702 546461
E-mail: info@hardymilestravel.co.uk
Web site: www.hardymilestravel.co.uk
Prop: Richard Jordan, Michael Chapman
Fleet: 3 - 2 double-deck bus 1 single-deck coach.
Chassis: 2 MCW. 1 Scania
Bodies: 1 Irizar. 2 MCW
Ops incl: excursions & tours, private hire.

HEDINGHAM & DISTRICT OMNIBUSES LTD
WETHERSFIELD ROAD, SIBLE HEDINGHAM CO9 3LB
Tel: 01787 460621
Fax: 01787 462852
E-mail: services@hedingham.co.uk
Man Dir: R J MacGregor **Dir**: D R MacGregor
Fleet: 105 - 42 double-deck bus, 44 single-deck bus, 19 coach.
Chassis: 12 Bristol. 23 Dennis. 21 Leyland. 49 Volvo.
Bodies: 27 Alexander. 22 ECW. 1 East Lancs. 4 Leyland. 8 Northern Counties. 28 Plaxton. 14 Transbus. 1 Willowbrook. 1 Wright.
Ops incl: local bus services, school contracts, excursions & tours, private hire.
Livery: Red/Cream.
Ticket System: Wayfarer

IMPERIAL BUS CO LTD
MARSH VIEW INDUSTRIAL ESTATE, FERRY LANE, RAINHAM RM13 9YN
Tel: 01708 553953
Fax: 01708 525602
Web site: www.imperialbus.co.uk
Man Dir: M Biddell
Fleet: 37 - 27 double-deck bus, 9 single-deck bus, 1 coach.
Livery: Green.

KINGS COACHES
364 LONDON ROAD, STANWAY, COLCHESTER CO3 8LT
Tel: 01206 210332
Fax: 01206 213861
E-mail: info@kings-coaches.co.uk
Web site: www.kings-coaches.co.uk
Prop: Andrew B Cousins
Fleet: 7 single-deck coach.
Chassis: 7 Bova.
Bodies: 7 Bova.
Ops incl: excursions & tours, private hire, continental tours.
Livery: Green/Cream

KIRBYS COACHES (RAYLEIGH) LTD
2 PRINCESS ROAD, RAYLEIGH SS6 8HR
Tel: 01268 777777
Fax: 01702 202555
E-mail: kirbyscoaches@hotmail.com
Web site: www.kirbyscoaches.co.uk
Dir: Edward Kirby **Co Sec**: Elizabeth Kirby
Fleet: 9 coach.
Chassis/bodies: 9 Setra.
Ops incl: excursions & tours, private hire, continental tours.
Livery: Lilac/Turquoise

LINKFAST LTD T/A S&M COACHES
93 ROSEBERRY AVENUE, BENFLEET SS7 4JF.
Tel/Fax: 01268 795763.
Props: B. W. Smith (Ch Eng), W. N. May (Sec)
Fleet: 10 - 9 double-deck bus, 1 coach.
Chassis: Daimler, Leyland.
Bodies: ECW, Northern Counties, Park Royal, Plaxton.
Ops incl: school contracts, private hire.
Livery: Mixed.

LODGE COACHES
THE GARAGE, HIGH EASTER, CHELMSFORD CM1 4QT
Tel: 01245 231262
Fax: 01245 231825
E-mail: administrator@lodgecoaches.co.uk
Web site: www.lodgecoaches.co.uk
Dirs: Robert Lodge, Andrew Lodge, Christopher Lodge.
Fleet: 20 - 6 double-deck, 1 single-deck bus 11 single-deck coach, 2 minicoach.
Chassis: Bedford. Dennis. Iveco. Layland. Mercedes. Scania. Setra.
Bodies: Duple. Leyland. Marshall/MCV. Mellor. Mercedes-Benz. Optare. Park Royal. Plaxton. Setra. Van Hool
Ops incl: local bus services, school contracts, excursions & tours, private hire, continental tours.
Livery: Blue/Cream

MIKES COACHES
THE GRANARY, PIPPS HILL ROAD NORTH, CRAYS HILL, BASILDON CM11 2UJ.
Tel: 01268 525900.
Fax: 01268 453654.
Ptnrs: M. Orphan, D. Orphan, P. Brown.
Fleet: 6 - 5 coach, 1 midicoach.
Chassis: 2 Bedford. 1 DAF. 3 Volvo.
Bodies: 5 Plaxton. 1 Van Hool.
Ops incl: local bus services, school contracts, private hire.

NETWORK COLCHESTER
UNIT 4 HEATH BUSINESS PARK, GRANGE WAY, COLCHESTER CO2 8GH
Tel: 01206 877620
Tel: 01206 766345
Web site: www.networkcolchester.co.uk
Fleetname: Network Colchester
Man Dir: Paul Cooper **Fleet Eng**: Steve Legate
Fleet: 46 - 16 double-deck bus, 30 single-deck bus.
Chassis: 3 DAF. 22 Dennis. 1 Mercedes. 3 Optare, 7 Scania, 10 Volvo.
Bodies: 11 East Lancs. 15 Plaxton. 6 Alexander, 7 Caetano 4 N Counties, Optare.
Ops incl: local bus services, excursions & tours, school contracts, private hire, continental tours.
Livery: Blue/Yellow on White base
Subsidiary of Burtons Coaches/TGM - part of Arriva

W. H. NELSON (COACHES) LTD
THE COACH STATION, BRUCE GROVE, WICKFORD SS11 8BZ.
Tel: 01268 767870
Fax: 01268 735307
E-mail: info@nibsbus.com
Web site: www.nibsbus.com
Fleetname: Nelsons Independent Bus Services.
Ops incl: local bus services, school contracts
Livery: Yellow.

OLYMPIAN COACHES LTD
TEMPLE BANK, RIVER WAY, HARLOW CM20 2DY
Tel: 01279 868868.
Fax: 01279 868867
Web site: www.olympiancoaches.com
Dirs: C. Marino. **Co Sec:** Mrs D. K. Higgins. **Ops Dir:** B. Gunton
Fleet: 40 - coach, minibus.
Ops incl: local bus services, school contracts, excursions & tours, private hire, continental tours.

P & M COACHES
74 CHURCHEND LANE, WICKFORD SS11 7JG.
Tel: 01268 763616.

PHILLIPS COACHES
117B HULLBRIDGE ROAD, SOUTH WOODHAM FERRERS CM3 5LL.
Tel/Fax: 01245 323039.
Prop: L. Phillips.
Fleet: 3 - 2 coach, 1 minibus.
Chassis: 1 Freight Rover. 2 Volvo.
Bodies: Plaxton. Van Hool.
Ops incl: excursions & tours, private hire, school contracts.
Livery: Cream/Maroon.

REGAL BUSWAYS LTD
LANDVIEW, COOKSMILL GREEN, CHELMSFORD CM1 3SR
Tel: 01702 291001
E-mail: info@regalbusways.com
Web site: www.regalbusways.com
Man Dir: Adrian McGarry **Ops Dir**: Lee Whitehead **Dir**: Mandy McGarry
Fleetname: Essex Pullman
Fleet: 14 - 4 double-deck bus, 9 single-deck bus, 1 double-deck coach
Chassis: 4 Dennis. 1 MCW. 3 Optare. 2 Transbus. 4 Volvo.
Bodies: 1 Alexander. 4 Marshall. 1 MCW. 3 Optare. 4 Plaxton. 2 Transbus.
Ops incl: local bus services, private hire, school contracts.
Livery: Maroon/Cream
Ticket system: ERG

RELIANCE LUXURY COACHES
54 BROOK ROAD, BENFLEET SS7 5JF
Tel/Fax: 01268 758426
Props: Martyn J Titchen
Fleet: 4 - 1 double-deck bus, 3 single-deck coach
Chassis: 1 Leyland. 3 Scania.
Ops incl: private hire, school contracts.
Livery: Yellow/White/Orange/Red.

STALLION COACHES
STACEYS FARM BUNGALOW, BROOMFIELD, CHELMSFORD CM1 7HF.
Tel/Fax: 01245 443500.
Ptnrs: D. A. Brewster, Miss J. C. Pinkerton.
Fleet: 2 midicoach.
Chassis: 1 Mercedes. 1 Toyota.
Bodies: 1 Caetano. 1 Reeve Burgess.
Ops incl: school contracts, private hire.

STAN'S COACHES
THE COACH-HOUSE, BECKINGHAM ROAD, GREAT TOTHAM, MALDON CM9 8DY.
Tel: 01621 891959.
Fax: 01621 891365.
Prop: S. J. Porter.
Fleet: 6 - 5 coach, 1 minibus.
Chassis: 1 Bedford. 3 Bova. 1 Mercedes. 1 Volvo.
Bodies: 3 Bova. 1 Duple. 1 Mercedes. 1 Plaxton.
Ops incl: excursions & tours, private hire, continental tours.
Livery: White with Blue/Grey stripes.

STANSTED TRANSIT
UNIT 7, 500 AVENUE WEST, GREAT NOTLEY GARDEN VILLAGE BUSINESS PARK, GREAT NOTLEY CM77 7AA
Tel: 01229 681786
Fleet: 33 - 5 double-deck bus, 22 single-deck bus, 6 midibus.
Chassis: 1 DAF, 12 Dennis, 1 Leyland National, 5 MCW. 7 Optare.
Bodies: 1 Alexander, 2 Caetano, 7 Leyland, 1 Leyland National, 5 MCW. 7 Optare. 7 Plaxton. 1 UVG. 2 Wright.
Ops incl: local bus services, school contracts, private hire.
Livery: White.
Ticket system: ERG.

ESSEX

STEPHENSONS OF ESSEX LTD
RIVERSIDE INDUSTRIAL ESTATE, SOUTH STREET, ROCHFORD SS4 1BS
Tel: 01702 541511
Fax: 01702 549461
Web site: www.stephensonsofessex.com
E-mail: sales@stephensonsofessex.com
Man Dir: Bill Hiron **Fin Dir**: Lyn Watson
Ops Man: Lee Shuttleworth **Eng Man**: Tony Wright
Fleet: 58 - 37 double-deck bus, 17 single-deck bus, 2 single-deck coach. 2 double-deck coaxh
Chassis: 8 Alexander Dennis. 3 Dennis. 34 Leyland. 6 Optare. 8 Volvo.
Ops incl: local bus services, school contracts, private hire.
Livery: White/Green
Ticket System: Wayfarer 3

SUPREME COACHES
THE OLD BT DEPOT, STOCK ROAD, SOUTH END ON SEA SS2 5QA
Tel: 01702 440230
Fax: 01702 616590
E-mail: mandy@supremecoaches.co.uk
Web site: www.supremecoaches.co.uk
Man Dir: John Bridge. **Dir**: Toby Bridge
Sec: Ray Osborne **Dir of Ops**: David Parrin **Chief Eng**: Steve Mitchell
Fleet: 24 - 12 double-deck bus, 2 single-deck bus, 8 single-deck coach, 2 minibus.
Chassis: 2 Ford Transit. 1 Inveco. 1 Layland. 12 MCW. 1 Mercees-Benz. 4 Scania. 1 Setra. 2 Volvo.
Bodies: 1 Berkhof. 1 Carlyle. 2 Irizar. 12 MCW. 1 Plaxton. 1 Setra. 3 Van Hool. 3 Other.
Ops incl: school contracts, excursions & tours, private hire, continental tours.
Livery: Red/White/Blue

SWALLOW COACH CO LTD
RAINHAM HOUSE, MANOR WAY, RAINHAM RM13 8RE.
Tel: 01708 630555.
Fax: 01708 555135.
Chmn: D. R. Webb. **Man Dir**: K. I. Webb.
Sec: Mrs. S. D. Webb.
Fleet: 26 - 17 coach. 5 midicoach. 4 minicoach.
Chassis: 1 DAF. 1 Dennis. 1 Ford. 1 Ford Transit. 3 Freight Rover. 3 Leyland. 1 MAN. 2 Mercedes. 1 Setra. 1 Toyota. 11 Volvo.
Bodies: 5 Caetano. 1 Carlyle. 4 Jonckheere. 2 Mercedes. 6 Plaxton. 1 Setra. 2 Van Hool. **Ops incl**: Private hire.
Livery: Various.

T. F. MINI COACHES
1 SCRATTONS TERRACE, RIPPLE ROAD, BARKING IG11 0TY.
Tel: 020 8593 6205.
Fax: 020 8592 7182.
Man Dir: T. Farrugia.
Fleet: 7 midicoach.
Chassis: 7 Renault.
Ops incl: excursions & tours, private hire, airport transfer.

VICEROY COACHES LTD
12 BRIDGE STREET, SAFFRON WALDEN CB10 1BU
Tel: 01799 508010
Fax: 01799 522311
Man Dir: A R Moore **Man Dir/Eng**: S A Moore **Ops Man**: A L Moore
Fleet: 7 - 1 dingle-deck bus, 4 single-deck coach, 1 midibus, 1 minicoach.
Chassis: 1 BMC. 1 DAF. 4 Mercedes.1 Scania.
Bodies: 1 BMC. 1 Bova. 2 Hispano. 1 Mercedes. 1 Plaxton.
Ops incl: school contracts, excursions & tours, private hire, continental tours.
Livery: White
Ticket System: Wayfarer 3

WALDEN TRAVEL LTD
126 THAXTED ROAD, SAFFRON WALDEN CB11 3BJ
Tel/Fax: 01799 516878
Man Dir: Peter Blanchard **Non-exec Dirs**: John Wilson, David Grimmett, James Raynham
Fleet: 7 - 4 single-deck coach, 2 midibus, 1 minicoach.
Chassis: 2 Dennis. 1 Ford. 2 Mercedes. 2 Volvo
Bodies: 1 Jonckheere. Plaxton. 1 other.
Ops incl: local bus services, school contracts, excursions & tours, private hire.
Livery: White
Ticket System: ERG

WEST'S COACHES LTD
See London

GLOUCESTERSHIRE

ALEXCARS LTD
LOVE LANE INDUSTRIAL ESTATE, CIRENCESTER GL7 1YG
Tel: 01285 653985
Fax: 01285 652964
E-mail: rod@alexcars.co.uk
Web: www.alexcars.co.uk
Man Dir: Rod Hibberd **Dir/Com Sec**: Jenny Jarvis, **Snr Dir**: Barbara Hibberd
Dir: Ben Jarvis **Dir/Tran Man**: Will Jarvis
Ch Eng: Steve Hall
Fleet: 22 - 14 single-deck coach, 2 midicoach, 4 minicoach, 2 minibus.
Chassis: 4 Alexander Dennis 1 Bedford. 3 MAN. 10 Scania. 3 Toyota. 1 Volkswagen.
Bodies: 4 Caetano. 1 Duple. 11 Irizar. 1 Marcopolo. 1 Noge. 3 Plaxton. 1 Wadham Stringer.
Ops incl: school contracts, excursions & tours, private hire, continental tours.
Livery: Duo Blue

BAKERS COACHES
COTSWOLD BUSINESS VILLAGE, MORETON-IN-THE-MARSH GL56 0JQ
Tel: 0845 688 7707
Fax: 0845 688 7660
E-mail: enquiries@bakerscoaches.co.uk
Web site: www.bakerscoaches.co.uk
Dir: Mike Baker **Ops Man**: Dave Goodall
Fleet: 17 - 14 coach, 2 midicoach, 1 minibus.
Chassis: 2 Dennis. 2 Iveco. 3 Mercedes. 1 Scania. 2 Transbus. 7 Volvo.
Bodies: Alexander. Irizar. Plaxton.
Ops incl: local bus services, excursions & tours, school contracts, private hire, continental tours.
Livery: White/Red

120

B. E. W. BEAVIS/BEAVIS HOLIDAYS
BUSSAGE GARAGE, BUSSAGE, STROUD GL6 8BA
Tel: 01453 882297
Fax: 01453 731019
E-mail: admin@beavisholidays.co.uk
Props/Ptnrs: Brian Beavis, Anita Baxter
Chief Eng: Chris Beavis
Fleet: 8 - 5 single-deck coach, 2 midicoach, 1 minibus.
Chassis: 1 DAF. 4 Neoplan. 1 Scania. 1 Toyota. 1 Volkswagen.
Bodies: 1 Caetano, 1 Irizar, 4 Neoplan. 2 other.
Ops incl: excursions & tours, private hire, school contracts, continental tours.
Livery: Gold/Red/Yellow.

BENNETT'S COACHES
EASTERN AVENUE, GLOUCESTER GL4 7LP.
Tel: 01452 527809.
Fax: 01452 384448.
Prop: Peter Bennett
Fleet: 24 - 5 double-deck bus, 7 signle-deck bus, 12 single-deck coach.
Chassis: 4 DAF. 1 MAN 9 Mercedes-Benz. 5 Neoplan, 5Volvo.
Bodies: 5 Alexander Dennis, 2 Ikarus, 9 Mercedes 5 Neoplan, 3 Van Hool.
Ops incl: local bus services, excursions & tours, private hire, continental tours.
Livery: Blue/Grey/Orange.

JAMES BEVAN (LYDNEY) LTD
THE BUS STATION, HAMS ROAD, LYDNEY GL15 5PE
Tel/Fax: 01594 842859
E-mail: jamesbevancoaches@tiscali.co.uk
Web: jamesbevancoaches.com
Man Dir: James Bevan **Ops Dir**: J Zimmerman **Eng Dir**: M Zimmerman
Fleet: 12 - 6 single-deck coach, 5 midbus, 1minicoach.
Chassis: 2 Dennis. 1 LDV. 3 Mercedes-Benz. 2 Optare. 4 Volvo.
Bodies: 2 Optare, 4 Plaxton, 2 Sunsundegui, 2 Wadham Stringer.
Ops incl: local bus services, school contracts, private hire.
Livery: Silver
Ticket System: Wayfarer

CASTLEWAYS LTD
CASTLE HOUSE, GREET ROAD, WINCHCOMBE GL54 5PU
Tel: 01242 603715
Fax: 01242 604454
Web: www.castleways.co.uk
Man Dir: John Fogarty **Co Sec**: Mrs Rowena McCubbin **Ch Eng**: Trevor Wood
Fleet: 12 - 3 single-deck bus, 8 coach, 1 midicoach
Chassis: 1 Dennis. 7 Mercedes. 1 Toyota. 1 VDL. 2 Volvo.
Bodies: 1 Alexander Dennis. 1 Bova. 1 Caetano. 2 Mercedes. 1 Plaxton. 5 Setra. 1 Sunsundegui
Ops incl: local bus services, school contracts, private hire.
Livery: Dark Blue/Silver/Gold
Ticket System: Wayfarer

CATHEDRAL COACHES LTD
18 QUAY STREET, GLOUCESTER GL1 2JS
Tel: 01452 524591
Fax: 01452 524595
E-mail: info@cathedralcoaches.fsnet.co.uk
Web: cathedralcoaches.co.uk
Proprietors: Irene Chandler, Paul Chandler
Fleet: 10 - 6 single-deck bus, 4 midicoach.
Chassis: 1 Bedford. 1 DAF. 3 Dennis. 3 Mercedes-Benz. 1 Toyota 1 Volvo.
Bodies: 2 Caetano. 1 Duple. 1 Mercedes-Benz. 1 Optare. 5 Plaxton.
Ops incl: school contracts, private hire.
Livery: Blue/Grey/Red/White

EAGLE LINE TRAVEL
ANDOVERSFORD TRADING ESTATE, ANDOVERSFORD GL54 4LB
Tel/Fax: 01242 820535
E-mail: brian@eaglelinetravel.co.uk
Web site: www.eaglelinetravel.co.uk
Man Dirs: Brian Davis Martin Davis Wayne Hodge **Ch Eng**: Tony Mezzone
Fleet: 22 - 10 coach, 2 double-deck coach, 2 midibus, 4 midicoach, 2 minicoach, 2 minibus.
Chassis: 2 DAF. 2 Dennis. 4 Ford Transit. 6 Mercedes. 1 Neoplan. 1 Scania. Setra.1 Toyota. 5 Volvo.
Bodies: 2 Autobus. 2 Berkhof. 1 Caetano. 2 Mercedes. 4 Ford Transit. 1 Neoplan. 2 Plaxton. 6 Van Hool. 2 VW.
Ops incl: school contracts, excursions & tours, private hire, continental tours.
Livery: Dark Blue/Silver/Silver Blue

EBLEY COACHES LTD
UNIT 27, NAILSWORTH MILLS ESTATE, AVENING ROAD, NAILSWORTH GL6 0BS
Tel/Fax: 01453 839333
Dirs: C C Levitt, G A Jones.
Fleet: 19 - 6 double-deck bus, 7 coach, 5 minibus, 1 minicoach.
Chassis: 6 Bristol. 5 DAF. 1 Leyland. 1 MAN. 6 Mercedes.
Bodies: 4 Alexander. 1 Duple. 6 ECW. 1 Plaxton. 2 Reeve Burgess. 5 Van Hool.
Ops incl: local bus services, school contracts, excursions & tours, private hire, continental tours.

DAVID FIELD
WHEATSTONE HOUSE, WATERY LANE, NEWENT GL18 1PY
Tel: 01531 820979
E-mail: dowfield@yahoo.co.uk
Web site: www.davidfieldtravel.co.uk
Prop: David Field
Fleet: 9 - 7 single-deck coach, 2 midicoach.
Chassis: 1 Bedford. 1 DAF. 1 Dennis. 1 Iveco. 1 Leyland. 2 Mercedes. 1 Setra. 1 Toyota.
Ops incl: school contracts,private hire.
Livery: Black/White

GRINDLES COACHES LTD
4 DOCKHAM ROAD, CINDERFORD GL14 2DD.
Tel: 01594 822110.
Fax: 01594 823189.
Man Dir: P. R. Grindle. **Co Sec**: W. H. R. Grindle.
Fleet: 7 coach.
Chassis: 3 Bedford. 1 Bova. 3 DAF.
Bodies: 1 Bova. 5 Plaxton. 1 Van Hool.
Ops incl: local bus services, private hire.

MARCHANTS COACHES
61 CLARENCE STREET, CHELTENHAM GL50 3LB
Tel: 01242 257714
Fax: 01242 251360
E-mail: sales@marchants-coaches.com
Web site: www.marchants-coaches.com
Man Dir: Roger Marchant **Dir/Ops/Tran Man**: Richard Marchant **Ch Eng**: Russell Marchant **Co Sec**: Mrs Jean Ellis
Fleet: 24 -5 double-deck bus, 5 single-deck bus, 11 coach, 2 double-deck coach, 1 midicoach.
Chassis: 2 Bristol. 3 Leyland. 1 Mercedes. 2 Neoplan. 16 Volvo.
Bodies: 1 Alexander. 4 ECW. 4 Jonckheere. 2 Neoplan. 10 Plaxton. 3 Wright.
Ops incl: local bus services, school contracts, excursions & tours, private hire, continental tours.
Livery: Red/Gold
Ticket System: Wayfarer

PULHAM & SONS (COACHES) LTD
STATION ROAD GARAGE, BOURTON ON THE WATER, GL54 2EN
Tel: 01451 820369.
E-mail: info@pulhamscoaches.com
Web site: www.pulhamscoaches.com
Ops incl: local bus services, school contracts, excursions & tours, private hire.
Livery: Red

GLOUCESTERSHIRE

ROVER EUROPEAN TRAVEL LTD

THE COACH HOUSE, HORSLEY, STROUD GL6 0PU
Tel: 01453 832121
Fax: 01453 832722
E-mail: rovereuropean@compuserve.com
Man Dir: David Hand **Dir**: Carol Hand
Fleet: 11 - 10 coach, 1 midicoach
Chassis: 7 Bova. 3 Dennis. 1 Toyota.
Bodies: 1 Berkhof. 7 Bova. 1 Caetano. 1 Plaxton. 1 Wadham Stringer.
Ops incl: school contracts, excursions & tours, private hire, continental tours.
Livery: Cream base with Light Blue/Dark Blue/Orange.

STAGECOACH WEST

3RD FLOOR, 65 LONDON ROAD, GLOUCESTER GL1 3HF
Tel: 01452 418630
Fax: 01452 304857
E-Mail: west@stagecoachbus.com
Man Dir: I Manning **Eng Dir**: P Sheldon
Ops Dir: S Thomas **Com Man**: Caig Lockely
Fleet: 242 - 80 double-deck bus, 28 single-deck bus, 8 single-deck coach, 106 midibus, 20 minibus.
Chassis: 154 Alexander Dennis. 1 AEC. 4 Leyland. 9 MAN. 3 Mercedes. 18 Optare. 5 Scania. 47 Volvo.
Bodies: 176 Alexander Dennis. 6 Caetano. 4 Leyland. 1 Marshall/MCV. 9 Northern Counties. 18 Optare. 1 Park Royal. 23 Plaxton. 3 Wright
Ops incl: local bus services, school contracts, private hire, express.
Livery: Red/Blue/White/Orange
Ticket System: Wayfarer

SWANBROOK TRANSPORT LTD

GOLDEN VALLEY, STAVERTON, CHELTENHAM GL51 0TE
Tel: 01452 712386
Fax: 01452 859217
E-mail: enquiries@swanbrook.co.uk
Web site: www.swanbrook.co.uk
Chmn: D J Thomas **Man Dirs**: K T Thomas, **Fleet Dir**: J A Thomas **Dir**; Mrs K J West **Ops Man**: M Dowle
Fleet: 29 - 9 double-deck bus, 3 single-deck bus, 4 single-deck coach, 4 midibus. 9 minbus.
Chassis: 2 Dennis. 5 Leyland. 4 MCW. 9 Mercedes. 4 Optare. 5 Volvo.
Bodies: 6 Alexander. 1 East Lancs. 2 Marshall. 4 MCW. 4 Optare. 10 Plaxton. 2 Wadham Stringer.
Ops incl: local bus services, school contracts, private hire.
Livery: White/Green/Purple
Ticket System: Wayfarer II

F R WILLETTS & CO (YORKLEY) LTD

DEAN RISE, MAIN ROAD, PILLOWELL GL15 4QY
Tel: 01594 562511
Fax: 01594 564373
Man Dir: Geoff Willetts **Sec**: Sue Willetts
Fleet: 6 - 4 coach, 1 minicoach, 1 minibus.
Chassis: 1 Dennis. 1 Leyland. 2 Mercedes. 1 Setra. 1 Volvo.
Bodies: 1 Mercedes. 4 Plaxton. 1 Setra.
Ops incl: local bus services, school contracts, excursions & tours, private hire.
Livery: Red
Ticket System: Setright

MAL WITTS EXECUTIVE TRAVEL

1 YEW TREE COTTAGE, BRISTOL ROAD, HARDWICKE, GLOUCESTER GL2 4QZ
Tel/Fax: 01452 724072
E-mail: mal@malwittstravel.co.uk
Web site: www.malwittstravel.co.uk
Owners: Mal Witts, Lynn Witts
Fleet: 4 - 2 minicoach, 2 people carrier
Bodies: 2 Mercedes, 2 VW
Ops incl: private hire, continental tours, excursions & tours, school contracts

---

	Vehicle suitable for disabled	Seat belt-fitted Vehicle	24 hour recovery service
	Toilet-drop facilities available	Coach(es) with galley facilities	Replacement vehicle available
	Recovery service available	Air-conditioned vehicle(s)	Vintage Coach(es) available
	Open top vehicle(s)v	Coaches with toilet facilities	

GLOUCESTERSHIRE

122

GREATER MANCHESTER (BOLTON, BURY, OLDHAM, ROCHDALE, SALFORD, TAMESIDE, WIGAN)

ADLINGTON TAXIS AND MINICOACHES
LODGE FARM, SANDY LANE, HORWICH BL6 6RS
Tel: 01204 697577
E-mail: frank@fjohnson7.wanado.co.uk
Fleet: 5 - 2 single-deck bus, 1 coach, 2 midicoach.
Chassis: 1 Bedford. 2 Freight Rover. 2 Iveco.
Ops incl: local bus services, private hire.
Ticket System: Wayfarer

ASHALL'S COACHES
UNIT 11, FROXMER STREET, GORTON, MANCHESTER M18 8EF
Tel: 0161 231 7777
Fax: 0161 231 7787
Web site: www.ashalls.co.uk
Prop: D S Ashall
Fleet: 20 - 6 double-deck bus, 4 single-deck bus, 8 single-deck coach, 2 midicoach.
Chassis: 15 Dennis. 2 Mercedes. 1 Scania. 2 Volvo.
Bodies: 2 Duple. 2 Mellor. 6 Northern Counties. 2 Plaxton.2 Transbus. 6 Wadham Stringer.
Ops incl: local bus services, school contracts, private hire.
Livery: Red
Ticket system: Wayfarer 2

BATTERSBY'S COACHES
73 BRIDGEWATER ROAD, WALKDEN M28 3AF
Tel/Fax: 0161 790 2842
Dirs: R W Griffiths, S. J. Griffiths
Fleet: 3 coach.
Chassis: 1 Leyland. 2 Setra.
Ops incl: private hire, school contracts.

BLUEBIRD BUS & COACH
ALEXANDER HOUSE, GREENGATE, MIDDLETON M24 1RU
Tel: 0161 653 1900
Fax: 0161 653 6602
Web site: www.bluebirdbus.co.uk
Gen Man: Michael T G Dunstan
Fleet: 45 single-deck bus.
Chassis: 42 Alexander Dennis. 3 MAN
Bodies: 29 Alexander. 3 Caetano. 3 East Lancs. 7 Marshall. 1 Optare. 2 Plaxton.
Ops incl: local bus services.
Livery: two tone Blue
Ticket system: ER6

A & H BOOTH LTD
S K(with driver)
GROSVENOR GARAGE, 100 DOWSON ROAD, HYDE SK14 5BN
Tel: 0161 368 2413
Dirs: D Mycock, J Mycock
Fleet: 3 - 2 coach, 1 minicoach.
Chassis: 1 DAF. 1 Ford. 1 LDV.
Bodies: 1 Caetano. 1 Plaxton. 1 other.
Ops incl: private hire

R BULLOCK & CO (TRANSPORT) LTD
COMMERCIAL GARAGE, STOCKPORT ROAD, CHEADLE SK8 2AG
Tel: 0161 428 5265
Fax: 0161 428 9074
Web site: www.bullockscoaches.co.uk
Livery: Red/White.

BU-VAL BUSES LTD
UNIT 5, PARAGON INDUSTRIAL ESTATE, WALSDEN OL15 8QF
Tel: 01706 372787
Tel: 01706 372121
Man Dir: Martin Bull **Co Sec**: David Beames
Fleet: 20 midibus.
Chassis: 11 Dennis. 7 Marshall. 2 Optare.
Bodies: 2 Caetano. 7 Marshall/MCV. 2 Optare. 6 Plaxton. 2 Transbus. 1 UVG.
Ops incl: local bus services
Livery: White/Red
Ticket System: Wayfarer 386

LES BYWATER & SONS LTD
SPARTH BOTTOMS ROAD, ROCHDALE OL11 4HT.
Tel: 01706 648573.
Man Dir: M. T. Bywater. **Dir**: N. L. Bywater.
Fleet: 3 - 1 coach, 1 midicoach, 1 minibus.
Chassis: 1 Dennis. 2 Iveco.
Bodies: 1 Duple. 2 Robin Hood.
Ops incl: private hire, school contracts.
Livery: White/Blue/Black.

CARSVILLE COACHES
51A HIGHER ROAD, URMSTON M41 9AP
Tel: 0161 748 2698
Fax: 0161 747 2694
E-mail: janetcarsville@hotmail.com
Man Dir: Dave Dickson
Fleet: 13 - 2 double-deck bus, 10 coach,1 midicoach.
Chassis: 1 Bedford. 2 Ford. 4 Scania. 3 Volvo.
Bodies: 1 Caetano. 1 East Lancs. 1 Leyland. 1 Marcopolo. 5 Plaxton. 1 Van Hool.
Ops incl: private hire, excursions & tours, school contracts.
Livery: White/Purple.

COACH OPTIONS LTD
768 MANCHESTER ROAD, CASTLETON, ROCHDALE OL11 3AW
Tel: 01706 713966
Fax: 01706 759996
E-mail: coach.options@freeuk.com
Dirs: Paul Stone, Adrian Duffey
Fleet: 9 - 5 single-deck coach, 1 midicoach, 1 midibus, 2 minicoach
Chassis: 2 Bova. 2 DAF. 2 Ford Transit. 1 Iveco. 1 Mercedes. 2 Scania.
Ops incl: excursions & tours, private hire,continental tours, school contracts.
Livery: Blue

CROPPER COACHES
316 BURY ROAD, TOTTINGTON BL8 3DT
Tel: 01204 885322.
Prop: L. Donnell.
Fleet: 7 minibus.
Chassis: 5 Ford Transit. 1 Freight Rover.
Ops incl: private hire, school contracts.

DAM EXPRESS
GROVE HOUSE, 27 MANOR STREET, ARDWICK GREEN M12 6HE.
Tel: 0161 273 1234.
Fax: 0161 274 4141.
Fleetname: Don Travel.
Prop/Ops Man: D. Francis.
Sales Man: W. Lee. **Co Sec**: Miss T. Wilding.
Fleet: 3 - 1 coach, 2 double-deck coach.
Ops incl: excursions & tours, private hire, express, continental tours.

ELLEN SMITH (TOURS) LTD
MANDALE PARK, CORPORATION ROAD, ROCHDALE OL11 4HJ
Tel: 01706 345000
Fax: 01706 345970
E-mail: p.targett@ellensmith.co.uk
Web site: www.ellensmith.co.uk
Man Dir: Paul Targett
Fleet: 6 - 4 coach, 2 minibus
Chassis: 2 Bova. 1 Iveco. 1 Mercedes. 2 VW.
Bodies: 1 Beulas. 2 Bova. 1 Mercedes.

ELITE SERVICES LTD
UNITS 3/6, ADSWOOD ROAD INDUSTRIAL ESTATE, ADSWOOD ROAD, STOCKPORT SK3 8LF.
Tel: 0161 480 0617
Fax: 0161 480 3099
Dirs: Dave Nickson
Fleet: 21 - 2 double-deck bus, 17 coach, 2 double-deck coach.
Chassis: 1 Ayats. 1 Ford. 15 Scania. 2 Volvo.
Ops incl: excursions & tours, private hire, continental tours, school contracts.
Livery: White/Purple/Pink

FINGLANDS COACHWAYS LTD
261 WILMSLOW ROAD, RUSHOLME, MANCHESTER M14 5LJ
Tel: 0161 224 3341
Fax: 0161 257 3154
E-mail: enquiry@finglands.co.uk
Web site: www.finglands.co.uk
Fleetname: Finglands
Chmn: Peter Shipp **Dirs**: David Shurden, Peter Harrison **Fleet Eng**: Tim Jenkins
Traff Man: Fred Walton
Fleet: 57 - 42 double-deck bus, 5 single-deck bus, 10 single-deck coach
Chassis: 5 Alexander Dennis. 4 Dennis. 49 Volvo.
Bodies: 23 Alexander. 15 Northern Counties. 15 Plaxton. 4 Wright. 1 Other
Ops incl: local bus services, school contracts, private hire.
Livery: White/Orange/Brown
Ticket System: Wayfarer TGX150

123

FIRST IN MANCHESTER
WALLSHAW STREET, OLDHAM
OL1 3TR
Tel: 0161 627 2929
Fax: 0161 627 5845
Fleetname: First
Man Dir: Andrew Scholey **Fin Dir**: Martin Wilson **Eng Dir**: Colin Stafford **Service Delivery Dir**: Robert Mason **Network Dir**: Simon Bennett
Fleet: 855 - 138 double-deck bus, 509 single-deck bus, 136 midibus, 34 articulated bus, 38 minibus.
Chassis: BMC. Dennis. Irisbus. Leyland. Mercedes-Benz. Optare. Scania. Volvo.
Bodies: BMC. ECW. East Lancs Irisbus. Leyland. Marshall. Mercedes-Benz. Northern Counties. Optare. Scania. Transbus. Wright.
Ops incl: local bus services, school contracts, private hire.
Livery: First - Magenta, Blue & Grey/White
Ticket System: ERG TP4004

FREEBIRD
REVERS STREET GARAGE, BURY
BL8 1AQ
Tel: 0161 797 6633
Fax: 08712 773124
E-mail: info@freebirdcoaches.co.uk
Web site: www.freebirdcoaches.co.uk
Proprietor: Paul Dart
Fleet: 15 - 10 single-deck coach, 2 midicoach 1 minibus, 2 minicoach.
Chassis: 3 DAF. 2 Dennis. 4 Irisbus. 3 LDV. 2 Mercedes. 1 Volvo.
Bodies: 1 Beulas. 1 Berkhof. 1 Jonkheere. 1 Marcopolo. 2 Optare. 1 Plaxton. 1 Van Hool. 7 other.
Ops incl: private hire, school contracts, ecxcursions & tours
Livery: White

FREEDOM TRAVEL NORTH LTD
SMITHS OF MARPLE
72 CROSS LANE, MARPLE SK6 7PZ
Tel: 0161 427 2825.
Fax: 0161 449 7731.
Dir: Anthony Vernon, Angela Vernon
Ch Eng: Keith Bridle
Fleet: 13-7 double deck bus, 4 coach, 1 mini bus, 1 mioni coach
Chassis: 6 Leyland, 2 Mercedes, 1 Scania, 1 Setra, 3 Volvo
Bodies: 7 ECW. 2 Mellor, 2 Plaxton, 1 Setra, 1 Van Hool.
Ops incl: local bus services, school contracts, excursions & tours, private hire, continental tours.
Livery: White/Orange-Rose.
(Part of the Elite Group)

GO-GOODWINS COACHES
LYNTOWN TRADING ESTATE, 186 OLD WELLINGTON ROAD, ECCLES, MANCHESTER M309QG
Tel: 0161 789 4545
Fax: 0161 789 0939
E-mail: gogoodwins@btinternet.com
Web site: www.gogoodwins.co.uk
Prop: Geoff Goodwin
Ops incl: Local bus service, school contracts, Private hire.

GPD TRAVEL
27 HARTFIORD AVENUE, HEYWOOD OL10 4XM
Tel: 01706 622297
Fax: 01706 361494
E-mail: janinedawson@hotmail.co.uk
Web site: www.gpdtravel.co.uk
Proprietor: Gary Dawson
Fleet: 5 - 4 single-deck coach, 1 midicoach.
Chassis: 1 Mercedes-Benz. 4 Volvo.
Ops incl: school contracts, excursions & tours, private hire, continental tours.
Livery: White with red lettering

GRAYWAY COACHES
237 MANCHESTER ROAD, INCE, WIGAN WN2 2AE
Tel: 01942 243165
Fax: 01942 824807
E-mail: graywayone@aol.com
Web site: www.grayway.co.uk
Proprietors: Janet Gray, Michael Gray
Fleet: 30 - 24 single-deck coach, 6 minicoach.
Chassis: 2 DAF 6 Mercedes-Benz. 22 Volvo.
Ops incl: school contracts, exciusions & tours, private hire, continental tours.
Livery: Cream/Orange/Red

HAYTON'S EXECUTIVE TRAVEL LTD
12 ACORN CLOSE, BURNAGE M19 2HS
Tel: 0161 223 3103
Fax: 0161 223 9528
Prop: Barry Hayton **Dir/Sec**: Barry A Hayton
Fleet: 17 - 3 double-deck bus, 3 single-deck bus, 10 coach, 1 midibus.
Chassis: 3 MAN. 1 Neoplan. 1 Optare. 1 Setra. 10 Volvo.
Bodies: 2 East Lancs. 2 Jonckheere. 1 Noge. 2 Optare. 4 Plaxton. 1 Setra. 4 Van Hool.
Ops incl: local bus services, school contracts, excursions & tours, private hire, express, continental tours.
Livery: White

HEALINGS INTERNATIONAL COACHES
251 HIGGINSHAW LANE, ROYTON, OLDHAM OL2 6HW
Tel: 0161 624 8975
Fax: 0161 652 0320
Ptnrs: Philip Healing, Richard Healing
Fleet: 7 - 5coach, 1 midicoach, 1 minicoach.
Chassis: 1 DAF. 1 Mercedes. 1 Scania. 1 Toyota. 1 Volvo. 2 Duple425
Ops incl: school contracts, excursions & tours, private hire, continental tours.
Livery: White with coloured decals

JONES EXECUTIVE COACHES LTD
THE COACH STATION, SHARP STREET, WALKDEN M28 3LX
Tel: 0161 790 9495
Fax: 0161 790 9400
Web site: www.jonesexecutive.co.uk
E-mail: simon@jonesexecutive.co.uk
Man Dir: Simon Jones
Fleet: 7 - 7 single-deck coach
Chassis: 2 Dennis. 1 Irisbus. 2 Scania. 2 Volvo.
Bodies: 1 Beulas. 1 Irizar. 1 Neoplan. 2 Plaxton. 2 Van Hool.
Ops incl: school contracts, private hire.
Livery: Blue/Red/Silver

LAMBS COACHES
2A BUXTON STREET, HAZEL GROVE, STOCKPORT SK7 4BB
Tel: 0161 456 1515
Fax: 0161 483 5011
E-mail: lambs139@aol.com
Web-site: www.lambscoaches.net
Man Dir: Geoff Lamb **Dir**: Graham Lamb
Comp Sec: Christine Lamb
Fleet: 7 - 7 single-deck coach
Chassis: 2 DAF. 3 Scania. 1 Setra. 1 Volvo.
Bodies: 1 Setra. 6 Van Hool.
Ops incl: private hire, school contracts.
Livery: Blue/White

LENDOR TAXIS & MINI COACHES
17 VALLEY CLOSE, MOSSLEY ASHTON U LYNE OL5 0NH
Tel/Fax: 01457 832845
Prop: Leonard E Glynn
Fleet: 6 minibus.
Chassis: 2 Ford Transit. 1 Iveco. 1 LDV. 1 Mercedes. 1 Vauxhall.
Ops incl: private hire, school contracts

MARPLE MINI COACHES
5 GROSVENOR ROAD, MARPLE SK6 6PR.
Tel: 0161 881 9111.
Owner: G. W. Cross.
Fleet: 2 minicoach.
Chassis: Ford Transit. LDV.
Ops incl: school contracts, private hire.
Livery: White/Gold.

MAYNE OF MANCHESTER
1000 ASHTON NEW ROAD, CLAYTON M11 4PD
Tel (coaches): 0161 223 8111
E-mail: coaches@mayne.co.uk
Web site: www.mayne.co.uk
Fleetname: Mayne
Chmn/Man Dir: S B Mayne
Dir: A A Mayne, **Dir**: D Mayne (**Co Sec**)
Ch Eng: C Pannell **Comm Man**: A K Nuttall
Fleet: 18 coach.
Ops incl: School contracts, excursions & tours, private hire, continental tours.
Livery: Red/Cream

METROLINK

METROLINK, METROLINK HOUSE,
QUEENS ROAD, MANCHESTER M8 0RY
Tel: 0161 205 8685
Fax: 0161 205 8699
Web site: www.gmpte.com
Man Dir: Phil Smith
Fleet: 28 - tram
Chassis: GEC Alstom
Bodies: Firema
Ops incl: tram service
(part of Stagecoach)

DAVID PLATT COACHES & MINITRAVEL OF LEES

8 THE WOODS, GROTTON,
SADDLEWORTH, OLDHAM OL4 4LP
Tel/Fax: 0161 633 4845
Props: David Platt
Fleet: 2 - 1 coach, 1 minicoach.
Chassis: 1 Bedford. 1 Toyota.
Bodies: 1 Caetano. 1 Plaxton.
Ops incl: private hire.
Livery: Aqua/White

SELWYNS TRAVEL SERVICES

BUILDING 77, TERMINAL 2,
MANCHESTER AIRPORT M90 1QX
Tel: 0161 489 5720
Fax: 0161 499 9157
Recovery: 01928 572108
E-mail: sales@selwyns.co.uk
Web site: www.selwyns.co.uk
Man Dir: Selwyn A Jones **Co Sec/Acct**: Richard E Williams **Gen Man**: Geoff Prince **Fleet Eng**: Pual Trill **Ops Man**: Alan Spilman
Fleet: 12 - 4 single-deck coach, 5 minicoach, 3 minicoach.
Chassis: 4 DAF. 8 Mercedes.
Bodies: 8 Mercedes. 4 Van Hool.
Ops incl: local bus services, school contracts, private hire.
Livery: White/Blue/Orange/Green
Ticket System: Wayfarer

SOUTH LANCS TRAVEL

UNIT 22/23, CHANTERS INDUSTRIAL
ESTATE, ATHERTON M46 9BP
Tel: 01942 888893
Fax: 01942 894010
Man Dir: Martin Bott **Eng Dir**: D A Stewart

Tran Man: W Peach
Fleet: 50 - double-deck bus, single-deck bus, midibus
Chassis: incl: 2 Optare
Bodies: incl: 2 Optare
Ops incl: local bus services, tram service, school contracts
Livery: Yellow/Blue
Ticket System: Wayfarer 3

STAGECOACH MANCHESTER

HEAD OFFICE, HYDE ROAD,
MANCHESTER M12 6JS
Tel: 0161 273 3377
Fax: 0161 271 2594
E-mail: manchester.enquiries@stagecoachbus.com
Web site: www.stagecoachbus.com/manchester
Man Dir: M Threapleton **Ops Dir**: E Tasker.
Comm Dir: R A Cossins **Eng Dir**: D Roe
Ser Performance Man: A Wilson **Network Man**: J K Young **Mktng Man**: K Coventry
Personnel man: J E Crenigan
Fleet: 653 - 366 double-deck bus, 213 single-deck bus, 1 coach, 45 midibus, 33 minibus.
Chassis: 260 Dennis. 4 Iveco. 44 Leyland. 124 MAN. 33 Mercedes. 35 Scania. 158 Volvo.
Bodies: 443 Alexander. 20 Duple. 7 East Lancs. 1 Neoplan. 89 Northern Counties. 94 Plaxton. 4 other.
Ops incl: local bus services.
Livery: Blue/Orange/Red/White
Ticket System: ERG

STOTT'S TOURS (OLDHAM) LTD

144 LEES ROAD, OLDHAM OL4 1HT
Tel: 0161 624 4200.
Fax: 0161 628 2969.
Prop: A. Stott.
Ops incl: school contracts.
Livery: Cream/Red/Black.

SWANS TRAVEL

STANLEY HOUSE, BROADGATE,
CHADDERTON, OLDHAM OL9 9XA
Tel: 0161 681 0999.
Fax: 0161 681 0777.
E-mail: enquiries@swanstravel.com
Web site: www.swanstravel.co.uk
Man Dir: Kieran Swindells
Ops incl: Local bus services, Private hire.
Livery: White.

VIKING COACHES

DOCTOR FOLD FARM, DOCTOR FOLD
LANE, BIRCH, HEYWOOD OL10 2QE.
Tel: 01706 368999.
Fax: 01706 620011.
E-mail: viking@coaches76.freeserve
Web site: www.coach-day-trips
Owners: A. Warburton, Ms A. Warburton.
Fleet: 4 coach.
Chassis: Volvo. Iveco.
Bodies: Beulas. Plaxton. Van Hool.
Ops incl: excursions & tours, private hire, continental tours, school contracts.
Livery: Viking Ship.

W A SHEARINGS LTD

MIRY LANE, WIGAN WN3 4AG
Tel: 01942 244246
Fax: 01942 242518
Web site: www.washearings.com
ChExec: Dennis Wormwell
Fin Dir: David Newbold
Coo: Vince Flower, **Com Dir:** Alan Mcclean, **H R dir:** Jane Burke
Fleet: 252 coach
Chassis: 252 Volvo.
Bodies: 62 Jonckheere. 81 Plaxton. 6 Sunsundegui. 103 Van Hool.
Ops incl: excursions & tours, private hire, continental tours.
Livery: Blue or Gold

WRIGLEY'S COACHES LTD

4 FIDDLERS LANE, IRLAM M44 6QE
Tel: 0161 775 2414
Fax: 0161 775 1558
E-mail: sales@wrigleyscoaches.com
Web site: www.wrigleyscoaches.com
Man Dir: Colin Wrigley **Co Sec/Dir**: Lesley Wrigley **Ops Man**: Alan Grice
Fleet: 8 - 1 double-deck bus, 4 coach, 2 double-deck coach, 1 minicoach.
Chassis: 1 Leyland. 2 MAN. 1 Neoplan. 1 Setra. 1 Toyota. 2 Volvo.
Bodies: 1 Alexander. 1 Caetano. 3 Neoplan. 1 Plaxton. 1 Setra. 1 Van Hool.
Ops incl: private hire, school contracts.
Livery: Blue/White

GREATER MANCHESTER (BOLTON, BURY, OLDHAM, ROCHDALE, SALFORD, TAMESIDE, WIGAN)

	Vehicle suitable for disabled		Seat belt-fitted Vehicle
T	Toilet-drop facilities available		Coach(es) with galley facilities
R	Recovery service available		Air-conditioned vehicle(s)
	Open top vehicle(s)v		Coaches with toilet facilities
R24	24 hour recovery service		
	Replacement vehicle available		
	Vintage Coach(es) available		

125

HAMPSHIRE

AIRLYNX TRAVEL
THE SYCAMORES, OAKLEY ROAD, SOUTHAMPTON SO16 4LJ
Tel: 023 8039 9078
Fax: 023 8077 7724
E-mail: us@airlynx.co.uk
Web site: www.airlynx.co.uk
Dir : Gary Gregory **Co Sec**: Sharon Lucas
Fleet: 9 - 1 single-deck bus, 1 midicoach, 8 minibus, 8 minicoach
Chassis: 3 Ford Transit. 4 Mercedes. 1 VW.
Ops incl: private hire, school contracts, local bus services.
Livery: Blue/Yellow

ALTONIAN COACHES
THE DEPOT, MILL LANE TRADING ESTATE, ALTON GU34 2QJ
Tel: 01420 84839
Fax: 01420 84803
Dirs: R Turner, S P Austen **Ops Man**: M Jones **Ch Eng**: K Tillin
Fleet: 17 -11 coach, 3 midicoach, 2 minibus, 1 minicoach.
Chassis: 1 DAF. 9 Dennis. 1 Ford Transit. 1 Leyland. 1 Mercedes. 1 Optare. 1 Renault. 2 Setra.
Bodies: 1 Autobus. 1 Caetano. 3 Duple. 1 Irizar. 4 Neoplan. 1 Optare. 2 Plaxton. 1 Reeve Burgess. 2 Van Hool. 1 Wadham Stringer.
Ops incl: local bus services, school contracts, excursions & tours, private hire, continental tours.
Livery: Orange (cream lettering)

AMK CHAUFFEUR DRIVE LTD
MILL LANE, PASSFIELD, LIPHOOK GU30 7RP
Tel: 01428 751675
Fax: 01428 751677
E-mail: info@amkxl.com
Web site: www.amkxl.com
Fleet: 78 - 65 minibus, 3 midibus, 10 minicoach.
Ops inc: local bus services, school contracts, excursions & tours, private hire.

AMPORT & DISTRICT COACHES LTD
EASTFIELD HOUSE, AMESBURY ROAD, THRUXTON, ANDOVER SP11 8ED
Tel: 01264 772307
Fax: 01264 773020
E-mail: tedd@onetel.net
Dirs: P J Tedd, A M Tedd, N B Tedd
Fleet: 10 - 9 coach, 1 midicoach
Chassis: 1 DAF. 1 Mercedes. 3 Scania. 1 Setra. 4 Volvo.
Bodies: 3 Berkhof. 1 Optare. 3 Plaxton. 2 Van Hool.
Ops incl: private hire, continental tours, school contracts.
Livery: White/Silver

ANGELA COACHES LTD
OAKTREE HOUSE, LOWFORD, BURSLEDON SO31 8ES
Tel: 023 8040 3170
Fax: 023 8040 6487
E-mail: robert@angelacoaches.com
Web site: www.angelacoaches.com
Man Dir: M Pressley **Co Sec**: Mrs H M Pressley **Ops Dir**: R Pressley
Ch Eng: D Evans **Ops Man**: J Davies
Fleet: 9 - 3 coach, 1 midicoach, 5 minicoach.
Chassis: 4 Irisbus. 2 MAN. 1 Mercedes. 2 Toyota.
Bodies: 2 Beulas. 2 Caetano. 2 Indcar. 2 Neoplan. 1 other.
Ops incl: private hire, school contracts, excursions & tours, continental tours
Livery: Maroon/White

AVENSIS COACH TRAVEL LTD
29 PREMIER WAY, ABBEY PARK, ROMSEY SO51 9DO
Tel: 01794 515260
Fax: 01794 512260
E-mail: info@avensiscoaches.co.uk
Web site: www.avensiscoaches.co.uk
Dirs: Graham Humby, Simon Humby
Fleet: 8 coach.
Chassis: 8 Scania..
Bodies: 8 Irizar.
Ops incl: excursions & tours, private hire, continental tours.
Livery: Yellow/Purple

BYNGS INTERNATIONAL COACHES
1B ANGERSTEIN ROAD, NORTH END, PORTSMOUTH PO2 8HJ.
Tel: 023 9266 2223
Fax: 023 9267 8464
Dirs: Paul Grant, Trevor Grant. **Fleet Eng**: John Hampton.
Fleet: 40 - 1 single-deck bus, 37 coach, 1 midicoach, 1 minicoach.
Chassis: 10 Bova. 2 DAF. 2 Dennis. 4 Leyland. 4 Mercedes. 7 Scania. 1 Toyota. 10 Volvo.
Bodies: 10 Bova. 2 DAF. 2 Dennis. 4 irizar. 2 Jonckheere. 4 mercedes. 11 Plaxton. 7 Van Hool.
Ops incl: excursions & tours, private hire, school contracts.
Livery: Silver/Brown.

A. S. BONE & SONS
LONDON ROAD, HOOK RG27 9EQ
Tel: 01256 761388, 762106
Fleetname: Newnham Coaches
Man Dir: J. E. Bone. **Co Sec:** Mrs M. Bone.
Fleet: 5 - 3 double-deck bus, 2 single-deck bus.
Chassis: 1 Bristol. 2 Daimler. 2 Leyland National.
Ops incl: private hire.
Livery: Cream/Blue.

BLACK VELVET TRAVEL
SUITE A, BINNINC HOUSE, 4A HIGH STREET EASTLEIGH S050 5LA
Tel: 023 8061 2288.
Fax: 023 8064 4881.
E-mail: info@blackvelvettravel.co.uk
Web site: www.velvetbus.info
Chairman: Terry Stockley **Comp Sec:** Rosalind Stockley **Man Dir:** Phil Stockley
Ops Man: Taz Keeley **Dir:** David Huber
Fleet: 10 - 6 double-deck bus. 4 single-deck bus
Chassis: 4 DAF. 3 Leyland. 3 Volvo
Bodies: 3 Alexander Dennis. 4 East Lancs. 3 Northern Counties.
Ops incl: local bus services, private hire.
Livery: Purple
Ticket System: Wayfarer 3

BLUESTAR
BARTON PARK, EASTLEIGH SO50 6RR
Tel: 023 8061 4459
Fax: 023 8061 4234
E-mail: enquiries@bluestarbus.co.uk
Web site: www.bluestarbus.com
Man Dir: A Whickham **Fin Dir**: A R Hiles
Ops Man: Alex Hornby **Comm Man**: P C Curtis **Eng Man**: Steve Prewett
Fleet: 72 - 45 double-deck bus, 19 single-deck bus, 2 open-top bus, 6 midibus.
Chassis: 2 Bristol. 24 Dennis. 6 Iveco. 20 Leyland. 20 Volvo.
Bodies: 5 Alexander. 22 ECW. 18 East Lancs. 14 Leyland. 2 Marshall/MCV. 4 Mellor. 7 Northern Counties. 2 Reeve Burgess. 12 Transbus.
Ops incl: local bus services
Livery: Blue
Ticket System: Wayfarer 3
(Part of the Go-Ahead Group)

BRIJAN TOURS LTD
R24
THE COACH STATION, UNITS 4/5, BOTTINGS INDUSTRIAL ESTATE, CURDRIDGE SO30 2DY
Tel: 01489 788138
Fax: 01489 789395
Recovery: 017711 435189
E-mail: sales@brijantours.com
Web: www.brijantours.com
Man Dir: Brian Botley **Co Sec**: Janet Botley **Ops Man**: Brian Bedford **Chief Eng:** Colin Batten
Fleet: 28 - 9 double-deck bus, 8 single-deck bus, 11 single-deck coach.
Chassis: 2 Alexander Dennis. 1 Iveco. 6 Leyland. 3 MCW. 6 Mercedes. 2 Scania. 1 Volvo.
Bodies: 1 Irizar. 1 Jockheere. 12 Plaxton. 2 Van Hool. 5 Other.
Ops incl: local bus services, school contracts, excursions & tours, private hire.
Livery: Cream/Burgundy.
Ticket system: Wayfarer

126

CLEGG & BROOKING COACHES
WHITE HORSE SERVICE STATION, MIDDLE WALLOP, STOCKBRIDGE SO20 8DZ
Tel: 01264 781283
Fax: 01264 781679
E-mail: cleggandbrooking@btconnect.com
Dirs: Kevin Brooking, Jeanette Cook, John Cook
Fleet: 11 - 8 single-deck coach, 3 midibus
Chassis: 2 Dennis. 1 Mercedes. 4 Scania. 2 Toyota. 2 Volvo.
Bodies: 1 Berkhof. 4 Caetano. 2 Irizar. 2 Plaxton. 1 Sunsundegui. 1 Other
Ops incl: local bus services, private hire, school contracts.
Livery: Blue/Grey

COLISEUM COACHES LTD
BOTLEY ROAD GARAGE, WEST END, SOUTHAMPTON SO30 3JA
Tel: 023 8047 2377
Fax: 023 8047 6537
E-mail: info@coliseumcoaches.co.uk
Web site: www.coliseumcoaches.co.uk
Man Dirs: David Pitter (**Sec**), Kerry Pitter
Ch Eng: Dave Rowsell
Fleet: 12 coach
Chassis: 12 MAN
Bodies: 11 Neoplan. 1 Noge.

COOPERS COACHES
31-35 LAKE ROAD, WOOLSTON SO19 9EB
Tel: 023 8039 3393
Fax: 023 8044 4929.
Prop: Stephen & Ellen Cooper
Fleet: 6 - 4 single-deck coach, 2 minibus.
Chassis: 1 Dennis. 1 Ford Transit. 1 LDV. 1 Scania. 3 Volvo.
Bodies: 1 Alexander Dennis 1 Ikarus. 1 Jonkheere. 2 Plaxton.
Ops incl: local bus services, school contracts, private hire.

COUNTRYWIDE TRAVEL (FLEET) LTD
BOWENHURST FARM, CRONDALL FARNHAM, GU10 5PP
Tel: 01252 851009
Fax: 01252 852009
E-mail: info@countrywidetravel.co.uk
Web: www.countrywide.co.uk
Porprietor: John C Chadwick
Fleet: 20 - 5 single-deck bus, 12 midibus. 3 minibus.
Chassis: 2 Dennis. 1 Iveco. 3 LDV. 3 MAN. 10 Mercedes. 1 Optare.
Bodies: 3 East Lancs. 2 Marshall/MCV. 1 Mellor. 1 Optare. 1 Park Royal. 10 Plaxton. 3 Other.
Ops incl: local bus services, school contracts,
Livery: Black & Yellow
Ticket system: Wayfarer II

EASSONS COACHES LTD
44 WODEHOUSE ROAD, ITCHEN SO19 2EQ
Tel: 023 8044 8153

Fax: 023 8044 1635
Dirs: D. A. Easson, D. H. Easson.
Fleet: 7 - 5 single-deck coach, 2 midicoach.
Chassis: 2 Mercedes. 1 Neoplan. 3 Setra. 2 Volvo.
Bodies: 1 Neoplan. 1 Plaxton. 3 Setra. 2 other.
Ops incl: excursions & tours, private hire.
Livery: Cream.

EMSWORTH & DISTRICT MOTOR SERVICES LTD
THE BUS GARAGE, CLOVELLY ROAD, SOUTHBOURNE PO10 8PE
Tel: 01243 378337
Web site: www.emsworthanddistrict.co.uk
Fleet: 31 - 2 double-deck bus, 20 single-deck bus, 7 single-deck coach, 2 midicoach
Chassis: Alexander Dennis. AEC. Bedford. Bova. DAF. Leyland. MAN. Mercedes. Volvo.
Bodies: Alexander. Berkhof. Bova. Leyland. Mercedes. Van Hool.
Ops incl: local bus services, school contracts, excursions & tours, private hire, continental tours
Livery: Green/Cream.
Ticket system: Wayfarer Saver

FIRST HAMPSHIRE & DORSET LTD
226 PORTSWOOD ROAD, SOUTHAMPTON SO17 2BE
Tel: 023 8058 4321
Fax: 023 8067 1448
Web site: www.firstgroup.com
E-mail: hampshire-dorset.csc@firstgroup.com
Man Dir: Richard Soper **Dep Man Dir**: Marc Reddy **Eng Dir**: David Toy **Fin Dir**: Ian Stone **Ops Dir**: Mike Smith **Ops Man**: Chris Bainbridge **Ops Eng**: Mike Britten **Comm Man**: Kenneth Cobb
Fleet: 444 - 83 double-deck bus, 76 single-deck bus, 11 coach, 5 open-top bus, 179 midibus, 90 minibus.
Chassis: 7 Bristol. 177 Dennis. 36 Iveco. 32 Leyland. 67 Mercedes. 7 Optare. 26 Scania. 92 Volvo.
Bodies: 33 Alexander. 7 ECW. 26 East Lancs. 9 Leyland. 47 Marshall. 20 Northern Counties. 7 Optare. 124 Plaxton. 11 Roe. 1 Van Hool. 79 Wright. 80 other.
Ops incl: local bus services, school contracts, private hire

FLYGHT TRAVEL
3A SPUR ROAD, COSHAM PO6 3DY.
Tel: 02392 327703.
Fax: 02392 361253.
Proprietor: Peter Sharp **Chief Eng**: Roger Willoughby **Ops Man**: Trevor Byng.
Fleet: 26 - 19 single-deck coach, 1 minibus, 3 midicoach, 3 minicoach.
Chassis: 1 DAF. 1 Ford Transit. 1 MAN. 6 Mercedes. 18 Scania.
Body: 14 Inzar. 3 Optare. 2 Plaxton. 5 Van Hool.
Ops incl: excursions & tours, private hire, continental tours, school contracts.
Livery: White/Yellow/Blue/Red.

GEMINI TRAVEL SOUTHAMPTON LTD
MARCHWOOD INDUSTRIAL PARK, NORTH ROAD, MARCHWOOD SO40 4BL
Tel: 023 8066 0066
Fax: 023 8087 1308
Dirs: Ken Hatch, Mark Bennett **Gen Man**: Nigel Smith
Fleet: 10 - 2 single-deck coach. 4 midicoach, 4 minibus.
Chassis: 4 LDV. 4 Mercedes. 2 Volvo.
Bodies: 3 Optare. 2 Plaxton, 5 other.
Ops incl: private hire, school contracts.
Livery: White/Blue

HERRINGTON COACHES LTD
MANOR FARM, SANDLEHEATH ROAD, ALDERHOLT, FORDINGBRIDGE SP6 3EG
Tel: 01425 652842
Props: A G Herrington, Mrs J Herrington
Fleet: 6 - 3 coach, 3 minibus.
Chassis: 1 Dennis. 3 Mercedes. 2 Volvo.
Bodies: 1 Crest. 1 Jonckheere. 2 Mercedes. 1 Plaxton. 1 Van Hool.
Ops incl: local bus services, school contracts, private hire.
Livery: Grey/Red.

HYTHE & WATERSIDE COACHES LTD
1A HIGH STREET, HYTHE SO45 6AG
Tel: 023 8084 4788
Fax: 023 8020 7284
E-mail: enquiries@watersidetours.co.uk
Web site: www.watersidetours.co.uk
Fleetname: Waterside Tours
Man Dir: Roy Barker **Dirs**: Pam Parker, Jackie Withey
Fleet: 7 - 4 single- deck coach, 1 minibus, 2 midicoach.
Chassis: 1 BMC. 2 Mercedes. 4 Volvo.
Bodies: 4 Berkhof. 1 BMC. 1 Esker. 1 Mercedes-Benz.
Ops incl: excursions & tours, private hire, continental tours, school contracts.
Livery: White/Burgundy/Gold.

LUCKETTS TRAVEL
BROADCUT, WALLINGTON, FAREHAM PO16 8TB
Tel: 01329 823755
Fax: 01329 823855
E-mail: info@lucketts.co.uk
Web site: www.lucketts.co.uk
Chmn: David Luckett **Joint Man Dirs**: Steven Luckett, Ian Luckett **Eng Dir**: Mark Jordan **Ops Man**: Tony Harper
Fleet: 33 - 29 coach, 2 double-deck coach, 2 minicoach.
Chassis: 1 DAF. 8 Dennis. 2 Neoplan. 18 Scania. 2 Toyota. 2 Volvo.
Bodies: 5 Berkhof. 1 Bova. 2 Caetano. 21 Irizar. 2 Neoplan. 4 Plaxton
Ops incl: excursions & tours, private hire, continental tours, school contracts.
Livery: Grey/White/Orange

HAMPSHIRE

127

MARCHWOOD MOTORWAYS
200 SALISBURY ROAD, TOTTON
SO40 3PE
Tel: 023 8066 3700
Fax: 023 8066 7762
Man Dir: A Carter **Ops Man**: A Hornby
Fleet: 25-18 coach, 3 double-deck coach, 3 midicoach, 2 minibus.
Bodies: 3 Caetano. 1 Duple. 7 Ikarus. 11 Optare. 10 Van Hool. 13 Wright. 7 other.
Ops incl: local bus services, school contracts, excursions & tours, private hire, continental tours.
Ticket system: Wayfarer
Subsiduary of Bluestar, Part of the Go-Ahead Group

MERVYN'S COACHES
THE NEW COACH HOUSE, INNERSDOWN, MICHELDEVER
SO21 3BW
Tel/Fax: 01962 774574
Email: mervynscoaches@btconnect.com
Web site: www.mervynscoaches.com
Ptnrs: Mervyn Annetts, Carol Annetts, Linda Porter, James Annetts.
Fleet: 6 - 5 single-deck coach, 1 midicoach
Chassis: 4 Bedford. 2 Volvo.
Chassis: 1 Duple. 4 Plaxton. 1 other
Ops incl: local bus services, school contracts, excursions & tours, private hire.
Livery: Brown/Cream
Ticket System: Setright

JOHN PIKE COACHES
77 SCOTT CLOSE, WALWORTH INDUSTRIAL ESTATE, ANDOVER
SP10 5NU.
Tel: 01264 334328.
Fax: 01264 334329.
Props: J. S. Pike, Jenny Pike, C. Pike, R. Pike.
Fleet: 15 - 4 double-deck bus, 5 coach, 2 midicoach, 4 minibus.
Chassis: Bristol. Ford Transit. Iveco. Mercedes. Volvo.
Bodies: Mercedes. Plaxton. ECW.
Ops incl: local bus services, school contracts, excursions & tours, private hire, continental tours.
Livery: White.
Ticket System: Setright.

PRINCESS COACHES LTD
PRINCESS COACHES GARAGE, BOTLEY ROAD, WEST END, SOUTHAMPTON SO30 3HA
Tel: 023 8047 2150
Fax: 023 8039 9944
E-mail: enquiries@princesscoaches.com
Web site: www.princesscoaches.co.uk
Dirs: Y B Barfoot, D K Brown, P A Brown
Fleet: 16 - 12 coach, 2 double-deck coach, 1 minibus. 1 minicoach.
Chassis: 1 Ford. 14 Scania. 1 Toyota.
Bodies: 2 Berkhof. 1 Caetano. 8 Irizar. 4 Jonckheere. 1 other.
Ops incl: private hire, school contracts, continental tours.
Livery: White with multi-coloured flashes

SOLENT COACHES LTD
BROOKSIDE GARAGE, CROW LANE, RINGWOOD BH24 3EA
Tel: 01425 473188
Fax: 01425 473669
Recovery: 0784 326 6720/1
E-mail: enquiries@solentcoaches.co.uk
Web site: www.solentcoaches.co.uk
Man Dir/Co Sec: John Skew **Dir/Ch Eng**: Paul Skew.
Fleet: 9 - 7 coach, 1 minibus, 1 midicoach.
Chassis: 1 Mercedes. 6 Scania. 1 SETRA. 1 Toyota.
Bodies: 1 Caetano. 2 Irizar. 1 Mercedes. 1 Setra. 4 Van Hool.
Ops incl: excursions & tours, private hire, continental tours, school contracts.
Livery: White/Blue

STAGECOACH HAMPSHIRE
THE BUS STATION, FESTIVAL PLACE, CHURCHILL WAY, BASINGSTOKE RG21 7BE
Tel: 0845 121 0180
Web site: www.stagecoachbus/com/hampshire
Man Dir: Andrew Dyer. **Eng Dir**: Richard Alexander. **Fin Dir**: Martin Stoggell. **Div Man**: Matthew Callow.
Fleet: 150 - 47 double-deck bus. 86 single-deck bus. 17 minibus.
Chassis: 4 Bristol, 53 Dennis, 16 Leyland, 15 Mercedes, 2 Optare. 60 Volvo.
Bodies: 138 Alexander. 4 ECW. 2 Optare. Plaxton.
Ops incl: local bus services, school contracts.
Livery: Blue/Red/Orange
Ticket System: Wayfarer.

STAGECOACH HANTS & SURREY
HALIMOTE ROAD, ALDERSHOT GU11 1NJ
Tel: 01256 464501.
Man Dir: Andrew Dyer. **Eng Dir**: Richard Alexander. **Fin Dir**: Martin Stoggell.
Fleet: 80 - 13 double-deck bus, 43 single-deck bus, 24 minibus.
Chassis: 37 Dennis. 6 Leyland. 24 Mercedes. 13 Volvo.
Bodies: Alexander. Plaxton.
Ops incl: local bus services, school contracts.
Livery: Blue/Red/Orange
Ticket System: Wayfarer

SUMMERFIELD COACHES LTD
247 ALDERMOOR ROAD, ALDERMOOR, SOUTHAMPTON SO16 5NU
Tel: 023 8077 8717
Fax: 023 8032 0327
E-mail: summerfield@tcp.co.uk
Dirs: Tracey Ralph, Colin Ralph **Tran Man**: Dave Wheeler
Fleet: 9 - 6 coach, 2 minibus, 1 minicoach.
Chassis: 2 LDV. 1 MAN. 1 Mercedes. 1 Toyota. 4 Volvo.
Bodies: 1 Berkhof. 3 Caetano. 2 Leyland. 2 Plaxton. 1 other.
Ops incl: school contracts, private hire, excursions & tours, continental tours.
Livery: Green/Gold

TEST VALLEY TRAVEL
See Wiltshire

TOP TRAVEL COACHES
169 NEW GREENHAM PARK, BASINGSTOKE RG19 6HN
Tel: 01256 397270
Fax: 01635 821128
Dirs: Simon Weaver
Fleet: 33 - 4 double-deck bus, 2 coach bus, 6 double-deck coach, 1 minicoach.
Chassis: 8 Bova. 4 DAF. 4 Dennis. 1 Mercedes. 10 Scania. 6 Volvo.
Bodies: 3 Berkhof. 8 Bova. 9 East Lancs. 7 Irizar. 1 MCW. 1 Plaxton. 4 Van Hool.
Ops incl: school contracts, private hire
Livery: Electric Blue
(Subsidiary of Weavaway Travel, Berkshire)

TRUEMANS COACHES (FLEET) LTD
Truemans End, Lynchford Road, Ash Vale, GU12 5PQ
Tel: 01252 373303
Fax: 01252 373393
Dirs: Richard Truemanr
Fleet: 15 - single deck coach.
Chassis: 5 Iveco. 10 MAN.
Bodies: 5 Beulas. 6 Neoplan. 4 Plaxton.
Ops incl: school contracts, private hire, excursions & tours.
Livery: Electric Blue

VISION TRAVEL INTERNATIONAL LTD
3 A SPUR ROAD, COSHAM, PORTSMOUTH
Tel: 02392 359168
Fax: 02392 361253
E-mail: visiontravels@aol.com
Web site: www.visiontravel.co.uk
Proprietor: Peter R Sharpe **Ops Man**: Trevor Byng **Chief Eng**: Roger Willoughby
Fleet: 26 - 19 single-deck coach, 5 midicoach, 1 minibus 1 minicoach
Chassis: 1 DAF. 1 Ford Transit. 1 MAN. 6 Mercedes. 17 Scania.
Bodies: 14 Irizar. 3 Optare. 2 Plaxton 5 Van Hool.
Ops incl: school contracts, excursions & tours, private hire, continental tours.
Ops incl: private hire, school contracts, continental tours.
Livery: Yellow/Red/White

WHEELERS TRAVEL LTD
UNIT 9, GROVE FARM, UPPDER NORTHAM DRIVE, HEDGE END, SOUTHAMPTON SO30 4BG
Tel: 02380 471800
Fax: 02380 470414
Recovery: 07917 170455
E-mail: sales@wheelerstravel.co.uk
Web site: www.wheelerstravel.co.uk
Dirs: D Wheeler **Gen Man**: Paul Barker
Fleet: 30 - 8 single-deck coach, 8 midicoach, 6 minibus, 3 70 seat single. 2 minicoach, 3 disabled bus.
Chassis: 1 Ayats. 1 Bova. 1 Ford transit. 2 Iveco. 5 LDV. 2 MAN. 8 Mercedes-benz. 1 Renault. 2 Scania. 3 Volvo.
Bodies: 1 Autobus. 1 Ayats. 1 Beulas. 3 Berkhof. 1 Bova.1 Esker. 2 Irizar. 5 Mercedes-Benz. 2 Marcopolo. 1 Plaxton.
Ops incl: private hire, school contracts, continental tours.
Livery: Blue/Orange

HEREFORDSHIRE

BOWYER'S COACHES
QUARRY GARAGE, PETERCHURCH HR2 0TF.
Tel: 01981 550206.
Prop: Fernley C. Anning, Anthony H. Anning.
Fleet: 9 - 5 coach, 4 minibus.
Chassis: Bedford. LDV.
Ops incl: private hire, school contracts.
Livery: White/Red.

BROMYARD OMNIBUS COMPANY
STREAMHALL GARAGE, LINTON TRADING ESTATE, BROMYARD HR7 4QL
Tel: 01885 482782
Fax: 01885 482127
Prop: Martin Perry **Fleet Eng**: Michael Simcock
Fleet: 11 - 6 single-deck bus, 3 coach, 1 midibus, 1 minicoach.
Chassis: 1 Bedford. 2 Leyland. 2 Mercedes. 4 Optare. 1 Volvo. 1 Trojan.
Bodies: 2 Autobus. 1 Caetano. 1 Duple. 4 Optare. 2 Plaxton. 1 Trojan.
Ops incl: local bus services, school contracts, privte hire.
Livery: Red/Cream
Ticket System: Wayfarer Saver

COACH COMPANIONS LTD
MAGNOLIA HOUSE, 12 ST BOTOLPH'S GREEN, LEOMINSTER HR6 8ER
Tel: 01568 620279
Fax: 01568 616906
E-mail: enquiries@coachcompanions.co.uk
Web site: www.coachcompanions.co.uk
Dir: Richard Asghar-Sandys
Fleet: 1 midicoach.
Chassis: 1 Mercedes.
Bodies: 1 other.
Ops incl: private hire.
Livery: White

D R M BUS AND CONTRACT SERVICES
THE COACH GARAGE, BROMYARD HR7 4NT
Tel: 01885 483219
Prop: David R. Morris
Fleet: 9 single-deck bus
Chassis: 3 Scania. 6 Volvo.
Bodies: 2 Alexander. 3 East Lancs. 1 Leyland National. 3 Omnicity.
Ops incl: local bus services, school contracts.
Livery: Blue/Silver-White
Ticket System: Wayfarer 3

GOLDEN PIONEER TRAVEL
BRANDON, REDHILL, HEREFORD HR2 8BH
Tel: 01432 274307
Fax: 01432 275809
Prop: Bryan Crockett **Dir**:J Crockett.
Fleet: 4 - 3 single-deck coach, 1 minicoach.
Chassis: incl. 1 Iveco. 1 Scania. 1 Toyota.
Bodies: 1 Beulas. 1 Caetano. 1 Irizar. 1 Van Hool.
Ops incl: school contracts, excursions & tours, private hire, continental tours.
Livery: Black/Gold/Red/Green/Yellow

GOLD STAR TRAVEL
See Worcestershire

P. W. JONES COACHES
HILBROY GARAGE, BURLEY GATE, HEREFORD HR1 3QL
Tel: 01432 820214
Fax: 01432 820521
Recovery: 01432 820214
E-mail: coaches@p.w.jones.com
Owner: Philip W Jones
Fleet: 18 - 16 single-deck coach, 1 midicoach, 1 minicoach.
Chassis: 1 Bedford. 1 Bova. 13 Dennis. 1 MAN. 1 Mercedes. 1 Neoplan. 1 Toyota.
Bodies: 1 Bova. 1 Caetano. 1 uple. 1 Marcopolo. 1 Neoplan. 14 Plaxton.
Ops incl: excursions & tours, private hire, continental tours, school contracts., express
Livery: White/Blue

LUGG VALLEY PRIMROSE TRAVEL
SOUTHERN AVENUE, LEOMINSTER HR6 OGX
Tel: 01432 344341
Fax: 01432 356206
E-mail: elain.lvpt@btconnect.com
Man Dirs: N D Yeomans, G H Yeomans
(Com Sec) F E Sankey
Gen Man: A O Jones **Ops Man**: I Davies
Chief Eng: D W Jones
Fleet: 23 -15 single-deck bus, 8 single-deck coach
Chassis: 1 BMC. 5 Dennis. 1 Marshall. 10 Optare. 1 Scania. 5 Volvo.
Bodies: 1 Berkhof, 1 BMC, 2 Duple, 1 Irizar, 1 Jonckheere, 1 Marshall/mcv, 1 Northern Counties, 10 Optare, 5 Plaxton.
Ops incl: local bus services, school contracts, excursions & tours, private hire
Livery: Cream/Green/Orange
Ticket System: ERG

M & S COACHES OF HEREFORDSHIRE LTD
CROFTWELL HOUSE, KIMBOLTON, LEOMINSTER HR6 0HD
Tel: 01568 612803
Dir: Maurice Peruffo
Fleet: 7 - 4 midicoach, 3 minicoach.
Chassis: 4 Mercedes. 2 Toyota. 1 Volvo.
Bodies: 2 Caetano. 2 Mercedes. 1 Optare. 1 Van Hool. 1 other.
Ops incl: school contracts, private hire

NEWBURY COACHES
LOWER ROAD TRADING ESTATE, LEDBURY HR8 2DJ.
Tel: 01531 633483.
Fax: 01531633650.
Livery: Blue/White.

SARGEANTS BROS LTD
MILL STREET, KINGTON HR5 3AL
Tel/Fax: 01544 230481
E-mail: mike@sargeantsbros.com
Web site: www.sargeantsbros.com
Prop: Michael Sargeant
Fleet: 24 - 1 double-deck bus, 3 single-deck bus, 6 single-deck coach, 7 midibus, 7 minibus.
Chassis: 1 Blue Bird, 1 DAF, 1 Dennis, 2 Ford Transit, 1 LDV, 3 Mercedes, 6 Optare, 2 Renault, 1Volkswagen, 4 Volvo, 2 Talbot.
Bodies: 1 Alexander, 2 Jonckheere, 8 Optare, 2 Plaxton, 1 Transbus. 2 Van Hool. 5 Other
Ops incl: local bus services, school contracts, private hire.
Livery: Red/Gold
Ticket System: Wayfarer

SMITHS MOTORS (LEDBURY) LTD
COACH GARAGE, HOMEND, LEDBURY HR8 1BA.
Tel: 01531 632953.
Dirs: F. W. B. Sterry, M. Sterry.
Fleet: 11 - 8 coach, 2 midicoach, 1 minibus.
Chassis: 3 Bedford. 1 Ford. 1 Iveco. 4 Leyland. 2 Mercedes.
Bodies: 1 Caetano. 3 Duple. 3 Plaxton. 2 Van Hool. 1 PMT. 1 Devon.
Ops incl: local bus services, continental tours.
Livery: White with Green/Blue/Red stripe.
Ticket System: Setright.

STAGECOACH IN SOUTH WALES
See Torfaen

YEOMANS CANYON TRAVEL LTD
21-23 THREE ELMS TRADING ESTATE, HEREFORD HR4 9PU
Tel: 01432 356201
Fax: 01432 356206
E-mail: nigelyeomans@aol.com
Dirs: N D & G H Yeomans **Gen Man**: A Jones **Ch Eng**: C Taylor
Ops Man: I Davies
Fleet: 41 - single-deck bus, coach, minibus.
Chassis: 2 BMC. 6 Dennis. 2 Ford Transit. 1 Leyland. 1 Neoplan. 12 Optare. 8 Scania. 6 Volvo 1 Transbus.
Bodies: 2 Berkhof. 2 BMC. 5 Caetano. 3 Carlyle. 1 Duple. 2 Marcopolo. 1 Neoplan. 12 Optare. 11 Plaxton. 1 Transbus. 1 Wadham Stringer.
Ops incl: local bus services, school contracts, excursions & tours, private hire, express, continental tours.
Livery: Cream/Green/Orange
Ticket System: ERG

HERTFORDSHIRE

ABBEY TRAVEL LTD
58 BURYMEAD ROAD, HITCHIN SG5 1RT
Tel: 01462 421777/421888
Fax: 01462 421999
E-mail: rich@abbeytravel.co.uk
Web site: www.abbeytravel.co.uk
Man Dir: Peter Malyon **Dir**: Patricia Malyon **Co Man**: Richard Window.
Co Sec: Leigh Featherstone
Fleet: 14 - 2 single-deck bus, 8 coach, 1 midibus, 2 minibus, 1 minicoach
Chassis: 1 Dennis. 1 Ford Transit. 4 Mercedes. 1 Peugeot. 7 Volvo.
Bodies: 1 Berkhof. 1 Duple. 2 Jonckheere. 1 Mercedes. 4 Plaxton. 3 Reeve Burgess. 1 Van Hool. 1 Peugeot.
Ops incl: excursions & tours, private hire, continental tours, school contracts.
Livery: White/Blue.

ALPHA PERSONALISED TRAVEL LTD
300 HIGH ROAD, LEAVESDEN WD25 7EB
Tel/Fax: 01923 202052.
Chmn: G. Picton. **Man Dir**: D. Green.
Co Sec: J. Foster.
Fleet: 3 - 1 midicoach, 2 minibus.
Chassis: 2 Ford Transit. 1 Toyota.
Bodies: 1 Caetano.
Ops incl: excursions & tours, private hire, continental tours.
Livery: Blue/Orange/White.

A R TRAVEL LTD
40 PERRY GREEN, HEMEL HEMPSTEAD HP2 7ND
Tel: 01442 408093
Fax: 01442 389899
E-mail: artravelltd@hotmail.com
Web site: www.artravelltd.co.uk
Dir: Terry Hill
Fleet: 3 minicoach.
Chassis/bodies: 2 Mercedes. 1 VW.
Bodies: 2 Optare. 1 Other.
Ops incl: excursions & tours, private hire, school contracts.
Livery: White /Silver

CANTABRICA COACH HOLIDAYS
9 ELTON WAY, WATFORD WD25 8HH
Tel: 01923 247444
Fax: 01923 817066
Web site: www.cantabricacoaches.co.uk
Dir: David Stewart
Fleet: incl single-deck coach
Chassis: Volvo.
Bodies: Berkhof
Ops incl: private hire, continental tours.
Livery: Blue/Red

CHAMBERS COACHES (STEVENAGE) LTD
38 TRENT CLOSE, STVENAGE SG1 3RT
Tel: 01438 352920
Fax: 01462 486616
E-mail: chamberscoaches@btconnect.com
Web site: www.chamberscoaches.com
Man Dire: C R Chambers **Dir**: M R Chambers **Comp Sec**: D C Tidey
Fleet: 27 - 25 single-deck coach, 2 minicoach
Chassis: 1 BMC. 12 Dennis. 3 Iveco. 1 LDV. 2 Mercedes-Benz. 2 Toyota. 1 VDL
Bodies: Beulas. BMC. Marcopolo. Mercedes-Benz. UGV. Wadham Stringer
Ops incl: school contacts, private hire, express, continental tours.
Livery: White/Red /Blue

GOLDEN BOY COACHES LTD
JOHN TERENCE HOUSE, GEDDINGS ROAD, HODDESDON EN11 0NT
Tel: 01992 465747
Fax: 01992 450957
E-mail: sales@goldenboy.co.uk
Web site: www.goldenboy.co.uk
Joint Man Dirs: G A McIntyre, T P McIntyre **Tran Man**: G Jaikens **Ch Eng**: P Murdoch
Fleet: 35 - 3 single-deck bus, 17 single-deck coach, 12 midicoach, 3 minicoach.
Chassis: 3 Dennis. 15 Mercedes. 17 Volvo.
Bodies: 3 Alexander. 2 Optare. 9 Plaxton. 17 Van Hool. 2 Sitcar, 1 Euro, 1 Crest
Ops incl: local bus services, private hire, school contracts.
Livery: Black/Red/Gold.
Ticket System: Wayfarer

GRAVES COACHES & MINIBUSES
134 WINFORD DRIVE DRIVE, BROXBOURNE EN10 6PN
Tel/Fax: 01992 445556
E-mail: m.graves@btinternet.com
Prop: Michael Graves
Fleet: 2 -1 minicoach, 1 minibus
Chassis: 1 Mercedes. 1 Toyota.
Bodies: 1 Caetano. 1 Mercedes.
Ops incl: private hire, school contracts.

GROVE COACHES
101 MANDEVILLE ROAD, HERTFORD SG13 8JL
Tel: 01992 583417
Fleetname: Pride of Hertford
Driver/operator: R A Bowers
Fleet: 1 coach.
Chassis: Volvo. **Body**: Plaxton.
Ops incl: private hire, school contracts.
Livery: Brown/Orange

KENZIES COACHES LTD
6 ANGLE LANE, SHEPRETH SG8 6QH
Tel: 01763 260288
Fax: 01763 262012
Fleet: 25 coach.
Chassis: 2 Bedford. 1 Scania. 22 Volvo.
Bodies: 6 Plaxton. 19 Van Hool.
Ops incl: private hire, school contracts.

LITTLE JIM'S
1 CASTLE STREET, BERKHAMSTED HP4 2BQ
Tel: 01442 870029
Fax: 01442 877217
E-mail: littlejimbuses@aol.com
Prop: James H Petty
Fleet: 2 - 1 midibus, 1 midicoach.
Chassis: 2 Mercedes.
Bodies: 2 Plaxton.
Ops incl: local bus services, excursions & tours, private hire.
Livery: White/Purple.
Ticket System: Almex A

MARSHALLS COACHES
FIRBANK WAY, LEIGHTON BUZZARD LU7 4YP
Tel: 01525 376077
Fax: 01525 850967
Recovery: 01525 375301
E-mail: info@marshalls-coaches.co.uk
Web site: www.marshalls-coaches.co.uk
Fleetname: MCE Ltd
Prop: G Marshall **Ops Man**: I White
Wkshp Man: R Winters
Fleet: 28 - 3 double-deck bus, 22 coach, 2 double-deck coach, 1 midicoach.
Chassis: 3 Ayats. 4 Dennis. 3 Iveco. 2 Leyland. 1 Mercedes. 15 Volvo.
Bodies: 3 Ayats. 3 Beulas. 1 Caetano. 3 East Lancs. 5 Jonckheere. 1 Mercedes. 10 Plaxton.
Ops incl: private hire, school contracts, continental tours.
Livery: Blue/Multicoloured.

MASTER TRAVEL COACHES
9-12 PEARTREE FARM, WELWYN GARDEN CITY AL7 3UW
Tel: 01707 334040
Fax: 01707 334366
E-mail: mastertravel@btclick.com
Ptnrs: R J Goulden, S Goulden
Fleet: 16-1 bus 13 coach 2 minibus
Chassis: 1 BMC. 4 Dennis. 2 Ford Transit. 3 Mercedes. 1 Neoplan. . 2 Scania. 1 Optare, 1 Autosan, 1 Volvo
Bodies: 1 Berkhof. 1 BMC. 2 Irizar. 2 Marcopolo. 1 Neoplan. 1 Northern Counties. 1 Optare. 4 other. 1 Caetano. 1 UGV
Ops incl: school contracts, private hire.
Livery: White/Blue, White

MINIBUS SERVICES LTD
773 ST ALBANS ROAD, WATFORD WD25 9LA
Tel: 01923 663432
Fax: 01923 337347
E-mail: minibusservices@btconnect.com
Prop: Russell Crowson, Gillian Crowson.
Fleet: 4 - 1 single-deck coach, 1minibus, 2 midicoach
Chassis: 1 Ford Transit. 1 Mercedes.1 Toyota. 1 Volvo.
Bodies: include Caetano, Plaxton
Ops incl: school contracts, private hire

PARKSIDE TRAVEL LTD
PARADISE WILDLIFE PARK,
WHITE STUBBS LANE, BROXBOURNE
EN10 7QA
Tel: 01992 444177
Fax: 01992 465441
Fleetname: Parkside Travel
Dirs: P C Sampson, G F Sampson
Fleet: 7 minibus.
Chassis: 7 Ford Transit.
Ops incl: school contracts, private hire.
Livery: Light Blue

PROVENCE PRIVATE HIRE (P.P.H. COACHES)
HEATH FARM LANE, ST ALBANS
AL3 5AE
Tel: 01727 864988
Fax: 01727 855275
E-mail: office@pphcoaches.com
Web site: www.pphcoaches.com
Dir: A. K. Hayes, **Ch Eng**: D. Higgins
Fleet: 30 - 2 double-deck bus, 20 coach, 2 double-deck coach, 3 midicoache, 2 minibus, 1 minicoach.
Chassis: 1 DAF. 4 Dennis. 2 LDV. 2 Leyland. 1 MCW. 3 Mercedes. 10 Scania. 2 Toyota. 4 Volvo. 1 other.
Bodies: 3 Caetano. 1 Duple. 4 East Lancs. 6 Irizar. 1 MCW. 2 Optare. 10 Plaxton. 2 Toyota. 4 Volvo.
Ops incl: excursions & tours, private hire, continental tours, school contracts.
Livery: Yellow.

REG'S COACHES LTD
113 - 115 CODICOTE ROAD, WELWYN
AL6 9TY
Tel: 01483 822000
Fax: 01483 822003
E-mail: www.regscoaches@btconnect.com
Web site: www.regscoaches.co.uk
Man Dir: T Hunt **Dir**: Mrs B Hunt **Ops Man**: Mick Mead
Fleet: 16 - 2 single-deck bus, 12 single-deck coach, 2 midicoach, .
Chassis: 7 Dennis. 2 Mercedes. 7 Volvo.

Bodies: 1 Birkof. 1 Nothern Counties. 1 Optare. 9 Plaxton. 2 Van Hool. 1 Wright. 1 Other
Ops incl: local bus services, school contracts, excursions & tours, private hire.
Livery: Black/Green/Orange
Ticket System: Wayfarer 2/Almex

REYNOLDS DIPLOMAT COACHES
285 LOWER HIGH STREET, WATFORD
WD17 2HY
Tel: 01923 296877
Fax: 01923 210020
E-mail: enquiries@reynoldscoaches.com
Web site: www.reynoldscoaches.com
Props: Richard Reynolds,
Susan Reynolds **Ops Dir**: Christopher Barker
Fleet: 18 - 13 coach, 3 double-deck coach, 2 midibus.
Chassis: 1 MAN. 3 Mercedes. 3 Scania. 3 Setra. 1 Volvo.
Bodies: 1 Caetano. 7 Jonckheere. 3 Neoplan. 1 Optare. 3 Setra. 3 Van Hool.
Ops incl: excursions & tours, private hire, continental tours, school contracts.
Livery: Gold

RICHMOND'S COACHES
THE GARAGE, BARLEY, ROYSTON
SG8 8JA
Tel: 01763 848226
Fax: 01763 848105
E-mail: postbox@richmonds-coaches.co.uk
Web site: www.richmonds-coaches.co.uk
Dirs: David Richmond, Michael Richmond, Andrew Richmond **Sales & Mktg Man**: Rick Ellis **Asst Ops Man**: Craig Ellis **Ch Eng**: Patrick Granville **Exc & Tours Man**: Natalie Richmond
Fleet: 26 - 19 single-deck coach, 1 midicoach, 6 midibus.
Chassis: 6 Bova. 2 DAF. 1 Dennis. 5 Mercedes. 2 Optare. 10 Volvo.
Bodies: 1 Berkhof. 6 Bova. 2 Optare. 4 Plaxton. 12 Van Hool. 1 other.
Ops incl: local bus services, school contracts, excursions & tours, private hire, express, continental tours.
Livery: Chocolate/Cream

SHIRE COACHES
PO BOX 862, ST ALBANS AL1 9BT
Tel: 01727 832519
Fax: 01727 832548
Subsidiary of Galleon Travel - see Essex

SMITH BUNTINGFORD
CLAREMONT, BALDOCK ROAD,
BUNTINGFORD SG9 9DJ
Tel/Fax: 01763 271516
Prop: Graham H Smith **Fleet Eng**: Stewart C Smith
Fleet: 6 minicoach.
Chassis: 1 Ford Transit. 3 Mercedes. 1 Renault. 1 Vauxhall
Bodies: 1 Autobus. 1 Courtside. 1 Ford. 1 Mellor. 1 Stanford.
Ops incl: private hire, school contracts
Livery: White/Orange

SMITHS OF TRING
THE GARAGE, WIGGINTON HP23 6EJ
Tel: 01442 322555
Fax: 08707 627292
Dirs: G. A. Smith (**Man Dir**),
Mrs S. N. Smith, J. Smith.
Fleet: 8 - 6 coach, 1 midicoach,
1 minicoach. **Chassis**: 2 Mercedes. 6 Volvo.
Bodies: 2 Mercedes. 1 Plaxton. 1 Reeve Burgess.
Ops incl: local bus services, excursions & tours, private hire, continental tours.
Livery: Red/Cream.

SOUTH MIMMS TRAVEL LTD
WARRENGATE ROAD, NORTH MIMMS
AL9 7TU
Tel: 01707 322555
Fax: 08707 627292
E-mail: info@southmimmstravel.com
Web site: www.southmimmstravel.co.uk
Man Dir: S. J. Griffiths.
Fleet: 10 coach.
Chassis: incl: Dennis, MCW, Neoplan, Volvo.
Bodies: incl: Berkhof, Bova, MCW, Neoplan, Plaxton.
Ops incl: school contracts, excursions & tours, private hire, continental tours.
Livery: Red/Black/Gold

SULLIVAN BUSES LTD
FIRST FLOOR, DEARDS HOUSE, ST ALBANS ROAD, POTTERS BAR
EN6 3NE
Tel: 01707 646803
Fax: 01707 646804
E-mail: admin@sullivanbuses.com
Web site: www.sullivanbuses.com
Man Dir: Dean Sullivan
Fleet: 36 - 26 double-deck bus, 10 single-deck bus
Chassis: 3 AEC.11 Leyland. 9 MCW. 10 Transbus. 2 Volvo.
Bodies: 7 Caetano. 1 Carlyle. 2 East Lancs. 11 Leicester. 9 MCW. 3 Park Royal. 3 Plaxton.
Ops incl: local bus services
Livery: Red
Ticket system: Wayfarer TGX

HERTFORDSHIRE

131

TATES COACHES
44 HIGH STREET, MARKYATE AL3 8PA
Tel: 01582 840297
Fax: 01582 840014
E-mail: info@tates-coaches.co.uk
Web site: www.tates-coaches.co.uk
Dirs: Alan Tate, Tony Tate, Stephen Tate
Fleet: 10 - 9 single-deck coach, 1 midicoach
Chassis: 1 Bova. 1 DAF. 1 EOS. 1MAN. 1 Mercedes. 2 Neoplan. 3 Scania.
Bodies: 1 Bova. 1 Caetano. 1 Hispano. 3 Irizar. 2 Neoplan. 1 Van Hool. 1 Wadham Stringer.
Ops incl: school contracts, excursions & tours, private hire, continental tours.
Livery: Cream/Blue/Orange

TERRY'S COACHES
45 HOMEFIELD ROAD,
HEMEL HEMPSTEAD HP2 4BZ
Tel: 01442 265850
Dirs: Terry Bunyan, Shirley Bunyan.
Fleet: 5 - 1 midibus, 2 midicoach, 2 minicoach.
Chassis: 1 Iveco. 1 LDV. 2 Mercedes.
Bodies: 1 Leicester. 2 Optare. 2 other.
Ops incl: school contracts, private hire.
Livery: Blue/White

TIMEBUS TRAVEL
See London

UNICORN COACHES LTD
PO BOX 45, HATFIELD AL9 5LD
Tel: 01707 269003
Tel: 01707 260039
E-mail: stsunicorn@aol.com
Web site: www.unicorncoaches.com
Man Dir: Mrs J E Pleshette **Gen Man**: S T Saltmarsh
Fleet: 2 minibus.
Chassis: 2 Ford Transit.
Ops incl: school contracts, private hire.
Livery: Red/White

UNO LTD
GYPSY MOTH AVENUE, HATFIELD BUSINESS PARK, HATFIELD AL10 9BS
Tel: 01707 255764
Web site: www.unobus.info
Man Dir: Bill Hiron
Fleet: 88-8 double deck bus, 80 single deck bus
Chassis: DAF, Dennis, Mercedes, Optare Scania, Mercedes.
Bodies: 4 Bluebird, 1 Mercedes, 1 East Lancs, 1 Leyland, 5 Marshall, 2 Northern Counties, 4 Optare, 1 Reeve Burgess, 20 Wright.
Ops incl: local bus services, school contracts.
Livery: Pink/Purple.
Ticket System: Wayfarer 3 Inform.

LEN WRIGHT BAND SERVICES LTD
9 ELTON WAY, WATFORD WD2 8HH.
Tel: 01923 238611.
Fax: 01923 230134.
E-mail: lwbs1@aol.com
Web site: www.lenwright.co.uk
Ops Dir: L. Collins.
Fleet: 13 - 6 coach, 5 double-deck coach (all sleeper), 2 minibus.
Chassis: 1 Bova. 2 Mercedes. 4 Scania. 6 Volvo.
Bodies: 1 Bova. 2 Irizar. 2 Jonckheere. 2 Plaxton. 4 Van Hool. 2 Autobus.
Ops incl: specialist private hire.
Livery: Grey.

ISLE OF WIGHT

AWAY DAYS
56 WILTON ROAD, SHANKLIN PO37 7BZ
Tel: 01983 862774
Fax: 01983 864215
E-mail: awaydays@supanet.com
Website: www.awaydaysiowco.uk
Props: Roy Townend, Hedda Townend
Fleet: 3 coach
Chassis: 2 Iveco. 1 Scania.
Bodies: 2 Beulas. 1 Berkhof.
Ops incl: school contracts, excursions & tours, private hire, continental tours.
Livery: White with orange lettering and multi-coloured kite.

GANGES COACHES
77 PLACE ROAD, COWES PO31 7AE
Tel: 01983 296666
Fax: 01983 296666
Prop: John Gange
Fleet: 9 - 4 coach, 3 midicoach, 1 minibus, 1 minicoach.
Chassis: 1 AEC. 1 Bedford. 1 Ford. 1 Leyland. 3 Mercedes. 1 Renault. 1 Peugeot/Talbot
Bodies: 2 Duple. 1 Mercedes. 3 Plaxton. 3 other.
Ops incl: private hire
Livery: Red/Cream and Blue/Cream

GRAND HOTEL TOURS LTD (KIM'S COACHES)
GRAND HOTEL, CULVER PARADE, SANDOWN PO36 8QA.

Tel: 01983 402236.
Fax: 01983 406784.
Fleetname: Grand Tours.
Prop: R. J. H. & M. A. Hayter.
Sec: Mrs Marilyn Gerrard. **Traf Man**: G. Worrall. **Gen Man**: R. H. J. Hayter.
Fleet: 3 coach.
Chassis: DAF. Dennis. Scania.
Bodies: Duple. Van Hool. LAG.
Ops incl: excursions & tours, private hire.
Livery: Yellow/White.

ISLAND COACH SERVICES LTD
UNIT D10, SPITHEAD BUSINESS CENTRE, NEWPORT ROAD, SANDOWN PO36 9PH
Tel: 01983 408080
Fax: 01983 408808
Website: www.islandcoachservices.co.uk
E-mail: info@islandcoachservices.co.uk
Dir: R J Long **Tran Man**: D Draper
Fleet: 11 coach
Chassis: 1 DAF. 1 Dennis. 1 Mercedes. 8 Volvo.
Bodies: 2 Caetano. 2 Jonckheere. 1 Mercedes. 1 Neoplan. 3 Plaxton. 2 Van Hool.
Ops incl: excursions & tours, private hire, continental tours, school contracts.
Livery: Blue flash/White.

ISLE OF WIGHT COUNTY TRANSPORT DEPARTMENT
21 WHITCOMBE ROAD, NEWPORT PO30 1YS

Tel: 01983 823784.
Fax: 01983 825818.
Fleetname: Wightbus.
Tran Man: A. A. Morris. **Ops Man**: J. Lamb.
Fleet: 27 - 1 double-deck bus, 13 single-deck bus, 2 coach, 11 midibus.
Chassis: 13 Dennis. 1 Ford. 2 Leyland. 11 Mercedes.
Bodies: 2 Caetano. 1 Duple. 1 ECW. 1 Reeve Burgess. 15 Wadham Stringer. 1 Wright. 2 LCB. 1 Mellor. 1 Steedrive. 2 Withey.
Ops incl: local bus services, school contracts, excursions & tours, private hire.
Livery: White with Orange and Blue stripes.
Ticket System: Setright.

KARDAN TRAVEL LTD
1ST FLOOR, 35A ST JAMES STREET, NEWPORT PO30 1LG
Tel: 01983 520995
Fax: 01983 821288
E-mail: info@kardan.co.uk
Web site: www.kardan.co.uk
Dir: Robert Hodgson
Fleet: 5 single-deck coach
Chassis: 3 Setra. 2 Volvo.
Bodies: 2 Plaxton. 3 Setra.
Ops incl: excursions &tours, private hire, continental tours
Livery: Yellow/White

SEAVIEW SERVICES LTD
SEAFIELD GARAGE, COLLEGE FARM, FAULKNER LANE, SANDOWN PO36 9AZ
Tel: 01983 407070
Fax: 01983 407045
Recovery: 0773 923 7361
E-mail: mail@seaview-services.com
Web site: www.seaview-services.com
Chmn: Phillip Robinson **Ops Man**: Lorraine Bunce **Ch Eng**: Peter Brand, Jim Wood **Fleet**: 10 - 9 single-deck coach, 1 minicoach.
Chassis: 1 Setra. 1 Toyota. 8 Volvo.
Bodies: 1 Caetano. 5 Plaxton. 1 Setra. 3 Van Hool.
Ops incl: excursions & tours, private hire, continental tours, express, school contracts.
Livery: Green/Red

THE SOUTHERN VECTIS OMNIBUS CO LTD
NELSON ROAD, NEWPORT PO30 1RD
Tel: 01983 522456
Fax: 01983 524961
Recovery: 01983 821135
E-mail: v.gibbs@southernvectis.com
Web site: www.islandbuses.info
Man Dir: Alex Carter **Ops Dir**: Andrew Wickham **Fin Dir**: Matt Dolphin **Acting Eng Dir**: Vernon Gibbs **Ops/Comm Man**: Marc Morgan-Huws
Fleet: 94 - 54 double-deck bus, 26 single-deck bus, 2 coach, 10 open-top bus, 2 midibus.
Chassis: 4 Bristol. 28 Dennis. 2 Iveco. 24 Leyland. 7 Mercedes. 26 Volvo. 3 other.
Bodies: 4 ECW. 15 Leyland. 1 Marshall. 1 Mellor. 7 Mercedes. 28 Northern Counties. 28 Plaxton. 2 Transbus. 6 UVG. 3 other
Ops incl: local bus services, school contracts, excursions and tours, private hire.
Livery: Green/Red/Blue/Orange
Ticket system: Wayfarer
(Part of the Go-Ahead Group)

WIGHTROLLER COACHES
UNIT C7, SPITHEAD BUSINESS CENTRE, NEWPORT ROAD, SANDOWN PO36 9PH
Tel: 01983 404028
Fax: 01983 404772
E-mail: wightrollers@supanet.com
Web site: www.wightrollers.co.uk
Dirs: P Steele, T Bryant **Ch Eng**: Colin Steele
Fleet: 14 - 12 single-deck coach, 1 minibus, 1 minicoach
Chassis: 6 Dennis. 1 Mercedes-Benz. 1 Renault. 6 Volvo.
Bodies: 4 Alexander Dennis. 1 Caetano. 3 Jonckheere. 3 Plaxton. 3 Van Hool.
Ops incl: excursions & tours, private hire, continental tours.

VINTAGE TOURS
WOODSTOCK, GROVE ROAD, RYDE PO33 3LH
Tel: 01983 812147
Web site: www.vintagetours.net
Prop: John Woodhams
Fleet: 2 single-deck coach.
Chassis: 2 Bedford.
Bodies: 2 Duple.
Ops incl: excursions & tours, private hire
Livery: Two tone Green

KENT

ARRIVA SOUTHERN COUNTIES
INVICTA HOUSE, ARMSTRONG ROAD, MAIDSTONE ME15 6TX
Tel: 01622 697000
Fax: 01622 697001
Web site: www.arriva.co.uk
Man Dir: Heath Williams
Fleet: 153 - double-deck bus, single-deck bus, minibus, midibus, coach.
Chassis: 20 DAF. 60 Dennis. 1 Mercedes. 6 Optare. 10 Scania. 28 Volvo. 21 other.
Ops incl: local bus services, school contracts, excursions & tours, express, continental tours, private hire.
Livery: Blue/Cream.
Ticket System: Wayfarer 3 & TGX150

ASM COACHES
8 THE OAZE, WHITSTABLE CT5 4TQ
Tel: 01227 280254
E-mail: asm.coaches@virgin.net
Web: www.asmcoaches.co.uk
Props: Steven R Morrish, Alison Morrish.
Fleet: 2 minicoach
Chassis: 1 LDV. 1 Mercedes.
Bodies: 1 Mercedes-Benz. 1 Other.
Ops incl: school contracts, private hire, continental trips.
Livery: Purple/White

AUTOCAR BUS & COACH SERVICES LTD
64 WHETSTED ROAD, FIVE OAK GREEN, TONBRIDGE TN12 6RT
Tel: 01892 833830
Fax: 01892 836977
Dir: Eric Baldock **Fleet Eng**: Ray Tompsett

Fleet: 8 - 4 single-deck bus, 2 coach, 1 double-deck coach, 1 midicoach.
Chassis: 1 DAF. 1 Dennis. 4 Leyland. 1 Mercedes. 1 Scania.
Bodies: 1 Alexander. 1 Duple. 2 East Lancs. 2 Plaxton. 1 Wadham Stringer. Wright.
Ops incl: local bus services, school contracts, private hire.
Livery: White/Purple (two shades)
Ticket System: Wayfarer 2

BRITANNIA COACHES
HOLLOW WOOD ROAD, DOVER CT17 0UB
Tel: 01304 228111
Fax: 01304 215350
E-mail: enq@britannia-coaches.co.uk.
Web site: www.britannia-coaches.co.uk.
Ptnrs: Barry Watson, Danny Lawson.
Fleet: 30 minicoach.
Chassis/bodies: 20 Mercedes. 10 Renault.
Ops incl: private hire, school contracts, excursions & tours.

BROWNS COACHES
OAKTREE COTTAGE, MANOR POUND LANE, BRABOURNE, ASHFORD TN25 5LG.
Tel: 01303 813555
Fax: 01303 812070
Prop: Patrick Browne
Fleet: 4 - 3 coach, 1 minibus.
Chassis: 1 LDV. . 3 Volvo.
Ops incl: school contracts, private hire

BUZZLINES
UNIT G1, LYMPNE INDUSTRIAL PARK, LYMPNE CT21 4LR
Tel: 01303 261870
Fax: 01303 230093
Recovery: 07767 475625
E-mail: sales@buzzlines.co.uk
Web site: www.buzzlines.co.uk
Dir: Mrs K Busbridge **Man Dir**: N. P. Busbridge **Eng Man**: D Lange **Ops Man**: G Creasey
Fleet: 56 - 2 single-deck bus, 28 coach, 3 double-deck coach, 3 midicoach, 15 minbus, 5 people carrier.
Chassis: 1 Dennis. 4 Ford Transit. 11 Mercedes. 11 Neoplan. 8 Scania. 2 Seat. 7 Setra. 4 Toyota. 5 Volvo. 3 Volkswagen.
Bodies: 4 Caetano. 4 Ford Transit. 6 Irizar. 11 Neoplan. 7 Setra. 11 Mercedes. 5 Volvo. 3 Volkswagen. 2 Seat. 2 PTS.
Ops incl: local bus services, school contracts, excursions & tours, private hire, continental tours.
Livery: Metallic blue.

CENTRAL MINI COACHES
177 LOWER ROAD, DOVER CT17 0RE.
Tel/Fax: 01304 823030.
Prop: P. Hull.
Fleet: 6 - 5 minibus, 1 minicoach.
Chassis: 3 Bedford. 1 Mercedes. 1 Renault.
Ops incl: private hire, school contracts.

CHALKWELL COACH HIRE & TOURS
195 CHALKWELL ROAD, SITTINGBOURNE ME10 1BJ
Tel: 01795 423982
Fax: 01795 431855
E-mail: coachhire@chalkwell.co.uk
Web site: www.chalkwell.com
Man Dir: Clive Eglinton **Ops Man**: Roland Eglinton **Financial Controller**: Louise Egllinton

133

Fleet: 42 - 1 double-deck bus, 2 single-deck bus, 17 single-deck coach, 14 midibus, 5 midicoach, 1 minibus. 2 minicoach.
Chassis: 12 Dennis. 1 Leyland. 16 Mercedes. 5 Optare. 1 Renault. 7 Volvo.
Bodies: 3 Alexander.1 Autobus. 1 East lancs. 4 Jonckheere. 5 Optare. 14 Plaxton. 3 UVG. 6 Wadham Stringer. 2 Wright. 3 other.
Ops incl: local bus services, excursions & tours, privet hire, expres, continental tours
Livery: White/Red/Black
Ticket System: Almex A90

COUNTRYWIDE TRAVEL SERVICES LTD
T/A ALAN DAWNEY HOLIDAYS, UNIT 7 TRANSIT WORKS, POWERSTATION ROAD, SHEERNESS ME12 3AD
Tel: 01795 662688
Fax: 01795 668692
E-mail: steve.mason@cwts.co.uk
Web site: www.alandawneyholidays.com
Man Dir: Steven Smith **Ops Man**: Steve Mason
Fleet: 6 - incl: single-deck coach, midicoach, minicoach
Chassis: incl: Iveco, Mercedes-Benz. Scania
Bodies: incl: irizar
Ops incl: excursions & tours,prvate hire, continental tours.
Livery: White/Green

CROSSKEYS COACHES
CROSSKEYS BUSINESS PARK, CAESARS WAY, FOLKESTONE CT19 4AL
Tel: 01303 272625
Fax: 01303 274085
E-mail: alan@crosskeys.uk.com
Web site: www.crosskeys.uk.com
Prop: Alan Johnson
Fleet: 24 - 2 single-deck bus, 19 coach, 3 minicoach.
Chassis: 9 Bova. 2 Leyland National. 3 Mercedes.
Bodies: 1 Jonckheere. 5 Plaxton. 1 Setra. 2 Van Hool.
Ops incl: school contracts, excursions & tours, private hire, continental tours.

EASTONWAYS LTD
MANSTON ROAD, RAMSGATE CT12 6HJ
Tel: 01843 588944
Fax: 01843 582300
E-mail: ele@eastonways.co.uk
Web site: www.eastonways.co.uk
Chmn/Co Sec E. L. Easton.
Man Dir: D. Austin **Dir**: Y. M. Easton.
Ops Man: S. Lee. **Eng**: E. Easton.
Fleet: 15 - 2 double-deck coach, 8 single-deck bus, 3 coach, 2 midicoach.
Chassis: 2 Bristol. 1 DAF. 1 Optare. 2 Toyota. 1 Volvo.
Bodies: 1 Caetano. 1 Duple. 2 Northern Counties. 8 Optare. 1 Van Hool.

Ops incl: local bus services, school contracts, private hire.
Livery: Coaches: Blue/Silver. Buses: Red.
Ticket System: Wayfarer.

EUROLINK FOKESTONE
GREATWORTH, CANTERBURY ROAD, ETCHINGHILL, FOLKESTONE CT18 8BS
Tel: 01303 862767
Fax: 01303 862484
E-mail: eurolinkcoaches@btconnect.com
Ptnrs: Andy Williams, Lyn Williams
Fleet: 9 - 5 midicoach, 4 minicoach.
Chassis: 1 Ford Transit. 2 MAN. 4 Mercedes. 1 Renault. 1 Toyota.
Bodies: 3 Caetano. 1 Esker. 1 Mercedes. 1 Optare. 3 other.
Ops incl: school contracts, private hire.
Livery: White/Grey/Orange

FARLEIGH COACHES
ST PETERS WORKS, HALL ROAD, WOULDHAM, ROCHESTER ME1 3XL
Tel: 01634 201065.
Fax: 01634 660350.
Prop: D R Smith
Livery: White/Yellow/Red/Black.

FERRYMAN TRAVEL
RECTORY LANE NORTH, LEYBOURNE ME19 5HD.
Tel/Fax: 01732 843396
Fleet: 4 minibus.
Chassis: 3 DAF. 1 Ford Transit.
Ops incl: school contracts, excursions & tours, private hire, continental tours.

G & S TRAVEL
14 PYSONS ROAD, RAMSGATE CT12 6TS
Tel: 01843 591105.
Fax: 01843 596274.
E-mail: shirleygstravel@fismail.net
Web: www.G-S-travel.co.uk
Dirs: Shirley Rimmer, George Rimmer
Ops Man: Malcolm Wood **Ch Eng**: Darren Doyle
Fleet: 12 - 8 single-deck coach, 2 minibus, 2 midicoach.
Chassis: 2 LDV. 2 Toyota. 8 Volvo.
Bodies: 5 Caetano. 5 Plaxton. 1 Van Hool. 2 other.
Ops incl: school contracts, excursions & tours, private hire, continental tours.
Livery: White.

GRIFFIN BUS
126 LONDON ROAD, DUNTON GREEN, SEVENOAKS

KENT COACH TOURS LTD
THE COACH STATION, MALCOLM SARGENT ROAD, ASHFORD TN23 6JW
Tel/Recovery: 01233 627330
Fax: 01233 612977
Web site: www.kentcoachtours.co.uk
Dirs: David Farmer, Ann Farmer, Andrew Farmer **(Co Sec)**, Brian Farmer **(Ch Eng)**

Fleet: 13 - 1 single-deck bus, 7 coach, 5 minibus.
Chassis: 1 MAN. 5 Mercedes. 1 Optare. 7 Volvo
Bodies: 1 Optare. 12 Plaxton.
Ops incl: local bus services, school contracts, excursions & tours, private hire.
Livery: Blue
Ticket System: Wayfarer

KENT COUNTY COUNCIL
COMMERCIAL SERVICES, PASSENGER SERVICES, FORSTAL ROAD, AYLESFORD ME20 7HB
Tel: 01622 605935.
Fax: 01622 790338.
Tran Man: Kenneth Cobb **Ops Contr**: Roger Faunch.
Asst Ops Contr: Mick Curd.
Fleet: 48 - 2 double-deck bus, 12 single-deck bus, 4 coach, 2 midibus, 1 midicoach, 27 minibus.
Chassis: 5 Dennis. 27 Iveco. 4 Leyland. 3 Mercedes. 4 Optare. 1 Volvo.
Bodies: 1 Alexander. 1 Caetano. 7 Leicester. 2 Leyland. 4 Optare. 6 Plaxton.27 Euromotive.
Ops incl: local bus services, school contracts, private hire.
Livery: Red on White.
Ticket System: Almex.

THE KINGS FERRY TRAVEL GROUP
THE TRAVEL CENTRE, GILLINGHAM ME8 6HW
Tel: 01634 377577
Fax: 01634 370656
E-mail: sales@thekingsferry.co.uk
Web site: www.thekingsferry.co.uk
Ops Dir: Ian Fraser **Com Dir**: Danny Elford **Financial Dir**: Stephen Hills
Fleet: 73 - 3 single-deck bus, 52 coach, 7 double-deck bus, 6 midicoach, 5 minicoach.
Chassis: 1 Bova. 1 DAF. 2 Dennis. 2 Iveco. 10 MAN. 9 Marshall. 2 Optare. 31 Scania. 4 Setra. 12 Volvo.
Bodies: 2 Alexander. 17 Berkhof. 1 Bova. 1 Castrosua. 2 Hispano. 2 Indcar. 11 Irizar. 3 Mercedes. 10 Noge. 5 Optare. 5 Setra. 5 Sunsundegui. 8 Van Hool.
Ops incl: local bus services, school contracts, excursions & tours, private hire, continental tours.
Livery: Yellow with green stripe
Part of the National Express Group

KINGSMAN INTERNATIONAL TRAVEL
57 BRAMLEY AVENUE, FAVERSHAM ME13 8LP
Tel: 01795 531553
Fax: 01795 536798
E-mail: jonathanamancini@tiscali.co.uk
Prosp: J A Mancini, J Mancini
Fleet: 8 - 4 single-deck bus, 3 coach, 1 midicoach.
Chassis: 6 Mercedes. 3Neoplan.
Bodies: 4 Mercedes. 3 Neoplan. 2 Plaxton.
Ops incl: local bus services, excursions & tours, private hire, continental tours.

LOGANS TOURS LTD
1 AND 2 THE COTTAGES, NORTHFLEET GREEN DA13 9PT
Tel: 01474 833876
E-mail: dave@loganstours.co.uk
Web site: www.loganstours.co.uk
Dir: David Logan
Fleet: 2 coach.
Chassis: 1 Dennis. 1 Raba.
Bodies: 1 Caetano. 1 Ikarus.
Ops incl: excursions & tours, private hire, continental tours
Livery: Pink/White

NEW ENTERPRISE COACHES
CANNON LANE, TONBRIDGE TN9 1PP.
Tel: 01732 355256.
Fax: 01732 357716.
Prop: Arriva Southern Counties.
Gen Man: Chris Lawrence.
Eng Man: Andy Weber.
Fleet: 24 - 5 double-deck bus, 2 single-deck bus, 17 coach.
Chassis: 8 DAF. 3 Leyland. 4 MCW. 3 Scania. 6 Volvo.
Bodies: 2 Caetano. 3 Duple. 4 MCW. 1 PMT. 11 Plaxton. 1 Reeve Burgess. 3 Van Hool.
Ops incl: local bus services, school contracts, excursions & tours, private hire, continental tours.
Livery: White/Red/Blue.
Ticket System: Wayfarer II.

NU-VENTURE COACHES LTD
UNIT 2F, DEACON TRADING ESTATE, FORSTAL ROAD, AYLESFORD ME20 7SP
Tel: 01622 882288
Fax: 01622 718070
E-mail: nuventurecoachesltd@yahoo.co.uk
Web site: www.nu-venture.co.uk
Dir: D Quick **Co Sec**: N Kemp
Fleet: 28 - 11 double-deck bus, 14 single-deck bus, 3 coach.
Chassis: 10 Dennis. 13 Leyland. 1 MAN. 1 Mercedes. 2 Optare. 1 Scania.
Bodies: 5 Alexander. 1 Caetano. 12 Leyland. 1 Marcopolo. 2 Marshall. 2 Optare. 1 Plaxton. 1 Reeve Burgess. 2 UVG. 1 Van Hool.
Ops incl: local bus services, school contracts, private hire, excursions & tours.
Livery: White/Blue
Ticket System: Wayfarer 3

POYNTERS COACHES LTD
WYE COACH DEPOT, WYE TN25 5BX
Tel: 01233 812002
Fax: 01233 813210
Recovery: 07770 874631
E-mail: poyntercoaches@aol.com
Man Dir: B Poynter **Ch Eng**: B Poynter
Fleet: 15 - 1 double-deck bus, 8 single-deck bus, 5 coach, 1 double-deck coach.
Chassis: 2 DAF. 3 Dennis. 2 Leyland. 1 MAN. 7 Volvo.
Bodies: 4 Alexander. 1 Berkhof. 1 Bova. 1 Jonckheere. 2 Leyland. 2 Neoplan. 1 Optare. 2 Reeve Burgess. 1 Van Hool
Ops incl: local bus services, school contracts, excursions & tours, private hire, continental tours.
Livery: White
Ticket System: Wayfarer

R. K. F. TRAVEL
R24
19 COBB CLOSE, STROOD ME2 3TY
Tel/Fax: 01634 715897.
Dir: Ray Fraser.
Fleet: 2 minibus.
Chassis: 1 LDV, 1 VW.
Ops incl: private hire.

THE RAINHAM COACH CO
1A SPRINGFIELD ROAD, GILLINGHAM ME7 1YJ
Tel : 01634 852020
Fax: 01634 582020
E-mail: info@rainhamcoach.co.uk
Web site: www.rainhamcoach.co.uk
Prop-Ptnrs: D Graham, C Graham **Gen Man**: A Lorentsen **Comp Sec**: C Graham
Fleet: 18 - 2 midicoach, 16 minicoach.
Chassis/Bodies: 1 Ford Transit. 17 Mercedes-Benz..
Ops incl: school contracts, private hire, excursions & tours.
Livery: White/Magenta

REDROUTE BUSES
GRANBY COACHWORKS, GROVE ROAD, NORTHFLEET DA11 9AX
Tel: 01474 353896
Web site: www.redroutebus.com
Fleet: 25 - 14 double-deck bus, 3 single-deck bus, 1 coach, 7 minibus.
Ops incl: local bus services
Livery: Red

REGENT COACHES
UNIT 16, ST AUGUSTINES BUSINESS PARK, WHITSTABLE CT5 2QJ
Tel: 01227 794345
Fax: 01227 795120
E-mail: info@regentcoaches.com
Web site: www.regentcoaches.co.uk
Ptnrs: Paul Regent, Kerry Regent **Tran Mans**: Colin MacDonald, Kenneth Bishop
Traff Assistant: Sam Regent **Fleet Eng**: Robert Wildish
Fleet: 25 - 8 minibus, 10 midicoach, 7 minicoach.
Chassis: 4 Iveco. 5 LDV. 12 Mercedes. 4 Renault.
Ops incl: local bus services, school contracts, private hire.
Livery: White/Red/Orange
Ticket system: Almex Electronic

SCOTLAND & BATES
HEATH ROAD, APPLEDORE TN26 2AJ
Tel: 01233 758325.
Fax: 01233 758611.
E-mail: info@scotlandandbates.co.uk
Web site: www.scotlandandbates.co.uk
Ptnrsl: R M Bates, G A Bates.
Fleet: 17 single-deck coach.
Chassis: 17 Volvo.
Bodies: 3 Plaxton. 14 Van Hool.
Ops incl: school contracts, private hire
Livery: Cream/Brown/Orange

SEATH COACHES
FIELDINGS, STONEHEAP ROAD, EAST STUDDAL CT15 5BU
Tel/Fax: 01304 620825.
Owner: P. Seath.
Fleet: 4 coach.
Chassis: Ford. Iveco. Leyland. Volvo.
Bodies: Caetano. Plaxton
Ops incl: school contracts, private hire.
Livery: Pink/White/Beige.

SPOT HIRE TRAVEL
STATION APPROACH, WARE STREET, BEARSTED RAILWAY STATION, MAIDSTONE ME14 4PH
Tel: 01622 738932
Fax: 01622 630406
Prop: R N Young
Fleet: 13 - 3 single-deck coach, 3 midicoach, 3 minicoach, 4 saloons.
Chassis: 1 Ford Transit. 1 Leyland. 11 Mercedes.
Ops incl: school contracts, excursions & tours, private hire, continental tours.
Livery: Cream with three stripes

STAGECOACH IN EAST KENT & HASTINGS
BUS STATION, ST GEORGE'S LANE, CANTERBURY CT1 2SY
Tel: 01227 828103
Fax: 01227 828150
Web site: www.stagecoachbus.com
Ch Exec: Brian Souter **Man Dir UK Bus**: L Warneford **Group Fin Dir**: M Griffiths
Co Sec: A Whitnall **Man Dir**: Paul Southgate **Ops Dir**: Neil Instrall **Eng Dir**: Jason Bush
Fleet: 302 - 143 double-deck bus, 45 single-deck bus, 17 coach, 45 midibus, 52 minibus.
Chassis: 48 Dennis. 3 Dodge. 1 Ford. 4 Ford Transit. 43 Leyland. 9 MAN. 52 Mercedes. 44 Scania. 106 Volvo.
Bodies: 182 Alexander. 4 Leyland. 7 Leyland. 74 Northern Counties. 40 Plaxton. 3 Wadham Stringer. 3 Wright.
Ops incl: local bus services, express.
Livery: Stagecoach (Blue,Orange,White,Red); National Express (White).
Ticket System: ERG/Wayfarer.

STREAMLINE
WEST STATION APPROACH, MAIDSTONE ME16 8RJ
Tel: 01622 750000
Fax: 01622 752978
Web site: www.streamlinetravel.co.uk
Fleet: 5 - 2 mincoach, 3 midicoach.
Chassis/Bodies: 1 Iveco. 4 Mercedes
Ops include: local bus services, excursions & tours, private hire, school contracts
Livery: Silver

THOMSETT'S COACHES
50 GOLF ROAD, DEAL CT14 6QB
Tel/Fax: 01304 374731
E-mail: thomsettscoaches@fsmail.net
Prop: S. J. Thomsett
Fleet: 4 - 3 single-deck coach, 1 midicoach.
Chassis: 1 MAN. 3 Scania.
Bodies: 1 Caetano. 3 Van Hool.
Ops incl: school contracts, private hire.
Livery: Burgandy/Red/White

KENT

TRACKS VEHICLE SERVICES LTD
THE FLOTS, BROOKLAND, ROMNEY MARSH TN29 9TG
Tel: 01797 344164
Fax: 01797 344135
E-mail: info@tracks-travel.com
Web site: tracks-travel.com
Man Dir: Andrew Toms.
Fleet: 7 single-deck bus
Chassis: 1 DAF. 1 Scania. 5 Volvo.
Bodies: 1 Caetano. 1 Jonckheere. 5 Van Hool.
Ops incl: continental tours.

TRAVELMASTERS
DORSET ROAD INDUSTRIAL ESTATE, DORSET ROAD, SHEERNESS ME12 1LT
Tel: 01795 660066
Fax: 01795 660088
Recovery: 07850 848008
E-mail: sales.travel@btconnect.com
Dirs: T Lambkin, C Smith

Fleet: 23 - 4 double-deck bus, 2 single-deck bus, 10 coach, 2 double-deck coach, 2 midibus, 1 midicoach, 3 minibus.
Chassis: 1 Dennis. 2 Leyland. 5 Mercedes. 4 Scania. 11 Volvo.
Bodies: 2 Alexander. 2 ECW. 3 Mercedes. 2 Northern Counties. 5 Plaxton. 9 Van Hool.
Ops incl: school contracts, excursions & tours, private hire, continental tours.

VIKING MINICOACHES
UNIT 1, LYSANDER CLOSE, PYSONS ROAD INDUSTRIAL ESTATE, BROADSTAIRS CT10 2YJ
Tel/Fax: 01843 860876
Fax: 01843 866975
Prop: Paul Troke
Fleet: 7 - 2 midicoach, 5 minibus.
Chassis/bodies: 2 Iveco. 1 LDV. 2 Mercedes. 1 Renault. 1 Toyota. 1 Caetano
Ops incl: school contracts, private hire.

WESTERHAM COACHES
See Surrey

WEST KENT BUSES
THE COACH STATION, LONDON ROAD, WEST KINGSDOWN TN15 6AR
Tel: 01474 855444
Fax: 01474 855454
E-Mail: info@westkentbuses.co.uk
Proprietor: Stuart Gilkes
Fleet: 7 - 5 double-deck bus, 2 single-deck bus.
Chassis: 1 AEC. 3 Leyland. 3 Volvo.
Bodies: 1 Alexander. 3 Leyland. 1 Park Royal. 2 Plaxton.
Ops incl: school contracts, private hire.
Livery: Dark Red/Cream

LANCASHIRE (BLACKBURN, DARWEN, BLACKPOOL, WIGAN)

ADLINGTON TAXIS & MINICOACHES
See Greater Manchester

ALFA TRAVEL
EUXTON LANE, EUXTON, CHORLEY PR7 6AF
Tel: 0845 130 5777
Fax: 0845 130 3777
E-mail: req@alfatravel.co.uk
Web site: www.alfatravel.co.uk
Fleetname: Alfa Travel
Man Dir: Paul Sawbridge **Fin Dir**: Peter Sawbridge **Head of Ops**: Neil McMurdy
Ops Man: Tom Smith
Fleet: 35 coach
Chassis: 6 DAF. 19 Dennis. 10 Volvo.
Bodies: 6 Ikarus. 29 Plaxton.
Ops incl: excursions & tours, private hire, continental tours.
Livery: Cream

J & F ASPDEN (BLACKBURN) LTD
LANCASTER STREET, BLACKBURN BB2 1UA.
Tel: 01254 52020.
Fax: 01254 57474.
Fleetname: Aspdens Coaches.
Fleet: 14 - 1 double-deck bus, 13 coach.
Chassis: 1 Bristol. 13 Leyland.
Bodies: 5 Duple. 1 Northern Counties. 8 Plaxton.
Ops incl: school contracts, excursions & tours, private hire, continental tours.
Livery: Yellow/Black.
Subsidiary of Holmeswood Coaches

BATTERSBY SILVER GREY COACHES
THE COACH STATION, MIDDLEGATE, WHITE LUND BUSINESS PARK, MORECAMBE LA3 3PE

Tel: 01524 380000
Fax: 01524 380800
E-mail: sales@battersbys.co.uk
Web: www.battersbys.co.uk
Chmn: J A Harrison **Sec**: M F Harrison
Ops Man: R Blaikie
Fleet: 35 - 25 single-deck coach, 10 midicoach.
Chassis: 10 Mercedes-Benz. 25 Volvo.
Bodies: 24 Plaxton. 1 Van Hool.
Ops incl: local bus services, excursions & tours, private hire, continental tours, school contracts.
Livery: White
Ticket system: Wayfarer

BLACKPOOL TRANSPORT LTD
RIGBY ROAD, BLACKPOOL FY1 5DD
Tel: 01253 473001
Fax: 01253 473101
E-mail: directors@blackpooltransport.com
Web site: www.blackpooltransport.com
Fleetname: MetroCoastlines
Man Dir: Steve Burd **Eng Dir**: Dave Hislop **Ops Dir**: Oliver Howarth **Fin Dir**: Sue Kennedy **Fleet**: 229 - 72 double-deck bus, 39 single-deck bus, 46 midibus, 72 tram.
Chassis: 30 DAF. 18 Dennis. 48 Leyland. 55 Optare. 6 Volvo.
Bodies: 10 ECW. 44 East Lancs. 15 Northern Counties. 85 Optare. 3 Roe. (also 8 Optare Solos jointly owned by Blackpool Borough Council and Lancashire County Council)
Ops incl: local bus services, tram services, school contracts, private hire.
Livery: Yellow plus route branded route colours.
Ticket System: Almex A90

BRADSHAWS TRAVEL
46 WESTBOURNE ROAD, KNOTT END

ON SEA, POULTON LE FYLDE FY6 0BS
Tel/Fax: 01253 810058
Proprietor: Mrs Jill Swift
Fleet: 7 - 5 single-deck coach, 1 midibus, 1 minibus.
Chassis: 2 Dennis. 2 Leyland. 1 Mercedes. 2 Volvo.
Bodies: 1 Berkhof. 1 Duple. 1 Mercedes-Benz. 3 Plaxton. 1 Van Hool
Ops incl: private hire, school contracts.
Livery: White/Yellow/Black
Ticket System: Almex

COACH OPTIONS
See Greater Manchester

COLRAY COACHES
14 PRESTBURY AVENUE, BLACKPOOL FY4 1PT
Tel: 01253 349481
Dirs: Geoffrey Shaw, V Shaw
Fleet: 4 - coach, midibus, midicoach.
Chassis: 1 Mercedes. 1 Setra. 2 Toyota. 1 Volvo.
Bodies: 1 Caetano. 1 Mercedes. 1 Plaxton. 1 Setra
Ops incl: excursions & tours, school contracts, private hire, continental tours.
Livery: White/Blue

EAVESWAY TRAVEL LTD
BRYN SIDE, BRYN ROAD, ASHTON-IN-MAKERFIELD WN4 8BT
Tel: 01942 727985
Fax: 01942 271234
E-mail: sales@eaveswaytravel.com
Web site: www.eaveswaytravel.com
Man Dir: Mike Eaves **Dir**: Phil Rogers
Ops Man: Tim Presley
Fleet: 26 coach, 14 single, 12 double-deck
Chassis: 23 DAF. 3 MAN.
Bodies: 26 Van Hool.
Ops incl: e express, private hire.
Livery: Silver/Blue/Green.

JOHN FISHWICK & SONS
GOLDEN HILL GARAGE, LEYLAND PR25 3LE.
Tel: 01772 421207.
Fax: 01772 622407.
E-mail: enquiries@fishwicks.co.uk
Web site: www.fishwicks.co.uk
Dir: J. C. Brindle. **Dir**: J. F. Hustler.
Ch Eng: J. Cave. **IT Man**: A Clenshaw
Coach Man: A Aldam.
Fleet: 41 - 7 double-deck bus, 28 single-deck bus, 6 coach,
Chassis: 23 DAF. 4 Dennis. 10 Leyland. 4 Leyland National.
Bodies: 5 Alexander. 2 ECW. 3 Leyland. 4 Leyland National. 4 Plaxton. 6 Van Hool. 17 Wright.
Ops incl: local bus services, school contracts, excursions & tours, private hire, continental tours.
Livery: Green.
Ticket System: Wayfarer.

FLIGHTS HALLMARK
See West Midlands

FRASER EAGLE
THE COACH HOUSE, SHUTTLEWORTH MEAD, BUSINESS PARK, PADIHAM BB12 7NG
Tel: 08700 842713
Fax: 08700 842726
Recovery: 01254 232700
E-mail: info@frasereagle.com
Web site: www.frasereagle.com
Fleetname: Fraser Eagle Coaching
Dirs: Neil Atkins, Alan Dyson, Steve Ellis
Fleet: 18
Chassis: 8 DAF. 1 MAN. 2 Mercedes. 2 Scania. 5 Volvo.
Bodies: 3 Bova. 3 Neoplan. 12 Van Hool.
Ops incl: school contracts, excursions & tours, private hire, express, continental tours.
Livery: Green front/Blue rear/White slash with Eagle in middle.

FREEBIRD
See Greater Manchester

GPD TRAVEL
27 HARTFORD AVENUE, HEYWOOD OL10 4XH
Tel: 01706 622297
Fax: 01706 361494
Web site: www.gpdtravel.freeserve.co.uk
E-mail: gary@gpdtravel.freeserve.co.uk
Props: Gary Dawson, Janine Dawson
Fleet: 7 - 3 coach, 2 minicoach. 2 midibus.
Chassis: 2 DAF. 4 Mercedes. 1 Volvo.
Bodies: 1 Autobus, 1 Caetano. 2 Plaxton.
Ops incl: school contracts, excursions & tours, private hire, continental tours.
Livery: Red/Gold stripes.

G-LINE COACH TOURS
54 ST DAVIDS ROAD SOUTH, ST ANNES FY8 1TS
Tel: 01253 725999

Fax: 01253 781843
Web: www.g-linecoaches.co.uk
E-mail: infor@g-linecoaches.co.uk
Prop: Mr E Bradshaw **Tours Man**: Mr A Nayler **Coach Man**: Mr P Smith **Office Man**: Mrs P Jenkinson
Fleet: 10 single-deck coach
Chassis: 6 DAF. 4 Volvo
Bodies: 1 Berkhof. 3 Plaxton. 6 Van Hool.
Ops incl: excursions & tours, private hire, continental tours.
Livery: Maroon/White/Gold

JEFF GRIFFITHS COACHES
22 MYERSCOUGH AVE, ST ANNES-ON-SEA FY8 2HY
Tel: 01253 714230
Fax: 01253 640560
E-mail: jeff-griffiths@comserve.com
Dir: Jeff Griffiths
Fleet: coach
Chassis: Volvo.
Bodies: Plaxton
Ops incl: excursions & tours, private hire.
Livery: White

RIGBY'S EXECUTIVE COACHES
MOORFIELD INDUSTRIAL ESTATE, MOORFIELD DRIVE, ALTHAM, ACCRINGTON BB5 5WG
Tel: 01254 388866
Fax: 01254 232505
Web: www.rigbyscoachcentre.co.uk
Man Dir: Derek Moorhouse **Eng Dir**: Mel Mellor **Tran Man**: Andrew Knowles **Ops Man**:Mr K Williamson
Fleet: 19 - 16 single-deck coach, 2 midibus, 1 minicoach
Chassis: 1 Ford Transit. 2 Mercedes-Benz. 1 Scania. 15 Volvo
Ops incl: school contracts, excursions & tours, private hire, continental tours
Livery: Orange
Ticket System: Almex

HEALINGS INTERNATIONAL COACHES
See Greater Manchester

HODDER MOTOR SERVICES LTD
3 ALDERFORD CLOSE, CLITHEROE BB7 2QP
Tel: 01200 422473
Fax: 01200 422590
E-mail: hodder@talk21.com
Dir: Paul Hodgson **Co Sec**: Janice Hodgson.
Fleet: 1 coach
Chassis: Volvo.
Body: Jonckheere.
Ops incl: private hire, excursions & tours.
Livery: Green/Blue/White

HOLMESWOOD COACHES LTD
SANDY WAY, HOLMESWOOD, ORMSKIRK L40 1UB
Tel: 01704 821245

Fax: 01704 822090
E-mail: sales@holmeswood.uk.com
Web site: www.holmeswood.uk.com
Dirs: J F Aspinall, M Aspinall, D G Aspinall, C H Aspinall, M F Aspinall, M J Aspinall
Fleet names: Bostock's Coaches, Congleton. Walkers Coaches, Northwich. Aspden's Coaches, Blackburn. John Flanagan, Warrington.
Fleet: 125 - 14 double-deck bus, 82 single-deck coach, 2 double-deck coach, 3 midibus, 14 midicoach, 10 minicoach.
Chassis: DAF. Dennis. Irisbus. Iveco. Leyland. MAN. Mercedes-Benz. Neoplan. Scania. VDL. Volvo.
Bodies: Alexander Dennis. Beulas. Caetano. ECW. East Lancs. Esker. Ikarus. Irizar. Jonckheere. Marcopolo. Neoplan. Northern Counties. Plaxton. Van Hool.
Ops incl: local bus services, school contracts, excursions & tours, private hire, continental tours.
Livery: Green
Ticket system: Wayfarer

J & Y COACHES
9 MILLTHORNE AVENUE, CLITHEROE BB7 2LE.
Tel/Fax: 01200 426269.
Web site: www.uk-coachtours.co.uk
Ptnrs: J. Robinson, Yvonne Robinson.
Fleet: 1 coach. **Chassis/body**: Setra.
Ops incl: excursions & tours, private hire, continental tours.
Livery: Blue/White.

JACKSONS COACHES
JACKSON HOUSE, BURTON ROAD, BLACKPOOL FY4 4NW
Tel: 01253 792222
Fax: 01253 692070
Ptnr: Jon Paul Jackson
Fleet: 6 single-deck coach.
Chassis: 1 Iveco. 3 Scania. 2 Volvo.
Bodies: 2 Irizar. 3 Plaxton. 1 Van Hool.
Ops incl: school contracts, private hire, excursions & tours, continental tours.
Livery: White/Blue.
Ticket System: Setright

JAMES HACKING (YELLOW ROSE COACHES) LTD
WEST LEA, DIXON'S FIELD, CRAG BANK, CARNFORTH LA5 9JN
Tel: 01524 735853
E-mail: www.yellowrosecoaches.co.uk
Web site: yellowrosecoaches@tiscali.co.uk
Dirs: G Brocken(**Co Sec**), **Dir**: Mrs C M Brocken **Fleet Eng**: C R Ardis
Fleet name: Yellow Rose Coaches
Fleet: 4 - 2 single-deck coach, 1 midicoach, 1 minicoach.
Chassis: 1 MAN. 1 Mercedes. 2 Volvo.
Bodies: 1 Caetano. 1 Mercedes. 2 Van Hool.
Ops incl: excursions & tours, private hire, school contracts.
Livery: Yellow/White
Ticket System: Almex

LANCASHIRE (BLACKBURN, DARWEN, BLACKPOOL, WIGAN)

137

KIRKBY LONSDALE COACH HIRE LTD
OLD STATION YARD, WARTON ROAD, CARNFORTH LA5 9EU
Tel: 01524 733831
Fax: 01524 733821
Web site: www.klcoachhire.com
E-mail: sutton@klch.bbfree.co.uk
Dirs: Mrs Jane Sutton, Stephen Sutton
Fleet: 20 - 5 single-deck coach, 11 midibus, 2 midicoach, 1 minicoach, 1 minibus.
Chassis: 1 Bova. 3 DAF. 15 Mercedes. 1 Optare.
Bodies: 1 Bova. 1 Caetano. 1 Marshall/MCV. 3 Optare. 13 Plaxton. 1 Van Hool.
Ops incl: local bus services, school contracts, excursions & tours, private hire.
Livery: Maroon/White/Blue
Ticket System: Wayfarer TGX, Almex

LENDOR TAXIS & LUXURY MINICOACH TRAVEL
See Greater Manchester

McLAUGHLIN'S TOURS
UNIT 1A PORTAKABIN, FACTORY LANE, PENWORTHAM PR1 9TZ
Tel/Fax: 01772 749358
Prop: Anthony McLaughlin
Fleet: 7 - 4 coach, 3 minibus.
Chassis: 2 Leyland, 3 Volvo.
Bodies: 3 Mercedes.
Ops incl: local bus services, school contracts, excursions & tours, continental tours.
Livery: Blue/White/Yellow.
Ticket System: Almex

NORTH WEST COACHES & LIMOS
HILLHOUSE INTERNATIONAL BUSINESS PARK, WEST ROAD, THORNTON CLEVELEYS FY5 4DQ
Tel: 01253 855000
Fax: 01253 522845
Recovery: 07850 500015
E-mail: stewart.farrel@tiscali.co.uk
Web site: www.northwestcoaches.co.uk
Owner/Operator: Stuart J Farrell **Ops Man**: Paul Portisman **Head Fitter**: John Keen
Fleet: 18 - 1 double-deck coach, 3 coach, 2 midibus, 5 midicoach, 7 minibus.
Chassis: 1 DAF. 1 Iveco. 5 Mercedes. 1 Neoplan. 8 Renault. 2 Volvo.
Ops incl: local bus services, excursions & tours, school contracts, private hire

OLYMPIA TRAVEL
44 ARGYLE STREET, HINDLEY WN2 3PH
Tel: 01942 522322
Fax: 01942 255845
E-mail: olympia@coach-hire.net
Web site: www.olympiatravel.co.uk
Props: Joseph Lewis, Shaun Lewis.
Fleet: 18 - 12 coach, 4 midicoach, 2 minibus.

Chassis: 1 Bedford. 6 Dennis. 1 Ford Transit. 1 LDV. 5 Volvo.
Bodies: 5 Duple. 2 Jonckheere. 2 Mercedes. 4 Plaxton. 1 Reeve Burgess.
Ops incl: local bus services, school contracts, private hire, continental tours.
Livery: White with blue stripes

PRESTON BUS LTD
221 DEEPDALE ROAD, PRESTON PR1 6NY
Tel: 01772 253671
Fax: 01772 555840
Recovery: 01772 253671
E-mail: enquiries@prestonbus.co.uk
Web site: www.prestonbus.co.uk
Man Dir: Peter Bell **Ops Dir**: John Asquith **Eng Dir**: Jack Hornby. **Fin Dir**: Margaret Ingram
Fleet: 124 - 56 double-deck bus, 16 single-deck bus, 52 minibus.
Chassis: 18 Dennis. 45 Leyland. 52 Optare. 9 Scania.
Bodies: 12 Alexander. 1 ECW. 33 East Lancs. 21 Leyland. 5 Northern Counties. 52 Optare.
Ops incl: local bus services, school contracts.
Livery: Blue/Cream
Ticket System: Wayfarer TGX150

REDLINE TRAVEL
25 GOWER GROVE, WALMER BRIDGE, PRESTON PR4 5QJ
Tel: 01772 611612.
Fax: 01772 611613.
E-mail: info@lancashirecoachhire.co.uk
Web site: www.lancashirecoachhire.co.uk
Prop: R. G. H. & S. R. Nuttall.

REEVES COACH HOLIDAYS
34 MONKS DRIVE, WITHNELL, CHORLEY PR6 8SG.
Tel/Fax: 01254 830545
E-mail: info@reevescoachholidays.com
Web site: www.reevescoachholidays.com
Partners: John Reeves, Kathryn Reeves
Fleet: 1 single-deck coach
Chassis/body: Setra.
Ops incl: excursions & tours, private hire, continental tours.
Livery: Artic Blue/Silver

ROBINSONS HOLIDAYS
PARK GARAGE, GREAT HARWOOD BB6 7SP
Tel: 01254 889900
Fax: 01254 884708
E-mail: info@robinsons-holidays.co.uk
Web site: www.robinsons-holidays.co.uk
Dirs: D D Lord, J E Bannister (**Sec**), J McMillan **Ops Man**: C Skeen **Engineer**: P Godwin **Off Man**: B Cooke **Sales Man**: G Holdsworth
Fleet: 17 - 15 coach, 2 minibus.
Chassis: 1 DAF. 4 MAN. 10 Volvo.
Bodies: 3 Jonckheere. 4 Noge. 7 Plaxton. 1 Van Hool.
Ops incl: excursions & tours, private hire, continental tours, school contracts.
Livery: Blue

ROSSENDALE TRANSPORT LTD
KNOWSLEY PARK WAY, HASLINGDEN BB4 4RS
Tel: 01706 390520
Fax: 01706 390530
Web site: www.rossendalebus.co.uk
E-mail: info@rossendalebus.co.uk
Man Dir: Edgar Oldham **Comm Dir**: Barry Drelincourt
Fleet: 107 - 15 double-deck bus, 92 single-deck bus.
Chassis: 43 Dennis. 5 Leyland. 4 Mercedes. 23 Optare. 26 Volvo. 6 other.
Ops incl: local bus services, school contracts, private hire, express, continental tours.
Livery: White/Red/Cream.
Ticket System: Wayfarer TGX

SANDGROUNDER COACHES
28 WARWICK STREET, SOUTHPORT PR8 5ES
Tel: 01704 541194
Recovery: 07734 003464
E-mail: gerry@dohe.wanadoo.co.uk
Dirs: Gerald Doherty, John Fairbank
Fleet: 3 coaches.
Chassis: 2 DAF. 1 Mercedes.
Ops incl: school contracts, excursions & tours, private hire.

TRANSDEV BURNLEY & PENDLE
QUEENSGATE BUS DEPOT, COLNE ROAD, BURNLEY BB10 1HH
Tel: 01282 427778
Web site: www.burnleyandpendle.co.uk
Prop: Blazefield Holdings Ltd.
Man Dir: Russell Revill. **Ops Dir**: John Threlfall, **Com Dir**: David Wilson
Fleet: 72 - double-deck buses, single-deck buses.
Chassis: Dennis, Leyland, Mercedes-Benz, Optare, Volvo.
Bodies: Alexander, ECW, Northern Counties, Optare, Plaxton, Wright.
Livery: Red/Cream.
Ticket System: ERG.
(Part of the Blazefield group which is owned by Transdev)

TRANSDEV LANCASHIRE UNITED LTD
INTACK GARAGE, BLACKBURN BB1 3JD.
Tel: 01254 260661
FAX: 01234 693964
Web site: www.lancashireunited.co.uk
Prop: Blazefield Holdings Ltd
Man Dir: RussellRevill **Ops Dir**: John Threlfall **Com Dir**: David Wilson
Fleet: 131 - 45 double-deck buses, 68 single-deck buses, 18 minibuses.
Chassis: Dennis, Leyland, Mercedes-Benz, Optare, Volvo.
Bodies: Alexander, Berkhof, East Lancs, National, Northern Counties, Plaxton, Wright.
Livery: Blue/Cream.
Ticket System: ERG.
(Part of the Blazefield group which is owned by Transdev)

TRANSDEV NORTHERN BLUE

UNIT 5, DEAN MILL, PLUMBE STREET,
BURNLEY BB11 3AG
Tel: 01282 456351
Fax: 01282 439386
E-mail: northernblue@btconnect.com
Web site: www.northernblue.co.uk
Man Dir: Russell Revill. **Ops Dir**:
John Threlfall, **Com Dir**: David Wilson
Fleet: 65 - 25 double-deck bus, 18 single-deck bus, 22 midibus
Chassis: 3 Dennis. 8 Leyland. 22 Optare. 18 Scania. 14 Volvo.
Bodies: 23 Alexander. 3 Duple. 1 ECW. 8 East Lancs. 4 Northern Counties. 22 Optare. 4 Plaxton
Ops incl: local bus services, school contracts, express, private hire.
Livery: Blue/White.
Ticket System: Wayfarer TGX
(Part of the Blazefield Group which is owned by Transdev)

THE TRAVELLERS CHOICE

THE COACH & TRAVEL CENTRE,
SCOTLAND ROAD, CARNFORTH
LA5 9RQ
Tel: 01524 720033
Fax: 01524 720044
E-mail: info@travellerschoice.co.uk
Web site: www.travellerschoice.co.uk
Chmn: R Shaw **Man Dirs**: J Shaw, D Shaw **Co Sec**: P Shaw **Dir**: M Shaw
Fleet: 74 - coach, midicoach, minicoach.
Chassis: 13 Mercedes. 6 Scania. 55 Volvo.
Bodies: 4 Berkhof. 6 Caetano. 2 Esker. 1 Irizar. 30 Jonckheere. 8 Mercedes. 1 Optare. 89 Plaxton. 13 Sunsundegui.
Ops incl: school contracts, excursions & tours, private hire, continental tours, express.
Livery: White with blue/yellow/red stripe

TYRER TOURS LTD

16 KIRBY ROAD, LOMESHAYE
INDUSTRIAL ESTATE, NELSON
LANCASHIRE BB9 6RS
Tel: 01254 611123
Fax: 01254 350575
Recovery: 01254 232700
E-mail: info@tyrertours.com
Web site: www.tyrertours.com
Chmn: Alan Dyson **Dir**: Kevin Dean
Principal: Howard Tyrer
Fleet: 34 - 6 double-deck bus 7 single deck bus 1 coach 18 midibus 2 minibus.
Chassis: DAF. Mercedes Optare, Dennis, Leyland, Scania, Volvo.
Bodies: Alexander, Esker, Irizar, Leyland, Mercedes, Marshall, Optare, Plaxton, Reave, Burgess, Transbus, Wright.
Ops incl: Local bus services, school contracts, excursions & tours, private hire, express, continental tours.
Livery: White with Blue/Red lettering

LEICESTERSHIRE, CITY OF LEICESTER, RUTLAND

ABBEY TRAVEL

RMC YARD, THURMASTON FOOTPATH,
HUMBERSTONE LANE, LEICESTER
LE6 0EW
Tel: 0116 246 1755
Fax: 0116 246 1755
Prop: Bryan A Garratt **Eng**: Paul Garratt
Fleet: 15 - 1 double-deck coach, 12 single-deck coach, 1 midibus, 1 midicoach.
Chassis: 3 Bova. 1 DAF. 2 Dennis. 1 Leyland. 1 MAN. 2 Mercedes-Benz. 3 Volvo.
Bodies: 1 Berkhof. 3 Bova. 2 Caetani. 2 Hispano. 1 Ikarus. 3 Plaxton. 1 Van Hool.
Ops incl: school contracts, excursions & tours, private hire, continental tours.
Livery: White/Red/Green

ARRIVA MIDLANDS

852 MELTON ROAD, LEICESTER
LE4 8BT
Tel: 0116 264 0400
Fax: 0116 260 5605
Web site: www.arriva.co.uk
Man Dir: R.A Hind **Fin Dir**: J. Barlow **Ops Dir**: A Lloyd **Eng Dir**: M Evans
Fleet: 774 - 216 double-deck bus, 144 single-deck bus, 15 single-deck coach, 361 midibus, 38 minibus.
Chassis: 270 Alexander. 127 DAF. 9 Leyland. 38 Mercedes-Benz. 19 Optare. 89 Scania. 42 VDL. 180 Volvo
Bodies: 87 Alexander. 6 Caetano. 1 Carlyle. 162 East Lancs. 1 Ikarus. 7 Marshall. 76 Northern Counties. 21 Optare. 227 Plaxton. 3 UVG. 9 Van Hool. 159 Wright. 15 Other.
Ops incl: local bus services.
Livery: Arriva
Ticket System: Wayfarer

ASMAL COACHES

70 KEDLESTONE ROAD, LEICESTER
LE5 5HW
Tel/Fax: 0116 249 0443
Man Dir: Mehboob M. Asmal.

AUSDEN CLARK LTD

DYSART WAY, LEICESTER LE1 2JY
Tel: 0116 262 9492
Fax: 0116 251 5551
E-mail: enquiries@ausdenclark.co.uk
Web Site: www.ausdenclark.co.uk
Man Dir: Paul Ausden-Clark.
Fleet: 60 - 44 coach, 8 double-deck coach, 8 minicoach.
Chassis: incl: Irizar. Mercedes. Scania.
Ops incl: local bus services, school contracts, excursions & tours, private hire, continental tours.

CENTREBUS LIMITED

37 WENLOCK WAY, LEICESTER
LE4 9HU
Tel: 0116 246 0030
Fax: 0116 276 7221
E-mail: centrebusltd@btconnect.com
Web Site: www.centrebus.co.uk
Dirs: Peter Harvey, Mark O Mahony
Fin Controller: Chris Holmes
Ops Inc: Local bus srevice
Livery: Blue/Orange

CONFIDENCE BUS & COACH LTD

30 SPALDING STREET, LEICESTER
LE5 4PH
Tel/Fax: 0116 276 2171
E-mail: confidencebus@btclick.com
Web site: www.confidencebus.co.uk
Dirs: K M Williams, A P Williams **Ops Man**: A Harris **Ch Eng**: R Allen
Fleet: 31 - 19 double-deck coach, 12 single-deck coach.
Chassis: 1 AEC. 26 Leyland. 4 Volvo.
Bodies: 1 Duple. 14 ECW. 1 East Lancs. 1 Optare. 1 Park Royal. 9 Plaxton. 3 Roe. 1 Van Hool.
Ops incl: school contracts, private hire.
Livery: Buses: Grey/Black, Coaches: Red/Black
Ticket System: Setright

COUNTY MINI COACHES

31 EDENHURST AVENUE, LEICESTER
LE3 2PH.
Tel/Fax: 0116 289 7205.
Owner: F. Bradshaw.
Fleet: 3 - 2 midicoach, 1 minibus.
Chassis: 1 DAF. 1 Freight Rover. 1 Iveco.
Ops incl: school contracts, private hire.

COUNTRY HOPPER

213 MELBOURNE ROAD, IBSTOCK
LE67 6NQ
Tel: 01530 260888

DUNN-LINE GROUP

See Nottinghamshire

FIRST LEICESTER

PO BOX 8324, LEICESTER LE41 9BF.
Tel: 0116 251 6691.
Fax: 0116 268 9198.
Acting Man Dir: Maurice Bulmer
Eng Dir: C. Stafford. **Fin Dir**: J. Hollis.
Gen Man Ops: C. Lara.
Fleet: 116 - double-deck bus, single-deck bus, coach, midibus, minibus.
Chassis: Bristol. Dennis. Mercedes. Optare. Scania. Volvo.
Bodies: 8 Alexander. 71 East Lancs. 10 Marshall. 20 Northern Counties. 19 Optare. 3 Plaxton. 1 Wright.
Ops incl: local bus services, school contracts, excursions & tours, private hire, express, continental tours.
Livery: Multicoloured.
Ticket System: Wayfarer 3

PAUL JAMES COACHES

UNIT 5, GRANGE FARM BUSINESS
PARK, GRANGE ROAD, HUGGLESCOTE
LE67 2BT
Tel: 01530 832399
Fax: 01530 836128
E-mail: info@pauljamescoaches.co.uk
Web site: www.pauljamescoaches.co.uk

139

Gen Man: Wayne Smith
Fleet: 35 - single-deck bus, coach, midibus.
Chassis: incl: 3 Bedford. 2 Bova. 1 Dennis. 2 Leyland. 6 Mercedes. 6 Optare. 1 Setra. 6 Volvo
Bodies: incl: 5 Alexander. 1 Autobus. 2 Bova. 6 Optare. 10 Plaxton. 2 Van Hool.
Ops incl: excursions & tours, private hire, local bus services, school contracts, continental tours.
Livery: Ivory
Ticket System: Wayfarer 3
(Part of the Veolia Group)

MACPHERSON COACHES LTD
See Derbyshire

NESBIT BROS LTD
BURROUGH ROAD, SOMERBY, MELTON MOWBRAY LE14 2PP
Tel: 01664 454284
Fax: 01664 454106
Dirs: I Foster, J Townsend
Fleet: 13 coach.
Chassis: 13 Volvo.
Bodies: 7 Plaxton. 6 Van Hool
Ops incl: school contracts, private hire

NIGEL JACKSON TRAVEL
5 NEW ZEALAND LANE, QUENIBOROUGH LE7 3FU
Tel: 0116 260 0839
Fax: 0116 276 1969
Prop: N Jackson
Fleet: 7 - 3 double-deck bus, 2 coach, 1 midicoach, 1 minibus
Chassis: 1 Dennis. 1 Leyland. 2 MCW. 1 Scania. 2 Toyota.
Bodies: 1 Alexander. 2 Caetano. 1 Duple. 2 MCW. 1 Plaxton
Ops incl: school contracts, private hire
Livery: coaches White, buses Blue/Red

ROBERTS COACHES LTD
THE LIMES, MIDLAND ROAD, HUGGLESCOTE LE67 2FX
Tel: 01530 817444
Fax: 01530 817666
Recovery: 07785 572526
E-mail: info@robertscoaches.co.uk
Web site: www.robertscoaches.co.uk
Man Dir: Jonathan Hunt **Sec**: Margaret Bunker
Fleet: 32 - 12 double-deck bus, 10 single-deck coach, 2 Double-deck coach, 3 open-top bus, 3 midibus, 1 minibus, 1 minicoach.
Chassis: 1DAF. 1 Ford Transit 1 LDV. 14 MCW. 3 Mercedes. 12 Volvo.

Bodies: 2 East Lancs. 4 Jonckheere.1 Marshall/MCV. 14 MCW. 3 Mercedes-benz. 7 Van Hool.
Ops incl: local bus services, school contracts, excursions & tours, private hire, continental tours
Livery: coaches-white. DD-Silver.
Ticket System: Wayfarer III

SCHOFIELD TRAVEL LTD
PRINCE WILLIAM ROAD, LOUGHBOROUGH LE11 OGU.
Tel: 01509 611045
Fax: 01509 611012
Man Dir: E. B. Mee **Dir/Ch Eng**: K. W. Greasley. **Gen Man**: R. A. Schofield.
Fleet: 6 - 4 coach, 2 midicoach.
Chassis: 1 Bedford. 2 Bova. 2 DAF. 1 Ford.
Bodies: 2 Bova. 4 Plaxton.
Ops incl: school contracts, private hire, express.
Livery: Blue/Pale Grey.

TRAVEL-WRIGHT
64 ROCKHILL DRIVE, MOUNTSORREL LE12 7DT.
Tel: 0116 230 2887.
Fax: 0116 230 2223.
E-mail: trwright@demon.co.uk
Dir: C. Wright.
Fleet: 5 minibus.
Chassis: 1 DAF. 2 Mercedes. 2 VW.
Bodies: 2 Crystals. 2 VW. 1 Advanced.
Ops incl: private hire, school contracts.

WEST END/RUTLAND TRAVEL
COACH & BUS CENTRE, DIXON DRIVE, LEICESTER ROAD, MELTON MOWBRAY LE13 0BS
Tel: 01664 563498
Fax: 01664 568568
Fleetname: Romdrive
Man Dirs: John Penniston, Peter Penniston
Fleet: 23 - 1 single-deck bus, 11 coach, 8 midibus, 2 minibus, 1 minicoach.
Chassis: 1 Dennis. 11 Mercedes. 1 Scania. 3 Setra. 4 Volvo.
Bodies: 4 Alexander. 2 Jonckheere. 5 Mercedes. 7 Plaxton. 1 Reeve Burgess. 3 Setra. 1 Wadham Stringer.
Ops incl: local bus services, school contracts, excursions & tours, private hire, continental tours.
Livery: Red/Blue/White
Ticket System: Wayfarer 3

WIDE HORIZON
48 COVENTRY ROAD, BURBAGE, HINCKLEY LE10 2HP
Tel: 01455 615915
Fax: 01455 230767
Ptnrs: Reg Clarke, Jon Clarke.
Fleet: 16 - 9 double-deck bus, 7 coach
Chassis: 1 Bova. 3 DAF. 1 Dennis. 1 Leyland. 1 MAN. 1 Mercedes. Neoplan. 1 Scania. 1 Volvo.
Bodies: 2 Berkhof. 1 Bova. 2 Plaxton. 2 Setra.
Ops incl: local bus services, excursions & tours, school contracts, private hire, continental tours.
Livery: White

PAUL S WINSON COACHES LTD
ROYAL WAY, LOUGHBOROUGH LE11 5XR
Tel: 01509 232354
Fax: 01509 265110
Recovery: 01509 237999
Web site: www.winsoncoaches.co.uk
E-mail: sales@winsoncoaches.co.uk
Chmn: Paul Winson **Ch Eng**: Paul B Winson **Dir**: Mrs M A Winson **Ops Man**: Anthony J Winson
Fleet: 28 - 6 double-deck bus, 18 coach, 4 minibus.
Chassis: 4 Bova. 1 DAF. 3 Dennis. 6 Leyland. 7 Mercedes. 8 Volvo.
Bodies: 1 Autobus. 4 Bova. 1 Caetano. 3 Jonckheere. 2 Northern Counties. 12 Plaxton. 3 Roe.
Ops incl: local bus services, school contracts, excursions & tours, private hire, continental tours.
Livery: Red/White/Blue.
Ticket system: Wayfarer

WOODS COACHES LTD
211 GLOUCESTER CRESCENT, WIGSTON LE18 4YH
Tel: 0116 278 6374
Fax: 0116 247 7819
E-mail: sales@woods-coaches.co.uk
Web site: www.woods-coaches.com
Chmn: Mark Wood **Man Dir**: Kevin Brown
Com Sec: Jacqui Bates **Eng Dir**: Ian Trigg **Traffic Manager**: Bill Tanser
Fleet: 17- 16 single-deck coach, 11 midibus.
Chassis: 1 Mercedes-Benz. 4 Neoplan. 12 Volvo.
Ops incl: school contracts, excursions & tours, private hire, continental tours.
Livery: Blue base – Orange/Yellow/White relief

	Vehicle suitable for disabled		Seat belt-fitted Vehicle		24 hour recovery service
T	Toilet-drop facilities available		Coach(es) with galley facilities		Replacement vehicle available
R	Recovery service available		Air-conditioned vehicles(s)		Vintage Coach(es) available
	Open top vehicle(s)v		Coaches with toilet facilities		

LEICESTERSHIRE, CITY OF LEICESTER, RUTLAND

LINCOLNSHIRE

BRYLAINE TRAVEL LTD
291 LONDON ROAD, BOSTON PE21 7DD
Tel: 01205 364087
Man Dir: Brian W Gregg, Elaine R Gregg
Co Sec: Susan E Bradshaw **Eng Dir**: Brian P Gregg **Ops Dir**: Malcolm P Wheatley
Fleet: 35 - 9 double-deck bus, 11 single-deck bus, 15 midibus.
Chassis: 3 BMC. 6 DAF. 2 Dennis. 1 Leyland. 2 MCW. 1 Mercedes. 14 Optare. 6 Volvo.
Ops incl: local bus services, school contracts
Livery: Red/Blue/Yellow
Ticket system: Wayfarer

J W CARNELL LTD
72 BRIDGE ROAD, SUTTON BRIDGE PE12 9UA.
Tel: 01406 350482.
Fax: 01406 350600.
E-mail: enquiries@carnellscoaches.co.uk
Web site: www.carnellscoaches.co.uk
Dirs: John Grindwood, Mervyn Emmet
Fleet: 22 - 3 double-deck bus, 16 coach, 2 midicoach, 1 minicoach.
Chassis: 2 Bedford. 1 Bova. 2 DAF. 5 Leyland. 1 MAN. 3 MCW. 2 Toyota 6 Volvo.
Bodies: 1 Bova. 3 Caetano. 8 Duple. 3 MCW. 6 Plaxton. 1 Van Hool.
Ops incl: local bus services, school contracts, excursions and tours.
Livery: Silver/Red/Orange.
Ticket system: Setright.

CROPLEY COACHES
MAIN ROAD, FOSDYKE, BOSTON PE20 2BH
Tel: 01205 260226
Fax: 01205 260246
Web site: www.cropleycoach.co.uk
E-mail: enquiries@cropleycoach.co.uk
Dirs: J R Cropley, Mrs S R Cropley
Fleet: 12 coach.
Chassis: 1 Setra, 11 Volvo.
Bodies: 1 Jonckheere. 7 Plaxton. 1 Setra. 3 Sunsundegui
Ops incl: school contracts, excursions & tours, private hire, continental tours.
Livery: White

DELAINE BUSES LTD
8 SPALDING ROAD, BOURNE PE10 9LE
Tel: 01778 422866
Fax: 01778 425593
Web site: www.delainebuses.com
Chmn: I Delaine-Smith **Man Dir**: A Delaine-Smith **Dirs**: M Delaine-Smith, K Delaine-Smith **Sec**: Mrs B P Tilley
Fleet: 20 - 16 double-deck bus, 4 single-deck bus.
Chassis: 20 Volvo.
Bodies: 17 East Lancs.1 Optare. 2 Wright.
Ops incl: local bus services
Livery: Light/Dark Blue Blue/Ivory.
Ticket System: Almex A90

DUNN-LINE (HOLDINGS) LTD
See Nottinghamshire

EAGRE COACHES LTD
CROOKED BILLET STREET, MORTON, GAINSBOROUGH DN21 3AG
Tel: 01427 612098
Fax: 01427 811340
Ch Eng: M Thrower **Tours Man**: Ann Lee
Fleet: 8 coaches
Chassis: incl: Irisbus. MAN.
Bodies: incl: Beulas. Noge. Marcopolo.
Ops incl: excursions & tours, private hire, continental tours
Livery: Multicolours
(Subsidiary of Wilfreda Beehive, South Yorkshire)

FOWLER TRAVEL
155 DOG DROVE SOUTH, HOLBEACH DROVE, SPALDING PE12 0SD
Tel: 01406 330232
Fax: 01406 330923
E-mail: andrew@fowlerstravel.com
Web site: www.fowlerstravel.com
Fleetname: Fowlers Travel
Fleet: 19 - 7 double-deck bus, 3 single-deck bus, 8 single-deck coach, 1 open-top bus.
Chassis: 1 Alexander Dennis. 2 DAF. 3 Leyland. 1 Mercedes. 11 Volvo
Bodies: Alexander. 2 Jonckheere. 3 Marshall. 9 Plaxton.
Ops incl: local bus services, school contracts, excursions & tours, private hire.
Livery: Cream/Orange
Ticket System: Wayfarer

GRAYSCROFT BUS SERVICES LTD
15A VICTORIA ROAD, MABLETHORPE LN12 2AF
Tel: 01507 473236
Fax: 01507 477073
Recovery: 01507 473236
E-mail: grayscroftltd@btconnect.com
Web site: www.grayscroft.co.uk
Dirs: C W Barker, N Barker, N W Barker, C S Barker
Fleet: 19 - 6 double-deck bus, 2 single-deck bus, 9 coach, 2 midibus.
Chassis: 2 Leyland. 2 Mercedes. 1 Optare. 12 Volvo.
Bodies: 2 Alexander. 1 Caetano. 4 East Lancs. 1 Hispano. 3 Jonckheere. 2 Mercedes. 1 Optare. 2 Plaxton. 3 Van Hool.
Ops incl: local bus services, school contracts, excursions & tours, private hire, express
Livery: White/Blue
Ticket system: Setright/Wayfarer

PHIL HAINES COACHES
RALPHS LANE, FRAMPTON WEST, BOSTON PE20 1QU.
Tel/Fax: 01205 722359.
Props: N. A. & F. E. Haines.

HODSON COACHES LTD
CHAPEL LANE, NAVENBY LN5 0ER
Tel: 01522 810262
Fax: 01522 810793
E-mail: sales@hodsoncoaches.co.uk
Web Site: www.hodsoncoaches.co.uk
Dirs: S Carter, J Carter.
Fleet: 10 - 5 single-deck coach, 1 midibus, 1 midicoach, 3 minicoach.
Chassis: 7 Mercedes. 3 Setra
Bodies: 6 Mercedes. 1 Optare. 3 Setra.
Ops incl: local bus services, school contracts, excursions & tours, private hire, continental tours.
Livery: Lemon/Purple
Ticket system: Almex

HORNSBY TRAVEL SERVICES LTD
See North Lincolnshire

F HUNT COACH HIRE LTD
2/3 WEST STREET, ALFORD LN13 9DG
Tel/Fax: 01507 463000
E-mail: travel.office@hunts-coaches.co.uk
Web site: www.hunts-coaches.co.uk
Fleetname: Hunts Travel
Dirs: Michael Hunt, Charles Hunt, Dave Eales
Fleet: 19 - 1 double-deck bus, 5 single-deck bus, 10 coach, 3 midibus.
Chassis: 3 Dennis. 1 Leyland. 3 Mercedes. 1 Optare. 11 Volvo.
Bodies: 2 Alexander. 3 Mercedes. 1 Optare. 10 Van Hool. 3 Wright.
Ops incl: local bus services, school contracts, excursions & tours, private hire, express, continental tours.
Livery: White/Red/Grey
Ticket System: Almex

R KIME & CO LTD
3 SLEAFORD ROAD, FOLKINGHAM, SLEAFORD NG34 0SB
Tel: 01529 497251
Fax: 01529 497554
E-mail: enquiries@kimesbuses.co.uk
Web site: www.kimesbuses.co.uk
Fleetname: Kimes Coaches.
Man Dir: Paul Brown **Dirs**: Geoff Blanchard, Angella Cliff
Fleet: 26 - 13 double-deck bus, 13 single-deck bus.
Chassis: DAF. Leyland. Mercedes. Volvo Optare Scania.
Bodies: Alexander. Leyland. Northern Counties. Optare. Plaxton Ikarus Wright.
Ops incl: local bus services, school contracts, excursions & tours, private hire.
Livery: Cream/Green
Ticket System: Almex

MEMORY LANE COACHES
ELM HOUSE, OLD BOLINGBROKE, SPILSBY PE23 4HF
Tel: 01790 763394
Prop: John B Dorey
Fleet: 5 - 3 coach, 2 midicoach.
Chassis: 2 Bedford. 1 Iveco. 1 Leyland. 1 Mercedes.
Bodies: 1 Carlyle. 3 Duple. 1 Plaxton.
Ops incl: school contracts, private hire.
Livery: White/Green/Red.

PC COACHES OF LINCOLN LTD
17 CROFTON ROAD, LINCOLN LN3 4NL
Tel: 01522 533605
Fax: 01522 560402
Man Dir: Peter Smith. **Ops Dir**: Miss Sarah Smith.
Dir International ops: Chris Bristow
Ops incl: local bus services, school contracts, private hire, continental tours.
Livery: White/Maroon/Red

PULFREYS COACHES
271 HARLAXTON ROAD, GRANTHAM NG31 7SL
Tel: 01476 564144
Dlr: Andrew Pulfrey.
Fleet: 3 - 2 coach, 1 midicoach.
Chassis: 1 Dennis. 1 Iveco. 1 Mercedes.
Bodies: 1 Beulas. 2 Plaxton.
Ops incl: local bus, school contracts, excursions & tours, private hire, continental tours.
Livery: Blue/White
Ticket System: Wayfarer

RADLEY COACH TRAVEL
THE TRAVEL OFFICE, 50 WRAWBY STEET, BRIGG DN20 8JB
Tel: 01652 653583
Fax: 01652 656020
E-mail: radleytravel@aol.com
Web Site: www.radleytravel.co.uk
Dirs: Kevin Radley
Fleet: 4 - 4 single-deck coach.
Chassis: 4 Scania
Bodies: 2 Berkof. 2 Irizar.
Ops incl: excursions & tours, private hire, continental tours.
Livery: gold/maroon

ROY PHILLIPS
69 STATION ROAD, RUSKINGTON NG34 9DF
Tel: 01526 832279
Prop: R Phillips.
Fleet: 6 coach.
Chassis: 1 Leyland. 5 Volvo.
Bodies: 3 Plaxton. 3 Van Hool.
Ops incl: private hire, school contracts.

SLEAFORDIAN COCHES
PRIDE PARKWAY, EAST ROAD, SLEAFORD NG34 7EH
Tel: 01529 303333
Fax: 01529 303324
E-mail: office@sleafordian.co.uk
Web site: www.sleafordian.co.uk
Fleetname: Sleafordian
Dirs: M Broughton, Mrs L Broughton
Fleet: 21 - 4 double-deck bus, 12 coach, 3 midibus, 1 minibus.
Chassis: Leyland. Mercedes. Neoplan. Optare. Renault. Volvo.
Bodies: Leyland. Neoplan. Optare. Plaxton. Renault. Van Hool.
Ops incl: private hire.
Livery: White/Orange
(part of Sleafordian Taxi Co Ltd)

SMITHS COACHES, CORBY GLEN
THE GREEN, CORBY GLEN NG33 4NR.
Tel: 01476 550285.
Fax: 01476 550032.
Ptnrs: H. J. and Mary J. Smith.
Fleet: 7 - 5 coach, 1 double-deck coach, 1 minibus.
Chassis: 1 Bedford. 1 Bova. 1 Ford. 1 Freight Rover. 2 MAN. 1 Mercedes.
Bodies: 1 Bova. 1 Carlyle. 1 Duple. 2 MAN. 1 Neoplan. 1 Plaxton.
Ops incl: excursions & tours, private hire, continental tours, school contracts.
Livery: Blue/White.

STAGECOACH LINCOLNSHIRE
PO BOX 15, DEACON ROAD, LINCOLN LN2 4JB
Tel: 01522 522555
Fax: 01522 538229
Web site: www.stagecoachbus.com
Chassis: 6 DAF. 2 Mercedes. 2 Volvo.
Bodies: 6 Bova. 2 Jonckheere. 2 Mercedes.
Ops incl: excursions & tours, private hire, continental tours, school contracts.
Livery: Cream/Beige.

Man Dir: Gary Nolan **Eng&Ops Dir**:
Fleet: 272 - 100 double-deck bus, 145 single-deck bus, 4 open-top bus, 20 midibus, 3 minibus.
Chassis: incl: DAF. Dennis. Mercedes. Optare. Renault. Scania. 80 Volvo.
Bodies: incl: Alexander. East Lancs. Optare. Plaxton. Wright.
Ops incl: local bus services, school contracts
Livery: Green/Yellow/White; Blue/Yellow/Red
Ticket System: Almex.
Part of Stagecoach

TRANSLINC
JARVIS HOUSE, 157 SADLER ROAD, LINCOLN LN6 3RS
Tel: 01522 503400
Fax: 01522 503406
E-mail: logistics@translinc.co.uk
Web site: www.translinc.co.uk
Man Dir: Paul Roberts **Sales & Mktg Dir**: John Soulby **Fin Dir**: Stephen Jago
Comm Dir: David Foulds.
Fleet: 193 - 18 coach, 19 midibus, 136 minibus, 20 minicoach (8 seats & under)
Chassis: 16 Citroen. 2 DAF. 10 Dennis. 8 Fiat. 104 Iveco. 7 LDV. 20 Mercedes. 2 Optare. 13 Renault. 2 Scania. 4 Toyota. 1 VW. 4 Volvo.
Ops incl: local bus services, school contracts, excursions & tours, private hire, express.

A C WILLIAMS LTD
ERMINE STREET, ANCASTER, GRANTAM NG32 3QN
Tel: 01400 230833
Fax: 01400 230296
E-mail: coaches@acwilliams.co.uk
Web site: www.acwilliams.co.uk
Man Dir: A D C Williams **Dir**: Mrs A Parker
Coach Man: I Mansell **Co Sec**: Mrs S Somerville
Fleet: 20- 5 Double-deck bus, 1 Single-deck coach, 1 Double-deck coach, 2 Midicoach.
Chassis: 1 DAF. 5 Leyland. 2 MAN. 1 Mercedez-Benz. 1 Neoplan. 6 Scania. 1 Setra. 1 Toyota. 3 Volvo.
Bodies: 2 Berkhof. 1 Caetano. 1 Duple. 5 East Lancs. 5 Irizar. 1 Neoplan. 1 Setra. 4 Van Hool.
Ops incl: school contracts, excursions & tours, continental tours.

LINCOLNSHIRE

LONDON

This section includes those operators in the London postal areas, as well as operators who have asked to appear under this heading. Other operators within Greater London with a non-London postal address, eg Kingston, Surrey; Bromley, Kent; Enfield, Middlesex, etc, may be found under their respective postal counties.

AA, KNIGHTS OF THE ROAD
WREN ROAD, SIDCUP DA14 4NA
Tel: 020 8309 7741
Prop: J. V. H. Knight. **Ch Eng**: D. Knight
Fleet: 10 - 6 coach, 2 double-deck coach, 2 minicoach.

ANDERSON TRAVEL LTD
178A TOWER BRIDGE ROAD, LONDON SE1 3LS
Tel: 020 7403 8118
E-mail: sales@andersontravel.co.uk
Web site: www.andersontravel.co.uk
Man Dir: Mark Anderson. **Comm Man**: Keith Payne. **Gen Man**: Steve Lee. **Eng Man**: Peter Gilbert. **Op Man**: Barry Nunn.
Fleet: 24 - 21 single-desck coach, 1 midicoach, 2 minicoach.
Chassis: 4 Mercedes. 4 Volvo 13 Bova.
Bodies: 13 Bova. 4 Mercedes Benz. 4 Plaxton.
Ops incl: school contracts, excursions & tours, private hire.
Livery: White/Green

ANGEL MOTORS (EDMONTON) LTD
1 CONSTABLE CRESCENT, LONDON N15 4QZ
Tel: 020 8808 2000
Fax: 020 8808 0008
Fleet: 19 - 17 coach, 2 minicoach.
Livery: White/Blue/Yellow.

142

ARRIVA LONDON
16 WATSONS ROAD LONDON N22 7TZ
Tel: 020 8271 0200
Web site: arrivabus.co.uk
Man Dir: Mark Yexley
Fleet: 1460 - incl: double-deck bus, single-deck bus, 157 articulated bus.
Chassis: incl: DAF. Dennis. Mercedes. Volvo.
Bodies: incl: Alexander. Mercedes. Plaxton. Wright
Ops incl: local bus services, excursions & tours, private hire.
Livery: Red

BACK ROADS TOURING CO LTD
14A NEW BROADWAY, LONDON W5 2XA.
Tel: 020 8566 5312
Fax: 020 8566 5457
E-mail: info@backroadstouring.co.uk
Web site: www.backroadstouring.co.uk
Man Dir: Bruce Cherry **Fin Dir**: Erika Harcz **Ops Dir**: Alex Newmann
Fleet: 22 minibus.
Chassis/Bodies: 16 Mercedes. 6 Renault
Ops incl: excursions & tours, private hire, continental tours.
Livery: White

BIG BUS COMPANY
GROSVENOR GARDENS HOUSE, 35-37 GROSVENOR GARDENS, LONDON SW1W 0BS
Tel: 020 7233 8722
Fax: 020 7233 8766
E-mail: info@bigbustours.com
Web site: www.bigbustours.com
Fleet: 72 open-top bus.
Chassis: 14 Dennis. 42 Leyland. 16 MCW.
Ops incl: local bus services, private hire, excursions & tours.
Livery: Maroon/Cream
Ticket system: Almex

BLUEWAYS GUIDELINE COACHES LTD
49 WINDERS ROAD, LONDON SW11 3HE
Tel: 020 7228 3515
Fax: 020 7228 0290
E-mail: blueways@clara.co.uk
Web site: www.bluewaysguideline.co.uk
Dirs: Philip Bruton, Janet Bruton, Thomas McKechnie.
Fleet: 6 - 4 coach. 2 minicoach.
Chassis: 1 Mercedes. 3 Scania. 2 Toyota
Bodies: 2 Caetano. 3 Irizar. 1 Mercedes.
Ops incl: excursions & tours, private hire, continental tours, school contracts.
Livery: 2 White/two-tone Blue, 2 White, 2 England sponsors.

BRENTONS OF BLACKHEATH
GREENWICH HIGH ROAD, LONDON SE10 8JL
Tel: 020 820 2020
Fax: 020 692 4932
E-mail: davee@brentonsofblackheath.co.uk
Web site: www.brentonsofblackheath.co.uk

Prop: C Clark **Coach Man**: D Eaton **Ch Eng**: I Powell
Fleet: 14 - 11 coach, 1 midicoach, 2 minicoach.
Chassis: 2 Dennis. 5 Leyland. 3 Mercedes. 5 Volvo.
Bodies: 1 Berkhof 2 Duple. 3 Mercedes. 7 Plaxton. 1 Van Hool.
Ops incl: private hire, school contracts, excursions and tours.
Livery: Red/Cream/Grey

BRYANS OF ENFIELD
19 WETHERLEY ROAD, ENFIELD EN2 0NS.
Fax: 020 8366 0062.
Owner: B. Nash.
Fleet: 6 - 3 double-deck bus, 1 single-deck bus, 1 coach, 1 double-deck coach.
Chassis: 1 AEC. 1 DAF. 2 Daimler. 1 Leyland. 1 MCW.
Bodies: 1 ECW. 2 MCW. 2 Park Royal. 1 Van Hool.
Ops incl: school contracts, private hire.
Livery: Red.

CENTAUR TRAVEL MINICOACHES
188 HALFWAY STREET, SIDCUP DA15 8DJ.
Tel: 020 8300 3001.
Fax: 020 8302 5959.
Man Dir: M. Sims. **Ch Eng**: R. Raison.
Ops Man: Kay Priestley.
Fleet: 14 - 2 midicoach, 5 minibus, 7 minicoach.
Chassis: 7 Freight Rover. 2 Mercedes. 5 Renault.
Ops incl: private hire, school contracts.

CALL-A-COACH
See Surrey

CAVALIER TRAVEL SERVICES
ASH COURT, LAND "C", PHOENIX DISTRIBUTION PARK, PHOENIX WAY, HESTON TW5 9NB
Tel: 0845 125 9379
Fax: 0845 833 2295
E-mail: bookings@cavaliercoaches.com
Web site: www.cavaliercoaches.com
Dirs: Andrew W Pagan, Denise H Pagan
Fleet: 12 - 7 double-deck coach, 2 midicoach, 2 minibus. 1 people carrier.
Chassis: 3 Iveco. 4 Mercedes. 2 Neoplan. 1 Scania. 1 Toyota.
Bodies: 3 Beulas. 1 Caetano. 1 Esker. 1 Irizar. 2 Neoplan. 3 Optare.
Ops incl: private hire
Livery: White, White/Blue

CHALFONT LINE LTD
See Middlesex

CLARKES OF LONDON
KANGLEY BRIDGE ROAD, LONDON SE26 5AT
Tel: 020 8778 6697
Fax: 020 8778 0389
E-mail: info@clarkescoaches.co.uk
Web site: www.clarkescoaches.co.uk

Man Dir: Mrs D Newman **Comm Dir**: J Devacmaker **Fin Dir**: S Reeve
Fleet: 51 - 46 coach, 5 minicoach.
Chassis: 22 Setra. 23 Scania . 5 Toyota. 1 Volvo.
Bodies: 5 Caetano. 23 Irizar. 1 Jonckheere. 22 Setra
Ops incl: excursions & tours, private hire, express, continental tours.
Livery: Green/Silver.

COLLINS COACHES LTD
UNIT 6, WATERSIDE TRADING CENTRE, TRUMPERS WAY, LONDON W7 2QD
Tel: 020 8843 2145
Fax: 020 8843 2375
E-mail: collinscoaches@aol.com
Web site: www.collins-coaches.co.uk
Man Dir: Eric Collins **Sec**: Pauline Collins
Dir: Alfred Collins
Fleet: 9 coach.
Chassis: 9 Volvo.
Bodies: 4 Jonckheere. 4 Plaxton. 1 Van Hool.
Ops incl: private hire, school contracts.
Livery: Red/White.

CONISTON COACHES LTD
88 CONISTON ROAD, BROMLEY BR1 4JB.
Tel/Fax: 020 8460 3432
E-mail: ricksmock@oal.com
Web site: www.conistoncoaches.co.uk
Dir: Richard Smock
Fleet: 5 coach - 5 single-deck coach
Chassis: 5 Volvo
Bodies: 1 Caetano. 4 Plaxton.
Ops incl: private hire, school contracts.
Livery: White/Red.

COUNTY COACHES
See Essex

DAVID CORBEL OF LONDON LTD
6 CAMROSE AVENUE, EDGWARE HA8 6EG
Tel: 020 8952 1300.
Fax: 020 8952 8641
E-mail: corbeloflondon@aol.com
Web site: www.corbel-coaches.com
Dir: Robert Whelan
Fleet: 9 coach
Chassis: 4 Dennis. 1 Setra. 4 Volvo.
Bodies: 4 Plaxton. 1 Setra. 4 UVG.
Ops incl: school contracts, private hire.
Livery: Pink/Blue.

CROWN COACHES
68 CANON ROAD, BICKLEY BR1 2SP
Tel: 020 8313 3020
Fax: 020 8464 2375
Fleet: 5 - 4 coach, 1 minibus.
Chassis: incl: 1 Ford Transit.
Bodies: incl: 2 Mercedes. 1 Setra. 1 Van Hool.
Ops incl: excursions & tours, private hire, continental tours.

CROYDON TRAMLINK
TRAMTRACK CROYDON LTD, COOMBER WAY, CROYDON CR0 4TQ
Tel: 020 8665 9695
Web site: www.tfl.gov.uk/trams
Ops Dir: John Ryman **Head of Safety**: C Tomlinson
Fleet: 24 Tram
Chassis/bodies: Bombardier
Ops incl: local tram services
Livery: Red/White

CRYSTALS COACHES LTD
HORTENSIA ROAD, LONDON SW10 0QP.
Tel: 020 7376 3015
Fax: 020 7376 3019
Ops Man: G. Betts.
Fleet: 30 - 15 minibus, 15 minicoach.
Chassis: Ford Transit. Freight Rover. Mercedes.
Ops incl: local bus services, school contracts, private hire.

DANS LUXURY TRAVEL LTD
ROYAL FOREST COACH HOUSE, 109 MAYBANK ROAD, LONDON E18 1EZ.
Tel: 020 8505 8833.
Fax: 020 8519 1937.
Man Dir: D. J. Brown. **Dir**: S. A. Brown.
Fleet: 43 mini/midicoaches
Chassis: 19 Ford Transit. 24 Mercedes
Bodies: 24 Mercedes. 7 Optare. 5 Reeve Burgess. 1 Ford
Ops incl: school contracts, excursions & tours, private hire, continental tours.

DAVIAN COACHES LTD
1-3 BECKET ROAD, EDMONTON, LONDON N18 3PN
Tel: 020 8807 1515
Fax: 020 8807 2323
Man Dirs: Darren Wardle, **Dir**: Judy Wardle (**Co Sec**) **Comp Man**: David Bee
Trans Man: Richard Window
E-mail: daviancoaches@btconnect.com
Fleet: 23 - 6 single-deck coach, 2 minicoach. 15 minibus.
Chassis: 2 Autosan 2 BMC. 11 DAF. 4 Mercedes. 4 Scania.
Bodies: 4 BMC. 4 Irizar. 11 Leyland. 4 Mercedes-Benz.
Ops incl: excursions & tours, school contracts, private hire, continental tours.
Livery: White/Orange/Blue

DOCKLANDS BUSES LTD
FACTORY ROAD, LONDON E16 2EW
Tel: 020 7474 8130
E-mail: enquiries@go-ahead-london.com
Web site: www.go-ahead-london.com
Fleetname: Docklands
Ch Exec: John Trayner **Eng Dir**: Phil Margrave **Fin Dir**: Paul Reeves.
Ops Dir: David Cutts
Fleet: 29 midibus
Chassis: 29 Dennis
Bodies: 29 Marshall/MCV
Ops incl: local bus services
(part of the Go Ahead Group)

EALING COMMUNITY TRANSPORT LTD
97 BOLLO LANE, LONDON W3 8QN
Tel: 020 8753 7810
Web site: www.ectgroup.co.uk
Pass Ops Dir: Anna Whitty
Fleet: 28 - 13 single-deck bus, 15 minibus
Ops incl: local bus services
Livery: Red/Yellow

EAST LONDON BUS GROUP
2 CLEMENTS ROAD, ILFORD IG1 1BA
Tel: 020 8477 7200
E-mail: pr.london@elbiz.com
Web-site: www.elbg.com
CEO: Nigel Barrett **Ch Fin Off**: Paul Cox
Eng Dir: Peter Sumner
Fleet: 1240 - 935 double-deck bus, 256 single-deck bus, 49 articulated bus
Chassis: 1160 Alexander Dennis. 7 AEC. 6 DAF. 49 Mercedes. 16 Scania. 2 Volvo.
Bodies: 7 Park Royal.
Ops incl: local bus services
Livery: Red

P & J ELLIS LTD
UNIT 3, RADFORD ESTATE, OLD OAK LANE, LONDON NW10 6UA
Tel: 020 8961 1141
Fax: 020 8965 5995
E-mail: enquiries@pjellis.co.uk
Web-site: www.pjellis.co.uk
Dir: Matthew Ellis
Fleet: 12 coach.
Chassis: 12 Volvo.
Bodies: 12 Jonckheere.
Ops incl: excursions & tours, private hire, continental tours.

ELTHAM EXECUTIVE CHARTER LTD
21-23 CROWN WOODS WAY, LONDON SE9 2NL
Tel: 020 8850 2011
Fax: 020 8850 5210
E-mail: enquiries@eec-minicoaches.co.uk
Web site: www.eec-minicoaches.co.uk
Dirs: Ray Lawrence, Jill Lawrence, Fiona Lawrence
Fleet: 6 - 3 midicoach, 1 minibus, 2 minicoach
Chassis: 1 Ford. 5 Iveco.
Bodies: 3 Indcar. 1 Optare. 2 other
Ops incl: private hire.
Livery: White with blue&gold graphics

EMPRESS MOTORS LTD
3 CORBRIDGE CRESCENT, LONDON E2 9DS.
Tel: 020 7739 5454 **Fax**: 020 7729 0237
E-mail: info@empresscoaches.co.uk
Web site: www.empresscoaches.co.uk
Fleetmane: Empress of London
Man Dir: P D Stanton **Co Sec**: T A Stanton **Dir**: L M R Stanton **Op Mans**: J C Stanton, M E Stanton
Fleet: 18 - 13 coach, 3 midicoach, 2 minibus.
Chassis/Bodies: 1 Caetano. 1 Jonckheere. 1 Mercedes. 1 Optare. 13 Plaxton. 1 Toyota.
Ops incl: private hire.
Livery: Cream/Maroon.

EXCALIBUR COACHES
709 OLD KENT ROAD, LONDON SE15 1JL
Tel: 020 7358 1441
Fax: 020 7358 1661
E-mail: bookings@excalibur-coach-hire.com
Web site: www.excalibur-coach-hire.com
Man Dir: Garby Zacca **Ch Eng**: C Patel

Fleet: 12 coach.
Chassis: 2 Iveco. 10 Scania.
Bodies: 2 Beulas. 10 Irizar.
Ops incl: excursions & tours, private hire, express, continental tours, school contracts.
Livery: Blue

FIRST LONDON & BERKSHIRE
3RD FLOOR, MACMILLAN HOUSE, PADDINGTON STATION, LONDON W2 1TY
Tel: 020 7298 7300
Fax: 020 7706 8789
Web site: www.firstgroup.co.uk
Man Dir: Adrian Jones.
Fleet: 1204 - 699 double-deck bus, 12 single-deck bus, 476 midibus, 15 minibus, 2 open-top bus.
Chassis: 59 AEC. 924 Dennis. 21 Leyland. 24 MCW. 24 Mercedes. 149 Volvo.
Bodies: 67 Alexander. 3 Carlyle. 49 East Lancs. 1 Leyland. 450 Marshall. 30 MCW. 14 Mercedes. 89 Northern Counties. 59 Park Royal. 429 Plaxton. 2 Reeve Burgess. 11 Wright.
Ops incl: local bus services, school contracts, private hire.
Livery: Red with Yellow/Grey stripes.
Ticket System: Prestige (TfL).

FLIGHTS HALLMARK
See West Midlands

FOREST COACHES
THE COACH HOUSE, NELSON STREET, LONDON E6 2QA.
Tel: 020 8472 5954.
Fax: 020 8472 6098.

FORESTDALE COACHES LTD
68 VINEY BANK, COURTWOOD LANE, FORESTDALE, ADDINGTON CR0 9JT
Tel/Fax: 020 8651 1359
Chmn/Man Dir: V Holub **Co Sec**: Mrs P R Holub
Fleet: 1 single-deck coach.
Chassis/Body: Bova.
Ops incl: excursions & tours, private hire, continental tours.
Livery: Red/Gold Signwriting

GOLDENSTAND (SOUTHERN) LTD
13 WAXLOW ROAD, LONDON NW10 7NY
Tel: 020 8961 9974/5
Fax: 020 8961 9949

Web site: www.goldenstand.co.uk
Chmn: J Chivrall **Sec**: J Kemp
Fleet: 8 - 5 coach, 3 minibus.
Chassis: 3 LDV. 5 Scania.
Bodies: 5 Jonckheere. 3 Leyland
Ops incl: school contracts, private hire, excursions & tours
Livery: Red/White

THE GOLD STANDARD

94A HORSENDEN LANE NORTH, GREENFORD UB6 7QH
Tel: 020 8795 0075.
Fax: 020 8900 9630.
E-mail: paul@luxuryminicoaches.co.uk
Web site: www.luxuryminicoach.co.uk
Prop: Paul Grant
Fleet: 1 minicoach.
Chassis: Optare.
Ops incl: excursions & tours, private hire.

A GREEN COACHES LTD

357A HOE STREET, WALTHAMSTOW, LONDON E17 9AP
Tel: 020 8520 1138
Fax: 020 8520 1139
E-mail: agreencoaches357@aol.com
Man Dir: Keith Richards **Tran Man**: Janis Grover **Gen Man**: Candice Connor
Fleet: 5 coach
Chassis: 1 Scania. 4 Volvo
Ops incl: private hire, school contracts.

HEARNS COACHES

801 KENTON LANE, HARROW WEALD HA3 6AH
Tel: 020 8954 0444
Fax: 020 8954 5959
E-mail: ged@hearns-coaches.co.uk
Web site: www.hearns-coaches.co.uk
Prop: R J Hearn **Ops Man**: Ged Newham
Ch Eng: Dave Berry **Contracts Man**: Dave Sharpe
Fleet: 38 - 34 coach, 3 minibus, 1 midicoach.
Chassis: 1 Leyland. 8 Mercedes. 2 Neoplan. 9 Scania. 11 Setra. 3 Volvo.
Ops incl: private hire, school contracts, excursions & tours, continental tours

HCT GROUP

ASH GROVE DEPOT, MARE STREET, LONDON, E8 4RH
Tel: 020 7275 2400
Fax: 020 7275 2450
E-mail: info@hctgroup.org
Web site: www.hctgroup.org
Ch Exec: Dai Powell **Group FD**: Stephen Mason
Fleet Inc: double deck bus, midibus, minibus
Ops inc: Local bus services

JOHN HOUGHTON LUXURY MINI COACHES

2 ELGAR AVENUE, EALING, LONDON W5 3JU
Tel: 020 8567 0056
Fax: 020 8567 5781
E-mail: john@luxuryminicoaches.co.uk
Web site: www.luxury-mini-coaches.co.uk
Man Dir: J Houghton **Co Sec**: M Houghton
Fleet: 3 minicoach.
Chassis/bodies: 3 Mercedes.
Ops incl: private hire
Livery: White

HOUNSLOW MINI COACHES

2 VINEYARD ROAD, HIGH STREET, FELTHAM TW13 4HQ.
Tel: 020 8890 8429
Fax: 020 8893 1736
Web site: www.hounslowminicoaches.co.uk
E-mail: hounslowminicoaches@btconnect.com
Fleet: 19 - 3 midicaoch, 4 minibus, 4 minicoach, 8 people carrier.
Chassis: 2 Ford Transit, 1 Iveco. 5 LDV. 7 Mercedes. 1 Toyota.
Bodies: 1 Caetano. 3 Mellor. 4 Mercedes. 5 Optare. 3 other.
Ops incl: school contracts, private hire.

HOUSTON'S OF LONDON

83 GLADESMORE ROAD, LONDON N15 6TL.
Tel/Fax: 020 8800 4576.
Prop: H. Jones.
Fleet: 2 coach. **Chassis**: Leyland.
Ops incl: school contracts, excursions & tours, private hire.

IMPACT OF LONDON

7-9 WADSWORTH ROAD, GREENFORD UB6 7JZ
Tel: 020 8579 9922
Fax: 020 8840 4880.
E-mail: info@impactgroup.co.uk
Web site: www.impactgroup.co.uk
Dir: A Hill **Gen Man**: A. Palmer. **Engs**: H Louis, L. Singh.
Fleet: 44 - 14 coach, 20 midicoach, 10 minibus.
Chassis: 2 Bova. 2 Dennis. 10 LDV. 20 Mercedes. 10 Volvo.
Bodies: 7 Berkhof. 2 Bova. 1 Caetano. 2 Mellor. 24 Mercedes. 3 Optare. 3 Plaxton. 2 Van Hool.
Ops incl: excursions & tours, private hire, express, continental tours, school contracts.
Livery: White.

INTERNATIONAL COACH LINES LTD

19 NURSERY ROAD, THORNTON HEATH CR7 8RE.
Tel: 020 8684 2995.
Fax: 020 8689 3483.
Dir: Mrs S. Bailey.
Fleet: 18 - 3 double-deck bus, 1 single-deck bus, 10 coach, 4 minicoach.
Ops incl: excursions & tours, private hire, express, continental tours.
Livery: Blue/White.

THE KINGS FERRY

See Kent

LEWIS TRAVEL UK PLC

2-10 DENHAM STREET, LONDON SE10 0RY
Tel: 020 8858 0031
Fax: 020 8858 7631
E-mail: sales@lewistravel.co.uk
Dir: T Legnor-Lewis **Gen Man**: J Harpic
Fleet: 29 - 20 coach, 4 midibus, 3 minibus, 2 minicoach.
Chassis: 1 Ayats. 1 Bova. 4 DAF. 3 Dennis. 4 Mercedes. 2 Neoplan. 2 Scania. 1 Setra. 6 Transbus. 6 Volvo.
Bodies: 1 Ayats. 1 Bova. 1 Duple. 4 Ikarus. 3 Irizar. 1 Jonckheere. 2 Mercedes. 1 Neoplan. 7 Plaxton. 1 Setra. 4Transbus. 3 Van Hool.
Ops incl: local bus services, school contracts, excursions & tours, private hire, continental tours.
Livery: incl. Red

LINK LINE COACHES LTD

1 WROTTESLEY ROAD, LONDON NW10 5XA.
Tel: 020 8965 2221.
Fax: 020 8961 3680.
E-mail: info@linkline-coaches.co.uk
Web site: wwwlinkline-coaches.co.uk
Man Dir: T. J. Russell
Fleet: 10 - 7 single-deck bus, 3 coach.
Chassis: 6 Dennis. 1 Mercedes. 3 Volvo.
Bodies: 8 Caetano. 1 Optare. 1 Plaxton.
Ops incl: private hire, continental tours, school contracts.
(Subsidiary of Tellings Golden Miller) Part of Arriva

THE LITTLE BUS COMPANY

HOME FARM, ALDENHAM ROAD, ELSTREE WD6 3AZ
Tel: 020 8953 0202
Fax: 020 8953 9553
E-mail: enquiry@littlebus.co.uk
Web site: www.littlebus.co.uk
Fleet: includes single deck coach, midicoach, minibus, minicoach
Chassis: LDV. Leyland. Mercedes.
Bodies: Mercedes.
Prop: Jeremy Reese
Fleet: 7 minibus.
Chassis: 5 LDV. 2 Ford Transit.
Ops incl: school contracts, private hire.

LONDON BUSES LTD t/a EAST THAMES BUSES

ASH GROVE, MARE STREET, LONDON E8 4RH
Tel: 020 7241 7220.
Fax: 020 7241 7239.
Fleet Name: East Thames Buses.
Man Dir: Alan Barrett **Fin Dir**: David Bowen. **Eng. Dir**: Gary Filbey. **Gen Man**: Norman Priestly.
Fleet: 128 - 77 double-deck bus. 51 single-deck bus.
Chassis: 12 DAF, 15 Dennis. 10 Optare. 14 Scania. 77 Volvo.
Bodies: 40 East Lancs. 10 Optare. 21 Plaxton. 3 Wright.
Ops incl: local bus services.
Livery: Red.
Ticket System: Prestige
(Part of Transport for London)

LONDON CENTRAL BUS CO LTD

18 MERTON HIGH STREET, LONDON SW19 1DN
Tel: 020 8545 6100
Fax: 020 8545 6101
E-mail: enquiries@go-ahead-london.com
Web site: www.go-ahead-london.com
Fleet Name: London Central
Ch Exec: John Trayner **Eng Dir**: Phil Margrave **Fin Dir**: Paul Reeves.
Ops Dir: David Cutts
Fleet: 622 - 429 double-deck bus, 130 single-deck bus, 63 articulated bus.
Chassis: 3 AEC. 6 DAF. 163 Dennis. 63 Mercedes. 387 Volvo.
Bodies: 189 Alexander. 20 Marshall. 10 Northern Counties. 3 Park Royal. 269 Plaxton. 62 Wright. 69 other.
Ops incl: local bus services, school contracts, private hire.
Livery: Red
(part of the Go Ahead Group)

LONDON GENERAL TRANSPORT SERVICES LTD

18 MERTON HIGH STREET, LONDON SW19 1DN
Tel: 020 8545 6100
Fax: 020 8545 6101
E-mail: enquiries@go-ahead-london.com
Web site: www.go-ahead-london.com
Fleet Name: London General
Ch Exec: John Trayner **Eng Dir**: Phil Margrave **Fin Dir**: Paul Reeves.
Ops Dir: David Cutts
Fleet: 719 - 516 double-deck bus, 172 single-deck bus, 31 articulated bus.
Chassis: 5 AEC. 240 Dennis. 31 Mercedes. 443 Volvo.
Bodies: 173 Alexander. 52 East Lancs. 17 Marshall/MCV. 30 Noge. 5 Park Royal. 200 Plaxton. 211 Wright. 31 other.
Ops incl: local bus services, school contracts, private hire.
Livery: Red
(part of the Go Ahead Group)

LONDON UNITED BUSWAYS LTD
See Middlesex

MARTINS COACHES

THE GAS WORKS, 709 OLD KENT ROAD, LONDON SE15 1JZ
Tel: 020 7732 1000
Fax: 020 7732 1011
E-mail: info@martinscoachesco uk
Web site: www.martinscoaches.co.uk
ManDir: Steve Martin
Fleet: 21 - 10 coach, 10 midicoach, 1 minibus
Chassis: 11 Mercedes. 10 Transbus.
Bodies: 11 Plaxton. 10 Transbus.
Ops incl: school contracts, excursions & tours, private hire, continental tours.
Livery: White/Purple

MARSHALLS COACHES

FIRBANK WAY, LEIGHTON BUZZARD LU7 4YP
Tel: 01525 376077
Fax: 01525 850967
Recovery: 01525 375301
E-mail: info@marshalls-coaches.co.uk
Web site: www.marshalls-coaches.co.uk
Fleetname: MCE Ltd
Prop: G Marshall **Ops Man**: I White **Ch Eng**: Bob Barnard
Fleet: 27 - 3 double-deck bus, 22 coach, 2 double-deck coach.
Chassis: 3 Ayats. 4 Dennis. 3 Iveco. 2 Leyland. 1 Mercedes. 15 Volvo.
Bodies: 3 Ayats. 2 Beulas. 1 Caetano. 3 East Lancs. 4 Jonckheere. 2 Leyland 1 Mercedes. 10 Plaxton 1 Van Hool.
Ops incl: private hire, school contracts, continental tours.
Livery: Blue/Multicoloured.

METROBUS
See West Sussex

METROLINE
See Middlesex

M&M COACHLINES
See Middlesex

M T P CHARTER COACHES

39 GROSVENOR ROAD, LONDON E11 2EW
Tel/Fax: 020 8989 0211
Prop: M Powis
Fleet: 2 - 1 coach, 1 mdnicoach.
Chassis/bodies: 1 Setra. 1 Caetano.
Ops incl: private hire, excursions & tours, continental tours.
Livery: White

NEW BHARAT COACHES LTD

1A PRIORY WAY, SOUTHALL UB2 5EB
Tel: 020 8574 6810
Fax: 020 8813 9555
E-mail: admin@newbharat.co.uk
Web site: www.newbharat.co.uk
Dir: Surjit Singh Dhaliwal **Ch Eng**: Alan Littlemore
Fleet: 4 coach
Chassis: 4 Volvo
Ops incl: school contracts, excursions & tours, private hire, express, continental tours.
Livery: Red/Yellow/Blue on white base.

NEWBOURNE COACHES

FIRBANK WAY, LEIGHTON BUZZARD LU7 4YP
Tel: 020 7837 6663
Fax: 01525 850967
Web site: www.marshalls-coaches.co.uk
E.mail: info@marshalls-coaches.co.uk
Props: G R Marshall, S J Marshall
Ops Man: Ian White **Ch Eng**: Bob Barnard
Fleet: See Marshalls Coaches
Ops incl: private hire, school contracts, local bus services.
Livery: Blue/Multicoloured.
(part of Marshalls Coaches)

OFJ CONNECTIONS LTD

BUILDING 16300, ELECTRA AVENUE, HEATHROW AIRPORT, HOUNSLOW MIDDLESEX, TW6 2DN
Tel: (0)20 8754 7375
Fax: (0)20 8759 6589
Email: enquiries@ofjbus.com
Web site: www.ofjbus.com
Ops Inc: Scholl contracts, private hire, Airport transfers
Livery: White
Subsidiary of Tellings Golden Miller, Part of Arriva

THE ORIGINAL LONDON TOUR

JEWS ROW, LONDON SW18 1TB
Tel: 020 8877 1722
Fax: 020 8877 1968
E-mail: info@theoriginaltour.com
Web site: www.theoriginaltour.com
Man Dir: Bob Scowen
Fleet: 94 - 24 double-deck bus, 70 open-top bus.
Chassis: 2 Dennis. 13 Leyland. 41 MCW. 14 Volvo.
Bodies: 13 Alexander. 41 MCW. 2 Northern Counties. 14 Transbus.
Ops incl: local bus services.
Livery: Red/Cream
Ticket system: Almex/Wayfarer
Subsidiary of Arriva

REDWING COACHES

10 DYLAN ROAD, LONDON SE24 0HL
Tel: 020 7733 1124
Fax: 020 7733 5194
E-mail: redwing@redwing-coaches.co.uk
Web site: www.redwing-coaches.co.uk
Man Dir: vacant **Ops Man**: Barry Nunn
Gen Man: John Fowler **Ch Eng**: Robbie

Hodgekiss **Reservations**: Jef Johnson
Fleet: 45 - 43 coach, 2 midicoach.
Chassis: 20 Iveco. 11 Mercedes. 14 Setra.
Bodies: 20 Beulas. 11 Caetano. 14 Setra
Ops incl: excursions & tours, private hire, continental tours.
Livery: Red/Cream
Part of Addison Lee

ROUNDABOUT BUSES
25 OLDFIELD ROAD, BEXLEYHEATH DA7 4DX
Tel: 020 8302 7551
E-mail: info@roundaboutbuses.co.uk
Web site: www.roundaboutbuses.co.uk
Man Dir: Glyn Matthews.
Fleet: 6 - 1 single-deck bus, 1 minibus.
Chassis: 1 AEC. 2 Iveco. 5 Leyland.
Bodies: 3 ECW. 1 Marshall. 1 Park Royal. 1 Roe. 1 Robin Hood.
Ops incl: local bus services, school contracts.
Livery: Green/Cream.
Ticket System: Wayfarer.

SILVERDALE LONDON LTD
UNIT 3, RADFORD ESTATE, OLD OAK LANE, LONDON NW10 6UA
Tel: 020 8961 1812
Fax: 020 8961 5677
Email: silverdalelondon@aol.com
Web site: www.silverdalelondon.com
Dir: Robert Green **Tran Man**: Richard Cassell
Fleet: 14 - coach, midibus.
Chassis: 1 Dennis. 1 MAN. 2 Mercedes. 10 Volvo.
Bodies: 10 Caetano. 1 Marcopolo. 2 Optare. 1 Plaxton.
Ops incl: school contracts, excursions & tours, private hire, express, continental tours.
Livery: White/Red
(part of the Silverdale Tours, Nottinghamshire)

SOUTHGATE & FINCHLEY COACHES LTD
231A COLNEY HATCH LANE, LONDON N11 3DG
Tel: 020 8368 0040
Fax: 020 8361 1934
Web site: www.coaches.org.uk
Man Dir: M. P. Rice. **Dirs**: Mrs V. M. Rice (**Co Sec**), P. M. Rice, Mrs E. B. Scrivens.
Fleet: 23 coach.
Chassis: 23 V.olvo.
Bodies: 23 Plaxton
Ops incl: school contracts, excursions and tours, private hire
Livery: Yellow/Blue/Orange

TELLINGS GOLDEN MILLER COACHES LTD
BUILDING 16300 MT2, ELECTRA AVENUE, HEATHROW AIRPORT, HOUNSLOW TW6 2DN
Tel: 020 8757 4700
Fax: 020 8757 4719
E-mail: info@tellings.co.uk

Web site: www.tellingsgoldenmiller.co.uk
Chmn: Stephen Telling **Group Ops Dir**: Richard Telling **Fin Dir/Co Sec**: Basil Taylor **Ops Dir**: Paul Cowell **Eng Man**: Ian Foster
Fleet: 75 - 58 coach, 14 minicoach, 3 minicoach.
Chassis: 2 Iveco. 15 Mercedes. 3 Setra. 2 Toyota. 53 Volvo.
Bodies: 2 Beulas. 6 Caetano. 3 Mercedes. 59 Plaxton. 3 Setra. 2 Van Hool.
Ops incl: school contracts, excursions & tours, private hire, express, continental tours.
Livery: White/Blue/Yellow
Subsidiary of Arriva

TIMEBUS TRAVEL
7 BOLEYN DRIVE, ST ALBANS AL1 2BP
Tel: 01727 866248
Web site: www.timebus.co.uk
Fleetname: Timebus
Prop: David Pring
Fleet: 12 - 8 double-deck bus, 2 single-deck bus, 2 open-top bus
Chassis: 11 Aec. 1 Leyland.
Bodies: 2 MCW. 9 Park Royal. 1 other.
Ops incl: private hire
Livery: Red with grey lining

TOMORROWS TRANSPORT
GIBBS STORAGE, GIBBS ROAD, LONDON N18 3PU
Tel: 020 8807 4555
Fax: 020 8807 4603
Prop: V A Daniels
Fleet: 3 - 2 coach, 1 midicoach
Chassis: 1 DAF. 1 Leyland. 1 Toyota.
Bodies: 1 Caetano. 1 Duple. 1 Van Hool.
Ops incl: private hire

TRAVEL LONDON LTD
301 CAMBERWELL NEW ROAD, LONDON SE5 0TF
Tel: 020 7805 3500
Fax: 020 7805 3510
Web site: www.travellondonbus.co.uk
Man Dir: Paul McGowan **Ops Dir**: Bill Weatherley **Eng Dir**: Steve Hamilton **Fin Dir**: Ross Hanley
Fleet: 433 - 198 double-deck bus, 223 single-deck bus, 12 midibus
Chassis: Dennis. Optare. Mercedes. Volvo.
Bodies: Alexander. Wright. East Lancs. Plaxton. Caetano.
Ops incl: local bus services
Livery: Red (London), Red and white (Surrey CC)
Ticket system: Wayfarer, Almex
(Subsidiary of National Express Group)

WESTBUS COACH SERVICES LTD
27A SPRING GROVE ROAD, HOUNSLOW TW3 4BE
Tel: 020 8572 6348
Fax: 020 8570 2234
Recovery: 020 8572 6348
E-mail: reservations@westbus.co.uk
Web site: www.westbus.co.uk
Gen Man: Tim Miles **Ops Man**: Chris Shaw **Ch Eng**: Graham Bessant
Chassis: 15 DAF. 4 Mercedes. 2 Setra. 5 Volvo.
Bodies: 2 Berkhof. 1 Hispano. 5 Plaxton. 2 Setra. 1 Sitcar. 15 Van Hool.
Ops incl: private hire, continental tours, excursions & tours, school contracts.
Livery: Red/Cream
(Part of the Comfort Delgro Corporation)

WEST'S COACHES LTD
198/200 HIGH ROAD, WOODFORD GREEN IG8 9EF
Tel: 020 8504 9747
Fax: 020 8559 1085
Dirs: R L West, E J M West, M M West
Ch Eng: P Faux
Fleet: 17- 15 coach, 1 open-top bus, 1 midibus.
Chassis: 1 AEC. 2 DAF. 3 Dennis. 1 Iveco. 1 MCW. 9 Volvo
Bodies: 1 Beadle. 2 Caetano. 2 Marcopolo. 1 MCW. 9 Plaxton. 2 UVG.
Ops incl: excursions & tours, private hire, school contracts, continental tours.
Livery: White/Red/Blue

147

WESTWAY COACH SERVICES
7A RAINBOW INDUSTRIAL ESTATE, STATION APPROACH, RAYNES PARK, LONDON SW20 0JY
Tel: 020 8944 1277.
Fax: 020 8947 5339.
E-mail: info@westway-coaches.co.uk
Web: www.westwaycoachservices.com
Prop: David West. **Gen Man:** Arthur Richardson. **Ops Man:** Kevin Pates
Fleet: 22 - 12 single-deck coach, 7 double-deck coach, 1 midicoach, 2 minicoach.
Chassis: 2 Mercedes-Benz. 1 Scania. 19 Volvo
Bodies: 7 Jonckheere. 2 Plaxton. 13 Van Hool.
Ops incl: school contracts, excursions & tours, private hire, continental tours.
Livery: Blue/Orange

WINGS LUXURY TRAVEL LTD
47 WALLINGFORD ROAD, UXBRIDGE UB8 2XS
Tel: 020 8573 8388
Fax: 020 8573 7773
Web site: www.wingstravel.co.uk
E-mail: info@wingstravel.co.uk
Chmn: F L Gritt **Gen Man:** W Gritt **Ops Man:** S Hughes
Fleet: 16 - 8 midicoach, 8 minicoach
Chassis/Bodies: 16 Mercedes
Ops Incl: school contracts, excursions and tours, private hire
Livery: White

MERSEYSIDE (ST HELENS, KNOWSLEY, LIVERPOOL, SEFTON, WIRRAL)

A1A LTD
373 CLEVELAND STREET, BIRKENHEAD CH41 4JW
Tel: 0151 650 1616
Fax: 0151 650 0007
Web site: www.a1atravel.co.uk
Props: John and Barbara Ashworth
Fleet: 26 - 7 single-deck bus, 8 midibus, 11 minibus.
Chassis: 7 Dennis. 8 LDV. 1 Mazda. 5 Mercedes. 1VW.
Ops incl: local bus services, school contracts, private hire.
Livery: White/Blue

A.2.B TRAVEL UK LTD
PRENTON WAY, NORTH CHESHIRE TRADING ESTATE, PRENTON CH43 3DU
Tel: 0151 609 0600
Fax: 0151 609 0601
E-mail: info@a2b-travel.com
Web site: www.a2b-travel.com
Dirs: G Evans, D Evans
Fleet: 26 - 2 single-deck coach, 2 midbus, 12 midiicoach, 10 minibus
Chassis: 1 Dennis. 4 Ford. 6 Ford Transit. 10 Freight Rover. 2 Iveco. 1 MAN. 1 Mercedes. 1 Renault.
Bodies: 1 Beulas. 1 Caetano. 2 Mercedes. 1 Plaxton.
Ops incl: school contracts, private hire, excursions & tours.
Livery: White/Blue

AINTREE COACHLINE
11 CLARE ROAD, BOOTLE L20 9LY.
Tel: 0151 922 8630.
Fax: 0151 933 6994.
Livery: Red/Cream.
Owns Helms of Eastham.

ALS COACHES LTD
400 CELEVELAND STREET, BIRKENHEAD, MERSEYSIDE CH41 8EQ
Tel: 0151 6530222
Fax: 0151 6700509
E-mail: dan@happyals.com
Web site: www.happyals.com
Fleetname: Happy Al's
Man Dir: T.A Cullinan **Gen Man:** M Cullinan **Tpt Man:** C Cullinan
Fleet: 48 - 25 double-deck bus, 8 single-deck bus, 15 single-deck coach.
Chassis: 13 DAF. 2 MAN. 8 Volvo.
Bodies: 1 Bova. 10 East Lancs. 11 Ikarus. 15 Leyland. 1 Plaxton. 2 Van Hool.
Ops incl: school contracts, private hire, excursions & tours.
Ticket System: Wayfarer

ARRIVA NORTH WEST AND WALES
73 ORMSKIRK ROAD, AINTREE L9 5AE.
Tel: 0151 522 2880
Fax: 0151 525 9556
Web site: www.arriva.co.uk
Man Dir: Phil Stone **Eng Dir:** Malcolm Gilkerson **Ops Dir:** John Rimmer
Ops Man: Tom Balshaw **Fin Dir:** Simon Mills
Fleet: 1322 - 159 double-deck bus, 1011 single-deck bus, 2 coach, 9 open-top bus, 137 midibus, 6 minibus.
Ops incl: local bus services, school contracts.
Livery: Arriva
Ticket System: Wayfarer

G. ASHTON COACHES
WATERY LANE, ST HELENS WA9 3JA
Tel: 01744 733275
Fax: 01744 454122
E-mail: enquiries@gashtoncoaches.f2s.com
Prop: George Ashton
Fleet: 7-6 coach, 1 Midicoach
Chassis/bodies: 2 DAF. 2 Scania. 1 Toyota.
Bodies: 1 Berkhof. 1 Caetano. 4 Irizar. 1 Vanhool.
Ops incl: excursions & tours, private hire, continental tours.

AVON COACH AND BUS COMPANY
10 BROOKWAY, NORTH CHESHIRE TRADING ESTATE, PRENTON CH43 3DT.
Tel: 0151 608 8000.
Fax: 0151 608 9955.
Props: Larry Smith, George Lewis
Ops Man: George Lewis
Fleet: 10 - 7 double-deck bus, 2 single-deck bus, 1 coach.
Chassis: 1 Bedford. 2 Daimler. 4 Leyland. 2 Leyland National. 1 Volvo.
Bodies: incl 3 Plaxton
Ops incl: local bus services, school contracts, excursions & tours, private hire.
Livery: Cream with Blue and Gold stripe.
Ticket System: Wayfarer.

BLUELINE TRAVEL
54 STATION ROAD, MAGHULL L31 3DB.
Tel/Fax: 0151 526 8888.
Prop: C. P. Carr.
Fleet: 12 - 3 coach, 4 midicoach, 5 minicoach.
Ops incl: private hire, school contracts.

CUMFYBUS LTD
178 CAMBRIDGE ROAD, SOUTHPORT PR9 7LW.
Tel: 01704 227321.
Fax: 01704 505781.
E-mail: info@cumfybus.co.uk
Web site: www.cumfybus.co.uk
Prop: M. R. Vickers. **Admin:** Mrs P. Lyon.
Fleet: 12 - 1 midicoach, 3 minibus, 8 minicoach.
Chassis: 1 Bedford. 3 Dodge. 1 Iveco. 1 Mercedes. 5 Renault.
Bodies: 1 Duple. 1 Wright. 3 Reeve Burgess. 6 van conversions.
Ops incl: Local bus services, school contracts.

FIRST IN CHESTER & THE WIRRAL
THE PEBBLES, LIVERPOOL ROAD, CHESTER CH2 1AE
Tel: 08708 500 868
Fax: 01782 592541
Web site: www.firstgroup.com
Man Dir: KEN POOLE
Fleet: 203 double-deck bus, single deck bus, coach, midibus.
Ops incl: local bus services

FIVE STAR GROUP TRAVEL
SNAPE GATE, FOXS BANK LANE, WHISTON, PRESCOTT L35 3SS
Tel: 0151 481 0000
Fax: 0151 493 9999
E-mail: phil@fivestar.freeserve.co.uk
Web site: www.fivestartravel.co.uk
Prop: Phil Riley
Fleet: 2 single-deck coach.
Chassis: 2 DAF
Bodies: 2 Bova.
Ops incl: excursions & tours, private hire, continental tours.
Livery: White

FORMBY COACHWAYS LTD
38 STEPHENSON WAY,
FORMBY L37 8EG
Tel: 01704 834448
Fax: 01704 878820
Fleetname: Freshfield Coaches.
Man Dir: K W Bradley **Sec**: D A Bradley
Fleet: 1 minicoach.
Chassis/bodies: Mercedes.
Ops incl: school contracts, private hire.
Livery: Green/Silver

HARDINGS TOURS LTD
CAVENDISH FARM ROAD, WESTON VILLAGE, RUNCORN WA7 4LU
Tel: 0151 647 7831
Fax: 0151 650 1033
Web site: www.hardingstours.co.uk
Man Dir: Selwyn A Jones **Ops Man**: Ken Pickavance **Fleet Eng**: Cledwyn Owen
Fleet: 13 - 11 coach, 1 minibus, 1 minicoach
Chassis: 1 Caetano. 2 Mercedes. 8 Scania. 2 Volvo.
Bodies: 1 Berkhof. 1 Caetano. 7 Irizar. 2 Mercedes. 2 Van Hool.
Ops incl: school contracts, excursions & tours, private hire, continental tours.
Livery: White/Red/Orange/Yellow.
Subsidiary of Selwyns Travel

LIVERPOOL CITY COACHES/CITY BUS
99-103 STANHOPE STREET,
LIVERPOOL L8 5RE.
Tel: 0151 708 6201.
Fax: 0151 708 7201.
Prop: J. Bleasdale.
Fleet: 13 - 2 double-deck bus, 6 single-deck bus, 2 coach, 1 midibus, 2 minibus.
Chassis: 2 Bristol. 1 Ford Transit. 1 Freight Rover. 4 Leyland. 5 Leyland National.
Bodies: 2 ECW. 1 Leyland. 5 Leyland National. 1 Optare. 2 Plaxton.
Ops incl: local bus services, private hire.
Livery: Blue/White.
Ticket System: Wayfarer.

MAYPOLE COACHES
SPENCERS LANE, MELLING L31 1HB
Tel: 0151 547 2713
Fax: 0151 548 2849
Prop: Andrew Donnelly
Fleet: 10 - 2 double-deck bus, 2 single-deck bus, 4 coach, 2 midicoach.
Chassis: 2 Bluebird. 1 DAF. 1 Ford Transit. 2 Leyland National. 4 Volvo.
Ops incl: school contracts, excursions & tours, private hire, **Livery**: White.
Livery: Blue/Green

GAVIN MURRAY & ELLISONS TRAVEL SERVICES
QUEENS GARAGE, 61 BOUNDARY ROAD, ST HELENS WA10 2LX.
Tel: 01744 22882.
Fax: 01744 24402.
Web-site: www.ellisonstravel.com
Dirs: A. Magowan, M. Magowan.
Fleet: 10 coach.
Chassis: 6 Bova. 3 Mercedes. 1 Volvo.
Bodies: 6 Bova. 3 Neoplan. 1 Van Hool.
Ops incl: private hire.
Livery: White/Red/Yellow.

DAVID OGDEN COACHES
BAXTERS LANE, SUTTON, ST HELENS WA9 3DH
Tel/Recovery: 01744 606176
Fax: 01744 850903
E-mail: ogdenssutton@btconnect.com
Web site: www.davidogdenholidays.co.uk
Dirs: David Ogden, Carol Ogden.
Fleet: 19 - 2 single-deck bus, 14 coach, 3 minibus.
Chassis: 16 DAF. 2 Ford Transit. 1 Mercedes.
Bodies: 3 Ikarus. 3 Plaxton. 10 Van Hool.
Ops incl: excursions & tours, private hire, express, continental tours.
Livery: Red/White/Blue.

STAGECOACH MERSEYSIDE
GILMOSS GARAGE, EAST LANCASHIRE ROAD, LIVERPOOL L11 0BB
Tel: 0151 330 6204
Email: enquiries.merseyside@stagecoachbus.com
Web site: www.stagecoachbus.com
Fleet: 173 - includes single-deck bus, double-deck bus.
Ops incl: local bus services

SUPERTRAVEL OMNIBUS LTD
STC HOUSE, SPEKE HALL ROAD, SPEKE L24 9HD
Tel: 0151 486 3994
Fax: 0151 448 1216
E-mail: 96.supertravel@btconnect.com
Man Dir: Graham Bolderson.
Fleet: 36 - 25 single-deck bus, 7 midicoach, 1 minibus, 3 minicoach.
Chassis: 12 Alexander Dennis. 10 Mercedes-Benz. 13 Optare. 1 Renault.
Bodies: 2 Alexander Dennis. 1 Mellor. 6 Mercedes-Benz. 16 Optare. 11 Plaxton.
Ops incl: local bus services, school contracts, private hire.

MIDDLESEX

ALLIED COACHLINES LTD
THE BULLS BRIDGE CENTRE, NORTH HYDE GARDENS, HAYES UB3 4QT
Tel: 020 8573 2626
Fax: 020 8561 6636
E-mail: sales@alliedcoachlines.co.uk
Web site: www.alliedcoachlines.co.uk
Dirs: R & R Charles
Fleet: 7 coach.
Chassis: 5 Mercedes. 2 Setra
Bodies: 5 Mercedes. 2 Setra.
Ops incl: private hire.

ARON COACHLINES LTD
THE BULLS BRIDGE CENTRE, NORTH HYDE GARDENS, HAYES UB3 4QT
Tel: 020 8569 2949
Fax: 020 8561 2829
E-mail: sales@aroncoachlines.co.uk
Web site: www.aroncoachlines.co.uk
Dirs: S. Robinson, R. Charles
Fleet: 6 - 4 coach, 2 minibus.
Chassis: 6 Mercedes.
Bodies: 6 Mercedes.
Ops incl: private hire.

ASHFORD LUXURY COACHES
373 HATTON ROAD,
FELTHAM TW14 9QS
Tel: 020 8890 6394
Fax: 020 8751 5054
Web site: www.ashfordluxurycoaches.co.uk
Man Dir: Martin Cornell
Fleet: 10 - 1 single-deck bus, 6 coach, 2 midicoach, 1 minicoach.
Chassis: 7 Dennis. 3 Mercedes.
Bodies: 3 Mellor. 7 Plaxton.
Ops incl: private hire, school contracts, local bus services.

ATBUS LTD
41 MANOR ROAD, ASHFORD TW15 2SL
Tel: 07949 140437
Web site: www.atbus.org.uk
Man Dir: Andrew Tanner **Co Sec**: Clifford Tanner
Ops Man: Mathew Downing
Fleet: 11- 6 double-deck bus, 5 single-deck bus.
Chassis: 3 Dennis. 2 Leyalnd. 3 Volvo.
Bodies: 3 MCW
Ops incl: school contracts.
Livery: Red/Grey
Ticket System: Wayfarer

BEECHES TRAVEL
23 POWDER MILL LANE, TWICKENHAM TW2 6EE.
Tel/Fax: 020 8898 7048.
Prop: C. Miller.
Fleet: 4 minicoach.
Chassis: Ford Transit. Freight Rover.
Ops incl: school contracts, excursions & tours, private hire.
Livery: White/Yellow.

BESSWAY TRAVEL
16 TINTERN WAY, WEST HARROW HA2 0SA.
Tel: 020 8422 3128.
Prop: Michael Heffernan.
Fleet: 6 - 1 coach, 3 midicoach, 2 minicoach.
Chassis: 1 Dennis. 5 Mercedes.
Bodies: 5 Autobus. 1 UVG.
Ops incl: private hire, school contracts.

149

CABIN COACHES
1 PARSONAGE CLOSE, HAYES UB3 2LZ
Tel: 020 8573 1100
Fax: 020 8573 8604
E-mail: cabincoaches@aol.com
Props: P Martin
Fleet: 5 - 4 coach, 1 midicoach.
Chassis: 1 Dennis. 1 Mercedes. 1 Scania. 2 Setra.
Bodies: 1 Duple. 1 Mercedes. 2 Setra. 1 Van Hool.
Ops incl: excursions & tours, school contracts, private hire.
Livery: White

CALL-A-COACH
See Surrey

CAVALIER TRAVEL SERVICES
See London

CARAVELLE COACHES
9 CHESTNUT AVENUE, EDGWARE HA8 7RA
Tel/Fax: 020 8952 4025
Dir: H Lawrence.
Fleet: 2 - 1 midibus, 1 minibus.
Chassis: 1 Iveco. 1 Mercedes.
Ops incl: school contracts, private hire.

CHALFONT COACHES OF HARROW LTD
200 FEATHERSTONE ROAD, SOUTHALL UB2 5AQ
Tel: 020 8843 2323
Fax: 020 8574 0939
E-mail: chalfont.coaches@btopenworld.com
Web site: www.chalfontcoaches.co.uk
Man Dir: C J Shears **Dirs**: I Shears, M Shears **Ops Man**: P Williams **Ch Eng**: R Arents **Co Sec**: G Shears
Fleet: 18 - 15 coach, 1 midicoach, 2 minibus.
Chassis: 2 LDV. 1 Mercedes. 15 Volvo.
Bodies: 3 Autobus. 15 Van Hool.
Ops incl: school contracts, excursions & tours, private hire, express, continental tours.
Livery: Mauve/White

CHALFONT LINE LTD
4 PROVIDENCE ROAD, WEST DRAYTON UB7 8HJ
Tel: 01895 459540
Fax: 01895 459549
E-mail: info@chalfont-line.co.uk
Web site: www.chalfont-line.co.uk
Chmn: T J Reynolds **Man Dir**: R Chadija
Dir: M Kerr **Tran Man**: Lynn Young
Fleet: 84 minibus.
Chassis: 64 DAF. 6 Ford Transit. 8 Mercedes. 6 Renault.
Ops incl: school contracts, excursions & tours, private hire, continental tours.
Livery: White/Green

CUMFI-LUX COACHES
69 CORWELL LANE, HILLINGDON UB8 3DE.

Tel: 020 8561 6948
Fax: 020 8569 3809.
Prop: N. R. Farrow (**Traf Man**).
Sec: Mrs T. K. Lovell.
Fleet: 3 - 1 coach, 1 minibus, 1 minicoach.
Chassis: 2 Mercedes. 1 Scania
Ops incl: excursions & tours, private hire.
Livery: Orange/White (coach); White (minibuses).

FALCON TRAVEL
123 NUTTY LANE, SHEPPERTON TW17 0RQ
Tel: 01932 787752
Fax: 01932 785521
Fleet: 6 - 5 coach, 1 midicoach.
Chassis: 1 Mercedes. 5 Volvo.
Bodies: 5 Van Hool. 1 other.
Ops incl: private hire, school contracts.
Livery: White/Black/Crimson

HAMILTON OF UXBRIDGE
589-591 UXBRIDGE ROAD, HAYES END UB4 8HP
Tel: 01895 232266
Fax: 01895 810454.
Ops Man: D. L. Bennett.
Fleet: 10 - 8 coach, 2 double-deck coach.
Chassis: 10 MAN.
Bodies: 5 Ayats. 4 Noge. 1 Marco Polo
Ops incl: private hire, express, continental tours.

HEARNS COACHES
See London

HOUNSLOW COMMUNITY TRANSPORT
9 MONTAGUE ROAD, HOUNSLOW TW3 1JY.
Tel: 020 8572 8204.
Fax: 020 8572 0997
E-mail: haightim@aol.com
Ch Officer: Tim Haigh **Flt Co-ord**: Steve Cann
Fleet: 9 minibus

HOUNSLOW MINI COACHES
See London

VIC HUGHES & SON LTD
61 FERN GROVE, FELTHAM TW14 9AY
Tel: 020 8831 0770
Fax: 020 8831 0660
Man Dir: V B Hughes.
Co Sec: Mrs V. Hughes. **Dir**: K. Hughes.
Fleet: 21 - 4 midicoach, 5 minibus, 12 ambulance.
Chassis: Ford, Mercedes.
Ops incl: school contracts, excursions & tours, private hire.
Livery: White/Black.

J & D EUROTRAVEL
58 WEALD LANE, HARROW WEALD HA3 5EX
Tel: 020 8861 1829
Fax: 020 8424 2585

E-mail: jdetravel@aol.com
Man Dir: J T Thomas
Fleet: 10 - 3 coach, 3 midicoach, 2 minibus, 2 minicoach.
Ops incl: school contracts, excursions & tours, private hire, express, continental tours.

LEOLINE TRAVEL
UPPER SUNBURY ROAD, HAMPTON TW12 2DW
Tel: 020 8941 3370
Fax: 020 8941 3372
E-mail: leolinecoaches@aol.com
Web site: www.leolinetravel.co.uk
Prop: David Baker **Ops Man**: Judy Dale
Fleet: 6 - 5 single-deck coach, 1 minibus.
Chassis: 2 Iveco. 1 Toyota. 3 Volvo.
Bodies: 2 Beulas. 1 Caetano. 1 Jonckheere. 2 Van Hool.
Ops incl: excursions & tours, private hire, school contracts.
Livery: Blue/Orange

LONDON SOVEREIGN
BUSWAYS HOUSE, WELLINGTON ROAD, TWICKENHAM TW2 5NX
Tel: 020 8400 6600
Web site: www.sovereignlondonbuses.co.uk
Man Dir: Nigel Stevens
Fleet: 100 - double-deck bus, single-deck bus.
Ops Incl: local bus services, private hire
Livery: TfL
Part of the Transdev Group

LONDON UNITED BUSWAYS LTD
BUSWAYS HOUSE, WELLINGTON ROAD, TWICKENHAM TW2 5NX
Tel: 020 8400 6605
Fax: 020 8943 2688
E-mail: customer@lonutd.co.uk
Web site: www.lonutd.co.uk
Man Dir: Nigel Stevens **Fin Dir**: Richard Casling **Human Res Dir**: Karen Fuller
Eng Dir: Les Birchley **Ops Dir**: Paul Matthews **Com Man**: Steffan Evans
Fleet: 781 - 420 double-deck bus, 361 single-deck bus.
Chassis: 503 Dennis. 88 Scania. 190 Volvo.
Bodies: 235 Alexander. 128 East Lancs. 400 Plaxton. 3 Reeve Burgess. 15 other.
Ops Incl: local bus services, private hire
Livery: Red
Ticket system: Oyster
(Part of the Transdev Group)

M&M COACHLINES
33 HITHERWELL DRIVE, HARROW WEALD HA3 6JD
Tel: 020 8863 2085
Fax: 020 8861 6175
Prop: M C Burcombe **Sec/Prop**: Mrs M M Burcombe **Ch Eng**: N Bassett
Fleet: 1 coach.
Chassis: Scania.
Body: Berkhof.
Ops incl: private hire, excursions & tours, continental tours.

METROLINE TRAVEL LTD
66 COLLEGE ROAD, HARROW HA1 1BE
Tel: 020 8218 8888
Fax: 020 8218 8899
E-mail: info@metroline.co.uk
Web site: www.metroline.co.uk
Chief Exec Off: Jaspal Singh **Ch Op Officer**: Sean O'Shea **Fin Dir**: Damian Rowbotham. **Eng Dir**: vacant
Fleet: 1231 - 810 double-deck bus, 416 single-deck bus, 1 open-top bus, 5 midibus.
Chassis: 3 AEC. 844 Alexander Dennis. 38 MAN. 1 MCW. 5 Optare. 33 Scania. 307 Volvo.
Bodies: 410 Alexander Dennis. 39 East Lancs. 41 Marshall/MCV. 1 MCW. 5 Optare. 3 Park Royal. 732 Plaxton.
Ops incl: local bus services, school contracts, private hire.
Livery: Red/Blue.
Ticket System: Wayfarer (London Buses spec)
Part of the Comfort Delgro Group

NCP CHALLENGER
TWICKENHAM TRADING ESTATE, RUGBY ROAD, TWICKENHAM TW1 1DU
Tel: 020 8892 5830
Fax: 0 20 8744 3893
Web site: www.ncpchallenger.co.uk
Head of Public transport: Matt Larkin
Fleet: 69 single deck bus
Chassis: Alexander Dennis
Bodies: Alexander Dennis
Ops incl: local bus services
Livery: /Red/Yellow
Ticket System: Wayfarer
(Subsidiary of National Car Parks Ltd)

SUNBURY COACHES
204A CHARLTON ROAD, SHEPPERTON TW17 0RG.
Tel: 01932 785153.
Fax: 01932 761923.
Dir: P. Jones.
Fleet: 5 coach.
Chassis: Irisbus, Leyland, Volvo.
Bodies: Berkhof, Beulas, Jonckheere.

Ops incl: excursions & tours, private hire.
Livery: White/Turquoise.

TELLINGS GOLDEN MILLER COACHES LTD
See London

VENTURE TRANSPORT (HENDON) (1965) LTD
307 PINNER ROAD, HARROW HA1 4HG.
Tel: 020 8427 0101.
Fax: 020 8427 1707.
Ops incl: private hire
Subsidiary of Hearns Coaches

WESTBUS COACH SERVICES LTD
See London

WINGS LUXURY TRAVEL LTD
See London

NORFOLK

AMBASSADOR TRAVEL (ANGLIA) LTD
JAMES WATT CLOSE, GAPTON HALL INDUSTRIAL ESTATE, GREAT YARMOUTH NR31 0NX
Tel: 01493 440350
Fax: 01493 440367
E-mail: ambassador-travel@hotmail.co.uk
Chmn: R H Green **Ops Man**: B Picton
Dep Ops Man: M Pleasants
Fleet: 43 - 1 double-deck bus, 2 single-deck bus, 36 coach, 4 midibus.
Chassis: 1 Leyland.3 Scania. 33 Volvo.
Bodies: 2 Caetano. 4 Jonckheere. 5 Optare. 23 Plaxton. 4 Sunsundegui. 5 Other.
Ops incl: local bus services, school contracts, private hire, express, excursions & tours.
Livery: White.
Ticket System: Setright/Almex/Wayfarer

ANGLIAN COACHES LTD
See Suffolk

CHENERY TRAVEL
THE GARAGE, DICKLEBURGH, DISS IP21 4NJ
Tel: 01379 741221
Fax: 01379 740728
Recovery: 01379 741656
E-mail: julia@chenerytravel.co.uk
Web site: www.chenerytravel.co.uk
Dir: Mrs P Garnhem **Gen Man**: Mrs J M McGraffin
Fleet: 20 coach.
Chassis: 1 Bedford. 1 Leyland. 18 Setra.
Bodies: 1 Duple. 1 Plaxton. 18 Setra.
Ops incl: school contracts, excursions & tours, private hire, express, continental tours.
Livery: Silver/Blue.

COACH SERVICES LTD
1A HOWLETT WAY, THETFORD IP24 1HZ
Tel: 01842 821509
Fax: 01842 766581
E-mail: info@coachservicesltd.co.uk
Web site: www.coachservicesltd.co.uk
Prop: A Crawford **Tran Man**: R Matin
Fleet: 27 - 1 double-deck bus, 21 coach, 3 midibus, 2 minibus.
Chassis: 1 AEC. 2 Bova. 3 DAF. 1 LDV. 1 Leyland. 2 Mercedes. 3 Optare. 3 Scania. 2 Transbus. 9 Volvo.
Bodies: 1 Routemaster. 2 Bova. 3 Irizar. 2 LDV. 7 Jonckheere. 3 Optare. 4 Plaxton. 1 Transbus. 3 Van Hool.
Ops incl: local bus services, school contracts, excursions & tours, private hire, continental tours
Ticket System: Almex

CRUSADER HOLIDAYS
See Essex

D-WAY TRAVEL
See Suffolk

A. W. EASTONS COACHES LTD
THE OLD COACH HOUSE, STRATTON STRAWLESS, NORWICH NR10 5LR
Tel/Fax: 01603 754253
E-mail: admin@eastonsholidays.co.uk
Web site: www.eastonsholidays.co.uk
Dirs: Robert Easton, Derek Easton
Fleet: 10 - 1 single-deck bus, 9 coach.
Chassis: 2 Bova. 1 Dennis. 1 Setra. 7 Val Hool.
Bodies: 2 Bova. 1 Optare. 1 Setra. 7 Van Hool.
Ops incl: local bus services, excursions & tours, school contracts, private hire, continental tours.
Livery: Purple
Ticket System: Almex

EUROSUN COACHES
UNIT 1, GREENWAYS, THORPE MARKET ROAD, SOUTH REPPS NR11 8NQ.
Tel: 01263 834483
Fax: 01263 834482
E-mail: eurosuncoaches@hotmail.com
Web site: www.eurosun.net
Ch Eng: Adam Goffin **Sales & Mktg Man**: Tony Porter **Dirs**: Phil Overy, Jack Overy
Fleet: 19 - 16 coach, 3 double-deck coach.
Chassis: 7 DAF. 4 Leyland. 3 MAN. 2 Mercedes. 5 Neoplan.
Bodies: 3 Bova. 2 Leyland. 5 Neoplan. 6 Plaxton. 2 Van Hool. 1 other.
Ops incl: school contracts, excursions & tours, private hire, continental tours.
Livery: Red and Gold

FARELINE COACH SERVICES
See Suffolk

FIRST EASTERN COUNTIES BUSES LTD
ROUEN HOUSE, ROUEN ROAD, NORWICH NR1 1RB
Tel: 08456 020 121
Fax: 01603 615439
Web site: www.firstgroup.com
Man Dir: Peter Iddon **Fin Dir/Co Sec**: Stephen Wickers **Ops Dir**: Colin Booth
Fleet: 335 - 77 double-deck bus, 94 single-deck bus, 31 single-deck coach. 17 double-deck coach, 113 Midibus, 3 minibus.
Chassis: 3 AEC. 107 Dennis. 35 Leyland. 2 Optare. 60 Scania. 108 Volvo.
Bodies: 45 Alexander Dennis. 7 Leyland. 3 Marshall. 11 Northern Counties. 2 Optare. 3 Park Royal. 131 Plaxton. 20 Transbus. 93 Wright.
Ops incl: local bus services, school contract, private hire.
Ticket System: Wayfarer 3

151

FREESTONES COACHES LTD
GREEN LANE, BEETLEY, DEREHAM NR20 4DL
Tel: 01362 860236
Fax: 01362 860276
Dir: Mrs Gloria Feeke **Ops Man**: Robert Tibbles **Co Sec**: Gary Feeke
Web: www.freestonescoaches.co.uk
E-mail: freestonescoachesltd@tiscali.co.uk
Fleet: 11 - 2 Single-deck bus 8 single-deck coach, 1 minibus.
Chassis: 1 Alexander Dennis. 1 DAF. 2 Iveco. 1 Mercedes-Benz. 1 Scania. 1 Volkwagen. 4 Volvo.
Bodies: 1 Alexander Dennis. 2 Beulas. 1 Hispano. 1 Optare. 4 Van Hool.
Ops incl: local bus services, excursions & tours, school contracts, private hire, continental tours.

D&H HARROD (COACHES) LTD
BEXWELL AERODROME, DOWNHAM MARKET PE38 9LU
Tel: 01366 381111
Fax: 01366 382010
E-mail: info@harrodscoaches.co.uk
Web site: www.harrodcoaches.co.uk
Man Dir: Derek Harrod **Co Sec**: Anne Harrod **Ops Man**: Paul Harrod.
Fleet: 12 coach
Chassis: 3 Dennis. 1 Iveco. 8 Volvo.
Bodies: 4 Jonckheere. 1 Plaxton. 3 Van Hool. 2 Wadham Stringer. 2 other.
Ops incl: local bus services, school contracts, excursions & tours, private hire, continental tours.
Livery: White

KONECTBUS LTD
JOHN GOSHAWK ROAD, DEREHAM NR19 1SY
Tel: 01362 851210
Fax: 01362 851215
E-mail: enquiries@konectbus.co.uk
Web site: www.konectbus.co.uk
Fleetname: Konectbus
Dirs: Julian Patterson, Steve Challis
Fleet: 35 - 6 double-deck bus, 29 single-deck bus.
Chassis: 1 Leyland. 29 Optare. 5 VDL.
Bodies: 1 Alexander. 29 Optare. 5 Wright.
Ops incl: local bus services
Livery: Blue/Yellow/Grey
Ticket System: Wayfarer TGX150

MATTHEWS COACHES
50 WESTGATE STREET, SHOULDHAM, KING'S LYNN PE33 0BN
Tel: 01366 347220
Fax: 01366 347293
E-mail: john@matthewscoaches.co.uk
Fleet: 6 - 5 single-deck coach, 1 minibus
Chassis: 2 DAF. 3 Dennis. 1 LDV.
Bodies: 1 Berkhof. 3 Plaxton. 2 Van Hool.
Ops incl: school contracts, excursions & tours, private hire.
Livery: White/Blue
Ticket system: Setright

NORFOLK GREEN
HAMLIN WAY, KINGS LYNN PE31 6HA
Tel: 01553 776980
Fax: 01553 770891
E-mail: enquiries@norfolkgreen.co.uk
Web site: www.norfolkgreen.co.uk
Man Dir: Ben Colson **Dir**: Keith Shayshutt
Fleet Eng: Nigel Firth **Ops Man**: Richard Pengelly **Accountant**: Simon Carr
Fleet: 44 - 8 single-deck bus, 29 midibus, 7 minibus
Chassis: 6 Dennis. 17 Mercedes. 21 Optare.
Bodies: 10 Alexander. 21 Optare. 13 Plaxton.
Ops incl: local bus services, school contracts
Livery: two-tone Green
Ticket System: Wayfarer TGX

PEELINGS COACHES
THE GARAGE, CLAY HILL, TITTLESHALL, KING'S LYNN PE32 2RQ
Tel/Fax: 01328 701531
Web: www.peelings-coaches.co.uk
E-mail: jonathon.joplin@btinternet.com
Prop: Jonathan Joplin **Comp Sec**: Ruth Joplin **Ch Eng**: Jonathan Sayer
Fleetname: Peelincs Coaches
Fleet: 6 - single-deck coach.
Chassis: 1 Dennis. 1 Iveco. 4 Volvo.
Bodies: 1 Beulas. 1 Jonckheere. 4 Plaxton.
Ops incl: local bus services, school contracts, excursions & tours, private hire, express.
Livery: White/Blue/Silver
Ticket System: Setright

REYNOLDS COACHES Ltd
THE GARAGE, ORMESBY ROAD, CAISTER-ON-SEA NR30 5QJ
Tel: 01493 720312
Fax: 01493 721512
E-mail: reynolds.coaches@gtyarmouth.co.uk
Man Dir: Charles Reynolds **Dir**: Mrs Julie Reynolds **Co Sec**: Mrs Grace Reynolds
Ch Eng: Jeffrey Buckle
Fleet: 16 -15 single-deck coach, 1 minicoach.
Chassis: 7 Alexander Dennis. 1 DAF. 1 Iveco. 1 MAN. 2 Mercedes-Benz. 3 Volvo.
Bodies: 2 Beulas. 1 Duple. 1 Neoplan. 7 Plaxton. 1 Reeve Burgess. 3 Van Hool. 1 Other.
Ops incl: school contracts, excursions & tours, private hire, continental tours.
Livery: Blue/Grey/Yellow.

SANDERS COACHES
HEATH DRIVE, HEMPSTEAD ROAD INDUSTRIAL ESTATE, HOLT NR25 6JU
Tel: 01263 712800
Fax: 01263 710920
E-mail: info@sanderscoaches.com
Website: www.sanderscoaches.com
Dir: Charles Sanders
Fleet: 85 - 8 double-deck bus, 24 single-deck bus, 36 coach, 14 midibus, 2 minicoach, 1 minibus.
Chassis: 10 Bedford. 43 DAF. 7 Dennis. 4 Leyland. 17 Mercedes. 2 Setra. 2 Volvo.
Bodies: 3 Duple. 4 ECW. 17 Ikarus. 2 Neoplan. 4 Northern Counties. 14 Optare. 20 Plaxton. 7 Reeve Burgess. 2 Setra. 12 Van Hool.
Ops incl: local bus services, school contracts, excursions & tours, private hire, continental tours.
Livery: Yellow/Blue/Orange
Ticket System: Wayfarer 3

H SEMMENCE & CO LTD
34 NORWICH ROAD, WYMONDHAM NR18 0NS
Tel: 01953 602135
Fax: 01953 605867
E-mail: sales@semmence.co.uk
Web site: www.semmence.co.uk
Chairm: R H Green **Man Dir**: Sean Green
Co Sec: Mark Green **Tran Man**: Brian Lafferty **Eng Man**: Kevin Hughes
Fleet: 30 - 26 coach, 4 minicoach.
Chassis: 15 Dennis. 4 Mercedes. 1 Scania. 10 Volvo.
Ops incl: local bus services, school contracts, excursions & tours, express, private hire
Livery: White
Ticket System: Wayfarer
(Subsidiary of Ambassador Travel)

SIMONDS COACH & TRAVEL
ROSWALD HOUSE, OAK DRIVE, DISS IP22 4GX
Tel: 01379 647300
Fax: 01379 647350
E-mail: info@simonds.co.uk
Web site: www.simonds.co.uk
Man Dir: M S Simonds **Chairman**: D O Simonds **Dirs**: R S Simonds, A Tant **Fleet**: 42 - 7 single-deck bus, 27 single-deck coach, 7 midibus, 1 minicoach.
Chassis: 1 DAF. 4 MAN. 8 Mercedes-Benz. 2 Transbus. 27 Volvo.
Bodies: 1 Alexander. 4 MCV. 1 Optare. 16 Plaxton. 2 Transbus. 18 Van Hool.
Ops incl: local bus services, school contracts, excursions & tours, private hire, continental tours.
Livery: White with Green/Red/Gold leaves
Ticket system: Wayfarer/Paycell

SPRATTS COACHES (EAST ANGLIAN & CONTINENTAL) LTD
THE GARAGE, WRENINGHAM, NORWICH NR16 1AZ
Tel: 01508 489262
Fax: 01508 489404
E-mail: sprattscoaches@btconnect.com
Web site: www.sprattscoaches.co.uk
Dirs: Richard Spratt, Christine Bilham
Fleet: 11 - 8 single-deck coach, 3 midicoach.
Chassis: 1 Bedford. 1 Bova. 2 MAN. 1 Mercedes-Benz. 5 Scania. 1 Volvo.
Bodies: 1 Autobus. 1 Berkhof. 1 Bova. 1 Caetano. 1 Duple. 5 Wadham Stringer.
Ops incl: private hire.
Livery: White

SUNBEAM COACHES LTD
WESTGATE STREET, HEVINGHAM, NORWICH NR10 5NH
Tel/Fax: 01603 754211
E-mail: sunbeamcoaches@aol.com
Dirs: G M Coldham, J M Cole , G J Coldham
Fleet: 5 - 4 single-deck coach, 1 minicoach.
Chassis: 1 Alexander Dennis. 2 MAN. 1 Toyota. 1 Volvo.
Bodies: 1 Caetano. 2 Neoplan. 1 Plaxton. 1 Van Hool.
Ops incl: local bus service, school contracts, private hire, excursions & tours.
Livery: White with Orange/Blue/Yellow

NORTH & NORTH EAST LINCOLNSHIRE

APPLEBYS COACHES
CONISHOLME, LOUTH LN11 7LT
Tel: 01507 357900
Fax: 01507 357910
E-mail: enquiries@applebyscoaches.co.uk
Web site: www.applebyscoaches.co.uk
Fleet: 14 coach
Ops incl: excursions & tours, continental tours.
(Subsidiary of L F Bowen Ltd, Staffordshire)

BEN GEORGE TRAVEL LTD
♿ 🪑 ▭ R24 🔧
BRICKHILLS, BROUGHTON, BRIGG DN20 0BZ
Tel: 01652 654681
Fax: 01652 350396
Dirs: S & J Easton
Fleet: 31 - 5 double-deck bus, 7 coach, 1 double-deck coach, 1 midicoach, 3 minibus.
Chassis: 3 AEC. 3 Bedford. 1 Bristol. 1 Daimler. 1 Dennis. 2 Leyland. 2 MAN. 3 Mercedes. 1 Neoplan.
Bodies: 1 Alexander. 3 Duple. 1 Jonckheere. 2 Leyland. 3 Mercedes. 1 Neoplan. 3 Plaxton.
Ops incl: local bus services, school contracts, excursions & tours, private hire, continental tours.
Livery: Red/White/Blue

EMMERSON COACHES LTD
♿ 🪑 ❄
BLUESTONE LANE, IMMINGHAM DN40 2EL.
Tel: 01469 578166
Fax: 01469 575278
Web site: www.emmersoncoaches.ukf.net
Dirs: Alan Brumby, O. M. Stocks, Allen Stocks.
Fleet: 12 - 11 coach, 1 minibus.
Chassis: 1 Bedford. 1 DAF. 1 Ford. 2 MAN. 3 Mercedes. 1 Scania. 3 Volvo.
Bodies: 2 Duple. 1 Ikarus. 1 Jonckheere. 2 Mercedes. 4 Plaxton. 1 other.
Ops incl: school contracts, private hire.
Livery: Cream with orange and brown stripes.

EXPERT COACH SERVICES LTD
♿ 🪑 ❄
2 PASTURE STREET, GRIMSBY DN31 1QD
Tel: 01472 350650
Fax: 01472 351926
E-mail: sales@expertcoaches.co.uk
Web site: www.expertcoaches.co.uk
Man Dir: L A Harniess **Dir**: C J Cator
Fleet: 2 coach
Chassis: 2 Scania.
Bodies: 1 Berkhof. 1 Plaxton.
Ops incl: excursions & tours, private hire, continental tours.
Livery: Blue/White.

HOLLOWAY COACHES LTD
COTTAGE BECK ROAD, SCUNTHORPE DN16 1TP.
Tel: 01724 282277, 281177.
Fax: 01724 289945.
Dirs: F. S. Holloway (**Man Dir**), P. A. Holloway.
Fleet: 14 - 7 double-deck bus, 6 coach, 1 minicoach.
Chassis: 1 Bedford. 2 Dennis. 11 Leyland.
Bodies: 7 Alexander. 6 Plaxton. 1 other.
Ops incl: excursions & tours, express.
Livery: Red/White/Blue.

HORNSBY TRAVEL SERVICES LTD
🪑 ♿ ❄ 🚻
51 ASHBY HIGH STREET, SCUNTHORPE DN16 2NB
Tel: 01724 282255
E-mail: office@hornsbytravel.co.uk
Man Dir: R Hornsby **Gen Man**: N Hornsby
Fleet: 30 - 4 double-deck bus, 17 single-deck bus, 9 coach, 1 minibus
Chassis: 1 BMC. 4 DAF. 13 Dennis. 2 Leyland. 2 MCW. 2 Plaxton. 1 Vauxhall. 2 Volvo.
Bodies: 3 Alexander. 1 BMC. 2 MCW. 19 Plaxton. 1 Transbus. 4 Wright. 1 other.
Ops incl: local bus services, excursions & tours, private hire, school contracts
Livery: Silver/Blue.
Ticket System: Almex

MILLMAN COACHES
♿ 🪑 🔧
17 WILTON ROAD, HUMBERSTON, GRIMSBY DN36 4AW
Tel: 01472 210297
Fax: 01472 595915
E-mail: enquiries@millmancoaches.co.uk
Web site: www.millmancoaches.co.uk
Ptnrs: Marjorie Millman, David Millman, Amanda J Millman
Fleet: 9 - 6 single-deck coach, 2 midicoach, 1 minibus.
Chassis: 2 Cummins. 1 Dennis. 2 Leyland. 1 Mercedes. 3 Volvo.
Bodies: 2 Duple. 2 Jonckheere. 1 Mercedes. 4 Plaxton.
Ops incl: private hire, school contracts.
Livery: White/Blue/Yellow

RADLEY COACH TRAVEL
🪑 ♿ ❄
THE TRAVEL OFFICE, 50 WRAWBY STREET, BRIGG DN20 8JB
Tel: 01652 653583
Fax: 01652 656020
E-mail: radleytravel@aol.com
Web site: www.radleytravel.co.uk
Owner: Kevin Radley.
Fleet: 4 coach
Chassis: 4 Scania.
Bodies: 2 Berkof. 2 Irizar.
Ops incl: excursions & tours, private hire, continental tours.
Livery: Gold/Maroon

SHERWOOD TRAVEL
🪑 ♿ ❄
19 QUEENS ROAD, IMMINGHAM DN40 1QR
Tel: 01469 571140
E-mail: enquiries@sherwoodtravel.co.uk
Web site: www.sherwoodtravel.co.uk
Dirs: Stuart Oakland
Fleet: 9 - 4 single-deck coach, 2 minicoach, 2 minibus, 1 minicoach.
Chassis: 4 Mercedes-Benz. 2 Scania. 3 Volvo.
Ops incl: school contracts, excursions & tours, private hire.

SOLID ENTERTAINMENTS
♿
46 WELLOWGATE, GRIMSBY DN32 0RA.
Tel: 01472 349222.
Fax: 01472 362275.
Prop: S. J. Stanley.
Fleet: 2 - 1 coach, 1 minibus.
Chassis: 1 Scania.
Bodies: 1 Irizar.
Ops incl: excursions & tours, private hire, continental tours.
Livery: Black.

♿	Vehicle suitable for disabled	🪑	Seat belt-fitted Vehicle
🚻	Toilet-drop facilities available	🍴	Coach(es) with galley facilities
R	Recovery service available	❄	Air-conditioned vehicle(s)
▭	Open top vehicle(s)v	♿	Coaches with toilet facilities
R24	24 hour recovery service	🔧	Replacement vehicle available
		▭	Vintage Coach(es) available

NORTH YORKSHIRE, YORK

G. ABBOTT & SONS
R24
AUMANS HOUSE, LEEMING, NORTHALLERTON DL7 9RZ
Tel: 01677 422858/422571
Fax: 01677 424971
Fleetname: Abbotts of Leeming
Ptnrs: David C Abbott, Clifford G Abbot.
Fleet: 61 - 1 double-deck bus, 3 single-deck bus, 50 coach, 6 midibus, 1 minicoach.
Chassis: 2 Bedford. 6 DAF. 6 Ford Transit. 1 Iveco. 10 Leyland. 3 Optare.
Bodies: 1 Caetano. 6 Duple. 10 Irizar. 3 Optare. 20 Park Royal. 10 Van Hool.
Ops incl: local bus services, school contracts, excursions & tours, private hire, express, continental tours.

H ATKINSON & SONS (INGLEBY) LTD
INGLEBY ARNCLIFFE NORTHALLERTON DL6 3LN
Tel: 01609 882222
Fax: 01609 882476
E-mail: h.atkinson@eurotelonline.com
Web site: www.atkinsoncoaches.co.uk
Dirs: Martin Atkinson, David Atkinson
Fleet: 11 - 10 single-deck coach, 1 midicoach
Chassis: 3 DAF. 1 EOS. 1 Iveco. 2 MAN. 2 Mercedes-Benz. 2 Setra. 3 Volvo.
Bodies: 1 Beulas. 3 Bova.1 Indcar. 1 Jonckheere. 1 Marcopolo. 1 Plaxton. 2 Setra. 1 other.
Ops Incl: schools contract, excursions & tours, private hire, continental tours.

BALDRY'S COACHES
R
LEYLANDII, SELBY ROAD, HOLME-ON-SPALDING-MOOR YO43 4HB.
Tel: 01430 860992.
Prop: A. Baldry.
Fleet: 9 - 8 coach, 1 midicoach.
Chassis: 1 AEC. 1 Bedford. 5 Ford.
Ops incl: school contracts, excursions & tours, private hire.
Livery: Two-tone Green.

BEECROFT COACHES
POST OFFICE, FEWSTON HG3 1SG.
Tel/Fax: 01943 880206.
Prop: D. Beecroft.
Fleet: 6 - 3 coach, 1 midicoach, 2 minibus.
Chassis: 1 DAF. 1 Dodge. 2 Freight Rover. 1 Scania. 1 Volvo.
Bodies: 1 Alexander. 1 Bova. 3 Carlyle. 1 Duple. 1 Plaxton. 1 Van Hool.
Ops incl: local bus services, school contracts, excursions & tours, private hire, continental tours.
Livery: Green/Orange/White.

BIBBY'S OF INGLETON
NE0W ROAD, INGLETON LA6 3NU.
Tel: 01524 241330
Fax: 01524 242216
E-mail: bibbys_travel@talk21.com
Man Dir: P Bibby **Co Sec**: Mrs S Holcroft
Ch Eng: M Stephenson.
Fleet: 22 - 17 coach, 5 minibus.
Chassis: 17 DAF. 3 LDV. 3 Mercedes.
Bodies: 6 Ikarus. 3 LDV. 2 Mercedes. 4 Plaxton. 7 Van Hool. 1 Ovi.
Ops incl: school contracts. excursions & tours, private hire, continental tours.
Livery: Blue/Grey/Red with white stripes.

BOTTERILLS
HIGH STREET GARAGE, THORNTON LE DALE YO18 7QW
Tel: 01751 474210
E-mail: botterills@hotmail.com
Web site: www.botterills.org
Fleet: 4 minibus
Chassis/bodies: 4 Mercedes
Ops incl: local bus services, school contracts, private hire.
Livery: White

BURRELLS (BARNARD CASTLE COACHES)
SOUTH VIEW GARAGE, NEWSHAM, RICHMOND DL11 7RA
Tel: 01833 621302
Fax: 01833 621431
E-mail: qlburrell@hotmail.com
Dirs: Alan Burrell, Mrs Sandra Burrell
Fleet: 6 - 5 single-deck coach, 1 midicoach
Chassis: 1 Leyland. 1 Mercedes-Benz. 4 Volvo.
Bodies: 1 Leyland. 1 Plaxton. 3 Van Hool. 1 Other.
Ops incl: school contracts, excursions & tours, private hire, continental tours.
Livery: Yellow/White

EDDIE BROWN TOURS LTD
BAR LANE, ROECLIFFE, YORK YO51 9LS
Tel: 01423 321240
Fax: 01423 326213
E-mail: enquiries@eddiebrowntours.com
Web site: www.eddiebrowntours.com
Dirs: Philip Brown, Deidree Brown.
Fleet: 49 - single-deck coach, midicoach, minicoach.
Chassis: Dennis. MAN. Mercedes. Neoplan. Scania. Setra. Toyota.Volvo.
Bodies: Irizar. Neoplan. Plaxton. Reeve Burgess. Setra. Van Hool.
Ops incl: school contracts, excursions & tours, private hire, continental tours.
Livery: White/Orange/Red
Ticket system: Wayfarer

CHARTER COACH LTD
THE CONTROL TOWER OFFICES, THE AIRFIELD, TOCKWITH YO26 7QF
Tel: 01423 359655.
Fax: 01423 359459.
E-mail: expert.coaches@btinternet.com
Dir: Antoni LaPilusa.

COASTAL AND COUNTRY COACHES
THE GARAGE, FAIRFIELD WAY, WHITBY BUSINESS PARK, WHITBY YO22 4PU
Tel: 01947 602922
Fax: 01947 600830
E-mail: enquiries@coastalandcountry.co.uk
Web site: www.coastalandcountry.co.uk
Prop: C Vasey, J Vasey.
Fleet: 20 - 1 double-deck bus, 13 single-deck coach, 1 open-top bus. 1 midicoach, 1 minibus, 1 minicoach, 2 midibus
Chassis: 1 Bedford. 1 Bristol. 1 Dennis. 2 Leyland. 5 Mercedes-Benz. 11 Volvo.
Bodies: 1 Duple. 1 ECW. 1 Jonckheere. 2 Mercedes-Benz. 11 Plaxton. 1 Roe. 3 Van Hool.
Ops incl: local bus services, school contracts, excursions & tours, private hire.
Livery: White/Blue.
Ticket system: Wayfarer

COLLINS COACHES
CLIFFE SERVICE STATION, YORK ROAD, CLIFFE, SELBY YO8 6NN
Tel: 01757 638591
Fax: 01757 630196
E-mail: collins@coaches.hotmail.co.uk
Web site: www.collinscoaches.co.uk
Prop: Alan Collins.
Fleet: 5 - 4 coach, 1 midicoach
Chassis: 1 Mercedes. 4 Volvo.
Ops incl: school contracts, private hire.
Livery: White

COUNTRYSIDE BUS SERVICES
SOUTH GOWLAND, GOWLAND LANE, CLOUGHTON, SCARBOROUGH YO13 0DU
Tel: 01723 870790
Fax: 01273 870790
Tran Man: Piers Turner **Ptnr**: Mrs Jasmin M Turner.
Fleet: 2 minicoach.
Chassis/bodies: 2 LDV
Ops incl: local bus services, school contracts.
Livery: Yellow/Blue

JOHN DODSWORTH (COACHES) LT'D
WETHERBY ROAD, BOROUGHBRIDGE YO5 9HS.
Tel: 01423 322236.
Fax: 01423 324682.
Dir: John Dodsworth.
Fleet: 17 - 10 coach, 2 midicoach, 1 minicoach.
Chassis: 3 Mercedes. 12 Volvo.
Bodies: 10 Plaxton. 2 Reeve Burgess. 1 Onyx.
Ops incl: excursions & tours, private hire, continental tours, school contracts.
Livery: Cream/Orange.

FIRST YORK
45 TANNER ROW, YORK YO1 6JP
Tel: 01904 883000
Fax: 01904 883057
Web site: www.firstgroup.com
Man Dir: Richard Eames
Fleet: 100 - 12 double-deck bus, 86 single-deck bus, 2 midibus, articulated bus.
Chassis: 98 Volvo, 2 Optare
Bodies: 12 Alexander. 2 Optare. 86 Wright.
Ops incl: local bus services, school contracts.
Livery: Grey/Magenta/Blue.
Ticket System: Wayfarer.

154

HANDLEY COACHES
NORTH ROAD, MIDDLEHAM, NEAR LEYBURN DL8 4PJ
Tel: 01969 623216
Fax: 01969 624546
Dirs: Mr M Anderson, Mrs J Anderson, Mrs L Cooke
Fleet: 11 - 6 single-deck coach, 1 Midibus, 2 Midicoach, 2 minibus.
Chassis: 1 Ford Transit. 1 Iveco. 2 Scania. 2 Volvo.
Bodies: 2 Leyland. 3 Mercedes.
Ops incl: local bus services, private hire, school contracts.
Livery: White with black/Red logo

HARGREAVES COACHES
BRIDGE HOUSE, HEBDEN, SKIPTON BD23 5DE
Tel: 01756 752567
Fax: 01756 753768
E-mail: hargreaves.coaches@ukonline.co.uk
Prop: Mr A C Howick
Fleet: 7 - 3 single-deck coach, 1 double-dek coach. 2 midicoach, 1 minibus.
Chassis: 1 DAF. 1 LDV. 2 MAN. 2 Mercedes-Benz. 1 Scania.
Bodies: 1 Berkhof. 1Neoplan. 1 Noge. 2 Plaxton. 1 Van Hool. 1 Other.
Ops incl: local bus services, school contracts, private hire, continental tours.
Livery: Silver Grey/French Pink

HARROGATE COACH TRAVEL LTD
6 ST THOMAS WAY GREEN HAMMERTON YORK YO26 8BE
Tel: 01423 399600
Fax: 01423 3330785
Web site: www.harrogatecoachtravel.co.uk
E-mail: harrolgatecoach@aol.com
Fleet: 14 - 5 double-deck bus, 6 single-deck bus, 1 single-deck coach, 2 midibus.
Chassis: 4 Leyland. 1 Mercedes-Benz. 1 Optare. 8 Scania.
Bodies: 3 Alexander Dennis. 2 East Lancs. 1 Leyland. 2 Northern Counties. 1 Optare.1 Plaxton. 1 Roe. 3 Wright.
Ops incl: local bus services, school contracts. private hire.
Livery: Green/White
Ticket System: Wayfarer

HARROGATE & DISTRICT TRAVEL LTD
PROSPECT PARK, BROUGHTON WAY, STARBECK, HARROGATE HG2 2NY
Tel: 01423 884020
Fax: 01423 885670
Web site: www.harrogateanddistrict.co.uk www.the36.co.uk
Fleetname: Harrogate & District.
Ch Exec: Martin Gilbert
Man Dir: Dave Alexander **Fin Dir**: Jim Wallace
Fleet: 66 - 8 double-deck bus, 45 single-deck bus, 13 coach.
Chassis: 13 Dennis. 6 Leyland. 47 Volvo.
Bodies: 7 Alexander. 4 Northern Counties. 13 Plaxton. 42 Wright.
Ops incl: local bus services, school contracts.
Livery: Red/Cream.
Ticket System: Wayfarer 3
Part of the Blazefield group which is owned by Transdev

HOPWOOD COACHES
22 MAIN STREET, ASKHAM BRYAN YO23 3QU
Tel: 01904 707394
Dirs: P Hopwood, R Baker.
Fleet: 2 single-deck coach.
Chassis: 2 Alexander Dennis
Ops incl: school contracts, private hire.

INGLEBY'S LUXURY COACHES LTD
24 HOSPITAL FIELDS ROAD, FULFORD ROAD, YORK YO10 4DZ
Tel: 01904 637620
Fax: 01904 612944
Dir: C Ingleby **Fleet Eng**: R Atkinson
Ops: A Evans
Fleet: 12 - 8 coach, 2 midicoach, 2 minibus.
Chassis: 1 Bova. 1 Dennis. 4 Mercedes. 6 Volvo.
Bodies: 1 Bova. 2 Mercedes. 2 Plaxton. 1 Sitcar. 6 Van Hool.
Ops incl: private hire.
Livery: Blue/Cream

J. R. TRAVEL
36 CALF CLOSE, HAXBY YO3 3NS.
Tel: 01904 766233.
Ptnrs: R. Flatt, J. Smith.
Fleet: 10 - 3 double-deck bus, 3 coach, 4 double-deck coach.
Chassis: 3 Daimler. 3 Mercedes. 4 Neoplan.
Bodies: 1 East Lancs. 2 Neoplan. 2 Northern Counties. 2 Plaxton. 3 Taz.
Ops incl: local bus services, school contracts, excursions & tours, private hire, continental tours.
Livery: White with green/red stripes. (associated with Compass Royston Travel, Durham)

KINGS LUXURY COACHES
FERRY ROAD, MIDDLESBROUGH TS2 1PL.
Tel: 01642 243687.
Prop: K. E. King.
Fleet: 5 - 2 double-deck bus, 3 coach.
Chassis: 2 Scania. 3 Setra.
Bodies: 1 Jonckheere. 3 Setra. 1 Van Hool.
Ops incl: private hire, continental tours.
Livery: Yellow/White.

METRO COACHES
THE CONIFERS, DARLINGTON RD, STOCKTON-ON-TEES TS21 1PE
Tel: 07970 826115
E-mail: info@coachiremiddlesbrough.co.uk

PERRY'S COACHES
RICCAL DRIVE, YORK ROAD INDUSTRIAL PARK, MALTON YO17 6YE.
Tel: 01653 690500
Fax: 01653 690800
Web site: www.perrystravel.com
E-mail: info@perrystravel.com
Ptnrs: D J Perry (**Gen Man/Ch Eng**) Mrs A Holtby (**Co Sec**)
Fleet: 19 - 11 coach, 6 midicoach, 2 minicoach.
Chassis: 1 Dennis. 7 Mercedes. 1 Toyota. 9 Volvo.
Bodies: 1 Caetano. 2 Crest. 1 Jonckheere. 9 Plaxton. 3 Van Hool. 2 Sitcar.
Ops incl: local bus services, school contracts, excursions & tours, private hire, continental tours.
Livery: Red/White.

PROCTERS COACHES (NORTH YORKSHIRE) LTD
TUTIN ROAD, LEEMING BAR INDUSTRIAL ESTATE, LEEMING BAR, NORTHALLERTON DL7 9UJ
Tel: 01677 425203
Fax: 01677 426550
E-mail: enquiries@procterscoaches.co.uk
Web site: www.procterscoaches.co.uk
Man Dir: Kevin Procter **Fleet Eng**: Philip Kenyon **Tran Man**: Andrew Fryatt
Fleet: 56 - 31 coach, 1 double-deck coach, 2 midicoach, 22 minibus.
Chassis: 1 DAF. 5 Dennis. 1 Ford Transit. 1 Leyland. 13 Mercedes. 9 Optare. 1 Setra. 1 Van Hool. 23 Volvo.
Bodies: 1 Alexander. 1 Autobus. 5 Berkhof. 3 Jonckheere. 1 Mercedes. 9 Optare. 29 Plaxton. 1 Setra. 2 Transbus. 2 Van Hool. 1 Wright.
Ops incl: local bus services, school contracts, private hire, continental tours.
Livery: White
Ticket System: Wayfarer 3

RELIANCE MOTOR SERVICES
RELIANCE GARAGE, YORK ROAD, SUTTON-ON-FOREST, YORK YO61 1ES
Tel/Fax: 01904 768262
Web: www.reliancemotorservice.co.uk
E-mail: reliance.motors@btconnnect.com
Prop: John H Duff
Fleet: 10 - 4 double-deck bus, 4 single-deck bus, 1 single-deck coach, 1 midicoach.
Chassis: 1 DAF. 1 Mercedes. 8 Volvo.
Bodies: 1 Alexander Dennis. 2 East lancs. 1 Optare. 1 Van Hool. 5 Wright.
Ops incl: local bus services, school contracts, private hire.
Livery: Cream/Green
Ticket System: Wayfarer TGX

RONDO TRAVEL
LEVENS HALL PARK, LUND LANE, KILLINGHALL, HARROGATE HG3 2BG
Tel: 01423 526800
Fax: 01423 527800
E-mail: sales@rondotravel.co.uk
Web site: www.rondotravel.co.uk
Man Dir: J D Bullock **Duty Man**: M A Wilson **Traff Man**: N T Chatterton
Fleet: 3 coach
Chassis: 1 Scania, 2 Setra
Bodies: 2 Setra, 1 Van Hool
Ops incl: private hire, excursions & tours, continental tours.
Livery: Red/Gold.

SCARBOROUGH & DISTRICT
BARRY'S LANE, SCARBOROUGH YO12 4HA
Tel: 01723 500064
Fax: 01723 370064
E-mail: sd@eyms.co.uk
Web site: www.eyms.co.uk
Chmn: P J S Shipp **Fin Dir**: P Harrson
Com Man: R Rackley **Eng&Ops Man**: R Graham
Ops incl: local bus services, school contracts, excursions & tours, private hire, express, continental tours.
Livery: Burgundy/Cream
Ticket system: Wayfarer TGX150
A division of East Yorkshire Motor Services Ltd

SIESTA HOLIDAYS
LAMPORT STREET, MIDDLESBROUGH TS1 3RB
Tel: 0845 271 2443
Web site: www.siestaholidays.co.uk
Dir: Paul R Herbert **Co Sec**: Julie Marsh
Traffic Man: Patrick Steel
Fleet: 13 - 3 single-deck bus, 6 double-deck coach, 4 minibus.
Chassis: incl - Ford. 9 Scania.
Bodies: incl - 9 Berkhof. 2 Mercedes-Benz.
Ops incl: excursions & tours, private hire, continental tours.
Livery: Blue.

JOHN SMITH & SONS LTD
R24
THE AIRFIELD, DALTON, THIRSK YO7 3HE
Tel: 01845 577250
Fax: 01845 577752
E-mail: admin@johnsmithandsons.net
Web site: www.johnsmithandsons.net
Dirs: A N Smith, J Smith, T G Smith, I Smith (**Ops Man**) **Sec**: B White
Fleet: 23 - 1 double-deck bus, 2 single-deck bus, 11 coach, 4 midibus, 2 midicoach, 1 minibus, 2 minicoach.
Chassis: 1 Bedford. 14 DAF. 1 Ford. 2 Ford Transit. 3 Leyland. 2 Mercedes. 2 Neoplan.
Bodies: 1 Duple. 1 Mercedes. 3 Neoplan. 8 Plaxton. 1 Reeve Burgess. 2 UVG. 6 Van Hool.
Ops incl: local bus services, school contracts, excursions & tours, private hire, continental tours.
Livery: Green/Cream/Gold/Black
Ticket system: Wayfarer

STEPHENSONS OF EASINGWOLD LTD
MOOR LANE INDUSTRIAL ESTATE, THOLTHORPE, YORK YO61 1SR
Tel: 01347 838990
Fax: 01347 830189
E-mail: sales@stephensonsofeasingwold.co.uk
Web site: www.stephensonsofeasingwold.co.uk
Chairman: H J Stephenson, **Man Dir/Co Sec**: D A Stephenson **Ops Man**: Jonathan Hill

Fleet: 55 - 6 double-deck bus, 10 single-deck bus, 35 single-deck coach, 4 minibus.
Chassis: 1 Alexander Dennis. 3 DAF. 3 Dennis. 3 Leyland. 1 Leyland National. 1 MAN. 3 Mercedes-Benz. 2 Optare. 2 Scania. 36 Volvo.
Bodies: 1 Alexander Dennis. 1 Caetano. 2 Duple. 6 East Lans. 1 Jonkheere. 1 Leyland National. 2 Optare. 38 Plaxton. 3 Van Hool.
Ops incl: local bus services, school contracts, excursions & tours, private hire.
Livery: Cream or gold/orange & gold stripe
Ticket system: Wayfarer

STEVE STOCKDALE COACHES
(t/a Validford Ltd)
76 GREEN LANE, SELBY YO8 9AW
Tel: 01757 703549
Fax: 01757 210956
Dirs: S. Stockdale, J. Stockdale
Dir/Co Sec: Julie O'Neill
Fleet: 6 - 2 double-deck bus, 4 coach
Chassis: 2 Bedford. 2 Bristol. 2 Leyland.
Bodies: 2 Alexander. 2 Duple. 2 Plaxton.
Ops incl: local bus services, school contracts, private hire.
Livery: Red/White.
Ticket System: Almex.

THORNES INDEPENDENT LTD
THE COACH STATION, HULL ROAD, HEMINGBROUGH, SELBY YO8 6QG
Tel: 01757 630777
Fax: 01757 630666
Web: www.thornes.info
E-mail: coaches@thornes.info
Man Dir: P Thornes **Ch Eng**: S Cotton
Co Sec: C Thornes **Ops Man**: L J Thornes
Fleet: 18 - 3 double-deck bus, 1 single-deck bus, 8 single-deck coach, 2 midicoach, 4 heritage coach
Chassis: 1 Bedford. 1 Bristol. 1 DAF. 3 Dennis 2 Leyland. 2 Mercedes-Benz. 1 Seddon. 6 Volvo. 2 Other.
Bodies: 1 Beadle. 1 Duple. 4 East Lancs. 1 Harrington. 1 Optare. 10 Plaxton.
Ops incl: local bus services, school contracts, tours, private hire, continental tours
Livery: Blue/Grey/Red
Ticket System: Wayfarer Saver

TRANSDEV YORK
(formerly Topline Travel of York)
23 HOSPITAL FIELDS ROAD, FULFORD INDUSTRIAL ESTATE, YORK YO10 4EW
Tel: 01904 655585
Fax: 01904 655587
Web: www.toplinetravelofyork.co.uk
Web: www.yorktourbuses.co.uk
Web: www.transdevyork.co.uk
E-mail: toplinetravel@aol.com
Fleetname: York City Sightseeing
Cheif Exec: Martin Gilbert **Man Dir**: David Alexander **Fin Dir**: Jim Wallace
District & Gen man: Peter Dew
Fleet: 23 - 5 double-deck bus, 8 single-deck bus, 10 open-top bus.
Chassis: 1 DAF. 3 Dennis. 6 Leyland. 5 MCW. 7 Optare. 1 Volvo
Bodies: 5 Alexander. 4 East Lancs. 5 MCW. 8 Optare. 1 Wright.
Ops incl: local bus services, school contracts.
Livery: Red
Ticket System: Almex A90/Wayfarer TX150
(Part of the Blazefield Group which is owned by Transdev)

WINN BROS
8 MILL HILL CLOSE, BROMPTON DL6 2QP.
Tel: 01609 773520.
Fax: 01609 775234.

WISTONIAN COACHES
PLANTATION GARAGE, CAWOOD ROAD, WISTOW YO8 0XB.
Tel: 01757 269303.
Props: John Firth, Gordon Firth.
Fleet: 3 coach, 1 midicoach.
Chassis: 1 Bedford. 3 Volvo. **Bodies**: 4 Plaxton.
Ops incl: school contracts, private hire.
Livery: Cream, Red/Orange/Yellow stripes.

YORKSHIRE COASTLINER LTD
BUS STATION, RAILWAY STREET, MALTON YO17 7NR.
Tel: 01653 692556.
Fax: 01653 695341.
Web site: www.yorkshirecoastliner.co.uk
Prop: Blazefield Holdings Ltd.
Ops Man: Brian Kneeshaw
Fleet: 19 - 12 double-deck bus, 7 single-deck bus.
Chassis: 26 Volvo.
Bodies: 11 Alexander. 1 Northern Counties. 3 Plaxton. 13 Wright.
Ops incl: local bus services.
Livery: Cream/Blue.
Ticket System: Wayfarer 3
(Part of the Blazefield group which is owned by Transdev)

YORK PULLMAN BUS CO LTD
WETHERBY ROAD RUFFORTH YO23 3QA
Tel: 01904 622992
Fax: 01904 622993
Recovery: 07753 670742
E-mail: sales@yorkpullmanbus.co.uk
Web site: www.yorkpullmanbus.co.uk
Man Dir: Tom James **Acnts Man**: Maxine James (**Ops Man**) Kevin Walker **Chief Eng**: Paul Hirst
Fleet: 45 - 10 double-deck bus, 1 single-deck bus, 25 single-deck coach, 6 open-top bus. 2 midicoach, 1 minibus.
Chassis: 2 AEC. 1 Bedford. 1 Bova. 3 Bristol. 2 DAF. 1 Dennis. 2 Ford. 2 Iveco. 6 Leyland. 2 MAN. 2 MCW. 3 Scania. 1 Toyota. 17 volvo.
Bodies: 2 Alexander Dennis. 1 Berkof. 1 Bova. 1 Caetano. 2 Duple. 2 ECW. 3 East Lancs. 3 Leyland. 2 MCW. 2 Neoplan. 1 Northern Counties. 2 Park Royal. 22 Plaxton. 1 Other.
Ops incl: local bus services, school contracts, excursions & tours, private hire, continental tours.
Livery: York Pullman
Ticket system: Wayfarer

NORTHAMPTONSHIRE

GEOFF AMOS COACHES LTD
THE COACH STATION, WOODFORD ROAD, EYDON, DAVENTRY NN11 3PL
Tel: 01327 260522
Fax: 01327 262883
Recovery: 01327 260522
E-mail: sales@geoffamos.co.uk
Web site: www.geoffamos.co.uk
Dir: Shirley Smith, Brian Amos **Ops Man**: Brian Ellard **Ch Eng**: Kevin Wilson
Fleet: 23 - 9 double-deck bus, 7 single-deck bus, 6 single-deck coach, 1 midibus
Chassis: 4 Alexander Dennis. 9 Leyland. 4 MAN. 1 Mercedes. 1 Optare. 6 Volvo.
Bodies: 1 Caetano. 2 East Lancs 2 Jonkheere. 9 Leyland. 5 Marshall/MCV. 1 Plaxton. 3 Sunsundegui.
Ops incl: local bus services, school contracts, excursions & tours, private hire, continental tours.
Livery: buses: Yellow, coaches: Metallic
Ticket system: Wayfarer

J F BOWEN T/A JEFFS COACHES LTD
STATION ROAD, HELMDON, BRACKLEY NN13 5QT
Tel: 01295 768292
Fax: 01295 760365
E-mail: admin@jeffscoaches.com
Web site: www.jeffscoaches.com
Ch Exec: Kevin Lower **Man Dir**: Bob Lyng
Ops Man: Sarah Bayliss **Sales Man**: Fred Eaton **Conracts Man**: Eddie Rainbow
Wkshp Man: Clive Faulkner
Fleet: 58 - 8 double-deck bus, 1 single-deck bus, 47 coach, 2 midicoach.
Fleet: 4 Dennis. 6 Iveco. 8 Leyland . 2 Toyota. 38 Volvo.
Bodies: 6 Beulas. 23 Caetano. 8 Jonckheere. 8 Leyland. 9 Plaxton. 2 Van Hool. 2 other.
Ops incl: school contracts, excursions & tours.
Livery: White /Red/Green/Silver

L F BOWEN t/a YORKS COACHES
SHORT LANE, COGENHOE NN7 1LE
Tel: 01604 890210
Fax: 01604 891153
E-mail: yorksta@yorks-travel.co.uk
Web site: www.yorkstravel.com
Chmn: A H Moseley **Ch Exec**: K Lower
Man Dir (coaching): R Lyng group
Eng Man: D Hoy **Group Ops Man**: N G Tetley **Dirs**: C J Padbury, K G York
Man Dir: (retail): M Stones
Property Dir: N Ellis
Fleet: 26 - 23 single-deck coach, 2 midicoach, 1 minibus.
Chassis: 3 Dennis. 2 Irisbus. 1 LDV. 7 MAN. 1 Neoplan. 2 Scania. 2 Setra. 6 Volvo.
Bodies: 2 Beulas. 2 Caetano. 2 Irizar. 4 Marcopolo. 6 Noge. 5 Plaxton. 2 Setra. 1 Van Hool. 1 other.
Ops incl: local bus services, excursions & tours, school contracts, private hire, express, continental tours.
Livery: Silver
Ticket System: Almex

BRITTAINS COACHES LTD
SOUTHBRIDGE, COTTON END, NORTHAMPTON NN4 8BS.
Tel: 01604 765708.
Fax: 01604 700481.
Dirs: W. J. Cunningham, Mrs P. M. Brittain, Mrs J. Cunningham.
Co Sec: Miss C. Brittain. **Off Man**: M. Kelly.
Fleet: 7 - 3 double-deck bus, 4 coach.
Chassis: 3 Bristol. 2 DAF. 2 Scania.
Bodies: 3 Alexander. 2 Caetano. 2 Van Hool.
Ops incl: private hire.
Livery: White with Black lettering.

BUCKBY'S COACHES
3 FOX STREET, ROTHWELL, KETTERING NN14 6AN
Tel: 01536 710344
Tel: 01536 712244
Recovery: 07887945564
Prop: Minesh Uka.
Fleet: 10 - 1 double-deck bus, 1 single-deck bus, 6 coach, 1 double-deck coach, 1 minicoach.
Chassis: 1 Bedford. 2 Dennis. 1 Mercedes. 6 Volvo.
Bodies: 1 Duple. 1 East Lancs. 1 Jonckheere. 7 Plaxton.
Ops incl: local bus services, school contracts, excursions & tours, private hire, continental tours.

COUNTRY LION (NORTHAMPTON) LTD
87 ST JAMES MILL ROAD, NORTHAMPTON NN5 5JP
Tel: 01604 754566
Fax: 01604 755800
Dirs: J S F Bull, A J Bull
Fleet: 40 - 8 coach, 2 single-deck bus, 22 coach, 8 midicoach
Chassis: 6 Dennis. 6 Irisbus. 4 Leyland National. 8 Mercedes. 2 Scania. 14 Volvo.
Bodies: 1 Alexander. 6 Beulas. 1 East Lancs. 2 Irizar. 1 Jonckheere. 3 Northern Counties. 1 Optare. 19 Plaxton. 1 Van Hool. 4 Wadham Stringer
Ops incl: local bus services, school contracts, excursions & tours, continental tours, private hire.
Livery: First Group Magenta/Blue/Grey/White

FIRST NORTHAMPTON
ST JAMES' ROAD, NORTHAMPTON NN5 5JD
Tel: 01604 751431.
Fax: 01604 590522
Interim Man Dir: Maurice Bulmer **Fin Dir**: A Bhimani
Fleet: 75 - 42 double-deck bus, 24 single-deck bus, 5 coach, 4 minibus.
Chassis: 3 Bristol. 9 MCW. 4 Renault. 6 Scania. 45 Volvo.
Bodies: Alexander, East Lancs, Northern Counties, Wright.
Ops incl: local bus services, school contracts, private hire.
Livery: Cream/Red.
Ticket System: Wayfarer 3

GOODE COACHES
47 BURFORD AVENUE, BOOTHVILLE, NORTHAMPTON NN3 6AF
Tel: 01604 862700
Prop: David Goode **Tran Man**: Andrew Wall
Fleet: 5
Chassis: 1 DAF.4 Leyland.
Bodies: 1 Ikarus. 2 Plaxton. 2 Van Hool.
Ops incl: school contracts, private hire.
Livery: Cream/Maroon.

JCS COACHES
2 THE JAMB, CORBY NN17 1AY
Tel: 01536 202660
Fax: 01536 406299
E-mail: jambtravel@yahoo.co.uk
Props: Jackie Burton, Michael Burton
Fleet: 5 - 4 coach, 1 midicoach.
Chassis: 2 Bova. 2 DAF. 1 Mercedes.
Bodies: 2 Bova. 1 Caetano. 1 Ikarus. 1 Marshall.
Ops incl: excursions & tours, private hire.

J. R. J. COACHES
24 STALBRIDGE WALK, CORBY NN18 0DT.
Tel: 01536 200317.
Fax: 01536 394387.
Prop: J. D. Judge.
Fleet: 6 - 3 coach, 1 midicoach, 2 minibus.
Chassis: 1 Bedford. 1 Ford Transit. 1 Mercedes.
Bodies: 1 Caetano. 1 Carlyle. 1 Duple. 1 Mercedes.
Ops incl: local bus services, school contracts, excursions & tours, private hire

MARTINS COACHES
6 HAZEL ROAD, KETTERING NN16 7AL.
Prop: G. H. Martin.

R B TRAVEL
ISHAM ROAD, PYTCHLEY NN4 1EW
Prop: Roger Bull
Tel/Fax: 01536 791066
Fleet: 10 coach
Chassis: 6 DAF. 4 MAN.
Bodies: 2 Plaxton. 8 Van Hool.

RODGER'S COACHES LTD
102 KETTERING ROAD, WELDON NN17 3JG
Tel: 01536 200500
Fax: 01536 407407
E-mail: rodgerscoaches@hotmail.com
Props: James Rodger, Linda Rodger
Fleet: 14 - 7 double-deck bus, 7 single-deck bus.
Chassis: 1 DAF. 1 Dennis. 1 Leyland. 1 Scania. 10 Volvo.
Bodies: 2 Alexander. 2 East Lancs. 1 Ikarus. 4 Jonckheere. 2 Northern Counties. 2 Van Hool.
Ops incl: private hire, excursions & tours, continental tours.
Livery: White/Red

SOUL BROTHERS
See: Buckinghamshire

STAGECOACH EAST
ROTHERSTHORPE AVENUE,
NORTHAMPTON NN4 8UT
Tel: 01604 662266
Fax: 01604 662260

E-mail:
eastenquiries@stagecoachbus.com
Web site: www.stagecoachbus.com
Ops Dir: Michelle Hargreaves **Eng Dir**: Keith Dyball
Fleet: 305 - 102 double-deck bus, 13 single-deck bus, 26 coach, 102 midibus, 62 minibus.
Chassis: 1 Bristol. 124 Dennis. 32 Leyland. 9 Mercedes. 53 Optare. 5 Scania. 81 Volvo
Bodies: 99 Alexander. 1 ECW. 5 East Lancs. 31 Northern Counties. 53 Optare. 116 Plaxton.
Ops incl: local bus services, school contracts.
Livery: Stagecoach Group
Ticket System: ERG

NORTHUMBERLAND

ADAMSON'S COACHES
8 PORLOCK TOWER, NORTHBURN CHASE, CRAMLINGTON NE23 3TT
Tel/Fax: 01670 734050
Recovery: 07721 633351
E-mail: adamsonscoaches@btconnect.com
Prop: Allen Mullen **Ch Eng**: Paul Mullen
Co Sec: Mrs Wendy Mullen
Fleet: 3 coach
Chassis: 3 DAF
Bodies: 3 Van Hool
Ops incl: excursions & tours, private hire
Livery: White

HENRY COOPER
See Tyne & Wear.

CRAIGGS TRAVEL EUROPEAN
1 CENTRAL AVENUE, AMBLE, MORPETH NE65 0NQ
Tel/Fax: 01665 710614
Admin: J Craiggs **Eng**: I C Craiggs **Man**: L Craiggs
Fleet: 5 coach.
Chassis: 1 DAF. 1 Leyland 2 Setra. 1 Volvo.
Bodies: 1 Leyland. Plaxton. 2 Setra. 1 Van Hool.
Ops incl: excursions & tours, private hire, continental tours, school contracts.
Livery: Silver

GO NORTH EAST
See Tyne & Wear.

HILLARYS COACHES
20 CASTLE VIEW, PRUDHOE NE42 6NG
Tel/Fax: 01661 832560
Props: Lawrence Hillary
Fleet: 5 - 1 single-deck coach. 2 midicoach, 2 midibus.
Chassis/Bodies: 1 Caetano. 1 Ford. 1 Mercedes-Benz. 1 Toyota. 1 Volkswagen.
Ops incl: school contracts, excursions & tours, private hire.

LONGSTAFF'S COACHES
UNIT 107, AMBLE INDUSTRIAL ESTATE, AMBLE, MORPETH NE65 0PE
Tel: 01665 713200
Fax: 01665 710987
Man Dir: Frederick Longstaff **Co Sec**: Alison Longstaff **Ops Man**: Frederick Longstaff

Fleet: 9 - 7 coach, 1 midicoach
Chassis: 1 Leyland. 1 Mercedes. 1 Neoplan. 7 Volvo
Bodies: 1 Jonckheere. 1 Neoplan. 3 Plaxton. 3 Van Hool. 1 other
Ops incl: local bus services, excursions & tours, private hire, continental tours, school contracts.
Livery: Blue/Cream/Yellow.

PERRYMAN'S BUSES
NORTH ROAD INDUSTRIAL ESTATE, BERWICK UPON TWEED TD15 1TX
Tel: 01289 308719
Fax: 01289 309970
Web site: www.perrymansbuses.com
Dirs: R J Perryman L M Perryman
Fleet: 35-20 single deck bus, 5 Coach, 6 Midicoach, 4 Minibus.
Ops Inc: Local bus services, school contracts, private hire
Ticket System: Wayfarer.

ROWELL COACHES
3B DUKES WAY, PRUDHOE NE42 6PQ
Tel: 01661 832316
Fax: 01661 834485
E-mail: sales@rowellcoaches.co.uk
Web site: www.rowellcoaches.co.uk
Dirs: Mrs Gardiner, Mrs B Gardiner
Fleet: 10 coach
Chassis: 6 Bova. 4 Duple.
Ops incl: school contracts, excursions & tours, private hire.
Livery: White

SERENE TRAVEL
86A FRONT STREET EAST, BEDLINGTON NE22 5AB.
Tel: 01670 829636.
Fax: 01670 827961.
Web site: www.yell.co.uk/sites/serenetravel
Man Dir: Mrs C. E. Fielding. **Flt Eng**: G. J. Balsdon. **Co Sec**: D. A. Fielding.
Fleet: 17 - 7 single-deck bus, 6 coach, 2 midicoach, 2 minibus.
Chassis: 1 AEC. 2 Bedford. 1 Ford Transit. 1 Iveco. 3 Leyland. 6 Leyland National. 2 MCW. 1 Volvo.
Bodies: 2 Carlyle. 2 Duple. 6 Leyland National. 2 Optare. 4 Plaxton. 1 Burlingham.
Ops incl: local bus services, school contracts, excursions & tours, private hire, express.
Livery: Blue/Cream.
Ticket System: Wayfarer II.

TRAVELSURE
STATION ROAD, BELFORD NE70 7DT
Tel: 01668 219291
Fax: 01668 213947
E-mail: travelsure@travelsure.co.uk
Web site: www.travelsure.co.uk
Owner: Barrie Patterson
Fleet: 24 - 7 single-deck bus, 13 single-deck coach, 1 minibus, 3 minicoach.
Chassis: 2 Bova. 2 DAF. 5 Dennis. 3 Irisbus. 1 LDV. 2 Leyland. 8 Mercedes-Benz. 1 Volvo.
Bodies: 4 ALexander Dennis. 3 Beulas. 2 Bova. 2 Caetano. 1 ECW. 2 Optare. 4 Plaxton. 1 Reeve Burgess. 1 Setra. 3 Van Hool. 1 other.
Ops incl: local bus services, school contracts, excursions & tours, private hire, continental tours.
Livery: Blue.
Ticket System: Wayfarer

TYNEDALE GROUP TRAVEL
TOWNFOOT GARAGE, HALTWHISTLE NE49 0EJ.
Tel: 01434 322944.
Fax: 01434 322955.
E-mail: admin@tynedalegrouptravel.co.uk
Web site: www.tynedalegrouptravel.co.uk
Ptnr: Andy Sinclair.
Fleet: 6 - 1 single-deck coach, 3 midibus, 2 midicoach.
Chassis: 5 Mercedes. 1 Volvo.
Bodies: 4 Plaxton, 1 Van Hool, 1 other.
Ops incl: local bus servcices, school contracts, excursions & tours, private hire, continental tours.

TYNE VALLEY COACHES LTD
ACOMB, HEXHAM NE46 4QT
Tel: 01434 602217
Fax: 01434 604150
Fleet: 20 - 1 single-deck bus, 18 single-deck coach, 1 midibus.
Chassis: 1 DAF. 12 Leyland. 1 Optare. 6 Volvo.
Bodies: 4 Duple. 2 Optare. 13 Plaxton. 1 Van Hool.
Ops incl: local bus services, school contracts, private hire
Livery: Blue/Silver
Ticket System: AES

NOTTINGHAMSHIRE, NOTTINGHAM

BAILEY'S COACHES LTD
EEL HOLE FARM, LONG LANE, WATNALL NG16 1HY.
Tel: 0115 968 0141
Fax: 0115 968 1101.
Dirs: T. Bailey (**Gen Man & Traf Man**), Mrs J. Bailey (**Sec**).
Ch Eng: G. Payne.
Fleet: 10 - 2 double-deck bus, 6 coach 2 double-deck coach.
Chassis: Bristol. DAF. Duple. Volvo.
Bodies: 10 Duple. 3 Others.
Ops incl: local bus services, school contracts, excursions & tours, private hire, continental tours.
Livery: White with Yellow/Brown/Orange stripes.

BUTLER BROTHERS COACHES
60 VERNON ROAD, KIRKBY IN ASHFIELD NG17 8ED
Tel: 01623 753260
Fax: 01623 754581
E-mail: butlerscoaches@btconnect.com
Dirs: Robert Butler, Anita Butler, James Butler.
Fleet: 9 - 1 double-deck bus, 7 coach, 1 midicoach.
Chassis: 2 DAF. 3 Dennis. 1 Leyland. 2 MAN. 1 Volvo.
Bodies: 1 Berkhof. 2 Caetano. 1 East Lancs. 2 Plaxton. 3 Van Hool.
Ops incl: school contracts, excursions & tours, private hire, continental tours.
Livery: Dual Blue
Ticket System: Wayfarer

DUNN-LINE (HOLDINGS) LTD
BEECHDALE ROAD, BEECHDALE, NOTTINGHAM NG8 3EU
Tel: 0115 916 9000
Fax: 0115 942 0578
Web site: www.veolia-transport.co.uk
Fleet: 230 - 54 double-deck bus, 22 single-deck bus, 66 coach, 1 double-deck coach, 1 open-top bus, 82 midibus, 4 minibus.
Chassis: 1 Bova. 1 DAF. 6 Dennis. 4 Leyland National. 5 MAN. 23 MCW. 42 Mercedes. 43 Optare. 9 Scania. 3 Transbus. 93 Volvo.
Bodies: 24 Alexander. 1 Bova. 16 Caetano. 1 Duple. 1 ECW. 19 East Lancs. 3 Irizar. 4 MCV/Marshall. 23 MCW. 4 Mellor. 3 Mercedes. 3 Northern Counties. 44 Optare. 68 Plaxton. 5 Sunsundegui. 3 Transbus. 8 Van Hool.
Ops incl: local bus services, school contracts, private hire, express, continental tours.
(part of the Veolia Group)

GOSPEL'S COACHES
27 ASCOT DRIVE, HUCKNALL NG15 6JA
Tel: 0115 963 3894
Dirs: T Gospel, G Gospel, G T Gospel
Fleet: 4 - 2 double-deck bus, 2 coach.
Chassis: 2 Leyland. 2 Volvo.

Bodies: 1 Alexander. 1 Northern Counties. 2 Plaxton.
Ops incl: excursions & tours, private hire, school contracts.
Livery: White/Blue.

HENSHAWS COACHES
57 PYE HILL ROAD, JACKSDALE NG16 5LR
Tel: 01773 607909
Prop: Paul Henshaw
Fleet: 6 - 5 coach, 1 midicoach
Chassis: Bova, DAF, Leyland, MAN, Mercedes
Bodies: Bova, Duple, Hispano, Noge, Van Hool.
Ops incl: excursions & tours, private hire, school contracts, continental tours.
Livery: Cream/Orange/Brown

JOHNSON BROS TOURS
GREEN ACRE, GREEN LANE, HODTHORPE, WORKSOP S80 4XR
Tel: 01909 720337 / 721847
Fax: 01909 722886
Recovery: 01909 720337
E-mail: lee@johnsonstours.co.uk
Web site: www.johnsonstours.co.uk
Fleetname: Redfern Travel
Dirs Tony Johnson, Lee Johnson, Anthony Johnson, Scott Johnson, Colleen Johnson, Sheila Johnson
Fleet: 111 - 65 double-deck bus, 1 single-deck bus, 35 single-deck coach, 3 double-deck coach, 1 midibus, 4 midicoach, 1 minibus, 1 minicoach.
Chassis: 4 Bova. 40 Bristol. 1 DAF. 2 Ford Transit. 5 Irisbus. 5 Iveco. 1 LDV. 10 Mercedes-Benz. 5 Neoplan. 1 Optare. 10 Scania. 10 Volvo.
Ops incl: local bus services, school contracts, excursions & tours, private hire, continental tours.
Livery: Blue/Green

K & S COACHES
21 CLIFTON GROVE, MANSFIELD NG18 4HY.
Tel/Fax: 01623 656768.
Prop: K. & Sue Burnside.
Fleet: 4 - 1 midicoach, 3 minicoach.
Chassis/bodies: Ford Transit. Mercedes. Renault. Talbot.
Ops incl: school contracts, excursions & tours, private hire.
Livery: White/Red/Grey.

KETTLEWELL (RETFORD) LTD
GROVE STREET, RETFORD DN22 6LA
Tel: 01777 860360
Fax: 01777 710351
E-mail: paulkettlewell@btconnect.com
Man Dir: Paul Kettlewell **Tour Man:** Christine Kettlewell **Senior Officer:** Margaret Burton **Ops Man:** Tony Bradley
Fleet: 15 - 1 double-deck coach, 12 single-deck coach, 1 double-deck coach, 1 minicoach.

Chassis: 1 MAN. 1 Mercedes-Benz. 1 Neoplan. 10 Scania. 2 Other.
Bodies: 1 East Lancs. 7 Irizar. 2 Neoplan. 1 Plaxton. 1 Van Hool. 3 Other.
Ops incl: school contracts, excursions & tours, private hire, continental tours.
Livery: White
Ticket System: Wayfarer

MARSHALLS OF SUTTON-ON-TRENT LTD
11 MAIN STREET, SUTTON-ON-TRENT NG23 6PF.
Tel: 01636 821138
Fax: 01636 822227
Recovery: 01636 821138
E-mail: office@marshallscoaches.co.uk
Web site: www.marshallscoaches.co.uk
Prop: J. A. Marshall. **Eng Dir:** P. J. Marshall **Financial Dir:** S E Sloan
Ops Man: K G Tagg
Fleet: 27 - 8 double-deck bus, 2 single-deck bus, 8 single-deck coach, 5 midibus, 2 midicoach,1 minibus, 1 minicoach
Chassis: 2 Dennis. 1 Irisbus. 3 Leyland. 1 MAN. 1 MCW. 2 Mercedes-Benz.1 Neoplan. 6 Optare. 10 Volvo.
Bodies: 5 Alexander. 1 Berkhof. 2 East Lancs.1 Indecar. 1 MCW. 1 Meercedes-Benz. 6 Optare. 9 Plaxton.
Ops incl: local bus services, school contracts, excursions & tours, private hire, continental tours.
Livery: Blue/Cream.
Ticket System: Almex & Wayfarer

MAUN CRUSADER TOURS
NEW CROSS HOUSE, 8-10 MANSFIELD ROAD, SUTTON-IN-ASHFIELD NG17 4GR.
Tel: 01623 555621.
Fax: 01623 555671.
Dirs: R. A. Read (**Gen Man/Traf Man**), N. G. Barks (**Sec**). **Ch Eng:** S. Palmer.
Fleet: 17 - 8 double-deck bus, 8 single-deck bus. 1 midicoach.
Chassis: 3 DAF, 1 Daimler. 5 Dennis. 2 Leyland. 1 MAN. 1 Mercedes. 4 Integral.
Bodies: 1 Alexander. 1 Caetano. 6 Duple. 1 East Lancs. 1 Jonckheere. 1 Marco Polo. 4 Northern Counties. 1 Plaxton. 1 SC.
Ops incl: private hire, continental tours, school contracts.
Livery: Multi-coloured.

C. W. MOXON LTD
MALTBY ROAD, OLDCOTES, WORKSOP S81 8JN.
Tel: 01909 730345.
Fax: 01909 733670.
Web site: www.moxons-tours.co.uk
Fleetname: Moxons Coaches.
Dirs: Mrs L. Marlow, Mrs M. Moxon, **Co Sec:** Mrs J. Holder, **Ch Eng:** M. Marlow.
Fleet: 15 - 3 double-deck bus, 12 coach.
Chassis: 2 Bedford. 3 Bristol. 7 DAF. 2 Leyland. 1 Iveco.
Bodies: 2 Bova. 1 Duple. 3 MCW. 5 Plaxton. 3 Van Hool. 1 Eos.
Ops incl: excursions & tours, private hire, continental tours, school contracts.
Livery: Cream/Red.

159

NOTTINGHAM CITY TRANSPORT

LOWER PARLIAMENT STREET, NOTTINGHAM NG1 1GG
Tel: 0115 950 5745
Fax: 0115 950 4425
E-mail: shiela.swift@nctx.co.uk, info@nctx.co.uk
Web site: www.nctx.co.uk
Chmn: Brian Parbutt **Man Dir**: Mark Fowles **Eng Dir**: Barry Baxter **Fin Dir/Co Sec**: Rob Hicklin **Mktg & Comms Dir**: Nicola Tidy **Comm Man**: Barrie Burch
Fleet Eng: Farrell Smith
Fleet: 335 - 161 double-deck bus, 74 single-deck bus, 5 articulated bus, 95 midibus
Chassis: 54 Dennis. 108 Optare. 149 Scania. 23 Volvo.
Bodies: 114 East Lancs. 51 Scania. 54 Transbus. 5 Wright.
Ops incl: local bus services
Livery: Multi-Branded
Ticket system: Almex

NOTTINGHAM EXPRESS TRANSIT

LAWRENCE HOUSE, TALBOT STREET, NOTTINGHAM NG1 5NT
Tel: 0115 915 6600
Web site: www.thetram.net, www.nottinghamcity.gov.uk, www.nottinghamexpresstransitco.uk, www.netphasetwo.com
Concession Co: Arrow Light Rail (Bombardier, Carillion, Transdev, Nottingham City Transport, Inisfree, CDC Projects)
Commercial Manager: Colin Lea
Fleet: 15 tram
Chassis/bodies: Bombardier
Ops incl: tram service
Livery: Green/White

PATRON TRAVEL

GLEBE COTTAGE, 1 FOSSE WAY, FLINTHAM NG23 5LH
Tel: 01636 525725
Fax: 01636 525731
Prop: Ron Todd
Fleet: 3 - 1 double-deck bus, 2 coach.
Chassis: 1 Leyland. 2 Volvo
Bodies: 1 Alexander. 2 Jonckheere.
Ops incl: continental tours, private hire, school contracts.
Livery: Cream

PREMIERE TRAVEL LTD

TRENT WHARF, MEADOW LANE, NOTTINGHAM NG2 3HR
Tel: 0115 985 1111
Fax: 0115 986 3366
E-mail: sales@premiere-travel.co.uk
Web site: www.premiere-travel.co.uk
Ops incl: Local bus service, private hire, school contracts.
Livery: Red/Silver

REDFERN COACHES (MANSFIELD) LTD

LINDLEY STREET, MANSFIELD NG18 1QE

Tel: 01623 27653
Fax: 01623 25787
E-mail: enquiries@johnsonstours.co.uk
Web site: www.johnsonstours.co.uk
Ops incl: local bus services, excursions & tours, private hire, express, continental tours, school contracts.
Livery: Green/Faded Green/Gold (Subsidiary of Johnsons Tours)

SHARPE & SONS (NOTTINGHAM) LTD

UNIT 10, CANALSIDE INDUSTRIAL PARK, CROPWELL BISHOP, NOTTINGHAM NG12 3BE
Tel: 0115 989 4466
Fax: 0115 989 4666
E-mail: trevor.sharpe@sharpesofnottingham.com
Web site: www.sharpesofnottingham.com
Man Dir: Trevor Sharpe **Ops Dir**: James Sharpe
Fleet: 20 - 1 double-deck bus, 3 single-deck bus, 16 coach, 1 double-deck coach.
Chassis: 2 Leyland. 1 Leyland National. 17 Volvo.
Bodies: 1 Alexander. 2 Leyland. 1 Leyland National. 16 Van Hool
Ops incl: local bus services, school contracts, private hire, continental tours, excursions & tours.
Livery: Silver Blue/Navy Blue

SILVERDALE TOURS LTD

LITTLE TENNIS STREET SOUTH, NOTTINGHAM NG2 4EU
Tel: 0115 912 1000
Fax: 0115 912 1558
E-mail: info@silverdaletours.co.uk
Web site: www.silverdaletours.co.uk
Dir: Shaun Doherty
Fleet: 39 - 6 double-deck bus, 3 single-deck bus, 26 coach, 2 double-deck coach, 2 midicoach
Chassis: 2 Ayats. 2 DAF. 3 Leyland National. 2 Mercedes. 30 Volvo.
Bodies: 5 Beulas. 19 Caetano. 3 Jonckheere. 3 Leyland National. 8 Plaxton. 1 Van Hool.
Ops incl: local bus services, private hire, express, school contracts, continental tours.
Livery: Yellow/Red/Black

SKILLS HOLIDAYS

BELGRAVE ROAD, NOTTINGHAM NG6 8LY
Tel: 0115 977 0080
Fax: 0115 977 7436
E-mail: pete.hallam@skillsholidays.co.uk
Web site: www.skillsholidays.co.uk
Man Dir: Nigel Skill **Fin Dir**: Simon Skill
Comm Dir: Roy Fitch **Ops Dir**: Pete Hallam
Fleet: 38 - 4 double-deck bus, 30 coach, 2 midibus, 2 midicoach.
Chassis: 2 MAN. 4 MCW. 18 Mercedes. 13 Volvo.
Bodies: 7 Jonckheere. 4 MCW. 1 Plaxton. 16 Setra. 6 Van Hool. 4 other.
Ops incl: school contracts, excursions & tours, private hire, continental tours.
Livery: Green
Livery: White with red and blue

TIGER EUROPEAN

UNIT E PRIVATE ROAD, NO 4 COLWICK INDUSTRIAL ESTATE, NOTTINGHAM NG2 2JT
Tel: 01159 404040
Fax: 01159 404030
E-mail: info@tiger-european.com
Web site: www.tiger-european.co.uk.
Dirs: Mr G Golaz, Mrs B Golaz.
Fleet: 15 - 2 double-deck bus, 3 single-deck bus, 3 single-deck coach, 1 double-deck coach, 1 midicoach, 5 minibus
Chassis: 4 Ford. 1 LDV. 3 Leyland. 1 MAN. 1 MCW. 2 Mercedes-Benz. 3 Volvo.
Bodies: 1 Caetano. 2 Jonkheere. 2 Leyland. 1 Marsahll/MCV. 1 Plaxton. 8 Other.
Ops incl: School contracts, private hire

TRANSIT EXPRESS TRAVEL

UNIT 7, EVANS BUSINESS PARK, RADMARSH ROAD, LENTON, NOTTINGHAM NG7 2GN
Tel: 0115 970 2900
Fax: 0115 970 5515
E-mail: garycrosby@hotmail.com
Prop: Gary M Crosby
Fleet: 8 - 4 coach, 2 midicoach, 2 minicoach.
Chassis: 1 Bedford. 2 Ford. 2 Ford Transit. 2 Leyland. 1 MAN.
Bodies: 1 Caetano. 1 Duple. 2 Plaxton. 1 Reeve Burgess. 3 other.
Ops incl: private hire.
Livery: Blue/White

TRAVEL WRIGHT LTD

BRUNEL BUSINESS PARK, JESSOP CLOSE, NEWARK NG24 2AG
Tel: 01636 703813
Fax: 01636 674641
E-mail: info@travelwright.fsnet.co.uk
Web site: www.travelwright.co.uk.
Dirs: Terry Wright, David Wright, Colin Wright, Paula Allen. .
Chassis: 1 Alexander Dennis. 8 Dennis. 7 MAN. 5 Mercedes-Benz. 1 Neoplan. 2 Optare. 1 Scania. 1 Setra. 2 Van Hool. 2 Volvo.
Bodies: 1 Aleaxander Dennis. 7 Caetano. 3 Jonckheere. 3 Neoplan. 2 Noge. 3 Optare. 3 Plaxton. 1 Setra 1 UVG. 3 Van Hool.
Ops incl: local bus services, school contracts, excursions & tours, private hire, continental tours.

UNITY COACHES

BECK GARAGE, CLAYWORTH DN22 9AG.
Tel: 07777 817556.
Ptnrs: F. Marriott, Mrs J. Marriott.
Livery: Blue/Grey/Cream.

WALLIS COACHWAYS

100 GRILLINGTON ROAD, BILSTHORPE NG22 8SP
Tel: 01623 870655
Fax: 01623 870655
Prop: Stephen Wallis
Fleet: 2 - 1 midibus, 1 midicoach.
Chassis/Bodies: 1 Mercedes. 1 Toyota
Ops incl: school contracts, private hire
Livery: White
Ticket system: Almex

OXFORDSHIRE

BAKERS COMMERCIAL SERVICES
UNIT 5A, ENSTONE BUSINESS PARK, ENSTONE OX7 4NP
Tel: 01608 677415/6
Fax: 01608 677150
E-mail: enquiries@bakerscoaches.co.uk
Web site: www.bakerscoaches.co.uk
Prop: Mike Baker **Ops Man:** Dave Goodall **Ch Eng:** Dave Nappin
Fleet: 12 - 11 coach, 1 minibus, 2 minicoach.
Chassis: 6 Dennis. 3 Mercedes. 5 Volvo.
Bodies: 1 Berkhof. 1 Caetano. 11 Plaxton.
Ops incl: local bus services, school contracts, excursions & tours, private hire, continental tours.
Livery: Red on White.

BANBURYSHIRE ETA LTD
UNIT 17, BEAUMONT BUSINESS CENTRE, BEAUMONT CLOSE, BANBURY OX16 7TN
Tel: 01295 263777
Fax: 01295 273086
E-mail: bcta@msn.com
Fleetname: Cherwell District Dial-A-Ride
Fleet: 3 minibus
Chassis/Bodies: 2 Mercedes. 1 Peugeot
Ops incl: local bus services, private hire

BLUNSDON'S COACH TRAVEL
73 GROVE ROAD, BLADON OX20 1RJ
Tel: 01993 811320
Fax: 01993 811416
E-mail: blunsdons-coaches@merlyn73.wanadoo.co.uk
Dirs: Merlyn H Blunsdon, Michael A Blunsdon
Fleet: 5 coach
Chassis: 5 Dennis.
Bodies: 2 Neoplan. 3 Plaxton.
Ops incl: private hire, school contracts, excursions & tours
Livery: White with Red/Green.

CHARLTON-ON-OTMOOR SERVICES
THE GARAGE, CHARLTON-ON-OTMOOR OX5 2UQ.
Tel: 01865 331249.
Fax: 01865 316189.

CHENEY COACHES LTD
THORPE MEAD, BANBURY OX16 4RZ
Tel: 01295 254254
Fax: 01295 271990
E-mail: travel@cheneycoaches.co.uk
Web site: www.cheneycoaches.co.uk
Chmn: G W Peace **Man Dir:** M R Peace
Co Sec: S A Peace **Dir:** A G Peace **Fleet Eng:** Tony Piotrowski
Fleet: 45 - 1 double-deck bus, 34 coach, 1 midicoach, 9 minibus.
Chassis: 2 DAF. 1 Dennis. 7 Ford Transit. 1 LDV. 2 Mercedes. 1 Neoplan. 4 Scania. 23 Volvo. 3 other.
Bodies: 1 Berkhof. 4 Caetano. 11 Jonckheere. 2 Mercedes. 1 Neoplan. 7 Plaxton. 10 Van Hool.
Ops incl: school contracts, private hire

GRAYLINE COACHES
STATION APPROACH, BICESTER OX26 6HU
Tel: 01869 246461
Fax: 01869 240087
E-mail: sales@grayline.co.uk
Web site: www.grayline.co.uk
Dirs: A Gray, B Gray **Ops Man:** P Gray
Traff Man: S Gray
Fleet: 17 - 8 single-deck coach, 9 midibus.
Chassis: 1 Bedford. 2 Dennis. 5 Iveco. 1 MAN. 4 Mercedes-Benz. 4 Optare.
Bodies: 5 Beulas. 1 Mercedes-Benz. 4 Optare. 7 Plaxton.
Ops incl: school contracts, local bus services, private hire, continental tours.
Livery: White/Red/Blue
Ticket System: Wayfarer 3

HEYFORDIAN TRAVEL LTD
MURDOCK ROAD, BICESTER OX26 4PP.
Tel: 01869 241500.
Fax: 01869 360011.
E-mail: info@heyfordian.co.uk
Web site: www.heyfordian.co.uk
Dir: Graham Smith
Fleet: 85 - 4 double-deck bus, 11 70 coach, 2 double-deck coach, 3 minibus. 3 minicoach.
Chassis: 8 Bova. 8 DAF. 2 Dennis. 27 Leyland. 1 MAN. 4 Optare. 20 Scania. 15 Volvo.
Bodies: 7 Alexander. 8 Bova. 4 Caetano. 31 Jonckheere. 2 Neoplan. 4 Optare. 25 Plaxton. 4 Van Hool.
Ops incl: local bus services, school contracts, excursions & tours, private hire, continental tours.
Livery: White/Red/Orange/Black.
Ticket System: Wayfarer.

McLEANS COACHES
UNIT 5, TWO RIVERS INDUSTRIAL ESTATE, STATION LANE, WITNEY OX28 6BH.
Tel: 01993 771445.
Fax: 01993 779556
Dirs: Roger Alder, Mark Hepden
Fleet: 18 - 14 coach. 4 midicoach.
Chassis: MAN. Mercedes. Neoplan. Volvo.
Bodies: incl. Sunsundegui
Ops incl: local bus services, school contracts, excursions & tours, private hire.
Livery: White/Red.

OXFORD BUS COMPANY
COWLEY HOUSE, WATLINGTON ROAD, OXFORD OX4 6GA
Tel: 01865 785400
E-mail: info@oxfordbus.co.uk
Web site: www.oxfordbus.co.uk
Man Dir: Philip Kirk **Ops Dir:** Louisa Weeks **Eng Dir:** Ray Woodhouse **Fin Dir/Comm Dir:** Helen Le Fevre
Fleet: 146 - 28 double-deck bus, 76 single-deck bus, 39 single-deck coach, 3 midibus.
Chassis: 31 Dennis. 48 Mercedes-Benz. 12 Scania. 55 Volvo.
Bodies: 20 Alexander. 12 Irizar. 6 Jonckheere. 48 Mercedes-Benz. 36 Plaxton. 24 Wright.
Ops incl: local bus services, express.
Livery: Red (local bus) Green (express/park & ride) Blue (airline)
Ticket System: Wayfarer
Subsidiary of the Go Ahead Group

PEARCES PRIVATE HIRE
TOWER ROAD INDUSTRIAL ESTATE, BERINSFIELD, WALLINGFORD OX10 7LN
Tel: 01865 340560.
Fax: 01865 341582.
Props: Clive Pearce, Martin Pearce.
Fleet: 12 - 8 coach, 2 midicoach, 2 minicoach.
Chassis: 1 Bova. 6 Dennis. 2 Mercedes. 1 Scania. 2 Toyota.
Bodies: 1 Bova . 2 Caetano. 2 Neoplan. 6 Plaxton. 1 Van Hool.
Ops incl: school contracts, excursions and tours, private hire.
Livery: Yellow/White

PLASTOWS COACHES
134 LONDON ROAD, WHEATLEY OX33 1JH
Tel: 01865 872270
Fax: 01865 875066
E-mail: plastowscoaches@btconnect.com
Web site: www.plastows.co.uk
Fleet: 9 coach.
Chassis: 9 Volvo.
Ops incl: private hire, school contracts.

STAGECOACH IN OXFORDSHIRE
HORSPATH ROAD, COWLEY OX4 2RY
Tel: 01865 772250
Fax: 01865 405500
E-mail: oxford.enquiries@stagecoachbus.com
Web site: www.stagecoachbus.com/warwickshire
Man Dir: Martin Sutton **Service Delivery Dir:** Paul O'Callaghan
Fleet: 176 - 38 double-deck bus, 57 single-deck bus, 5 coach, 25 double-deck coach, 21 minibus, 30 midibus.
Chassis: 49 Dennis. 44 MAN. 33 Mercedes. 25 Neoplan. 18 Optare. 5 Scania. 32 Volvo.
Bodies: 106 Alexander. 5 Caetano. 25 Neoplan. 18 Optare. 21 Plaxton. 1 UVG.
Ops incl: local bus services, express, school contracts.
Livery: Stagecoach corporate
Ticket system: Wayfarer 3

TAPPINS COACHES
COLLETT ROAD, SOUTHMEAD PARK, DIDCOT OX11 7ET
Tel: 01235 819393
Fax: 01235 816464
E-mail: coaches@tappins.co.uk
Web site: www.tappins.co.uk
Man Dir: G Smith **Comp Sec**: Jeremy Smith **Dirs**: Andrew Smith, Roland Smith
Fleet: 45 - 1 double-deck bus, 2 single-deck bus, 39 single-deck coach, 1 double-deck coach, 2 minicoach.
Chassis: incl - Neoplan. Volvo.
Bodies: incl - Caetano. Plaxton. Van Hool.
Ops incl: local bus services, school contracts, excursions & tours, private hire, express.
Livery: Orange/Black
Ticket System: Wayfarer.
Subsidiary of Heyfordian Travel

THAMES TRAVEL
WYNDHAM HOUSE, LESTER WAY, WALLINGFORD OX10 9TD
Tel: 01491 837988
Fax: 01491 838562
E-mail: office@thames-travel.co.uk
Web site: www.thames-travel.co.uk
Dirs: John Wright, Barbara Wood
Fleet: 33 - 4 double-deck bus, 29 single-deck bus
Chassis: 5 Alexander Dennis. 18 MAN. 2 Optare. 7 Scania. 1 Volvo.
Bodies: 5 Alexander Dennis. 5 East Lancs. 18 Marsahll/MVC. 2 Optare. 3 Other
Ops incl: local bus services
Livery: Green/Blue
Ticket system: Wayfarer

WORTHS MOTOR SERVICES LTD
ENSTONE, CHIPPING NORTON OX7 4LQ
Tel: 01608 677322
Fax: 01608 677298
E-mail: worths.coaches@ukonline.co.uk
Web site: www.worthscoaches@ukonline.co.uk
Dirs: Richard Worth, Paul Worth **Ch F**: Mike Florey **Comp Sec**: Mrs P North
Fleet: 21 - 2 double-deck bus, 2 single-deck bus, 16 single-deck coach, 1 midicoach
Chassis: 1 Alexander Dennis. 2 Leyland. 1 Mercedes-Benz. 1 Optare.
Bodies: 1 Caetano. 1 Jonckheere. 2 Leyland. 1 Optare 19 Plaxton.
Ops incl: local bus services, school contracts, continental tours, private hire.
Livery: Silver/Blue
Ticket System: Wayfarer

SHROPSHIRE

ASTONS OF NEWPORT
STATION GARAGE, NEWPORT TF10 7EN
Tel/Fax: 01952 811285
Dirs: E. H. Aston, J. E. Aston, P. T. H. Aston
Fleet: 4 - 1 single-deck bus, 2 coach, 1 minibus.
Chassis: 2 Bedford. 1 Ford Transit. 1 Renault
Bodies: 1 Duple. 1 Northern Counties. 1 Plaxton. 1 Ford.
Ops incl: school contracts, private hire.

BOULTONS OF SHROPSHIRE LTD
SUNNYSIDE, CARDINGTON, CHURCH STRETTON SY6 7JZ
Tel: 01694 771226
Fax: 01694 771296
Dirs: M Boulton, G Boulton
Fleet: 17 - 6 single-deck bus, 6 coach, 5 midicoach
Chassis: 6 Bova. 1 BMC. 5 Mercedes
Bodies: 1 BMC. 6 Bova. 5 Mercedes
Ops incl: local bus services, school contracts, excursions & tours, private hire, continental tours.
Livery: Cream/Orange/Brown
Ticket System: Microfare

A T BROWN (COACHES) LTD
FREEMAIN HOUSE, HORTON ENTERPRIS E PARK, HORTON WOOD, TELFORD TF1 6PY
Tel: 01952 605331
Fax: 01952 608011
E-mail: atbrowncoaches@aol.com
Web site: www.atbrowncoaches.co.uk
Dirs: Nina Macleod, Ewen Macleod
Fleet: 12 - 10 coach, 2 midicoach
Chassis: 9 DAF. 1 Dennis. 2 Mercedes.
Bodies: 1 Autobus. 3 Caetano. 1 Ikarus. 5 Plaxton. 2 Van Hool.
Ops incl: school contracts, private hire, excursions & tours.
Livery: Sky Blue/Navy

BUTTERS COACHES LTD
LEWELLYN ROBERTS WAY, (OFF MAER LANE), MARKET DRAYTON TF9 1QS
Tel: 01630 658470
Fax: 01630 658490
E-mail: butterscoaches@hotmail.com
Dirs:
Erica Mackintosh, Lesley Mackintosh, Barry Managh.
Fleet: 10 - 9 coach, 1 minibus.
Chassis: 6 DAF. 1 Dennis. 1 LDV. 1 Leyland. 1 Volvo.
Bodies: 1 Jonckheere. 7 Van Hool. 2 other.
Ops incl: local bus services, school contracts, excursions & tours, private hire.
Livery: Blue lettering on White

CARADOC COACHES
UNIT 3, CROSSWAYS INDUSTRIAL ESTATE, CHURCH STRETTON SY6 6PQ
Tel/Fax/Recovery: 01694 724522
Prop: G Gough
Fleet: 9 - 2 coach, 2 midicoach, 4 minibus, 1 minicoach
Chassis: 1 Iveco. 4 LDV. 1 Leyland. 1 Mercedes. 1 Toyota. 1 Volvo.
Bodies: 1 Caetano. 1 Mercedes. 3 Plaxton. 4 other.
Ops incl: local bus services, school contracts, excursions & tours, private hire.

COURTESY TRAVEL
2 WOODFIELD AVENUE, SHREWSBURY SY3 8HT
Tel/Fax: 01743 358209
E-mail: courtesy@tiscali.co.uk
Prop: John Amies.
Fleet: 2 - 1 minicoach, 1 midicoach.
Chassis: 1 LDV. 1 Mercedes.
Bodies: 1 Autobus. 1 other.
Ops incl: excursions & tours, private hire.
Livery: Blue/White

ELCOCK REISEN
THE MADDOCKS, MADELEY, TELFORD TF7 5HA
Tel: 01952 585712
Fax: 01952 582577
Man Dir: J C Elcock **Dirs**: J H Prince, J D Ashley **Ops Man**: Mark Perkins **Gen Man**: Pete Taylor
Fleet: 35 - 28 coach, 4 midicoach, 3 minicoach.
Chassis: 7 Mercedes. 28 Volvo.
Bodies: 2 Autobus. 2 Esker. 31 Plaxton.
Ops incl: school contracts, excursions & tours, private hire, continental tours.
Livery: Silver/Red/Gold

HAPPY DAYS COACHES
See Staffordshire

HOLMES GROUP TRAVEL
CHAPEL HOUSE, 6 STAFFORD ROAD, NEWPORT TF10 7LY
Tel: 01952 820477
Fax: 01952 270607
Fax: 07831 258084
Dir: C Holmes
Fleet: 3 - coach
Chassis: includes 1 Mercedes, 1 Volvo.
Bodies: 1 Mercedes. 1 Plaxton.
Ops incl: excursions & tours, private hire.
Livery: White with flag emblem

HORROCKS
IVY HOUSE, BROCKTON, LYDBURY NORTH SY7 8BA.
Tel: 01588 680364
Prop: A P Horrocks
Fleet: 9 - 2 double-deck bus, 2 single-deck bus, 5 midibus.
Chassis: 1 Bedford. 1 Bristol. 1 Daimler. 1 Dodge. 1 LDV. 4 Mercedes. 1 Volvo.
Ops incl: school contracts, private hire
Livery: White/Blue

LAKESIDE COACHES LTD
THE COACH CENTRE, ELLESMERE BUSINESS PARK, ELLESMERE SY12 0EW
Tel: 01691 622761
Fax: 01691 623694
E-mail: mailbox@lakesidecoaches.co.uk
Web site: www.hiremeacoach@lakesidecoaches.co.uk
Man Dir: John Davies **Dirs**: Dorothy Davies, Gareth Davies **Man**: Neal Hall
Fleet: 20 - 15 single-deck coach, 4 midicoach, 1 minicoach
Chassis: 1 DAF. 2 Dennis. 3 Mercedes-Benz. 3 Toyota. 11 Volvo.
Bodies: 5 Caetano. 3 Mercedes-Benz. 11 Plaxton. 1 Van Hool.
Ops incl: local bus service, excursions & tours, private hire, school contracts.
Livery: Green/White

LONGMYND TRAVEL LTD
THE COACH DEPOT, LEA CROSS, SHREWESBURY SY5 8HX
Tel: 01743 861999
Fax: 01743 861901
E-mail: info@longmyndtravel.co.uk
Dirs: T G Evans, F J Evans, V Sheppard-Evans, D M Sheppard.
Fleet: 22 - 19 coach, 2 midicoach, 1 minibus
Chassis: 2 DAF. 1 Iveco. 1 Mercedes. 1 Toyota. 17 Volvo.
Bodies: 1 Berkhof. 2 Bova. 2 Caetano. 16 Jonckheere.
Ops incl: school contracts, private hire.
Livery: Red/White

M & J TRAVEL
COACH GARAGE, NEWCASTLE, CRAVEN ARMS SY7 8QL.
Tel: 01588 640273.
Prop: W. M. Price.
Fleet: 13 - 7 coach, 1 midicoach, 5 minibus.
Chassis: 4 Bedford. 2 Dennis. 1 Toyota. 1 Talbot.
Bodies: 1 Caetano. 2 Duple. 4 Plaxton.
Ops incl: school contracts, excursions & tours, private hire, continental tours.
Livery: White/Black/Gold.
Ticket System: Setright.

M P MINICOACHES
14 REDBURN CLOSE, KETLEY GRANGE TF2 0EE
Tel: 01952 415607
Fax: 01952 619188
Dir: Mark Perkins
Fleet: 3 minicoach.
Chassis: 3 Mercedes.
Bodies: 3 other

Ops incl: school contracts, private hire.
Livery: Two-tone Blue

MINSTERLEY MOTORS SERVICES LTD
STIPERSTONES, MINSTERLEY, SHREWSBURY SY5 0LZ
Tel: 01743 791208
Fax: 01743 790101
E-mail: john@minsterleymotors.co.uk
Web site: www.minsterleymotors.co.uk
Man Dir: John Jones
Fleet: 25 - 8 single-deck bus, 18 single-deck coach, 1 midibus, 2 midicoach.
Chassis: 5 Bedford. 6 Scania. 7 Volvo.
Bodies: 2 Mercedes-Benz. 5 Plaxton.
Ops incl: local bus services, school contracts, excursions & tours, private hire, continental tours.
Livery: Blue/White
Ticket system: Wayfarer

N.C.B. MOTORS LTD
EDSTASTON GARAGE, WEM, SHREWSBURY SY4 5RF
Tel: 01939 232379
Fax: 01939 234892
E-mail: mail@ncb-motors.co.uk
Web site: www.ncb-motors.co.uk
Dirs: Paul Brown (**Comp Sec**), Derek Brown
Fleet: 14 single-deck coach
Chassis: 14 Volvo.
Bodies: 1 Duple. 6 Jonckheere. 6 Plaxton. 1 Van Hool
Ops incl: private hire, school contracts.
Livery: Brown/Cream

OWENS COACHES LTD
36 BEATRICE STREET, OSWESTRY SY11 1QG
Tel: 01691 652126
Fax: 01691 670047
Web site: www.owenstravel.co.uk
Recovery: 01691 839944
Dir: Michael Owen **Co Sec**: Joyce Horton
Ops Man: Peter Worthy
Fleet name: Travelmaster
Fleet: 21 - 4 single-deck bus, 14 coach, 1 midicoach, 2 minibus.
Chassis: 2 Ayats. 1 DAF. 2 Dennis. 1 Irisbus. 1 Iveco. 3 MAN. 3 Mercedes. 2 Toyota. 6 Volvo.
Bodies: 2 Ayats. 2 Berkhof. 1 BMC. 3 Caetano. 1 Jonckheere. 1 Marcopolo. 1 Mercedes. 1 Noge. 7 Plaxton. 1 UVG. 1 Wright.
Ops incl: local bus services, excursions & tours, private hire, continental tours, school contracts.

R & B TRAVEL
PLEASANT VIEW, KNOWLE, LUDLOW SY8 3NE.

Tel/Fax: 01584 890770.
Prop: A T Radnor, L Radnor.
Fleet: 11 - midibus,
Chassis: 2 Bedford. 2 Leyland DAF. 1 Ford Transit. 2 VW. 1 Iveco. 2 Volvo.
Bodies: Duple. Optare. Plaxton. Robin Hood. Wright.
Ops incl: Local bus services, school contracts, private hire, excursions & tours.
Livery: Silver/Red/Orange/White

RIVERSIDE COACHWAYS LTD
HEATH HILL, DAWLEY TF4 2JU
Tel: 01952 505490
Fax: 01952 505590
Prop: K H Pollen
Fleet: 13 - included 2 double-deck buses, 1 double-deck coach
Chassis: includes - Bristol. Ford. Volvo.
Ops Incl: private hire, school contracts
Livery: Blue/Silver and Blue/White

SHROPSHIRE COUNTY COUNCIL
INTEGRATED TRANSPORT UNIT, 107 LONGDEN ROAD, SHREWSBURY SY3 9DS.
Tel: 01743 245300
Fax: 01743 253279
E-mail: peter.ralphs@shropshire-cc.gov.uk
Web site: www.shropshireonline.gov.uk
Fleetname: Fleet Operations
Ch Exec: Carolyn Downs **Gen Man Transp**: Adrian Millard **Fleet Ops Off**: Peter Ralphs.
Fleet: 55 - 1 single-deck bus, 51 minibus, 2 midicoach, 1 midibus.
Chassis: 1 Ford Transit. 30 Iveco. 13 LDV. 8 Mercedes. 1 Optare. 2 Renault.
Ops incl: local bus services, school contracts.
Livery: White
Ticket system: Almex

WORTHEN TRAVEL
ALDERBURY ROAD, SHREWSBURY SY5 9NA
Tel: 01743 792622
Fax: 01743 791053
Recovery: 01743 792622
E-mail: jackie@worthentravel.freeserve.co.uk
Prop: D A Pye **Gen Man**: C L Robinson **Sec**: J Davies
Fleet: 20 - 2 single-deck bus, 15 coach, 3 minibus.
Chassis: 5 DAF. 1 Ford Transit. 7 other.
Bodies: 3 Caetano. 4 Leyland. 3 Van Hool.
Ops incl: local bus services, school contracts, excursions & tours, private hire, express, continental tours.
Livery: White/Blue
Ticket system: Wayfarer 2

	Vehicle suitable for disabled		Seat belt-fitted Vehicle
T	Toilet-drop facilities available		Coach(es) with galley facilities
R	Recovery service available		Air-conditioned vehicle(s)
	Open top vehicle(s)v		Coaches with toilet facilities
R24	24 hour recovery service		Replacement vehicle available
			Vintage Coach(es) available

SHROPSHIRE

SOMERSET (ALSO BATH & N E SOMERSET, N SOMERSET)

A1 TRAVEL
80 HIGHFIELD ROAD, YEOVIL BA21 4RJ
Tel/Fax: 01935 477722
Web site: www.a1travelservices.com
Dir: Ian Watson
Fleet: 5 - 2 midibus, 3 minibus.
Chassis: 1 Ford. 2 Freight Rover. 2 LDV. 1 Mercedes. 1 Setra.
Bodies: include 1 Plaxton. 1 Setra.
Ops incl: school contracts, private hire.

ARLEEN COACH HIRE & SERVICES LTD
14 BATH ROAD, PEASEDOWN ST JOHN, BATH BA2 8DH
Tel: 01761 434625
Fax: 01761 436578
E-mail: arleen.coach-hire@virgin.net
Web site: www.arleen.co.uk
Dir: A W Spiller **Co Sec**: Mrs M K Spiller
Dir: A A Spiller **Ops Man**: J C Spiller **Ch Eng**: K T Spiller
Fleet: 23 - 20 single-deck bus, 3 minicoach.
Chassis: 2 Bedford. 3 DAF. 2 Dennis. 1 Ford. 1 LDV. 2 Leyland. 2 MAN. 6 Mercedes. 2 Neoplan. 2 Volvo.
Bodies: 1 Berkhof. 3 Duple. 6 Mercedes. 5 Plaxton. 3 Van Hool. 1 Wadham Stringer. 2 other.
Ops incl: school contracts, excursions & tours, private hire.
Livery: Red/White/Blue

AXE VALE COACHES
BIDDISHAM, AXBRIDGE BS26 2RD
Tel: 01934 750321
Fax: 01934 750334
Ptnrs: A L Bailey, C P Bailey (**Ops**), J Bailey **Ch Eng**: J Bailey
Fleet: 12 - 10 coach, 1 midicoach, 1 minibus.
Chassis: 7 Bova. 2 DAF. 1 Ford. 1 LDV. 1 Mercedes.
Bodies: incl: 7 Bova. 1 Leyland. 3 Plaxton.
Ops incl: local bus services, school contracts, excursions & tours, private hire, express, continental tours.
Livery: White
Ticket system: Setright

BAKERS COACHES YEOVIL
8 BUCKLAND ROAD, YEOVIL BA21 5EA.
Tel: 01935 428401.
Fax: 01935 410423
Recovery: 01935 428401
E-mail: bakers@bakerscoaches.1global.org.uk
Dirs: S Baker
Fleet: 13 - 10 single-deck coach, 2 midicoach, 1 minicoach.
Chassis: DAF. Ford Transit. Iveco. Volvo
Bodies: Beulas. Jonckheere. Mercedes-Benz. Van Hool.
Ops incl: school contracts, excursions & tours, private hire, continental tours.
Livery: White

BAKERS DOLPHIN COACH TRAVEL
48 LOCKING ROAD, WESTON-SUPER-MARE BS23 3DN
Tel: 01934 635635.
Fax: 01934 641162.
E-mail: coach.hire@bakersdolphin.com
Web site: www.bakersdolphin.com
Chmn: John Baker **Man Dir**: Tim Newcombe **Ch Eng**: Mark Vearncombe
Mktg Dir: Amanda Harrington **Ops Dir**: Max Fletcher **Ops Man**: Chris Rubery
Fin Controller: Steve Hunt
Fleet: 75 - 68 single-deck coach, 3 double-deck coach, 1 midicoach, 2 minibus, 1 minicoach
Chassis: 4 Bedford. 1 Bova. 1 Dennis. 5 Iveco. 2 LDV. 15 Leyland. 2 Mercedes. 45 Volvo.
Bodies: 5 Beulas. 1 Bova. 3 Jonckheere. 2 LDV. 1 Mercedes. 1 Optare. 34 Plaxton. 28 Van Hool.
Ops incl: local bus services, excursions & tours, private hire, express, continental tours, school contracts.
Livery: Blue/White/Green/Yellow.
Ticket System: Setright

BATH BUS COMPANY
6 NORTH PARADE, BATH BA1 1LF.
Tel: 01225 330444.
Fax: 01225 330727.
E-mail: hq@bathbuscompany.com
Web site: www.bathbuscompany.com
Chmn: Peter Newman **Man Dir**: Martin Curtis. **Dir**: Dr. Mike Walker. **Eng Dir**: Collin Brougham-Field. **Co Sec/Dir**: Rob Bromley. **Com Dir**: Keith Tazewell.
Fleet: 11 double-deck bus, 7 single-deck bus, 3 minibus.
Chassis: 1 AEC, 6 Bristol, 6 Dennis, 3 Leyland-DAB, 3 Leyland, 3 MCW. 4 Mercedes.
Bodies: 1 Alexander. 6 ECW. 1 Leyland. 3 MCW. 1 Park Royal. 3 Plaxton. 6 Wright.
Ops incl: local bus services, excursions & tours, private hire.
Livery: Red/Primrose.
Ticket System: Wayfarer/BBC punch system.
Subsidiary of Ensignbus

BERRY'S COACHES (TAUNTON) LTD
CORNISHWAY WEST, NEW WELLINGTON ROAD, TAUNTON TA1 5NA
Tel: 01823 331356
Fax: 01823 322347
E-mail: info@berryscoaches.co.uk
Web site: www.berryscoaches.co.uk
Dirs: S A Berry, P I Berry
Fleet: 30 - 25 coach, 5 double-deck coach.
Chassis: 30 Volvo.
Bodies: 3 Jonckheere. 7 Plaxton. 20 Van Hool.
Ops incl: local bus services, school contracts, excursions & tours, private hire, express, continental tours.
Livery: White/Red/Orange
Ticket system: Setright

BLAGDON LIONESS COACHES LTD
MENDIP GARAGE, BLAGDON BS40 7TL
Tel: 01761 462250
Fax: 01761 463237
Recovery: 01761 462250
Dir: T M Lyons **Gen Man**: M A Lyons
Fleet: 3 - 2 coach, 1 minibus
Chassis: 1 Bova. 1 Leyland. 1 Mercedes
Bodies: 1 Bova. 2 Plaxton.
Ops incl: local bus services, excursions & tours, private hire, school contracts.
Livery: White
Ticket System: Wayfarer

BLUE IRIS COACHES
See Bristol

BUGLERS COACHES LTD
29 VICTORIA BUILDINGS, LOWER BRISTOL ROAD, BATH BA2 3EH
TEL: 01225 444422
Fax: 01225 466665
E-mail: info@buglercoaches.co.uk
Website: www.buglercoaches.co.uk
Prop: Computer Village Group
Ops Incl: Local bus service, Private hire, School Contracts
Livery: Red/White/Yellow

CENTURION TRAVEL LTD
WEST ROAD GARAGE, WELTON, MIDSOMER NORTON, RADSTOCK BA3 2TP
Tel: 01761 417392
Fax: 01761 417369
E-mail: coach-hire@centuriontravel.co.uk
Web site: www.centuriontravel.co.uk
Man Dir: Martin Spiller
Fleet: 23 - 17 coach, 1 minibus, 4 minicoach.
Chassis: 2 Bedford. 2 Bova. 4 DAF. 3 Dennis. 6 Mercedes. 1 Scania. 2 Volvo. 1 Ford limo.
Bodies: 1 Autobus. 1 Berkhof. 2 Bova. 1 Caetano. 3 Duple. 1 Esker. 1 Irizar. 2 Jonckheere. 1 Marcopolo. 1 Mercedes. 3 Optare. 2 Plaxton. 2 Van Hool
Ops incl: school contracts, private hire, continental tours, excursions & tours.
Livery: Red/Cream/Burgundy

CLAPTON COACHES
1 HAYDON ESTATE, RADSTOCK BA3 3RD
Tel: 01761 431936
Fax: 01761 431935
E-mail: claptonholidays@btconnect.com
Dirs: S C Lippet, M C Lippet.
Fleet: 12 - 6 coach, 5 minicoach.
Bodies: 6 Bova.
Ops incl: excursions & tours, private hire, continental tours.
Livery: Lilac

COOKS COACHES
VICTOR HOUSE, GREENHAM BUSINESS PARK, WELLINGTON TA21 0LR
Tel: 01823 672247
Fax: 01823 673101
E-mail: landylines@aol.com
Web site: www.cookscoaches-somerset.co.uk
Man Dir: Paul Landymore
Ops Dir: Nigel Billinger.
Fleet: 60 - 21 single-deck bus, 1 coach, 8 midicoach, 12 midibus, 14 minibus, 4 minicoach.
Chassis: 1 Dennis. 1 Iveco. 16 LDV. 21 Mercedes. 21 Optare.
Bodies: 4 Alexander. 3 Autobus. 1 Berkhof. 21 Optare. 9 Plaxton. 2 UVG. 1 Wadham Stringer.
Ops incl: local bus services, school contracts, private hire.
Livery: White with Red/Blue
Ticket System: Almex Optima (Part of Stagecoach)

COOMBS TRAVEL
COOMBS HOUSE, SEARLE CRESCENT, WESTON-SUPER-MARE BS23 3YX
Tel: 01934 428555
Fax: 01934 428559
E-mail: coombscoaches@aol.com
Proprietors: B. F. Coombs, R Coombs
Traffic Man: Mrs J E Carroll **Ass Traf Man**: C Winser **Comp Sec**: Mrs M Lillie **Ch Eng**: J Ellis
Fleet: 30 - 1 double-deck bus, 15 single-deck coach, 5 midibus, 2 midicoach, 5 minibus, 2 minicoach.
Chassis: 3 Aleaxander Dennis. 3 Dennis. 6 Ford Transit. 5 LDV. 7 Mercedes-Benz. 10 Scania. 1 Toyota.
Bodies: 1 Alexander Dennis. 1 Caetano. 1 ECW. 2 Irizar. 10 Plaxton. 1 Reeve Burgess. 1 UGV. 3 Van Hool.
Ops incl: local bus services, school contracts, private hire.
Livery: Yellow/White
Ticket system: Setright

FIRST SOMERSET & AVON LTD
OLDMIXON CRESCENT, WESTON-SUPER-MARE BS24 9AY
Tel: 01934 620122
Fax: 01934 415859
Recovery: 0117 955 4442
Web site: www.firstgroup.com
Man Dir: Justin Davies
Fin Dir: Mike Gahan
Fleet: 460 - 85 double-deck bus, 10 articulated single-deck bus, 106 single-deck bus, 8 coach, 124 midibus, 127 minibus.
Ops incl: local bus services, school contracts, excursions & tours, express, private hire.
Livery: First
Ticket System: Wayfarer

LANGSON VIP LTD
5 TWEED ROAD, CLEVEDON BS21 6RR
Tel: 01275 340053
Fax: 01275 343035
E-mail: enquires@langsonvip.com
Web site: www.langsonvip.com
Proprietor: Chris Langson.
Fleet: 5- 2 double-deck bus, 3 single-deck bus.

HUTTON COACH HIRE
95 MOORLAND ROAD, WESTON-SUPER-MARE BS23 4HS
Tel: 01934 618292
Fax: 01934 641362
E-mail: hutton-coach-hire.co.uk
Owner: John Lawrence **Man**: Wendy Dover
Fleet: 4 - 2 coach, 1 minibus, 1 midicoach.
Chassis: 1 Dennis. 1 MAN. 1 Mercedes. Volvo.
Ops incl: private hire, school contracts.
Livery: Maroon with orange/green logo

QUANTOCK MOTOR SERVICES LTD
UNIT 13A, TAUNTON TRADING ESTATE, NORTON FITZWARREN TA2 6RX
Tel: 01823 251140
Fax: 01823 251833
E-mail: sales@quantockmotorservices.co.uk
Web site: www.quantockmotorservices.co.uk
Man Dir: Steve Morris **Dir**: Liz Ranson
Fleet Eng: Paul Smith **Trans Man**: Jonathan Pratt **Supervisor**: Willaim Ricketts
Fleet: 69 - 12 double-deck bus, 30 single-deck bus, 18 single-deck coach, 1 double-deck coach, 6 open-top bus, 2 minbus.
Chassis: incl - 14 Bristol. 2 Dennis. 2 Volo.
Bodies: 20 ECW. 2 Esker. 14 Van Hool.
Ops incl: local bus services, private hire, school contracts, excursions & tours.
Livery: Red with Gold lettering
Ticket system: Wayfarer 3

RIDLERS LTD
JURY ROAD GARAGE, DULVERTON TA22 9EJ
Tel: 01398 323398
Fax: 01398 324398
E-mail: info@ridlers.co.uk
Web site: www.ridlers.co.uk
Dirs: G Ridler, S Ridler **Ops Man**: M E Jamieson
Fleet: 16 - 14 single-deck coach, 2 midicoach.
Chassis: 6 Dennis. 1 Iveco. 2 Leyland. 5 Scania. 2 Toyota.
Bodies: 1 Berkhof. 2 Caetano. 5 Duple. 2 Irizar. 4 Plaxton. 2 Van Hool.
Ops incl: local bus services, school contracts, excursions & tours, continental tours, private hire
Livery: White/Red/Silver.
Ticket system: Almex

D. W. SKELTON
90 BROADWAY, CHILTON POLDEN TA7 9EQ.
Tel: 01278 722066.
Fax: 01278 722608.
Fleetname: Skelton Tours.
Prop: D. W. Skelton.
Fleet: 3 coach.
Chassis: 1 Ford. 2 MAN.
Bodies: 1 Neoplan. 1 Plaxton. 1 MAN.
Ops incl: excursions & tours, private hire, continental tours.
Livery: Black/Green/Gold.

SMITH'S COACHES (B.E. & G.W. SMITH)
BYFIELDS, PYLLE BA4 6TA.
Tel: 01749 830126
Fax: 01749 830888
Prop: Graham Smith
Fleet: 14 coach.
Chassis: 3 Bedford. 3 Leyland. 8 Volvo.
Bodies: 14 Plaxton.
Ops incl: school contracts, private hire.
Livery: Maroon/Cream

SOMERBUS LIMITED
64 BROOKSIDE, PAULTON, BRISTOL BS39 7YR
Tel: 07831 234616

SOMERSET (ALSO BATH & N E SOMERSET, N SOMERSET)

165

Fax: 01761 415456
Web site: www.somerbus.co.uk
E-mail: somerbus@tinyworld.co.uk
Man Dir: Tim Jennings
Fleet: 4 - 4 single-deck bus.
Chassis: 1 Mercedes. 3 Optare.
Bodies: 3 Optare. 1 Plaxton.
Ops incl: local bus services, school contracts
Livery: Orange/White
Ticket system: Wayfarer Saver

SOUTH WEST COACHES LTD/SOUTH WEST TOURS LTD
SOUTHGATE ROAD, WINCANTON BA9 9EB
Tel: 01963 33124
Fax: 01963 31599
E-mail: info@southwestcoaches.co.uk
Web site: www.southwestcoaches.co.uk
Man Dir: A M Graham **Co Sec**: S Graham
Comm Dir: S Caine **Eng Man**: K Jeffrey
Traff Man: J A Hiscock **Tours Man**: D Green
Fleet: 72 - 11 single-deck bus, 34 coach, 8 midibus, 2 midicoach, 17 minibus.
Chassis: 3 Bedford. 1 BMC. 1 DAF. 3 Dennis. 1 Ford. 10 Ford Transit. 2 LDV. 13 Leyland. 10 Mercedes. 4 Optare. 5 Setra. 2 VW. 17 Volvo.
Bodies: Alexander. Berkhof. BMC. Caetano. Duple. East Lancs. Jonckheere. Leyland. Mercedes. Optare. Plaxton. Setra. Van Hool.
Ops incl: local bus services, school contracts, excursions & tours, private hire, continental tours.

Livery: White with Red/Blue stripes
Ticket System: Paycell/Wayfarer

STONES OF BATH
LOWER BRISTOL ROAD, BATH BA2 3DR
Tel: 01225 422267
Fax: 01225 442209
E-mail: stonescoaches@compuserve.com
Senior Ptnr: D G Stone, **Ops Man**: C G Stone, **Ch Eng**: S M Stone, **Sec/Fin**: Mrs N R Russell
Fleet: 13 - 10 double-deck coach, 3 midicoach
Chassis: DAF. Neoplan. Scania. Toyota.
Bodies: Bova. Irizar. Neoplan. Van Hool.
Ops incl: excursions & tours, school contracts, private hire, continental tours.
Livery: Cream/Red

TAYLORS COACH TRAVEL LTD
PLOT 10, BYMPTON WAY, LYNX WEST TRADING ESTATE, YEOVIL BA20 2HP
Tel: 01935 427556
Fax: 01935 423177
E-Mail: taylorscoachtravel@tintinhull.fsworld.co.uk
Web site: www.taylorscoachtravel.co.uk
Man Dir: D D J Elliott **Co Sec**: Mrs T R Elliott **Eng Dir**: D Porter **Ops Dir**: M D Kirkland
Fleet: 46 - 34 coach, 7 midicoach, 5 minibus.
Chassis: 2 Autosan. 2 Bova. 4 BMC. 3 DAF. 3 Dennis. 4 Irisbus. 4 Iveco. 2 LDV. 6 Leyland. 1 Mercedes. 15 Volvo.
Bodies: 2 Autosan. 3 Alexander. 4 BMC. 2

Bova. 2 Duple. 3 Indcar. 2 Leyland. 1 Mercedes. 10 Plaxton. 1 Reeve Burgess. 12 Van Hool. 1 Wadham Stringer. 3 Vehixel.
Ops incl: local bus services, private hire, school contracts, excursions & tours, continental tours
Livery: Burgundy/White/Yellow/Gold
Ticket system: Wayfarer

TRAVELINE
SUMMERLAND CAR PARK, MINEHEAD TA24 5BN.
Tel: 01643 704774, 821883.
Fax: 01643 821883.
Dirs: D. C. & P. A. Grimmett.
Fleet: 1 coach. **Chassis/Body**: Bova.
Ops incl: excursions & tours, private hire, continental tours.

WEBBER BUS
BRUE AVENUE, BRIDGWATER TA6 5LT
Tel: 01278 452086
Fax: 01278 455250
E-mail: sales@webberbus.com
Web site: www.webberbus.com
Man Dir: Tim Webber **Ops Dir**: David Webber
Fleet: 38 - 25 coach, 3 midicoach, 7 minibus, 3 midibus.
Chassis: incl: 2 Bova. 1 DAF. 5 Ford Transit. 5 Irisbus. 2 LDV. 4 Optare.
Bodies: incl: 2 Bova. 4 Optare. 11 Plaxton. 4 Van Hool.
Ops incl: local bus services, school contracts, excursions & tours, private hire
Ticket system: Wayfarer

SOUTH YORKSHIRE

ANDERSON COACHES LTD
4 HOLLY BANK AVENUE, SHEFFIELD S12 2BL
Tel: 0114 239 9231
Fax: 01709 364750
Fleet: 5 - 3 coach, 2 minibus.
Chassis: 2 Dennis. 1 Ford Transit. 1 LDV. 1 Neoplan.
Ops incl: excursions & tours, private hire

ASHLEY TRAVEL LTD t/a GRANT & McALLIN
8A STATION ROAD, MOSBOROUGH, SHEFFIELD S19 5AD.
Tel: 0114 251 1234.
Fax: 0114 251 1900.
Dirs: R. Atack (**Gen Man/Traf Man**), T. F. Atack (**Ch Eng/Sec**).
Fleet: 3 coach.
Chassis: 1 Bedford. 2 Volvo.
Bodies: 3 Plaxton.
Ops incl: excursions & tours, private hire.
Livery: Turquoise/Blue/White.

BUCKLEYS TOURS LTD
STONEHAVEN, GATEHOUSE LANE, AUCKLEY, DONCASTER DN9 3EJ
Tel: 01302 770379.
Man Dir: Richard Buckley.
Fleet: 2 double-deck coach.
Chassis/Bodies: Mercedes/Neoplan.
Ops incl: excursions & tours.

BURDETTS COACHES LTD
8 STATION ROAD, MOSBOROUGH, SHEFFIELD S20 5AD
Tel: 0114 248 2341
Fax: 0114 247 5733
Dir: F. Burdett
Fleet: 12 coach.
Chassis: 2 Leyland. 10 Volvo.
Bodies: 2 Plaxton. 10 Van Hool.
Ops incl: private hire

BYRAN TOURS LTD
31 SUSSEX STREET, SHEFFIELD S4 7YY
Tel/Fax: 0114 270 0060
Dir/Owner: Julie Scott **Dir**: Dennis Heaton
Fleet: 6 - 3 minibus, 3 minicoach.
Chassis: 1 Ford. 4 Mercedes.
Bodies: include 1 Setra.
Ops incl: school contracts, excursions & tours, private hire.
Livery: White/Jade/Black.

CLARKSONS HOLIDAYS
See West Yorkshire

COOPERS TOURS LTD
ALDRED CLOSE, NORWOOD INDUSTRIAL ESTATE, KILLAMARSH S21 2JH
Tel: 0114 248 2859.
Fax: 0114 248 3867.
E-mail: sales@cooperstours.co.uk
Web site: www.cooperstours.co.uk
Dirs: Alan Cooper, Graham Cooper.
Fleet: 8 coach.
Chassis: 1 AEC. 2 Leyland. 1 MAN. 3 Volvo.
Bodies: 2 Berkhof. 4 Plaxton. 2 Van Hool.
Ops incl: excursions & tours, private hire, continental tours.
Livery: Yellow/White.

ELLENDERS COACHES
71 HURLFIELD AVE, SHEFFIELD S12 2TL.
Tel: 0114 264 1837.
Ptnrs: rs P. J. D. Ellender, C. S. Ellender.
Fleet: 2 coach.
Chassis: Volvo. **Bodies**: Jonckheere.
Ops incl: excursions & tours, private hire, continental tours, school contracts.

166

EXPRESSWAY COACHES
DERWENT WAY, WATH WEST INDUSTRIAL EASTATE, WATH ON DEARNE, ROTHERHAM S63 6EX
Tel: 01709 875358 **Fax**: 01709 879919
E-mail:expresswaycoaches@btconnect.com
Dirs: Peter Regan
Fleet: 16 - 1 single-deck bus 4 single-deck coach, 5 midicoach, 6 minicoach.
Chassis: 1 Alexander Dennis. 1 MAN. 11 Mercedes. 1 Volkswagen. 2 Volvo.
Bodies: 1 Alexander Dennis. 8 Mercedes-Benz. 1 Neoplan. 5 Plaxton. 1 Other.
Ops incl: local bus service, private hire, continental tours, school contracts, excursions & tours.
Livery: Orange/Yellow/White
Ticket system: Wayfarer II

FIRST SOUTH YORKSHIRE
MIDLAND ROAD, ROTHERHAM S61 1TF.
Tel: 01709 566000
Fax: 01709 566063
E-mail: enquiries@firstgroup.com
Web site: www.firstgroup.com
Man Dir: Bob Hamilton **Eng Dir**: John Clayton **Comm Dir**: Brandon Jones **Ops Dir**: Dennis Hajdukiewicz
Fleet: 623 - 151 double-deck bus, 318 single-deck bus, 112 midibus, 42 minibus.
Chassis: 111 Dennis. 30 Mercedes. 12 Optare. 12 Scania. 458 Transbus.
Bodies: 164 Alexander. 134 Northern Counties. 12 Optare. 113 Plaxton. 200 Wright.
Ops incl: local bus services
Livery: FirstGroup corporate livery
Ticket System: Wayfarer 3

L. FURNESS & SONS
48 THOMPSON HILL, HIGH GREEN, SHEFFIELD S30 4JU.
Tel: 0114 284 8365.
Ptnrs: G. Furness, A. Furness.
Ch Eng: P. Hayes.
Fleet: 8 - 7 coach 1 minicoach.
Chassis: 3 DAF. 3 Ford. 1 Leyland. 1 Mercedes.
Bodies: 1 Duple. 7 Plaxton.
Ops incl: excursions & tours, private hire.
Livery: Red/Cream.

GEE-VEE TRAVEL
173 DONCASTER ROAD, BARNSLEY S70 1UF
Tel: 01226 287403
Fax: 01226 284783
Owner: G Clark
Fleet: 14 - 13 single-deck coach, 1 minibus.
Chassis: 13 DAF. 1 MAN
Bodies: 13 Bova. 1 Mercedes-Benz.
Ops incl: excursions & tours, private hire, continental tours.

W GORDON & SONS
EASTWOOD TRADING ESTATE, CHESTERTON ROAD, ROTHERHAM S65 1SU
Tel: 01709 363913
Fax: 01709 830570
Dir: D Gordon
Fleet: 16 coach
Chassis: 2 Dennis. 1 Mercedes. 12 Volvo.
Bodies: incl: 15 Plaxton
Ops incl: school contracts, excursions & tours, private hire, express.
Livery: Red/Ivory

GRAYS LUXURY TRAVEL
30-32 SHEFFIELD ROAD, HOYLAND COMMON S74 0DQ.
Tel: 01226 743109.
Fax: 01226 749430.
E-mail: stephen@grays-travel.co.uk
Web site: www.grays-travel.co.uk
Man Dir: S. Gray. **Ch Eng**: P. Winter.
Fleet: 10 - 7 coach 1 midicoach, 1 minibus, 1 minicoach.
Chassis: 1 Bova. 6 DAF. 2 Dennis. 1 Toyota.
Bodies: 1 Berkhof. 1 Caetano. 2 Duple. 6 Plaxton.
Ops incl: excursions & tours, private hire, school contracts.
Livery: White/Blue/Yellow.

HAGUES COACHES
C/O W GORDON & SONS, CHESTERTON ROAD, EASTWOOD TRADING ESTATE, ROTHERHAM S65 1SU
Tel: 01709 382912
Fax: 01709 382570
Ops incl: excursions & tours.

HEATON'S OF SHEFFIELD LTD
31 SUSSEX STREET, SHEFFIELD S3 7YY
Tel/Fax: 0114 230 9184
Fleet: 10 - 4 coach, 2 midicoach, 4 minicoach.
Chassis: 1 Ford. 4 Mercedes. 5 Setra.
Bodies: 4 Mercedes. 1 Plaxton. 5 Setra.
Ops incl: school contracts, excursions & tours.
Livery: White.

ISLE COACHES
97 HIGH STREET, OWSTON FERRY DN9 1RL
Tel: 01427 728227.
Props: J. & C. Bannister.
Ch Eng: E. Scotford. **Sec**: Jill Bannister.
Fleet: 12 - 2 double-deck bus, 3 single-deck bus, 6 coach 1 minibus.
Chassis: 2 Daimler. 1 Ford. 4 Leyland. 3 Leyland National. 1 Mercedes. 1 Volvo.
Bodies: 1 Alexander. 1 Duple. 3 Leyland National. 4 Plaxton. 1 Reeve Burgess. 1 Roe. 1 Van Hool.
Ops incl: local bus services, excursions & tours, private hire.
Livery: Blue/Cream.
Ticket System: Almex.

JEMS TRAVEL
27 BOYBTON ROAD, SHIRECLIFFE, S5 7HJ
Tel: 0800 298 1938.
Fax: 0114 242 0885.
E-mail: info@jemstravel.co.uk
Web Site: www.jemstravel.co.uk
Prop: Malcolm S Mallender.
Fleet: 1 minibus.
Chassis: 1 LDV
Bodies: 1 other
Ops incl: school contracts, excursions & tours, private hire.

JOHN POWELL TRAVEL LTD
UNIT2, 6 HELLABY LANE, HELLABY S66 8HA
Tel: 01709 700900
Fax: 01709 701521
E-mail: jane@johnpowelltravel.co.uk
Dirs: Ian Powell, Jane Powell, John Powell, Pauline Powell **Chief Eng**: Ian Slater **Office Man**: Lynn Oliver
Supervisor: Jerry Smith
Fleet: 33 – 6 double-deck bus, 18 single-deck bus, 8 single-deck coach, 1 minicoach
Chassis: 1 BMC. 15 Daimlier. 5 Leyland. 4 MCW. 2 Optare. 1 Scania. 5 Volvo.
Ops incl: local bus services, school contracts, excursions & tours, private hire,
Livery: Blue/Yellow/Red/Orange
Ticket system: Wayfarer III

JOHNSON'S TOURS
See Nottinghamshire

K. M. MOTORS LTD
WILSON GROVE, LUNDWOOD, BARNSLEY S71 5JS
Tel: 01226 245564
Fax: 01226 213004
Man Dir: Keith Meynell
Fleet: 10 - 8 coach, 1 minicoach, 1 midicoach.
Chassis/bodies: incl: 2 Bova. 1 Mercedes. 4 Scania.
Ops incl: excursions & tours, continental tours, private hire.
Livery: Gold/Maroon/White.

LADYLINE
47 BERNARD STREET, RAWMARSH S62 5NR.
Tel: 01709 522422.
Fax: 01709 525558.
Owner: C. B. Goodridge.
Fleet: 6 coach.
Chassis: 2 AEC. 3 Bova. 1 DAF.
Bodies: 3 Bova. 1 Caetano. 2 Plaxton.
Ops incl: local bus services, school contracts, excursions & tours, private hire, continental tours.
Livery: Blue/White.

MALCYS
27 BOYNTON ROAD, SHIRECLIFFE, SHEFFIELD S5 7HJ
Tel: 0800 298 1938
Fax: 0114 242 0885
E-mail: malcystravel@aol.com
Prop/Transport Man: Malcolm S Mallender
Fleet: 1 minicoach.
Chassis: 1 Iveco.
Bodies: 1 other.
Ops incl: school contracts, excursions & tours, private hire.

SOUTH YORKSHIRE

WALTER MARTIN COACHES
57 OLD PARK AVENUE, GREENHILL, SHEFFIELD S8 7DQ
Tel: 0114 274 5004
Prop: John Martin, June Martin.
Fleet: 3 coach.
Chassis: 3 Volvo.
Ops incl: excursions & tours, private hire.

MASS BRIGHT BUS
HOUGHTON ROAD, ANSTON, SHEFFIELD S25 4JJ.
Tel: 01909 550480.
Fax: 01909 550486.
Recovery: 01909 550480
Web: www.brightbus.co.uk
Fleetname: Brightbus
Man Dir: Mick Strafford. **Co Sec**: Carol Morton **Eng Man**: Richard Harrison
Fleet: 50 - 48 double-deck bus, 2 single-deck bus.
Chassis: 11 Alexander Dennis. 12 DAF, 27 Leyland.
Bodies: 14 Alexander Dennis. 7 Duple. 17 Leyland. 12 Optare.
Ops incl: local bus services, school contracts.

J A MAXFIELD& SONS LTD
172 AUGHTON ROAD, AUGHTON, SHEFFIELD S26 3XE
Tel: 0114 287 2622
Fax: 0114 287 5003
E-mail: info@maxfieldstravel.co.uk
Web site: www.maxfieldstravel.co.uk

MOSLEYS TOURS
LEES HALL ROAD, THORNHILL LEES, DEWSBURY WF12 9EQ.
Tel: 01226 382243.
Fax: 01924 458665.
Dirs: A. Gath-Bragg, J. R. Bragg. **Gen Man**: P. R. Emerton.
Fleet: 3 - 2 coach, 1 midicoach.
Chassis: 1 Dennis, 1 Leyland, 1Volvo.
Ops incl: school contracts, private hire, continental tours, excursions and tours, express
Livery: Grey/Cream

NIELSEN TRAVEL SERVICE
23 WINN GROVE, MIDDLEWOOD, SHEFFIELD S6 1UW
Tel/Fax: 0114 234 2961
E-mail: niel@nielsenstravel.co.uk
Web site: www.nielsenstravel.co.uk
Fleet: 2 minibus
Chassis: 2 Mercedes.
Ops incl: school contracts, private hire, excursions & tours

COLLIN PHILLIPSON
1 HILLCREST, OUSEFLEET, GOOLE DN14 8HP.
Tel: 01405 704394.
Prop: C. Phillipson. **Traf Man**: Miss T. Phillipson.
Fleet: 1 minicoach.

Chassis: Mercedes.
Bodies: Autobus Classique.
Ops incl: excursions & tours, private hire.
Livery: White.

ROYLES TRAVEL
114 TUNWELL AVENUE, SHEFFIELD S5 9FG
Tel: 0114 245 4519
Fax: 0114 257 8585
E-mail: info@roylestravel.co.uk
Web site: www.roylestravel.co.uk
Ptnrs: Ricky Eales, Roy Eales.
Fleet: 2 coach.
Chassis: 1 Bova. 1 Iveco.
Bodies: 1 Beulas. 1 Bova.
Ops incl: excursions & tours.

SLEIGHTS COACHES
87 STATION STREET, SWINTON S64 8PZ.
Tel: 01709 584561.
Fax: 01709 582016.
Owner: J. Sleight.
Fleet: 3 coach.
Chassis: DAF. **Bodies**: Jonckheere.
Ops incl: excursions & tours, private hire, continental tours, school contracts.
Livery: Orange/Cream

STAGECOACH YORKSHIRE
UNIT 4 ELDON ARCADE, BARNSLEY S70 4PP
Tel: 01226 202555
Fax: 01226 282313
E-mail: yorkshire@stagecoach.com
Web site: www.stagecoachbus.com
Man Dir: Paul Lynch **Eng Dir**: Joe Gilchrist **Ops Dir**: Sue Hayes **Comm Dir**: Rupert Cox
Fleet: 551 – 66 double-deck bus, 157 single-deck bus, 37 coach, 2 double-deck coach, 1 open-top bus, 242 midibus. 46 minibus.
Chassis: 6 BMC. 16 DAF. 125 Dennis. 61 MAN. 2 MCW. 7 Mercedes. 40 Optare. 48 Scania. 46 Transbus. 232 Volvo.
Bodies: Alexander. BMC. East Lancs. Hispano. Jonckheere. Marshall/MCV. MCW. Mercedes. Northern Counties. Optare. Plaxton. Reeve Burgess. Transbus. Wright.
Ops incl: local bus services, school contracts, excursions & tours, private hire, express, continental tours.
Livery: Stagecoach
Ticket system: Wayfarer

STAGECOACH SHEFFIELD
GREEN LANE, ECCLESFIELD, SHEFFIELD S35 9WY
Tel: 014 247 0777
E-mail: sheffield@stagecoachbus.com
Web site: www.stagecoachbus.com
Man Dir: Paul Lynch, **Eng Dir**: Joe Gilchrist, **Ops Dir**: Sue Hayes, **Com Dir**: Rupert Cox
Fleet: See Stagecoach Yorkshire

Livery: Stagecoach
Ticket machines: Wayfarer

STAGECOACH SUPERTRAM
NUNNERY DEPOT, WOODBOURN ROAD, SHEFFIELD S9 3LS
Tel: 0114 275 9888
Fax: 0114 279 8120
E-mail: enquiries@supertram.com
Web site: www.supertram.com
Man Dir: A Morris
Fleet: 25 tramcars
Chassis/bodies: Siemens
Ops incl: tram services.
Livery: White/Orange/Red

SWIFTS HAPPY DAYS TRAVEL
HAPPY DAYS, THORNE ROAD, BLAXTON DN9 3AX
Tel/Fax: 01302 770999
Ptnrs: S J Swift, J E Swift
Fleet: 3 coach.
Chassis: 3 DAF.
Bodies: 3 Van Hool.
Ops incl: private hire.
Livery: Red/White/Blue

TM TRAVEL
HALFWAY BUS GARAGE, STATION ROAD, HALFWAY S20 3GZ
Tel: 0114 263 3890
Fax: 0114 263 3899
Web site: www.tmtravel.co.uk
E-mail: info@tmtravel.co.uk
Man Dir: Tim Watts **Ops Dir**: Paul Hopkinson **Comp Sec**: Catherine Watts.
Ops Man: Paul Harding **Chief Eng**: John Burton
Fleet: 101 - 24 Double-deck bus, 25 single-deck bus, 8 single-deck coach, 2 double-deck coach, 40 midibus, 2 midicoach.
Chassis: 13 DAF. 3 Dennis. 2 Enterprise. 24 Leyland. 4 MAN. 9 Mercedes-Benz. 38 Optare. 4 Scania. 4 Volvo.
Bodies: 11 Alexander Dennis. 4 ECW. 8 East Lancs. 1 Jockenheere. 1 Nothern Counites. 38 Optare. 30 Plaxton. 2 Van Hool
Ops incl: local bus services, school contracts, private hire, express, continental tours.
Livery: Maroon/Red/Cream
Ticket system: Wayfarer 3

TRAVELGREEN COACHES
CANDA LODGE, HAMPOLE BALK LANE, SKELLOW, DONCASTER DN6 8LF
Tel: 01302 722227
Web: www.travelgreen.co.uk
E-mail: travelgreen@btconnect.com
Owner: David Green
Fleet: 6 - 2 midicoach, 4 minicoach.
Chassis: 6 Mercedes. 2 Optare.
Bodies: 2 Plaxton.
Ops incl: private hire
Livery: Maroon/White

SOUTH YORKSHIRE

168

WILFREDA BEEHIVE
APEX HOUSE, CHURCH LANE, ADWICK-LE-STREET DN6 7AY
Tel: 01302 330330
Fax: 01302 330204
E-mail: sales@wilfreda.co.uk
Web site: www.wilfreda.co.uk
Chmn: W A Scholey **Man Dir:** Mrs S M Scholey **Dirs:** P G Haxby, N G Haxby
Ops Man: I Kaye **Ch Eng:** P Whitaker
Fleet: 36 - 5 double-deck bus, 17 single-deck bus, 9 coach, 5 minicoach.
Chassis: 4 BMC.
Bodies: 4 BMC. 6 Irizar.
Ops incl: local bus services, school contracts, excursions & tours, private hire, continental tours.
Livery: Blue/White/Yellow
Ticket System: Wayfarer TGX150

WILKINSONS TRAVEL
2 REDSCOPE CRESCENT, KIMBERWORTH PARK, ROTHERHAM S61 3LX
Tel: 01709 553403
Fax: 01709 550550
Owner: M. D. Wilkinson.
Fleet: 9 - 2 coach 3 minibus, 4 minicoach.
Chassis: AEC. Volvo.
Bodies: Berkhof. Duple. Ikarus. Jonckheere.
Ops incl: excursions & tours, private hire, continental tours, school contracts.

WILLIAMSONS OF ROTHERHAM
19 VICTORIA STREET, CATCLIFFE S60 5SJ.
Tel: 01709 366856.
Fax: 01709 828241.
Prop: P. Williamson.
Fleet: 3 coach.
Chassis: 1 Bedford. 1 DAF. 1 Leyland.
Bodies: 1 Duple. 1 Leyland. 1 Van Hool.
Ops incl: school contracts, excursions & tours, private hire, continental tours.
Livery: White.

WILSON'S COACHES
PLOT 5, BANKWOOD LANE INDUSTRIAL ESTATE, ROSSINGTON, DONCASTER DN11 0PS.
Tel: 01302 866193
Recovery: 07836 757618
Fleet: 3 coach.
Chassis: 3 Volvo.
Bodies: 1 Berkhof. 2 Van Hool.
Ops incl: excursions & tours, private hire.

STAFFORDSHIRE

ACE TRAVEL
10 BIDDULPH PARK, IRONSTON ROAD, BURNTWOOD WS7 8LG.
Tel: 01543 279068.
Prop: G. E. Elson.
Fleet: 1 midicoach. **Chassis:** Toyota.
Ops incl: excursions & tours, private hire, continental tours, school contracts.

ARRIVA MIDLANDS LTD
DELTA WAY, CANNOCK WS11 3XB.
Tel: 01543 466123.
Fax: 01543 570900.
Web site: www.arriva.co.uk
Fleetname: Arriva Serving the North Midlands.
Man Dir: R A Hind **Fin Dir:** J Barlow.
Eng Dir: M Evans. **Ops Dir:** A Lloyd.
Fleet: 774 - 216 double-deck bus, 144 single-deck bus, 361 midibus 15 coach, 38 minibus.
Chassis: 127 DAF. 270 Dennis. 9 Leyland. 35 Mercedes. 19 Optare. 89 Scania. 180 Volvo.
Bodies: Alexander. Carlyle. East Lancs. Leyland. Marshall. Northern Counties. Optare. Plaxton. Wright. Caetano. Ikarus. Van Hool.
Ops incl: local bus services, school contracts.
Livery: Aquamarine/Cotswold Stone.
Ticket System: Wayfarer 3.

BAKERS COACHES
THE COACH TRAVEL CENTRE, PROSPECT WAY, VICTORIA BUSINESS PARK, BIDDULPH ST8 7PL
Tel: 01782 522101
Fax: 01782 522363
E-mail: sales@bakerscoaches.com
Web site: www.bakerscoaches.com
Man Dir: Philip Baker **Ops Man:** David Machin, **Co Sec:** Susan Baker
Fleet: 42 - 5 single-deck bus, 17 coach, 18 midibus, 2 midicoach.
Chassis: 2 DAF. 11 Mercedes. 4 Optare. 5 Plaxton. 5 Scania. 3 VDL. 12 Volvo.
Bodies: 2 Berkhof. 3 Caetano. 2 Irizar. 4 Optare. 27 Plaxton. 1 Van Hool. 3 Wright.
Ops incl: local bus services, school contracts, excursions & tours, private hire, continental tours.
Livery: Green/White

BENNETTS TRAVEL (CRANBERRY) LTD
CRANBERRY, COTES HEATH ST21 6SQ.
Tel: 01782 791468
Prop/Gen Man: J. P. McDonnell.
Fleet: 27
Chassis: Bedford. Ford Transit. Leyland. Mercedes.
Bodies: Mercedes. Plaxton.
Ops incl: local bus services, excursions & tours, private hire.
Livery: Blue/White

L F BOWEN LTD
104 MARINER, LICHFIELD ROAD INDUSTRIAL ESTATE, TAMWORTH B79 7UL
Tel: 01827 300000
Fax: 01827 300009
E-mail: coachhire@bowenstravel.com
Web site: www.bowenstravel.com
Chmn: A R Moseley **Ch Exec:** Kevin Lower **Man Dir:** Bob Lyng **Group Ops Man:** Nick Tetley **Traff Man:** Tony York **Group Ch Eng:** David Hoy
Fleet: 39 - 27 coach, 2 midicoach, 10 minibus
Chassis: 10 MAN, 15 Scania, 2 Toyota. 10 Volkswagen. 2 Volvo
Bodies: 15 Irizar, 2 Marcopolo. 8 Noge, 2 Plaxton.
Ops incl: school contracts, private hire, express, continental tours, excursions & tours.
Livery: Silver/sun emblem

TERRY BUSHELL TRAVEL
13 DERBY STREET, BURTON-ON-TRENT DE14 2LA
Tel/Fax: 01283 538242
E-mail: info@terrybushelltravel.co.uk
Web: www.terrybushelltravel.co.uk
Prop: Terry Bushell

Fleet: 3 - 2 single-deck coach, 1 minicoach.
Chassis: 2 Volvo. 1 Mercedes-Benz.
Bodies: 1 Mercedes-Benz. 1 Volvo.
Ops incl: excursions & tours, private hire, continental tours.
Livery: Red/Poppy/Gold

CLOWES COACHES
See Derbyshire

COPELAND TOURS (STOKE-ON-TRENT) LTD
1009 UTTOXETER ROAD, MEIR, STOKE-ON-TRENT ST3 6HE.
Tel: 01782 324466
Fax: 01782 319401
Recovery: 01782 324466
E-mail: mb@copelandtours.co.uk
Web site: www.copelandtours.co.uk
Chmn/Man Dir: J E M Burn **Dir:** Mrs P Burn **Ch Eng:** J C Burn **Co Sec:** J E M Burn
Fleet: 26 - 1 single-deck bus, 22 coach, 2 midibus, 1 midicoach.
Chassis: 1 AEC. 14 DAF. 1 Dennis. 7 Leyland. 1 MAN. 2 Mercedes.
Bodies: 1 Duple. 1 Jonckheere. 1 Marshall. 17 Plaxton. 4 Van Hool. 2 Wadham Stringer.
Ops incl: local bus services, school contracts, excursions & tours, private hire, express, continental tours.
Livery: Blue-Blue/Orange.
Ticket System: Wayfarer.

CRUSADE TRAVEL LTD
THE COACHYARD, BUXTON ESTATES, PINFOLD LANE, PENKRIDGE ST19 5AS
Tel: 01785 714124
Fax: 01543 579678
E-mail: crusade-tvl@tiscali.co.uk
Web site: www.crusade-travel.com
Ops Man: Gavin Pardoe
Fleet: incl - single-deck coach, midicoach, minibus, minicoach.
Chassis: 1 Dennis. 3 Mercedes. 2 Volvo.
Ops incl: school contracts, excursions & tours, private hire.

STAFFORDSHIRE

STAFFORDSHIRE

D & G COACH AND BUS LTD
MOSSFIELD ROAD, ADDERLEY GREEN ST3 5BW
Tel: 01782 332337
Fax: 01782 337864
E-mail: dreeves@dgbus.co.uk
Man Dir: D Reeve **Fleet Eng**: M Johnson
Depot Eng: K Mitchell
Fleet: 49 - 14 coach, 35 midibus.
Chassis: 10 Dennis. 1 Ford. 33 Mercedes. 5 Optare.
Bodies: 7 Alexander. 2 Carlyle. 3 East Lancs. 1 Marshall. 6 Optare.12 Plaxton. 2 Reeve Burgess. 1 Wadham Stringer. 4 Wright. 11 other.
Ops incl: local bus services, school contracts.
Livery: Cream/Blue
Ticket system: Wayfarer

D H CARS OF DENSTONE LTD
9 HAWTHORN CLOSE, DENSTONE, UTTOXETER ST14 5HB
Tel: 01889 590819
Fax: 01889 591888
Dir: Donald Handley **Sec**: Alison Williams
Fleet: 2 - 1 single-deck coach, 1 minicoach.
Chassis: 1 Bova. 1 Mercedes-Benz.
Bodies: 1 Bova. 1 Other.
Ops incl: private hire
Livery: White/Ivory

DUNN-LINE GROUP
See Nottinghamshire

EAGLE TRAVEL
3A NEWPORT ROAD, STAFFORD ST16 2HH
Tel: 01785 220777
Fax: 01785 220666
Recovery: 07931 828762
E-mail: mikegilmore@btconnect.com
Dirs: M W Gilmore, D E Kaminski
Fleet: 11 - 3 coach, 3 midibus, 5 minibus.
Chassis: 1 DAF. 4 LDV. 3 Mercedes. 1 Talbot. 2 Volvo.
Bodies: incl: 3 Alexander. 2 Duple. 1 LAG.
Ops incl: private hire, school contracts.
Livery: Gold eagle/Burgundy and Gold stripes and lettering

FIRST IN NORTH STAFFORDSHIRE
ADDERLEY GREEN GARAGE, DIVIDY ROAD, STOKE-ON-TRENT ST3 0AJ
Tel: 01782 592500
Fax: 01782 592541
Man Dir: Ken Poole
Fleet: 490 (274 in Staffs)
Ops inc: Local bus services
Livery: First Group

HAPPY DAYS COACHES
GREYFRIARS COACH STATION, GREYFRIARS WAY, STAFFORD ST16 2SH
Tel: 01785 229797
Fax: 01785 229790
E-mail: info@happydayscoaches.co.uk
Web site: www.happydayscoaches.co.uk
Man Dirs: Richard Austin, Neil Austin **Dirs**: Brian Austin.
Fleet: 26 - 23 single-deck coach, 1 minicoach, 2 minibus.
Chassis: 3 DAF. 3 Mercedes-Benz. 1 Neoplan. 4 Scania. 15 Volvo.
Bodies: 2 Bova. 3 Irizar. 1 Jonkheere. 1 Mellor. 1 Neoplan. 9 Plaxton. 9 Van Hool.
Ops incl: excursions & tours, private hire, express, school contracts. continental tours

HOLLINSHEAD COACHES LTD
WHARF ROAD, BIDDULPH ST8 6AQ.
Tel: 01782 512209.
Man Dir: David Haydon
Fleet: 10 coach
Chassis: 1 DAF. 2 Leyland. 7 Volvo.
Ops incl: school contracts, excursions & tours, private hire

JOSEPHS MINI COACHES
171 CRACKLEY BANK, CHESTERTON, NEWCASTLE-UNDER-LYME ST5 7AB
Tel: 01782 564944
Dir: Joseph Windsor
Fleet: 1 minicoach.
Chassis/bodies: 1 Mercedes-Benz.
Ops incl: Excursions & tours, private hire
Livery: White

LEONS COACH TRAVEL LTD
DOUGLAS HOUSE, TOLLGATE, BEACONSIDE, STAFFORD ST16 3EE
Tel: 01785 244575
Fax: 01785 258444
Web site: www.leonsholidays.co.uk
Man Dir: L H Douglas **Co Sec**: S Douglas
Dirs: R L Douglas, A Douglas
Fleet: 26 - 23 coach, 2 midicoach, 1 minicoach.
Chassis: 6 Bova. 3 Ford. 8 Scania. 3 Setra. 3 Volvo.
Bodies: 5 Berkhof. 6 Bova. 3 Irizar. 6 Plaxton. 3 Setra.
Ops incl: excursions & tours, school contracts, private hire, continental tours.
Livery: Red/Yellow/Orange/Purple

PARAGON TRAVEL LTD
THE GARAGE, SPATH ST14 5AE
Tel: 01889 569899
Fax: 01889 563518
Recovery: 01889 569899
E-mail: phil@paragontravel.co.uk
Web site: www.paragontravel.co.uk
Dir: P L Smith **Ops Man**: www.paragontravel.co.uk
Fleet: 14 coach
Chassis: 1 Leyland. 1 Mercedes. 2 Scania. 10 Volvo
Bodies: 1 Alexander. 3 Jonckheere. 4 Plaxton. 6 Van Hool.
Ops incl: local bus services, school contracts, excursions & tours, continental tours, private hire.
Livery: White with Blue/Red lettering.
Ticket system: Setright

PARRYS INTERNATIONAL TOURS LTD
LADYWOOD GREEN, CHESLYN HAY WS6 7QX
Tel: 01922 414576.
Fax: 01922 413416
E-mail: info@parrys-international.co.uk
Web site: www.parrys-international.co.uk
Man Dir: David Parry
Fleet: 11 coach.
Chassis: 11 Neoplan.
Bodies: 11 Neoplan.
Ops incl: excursions & tours
Livery: Red/Gold

PLANTS LUXURY TRAVEL LTD
167 TEAN ROAD, CHEADLE ST10 1LS
Tel: 01538 753561
Fax: 01538 757025
E-mail: julie.plant@plantsluxurytravel.co.uk
Web site: www.plantsluxurytravel.co.uk
Ptnrs: T J Plant, M P Plant
Fleet: 4 - 1 midicoach, 3 minicoach.
Chassis: 3 Mercedes-Benz. 1 Toyota.
Bodies: incl: 1 Optare.
Ops incl: private hire, school contracts.
Livery: Silver with Burgundy/Gold/Mustard stripes

F PROCTER & SON LTD
DEWSBURY ROAD, FENTON ST4 2HS.
Tel: 01782 846031.
Fax: 01782 744732.
Dirs: R Walker, J Walker.
Fleet: 16
Chassis: 2 Bova. 5 DAF. 1 Iveco. 6 Leyland. 2 Scania.
Ops incl: local bus services, school contracts, excursions & tours, private hire.
Livery: Blue/White
Ticket System: Wayfarer

ROBIN HOOD TRAVEL LTD
HIGHWAY GARAGE, MACCLESFIELD ROAD, LEEK ST13 8PS
Tel: 01538 306618
Fax: 01538 306079
Web site: www.robinhoodtravel.co.uk
Fleet: 12 - 3 single-deck bus, 7 single-deck coach, 1 midicoach, 1 mincoach.
Chassis: incl: 6 Bova
Ops incl: school contracts, excursions & tours, private hire,continental tours
Livery: Green/Gold stars

SHIRE TRAVEL INTERNATIONAL LTD
UNIT 4:02 CANNOCK ENTERPRISE CENTRE, WALKERS RISE, HEDNESFORD WS12 0QU
Tel/Fax: 01543 871605
E-mail: hire@shiretravel.co.uk
Web site: www.shiretravel.co.uk
Dir: Robert Garrington **Comp Sec**: Michelle Wassell
Fleet: 9 - 3 single-deck coach, 1 midibus, 5 minibus.
Chassis: incl: 1 Scania. 2 Setra.
Bodies: 1 Irizar. 6 Mercedes-Benz. 2 Setra.
Ops incl: private hire, school contracts, excursions & tours, continental tours.
Livery: White/Red + end three lions flag

170

SOLUS COACH TRAVEL LTD
VENTURA PARK, TAMWORTH STAFFS B79 8NH
Tel: 01827 51736
Fax: 0871 900 4124
Recovery: 07773 785143
E-mail: sales@soluscoaches.co.uk
Web site: www.soluscoaches.co.uk
Dir: Andy Garratt **Comp Sec**: Lucy Garratt **Comp Eng**: Graham Hopkins
Fleet: 18 incl - 9 single-deck coach, 1 double-deck bus, 5 minicoach
Chassis: incl - 2 Bova. 5 Ford Transit. 5 Scania. 3 Temsa. 1 Volvo
Bodies: incl - 1 Bova. 5 Irizar. 2 Van Hool
Ops incl: school contracts, excursions & tours, pirvate hire, express, continental tours
Livery: Red/White/Black

STANWAYS COACHES
THE GASWORKS INDUSTRIAL ESTATE, HARDINGSWOOD ROAD, KIDSGROVE ST7 1EF
Tel: 01782 786232
Fax: 01782 786040
Recovery: 07967 377270
E-mail: stanwayscoaches@yahoo.co.uk
Ptnrs: David Elliot, Paul Richman,
Fleet: 13 - 1 double-deck bus, 10 single-deck coach, 1 midicoach, 1 minibus.
Chassis: incl - 2 Dennis. 1 Ford. 2 Leyland.
Bodies: incl - 1 Beulas. 1 Berkhof. 1 Duple. 1 Marshall/MCV. 2 Mercedes-Benz. 1 Setra. 2 Van Hool.
Ops incl: local bus service, excursions & tours, private hire, school contracts.
Livery: various
Ticket System: Wayfarer

STODDARDS LTD
GREENHILL GARAGE, LEEK ROAD, CHEADLE ST10 1JF
Tel: 01538 754420
Fax: 01538 750375
Web: www.stoddards.co.uk
Man Dir: Judith Myatt **Fleet**: Paul Stoddard **Ops**: Peter Stoddard **Comp Sec**: Brian Stoddard
Fleet: 6 - 2 single-deck bus, 4 single-deck coach.
Chassis: 6 DAF
Bodies: 6 Bova.
Ops incl: excursions & tours, private hire, school contracts.
Livery: Silver/Blue flashes

SWIFTSURE TRAVEL
3 GUILD STREET, BURTON-UPON-TRENT DE14 1NA.
Tel: 01283 512974
Fax: 01283 516728
E-mail: info@swiftsure-travel.co.uk
Web site: www.swiftsure-travel.co.uk
Man Dir: Richard Hackett **Co Sec**: Kathleen Hackett **Dirs**: Brian Kershaw, Julian Peddle
Fleet: 7 - 3 single-deck coach, 3 midicoach, 1 minibus.
Chassis: 1 Bova. 1 DAF. 1 LDV. 2 Mercedes-Benz. 1 Scania. 1 Toyota.
Bodies: 1 Bova. 1 Caetano. 1 Irizar. 2 Optare. 1 Van Hool. 1 other.
Ops incl: scholl contracts, excursions & tours, express, private hire,
Livery: White/Blue/Green

WARRINGTON COACHES
See Derbyshire

WARSTONE MOTORS LTD
THE GARAGE, LANDYWOOD WS6 6AD.
Tel: 01922 414141.
Fleetname: The Green Bus Service.
Dir: G. Martin
Fleet: 25 - 3 double-deck bus, 18 single-deck bus, 4 minibus.
Chassis: Leyland, Mercedes.
Bodies: Alexander. Carlyle. Duple. East Lancs. Massey. Roe.
Ops incl: local bus services.
Livery: Green/Cream.
Ticket System: Wayfarer.

WINTS COACHES
MONTANA, WETTON ROAD, BUTTERTON ST13 7ST
Tel/Fax: 01538 304370
Props: Andrew Wint, Maxine Wint.
Fleet: 10 - 8 coach, 2 minicoach.
Chassis: 1 DAF. 1 Dennis. 6 Mercedes. 1 Optare. 1 Volvo.
Bodies: 1 Bova. 6 Mercedes. 1 Neoplan. 1 Optare. 1 Plaxton.
Ops incl: school contracts, excursions & tours, private hire, continental tours.

J. P. A. WORTH
GOLDEN GREEN GARAGE, LONGNOR SK17 0QP.
Tel: 01298 83583.
Fleet: 2 - 1 midicoach, 1 minicoach.
Chassis: 1 Leyland. 1 Mercedes.
Ops incl: school contracts, private hire.

SUFFOLK

ANGLIAN BUS & COACH LTD
BECCLES BUSINESS PARK, BECCLES NR34 7TH
Tel: 01502 711109
Fax: 01502 711161
E-mail: office@angliancoaches.co.uk
Web site: www.anglianbus.co.uk
Fleet: 55 - 5 double-deck bus, 8 single-deck bus, 9 single-deck coach, 33 minibus.
Chassis: 2 Leyland. 36 Mercedes. 9 Optare. 8 Volvo.
Bodies: 1 ECW. 3 East Lancs. 7 Mercedes. 1 Northern Counties. 9 Optare. 31 Plaxton. 1 Van Hool. 2 Wadham Stringer.
Ops incl: local bus services, school contracts.
Livery: Yellow with blue stripes
Ticket System: Wayfarer 3

BEESTONS (HADLEIGH) LTD
THE COACH DEPOT, IPSWICH ROAD, HADLEIGH IP7 5DB
Tel: 01473 823243
Recovery: 07769 978191
E-mail: info@beestons.co.uk
Web site: www.beestons.co.uk
Man Dir: P Munson **Dir**: S Munson **Ops Man**: T Munson
Fleet: 37 - 9 double-deck bus, 5 single-deck bus, 14 single-deck bus, 1 double-deck coach, 8 minibus.
Chassis: 4 Leyland. 7 Mercedes. 1 Optare. 13 Scania. 11 Volvo. 1 Other
Bodies: 3 Alexander Dennis. 5 East Lancs. 1 Northern Counties. 1 Optare. 7 Plaxton. 15 Van Hool. 2 Wright. 3 Other.
Ops incl: local bus services, school contracts, excursions & tours, private hire.
Livery: coach - Gold/Black, bus - Blue/White
Ticket System: Wayfarer 3

BURTONS COACHES LIMITED
DUDDERY HILL, HAVERHILL CB9 8DR
Tel: 01440 702257
Fax: 01440 713287
E-mail: hire@burtons-bus.co.uk
Web site: www.burtoncoaches.com
Fleetname: Burtons
Man Dir: Paul Cooper **Fleet Eng**: Steve Legate
Fleet: 66 - 9 double-deck bus, 16 single-deck bus, 30 coach, 10 midibus, 1 midicoach.
Chassis: 3 Bova. 16 Dennis. 1 Iveco. 3 Leyland. 10 Mercedes. 33 Volvo.
Bodies: 5 Alexander. 1 Beulas. 3 Bova. 15 Caetano. 3 ECW. 3 East Lancs. 36 Plaxton
Ops incl: local bus services, school contracts, excursions & tours, private hire, express, continental tours.
Livery: Blue/Yellow on white base.
Ticket system: Almex A90
Subsidiary of Tellings Golden Miller part of Arriva.

H C CHAMBERS & SON LTD
HIGH STREET, BURES CO8 5AB
Tel: 01787 227233
Fax: 01787 227042
Recovery: 07770 886834
E-mail: info@chamberscoaches.co.uk
Web site: www.chamberscoaches.co.uk
Op Dir: Alex Chambers, **Eng Dir**: Robert Chambers, **Ops Dir**: Clive Bartholomey
Fleet: 29 - 18 double-deck bus, 2 single-deck bus, 5 coach, 4 minibus
Chassis: 2 MAN. 6 Mercedes. 21 Volvo.
Bodies: 8 Alexander. 4 East Lancs. 5 Marshall. 7 Northern Counties. 1 Plaxton. 2 Van Hool 2 Mercedes.
Ops incl: local bus services, excursions & tours, private hire.
Livery: Red
Ticket System: Wayfarer

D-WAY TRAVEL
GREENWAYS, THE STREET, EARSHAM, BUNGAY NR35 2TZ
Tel: 01986 895375
Fax: 05600 751425
E-mail: david@dwaytravel.com
Web site: www.dwaytravel.com
Prop: David Thompson **Eng**: Michael Gray
Fleet: 10 - 7 single-deck coach, 1 minicoach, 2 midicoach.
Chassis: 1 Ford Transit. 7 MAN. 2 Mercedes-Benz.
Bodies: incl: 10 Other
Ops incl: school contracts, excursions & tours, private hire.

FARELINE BUS & COACH SERVICES
OLD ROSES, SYLEHAM ROAD, WINGFIELD, EYE IP21 5RF
Tel: 01379 668151
Mobile: 07850 940445
Prop: Jeff Morss
Fleet: 1 coach
Chassis: 1 Bedford.
Body: 1 Plaxton
Ops incl: local bus services, school contracts, excursions & tours, private hire.
Livery: Blue/Cream
Ticket System: Setright Mk 3

FORGET-ME-NOT (TRAVEL) LTD
CHAPEL ROAD, OTLEY, IPSWICH IP6 9NT
Tel: 01473 890268
Fax: 01473 890748
E-mail: sales@forgetmenot-travel.co.uk
Web site: www.forgetmenottravel.co.uk
Fleetname: Soames
Dirs: A F Soames, Mrs M A Soames, A M Soames **Ch Eng**: A M Soames
Fleet: 17 - 16 single-deck coach, 1 midicoach.
Chassis: 1 Mercedes-Benz. 16 Volvo.
Bodies: 1 Esker. 1 Jonkheere. 13 Plaxton. 2 Van Hool.
Ops incl: private hire, school contracts.
Livery: three-tone Blue

GALLOWAY EUROPEAN COACHLINES
DENTERS HILL, MENDLESHAM, STOWMARKET IP14 5RR
Tel: 01449 766323
Fax: 01449 766241
E-mail: coach@gallowayeuropean.co.uk
Web: www.gallowayeuropean.co.uk
Man Dirs: D Cattermole **Dirs**: J Miles, R Stedman,
Fleet: 44 - 2 double-deck bus, 7 single-deck bus, 25 single-deck coach, 7 midibus, 3 minicoach.
Chassis: 1 Alexander Dennis. 15 DAF. 1 Dennis. 2 Ford Transit. 1 Iveco. 1 Leyland. 12 Mercedes-Benz. 1 Scania. 2 Setra. 2 Temsa. 6 VDL
Bodies: 1 Alexander Dennis. 1 Autobus. 1

Beulas. 1 East Lancs. 3 Ikarus. 2 Mercedes-Benz. 12 Plaxton. 2 Setra. 1 UVG. 14 Van Hool. 4 Wright. 2 Other.
Ops incl: local bus services, school contracts, excursions & tours, private hire, express, continental tours.
Ticket System: Wayfarer.

GEMINI TRAVEL
UNIT 20, STERLING COMPLEX, FARTHING ROAD, IPSWICH IP1 5AP
Tel: 01473 462721
Fax: 01473 462731
E-mail: info@geminiofipswich.co.uk
Web site: www.geminiofipswich.co.uk
Man Dir: E Nicholls **Co Sec**: K Nicholls
Tran Man: S Middlemas
Fleet: 7 - 4 midicoach, 1 minibus, 2 minicoach
Chassis: 1 BMC. 6 Mercedes.
Bodies: 1 BMC. 3 Optare. 2 Plaxton.
Ops incl: excursions & tours, private hire, school contracts, continental tours
Livery: Red/White

HARLEQUIN TRAVEL
77 LANERCOST WAY, IPSWICH IP2 9DP
Tel: 01473 407408
E-mail: paul.lewis80@ntlworld.com
Web site: www.harlequin-travel.co.uk
Dirs: P D Lewis, Mrs L M Lewis
Fleet: 3 - 2 midicoach, 1 minibus.
Chassis: 2 Mercedes. 1 Peugeot
Bodies: incl: 1 Autobus. 1 Plaxton.
Ops incl: school contracts, private hire
Livery: Maroon/White

IPSWICH BUSES LTD
7 CONSTANTINE ROAD, IPSWICH IP1 2DL.
Tel: 01473 232600
Fax: 01473 232062
E-mail: info@ipswichbuses.co.uk
Web site: www.ipswichbuses.co.uk
Man Dir: Malcolm Robson
Fleet: 98 - 28 double-deck bus, 1 open-top bus, 54 single-deck bus, 15 midibus.
Chassis: 7 DAF. 28 Dennis. 12 Leyland. 39 Optare. 9 Scania. 3 Volvo.
Bodies: 2 Alexander. 8 ECW. 41 East Lancs. 41 Optare. 1 Roe. 6 Scania Omnicity
Ops incl: local bus services, school contracts, private hire.
Livery: White/Green/Cream
Ticket System: Wayfarer TGX150

LAMBERT'S COACHES (BECCLES) LTD
UNIT 4A, MOOR BUSINESS PARK, BECCLES NR34 7TQ
Tel: 01502 717579
Fax: 01502 711209
E-mail: office@lambertscoaches.co.uk
Web site: www.lambertscoaches.co.uk
Man Dir: D M Reade **Dir**: Miss L K Reade
Fleet: 7 coach.
Chassis: 4 DAF. 3 Volvo.
Bodies: 2 Plaxton. 5 Van Hool.
Ops incl: private hire, school contracts.
Livery: Blue/White

MIL-KEN TRAVEL LTD
GRASSMERE, BURY ROAD, KENTFORD, NEWMARKET CB8 7PZ
Tel: 01638 750201
Fax: 01638 750439
E-mail: milkenkentford@btconnect.com
Web site: www.milkentravel.com
Gen Man: Mark Rogers **Man Dir**: Jason Miller **Fleet Man**: Ian Martin
Fleet: 39 - 37 single-deck coach, 2 minibus.
Chassis: 2 DAF. 5 Dennis. 2 LDV. 30 Volvo.
Bodies: 1 Berkhof. 3 Duple. 3 Jonckheere. 25 Plaxton. 4 Van Hool. 3 other.
Ops incl: private hire, excursions & tours, continental tours, school contracts.

MINIBUS & COACH HIRE
LINGS FARM, BLACKSMITHS LANE, FORWARD GREEN, EARL STONHAM IP14 5ET.
Tel: 01449 711117.
Fax: 01449 711977.
Owner: Mrs L. J. Eustace.
Fleet: 11 - 3 coach, 8 minibus.
Chassis: 3 Bedford, 1 Iveco. 6 LDV. 1 Nissan.
Bodies: Plaxton.
Ops incl: local bus services, school contracts, excursions & tours, private hire.

MULLEYS MOTORWAYS LTD
STOW ROAD, IXWORTH, BURY ST EDMUNDS IP31 2JB.
Tel: 01359 230234
Fax: 01359 232451
E-mail: enquiries@mulleys.co.uk
Web site: www. mulleys.co.uk
Dir/Co Sec: Jayne D Munson **Man Dir**: David J Munson **Ops Man**: Daniel Munson
Fleet: 44 - 8 double-deck bus, 5 single-deck bus, 22 single-deck coach, 2 double-deck coach, 1 midicoach, 6 midibus.
Chassis: 3 BMC. 3 Iveco. 9 Leyland. 7 Mercedes-Benz. 4 Scania. 4 Setra. 14 Volvo.
Bodies: 3 BMC. 1 ECW. 3 East Lancs.1 Indcar. 1 Irizar. 9 Jonckheere. 7 Plaxton. 4 Setra. 5 Van Hool. 7 Other.
Ops incl: local bus services, school contracts, excursions & tours, private hire,continental tours.
Livery: Orange/Silver.
Ticket System: Wayfarer.

ROUTESPEK COACH HIRE LTD
3 ELMS CLOSE, EARSHAM, NR BUNGAY NR35 2TD
Tel/Fax: 01968 893035
Director: Mr K Reeve **Comp Dir**: Mrs R Reeve
Fleet: 4 - 1 double-deck bus, 3 single-deck coach.
Chassis: 1 Bristol. 2 Leyland. 1 Volvo.
Bodies: 1 ECW. 3 Van Hool.
Ops incl: local bus service,school contracts, private hire.
Livery: Fawn
Ticket System: hand m/c

B R SHREEVE & SONS LTD
RIVERSIDE ROAD, LOWESTOFT NR33 0TU
Tel: 01502 532000
Fax: 01502 532009
E-mail: robert@bellecoaches.co.uk
Web site: www.bellecoaches.co.uk
Fleetname: Belle Coaches.
Man Dirs: Ken Shreeve, Robert Shreeve
Dir: John Shreeve **Co Sec**: Susan Speed
Fleet: 42 - 37 single-deck coach, 3 midicoach, 2 minibus
Chassis: 3 DAF. 3 MAN. 2 Mercedes-Benz. 9 Scania. 14 Setra. 1 Toyota. 2 Volkwagen. 8 Volvo.
Bodies: 2 Berkhof. 1 Caetano. 1 Duple. 9 Plaxton. 17 Setra. 9 Van Hool. 3 other.
Ops incl: local bus services, school contracts, excursions & tours, private hire, continental tours.
Livery: Blue/Yellow
Ticket System: Setright

SQUIRRELL'S COACHES
OLD MILL GARAGE, HITCHAM, IPSWICH IP7 7NF
Tel/Fax: 01449 740582
E-mail: squirrells@btconnect.com
Fleet: 7 - 5 coach, 2 midicoach.
Chassis: 1 Leyland. 2 Mercedes. 4 Volvo.
Bodies: 1 Autobus. 1 Reeve Burgess. 5 Van Hool.
Ops incl: school contracts, private hire.

THOMPSON'S REMOVALS & COACH HIRE
DORMICK HOUSE, NEW STREET, FRAMLINGHAM IP13 9RF.
Tel: 01728 723403.
Prop: M. A. Rogers, D. J. Rogers (**Sec**).
Fleet: 3 coach.
Chassis: 1 Ford. 2 Volvo.
Bodies: 1 Duple. 2 Jonckheere.
Ops incl: local bus services, excursions & tours, private hire, continental tours.
Livery: Blue/White.

SURREY

ARRIVA SURREY & WEST SUSSEX
FRIARY BUS STATION, GUILDFORD GU1 4YP
Tel: 01483 505693
Fleetname: Arriva serving Guildford & West Surrey.
Man Dir: Kevin Hawkins
Eng Dir: I. Tarran. **Fin Dir**: Ms E. Limm.
Gen Man: R. Thornton.
Fleet: 59 - 3 double-deck bus, 56 single-deck bus.
Chassis: 29 DAF. 39 Dennis.
Bodies: East Lancs. Plaxton. Wright.
Ops incl: local bus services.
Livery: Aquamarine and Stone.
Ticket System: Wayfarer 3

BANSTEAD COACHES LTD
1 SHRUBLAND ROAD, BANSTEAD SM7 2ES
Tel: 01737 354322
Fax: 01737 371090
E-mail: sales@bansteadcoaches.co.uk
Web site: www.bansteadcoaches.co.uk
Dirs: D C Haynes, C J Haynes, M C Haynes.
Fleet: 16 coach.
Chassis: 1 Bedford. 11 Dennis. 3 Mercedes. 1 Volvo.
Bodies: 4 Berkhof. 1 Caetano. 3 Mercedes. 8 Plaxton.
Ops incl: school contracts, private hire.

BUSES4U
EAST SURREY RURAL TRANSPORT PARTNERSHIP, TANDRIDGE DISTRICT COUNCIL, STATION ROAD EAST, OXTED RH8 0BT
Tel: 01730 815518
Web site: www.buses4u.org.uk

CALL-A-COACH
CAPRI HOUSE, WALTON-ON-THAMES KT12 2LY
Tel: 01932 223838
Fax: 01932 269109
E-mail: callacoach@aol.com
Prop: Arthur Freakes
Fleet: 10 - 4 single-deck coach, 2 midicoach, 4 minibus.
Chassis: incl - 4 DAF. 4 LDV.
Bodies: incl - 2 Mercedes-Benz.
Ops incl: school contracts, excursions & tours, private hire.
Livery: CALL-A-COACH

CHEAM COACHES
11 FREDERICK CLOSE, CHEAM SM1 2HY
Tel: 01372 742527
Fax: 01372 742528
E-mail: cheamco@aol.com
Web site: www.cheamcoaches.co.uk
Props: Michael Mower, Lise Cyr-Mower
Fleet: 6 - 2 coach, 4 minibus.
Chassis: 4 Mercedes. 1 Setra. 1 Volvo.
Bodies: 1 Jonckheere. 4 Mercedes. 1 Setra.
Ops incl: private hire, school contracts.

CHIVERS COACHES LTD
13A ROSS PARADE, WALLINGTON SM6 8QG
Tel: 020 8647 6648
Fax: 020 8647 6649
E-mail: chivlyn@aol.com
Dirs: Lynne Lucas, Melanie Chivers
Fleet: 4 - 2 coach, 1 midicoach, 1 minibus.
Chassis: 1 LDV. 1 Mercedes. 2 Volvo.
Bodies: incl: 2 Van Hool.
Ops Incl: private hire, school contracts.
Livery: White with blue graphics

COUNTRYLINER COACH HIRE LTD
GB HOUSE, MERROW LANE, GUILDFORD GU4 7BQ
Tel: 01483 506919
Fax: 01483 506913
E-mail: info@countryliner-coaches.com
Web site: www.countryliner-coaches.co.uk
Dirs: R Hodgetts, R Belcher, B King **Gen Man**: N Hatcher **Ops Mans**: M Lambley, M Chadwick, J Rees
Fleet: 40 - 5 double-deck bus, 21 single-deck bus, 10 coach, 2 double-deck coach, 1 midibus, 1 midicoach.
Chassis: 2 DAF. 19 Dennis. 6 Leyland. 5 Mercedes. 1 Neoplan. 2 Optare. 5 Volvo.
Bodies: 1 Alexander. 1 Caetano. 1 Duple. 5 ECW. 1 Ikarus. 1 Neoplan. 2 Optare. 21 Plaxton. 2 Van Hool. 5 other.
Ops incl: local bus services, school contracts, excursions & tours, private hire.
Livery: Green/White.
Ticket System: Wayfarer 2

CRUISERS LIMITED
UNIT M, KINGSFIELD BUSINESS CENTRE, REDHILL RH1 4DP
Tel: 01737 770036
Fax: 01737 770046
E-mail: enq@cruisersltd.co.uk
Web site: www.cruisersltd.co.uk
Dir: M J Walter
Fleet: 16 - 3 single-deck bus, 3 single-deck coach, 8 midicoach, 2 minicoach,
Chassis: inc: Dennis. Mercedes-Benz. Volvo.
Bodies: Optare. Plaxton. Wadhan Stringer.
Ops incl: local bus services, school contracts, private hire.
Livery: multi - metallic
Ticket System: Almex

EPSOM COACHES GROUP
21 BLENHEIM ROAD, LONGMEAD BUSINESS PARK, EPSOM KT19 9AF
Tel: 01372 731700
Fax: 01372 731740
E-mail: sales@epsomcoaches.com
Web site: www.epsomcoaches.com
Man Dir: A J Richmond **Comm Dir**: S Whiteway **Coach Hire Man**: J Fowler
Bus Services Man: J Ball **Service Man**: I Norman **Mktg Man**: A Scott
Fleet: 80 - 10 double-deck bus, 51 single-deck bus, 17 single-deck coach, 2 minibus.
Chassis: 39 Alexander Dennis. 5 Mercedes-Benz. 21 Optare. 15 Setra.
Bodies: 22 Alexander Dennis 1 Caetano. 16 East Lancs. 3 Mercedes-Benz. 21 Optare. 2 Plaxton. 15 Setra
Ops incl: local bus services, excursions & tours, private hire, express, continental tours.
Livery: Red/Cream
Ticket system: Wayfarer

FARNHAM COACHES

ODIHAM ROAD, FARNHAM GU10 5AE
E-mail: sales@farnhamcoaches.co.uk
Web site: www.farnhamcoaches.co.uk
Ops incl: school contracts, private hire
Livery: Red/Cream
(Fleet etc - see Safeguard Coaches)

G J TRAVEL LTD

135A BROX ROAD, OTTERSHAW KT16 0LG
Tel: 01932 560196
Fax: 01460 66967
Dirs: StephenAdams, Barbara M Adams.
Fleet: 6 - 2 minibus, 4 midicoach.
Chassis: 1 Leyland. 5 Mercedes.
Bodies: 2 Autobus. 1 Leyland. 2 Mercedes. 1 Optare.
Ops incl: private hire.
Livery: Red/Blue on White

HARDINGS COACHES

WELLWOOD, WELLHOUSE LANE, BETCHWORTH RH3 7HH
Tel: 01737 842103
Fax: 01737 842831
E-mail: sales@hardings-coaches.co.uk
Fleet: 13 - 6 coach, 3 midicoach, 4 minicoach.
Chassis: 1 MAN. 5 Mercedes. 2 Scania. 4 Volvo.
Bodies: 2 Berkhof. 2 Autobus. 1 Caetano. 3 Esker. 2 Irizar. 3 Plaxton.
Ops incl: private hire

HARWOOD COACHES

51 ELLESMERE ROAD, WEYBRIDGE KT13 0HW.
Tel: 01932 842073, 227272.
Prop: G. A. Harwood.
Fleet: 5 coach.
Chassis: 2 Bedford. 3 Volvo.
Bodies: 2 Duple. 3 Van Hool.
Ops incl: private hire.
Livery: Beige/Red/Brown.

HILLS OF HERSHAM

129 BURWOOD ROAD, HERSHAM KT12 4AN
Tel: 01932 254795
Fax: 01932 222671
Dir: D Hill
Fleet: 6 inc:- single-deck coach, midicoach, minicoach, minibus.
Chassis: 1 Iveco. 1 LDV. 1 Mercedes-Benz. 1 Renault. 2 Volvo.
Bodies: 1 Beulas. 1 Jonckheere. 1 Mercedes-Benz. 1 Van Hool.
Ops incl: school contracts, private hire
Livery: White/Red

MAYDAY TRAVEL

SUITE 7, UNIT 8, MILL LANE TRADING ESTATE, MILL LANE, CROYDON CR0 4AA
Tel: 020 8680 5111

Web site: www.coachhirelondon.co.uk
Fleet: coach, midibus, minibus.
Ops incl: private hire, excursions & tours.
Livery: Silver/White/Blue

M&E COACHES

11 VAUX CRESCENT, HERSHAM KT12 4HE.
Tel: 01932 244664.
Prop/Gen Man: M. W. Oram.
Sec: Mrs A. E. Oram.
Fleet: 3 coach.
Chassis: 1 MAN. 2 Mercedes.
Ops incl: school contracts, excursions & tours, private hire.
Livery: Blue/White.

MERTON COMMUNITY TRANSPORT

JUSTIN PLAZA 3, SUITE 3, LONDON ROAD, MITCHAM CR4 4BE
Tel: 020 8648 7727
E-mail: mertonct@ukonline.co.uk

PICKERING COACHES

12 HAYSBRIDGE COTTAGES, WHITE WOOD LANE, SOUTH GODSTONE RHG 8JN.
Tel/Fax: 01342 843731.
Props: R. Pickering, Ms D. Pickering.
Fleet: 5 coach.
Chassis: Volvo.
Bodies: 2 Duple. 1 Jonckheere. 2 Plaxton.
Ops incl: private hire, school contracts.

SAFEGUARD COACHES LTD

GUILDFORD PARK ROAD, GUILDFORD GU2 7TH
Tel: 01483 561103
Fax: 01483 455865
E-mail: sales@safeguardcoaches.co.uk
Web site: www.safeguardcoaches.co.uk
Man Dir/Co Sec: A J Halliday **Ops Man**: C S West **Non Exec Dirs**: Mrs E G Newman, Mrs J C Newman, D K Newman,

M G Newman, **Eng Man**: B J Lambley
Fleet: 36 - 7 single-deck bus, 25 single-deck coach, 4 midicoach.
Chassis: 1 AEC. 6 Dennis. 5 Mercedes-Benz. 4 Optare. 2 Setra. 18 Volvo.
Bodies: 1 Carlyle. 1 Hispano. 1 Mercedes-Benz. 1 Northern Counties. 5 Optare. 18 Plaxton. 2 Setra. 6 Van Hool. 1 other.
Ops incl: local bus services, school contracts, private hire.
Livery: Red/Cream.
Ticket System: Almex A90

SKINNERS OF OXTED

15 BARROW GREEN ROAD, OXTED RH8 0NJ
Tel: 01883 713633
Fax: 01883 730079
E-mail: info@skinnerstravel.co.uk
Web site: www.skinnerstravel.co.uk
Dirs: Stephen Skinner, Deborah Skinner.
Fleet: 14 - 13 single-deck coach, 1 minicoach.
Chassis: 5 Alexander Dennis. 1 MCW. 2 Mercedes-Benz. 6 Setra.
Bodies: 2 Duple. 1 Mercedes-Benz. 3 Neoplan. 1 Optare. 6 Setra. 1 Other.
Ops incl: excursions & tours, private hire, school contracts, continental tours.

SUNRAY TRAVEL LTD

79 ASHLEY RD, EPSOM KT18 5BN
Tel: 01372 740400
Fax: 01372 800778
E-mail: enquiries@gosunray.com
Web site: www.sunraytravel.co.uk
Fleetname: Go Sunray.com
Dir: Noel Millier
Fleet: 7 - 4 bus, 3 coach
Chassis: 3 Dennis. 1 Leyland. 3 Volvo
Bodies: include: 2 Alexander. 2 Carlyle. 4 Plaxton
Ops incl: local bus services, school contracts, excursions & tours, private hire, continental tours.
Livery: Blue with yellow/orange/red sun rays

SURELINE COACHES
UNIT 8, MARTLANDS INDUSTRIAL ESTATE, SMARTS HEATH LANE, MAYFORD, WOKING GU22 0RQ
Tel: 01483 234649
Fax: 01483 236464
E-mail: sureline@btclick.com
Prop: John McCracken
Fleet: 10 - 8 single-deck coach, 2 midicoach.
Chassis: 4. Bova. 2 MAN. 1 Mercedes-Benz. 2 Setra. 1 Toyota.
Bodies: 4 Bova. 2 Caetano. 1 Neoplan. 2 Setra. 1 other.
Ops incl: excursions & tours, private hire, school contracts, continental tours.
Livery: White with red signage

SURREY CONNECT
GATWICK COACH CENTRE, OLD BRIGHTON ROAD, LOWFIELD HEATH, CRAWLEY RH4 0PR
Tel: 01293 596831
E-mail: buses@connectbuses.com
Web site: www.connectbuses.com
Subsidiary of Flights Hallmark, part of Rotala PLC

SUTTON COMMUNITY TRANSPORT
HALLMEAD DAY CENTRE, ANTON CRESCENT, COLLINGWOOD ROAD, SUTTON SM1 2NT
Tel: 020 8644 6001
Fax: 020 8644 2247
Web site: www.suttonct.co.uk
Ch Exec: Turner Duff **Ops Man**: Malcolm Sailing **Chmn**: P Hewitt **Dirs**: D Mason, P Bloxham, Tony Pattison, Inger Wilson, Pam Wilson, Lal Hussain MBE
Fleet: 15 minibus.
Chassis/bodies: Ford Transit. Iveco. VW. LDV. Mercedes. Optare.
Ops incl: school contracts, excursions & tours, private hire.
Livery: White with purple logo

TELLINGS GOLDEN MILLER COACHES LTD
See Middlesex

EDWARD THOMAS & SON
442 CHESSINGTON ROAD, EPSOM, SURREY KT19 9EJ
Tel: 020 8397 4276
Fax: 020 8397 5276
E-mail: edwardthomasandson@btconnect.com
Web: www.edwardthomasandson.com
Owner: Ivan Thomas **Ch Eng**: Manny Seager **Ops Man**: Neil Seager
Comp Sec: Sharman Grey
Fleet: 24 - incl: double-deck bus, single-deck bus single-deck coach
Chassis: 8 Leyland. 16 Volvo.
Ops incl: local bus services, school contracts, private hire.
Livery: Green/Cream

TRAVEL SURREY
301 CAMBERWELL ROAD, LONDON SE5 0TF
Tel: 020 7805 3535
Fax: 020 7805 3502
Web: www.travellondonbus.co.uk
Ops incl: Local bus service.
A division of Travel London, part of National Express Group

W H MOTORS
See West Sussex.

WESTERHAM COACHES
15 BARROW GREEN ROAD, OXTED RH8 ONJ
Tel: 01883 713633
Fax: 01883 730079
Web: www.skinnerstravel
E-mail:info@skinnners.travel
Ptnrs: Stephen Skinner, Deborah Skinner.
Fleet: 14 - 13 single-deck coach, 1 minicoach.
Chassis: 5 Alexander Dennis. 1 MCW. 2 Mercedes-Benz. 6 Setra.
Bodies: 2 Duple. 1 Mercedes-Benz. 3 Neoplan. 6 Setra. 1 Other
Ops incl: excursions & tours, private hire, school contracts, continental tours.

TYNE & WEAR

A & J COACHES OF WASHINGTON
6 SKIRLAW CLOSE, GLEBE VILLAGE, WASHINGTON NE38 7RE
Tel: 0191 417 2564
Fax: 0191 415 4672
Recovery: 07702 068 063
E-mail: jean@ajcoaches.fsnet.co.uk
Dir: Ian Ashman **Co Sec**: Jean Ashman
Fleet: 1 coach
Chassis: 1 Volvo
Bodies: 1 Plaxton
Ops incl: school contracts, private hire.
Livery: Blue/White

A LINE COACHES
UNIT 1, PELAW INDUSTRIAL ESTATE, GATESHEAD NE10 0UW
Tel/Fax: 0191 495 2424
E-mail: les@a-linecoaches.co.uk
Web site: www.a-linecoaches.co.uk
Ptnrs: D C Annis, L B Annis **Sec**: Mrs S Reay **Wkshp**: B Jennings, S King
Fleet: 8 - 2 single-deck bus, 2 coach, 4 midibus.
Chassis: 1 DAF. 4 Dennis. 1 Leyland. 1 Mercedes. 1 Optare.
Bodies: 1 Duple. 1 Leyland. 1 Mellor. 1 Optare. 2 Plaxton. 1 Van Hool. 1 Wright.
Ops incl: local bus services, school contracts, excursions & tours, private hire, continental tours.
Livery: Red/White
Ticket System: AES 2000

ALTONA COACH SERVICES & TRAVEL CONSULTANT
UNIT K4, SKILLION BUSINESS CENTRE, GREEN LANE, FELLING NE10 0QW.
Tel: 0191 469 2193.
Fax: 0191 469 3025.
Fleetname: Altona Travel.
Prop: A. C. Hunter. **Ops Man**: A. I. Hunter.
Office Man: R. Dudding.
Fleet: 9 - 5 coach, 2 midicoach, 2 minicoach.
Chassis: 1 DAF. 1 Dennis. 2 Mercedes. 1 Toyota. 3 Volvo.
Bodies: 2 Caetano. 2 Duple. 1 LAG. 2 Plaxton. 1 Robin Hood. 1 Bus Craft Impala.
Ops incl: excursions & tours, private hire, continental tours.
Livery: Two tone Blue and Orange.

ARRIVA NORTH EAST
ADMIRAL WAY, DOXFORD INTERNATIONAL BUSINESS PARK, SUNDERLAND SR3 3XP
Tel: 0191 520 4200
Fax: 0191 520 4222
Web site: www.arriva.co.uk
Man Dir: Jonathon May **Eng Dir**: J Greaves **Fin Dir**: Sue Richardson
Ops Dir: I McInroy
Fleet: 650 - 117 double-deck bus, 326 single-deck bus, 8 coach, 199 minibus.
Chassis: DAF. Dennis. Iveco. Leyland. MCW. MAN. Mercedes. Optare. Scania. Transbus. Volvo.
Bodies: Alexander. ECW. East Lancs. Ikarus. Leyland. MCW. Mercedes. Northern Counties. Optare. Plaxton. Transbus. Van Hool. Wright.
Ops incl: local bus services, school contracts, private hire, express.
Livery: Aquamarine/Stone
Ticket System: Wayfarer 3

ASHLEY COACHES/ ROWLANDS GILL TAXIS
1 THORNLEY VIEW, ROWLANDS GILL, TYNE & WEAR NE39 1QL
Tel: 01207 543118
E-mail: ashleycoaches@aol.com
Web: www.ashleycoaches.aol.com
Dir: David Murphy
Fleet: 3 single-deck coach, 3 midicoach.
Chassis: 1 Leyland. 3 Renault, 2 Volkswagen.
Bodies: 3 Plaxton.
Ops incl: school contracts, private hire, express.
Livery: Blue

TYNE & WEAR

COACHLINERS OF TYNESIDE
16 BRANDLING COURT, SOUTH SHIELDS NE34 8PA
Tel/Fax: 0191 427 1515
E-mail: coachliners@yahoo.co.uk
Prop: John Dorothy
Fleet: 2 midicoach
Chassis: 2 Mercedes-Benz.
Bodies: 2 Plaxton.
Ops incl: school contracts, excursions & tours, private hire.
Livery: White with red stripes

HENRY COOPER COACHES
LANE END GARAGE, ANNITSFORD NE23 7BD
Tel: 0191 250 0260
Fax: 0191 250 1820
E-mail: ggpam@tiscali.co.uk
Ptnrs: Graham Greaves
Fleet: 7 single-deck bus
Chassis: 1 Leyland. 7 Volvo.

DERWENT COACHES LTD
MORRISON ROAD, ANNFIELD PLAIN DH9 7RX
Tel: 0191 488 7248.
Fax: 01207 281333.
E-mail: derwentc@aol.com
Man Dir: I. Shipley. **Dir**: A. Fox.
Comm Exec: D. Allan.
Garage Foreman: B. Thurgood.
Fleet: 10 coach.
Chassis: Volvo.
Bodies: 5 Plaxton. 5 Van Hool.
Ops incl: local bus services, school contracts, excursions & tours, private hire, express, continental tours.
Livery: White, Red & Blue.
Ticket System: Almex.

ERB SERVICES LTD
HANNINGTON PLACE, BYKER, NEWCASTLE UPON TYNE NE6 1JU
Tel: 0191 224 0002
Fax: 0191 224 0030
E-mail: sales@erb.entadsl.com
Web site: www.erbservices.co.uk
Man Dir: Edmund Brown **Dirs**: Edmund Brown(jnr), David R Brown
Fleet: 13 - 1 single-deck bus, 3 coach, 2 midicoach, 7 minibus
Chassis: 1 Dennis. 1 Ford. 9 Mercedes. 2 Volvo.

Bodies: 1 Jonckheere. 7 Mercedes. 1 Neoplan. 2 Optare. 1 Van Hool. 1 other
Ops incl: school contracts, excursions & tours, private hire
Livery: White

GO NORTH EAST
117 QUEEN STREET, GATESHEAD NE8 2UA
Tel: 0191 420 5050
Fax: 0191 420 0225
E-mail: customerservices@gonortheast.co.uk
Web site: www.simplygo.co.uk
Man Dir: P G Huntley **Ops Dir**: K Carr
Fin Dir: G C McPherson
Comm Dir: M P Harris
Fleet: 668 - 131 double-deck bus, 376 single-deck bus, 20 single-deck coach, 141 minibus.
Chassis: 1 Blue Bird. 60 DAF. 216 Dennis. 21 Leyland. 35 Mercedes-Benz. 16 Optare. 137 Scania. 26 Transbus. 6 VDL. 150 Volvo.
Bodies: 18 Alexander. 22 Cetano. 30 East Lancs. 3 Leyland. 24 Marshall/MCV. 35 Mercedes-Benz. 92 Northern Counties. 23 Optare. 123 Plaxton. 70 Transbus. 187 Wright. 41 other.
Ops incl: local bus services, school contracts, express.
Livery: Various route brands
Ticket System: Wayfarer 3

JIM HUGHES COACHES LTD
WEAR STREET, LOW SOUTHWICK, SUNDERLAND SR5 2BH
Tel: 0191 548 9600
Fax: 0191 549 3728
Man Dir: James Hughes **Dir**: V Hughes
Fleet: 6 single-deck coach
Chassis: 6 Volvo.
Bodies: 3 Plaxton. 3 Van Hool.
Ops incl: excursions & tours, private hire, continental tours

KINGSLEY COACHES
UNIT 20, PENSHAW WAY, PORTOBELLO INDUSTRIAL ESTATE, BIRTLEY DH3 2SA
Tel: 0191 492 1299
Fax: 0191 410 9281
E-mail: accounts@kingsleycoaches.co.uk
Dirs: David Kingsley (senior), David Kingsley (junior), Mrs Eileen Kingsley (Co Sec)
Fleet: 26 - 13 double-deck bus, 3 single-deck bus, 2 double-deck coach, 7 coach, 2 minibus.
Chassis: 1 Freight Rover. 5 Leyland. 2 MAN. 14 MCW. 1 Mercedes. 1 Optare. 1 Scania. 1 Volvo.
Bodies: 1 Berkhof. 1 Duple. 2 Marshall/MCV. 14 MCW. 1 Mercedes. 1 Optare. 4 Plaxton. 2 Van Hool.
Ops incl: school contracts, excursions & tours, private hire
Livery: Blue/White.
Ticket System: Wayfarer 3

PRIORY MOTOR COACH CO LTD
59 CHURCHWAY, NORTH SHIELDS NE29 0AD.
Tel/Fax: 0191 257 0283.
E-mail: sales.priorycoaches@btconnect.com
Dirs: S Kirkpatrick, P.Harris, I Fenwck, L Stewart.
Fleet: 10 - 9 single-deck coach, 1 minbus.
Chassis: 1 LDV. 1 Leyand. 8 Volvo.
Bodies: 1 Berkhof. 1 Caetano. 1 Jonkheere. 2 Plaxton. 4 Van Hool.
Ops incl: excursions & tours, private hire, school contracts.
Livery: White/Blue

STAGECOACH NORTH EAST
WHEATSHEAF, SUNDERLAND SR5 1AQ
Tel: 0191 567 5251
Fax: 0191 566 0202
E-mail: infonortheast@stagecoachbus.com
Web site: www.stagecoachgroup.com
Man Dir: John Conroy **Ops Dir**: Nigel Winter **Eng Dir**: David Kirsopp **Com Dir**: Robin Knight
Fleet: 526 - 93 double-deck bus, 262 single-deck bus, 4 double-deck coach, 9 minibus.
Chassis: 182 Dennis. 6 Leyland. 181 MAN. 9 Mercedes. 158 Volvo. 10 other.
Bodies: 454 Alexander. 42 Northern Counties. 20-Plaxton. 10 other
Ops incl: local bus services, school contracts.
Livery: White/Blue/Orange/Red
Ticket System: ERGsystem4000

	Vehicle suitable for disabled		Seat belt-fitted Vehicle
T	Toilet-drop facilities available		Coach(es) with galley facilities
R	Recovery service available		Air-conditioned vehicle(s)
	Open top vehicle(s)v		Coaches with toilet facilities
R24	24 hour recovery service		Replacement vehicle available
			Vintage Coach(es) available

176

WARWICKSHIRE

CATTERALLS OF SOUTHAM
74 COVENTRY STREET, SOUTHAM CV47 0EA
Tel: 01926 813840/3192
Fax: 01926 813915
Recovery: 01926 817442
E-mail: paul@travelcatteralls.co.uk
Web site: www.travelcatteralls.co.uk
Dir: Paul Catterall **Tran Man**: Stan Griffin
Eng: Paul Rhodes **Garage Man**: Dave Ould **Operations (Tours)**: Maureen Allison **Admin**: Richard Wilderspin
Fleet: 20 - 16 coach, 3 double-deck coach, 1 midicoach
Chassis: 3 MAN. 2 Mercedes. 2 Scania. 13 Volvo.
Bodies: 1 Irizar. 3 Jonckheere. 1 Marcopolo. 2 Noge. 10 Plaxton. 1 Setra. 2 Van Hool.
Ops incl: local bus services, school contracts, excursions & tours, private hire, continental tours.
Livery: Blue/Yellow stripes on White

CHAPEL END COACHES
WILSON HOUSE, 3 OASTON ROAD, NUNEATON CV11 6JX
Tel: 024 7635 4588
Fax: 024 7635 6406
Web site: www.chapelendcoaches.co.uk
E-mail: cecoaches@ukonline.co.uk
Man Dir/Trans Man: Ian Wilson **Dir/Sec**: Mrs Tracey Wilson
Fleet: 11- single-deck coaches.

Ops incl: local bus services, excursions & tours, private hire, continental tours, school contracts.
Livery: White/Red/Black

L. S. COURT LTD
RED HILL, FILLONGLEY CV7 8DA
Tel: 01676 540282
Fax: 01676 541110
Dirs: G Purchase, Mrs J Purchase.
Co Sec: J Purchase **Ch Eng**: D Purchase
Fleet: 14 - 2 double-deck bus, 1 single-deck bus, 7 coach, 3 midicoach, 1 minibus
Chassis: 1 Bedford. 1 Iveco. 3 Leyland. 2 MCW. 4 Mercedes. 3 Scania.
Bodies: 1 Beulas. 1 Jonckeere. 2 MCW. 4 Mercedes. 3 Plaxton. 3 Reeve Burgess. 1 Van Hool.
Ops incl: local bus services, school contracts, private hire.

MIKE DE COURCEY TRAVEL LTD
See West Midlands.

MARTIN'S OF TYSOE
20 OXHILL ROAD, MIDDLE TYSOE CV35 0SX
Tel: 01295 680642.
Prop: Martin Thomas.

SKYLINERS LTD
19 BOND STREET, NUNEATON CV11 4NX.

Tel: 024 7632 5682
Fax: 024 7635 4626
E-mail: haydn@skyliners.co.uk
Dir: Haydon J. Dawkins
Fleet: 1 double-deck coach.
Body: Neoplan.
Ops incl: excursions & tours, private hire, continental tours.

STAGECOACH IN WARWICKSHIRE
RAILWAY TERRACE, RUGBY CV21 3HS
Tel: 01788 562036
Fax: 01788 566094
E-mail: warksenquiries@stagecoachbus.com
Web site: www.stagecoachbus.com/warwickshire
Man Dir: Phil Medlicott **Eng Dir**: Mike Bishop
Fleet: 187 - 41 double-deck bus, 40 single-dek bus, 5 coach, 68 midibus, 33 minibus.
Chassis: 1 AEC. 53 Dennis. 16 Leyland. 6 MCW. 5 Mercedes. 28 Optare. 5 Scania. 73 Volvo.
Bodies: 114 Alexander. 3 ECW. 5 Jonckheere. 6 MCW. 2 Northern Counties. 28 Optare. 1 Park Royal. 16 Plaxton. 7 Transbus. 5 other.
Ops incl: local bus services, school contracts, private hire, express
Livery: Stagecoach
Ticket System: ERG

WEST MIDLANDS

ADAMS TOURS
75 SANDBANK, BLOXWICH WS3 2HL
Tel: 01922 406469
Fax: 01922 406469
Ptnr: David Adams
Fleet: 8 - 4 coach, 2 midicoach, 2 minibus.
Chassis: 4 DAF. 4 Mercedes.
Bodies: 2 Autobus. 1 Mellor. 1 Plaxton. 4 Van Hool.
Ops incl: private hire, school contracts, excursions & tours
Livery: Cream/Green/Orange

AIRPARKS SERVICES LTD
WILLOW HOUSE, PINEWOOD BUSNIESS PARK, COLESHILL ROAD, MARSTON GREEN, BIRMINGHAM B37 7HJ
Tel: 0121 717 5300
Fax: 0121 788 0778
E-mail: david.rowe@airparks.co.ik
Web site: www.airparks.co.uk
Ops Dir: Paul Humphrey **Group Fleet Man**: David Rowe **Trans Man**: Matt Lawton **Com Sec**: Elisabeth Hirlemann
Fleet: 32 - 27 single-deck bus, 5 minibus.
Chassis: 11 Alexandra Dennis, 4 Ford Transit, 16 MAN, 1Volkswagen.
Bodies: 11 Alexander Dennis. 16 MCV
Ops incl: private hire, - car park to aiport shuttle.

B B COACHES LTD
22 VICTORIA AVENUE, HALESOWEN B62 9BL
Tel: 0121 422 4501
Fax: 0121 602 2040
Dirs: Barbara, Mick
Fleet: 2 coach.
Chassis: 2 Volvo
Bodies: 2 Plaxton
Ops incl: excursions & tours, private hire.

BEACON COACHES
24 CHICHESTER GROVE, CHELMSLEY WOOD B37 5RZ.
Tel: 0121 783 2221
Fax: 0121 680 2582
E-mail: enquiries@beaconcoaches
Web site: www.beaconcoaches.co.uk
Fleet: 6 - 2 double-deck coach, 1 midicoach, 1 minicoach, 2 minibus.
Chassis: 1 MAN, 2 Scania, 1 Toyota. LDV.
Bodies: 3 Jonckheere.
Ops incl: excursions & tours, private hire, school contracts, continental tours.
Livery: White /Red/Grey.

L F BOWEN LTD
See Staffordshire

BIRMINGHAM INTERNATIONAL COACHES
10 FORTNUM CLOSE, TILE CROSS, BIRMINGHAM B33 0JT
Tel/Fax: 0121 783 4004
E-mail: birminghamintl@btconnect.com
Web site: www.birminghaminternationalcoaches.co.uk
Dirs: A Watkiss, M Watkiss, N Watkiss **Co Sec**: M Watkiss
Fleet: 10 - 9 coach, 1 midicoach.
Chassis: incl 9 Bova.
Bodies: incl 1 Caetano.
Ops incl: excursions & tours, private hire, continental tours, school contracts.
Livery: Dark Silver/Red

CENTRAL BUSES LTD
177 NEW TOWN ROW, NEWTOWN BIRMINGHAM B6 4QT
Tel: 07841 917846
Fax: 0870 199 2923
E-mail: email@centralbuses.com
Web site: www.centralbuses.com
Dirs: Geoff Cross, Stephen Cross
Fleet: 10 - single-deck bus
Chassis: 8 Dennis. 2 Optare.
Bodies: 2 Optare. 8 Plaxton
Ops incl: Local Bus services.
Livery: Red/Grey
Ticket System: Almex A90

WEST MIDLANDS

CENTRAL CONNECT
SHADY LANE, GREAT BARR, BIRMINGHAM B44 9ER
Tel: 0121 322 2717
Fax: 0121 360 2862
Recovery: 07973 939103
E-mail: buses@connectbuses.com
Web site: www.connectbuses.com
Fleet: 46 - 24 single-deck bus, 14 coach, 12 minibus.
Chassis: 30 Dennis. 9 LDV. 1 MAN. 1 Neoplan. 1 Setra. 8 Volvo.
Bodies: 4 Caetano. 1 Duple. 1 Neoplan. 2 Plaxton. 1 Setra. 6 Van Hool.
Ops incl: local bus services, school contracts, excursions & tours, private hire, express, continental tours
Livery: various
Ticket System: Wayfarer TGX
Part of Rotala PLC - Incorporating Birmingham Motor Traction, North Birmingham Busways & Zak's Bus & Coach Services.

COURTESY TRAVELS
2 WOODFIELD AVE, SHREWSBURY
Tel: 01743 358209
E-mail: courtesy@tiscalli.co.uk
Propritor: John Amies
Fleet: 2 - 1 midicoach, 1 minicoach
Chassis: 1 LDV, 1 Mercedes-Benz
Bodies: 1 Autobus. 1 Other
Ops incl: excursions & tours, private hire
Livery: Blue/White

DEN CANEY COACHES LTD
THE COACH STATION, STONE HOUSE LANE, BARTLEY GREEN, BIRMINGHAM B32 3AH
Tel: 0121 427 2078
Fax: 0121 427 8905
E-mail: enquiry@dencaneycoaches.co.uk
Web site: www.dencaneycoaches.co.uk
Man Dir: D Stevens **Dir**: M Stevens **Ch Eng**: A Doggett **Ops Man**: J Clarke
Administrator: Mrs D Johnston
Fleet: 9 coach
Chassis: 1 Dennis. 1 Leyland. 2 Toyota. 7 Volvo
Ops incl: private hire, school contracts

CHAUFFEURS OF BIRMINGHAM
CREST HOUSE, 7 HIGHFIELD ROAD, EDGBASTON, BIRMINGHAM B15 3ED.
Tel: 0121 456 3355.

CLARIBEL COACHES
10 FORTNUM CLOSE, TILE CROSS, BIRMINGHAM B33 0JT
Tel: 0121 789 7878
Fax: 0121 785 0967
Dirs: A Watkiss, M Watkiss, N Watkiss, M Watkiss
Fleet: 21 - 1 double-deck bus, 20 single-deck bus.
Chassis: 14 DAF. 1 Dennis. 6 Optare.
Ops incl: local bus services, school contracts, private hire, excursions & tours
Livery: Blue/White.
Ticket System: Wayfarer 3

N N CRESSWELL
See Worcestershire

DAIMLER
99 SAREHOLE ROAD, BIRMINGHAM B28 8ED
Tel: 0121 778 2837
Fax: 0121 702 2843
E-mail: roy@daimlertours.wanadoo.co.uk
Prop: Roy Picken
Fleet: 1 coach
Chassis/Body: 1 Neoplan
Ops incl: excursions & tours
Livery: White/Burgundy

DIAMOND BUS LTD
CROSS QUAYS BUSINESS PARK, HALLBRIDGE WAY, TIVDALE, OLDBURY, WEST MIDLANDS B69 3HW
Tel: 0121 557 7337
Fax: 0121 520 4999
Ops incl: Local bus service
Livery: Red/Black
Part of Rotala PLC

MIKE DE COURCEY TRAVEL LTD
ROWLEY DRIVE, COVENTRY CV3 4FG
Tel: 024 7630 2656
Fax: 024 7663 9276
E-mail: contactus@traveldecourcey.com
Web site: www.traveldecourcey.com
Fleetname: Travel De Courcey
Man Dir: Mike de Courcey **Co Sec**: Adrian de Courcey **Gen Man**: Bob Wildman **Fleet Eng**: Neville Collins
Fleet: 73 - 24 double-deck bus, 31 single-deck bus, 15 double-deck coach, 3 minibus.
Chassis: 1 Daimler. 1 LDV. 2 Leyland. 33 MAN. 17 MCW. 5 Mercedes-Benz. 14 Volvo.
Bodies: 4 Alexander Dennis. 2 Jonckheere. 4 Marcopolo. 29 Marshall/MCV. 17 MCW. 3 Mercedes-Benz. 4 Northern Counties. 6 Plaxton 2 Van Hool, 2 Other.
Ops incl: local bus services, school contracts, private hire.
Livery: White/Blue/Orange.
Ticket System: Wayfarer TGX

DIRECT COACH TOURS
68 BERKELEY ROAD EAST, HAY MILLS, BIRMINGHAM B25 8NP
Tel: 0121 772 0664.
Fax: 0121 773 8649.
Tours Man: Brian Bourne.
Fleet: 7 - 6 coach, 1 midicoach.
Chassis: 1 Toyota. 6 Volvo.
Bodies: 1 Caetano. 6 Plaxton.
Ops incl: excursions & tours, private hire.

FLIGHTS HALLMARK LTD
BEACON HOUSE, LONG ACRE, NECHELLS, BIRMINGHAM B7 5JJ
Tel: 0121 322 2222
Fax: 0121 322 2224
Recovery: 0121 322 2710
E-mail: sales@flightshallmark.com
Web site: www.flightshallmark.com
Chmn: John Dunn **Ch Exec**: Kim Taylor
Man Dir: Simon Dunn **Dir**: Geoff Flight
Eng Man: Dave Russell **Bus Dev Man**: Anthony Goozee **Com Man**: Ian Pollard
Ops Mans: Paul Williams (coach), Steve Elms (bus)
Fleet: 232 - 20 double-deck bus, 170 single-deck bus, 30 single-deck coach, 12 midicoach.
Chassis: 5 DAF. 69 Dennis. 6 LDV. 5 MAN. 10 Mercedes. 5 Optare. 2 Toyota. 100 Volvo.
Bodies: 10 Alexander. 3 Caetano. 2 Jonckheere. 2 MCW. 6 Mercedes. 2 Neoplan. 5 Optare. 190 Plaxton. 2 Sunsundegui. 1 Van Hool. 15 Wright.
Ops incl: local bus services, school contracts, excursions & tours, private hire, express, continental tours.
Ticket system: Wayfarer, ERG
Part of Rotala PLC

ENDEAVOUR COACHES LTD
30 PLUME STREET, ASTON, BIRMINGHAM B6 7RT
Tel: 0121 326 4994
Fax: 0121 326 4999
Dirs: J Mitchell, G Mitchell, D Mitchell
Fleet: single-deck coach, midibus.
Chassis: 1 Bova. 1 DAF. 1 MAN. 5 Volvo.
Bodies: 1 B`ova. 1 Marcopolo. 2 Plaxton. 5 Van Hool.
Ops incl: excursions and tours, school contracts, express.

EUROLINERS
1631 BRISTOL ROAD SOUTH, REDNAL, BIRMINGHAM BH45 9UA
Tel: 0121 453 5151
Fax: 0121 453 5504
Prop: Anthony Armstrong **Man**: Glen Styles
Fleet: 14 - 4 single-deck coach, 1 midibus, 2 midicoach, 7 minicoach.
Chassis: 5 LDV. 9 Mercedes-Benz.
Bodies: 2 Caetano. 6 Mellor, 4 Mercedes-Benz. 1 Optare. 1 Plaxton.
Ops incl: local bus services, school contracts, private hire, continental tours.

GOODE'S COACHWAYS
150 CRANKHALL LANE, WEDNESBURY WS10 0ED
Tel: 0121 556 0706
Fax: 0121 505 1619
E-mail: info@goodebus.com
Web site: www.goodebus.com
CEO: P W Goode **Ops Man**: K Goode
Fleet: 10 - 8 single-deck bus, 2 midicoach.
Chassis: 1 Mercedes-Benz. 8 Volvo. 1 Toyota. .
Bodies: 5 Jonckheere. 2 Optare. 2 Plaxton. 1 Van Hool.
Ops incl: excursions & tours, private hire, continental tours.

HARDINGS INTERNATIONAL
See Worcestershire

J. R. HOLLYHEAD INTERNATIONAL
32 CROSS STREET, WILLENHALL WV13 1PG.
Tel: 01902 607364.
Fax: 01902 609772.
Owner: J. R. Hollyhead.
Fleet: 5 coach.
Chassis: 2 Bova. 3 Volvo.
Bodies: 2 Bova. 3 Plaxton.
Ops incl: excursions & tours, private hire, express, continental tours.
Livery: White.

JOHNSONS COACH & BUS TRAVEL
LIVERIDGE HOUSE, LIVERIDGE HILL, HENLEY-IN-ARDEN B95 5QS
Tel: 01564 797000
Fax: 01564 797050
E-mail: info@johnsonscoaches.co.uk
Web site: www.johnsonscoaches.co.uk
Dirs: P G Johnson, J R Johnson **Co Sec**: J M Johnson
Fleet: 60 - 23 single-deck bus, 34 coach, 3 minicoach.
Chassis: Bova. Mercedes. Toyota.
Bodies: Bova. East Lancs. Optare.
Ops incl: local bus services, school contracts, excursions & tours, private hire, continental tours.
Livery: Blue/Yellow
Ticket system: Wayfarer
Bodies: 28 Bova. 1 Irizar. 1 Leyland. 2 Mercedes. 8 Plaxton.
Ops incl: school contracts, excursions & tours, private hire, continental tours.
Livery: Yellow/Blue/White.
Ticket System: Setright.

JOSEPHS MINI COACHES
See Staffordshire

KEN MILLER TRAVEL
10 CHURCHILL ROAD, SHENSTONE WS14 0LP
Tel: 01827 60494
Fax: 01827 60494
Recovery: 07976 303951
E-mail: ken.m.traveluk@amserve.net
Fleetname: Ken Miller Recovery
Prop: Ken Miller
Fleet: 2 single-deck bus, 2 minibus.
Chassis: LDV. Volvo.
Ops incl: school contracts, private hire, express, continental tours.
Livery: Blue/Silver
Ticket system: Wayfarer.

KINGSNORTON COACHES
40 BISHOPS GATE, NORTHFIELD, BIRMINGHAM B31 4AJ
Tel: 0121 550 8519
Fax: 0121 501 6554
Web site: www.kingsnortoncoaches.co.uk
Props: Richard Egan, Malcolm Stanley
Fleet: 15 - 2 coach, 13 minibus.
Ops incl: school contracts, excursions & tours, private hire.

KINGSWINFORD COACHWAYS
HIGH STREET, PENSNETT, BRIERLEY HILL DY6 8XB
Tel: 01384 401626
Fax: 01384 401580
Recovery: 07831 148626
Dir: David William Edmunds **Ch Eng**: Robert Lamesdale **Sec**: Robert Morgan
Advisor: David Moor
Fleet: 7 - 6 single-deck coach, 1 midibus.
Chassis: 6 Volvo.
Body: 2 Plaxton. 1 Reeve Burgess. 4 Van Hool
Ops incl: school contracts, private hire.
Livery: White/Yellow/Red.

LAKESIDE COACHES LTD
See Shropshire

LUDLOWS OF HALESOWEN LTD
COOMBS ROAD, HALESOWEN B62 8AA.
Tel: 0121 559 7506.
Fax: 0121 561 4503.
Dirs: Mrs P. C. Ludlow, A. S. Ludlow.
Fleet: 32 - 22 single-deck bus, 7 coach, 2 minibus, 1 minicoach.
Chassis: 8 Dennis. 11 Leyland National. 2 Mercedes. 5 Scania. 4 Volvo. 2 Irizar.
Bodies: 2 Duple. 11 Leyland National. 2 Plaxton. 3 Van Hool. 9 Wright.
Ops incl: local bus services, school contracts, private hire.
Livery: Base White and multi-colour.
Ticket System: Wayfarer 3
Part of Rotala PLC

MEADWAY PRIVATE HIRE LTD
MEADWAY COACHES, 28-32 BERKELEY ROAD, HAY MILLS, BIRMINGHAM B25 8NG
Tel: 0121 773 8389
Fax: 0121 693 7171
Fleet: single-deck bus, coach, midicoach, minibus.
Chassis: Bedford. Dennis. Leyland. Mercedes. Transbus. Volvo.
Bodies: Caetano. Leyland. Mercedes. Plaxton. Transbus.
Ops incl: private hire, school contracts.

MIDLAND RIDER
UNIT 6, CMT TRADING ESTATE, BROADWELL ROAD, OLDBURY B69 4BQ
Tel/Fax: 0121 541 1954
E-mail: midlandrider@btconnect.com
Web: www.midlandrider.co.uk
Dir/Traffic Man: Matthew Hidson
Dir/Comp Sec: Andrew Rysztogi
Fleet: 16 single deck bus
Chassis: 1 DAF. 12 Dennis. 1 Leyland. 2 Volvo
Body: 1 Carlyle. 1 Leyland. 1 Optare. 13 Wright.
Ops incl: local bus service, school contracts, private hire
Livery: Yellow/two tone Blue
Ticket System: Wayfarer

WEST MIDLANDS

179

NASH COACHES LTD
83 RAGLAN ROAD, SMETHWICK
B66 3TT
Tel: 0121 558 0024
Fax: 0121 558 0907
E-mail: info@nashscoaches.co.uk
Web site: www.nashscoaches.co.uk
Dirs: I F Powell, Miss L Powell, G S Powell
Fleet: 8 - 6 single-deck coach, 2 minicoach.
Chassis: 5 Mercedes. 1 Toyota. 2 Volvo.
Bodies: 1 Berkhof. 1 Caetano. 1 Neoplan. 1 Plaxton. 3 Setra. 1 Van Hool.
Ops incl: excursions & tours, private hire, express, continental tours, school contracts.
Livery: Blue-firework

NATIONAL EXPRESS LTD
1 HAGLEY ROAD, EDGBASTON, BIRMINGHAM B16 8TG
Tel: 0121 625 1122
Fax: 0121 456 1397
E-mail: reception@nationalexpress.com
Web site: www.nationalexpress.com
Ch Exec: Paul Bunting
Chassis: Bova. DAF. MAN. Marshall. Mercedes. Neoplan. Scania. Volvo.
Bodies: Berkhof. Bova. Caetano. Irizar. Jonckheere. Marshall/MCV. Mercedes. Neoplan. Plaxton. Van Hool.
Ops incl: express.
Livery: Red/White/Blue.
Ticket System: Pre-sale, Wayfarer.

NEWBURY TRAVEL
NEWBURY LANE, OLDBURY B69 1HF
Tel: 0121 552 3262
Fax: 0121 552 0230
E-mail: newburytravel@aol.com
Web site: www.newburytravel.co.uk
Man Dir: David Greenhouse **Ch Eng**: Chris Phillips
Fleet: 11 - 5 coach, 3 midicoach, 3 minicoach.
Chassis: 1 Ford Transit. 2 LDV. 3 Mercedes. 5 Volvo.
Bodies: 1 Berkhof. 3 Mercedes. 4 Van Hool.
Ops incl: school contracts, private hire.
Livery: White

PROSPECT COACHES WEST LTD
81 HIGH STREET, LYE, STOURBRIDGE DY9 8NG
Tel: 01384 895436
Fax: 01384 898654
E-mail: sales@prospectcoaches.co.uk
Web site: www.prospectcoaches.co.uk
Man Dir: Geoffrey Watts **Dir**: Roslynd A D Hadley **Ops Man**: D Price **Personnel Man**: Nathan Hadley
Fleet: 30 coach.
Chassis: 3 DAF. 23 Dennis. 1 Neoplan. 3 Volvo
Bodies: 3 Duple. 1 Neoplan. 26 Plaxton.
Ops incl: school contracts, private hire.
Livery: Silver

HARRY SHAW
MILL HOUSE, MILL LANE, BINLEY, COVENTRY CV3 2DU.
Tel: 024 7665 0650
Fax: 024 7663 5684
E-mail: john@harryshaw.co.uk
Web site: www.harryshaw.co.uk
Fleet: 15 coach
Chassis: 1 Scania, 3 Setra, 11 Volvo
Ops incl: local bus services, excursions & tours, school contracts, private hire, continental tours.
Livery: Orange

SILVERLINE LANDFLIGHT LTD
ARGENT HOUSE, VULCAN ROAD, SOLIHULL B91 2JY
Tel: 0121 711 7799
Fax: 0121 709 0556
E-mail: silverline@landflight.co.uk
Web site: www.landflight.co.uk
Man Dir: M E Breakwell **Dirs**: W J Matthews, R G Knott **Comp Sec**: A Cakebread
Fleet: 17 - 3 single-deck bus, 8 single-deck coach, 5 midicoach, 1 mincoach.
Chassis: 2 MAN. 7 Mercedes-Benz. 2 Neoplan. 5 Optare. 3 Scania. 5 Toyota. 5 Volkswagen
Bodies: 5 Caetano. 2 Esker. 3 Irizar. 2 Neoplan. 5 Optare.
Ops incl: local bus services, private hire.

SOLUS COACH TRAVEL LTD
See Staffordshire

T. N. C. COACHES
257 CHESTER ROAD, CASTLE BROMWICH B36 0ET
Tel: 0121 747 5722
Fax: 0121 747 5722
Dirs: N T Cunningham, K M Cunningham.
Fleet: 5 - 2 coach, 3 minibus.
Chassis: 1 DAF. 1 Leyland. 3 LDV.
Bodies: Duple. Van Hool
Ops incl: school contracts, excursions & tours, private hire.

TERRYS COACH HIRE
21 PANDORA ROAD, WALSGRAVE, COVENTRY CV2 2FU
Tel/Fax: 024 7636 2975
E-mail: enquiries@terrys-coaches.co.uk
Web site: www.terrys-coaches.co.uk
Prop: T Hall **Ops Man**: L Hall **Cheif Eng**: J Hall **Co Sec**: S Hall
Fleet: 10 - 1 double-deck bus, 1 single-deck bus, 8 single-deck coach
Chassis: 1 DAF. 2 Leyland. 4 MAN. 1 Neoplan. 2 Volvo.
Bodies: 1 Neoplan. 4 Noge. 4 Plaxton. 1 Van Hool
Ops incl: excursions & tours, private hire, continental tours, school contracts.
Livery: Gold/green motif

THE TRANSPORT MUSEUM, WYTHALL
See Worcestershire

TRAVEL EXPRESS LTD
30 COTON ROAD, PENN, WOLVERHAMPTON WV41 5AT
Tel/Fax: 01902 330653
E-mail: kisha.chumbers&sky.com
Props: Kishan Chumber, Nirmal Chumber
Fleet: 10 - 10 single-deck bus
Chassis: 9 Alexander Dennis
Bodies: 6 Carlyle, 3 Duple. 1 Reeve Burgess
Ops incl: local bus service.
Livery: mixed
Ticket System: Wayfarer

TRAVEL WEST MIDLANDS
51 BORDESLEY GREEN, BIRMINGHAM B9 4BZ
Tel: 0121 254 7200 **Fax**: 0121 254 7277
Web site: www.travelwm.co.uk
Acting Ch Exec/Ops Dir: Neil Barker **Fin Dir**: Peter Coates **Eng Dir**: Jack Henry **Mktg & Dev Dir**: Maryin Hancock
Fleet: 1700 - 929 double-deck bus, 31 articulated bus, 689 single-deck bus, 51 minibus.
Chassis: 21 DAF. 434 Dennis. 150 MCW. 213 Mercedes. 100 Optare. 705 Volvo. 77 Scania.
Bodies: 529 Alexander. 150 MCW. 213 Mercedes. 121 Optare. 106 Plaxton. 504 Wright. 77 Scania.
Ops incl: local bus services, school contracts, private hire.
Livery: Red/White/Blue

TRAVEL MIDLAND METRO
METRO CENTRE, POTTERS LANE, WEDNESBURY WS10 0AR
Tel: 0121 502 2006
Fax: 0121 556 6299
Web site: www.centro.org.uk
Fleet: 16 articulated tramcars
General Manager: Fred Roberts
Chassis/Bodies: Ansaldo
Ops incl: tram service
Part of Travel West Midlands

W A SHEARINGS LTD
BAYTON ROAD, EXHALL CV7 9EJ.
Tel: 024 7664 4633.
Fax: 024 7636 0304.
Gen Man: Carol Carpenter.
See also W A Shearings Ltd, Greater Manchester.

WEST MIDLANDS SPECIAL NEEDS TRANSPORT
218-220 WINDSOR STREET, NECHELLS, BIRMINGHAM B7 4NE
Tel: 0121 333 3107 **Fax**: 0121 333 3345
E-mail: enquiries@wmsnt.org
Web site: www.wmsnt.org
Ch Exec: E B Connor **Ops Man**: D Rogers **Co Sec**: J Frater
Fleet: 260 minibus.
Chassis: 260 Volkswagen.
Bodies: 260 Concept.
Ops incl: local bus services, school contracts.
Livery: Red/White/Blue Blue/Yellow
Ticket system: manual/receipts

WHITTLE COACH & BUS LTD
See Worcestershire

WICKSONS TRAVEL
COPPICE ROAD, BROWNHILLS WS8 7DG
Tel: 01543 372247
Fax: 01543 374271
Web site: www.wicksons.co.uk
Fleet: 11 - 8 coach, 1 midibus, 2 midicoach
Chassis: 5 DAF. 1 MAN. 1 Mercedes. 4 Volvo
Bodies: 1 Autobus. 1 Noge. 9 Van Hool.
Ops incl: school contracts, excursions & tours, private hire, continental tours.
Livery: White/Blue/Orange

WINDSOR-GRAY TRAVEL
186 GRIFFITHS DRIVE, WEDNESFIELD, WOLVERHAMPTON WV11 2JR
Tel: 01902 722392
Fax: 01902 722339
E-Mail: grahamwgt@hotmail.co.uk
Owner: Graham Williams
Fleet: 2 midicoach.
Chassis: 1 Bedford.1 Dennis.
Bodies: 1 Duple. 1 Plaxton.
Ops incl: private hire, excursions & tours.

YARDLEY TRAVEL LTD
68 BERKELEY ROAD EAST, HAY MILLS, BIRMINGHAM B25 8MP
Tel: 0121 772 3700. **Fax**: 0121 773 8649
Dirs: R A Meddings, R W Meddings, W J A Meddings
Fleet: 9 - 8 coach, 1 midicoach
Chassis: 1 Toyota. 8 Volvo.
Bodies: 2 Caetano. 7 Plaxton.
Ops incl: excursions & tours, private hire.
Livery: White/Yellow/Black.

YOUNGS OF ROMSLEY
MALVERN VIEW, DAYHOUSE BANK, ROMSLEY, HALESOWEN B62 0EU
Tel/Fax: 01562 710717
Prop: R Young
Fleet: 3 - 1 coach, 2 minicoach
Chassis: 3 Mercedes.
Bodies: 3 Mercedes
Ops incl: excursions & tours, private hire, continental tours.
Livery: Bronze

WEST SUSSEX

ARUN COACHES/FAWLTY TOURS
1 NORFOLK TERRACE, HORSHAM RH12 1DA.
Tel: 01403 272999.
Fax: 01403 272777.
Prop/Ch Eng: H. Miller.
Fleet: 4 coach.
Chassis: 1 AEC. 1 Bristol. 2 Hestair/Duple.
Bodies: 2 Duple. 1 ECW. 1 Plaxton
Ops incl: private hire.
Livery: Red/Gold.

C. L. COACHES
UNIT 13, CHARTWELL ROAD, LANCING BN15 8TU.
Tel: 01903 752555
Fax: 01903 752777
Man Dir: D Brown **Dir**: G Brown, D Brown
Man: H Ticehurst.
Fleet: 15 - 1 double-deck bus, 14 coach
Chassis: 15 Volvo
Bodies: 1 Alexander. 14 Plaxton
Ops incl: private hire, school contracts.
Livery: Cream/Green/Grey

COMPASS TRAVEL
FARADAY CLOSE, WORTHING BN13 3RB
Tel: 01903 690025
Fax: 01903 690015
E-mail: office@compass-travel.co.uk
Web site: www.compass-travel.co.uk
Man Dir: Chris Chatfield **Eng Dir**: Malcolm Gallichan **Co Sec**: Roger Cotterell
Fleet: 39 - 4 single-deck bus, 6 single-deck coach, 25 midibus, 2 midicoach, 2 minibus
Chassis: 18 Alexander Dennis. 4 DAF. 1 Ford transit. 9 Mercedes-Benz. 5 Optare. 1 Scania. 1 Volvo.
Bodies: 16 Alexander Dennis. 4 Autobus. 1 Ikarus. 1 MCW. 2 Plaxton. 1 Reeve Bugess 5 Van Hool. 5 Other
Ops incl: local bus services, school contracts, private hire.
Livery: White/Burgundy.
Ticket System: Wayfarer

CRAWLEY LUXURY
STEPHENSON WAY, THREE BRIDGES RH10 1TN.
Tel: 01293 521002
Fax: 01293 522450
E-mail: crawleylux@aol.com
Fleetname: Crawley Luxury Coaches.
Dirs: David Brown, Darren Brown, Gavin Brown **Ops Mans**: Stephen Burse, Howard Ticehurst
Fleet: 37 - 2 double-deck bus, 35 coach.
Chassis: 37 Volvo.
Bodies: 2 Alexander. 1 Duple. 1 Jonckheere. 33 Transbus.
Ops incl: private hire, school contracts.
Livery: Cream/Green/Grey.

METROBUS LTD
WHEATSTONE CLOSE, CRAWLEY RH10 9UA
Tel: 01293 518292
Web site: www.metrobus.co.uk
Man Dir: Alan Eatwell **Finance Dir**: Kevin Lavender **Ops Dir**: Kevin Carey **Eng Dir**: Dominic Moorhouse
Fleet: 399 - 144 double-deck bus, 255 single-deck bus.
Chassis: 1 AEC. 166 Dennis. 5 MAN. 2 Optare. 199 Scania. 26 Volvo.
Bodies: 9 Alexander Dennis. 18 Caetano. 180 East Lancs. 36 Marshall/MCV. 11 Northern Counties. 4 Optare. 1 Park Royal. 42 Plaxton. 38 Tansbus. 60 Other.
Ops incl: local bus services
Part of the Go-Ahead Group

PAVILION COACHES
See East Sussex

RICHARDSON TRAVEL LTD
RUSSELL HOUSE, BEPTON ROAD, MIDHURST GU29 9NB
Tel: 01730 813304
Fax: 01730 815985
E-mail: sales@richardson-travel.co.uk
Web site: www.richardson-travel.co.uk
Dirs: R W Richardson
Fleet: 15 - 7 double-deck bus. 7 single-deck coach. 1 midicoach
Chassis: 1 Mercedes-Benz. 14 Volvo
Bodies: 5 Alexander Dennis. 2 East Lancs. 8 Plaxton.
Ops incl: local bus services, school contracts, excursions & tours, private hire, continental tours.
Livery: Blue

ROADMARK TRAVEL LTD
UNIT 15 GERSTON BUSINESS PARK, GREYFRIARS LANE, STORINGTON, PULBOROUGH RH20 4 HE
Tel: 01903 741233
Fax: 01903 741232
E-mail: coaches@roadmarktravel.co.uk
Web site: www.roadmarktravel.co.uk
Man Dir: David Coster **Co Sec**: Les Anderson
Fleet: 2 - 2 single-deck coach
Chassis: 1 Mercedes-Benz. 1 Neoplan
Bodies: 1 Mercedes-Benz. 1 Neoplan
Ops incl: excursions & tours, private hire, continental tours.
Livery: White/Blue

RUTHERFORDS INTERNATIONAL
BRAMFIELD HOUSE, CHURCH LANE, EASTERGATE, CHICHESTER PO20 3UZ
Tel: 01243 543673
Fax: 01403 782028
Owner: G R Bell
Fleet: coach
Chassis: Leyland. Neoplan. Scania.
Bodies: Irizar. Noge. Plaxton
Ops incl: private hire, school contracts.
Livery: White

SOUTHDOWN PSV LTD
SILVERWOOD, SNOW HILL, COPTHORNE RH10 3EN
Tel: 01342 719619
Fax: 01342 719617
E-mail: info@southdownpsv.co.uk
Web site: www.southdownpsv.co.uk
Man Dir: Steve Swain **Eng Dir**: Simon Stanford **Fin Dir**: Peter Larking **Ops Dir**: Gary Wood
Fleet: 20 - 4 double-deck bus, 16 single-deck bus.
Chassis: 2 Alexander Dennis. 4 DAF. 13 Dennis. 1 Volvo.
Ops incl: local bus services, school contracts
Livery: White/Blue/Green
Ticket System: Wayfarer TGX

181

STAGECOACH (SOUTH) LTD
BUS STATION, SOUTHGATE, CHICHESTER PO19 8DG
Tel: 01243 536161
Fax: 01243 528743
E-mail: enquiries.south@stagecoachbus.com
Web site: www.stagecoachbus.com/south
Man Dir: Andrew Dyer **Eng Dir**: Richard Alexander **Ops Dir**: Andrew Jarvis **Com Dir**: Edward Hodgson
Fleet: 442 – 99 double-deck bus, 43 single-deck bus, 9 single-deck coach, 6 double-deck coach, 244 midibus, 42 minibus.
Chassis: 265 Alexander Dennis. 21 Leyland. 6 Mann. 16 Mercedes-Benz,. 26 Optare. 114 Volvo.
Ops incl: local bus services, school contracts, private hire.
Livery: Red/Blue/Orange/White
Ticket system: Wayfarer

SUSSEX COUNTRY COACH HIRE
TERMINAL BUILDING, SHOREHAM AIRPORT BN43 5FF
Tel: 01273 465500
Fax: 01273 453040
E-mail: sxcountry@tiscali.co.uk
Web site: www.sussex-country.co.uk
Dirs: A Wright, Mrs M Keats
Fleet: 4 - 2 single-deck coach, 1 midicoach, 1 minibus
Chassis: 1 LDV. 1 Mercedes-Benz. 2 Volvo
Bodies: 1 Plaxton. 1 Van Hool. 1 other

Ops incl: private hire, school contracts, excursions & tours.
Livery: BLue/Yellow/Green on White

W+H MOTORS
KELVIN WAY, CRAWLEY RH10 9SF
Tel: 01293 510220
Fax: 01293 513263
Recovery: 01293 548111
E-mail: coach@wandhgroup.co.uk
Web site: www.wandhgroup.co.uk
Man Dir: G M Heron **Co Sec**: Peter Phillips
Fleet: 16 - 10 coach, 2 double-deck coach, 4 midibus.
Chassis: 2 Ayats. 2 Iveco. 6 MAN. 6 Volvo.
Bodies: 3 Caetano. 2 Jonckheere. 1 Marshall/MCV. 3 Noge. 6 Sunsundegui. 1 Van Hool.
Ops incl: excursions and tours, private hire, school contracts, continental tours
Livery: White/Blue

WESTRINGS COACHES LTD
53 STOCKS LANE, EAST WITTERING, CHICHESTER PO20 8NH
Tel: 01243 672411
Fax: 01243 671366
E-mail: westringscoaches@btconnect.com
Web site: www.westringscoaches.co.uk
Dir: W J Buckland **Co Sec**: T S West
Fleet: 7 - 1 single-deck bus, 5 coach, 1 midicoach.
Chassis: 1 Dennis. 1 Scania. 1 Toyota. 3 Volvo.

Bodies: 1 Caetano. 1 East Lancs. 3 Jonckheere. 2 Plaxton.
Ops incl: school contracts, excursions & tours, private hire.

WOODS TRAVEL LTD
PARK ROAD, BOGNOR REGIS PO21 5NF
Tel: 01243 868080
Fax: 01243 871669
E-mail: info@woodstravel.co.uk
Web: www.woodstravel.co.uk
Dir: R Elsmere **Transport**: G Hawkes **Excursions**: L Glen **Tours**: S Edwards
Fleet: 13 - 12 single-deck coach, 1 minicoach.
Chassis: 12 DAF. 1 Mercedes-Benz
Bodies: 1 Autobus 12 Bova.
Ops incl: excursions & tours, private hire, continental tours, school contracts, private hire
Livery: Red/White/Blue.

WORTHING COACHES
117 GEORGE V AVENUE, WORTHING BN11 5SA.
Tel: 01903 505805
Prop: Lucketts of Fareham
Fleet: 7 coach.
Chassis: Volvo.
Bodies: incl: Irizar. Plaxton. Van Hool.
Ops incl: excursions & tours, private hire, continental tours.
Livery: Red/White/Yellow
Subsidiary of Lucketts, Hampshire

WEST YORKSHIRE, BRADFORD, CALDERDALE

ANDERSON'S COACHES
HOLMFIELD HOUSE, STRANGLANDS LANE, FERRYBRIDGE WF11 8SD
Tel: 01977 552980
Fax: 01977 557823
E-mail: paulanthonyanderson@btinternet.com
Props: Paul Anderson, Gillian Anderson
Fleet: 2 coach
Chassis: 2 Setra.
Bodies: 2 Setra.
Ops incl: excursions & tours, private hire, continental tours

ARRIVA YORKSHIRE LTD
24 BARNSLEY ROAD, WAKEFIELD WF1 5JX
Tel: 01924 231300
Fax: 01924 200106
Man Dir: Nigel Featham **Eng Dir**: Philip Cummins **Fin Dir**: David Cocker
Ops Dir: Paul Adcock
Fleet: 358 - 123 double-deck bus, 159 single-deck bus, 76 midibus.
Chassis: 149 DAF. 114 Dennis. 2 Leyland. 93 Volvo.
Bodies: 162 Alexander. 1 ECW. 35 East Lancs. 23 Ikarus. 14 Northern Counties. 42 Optare. 52 Plaxton. 2 Reeve Burgess. 1 UVG. 24 Wright.
Ops incl: local bus services.

B & J TRAVEL
3 SANDY LANE, MIDDLESTOWN, WAKEFIELD WF4 4PW.
Tel: 01924 263334.
Prop: J. S. Bendle.
Fleet: 2 coach.
Chassis: DAF. Volvo.
Bodies: Jonckheere. Plaxton.
Ops incl: school contracts, excursions & tours, private hire.
Livery: Red/White/Blue.

B L TRAVEL
10 GRANGE VIEW, HEMSWORTH, NR PONTEFRACT WF9 4ER
Tel: 01977 610313
Fax: 01977 613999
E-mail: bltravelcoaches@aol.com
Proprietors: Brian Lockwood, Paul Lockwood
Fleet: 14 - 8 single-deck bus, 2 single-deck coach, 4 minibus.
Chassis: incl - 2 Ford. 2 Mercedes-Benz. 2 Optare.
Bodies: incl - 1 Plaxton. 1 Van Hool. 6 Wright.
Ops incl: local bus service, school contracts, excursions & tours, private hire, express.

BRITANNIA TRAVEL
113 WESTON LANE, OTLEY LS21 2DX.
Tel/Fax: 01943 465591
Prop: A. Broome, Mrs S. Eastwood.
Fleet: 1 coach.
Chassis: Iveco. **Body**: Beulas.
Ops incl: excursions & tours, continental tours.
Livery: Silver/Red/Blue.

BROWNS COACHES(SK) LTD
WHITE APRON STREET, SOUTH KIRKBY WF9 3HQ
Tel: 01977 644777
Fax: 01977 643210
E-mail: sales@brownscoaches.com
Web site: www.brownscoaches.com
Fleetname: Browns
Man Dir: Mrs J M Brown **Co Sec**: Miss M Brown **Gen Man**: A Griffith **Eng Dir**: D Brown **Ops Man**: S Covell
Fleet: 16 - 5 coach, 7 midicoach, 4 minibus.
Chassis: 2 Ford Transit. 3 Iveco. 8 Mercedes. 3 Scania.
Bodies: 2 Beulas. 1 Esker. 3 Irizar. 3 Plaxton. 7 other.
Ops incl: private hire, school contracts, continental tours.
Livery: Red/White/Blue

CENTRAL GARAGE
STANSFIELD ROAD, TODMORDEN
OL14 5DL
Tel/Fax: 01706 813909
E-mail: tonygled@hotmail.co.uk
Man Dir: David Paul Guest **Man**: A J Gledhill.
Fleet: 3 - 2 midibus, 1 minicoach.
Chassis/bodies: 3 Mercedes-Benz.
Ops incl: scholl contracts, private hire.

CITY TRAVEL YORKSHIRE
10A MANYWELLS IND EST,
CULLINGWORTH,
BRADFORD BD13 5DX
Tel: 01535 275522
Fax: 01533 274400
E-mail: enquires@citytravel.com
Web. www.citytravel.co.uk
Fleet: 10 - 6 double-deck bus, 3 single-deck coach, 1 minbus.
Chassis: 6 BMC. 1 DAF. 1 Ford Transit. 1 Iveco. 1 Man.
Bodies: 1 Berkof. 6 BMC. 1 Noge. 1 Van Hool.
Ops incl: school contracts, private hire.

CLARKSONS HOLIDAYS
52 DONCASTER ROAD, SOUTH ELMSALL, PONTEFRACT WF9 2JN
Tel: 01977 642385
Fax: 01977 640158
E-mail: info@clarksonscoaches.co.uk
Web site: www.clarksoncoaches.co.uk
Chmn: Ken Clarkson **Dir/Co Sec**: JohnHancock **Dir**: Paul Clarkson
Fleet: 9 - 7 coach, 1 minicoach, 1 midicoach.
Chassis: 4 Mercedes. 5 Neoplan.
Bodies: 5 Mercedes. 4 Neoplan.
Ops incl: excursions & tours, continental tours.
Livery: Blue

DALESMAN
VICTORIA ROAD, GUISELEY LS20 8DG
Tel: 01943 870228
Fax: 01943 878227
Web: www.dalesmancoaches.co.uk
E-mail: dalesmancoaches@btconnect.com
Dir: K Hartshorne
Fleet: 13 - 6 single-deck coach, 3 midibus. 2 midicoach, 3 minibus.
Chassis: 2 DAF. 7 Mercedes-Benz. 4 VDL
Bodies: 3 Autobus. 3 Optare. 6 Van Hool. 1 Other

DEWHIRST COACHES LTD
TRAVEL TECH HOUSE, THORNCLIFFE ROAD, BRADFORD BD8 7DD
Tel/Fax: 01274 481208
E-mail: dewhirstcoaches@hotmail.co.uk
Dirs: S Dewhirst, Miss L Dewhirst
Fleet: 6 - 3 double-deck bus, 3 single-deck coach.
Chassis: 2 DAF. 2 EOS. 1 Scania. 1 Volvo.
Bodies: 1 Alexander Dennis. 2 East Lancs. 3 Van Hool.
Ops incl: school contracts, excursions & tours, private hire.
Livery: Blue/White

FIRST BRADFORD
BOWLING BACK LANE, BRADFORD BD4 8SP
Tel: 01274 734833
Fax: 01274 736768
E-mail: contact.us@firstgroup.com
Web site: www.firstgroup.com
Man Dir: Ian Humphrreys
Fleet: includes double-deck bus, single-deck bus, minibus.
Chassis: Leyland. Optare. Volvo.
Bodies: Alexander. Leyland.Optare. Wright.
Ops incl: local bus services, school contracts.
Ticket System: Wayfarer

FIRST IN CALDERDALE & HUDDERSFIELD
SKIRCOAT ROAD, HALIFAX HX1 2RF.
Tel: 01422 305426
Fax: 01422 346323
Web site: www.firstgroup.com
Man Dir: Alan Pilbeam **Ops Dir**: Graham Riley **Comm Dir**: Nigel Winter **Fin Dir**: Christine Haigh, **Eng Dir**: Mark Hargreaves, **Ops Man**: Adrian Arthur.
Fleet: 221 - 85 double-deck bus, 109 single-deck bus, 27 minibus.
Chassis: 2 Bluebird. 60 Dennis. 51 Leyland. 16 MCW. 27 Mercedes. 65 Volvo.
Bodies: Alexander. Bluebird. ECW. MCW. Optare. Plaxton. Roe. Wright.
Ops incl: local bus services, school contracts.
Livery: FirstGroup.
Ticket System: Wayfarer 3.

FIRST IN LEEDS
HUNSLET PARK, DONISTHORPE STREET, LEEDS LS10 1PL
Tel: 0113 381 5000 **Fax**: 0113 242 9721
Web site: www.firstgroup.com
www.firstleeds.co.uk
Fleetname: First in Leeds
Man Dir: Steve Graham
Fleet: 487 - 268 double-deck bus, 182 single-deck bus, 15 articulated bus, 22 minibus.
Chassis: 84 Dennis. Ford Transit. 33 MCW. 8 Mercedes. 14 Optare. 65 Leyland. 150 Scania. 133 Volvo.
Bodies: Alexander. MCW. Optare. Plaxton. Roe. Wright.
Ops incl: local bus services, school contracts.
Livery: FirstGroup
Ticket System: Wayfarer 3.

GAIN TRAVEL
EXPERIENCE
6 FAIR ROAD, WIBSEY, BRADFORD BD6 1QN
Tel: 01274 603224
Fax: 01274 678274
E-mail: gail@gaintravel.co.uk
Web site: www.gaintravel.co.uk
Man Dir: Gail Bottomley **Dirs**: Ian Bottomley, Darren Bottomley **Man**: Beryl LeaRoyd
Fleet: 5 - 4 coach, 1 minibus.
Chassis: 3 DAF. 1 MAN.
Bodies: 4 Van Hool.
Ops incl: excursions & tours, private hire

STANLEY GATH (COACHES) LTD
UNIT 6 DARTON BUSINESS PARK, BARNSLEY ROAD, DARTON S75 5NH
Tel: 01924 466766
Fax:01226 390048
E-mail: info@stanley-gath.co.uk
Web site: www.stanley-gath.co.uk
Fleet: 13 - 11 coach, 1 midibus, 1minicoach.
Chassis: 1 DAF. 1 LDV. 11 Volvo.
Ops incl: excursions & tours, private hire, school contracts
Livery: Grey/Cream

J D GODSON
3 SANDBED LANE, CROSSGATES LS15 8JH
Tel: 0113 264 6166. **Fax**: 0113 390 9669.
E-mail: godsonscoaches@hotmail.com
Man Dir: David Godson
Fleet: 8
Chassis: 2 Bova. 3 DAF. 3 Volvo
Bodies: 2 Bova. 1 Caetano. 5 Plaxton.
Ops incl: school contracts, private hire.
Livery: Pink/White/Brown

G. W. GOULDING W
64 THE RIDGEWAY, KNOTTINGLEY WF11 0JS.
Tel: 01977 672265, 672059.
Fax: 01977 670276.
Fleetname: B. Goulding.
Prop: G. W. Goulding.
Fleet: 5 - 3 coach, 1 midicoach, 1 minicoach.
Chassis: 1 Bristol. 1 Leyland. 1 Toyota. 2 Volvo.
Bodies: 1 Caetano. 4 Plaxton.
Ops incl: excursions & tours, continental tours.
Livery: White with Red/Yellow/Blue stripes.

INDEPENDENT COACHWAYS LTD
LOW FOLD GARAGE, NEW ROAD SIDE, HORSFORTH LS18 4DR
Tel: 0113 258 6491
Fax: 0113 259 1125
Dirs: P & C Thornes **Gen Man**: Barry Rennison **Traf Man**: Peter Seaward
Fleet: 8 - 1 single-deck bus, 7 single-deck coach
Chassis: 1 DAF. 7 Volvo.
Bodies: 1 Optare. 6 Plaxton. 1 Van Hool.
Ops incl: private hire, school contracts.
Livery: Blue/Grey

LONGSTAFF OF MIRFIELD
EASTFIELD GARAGE, STONEY LANE, MIRFIELD WF14 0DX2
Tel: 01924 463122
Web site: www.longstaffofmirfield.com
E-mail: jjlongstaff@btconnect.com
Co Sec: S Kaye **Ops Man**: G Kaye
Fleet: 2 - 2 single-deck bus.
Chassis: 2 Volvo.
Bodies: 2 Wright.
Ops incl: local bus services, school contracts.
Livery: Blue/Blue-Grey/White

A. LYLES & SON
156 COMMONSIDE, BATLEY WF17 6LA
Tel: 01924 464771
Fax: 01924 469267
E-mail: alyles&son@aol.com
Senior Ptnr: Terence Lyles
Ptnr: Howard Lyles
Fleet: 6 - 1 single-deck bus, 5 coach
Chassis: 2 DAF. 4 MAN.
Bodies: 1 Berkhof. 1 Duple. 1 Indcar. 1 Optare. 2 Van Hool
Ops incl: local bus services, school contracts, excursions & tours, private hire, continental tours.
Livery: Beige/Brown/Red

DAVID PALMER COACHES LTD
THE TRAVEL OFFICE, WAKEFIELD ROAD, NORMANTON WF6 2BT
Tel: 01924 895849
Fax: 01924 897750
E-mail: info@davidpalmercoaches.co.uk
Web site: www.davidpalmercoaches.co.uk
Dirs: Andrew Palmer, Lisa Palmer, David Palmer, Margaret Palmer.
Fleet: 7 - 4 coach, 1 midicoach, 2 minibus.
Chassis: 2 DAF. 1 LDV. 2 MAN. 1 Mercedes. 1 Toyota.
Bodies: incl: 1 Mercedes. 4 Van Hool.
Ops incl: excursions & tours, private hire, continental tours.
Livery: Silver

PULLMAN DINER
THE HAWTHORNES, GREAT NORTH ROAD, KNOTTINGLEY WF11 0BS
Tel: 07860 302018
Fax: 07860 677554
Web site: www.pullmandiner.co.uk
Prop: Michael Hartley
Fleet: 1 coach
Chassis: 1 MAN
Bodies: 1 Van Hool.
Ops incl: excursions & tours, private hire, continental tours

RED ARROW COACHES LTD
ASPLEY HOUSE, LINCOLN STREET, HUDDERSFIELD HD1 6RX.
Tel: 01484 420993.
Fax: 01484 540409.
E-mail: info@redarrowcoaches.co.uk
Web site: www.redarrowcoaches.co.uk
Dirs: Steven R. Moore, Suichwant Singh.
Fleet: 10 - 9 coach, 1 midicoach.
Chassis: 1 Ayats. 2 Bova. 2 DAF. 1 Dennis. 2 MAN. 2 Scania.
Bodies: 1 Ayats. 2 Bova. 1 Caetano. 2 Plaxton. 4 Van Hool.
Ops incl: excursions & tours, private hire, continental tours, school contracts.

JOHN RIGBY TRANSPORT & TRAVEL
SPRINGWELL MILLS, 231 BRADFORD ROAD, BATLEY WF17 6JL
Tel: 01924 485151
E-mail: rigbytransport@hotmail.co.uk
Web site: www.johnrigby.co.uk

Prop: John Rigby **Tran Man**: Steve Clayton
Fleet: 8 - 5 coach, 2 midicoach, 1 minicoach.
Chassis: 2 DAF. 1 Dennis. 2 MAN. 1 Mercedes. 2 Volvo.
Bodies: 3 Caetano. 1 Marcopolo. 1 Mercedes. 1 Plaxton. 2 Van Hool.
Ops incl: private hire, school contracts.
Livery: White

ROLLINSON SAFEWAY LTD
65 HALL LANE, LEEDS LS12 1PQ
Tel: 0113 231 1355
Fax: 0113 231 1344
Man Dir: Paul Rollinson. **Dir**: Peter Rollinson. **Contracts Man**: M. J. Joyce.
Fleet: 72 minibus.
Chassis: 1 Fiat. 3 Ford Transit. 3 Iveco. 20 Mercedes. 45 Renault.
Ops incl: private hire, school contracts.
Livery: Brown/Gold.

ROSS TRAVEL GROUP
THE GARAGE, ALLISON STREET, FEATHERSTONE WF7 6BB
Tel: 01977 791738
Fax: 01977 690109
E-mail: info@rosstravelgroup.co.uk
Web Site: www.rosstravelgroup.co.uk
Props: Peter Ross, Mary Ross.
Fleet: 17 - 10 single-deck bus, 5 single-deck coach, 1 midicoach, 1 minibus.
Chassis: 1 Alexander Dennis. 2 DAF. 7 Mercedes-Benz. 4 Optare. 1 Scania. 2 Volvo.
Bodies: 1 Alexander Dennis. 2 Bova. 1 Mercedes-Benz. 4 Optare. 5 Plaxton. 3 Van Hool. 1 other.
Ops incl: local bus services, excursions & tours, private hire, school contracts, continental tours.
Livery: Ross Travel Group
Ticket System: Almex

STEELS LUXURY COACHES LTD
61 MAIN STREET, ADDINGHAM LS29 0PD
Tel: 01943 830206
Fax: 01943 831499
E-mail: info@steelscoaches.co.uk
Web site: www.steelscoaches.co.uk
Dir: T Steel **Co Sec**: Mrs J Steel
Fleet: 6 - 2 single-deck coach, 3 midicoach, 1 minicoach.
Chassis: 1 Iveco. 4 Mercedes-Benz. 1 Volvo.
Bodies: 4 Plaxton. 2 other.
Ops incl: excursions & tours, private hire, school contracts, continental tours.
Livery: White/Red/Black

E STOTT & SONS LTD
COLNE VALE GARAGE, SAVILE STREET, MILNSBRIDGE, HUDDERSFIELD HD3 4PG
Tel: 01484 460463
Fax: 01484 461463
E-mail: info@stottscoaches.co.uk
Web site: www.stottscoaches.co.uk

Dirs: Mark Stott, Carl Stott
Fleet: 25 - 4 single-deck bus, 11 coach, 10 minibus.
Chassis: 4 Leyland. 10 Mercedes. 11 Volvo.
Bodies: 4 Leyland. 7 Plaxton. 4 Sunsundegui.
Ops incl: local bus services, school contracts, private hire.
Livery: White/Red/Black/Silver
Ticket System: Wayfarer

STRINGERS PONTEFRACT MOTORWAYS
102 SOUTHGATE, PONTEFRACT WF8 1PN
Tel: 01977 600205
Fax: 01977 704178
E-mail: enquires@stringerscoaches.co.uk
Web: www.stringerscoaches.co.uk
Ptnrs: Sydney Stringer, Mark G Stringer
Tran Man: Mark E Stringer **Sec**: Sonia Stringer **Ch Eng**: Chris Palmer
Fleet: 8 - 4 single-deck bus, 3 single-deck coach, 1 midicoach.
Chassis: 1 Mercedes-Benz. 4 Optare. 3 Volvo.
Bodies: 1 Jonkheere. 4 Optare. 1 Plaxton. 2 Van Hool.
Ops incl: local bus services, school contracts, excursions & tours, private hire.
Livery: Red/Black/White
Ticket system: Almex

T & S TRAVEL
LANGTHWAITE GRANGE INDUSTRIAL ESTATE, SOUTH KIRKBY, PONTEFRACT WF9 3NR.
Tel: 01977 644992.
Fax: 01977 608652.
Ptnrs: Mrs L. Stevenson, J. Tebbett.
Fleet: 9 - 4 midicoach, 5 minibus.
Chassis: 2 Ford Transit. 1 Freight Rover. 1 MCW. 3 Mercedes.
Ops incl: local bus services, excursions & tours.

TETLEYS MOTOR SERVICES LTD
76 GOODMAN STREET, LEEDS LS10 1NY
Tel: 0113 276 2276
Fax: 0113 276 2277
E-mail: sales@tetleyscoaches.com
Web site: www.tetleyscoaches.com
Dir: Ian Tetley **Co Sec**: Angela Tetley **Ch Eng**: David Leach **Ops Man**: Stephen Cunniff
Fleet: 17 - 13 single-deck coach. 2 midicoach. 2 minicoach
Chassis: 1 Dennis. 1 Iveco. 2 Mercedes. 2 Renault. 11 Volvo.
Bodies: 12 Plaxton. 3 Van Hool. 2 other.
Ops incl: private hire, school contracts, express.
Livery: Blue I on White

TRANSDEV KEIGHLEY & DISTRICT
CAVENDISH HOUSE, 91-93 CAVENDISH STREET, KEIGHLEY BD21 3DG
Tel: 01535 603284
Fax: 01535 610065
Web site: www.keighleyanddistrict.co.uk

Fleet name: The Zone
Chief Exec: Martin Gilchrist,
Man Dir: Dave Alexander
Fleet: 103 - 40 double-deck bus, 63 single-deck bus.
Chassis. Dennis. Volvo.
Bodies: Alexander. Plaxton. Wright.
Ops incl: local bus services, school contracts
Livery: Blue/White, Blue/Red
Part of the Blazefield group which is owned by Transdev

TWIN VALLEY COACHES
INDUSTRIAL ROAD, SOWERBY BRIDGE HX6 2RA.
Tel/Fax: 01422 833358.

Dirs: D Pilling, E Pilling.
Fleet: 5 - 2 coach, 2 midicoach, 1 minicoach.
Chassis: 2 Dennis. 1 LDV. 1 MAN. 2 Mercedes.
Bodies: 1 Caetano. 2 Optare. 1 Plaxton.
Ops incl: private hire, school contracts.
Livery: Green/White.

W A SHEARINGS LTD
MILL LANE, NORMANTON WF6 1RF
Tel: 01977 603088
Fax: 01977 603114
Ops Man: Martin Guy
See also W A Shearings Ltd, Greater Manchester

WELSH'S COACHES LTD
FIELD LANE, UPTON, PONTEFRACT WF9 1BH
Tel: 01977 643873
Fax: 01977 648143
E-mail: judy@welshscoaches.com
Web site: www.welshscoaches.co.uk
Dir: John Welsh **Co Sec**: Judy Welsh
Fleet: 7 - 5 single-deck coach, 2 minicoach.
Chassis: 2 Mercedes-Benz. 5 Setra.
Bodies: 2 Mercedes-Benz. 5 Setra.
Ops incl: excursions & tours, private hire, continental tours.
Livery: White/Red/Green

WILTSHIRE

ADRAINS OF BRINKWORTH
THE COACH YARD, THE COMMON, BRINKWORTH SN15 5DX
Tel: 01666 510874 5
Recovery: 07831 303295
Prop: Adrain Griffiths
Ops Man: Colin Minchin
Fleet: 8 - 3 single-deck bus, 4 coach, 1 minibus.
Chassis: 1 LDV. 2 Leyland. 3 Mercedes. 2 Volvo.
Bodies: 7 Plaxton. 1 Reeve Burgess.
Ops incl: local bus services, school contracts, private hire.
Livery: White/Blue/Yellow
Ticket system: Wayfarer

ANDREW JAMES QUALITY TRAVEL (ANDYBUS AND COACH LTD)
UNIT 6, WHITEWALLS, EASTON GREY, MALMESBURY SN16 0RD
Tel: 01666 825655
Fax: 01666 825651
Recovery: 07740 88710
E-mail: ajcoaches@andrew-james.co.uk
Web site: www.andrew-james.co.uk
Dir: Andrew James
Fleet: 16 - 3 coach, 6 single-deck bus, 6 midibus, 1 midicoach.
Chassis: 3 Bova. 2 DAF. 4 Dennis. 1 Leyland. 2 MAN. 1 Marshall. 5 Mercedes. 1 Optare. 1 Toyota.
Bodies: 3 Bova. 1 Caetano. 1 East Lancs. 1 Ikarus. 1 Marshall/MCV. 2 Optare. 8 Plaxton
Ops incl: local bus services, school contracts, private hire.
Livery: Bus - Cream/Orange, Coach - Yellow/Black
Ticket System: Wayfarer

APL TRAVEL LTD
PEAR TREE COTTAGE, CRUDWELL SN16 9ES
Tel: 01666 577774
Fax: 01249 721402
E-mail: apltravel@btconncet.com
Web: www.apltravel.co.uk
Dir: Alan Legg, Shane Legg
Fleet: 15-6 single-deck bus, 6 single-deck

coach, 2 midicoach, 1 mincoach.
Chasis: 3 Alexander Dennis. 1 Bedford. 1 DAF. 2 Dennis. 1 Iveco. 1 Leyland. 3 MAN. 3 Mercedes-Benz.
Bodies: 2 Berkhof. 1 Bova. 2 Ikarus. 2 Mercedez-Benz. 1 Noge. 3 Optare. 2 Plaxton.
Ops incl: local bus services, school contracts, excursions & tours, private hire.
Livery: White
Ticket System: Wayfarer

BARNES COACHES
UNIT E, WOODSIDE ROAD, SOUTH MARSTON BUSINESS PARK, SWINDON SN3 4AQ
Tel: 01793 821303
Fax: 01793 828486
E-mail: travel@barnescoaches.co.uk
Web site: www.barnescoaches.co.uk
Dirs: Lionel Barnes, Terry Barnes, Luke Barnes, Matt Barnes
Fleet: 25 - 25 single-deck coaches
Chassis: 10 Bova.15 Volvo.
Bodies: 10 Bova. 2 Jonckheere. 13 Van Hool
Ops incl: excursions & tours, school contracts, private hire, continental tours
Livery: Green

BEELINE (R & R) COACHES LTD
BISHOPSTROW ROAD, WARMINSTER BA12 9HQ
Tel: 01985 213503
Fax: 01985 213922
Dirs: M N Hayball, A D Hayball
Gen Man: N Ennis
Fleet: 32 - 22 coach, 6 midicoach, 4 minibus.
Chassis: 4 LDV. 12 Mercedes. 16 Volvo.
Bodies: 2 Optare. 26 Plaxton. 4 other.
Ops incl: local bus services, school contracts, private hire
Livery: Beige/White
Ticket system: Setright

BELLS LUXURY COACHES
162 CASTLE STREET, SALISBURY SP1 3UA.

Tel: 01722 339422
Fax: 01722 412681
Web site: bellscoaches.co.uk
Man Dir: A Carter **Eng Dir**: S Hamilton
Man: Chris Mills **Ops Dir**: A Wickham.
Fleet: 9 - 1 midicoach, 2 minicoach, 6 single-deck coach..
Chassis: 1 DAF. 1 Dennis. 2 Mercedes. 4 Volvo. 1 Toyota.
Bodies: 1 Caetano. 1 Jonckheere. 4 Plaxton. 1 Van Hool. 2 other.
Ops incl: excursions & tours, private hire, school contracts, continental tours.
Livery: Green/Cream
(Subsidiary of Wilts & Dorset)

BETTER MOTORING SERVICES
104A SWINDON ROAD, STRATTON-ST MARGARET SN3 4PT
Tel: 01793 823747
Fax: 01793 831898
E-mail: bmscoaches@btconnect.com
Fleetname: BMS Coaches.
Prop: D G Miles **Fleet Eng**: M J Hopkins
Sec: Mrs M Mulhern
Fleet: 10 - 8 midicoach, 2 minicoach. .
Bodies: 4 Autobus. 1 Esker. 2 Mellor. 1 Mercedes-Benz. 2 Other.
Ops incl: school contracts, excursions & tours, private hire, continental tours.
Livery: Coffee/Cream

BODMAN COACHES
88 HIGH STREET, WORTON, DEVIZES SN10 5RU
Tel: 01380 722393
Fax: 01380 721969
E-Mail: bodmancoaches@btconnect.com
Tran Man: John Hallett **Ops Man**: Graham Carter
Fleet: 39 - 20 single-deck bus, 19 single-deck coach.
Chassis: 4 Alexander Dennis. 2 DAF. 16 Dennis. 1 Leyland. 2 MAN. 4 Mercedes-Benz. 7 Volvo.
Bodies: 4 Alexander Dennis. 2 Berkhof. 2 Ikarus. 1 Marshal/MCV. 26 Plaxton.1 Van Hool. 1 Wadham Stringer.
Ops incl: local bus services, school contracts, private hire.
Ticket System: Wayfarer

185

CHANDLERS COACH TRAVEL
158 CHEMICAL ROAD, WEST WILTS TRADING ESTATE, WESTBURY BA13 4JN
Tel: 01373 824500
Fax: 01373 824300
E-mail: info@chandlerscoach.co.uk
Web site: www.chandlerscoach.co.uk
Prop: Margaret l'Anson **Fleet Eng**: Christopher l'Anson
Fleet: 10 - 9 coach, 1 minibus.
Chassis: 1 Renault. 9 Volvo.
Bodies: 4 Plaxton. 1 Renault. 5 Van Hool.
Ops incl: school contracts, excursions & tours, private hire, continental tours.
Livery: White/Burgundy/Gold

COACHSTYLE LTD
HORSDOWN GARAGE, NETTLETON, CHIPPENHAM SN14 7LN
Tel/Fax: 01249 782224
Owners: Andrew Jones, Mrs A L Jones
Fleet: 15 - 2 single-deck bus, 13 coach.
Chassis: 4 DAF. 3 Leyland. 1 Scania. 6 Volvo.
Bodies: 3 Berkhof. 1 Caetano. 2 Duple. 3 Jonckheere. 2 Mercedes. 3 Van Hool.
Ops incl: local bus services, school contracts, excursions & tours, private hire, continental tours.

ELLISON'S COACHES
THE GARAGE, HIGH ROAD, ASHTON KEYNES, SWINDON SN6 6NX
Tel: 01285 861224 **Fax**: 01285 862115
E-mail: sales@ellisonscoaches.co.uk
Web site: www.ellisonscoaches.co.uk
Prop: Alan Ellison
Fleet: 18 coach - 2 single-deck bus, 16 coach
Chassis: 2 BMC. 16 Neoplan.
Ops incl: school contracts, private hire.

FARESAVER BUSES
THE COACH YARD, VINCIENTS ROAD, BUMPERS FARM INDUSTRIAL ESTATE, CHIPPENHAM SN14 6AS
Tel: 01249 444444 **Fax**: 01249 448844
E-mail: sales@faresaver.co.uk
Web site: www.faresaver.co.uk
Prop: J V Pickford **Eng Dir**: J M Pickford
Ops Dir: D J Pickford **Ops Man**: D Beard
Ch Eng: D Watts
Fleet: 32 - 2 single-deck bus, 20 midibus, 10 minicoach
Chassis: 2 Dennis. 30 Mercedes.
Bodies: 32 Plaxton.
Ops incl: local bus services, school contracts, private hire.
Livery: White/Mauve.
Ticket System: Wayfarer 3

G-LINE MINICOACHES
MARSHGATE TRADING ESTATE, 107 STRATTON ROAD, SWINDON SN41 2NY.
Tel/Fax: 01793 814336.
E-mail: gline@btinternet.com
Chmn: P. McGarry. **Man Dir**: N. McGarry.
Service Dir: J. McGarry.
Tpt Man: N. McGarry.
Fleet: 30 - 4 minicoach, 26 minibus.
Chassis: 4 Ford Transit. 2 Iveco. 10 LDV. 5 Mercedes.
Ops incl: private hire, school contracts.

HATTS TRAVEL
FOXHAM, CHIPPENHAM SN15 4NB
Tel: 01249 740444 **Fax**: 01249 740447
E-mail: info@hattstravel.co.uk
Web site: www.hattstravel.co.uk
Man Ptnr: Adrian Hillier **Ops Man**: Andy Bridgeman **Traff Man**: Phil Turner
Wkshp Man: Mike Henderson
Accts: Lynne Peglar
Fleet: 53 - 22 single-deck coach, 2 double-deck coach. 4 midibus, 14 midicoach, 7 minibus. 4 minicoach.
Chassis: 1 Alexander Dennis. 2 Bova. 2 DAF. 18 MAN. 14 Mercedes-Benz. 1 Renault. 1 Toyota. 2 Volkswagen. 12 Volvo.
Bodies: 2 Ayats. 2 Berkhof. 2 Bova. 1 Caetano. 1 Esker. 1 Jonckheere. 2 Marcopolo. 4 Mellor. 8 Mercedes-Benz. 1 Neoplan. 2 Noge. 4 Optare. 8 Reeve Burgess. 1 UVG. 8 Van Hool. 1 Wadham Stringer. 7 Other.
Ops incl: local bus services, excursions & tours, private hire, continental tours, school contracts.
Ticket System: Wayfarer

KINGSTON COACHES
162 CASTLE STREET, SALISBURY SP1 3UA
Tel: 01722 337311 **Fax**: 01722 412681
Man: C Mills **Ops Man**: S Hursthouse
Fleet: 4 coach.
Chassis: 2 DAF. 1 Dennis. 1 Volvo.
Bodies: 3 Plaxton. 1 Van Hool.
Ops incl: private hire, continental tours, school contracts.
Livery: Red/Cream
(Subsidiary of Wilts & Dorset)

LEVER'S COACHES
162 CASTLE STREET, SALISBURY SP1 3UA
Tel: 01722 417229 **Fax**: 01722 412681
Man: C Mills **Asst Man**: I Bassindale
Fleet: 6 - 5 coach, 1 midicoach.
Chassis: 3 DAF. 1 Dennis. 1 Mercedes. 1 Volvo.
Bodies: 1 Autobus. 1 Jonckheere. 1 Plaxton. 3 Van Hool.
Ops incl: local bus services, school contracts, private hire.
Livery: Cream/Blue.
Ticket system: Almex
(Subsidiary of Wilts & Dorset)

MANSFIELD'S COACHES
27 FINCHDALE, COVINGHAM, SWINDON SN3 5AL.
Tel/Fax: 01793 525375.
Prop: R. E. Mansfield. **Man**: A. Mansfield.
Tran Man: P. Mansfield.
Sec: Mrs M. S. Mansfield.
Fleet: 6.
Chassis: 3 MAN. 2 Mercedes. 1 Toyota.
Ops incl: excursions & tours, private hire, express, school contracts.
Livery: Yellow/Green/Red.
Ticket System: Setright.

PEWSEY VALE COACHES
HOLLYBUSH LANE, PEWSEY SN9 5BB
Tel/Fax: 01672 562238
E-mail: pewseyvalecoaches@aol.com
Dirs: Andrew Thorne, Dawn Thorne, Anne Thorne
Fleet: coach, minicoach.
Chassis: Bova. Leyland. Mercedes. Volvo.

Bodies: Bova. Plaxton. Van Hool.
Ops incl: local bus services, school contracts, excursions & tours, private hire, continental tours
Livery: White/Blue/Red
Ticket system: Almex

SEAGER'S COACHES LTD
EASTON LANE, CHIPPENHAM SN14 0RW.
Tel: 01249 654949 **Fax**: 01249 652581
E-mail: seagerscoaches@hotmail.com
Web site: www.seagerscoaches.co.uk
Dirs: Ms J Seager, T Woods, A Watts, Ms A Truscott
Fleet: 19 - 1 coach, 14 minibus, 2 midicoach
Chassis: 1 DAF. 9 Ford Transit. 4 Iveco. 3 LDV. 2 Mercedes.
Ops incl: private hire, school contracts.
Livery: White

STAGECOACH WEST
See Gloucestershire

TEST VALLEY TRAVEL LTD
BANISTER BARN, NEWTON LANE, WHITEPARISH SP5 2QQ
Tel: 01794 884555
Man Dir: J M Norman **Co Sec**: Mrs A N Norman
Fleet: 3 - 2 minibus 1 minicoach.
Chassis/bodies: 2 LDV. 1 Renault.
Ops incl: private hire, school contracts.
Livery: Green/White

THAMESDOWN TRANSPORT
BARNFIELD ROAD, SWINDON SN2 2DJ
Tel: 01793 428400
Fax: 01793 428405
Recovery: 01793 428432
Web site: www.thamesdown-transport.co.uk
Man Dir: Paul Jenkins **Eng Dir**: Nigel Mason **Fin Controller/Co Sec**: Cliff Connor **Ops Dir**: David Burch
Fleet: 109 - 25 double-deck bus, 84 single-deck bus.
Chassis: 1 Daimler. 65 Dennis. 9 Leyland. 22 Scania. 12 Volvo
Bodies: 20 Alexander Dennis. 1 ECW. 3 East Lancs. 1 Northern Counties. 62 Plaxton. 22 Wright.
Ops incl: local bus services, school contracts.
Livery: Blue/Green
Ticket System: Wayfarer TGX

TOURIST COACHES LTD
162 CASTLE STREET, SALISBURY SP1 3UA
Tel: 01722 338359
Fax: 01722 412681
Man Dir: A Carter **Ops Dir**: A Wickham
Eng Dir: S Hamilton **Man**: C Mills **Ops Man**: S Hursthouse
Fleet: 32 - 21 coach, 4 midibus, 3 midicoach, 2 minicoach, 2 minibus
Chassis: 9 DAF. 5 Dennis. 2 LDV. 5 Mercedes. 3 Optare. 11 Plaxton. 7 Volvo.
Bodies: 1 Autobus. 1 Caetano. 2 Ferqui. 1 Mercedes. 3 Optare. 11 Plaxton. 1 Reeve Burgess. 8 Van Hool. 5 other.
Ops incl: local bus services, school contracts, excursions & tours, private hire, continental tours
Livery: Orange/Cream.

WORCESTERSHIRE

ASTONS COACHES
CLERKENLEAP, BROOMHALL, WORCESTER WR5 3HR
Tel: 01905 820201
Fax: 01905 829249
Recovery: 01905 820201
E-mail: info@astons-coaches.co.uk
Web site: www.astons-coaches.co.uk
Gen Man: Richard Conway **Sales Man**: Anna Woodward
Fleet: 35 - 4 double-deck bus, 11 single-deck bus, 15 coach, 2 midicoach, 3 minibus.
Chassis: 2 Dennis. 1 EOS. 4 Mercedes. 6 Optare. 13 Scania. 1 Setra. 4 Volvo.
Bodies: 1 Alexander. 4 East Lancs. 3 Irizar. 1 Jonckheere. 1 Mercedes. 6 Optare. 1 Plaxton. 1 Reeve Burgess. 1 Setra. 6 Van Hool.
Ops incl: local bus services, school contracts, private hire, continental tours.
Ticket system: ERG Subsidiary of Veolia

N N CRESSWELL COACH HIRE
WORCESTER ROAD, EVESHAM WR11 4RA
Tel: 01386 48655
Fax: 01386 48656
Props: Mrs Mary Shephard, Mrs Sue Everatt **Ch Eng**: W Fairbrother
Fleet: 21 - 14 coach, 5 minibus, 2 midicoach.
Chassis: 3 Bedford. 11 Dennis. 7 Mercedes-Benz.
Bodies: 21 Plaxton.
Ops incl: local bus services, school contracts, excursions & tours, private hire.
Livery: Bus/White
Ticket System: Setright/Wayfarer.

DUDLEY'S COACHES
POPLAR GARAGE, ALCESTER ROAD, RADFORD, WORCESTER WR7 4LS
Tel: 01386 792206
Fax: 01386 793373
Fleet: 17 - 16 single-desk coach, 1 minibus.
Chassis: 1 Leyland. 1 Toyota. 15 Volvo.
Bodies: 1 Caetano. 1 Jonckheere. 10 Plaxton. 5 Van Hool.
Ops incl: local bus services, school contracts, excursions & tours, private hire
Livery: Green/Cream.

FIRST WYVERN
HERON LODGE, LONDON ROAD, WORCESTER WR5 2EU.
Tel: 01905 359393.
Fax: 01905 351104.
Man Dir: Maurice Bulmer
Fleet: 240 - 119 single-deck bus, 7 coach, 114 minibus.
Chassis: Dennis. Leyland. Mercedes. Optare. Volvo
Bodies: Alexander. Leyland. Marshall. Optare. Plaxton. Wright
Ops incl: local bus services, school contracts.
Livery: White/Magenta/Blue
Ticket System: Wayfarer

GOLD STAR TRAVEL
COOKSEY LODGE FARM, UPTON WARREN, BROMSGROVE B61 9HD
Tel/Fax: 01527 861685
Prop: Mrs Dorothy Homer.
Fleet: 1 single-deck bus
Chassis/Bodies: 1 Volvo/Van Hool.
Ops incl: private hire, excursions and tours
Livery: White/Gold

HARDINGS INTERNATIONAL
OXLEASOW ROAD, REDDITCH B98 0RE
Tel: 01527 525200
Fax: 01527 523800
E-mail: john@hardingscoaches.com
Web site: www.hardingscoaches.co.uk
Man Dir: John Dyson
Co Sec: Malcolm Playford **Fleet Eng**: Malcolm Chance
Fleet: 43 - 5 single-deck bus, 35 coach, 4 minibus.
Chassis: 3 DAF. 5 Leyland. 4 MAN. 9 Mercedes. 20 Scania. 3 Volvo.
Bodies: 2 Berkhof. 1 East Lancs. 1 Ikarus. 13 Irizar. 5 Leyland. 9 Mercedes. 13 Van Hool.
Ops incl: local bus services, school contracts, excursions & tours, private hire, continental tours
Livery: Silver/Red/Blue

HARRIS EXECUTIVE TRAVEL
58 MEADOW ROAD, CATSHILL, BROMSGROVE B61 0JL
Tel: 01527 872857
Fax: 01527 872708
E-mail: steve@harriscoaches.fsnet.co.uk
Dirs: J G Harris, S W Harris
Fleet: 7 - 6 coach, 1 mdnicoach.
Chassis: 7 Mercedes.
Bodies: 1 Caciamali. 6 Neoplan
Ops incl: excursions & tours, private hire, continental tours.
Livery: White/Red/Orange/yellow

J B C MALVERNIAN TOURS
NEWTOWN ROAD TRAVEL CENTRE, NEWTOWN ROAD, MALVERN WR14 1PJ.
Tel: 01684 575082.
Fax: 01684 568870.
Fleetname: Jones Bros Coaches
E-mail: info@malverncoaches.co.uk
Web site: www.malverncoaches.co.uk
Prop: M. A. Crump. **Gen Man**: Michael Yates. **Ch Eng**: A. Jackson.
Fleet: 11 - 10 coach, 1 midicoach.
Chassis: 2 Bova. 1 DAF. 2 Dennis. 2 Leyland. 1 MAN. 1 Toyota. 2 Volvo.
Bodies: 2 Bova. 3 Duple. 3 Plaxton. 1 Van Hool.
Ops incl: local bus services, school contracts, excursions & tours, private hire, continental tours.
Livery: Off-white/Orange.

KESTREL COACHES
UNITS 1&2, BARRACKS ROAD, SANDY LANE, STOURPORT-ON-SEVERN DY13 9QB
Tel/Fax: 01299 829689
Prop: M Wood.
Fleet: 10 - 4 coach, 3 midicoach, 3 minibus.
Chassis: 1 Bedford. 2 Bova. 1 DAF. 1 LDV. 2 Mercedes. 2 Toyota. 1 Citroën.
Bodies: 2 Bova. 3 Caetano. 1 Leyland. 2 Mercedes. 1 Van Hool. 1 Relay
Ops incl: local bus services, school contracts, private hire.
Livery: White
Ticket System: Almex

WHITTLE COACH & BUS LTD
FOLEY BUSINESS PARK, STOURPORT ROAD, KIDDERMINSTER DY11 7QL
Tel: 01562 820002 **Fax**: 01562 820027
E-mail: webenquiries@whittlecoach.co.uk
Web site: www.whittlecoach.co.uk
Chmn: Peter Shipp **Man Dir**: David Shurden **Dir**: Peter Harrison
Fleet: 34 - 13 single-deck bus, 6 midibus, 14 minibus. 1 minicoach.
Chassis: 15 Dennis. 2 Mercedes Benz. 2 Optare. 15 Volvo.
Bodies: 5 Alexander Dennis. 2 Optare. 24 Plaxton. 2 Wright. 1 Other.
Ops incl: local bus services, school contracts, excursions & tours, private hire, continental tours.
Livery: White/Blue/Yellow.
Ticket system: Wayfarer III
Part of EYMS Group

WOODSTONES COACHES LTD
ARTHUR DRIVE, HOO FARM INDUSTRIAL ESTATE, WORCESTER ROAD, KIDDERMINSTER DY11 7RA
Tel: 01562 823073
Fax; 01562 827277
Man Dir: Ivan Meredith
Dir: Richard Meredith
Fleet: 6 single-deck coach
Bodies: 6 Plaxton.
Chassis: 6 Volvo
Ops incl: school contracts, excursions & tours, private hire
Livery: White/Orange/Yellow/Red

YARRANTON BROS LTD
EARDISTON GARAGE, TENBURY WELLS WR15 8JL.
Tel: 01584 881229.
Dirs: A. L. Yarranton (**Gen Man**), M. L. Yarranton, D. A. Yarranton.
Fleet: 12 - 10 coach, 1 minibus, 1 minicoach.
Chassis: 3 Bedford. 3 Dennis. 3 Mercedes. 2 Volvo. 1 Toyota.
Bodies: 2 Berkhof. 2 Caetano. 1 Jonckheere. 2 Mercedes. 4 Plaxton. 1 Duple.
Ops incl: local bus services, school contracts, excursions & tours, private hire, continental tours.
Livery: Green/White/Orange.

CHANNEL ISLANDS

ALDERNEY

RIDUNA BUSES
40C HIGH STREET, ALDERNEY GY9 3TG
Tel: 01481 823760
Fax: 01481 823030
Prop: A. J. Curtis.
Fleet: 5 - 2 single-deck bus, 2 coach, 1 minibus.
Chassis: 3 Bedford. 1 Freight Rover.
Bodies: 2 Duple. 1 Pennine. 1 Heaver.
Ops incl: local bus services, excursions & tours, private hire.
Livery: Cream/Maroon

GUERNSEY

ISLAND COACHWAYS LTD
THE TRAMSHEDS, LES BANQUES, ST PETER PORT GY4 6SF
Tel: 01481 720210
Fax: 01481 710109
E-mail: sales@island-coachways.demon.co.uk
Web site: www.island-coachways.demon.co.uk
Man Dir: Mrs Hannah Beacom
Co Sec/Dir: George Boucher
Works Man/Dir: Ben Boucher **Traf Man**: John Drillot **Off Man**: Mrs Jenny Down **Customer Care Man**: Mrs Ann Belben
Fleet Man: Tom Wilson
Fleet: 56 - 38 single-deck bus, 14 coach, 1 midicoach, 3 minibus.
Chassis: 1 Cannon. 33 Dennis. 4 Iveco. 9 Leyland. 4 Optare. 4 Renault. 1 Toyota.
Bodies: 1 Caetano. 4 Camo. 33 East Lancs. 3 Elme. 3 Iveco. 2 Leicester. 4 Optare. 6 Wadham Stringer.
Ops incl: local bus services, school contracts, excursions & tours, private hire
Livery: Bus: Green/Yellow Coach: Cream/Gold
Ticket System: Almex Smartfare.

JERSEY

CONNEX TRANSPORT (JERSEY) LTD
1A COLLETTE STREET, ST HELIER JE2 3NX
Tel: 01534 877772
FAX: 01534 723999
Gen Man: Phillipe Juhles
Fleetname: Connex
Fleet: 46 single-deck buses
Chassis: 46 Dennis
Bodies: 46 Caetano.

TANTIVY BLUE COACH TOURS
70/72 LA COLOMBERIE, ST HELIER JE2 4QA
Tel: 01534 706706
Fax: 01534 706705
E-mail: info@tantivybluecoach.com
Web site: www.jerseycoaches.com
Man Dir: Mike Cotilard **Ops Dir**: Paul Young
Fleet: 66 - 4 single-deck bus, 60 coach, 2 mdnicoach.
Chassis: 7 Bedford. 3 Cannon. 1 Iveco. 50 Leyland. 2 Optare.
Bodies: 2 Caetano. 6 Carlyle. 7 Duple. 3 Leicester. 2 Optare. 40 Wadham Stringer.
Ops incl: school contracts, excursions & tours, private hire.
Livery: Blue.

WAVERLEY COACHES LTD
UNIT 3, LA COLLETTE, ST HELIER JE2 3NX
Tel: 01534 758360
Fax: 01534 732627
Dir/Gen Man: S. E. Pedersen.
Ch Eng: Peter Evans.
Fleet: 18 - 12 coach, 2 midicoach, 4 minibus.
Chassis: 7 Bedford. 5 Leyland. 2 Mercedes. 1 Renault. 3 VW.
Bodies: 7 Duple. 5 Wadham Stringer. 4 other.
Ops incl: excursions & tours, private hire.
Livery: Yellow/White.

ISLE of MAN

DOUGLAS CORPORATION TRAMWAY
STRATHALLAN CRESCENT, DOUGLAS IM2 4NR
Tel: 01624 696420
E-mail: pcannon@douglas.gov.im
Fleet: 20 tramcars
Ops incl: tram services, private hire.

ISLE OF MAN TRANSPORT
TRANSPORT HEADQUARTERS, BANKS CIRCUS, DOUGLAS IM1 5PT
Tel: 01624 663366
Fax: 01624 663637
E-mail: info@busandrail.dtl.gov.im
Fleet: 109 - 75 double-deck bus, 10 single-deck bus, 24 tram.
Chassis: 33 DAF. 34 Dennis. 18 Leyland.
Bodies: 54 East Lancs. 8 Leyland. 10 Marshall. 10 Northern Counties. 3 Optare.
Ops incl: local bus/tram services, private hirwe
Livery: Red/Cream.
Ticket System: Wayfarer.

PROTOURS ISLE OF MAN LTD
SUMMERHILL, DOUGLAS IM2 4PF
Tel: 01624 674301
Fax: 01624 675656
Email: info@protours.co.im
Web: www.protours.co.im
Chmn & Man Dir: Roy Lightfoot **Dir**: S F Cairns, F B Kinnear **Traffic Man**: Dave Bennett **Ch Eng**: Alan Lancaster
Fleet: 28 - 2 two-deck bus, 17 single-deck coach, 2 midibus, 4 midicoach, 3 minibus.
Chassis: 5 Bedford. 1 BMC. 3 DAF. 5 Iveco.1 LAG. 3 Leyland. 1 MAN. 1 Mercedes-Benz. 4 Scania. 1 Toyota. 2 Volvo. 2 LAG.
Bodies: 1 Berkhof. 1 BMC. 1 Caetano. 5 Duple. 3 Irizar. 2 Jonkheere. 4 Leicester. 5 Plaxton. 1 Reeve Burgess. 3 Van Hool. 1 Wadham Stringer. 1 other.
Ops incl: local bus services, excursions & tours, private hire, express, continental tours, school contracts.
Livery: White/Blue/Yellow

ISLES OF SCILLY

HERITAGE TOUR
SANTAMANA, 9 RAMS VALLEY, ST MARY'S TR21 0JX
Tel: 01720 422387
Props: G. Twynham, Mrs P. Twynham.
Fleet: 1 single-deck bus (1948 vehicle).
Chassis: Austin K2. **Body**: Barnard.
Ops incl: excursions & tours, private hire.
Livery: Blue/Cream.

ISLAND ROVER
THE NOOK, CHURCH STREET, ST MARYS TR21OJT
E-mail: admin@islandrover.co.uk
Web-site: www.islandrover.co.uk
Props: Glynne Lucas
Tel: 01720 422131

SCOTTISH OPERATORS

ABERDEEN, CITY OF

BLUEBIRD BUSES LTD
THE BUS STATION, GUILD STREET, ABERDEEN AB11 6GR
Tel: 01224 591381
Fax: 01224 584202
Recovery: 01224 591381
E-mail: eastscotland@stagecoachbus.com
Web site: www.stagecoachbus.com
Fleetname: Stagecoach Bluebird
Man Dir: Charlie Mullen **Ops Dir**: Robert Hall **Eng Dir**: John MacPherson **Ops Man**: George Devine **Depot Eng**: Dave Cabine **Comm mgr**: Jim Gardner
Fleet: 369 - 65 double-deck bus, 141 single-deck bus, 17 coach, 61 midibus, 85 minibus.
Chassis: 42 Dennis. 52 Leyland. 38 MAN. 50 Mercedes. 25 Optare. 7 Scania. 155 Volvo.
Bodies: 268 Alexander. 5 Jonckheere. 11 Leyland. 10 Neoplan. 25 Optare. 43 Plaxton. 7 Wright.
Ops incl: local bus services, tram service, school contracts, excursions & tours, private hire, express.
Livery: Stagecoach/Megabus/Citylink
Ticket System: ERG

FIRST IN ABERDEEN
395 KING STREET, ABERDEEN AB24 5RP
Tel: 01224 650100
Web site: www.firstgroup.com
Man Dir: G Mair
Fleet: 185 - 34 double-deck bus, 107 single-deck bus, 12 coach, 20 articulated bus, 4 open top bus, 2 vintage, 6 minicoach.
Ops incl: local bus services, school contracts, excursions & tours, private hire, express, continental tours.
Livery: Coaches: Silver or White, Buses: Group Magenta Blue/Grey.

FOUNTAIN EXECUTIVE
HILL OF GOVAL, DYCE, ABERDEEN AB21 7NX
Tel: 01224 729090
Fax: 01224 729191
E-mail: info@fountainexecutive.co.uk
Web site: www.fountainexecutive.co.uk
Prop: Michael Ewen
Fleet: 10 - 4 coach, 1 midicoach, 5 minicoach.
Chassis: 6 Mercedes. 4 Scania.
Bodies: incl: 4 Jonckheere. Unvi
Ops incl: private hire, continental tours.
Livery: Gold

GRAMPIAN COACHES
FIRST ABERDEEN LTD,
395 KING STREET, ABERDEEN AB24 5RP
Tel: 01224 650151
Fax: 01224 650123
E-mail: tom.gordon@firstgroup.com
Web site: www.grampian-coaches.co.uk
Man Dir: George Mair **Sec**: Alan Paterson
Coaching Man: Tom Gordon
Fleet: 28 - 3 single-deck bus, 17 coach, 2 midicoach, 6 minibus.
Chassis: 1 Bluebird. 2 BMC. 1 Dennis. 6 Mercedes.1 Optare. 6 Scania. 11 Volvo.
Bodies: 6 Alexander. 2 BMC. 1 Duple. 6 Irizar. 5 Jonckheere. 1 Optare. 4 Plaxton. 2 Van Hool.
Ops incl: school contracts, excursions & tours, private hire, continental tours.
Livery: First ("Barbie")
Ticket System: Setright
subsidiary of First Group

MAIRS COACHES
395 KING STREET, ABERDEEN AB24 5RP.
Tel: 01224 650150.
Fax: 01224 650123.
Man Dir: G. Mair. **Eng Sup**: R. Elrick.
Comm Dir: J. Mackie
Fleet: 26 - 2 double-deck bus, 14 coach, 10 midicoach.
Chassis: 1 DAF. 1 Dennis. 3 Leyland. 8 Mercedes. 3 Renault. 1 Scania. 7 Volvo.
Bodies: 2 Alexander. 2 Duple. 8 Mercedes. 1 Irizar. 6 Plaxton. 2 Van Hool. 3 Dodge.
Ops incl: school contracts, excursions & tours, private hire, express, continental tours.
Livery: Silver/Grey or Maroon/Gold.
Ticket System: Wayfarer/Setright.
Part of FirstGroup.

WHYTES COACH TOURS
SCOTSTOWN ROAD, NEWMACHAR, ABERDEEN AB21 7PP
Tel: 01651 862211
Fax: 01651 862918
Recovery: 01651 862724
E-mail: sales@whytescoachtours.co.uk
Web Site: www.whytescoachtours.co.uk
Ops incl: school contracts, excursions & tours, private hire, continental tours.
Livery: Two-tone Green

ABERDEENSHIRE

AMBER TRAVEL
CROSSFIELDS FARMHOUSE, TURRIFF AB53 7QY.
Tel: 01888 563474.
Fax: 01888 563474.
Props: D. Cheyne, S. Cheyne.
Fleet: 5 - 4 coach, 1 midibus.
Chassis: 1 Bedford. 1 Mercedes. 3 Volvo.
Ops incl: school contracts, private hire.
Livery: White/Red/Amber

CHEYNES COACHES
ALLANDALE, DAVIOT, INVERURIE AB51 0EJ
Tel: 01467 671400
Fax: 01467 671479
E-mail: lesley@cheynescoaches.co.uk
Web site: www.cheynescoaches.co.uk
Ptnrs: W A Cheyne, R Cheyne, L A Cheyne, M F Cheyne.
Fleet: 10 - 3 single-deck bus, 3 single-deck coach, 1 minibus, 3 minicoach.
Chassis: 1 DAF. 1 Ford Transit. 3 Leyland.2 Volvo.
Bodies: 1 Bova. 2 Optare. 4 Plaxton. 2 Van Hool.
Ops incl: school contracts, excursions & tours, private hire.
Livery: Silver/Pink/Purple

J D PEACE CO ABDN LTD
FARE PARK, ECHT, WESTHILL. ABERDEENSHIRE AB32 27AL.
Tel: 01330 860542
Fax: 01330 860543
Web: peacescoches.co.uk
E-mail: info@peachescoaches.co.uk
Dirs: David J Collie, Kathleen Collie.
Fleet: 12 - incl: single-deck coach, midicoach, minicoach.
Chassis: incl: DAF. Ford Transit. Mercedes-Benz. Volvo.
Bodies: incl: Bova. Mercedes-Benz. Van Hool.
Ops incl: school contracts, private hire.

J W COACHES LTD
DYKEHEAD GARAGE, BLACKHALL, BANCHORY AB31 6PS.
Tel/fax: 01330 823300.
Fleet: 15 - 5 coach, 6 midibus, 1 midicoach, 3 minibus.
Chassis: 1 Bedford. 6 Freight Rover. 1 Iveco. 4 Leyland. 1 MAN. 2 Mercedes.
Bodies: 5 Carlyle. 3 Duple. 2 Plaxton. 2 Reeve Burgess. 1 Devon. 2 Dormobile.
Ops incl: local bus services, school contracts, excursions & tours, private hire.
Livery: Blue/Turquoise/White.
Ticket System: Setright.
subsidiary of Bluebird Buses.

KINEIL COACHES LTD
ANDERSON PLACE, WEST SHORE INDUSTRIAL ESTATE, FRASERBURGH AB43 9LG
Tel: 01346 510200
Fax: 01346 514774
Man Dir: Ian Neilson
Fleet: 27 - 19 single-deck bus, 1 midibus, 3 midicoach, 4 minibus.
Chassis: 1 DAF. 8 Mercedes-Benz. 1 Scania. 17 Van Hool.
Bodies: 1 Jonkheere. 5 Mercedes-Benz. 1 Scania. 17 Volvo.
Ops incl: local bus services, school contracts, excursions & tours, private hire, continental tours.
Livery: Blue/White/Red

ALEX MILNE COACHES
THE GARAGE, 4 MAIN STREET, NEW BYTH AB53 5XD
Tel: 01888 544340
Tel: 01888 544154
E-mail: info@alexmilnecoaches.co.uk
Web site: www.alexmilnecoaches.co.uk
Ptnrs: Alex Milne Brian Milne
Fleet: 14 - 1 single-desck bus, 4 coach, 3 minicoach, 6 minibus.
Chassis: 6 Ford Transit. 2 Volvo.
Bodies: 2 Esker. 4 Mercedes-Benz.
Ops incl: local bus services, school contracts, private hire, excursions & tours
Livery: Blue/White
Ticket system: Wayfarer

MAYNES COACHES LTD
4 MARCH ROAD WEST, BUCKIE AB56 4BU.
Tel: 01542 831219.
Fax: 01542 833572
Recovery: 01542 831219.
Web: www.maynes.co.uk
E-mail: info@maynes.co.uk
Proprietors: David Mayne, Kevin Mayne, Gordon Mayne
Fleet: 23 - 17single-deck coach, 5 midicoach, 1 minibus.
Chassis: 2 Bova. 5 MAN. 5 Mercedes-Benz.1 Optare. 1 Renault. 10 Volvo.
Bodies: 2 Bova. 1 Esker. 3 Marcopolo. 1 Mercedes-Benz. 2 Noge. 1 Optare. 2 Plaxton. 10 Van Hool. 1 other
Ops incl: local bus service, school contracts, excursions & tours, private hire, continental tours.
Livery: Blue/White/Gold.
Ticket System: Setright.

M W NICOLL'S COACH HIRE
THE BUSINESS PARK, ABERDEEN ROAD, LAURENCEKIRK AB30 1EY
Tel: 01561 377262.
Fax: 01561 378822.
E-mail: malcolm.nicoll@lineone.net
Web site: www.nicoll-coaches.co.uk
Man Dir: M. W. Nicoll. **Dir:** I. J. Nicoll.
Service Man: A. Gordon. **Office Man:** M Forrest
Fleet: 24 - 2 single-deck bus, 6 coach, 3 midibus, 6 midicoach, 2 minibus, 5 minicoach.
Chassis: 1 Bova, 4 Ford Transit, 1 Leyland, 9 Mercedes, 1 Optare, Setra, 2 Toyota, 6 Volvo.
Bodies: 1 Bova, 2 Caetano, 1 Duple, 10 Mercedes, 1 Solo, 6 Van Hool, 4 others.
Ops incl: local bus services, private hire.

Livery: White.
Ticket System: Almex.

REIDS OF RHYNIE
22 MAIN STREET, RHYNIE, BY HUNTLY AB54 4HB
Tel/Fax: 01464 861212
Recovery: 07831 173681
Owner: Colin Reid.
Fleet: 14 - 4 coach, 2 midibus, 1 midicoach, 7 minibus.
Chassis: 4 Ford Transit. 4 LDV. 3 Mercedes. 4 Volvo.
Bodies: include: 3 Caetano. 2 Mercedes. 1 Van Hool.
Ops incl: local bus services, school contracts, private hire.
Livery: White/Blue/Water Green
Ticket system: Wayfarer 3

SHEARER OF HUNTLY LTD
OLD TOLL ROAD, HUNTLY AB54 6JA.
Tel: 01466 792410
Fax: 01466 793926
Dlrs: James W Shearer, Irene E Shearer.
Fleet: 10 - 1 coach, 1 midicoach, 6 minibus, 2 mincoach
Chassis: 1 Dennis. 6 Ford Transit. 2 LDV. 1 Mercedes.
Bodies: incl: 1 UVG. 1 Wadham Stringer
Ops incl: school contracts, private hire.

SIMPSON'S COACHES
21 UNION STREET, ROSEHEARTY, FRASERBURGH AB43 7JQ
Tel: 01346 571610
Fax: 01346 571070
E-mail: info@simpsonscoaches.co.uk
Web site: www.simpsonscoaches.co.uk
Prop: Ron Simpson. Pat Simpson
Fleet: 6 coach.
Chassis: 1 Iveco. 5 Volvo.
Bodies: 1 Beulas. 2 Berkhof. 3 Caetano.
Ops incl: excursions & tours, private hire, continental tours.
Livery: Silver/Blue.

ANGUS

RIDDLER'S COACHES LIMITED
CAIRNIE LOAN, ARBROATH DD11 4DS
Tel: 01241 873464
Fax: 01241 873504
Dirs: C W Riddler, Mrs G M Riddler
Fleet: 6 single-deck coach.
Chassis: 6 Volvo.
Ops incl: excursions & tours, private hire

SIDLAW EXECUTIVE TRAVEL (SCOTLAND) LTD
UNIT 5 ARDYLE INDUSTRIAL ESTATE, PERRY STREET, DUNDEE DD2 2RD
Tel: 01382 610410
Fax: 01382 624333
E-mail: travel@sidlaw.co.uk
Web site: www.sidlaw.co.uk
Dir: Bob Costello **Fleet Eng:** Jamie Costello
Fleet: 14 - 2 coach, 4 minicoach, 4 midicoach, 4 minicoach.
Chassis: 1 MAN. 13 Mercedes.
Ops incl: school contracts, excursions & tours, private hire.
Livery: White/Silver.

ARGYLL & BUTE

BOWMAN'S COACHES (MULL) LTD
SCALLACASTLE, CRAIGNURE, ISLE OF MULL PA65 6BA.
Tel: 01680 812313.
Web site: www.bowmanstours.co.uk
Prop: A. Bowman, S. Bowman, I. Bowman, I. Bowman. **Gen Man:** A. Bowman.
Fleet: 12 coach.
Chassis: Bedford. Dennis. Ford. Leyland.
Bodies: Duple. Jonckheere. Plaxton.
Ops incl: local bus services, excursions & tours, private hire.
Livery: Cream/Red.
Ticket System: Setright, Almex.

CRAIG OF CAMPBELTOWN LTD
BENMHOR, CAMPBELTOWN PA28 6DN
Tel: 01586 552319.
Fax: 01586 552344
E-mail: enquiries@westcoastmotors.co.uk
Web site: www.westcoastmotors.co.uk
Fleetname: West Coast Motors
Chmr/Man Dir: W G Craig **Dir:** C R Craig
Co Sec: J M Craig **Tran Man:** D M Halliday
Fleet Eng: D Martin
Fleet: 71 - 6 double-deck bus, 28 single-deck bus, 30 coach, 2 midibus, 3 midicoach, 1 minibus.
Chassis: 1 Bedford. 26 DAF. 17 Dennis. 1Freight Rover. 5 Leyland. 1 MAN. 5 Mercedes. 5 Optare. 9 Volvo.
Bodies: 15 Alexander. 1 Ikarus. 1 Jonckheere. 1 Mellor. 1 Onyx. 5 Optare. 4 Park Royal. 13 Plaxton. 27 Van Hool. 2 Wright.
Ops incl: local bus services, school contracts, excursions & tours, private hire, express.
Livery: Multi-coloured
Ticket System: Wayfarer.

GARELOCHHEAD COACHES
WOODLEA GARAGE, MAIN ROAD, GARELOCHHEAD PA65 6BA
Tel: 01436 810200.
Fax: 01436 810050.
Prop: Stuart McQueen

HIGHLAND HERITAGE COACH TOURS
CENTRAL ADMINISTRATION OFFICE, DALMALLY PA33 1AY
Tel: 01838 200453
E-mail: info@highlandheritage.co.uk
Web site: www.highlandheritage.co.uk
Man Dir: Ian Cleaver
Fleet: 15 coach.
Chassis: 15 Volvo.
Bodies: 15 Van Hool.
Ops incl: excursions & tours
Livery: Gold

HIGHLAND ROVER COACHES
TAYNUILT PA35 1HT
Tel/Fax: 01866 822612
E-mail: angus.douglas@freeuk.com
Prop: Angus Douglas.
Fleet: 3 - 1 coach, 2 minibus.
Chassis: 1 Ford. 2 Mercedes.
Bodies: 2 Mercedes. 1 other
Ops incl: local bus services, school contracts, private hire
Ticket system: Setright.

Scottish Operators

190

McCOLLS OF ARGYLL LTD
MCCOLLS HOTEL, WEST BAY, DUNOON PA23 7HN
Tel: 01369 702764
Fax: 01369 702764
Web site: www.mccollshotel.co.uk
Dir: David Wilkinson
Fleet: 8 coach
Chassis: 8 Iveco
Bodies: 8 Beulas
Ops incl: excursions & tours
Livery: Red/yellow

OBAN & DISTRICT BUSES LTD
GLENGALLAN ROAD, OBAN PA34 4HH
Tel: 01631 570500
Fax: 01631 567152
E-mail: enquiries@westcoastmotors.co.uk
Web site: www.westcoastmotors.co.uk
Fleetname: Oban & District.
Man Dir: Colin Craig **Dir:** W. G. Craig
Depot Controllers: David Hannah, Donnie McDougal **Workshop Supervisor:** Iain McDonald
Fleet: 23 - 16 single-deck bus, 2 coach, 2 midicoach, 2 minibus, 1 midibus.
Chassis: 4 DAF. 3 Dennis. 2 LDV. 10 Leyland. 2 Mercedes. 1 Optare. 1 Volvo.
Bodies: 10 Alexander. 1 Optare. 5 Plaxton. 4 Wright. 1 Onyx. 1 KL Conversion.
Ops incl: local bus services, school contracts, private hire, express.
Livery: Red/Blue/Honeysuckle
Ticket System: Wayfarer 3
Subsidiary of West Coast Motors

L. F STEWART & SON LTD
DALAYICH, BY TAYNUILT PA35 1HN.
Tel: 01866 833342.
Fax: 01866 833237.
Dirs: R. Maceachen, M. A. Stewart.
Fleet: 4 - 2 coach, 2 minibus.
Chassis: 2 Mercedes. 2 Volvo.
Bodies: 1 Plaxton. 2 Reeve Burgess. 1 Berkhof.
Ops incl: local bus services, school contracts, private hire.
Livery: Red/White/Yellow.

BORDERS

AUSTIN TRAVEL
STATION ROAD, EARLSTON TD4 6BZ
Tel: 01896 849360
Fax: 01896 849623
E-mail: austin@travel.gbtbroadband.co.uk
Web site: www.scotlnetours.co.uk
Ptnrs: Douglas Austin, Barry Austin.
Fleet: 7 - 4 coach, 2 midicoach, 1 minicoach.
Chassis: 2 Bova. 3 Mercedes. 2 Setra.
Bodies: 2 Bova. 2 Esker. 2 Setra. 1 other.
Ops incl: school contracts, excursions & tours, private hire, continental tours.
Livery: Pearlescent white

FIRST EDINBURGH LTD
SEE STIRLING

JAMES FRENCH & SON
THE GARAGE, COLDINGHAM, EYEMOUTH TD14 5NS.
Tel/Fax: 01890 771283.
Fleet: 12 coach.
Chassis: Volvo.
Bodies: Van Hool.
Ops incl: excursions & tours.

MUNRO'S OF JEDBURGH LTD
OAKVALE GARAGE, BONGATE, JEDBURGH TD8 6DU
Tel: 01835 862253
Fax: 01835 864297
Recovery: 01835 864844
E-mail: info@munrosofjedburgh.co.uk
Web site: www.munrosofjedburgh.co.uk
Ops Dir: Ewan Farish **Eng Dir:** Bruce Campbell
Fleet: 34 - 14 single-deck bus, 5 single-deck coach, 9 midibus, 4 midicoach, 2 minicoach.
Chassis: 3 Alexander Dennis. 2 DAF. 3 Dennis. 2 Enterprise. 4 EOS. 2 Iveco. 7 MAN. 4 Mercedes-Benz. 7 Optare.
Bodies: 2 Alexander Dennis. 1 Ikarus. 7 Marshall/MCV. 7 Optare. 6 Park Royal. 5 Plaxton. 1 Transbus. 5 Van Hool.
Ops incl: local bus services, school contracts, private hire.
Livery: White/Red
Ticket System: Wayfarer TGX

PERRYMAN BUSES
NORTH ROAD INDUSTRIAL ESTATE, BERWICK UPON TWEED TD15 1UN.
Tel: 01289 308719
Fax: 01289 309970.
Web site: www.perrymansbuses.com
Man Dir: R J Perryman, L M Perryman.
Fleet: 35 - 20 double-deck bus, 5 single-deck coach, 6 midicoach, 4 minibus
Chassis: 4 MAN. 2 Mercedes-Benz. 12 Optare. 3 Renault. 5 Volvo
Bodies: incl: 1 Aleaxander Dennis. 4 Plaxton. 1 Wright.
Ops incl: local bus services, school contract, private hire
Ticket System: Wayfarer

TELFORD'S COACHES LTD
TWEEDEN BRAE, NEWCASTLETON TD9 0TL
Tel/Fax: 01387 375677
Recovery: 07711 280475
E-mail: alistair@telfordcoaches.com
Web site: www.telfordscoaches.com
Man Dir: Alistair S Telford **Ch Eng:** Rod Swan
Fleet: 16 - 9 single-deck coach, 4 midicoach, 3 minibus.
Chassis: 1 Ford. 1 Ford Transit. 6 Mercedes-Benz. 8 Volvo.
Bodies: 2 Jonckheere. 3 Mercedes-Benz. 11 Plaxton.
Ops incl: local bus services, school contracts, excursions & tours, private hire, continental tours.
Livery: White with Blue vinyls

CLACKMANNANSHIRE

M.LINE
THE COACH HOUSE, KELLIEBANK, ALLOA FK10 1NT.
Tel: 01259 212802.
E-mail: info@m-line.co.uk.
Web Site: www.m-line.co.uk.
Ops Man: Tom Matchett, Andy Mclellan.
Comp Eng: Dave Craig
Fleet: 16 - 7 double-deck bus, 1 single-deck bus, 5 single-deck coach, 1 middcoach, 2 minibus..
Chassis: 1 Alexander Dennis. 1 Ford. 2 Scania.12 Volvo.
Ops incl: local bus services, school contracts, excursions & tours, private hire, continental tours.
Livery: Cream/Beige.

MACKIE'S COACHES
32 GLASSHOUSE LOAN, ALLOA FK10 1PE.
Tel/Fax: 01259 216180
E-mail: enquiries@mackiescoaches.com
Web site: www.mackiescoaches.com
Fleet: 18 - 6 single-deck bus,12single-deck coach
Chassis: 5 Bova. 1 Dennis. 12 Volvo.
Bodies: 5 Bova. 1 Duple. 2 Jonckheere. 4 Van Hool. 1 Van Hool. 1 Wadham Stringer. 5 Wright.
Livery: White/Brown/Beige.
Ticket System: Wayfarer.

WOODS COACHES
2 GOLF VIEW, TILLICOULTRY FK13 6DH
Tel: 01259 751753
Fax: 01259 751824
Fax: 07836 662919
E-mail: jwcoaches@btinternet.com
Web site: www.woodscoaches.net
Owner: James Woods **Ops Man:** John Woods.
Fleet: 10 - coach, midicoach, minicoach
Chassis: 2 Bova, 8 Mercedes.
Bodies: 2 Bova. 2 Esker. 6 Mercedes.
Ops incl: school contracts, excursions & tours, private hire
Livery: Silver

DUMFRIES & GALLOWAY

ANDERSON'S COACHES
BLUE BELL HILL, SKIPPERS, LANGHOLM DG13 0LH.
Tel: 01387 380553.
Fax: 01387 380553.
Ptnrs: I. R. Anderson, K. Irving.
Ch Eng: C. Anderson.
Fleet: 6 - 2 single-deck bus, 2 minibus, 2 minicoach.
Chassis: 1 AEC. 3 Ford Transit. 1 Freight Rover. 1 Leyland.
Bodies: 2 Plaxton. 1 Robin Hood. 1 PMT. 1 N/S Transit.
Ops incl: local bus services, school contracts, private hire.
Livery: Red/Orange/Yellow stripe.
Ticket System: Almex.

R. K. ARMSTRONG COACHES
THE PARK, BRIDGE-OF-DEE, CASTLE DOUGLAS DG7 1TR.
Tel: 01556 503391
Fax: 01556 504656
Recovery: 01556 503391
E-mail: rkarmstrong8@aol.com
Web site: www.armstrongcoaches.com
Prop: R. K. Armstrong.
Fleet: 14 - 1 single-deck bus, 5 coach, 4 midibus, 2 midicoach, 1 minibus, 1 minicoach.
Chassis: 5 mercedes. 2 Optare. 1 Scania. 1 Toyota. 2 Volvo.
Bodies: 1 Jonckheere. 1 Leyland. 5 Mercedes. 2 Optare. 1 Plaxton. 2 Reeve Burgess. 1 Van Hool.
Ops incl: local bus services, school contracts, excursions and tours, private hire, continental tours.

WILLIAM BROWNRIGG

GARAGE, THORNHILL DG3 5LZ.
Tel/Fax: 01848 330203
Fleet: 8 - 4 single-deck coach, 4 minibus
Chassis: 1 Bova. 1 LDV. 3 Mercedes-Benz. 1 Scania. 2 Volvo.
Bodies: 1 Bova. 1Duple. 1 Plaxton. 1 Van Hool.
Ops incl: local bus services, school contracts, excursions and tours, private hire
Livery: Orange/White

JAMES KING COACHES

36 MAIN STREET, KIRKCOWAN, NEWTON STEWART DG8 0HG
Tel: 01671 830284
Fax: 01671 830499
E-mail: enquiries@kingscoachhire.com
Web: www.kingscoachhire.com
Fleet: 25 - 8 single-deck bus, 12 single-deck coach, 5 midicoach.
Chassis: 5 Optare. 12 Volvo.
Bodies: 1 Caetano. 2 Jonckheere. 5 Optare. 5 Plaxton. 12 Van Hool.
Ops incl: local bus services, school contracts, excursions & tours, private hire.
Livery: White.
Ticket System: Wayfarer

KIWI LUXURY TRAVEL

80 QUEEN STREET, NEWTON STEWART DG8 6JL
Tel: 01671 404294
Fax: 01671 403310
E-mail: kiwitravel@btconnect.com
Web site: www.kiwitravelltd.co.uk
Dirs: Ian Allison, Janet Allison
Fleet: 4 - 3 coach, 1 minicoach
Chassis: incl: 3 Volvo
Bodies: incl: 1 Caetano.
Ops incl: local bus services, school contracts, excursions & tours, private hire.

MacEWAN'S COACH SERVICES

JOHNFIELD, AMISFIELD, DUMFRIES DG1 3LS
Tel: 01387 256533
Fax: 01387 711123
Prop: John MacEwan **Ch Eng**: Peter Maxwell
Fleet: 65 - 5 double-deck, 22 single-deck bus, 9 coach, 1 double-deck coach, 12 midibus, 4 midicoach, 12 minibus
Chassis: 1 AEC. 2 Bedford. 1 Bristol. 1 DAF. 3 Dennis. 3 Ford Transit. 1 Iveco. 4 LDV. 2 Leyland. 5 MAN. 5 MCW. 18 Mercedes. 3 Optare. 5 Scania. 2 Transbus. 9 Volvo.
Bodies: 10 Alexander. 2 Autobus. 2 Duple. 1 ECW. 1 East Lancs. 1 Irizar. 1 Jonckheere. 4 LDV. 4 Marshall/MCV. 5 MCW. 3 Optare. 17 Plaxton. 3 Crystal. 2 Drinkwater. 2 Transbus. 1 Van Hool. 3 Wright. 1 DAB. 2 Montano.
Ops incl: local bus services, school contracts
Livery: White/Red/Blue
Ticket system: ERG Transit 400

MCCULLOCH AND SON

MAIN ROAD, STONEYKIRK, STRANRAER DG9 9DH.
Tel/Fax: 01776 830236.
E-mail: mcculloch.coaches@virgin.net
Fleetname: McCulloch Coaches
Ptnrs: D F McCulloch, E A McCulloch
Fleet: 8 - incl: 1 single-deck bus, 3 coach, 1 midibus, 1 midicoach, 1 minicoach.
Chassis: 1 Bedford. 4 Mercedes. 2 Optare. 3 Volvo.
Bodies: 1 Caetano. 1 Duple. 2 Optare. 4 Plaxton.
Ops incl: local bus services, excursions & tours, school contracts, private hire
Livery: White/Blue lettering
Ticket System: Ticket books

DUNDEE CITY

FISHERS TOURS

MID CRAIGIE TRADING ESTATE, MID CRAIGIE ROAD, DUNDEE DD1 5EP
Tel/Fax: 01382 455177
E-mail: fisherstours@btconnect.com
Web site: www.fisherstours.co.uk
Ptnrs: James Cosgrove, Catherine Cosgrove
Fleet: 16 - 3 single-deck bus (70seat), 11 coach, 1 midicoach, 1 midibus, 2 minibus.
Chassis: 3 Iveco. 7 Leyland. 4 Mercedes. 2 Volvo.
Bodies: 1 Beulas. 2 ECW. 1 Marshall. 3 Mercedes. 1 Optare. 6 Plaxton. 2 Van Hool.
Ops incl: school contracts, excursions & tours, private hire, continental tours.
Livery: White/Blue/Turquoise/Yellow.

SIDLAW EXECUTIVE TRAVEL (SCOTLAND) LTD

UNIT 5 ARDYLE IND ESTATE, PERRIE STREET, DUNDEE DD2 2RD
Tel: 01382 610410
Fax: 01382 624333
E-mail: travel@sidlaw.co.uk
Web site: www.sidlaw.co.uk
Dir: Bob Costello **Fleet Eng**: Jamie Costello
Fleet: 14 - 2 coach, 4 minicoach, 4 midicoach, 4 minicoach.

Chassis: 1 MAN. 13 Mercedes.
Ops incl: school contracts, excursions & tours, private hire.
Livery: White/Silver

STRATHTAY SCOTTISH OMNIBUSES LTD

SEAGATE BUS STATION, DUNDEE DD1 2HR.
Tel: 01382 228345
Fax: 01382 202267
Recovery: 01382 228345
E-mail: eastscotland@stagecoachbus.com
Web site: www.stagecoachbus.com
Fleet Name: Stagecoach Strathtay
Man Dir: Doug Fleming **Ops Dir**: Steve Walker **Chief Eng Dir**: Jim Penrose **Ops Man**: Martin Hall **Depot Eng**: Alan Hughes
Fleet: 164 - 40 double-deck bus, 31 single-deck bus, 15 single deck coach, 18 midibus, 50 minibus.
Bodies: 58 Alexander. 33 East Lancs. 13 Northern Counties. 17 Optare. 18 Plaxton. 12 Wright. 3 Other.
Ops incl: local bus services, school contracts, excursions & tours, private hire, express.
Livery: Stagecoach/City Link/Megabus
Ticket System: ERG

TRAVEL DUNDEE

44-48 EAST DOCK STREET, DUNDEE DD1 3JS
Tel: 01382 201121
Fax: 01382 201997
E-mail: mailbox@traveldundee.co.uk
Web site: www.traveldundee.co.uk
Traff Man: William Murphy **Ch Eng**: Frank Sheach **Business Man**: Elsie Turbyne
Fleet: 127 - 18 double-deck, 88 single-deck, 19 coach, 2 double-deck coach
Chassis: 7 Dennis. 2 Leyland. 7 Mercedes. 12 Optare. 6 Scania. 93 Volvo.
Bodies: 3 East Lancs. 2 Leyland. 3 Mercedes. 12 Optare. 17 Plaxton. 90 Wright
Ops incl: local bus services, school contracts, excursions & tours, private hire.
Livery: Travel Dundee/Travel Greyhound (Part of the National Express Group)

EAST AYRSHIRE

LIDDELL'S COACHES
1 MAUCHLINE ROAD,
AUCHINLECK KA18 2BJ.
Tel: 01290 424300/420717.
Fax: 01290 425637.
Prop: J. Liddell. **Ch Eng**: J. Quinn. **Co Sec**:
Ms J. Samson. **Ops Man**: Ms M. Milroy.
Fleet: 24 - 8 double-deck bus, 10 coach,
4 midicoach, 2 minibus.
Chassis: 1 Bova. 3 DAF. 2 Dodge. 2 Freight
Rover. 10 Leyland. 6 Volvo.
Bodies: 8 Alexander. 1 Bova. 1 Caetano.
3 Duple. 1 ECW. 1 East Lancs.
2 Jonckheere. 4 Plaxton. 2 Reeve Burgess.
1 Wright.
Ops incl: local bus services, school
contracts, excursions & tours, private hire,
express.
Livery: White with Brown/Orange/Lemon
stripes.
Ticket System: Setright.

MILLIGAN'S COACH TRAVELL LTD
LOAN GARAGE, 20 THE LOAN,
MAUCHLINE, EAST AYRESHIRE
KA5 6AN.
Tel: 01290 550365.
Fax: 01290 553291.
Dir: W J Milligan. **Ops Man**: M Milligan
Fleet: 17 - 15 single -deck coach, 1
midicoach, 1 minicoach.
Chassis: 19 DAF. 4 Leyland. 1 Mercedes-
Benz. 3 Scania.
Bodies: 9 Bova. 3 Irizar. 5 Plaxton
Ops incl: school contracts, excursions &
tours, private hire, express.
Livery: Black/Silver/Red.

ROWE & TUDHOPE
WEST HILLHEAD, FARM ROAD,
KILMARNOCK KA3 1PH
Tel: 01563 525631
Fax: 01563 571489
E-mail: geo.rowe@fsmail.net
Web site: www.roweandtudhope.com
Dir: George Rowe
Fleet: 14 - 2 double-deck bus, 7 single-deck
coach, 1 midicoach, 3 minibus, 1 party
coach.
Chassis: 3 Bova. 3 Ford Transit. 2 Leyland.
1 Mercedes-Benz. 1 Scania. 4 Volvo.
Bodies: 2 Alexander. 1 Berkhof. 3 Bova. 1
Irizar. 1 Jonckheere. 2 Plaxton. 1 Van Hool.
Ops incl: school contracts, private hire.
Livery: White/Blue flag

EAST LOTHIAN

EVE CARS & COACHES
SPOTT ROAD, DUNBAR EH42 1RR.
Tel: 01368 865500.
Fax: 01368 865400.
E-mail: admin@eveinfo.co.uk
Web site: www.eveinfo.co.uk
Ptnrs: Gary Scougall, Vona Scougall.

FIRST EDINBURGH LTD
SEE STIRLING

EAST RENFREWSHIRE

HENRY CRAWFORD COACHES LTD
SHILFORD MILL, NEILSTON,
GLASGOW G78 3BA
Tel: 01505 850456
Fax: 01505 850479
E-mail: henrycrawford@talk21.com
Web site: www.henrycrawford.coaches.co.uk
Ops Man: James Crawford(**Dir**) **Ch Eng**:
John Crawford(**Dir**) **Co Sec**:
Isobel Crawford(**Dir**)
Fleet: 26 - 21 coach, 5 minicoach.
Chassis: 1 Bova. 2 Leyland. 5 Mercedes. 18
Volvo.
Bodies: 1 Bova. 2 Duple. 1 Indcar. 1 Optare.
3 Plaxton. 16 Van Hool. 2 other.
Ops incl: private hire, school contracts.
Livery: White/Red

SOUTHERN COACHES (NM) LTD
LOCHIBO ROAD, BARRHEAD G78 1LF.
Tel: 0141-881 1147.
Fax: 0141 881 1148.
E-mail:
reservations@southerncoaches.co.uk
Web site: southerncoaches.co.uk
Dirs: R. Wallace, D. Wallace, Mary Wallace.
Fleet: 19 - 17 coach, 2 minicoach.
Chassis: 2 DAF. 2 Toyota. 15 Volvo.
Bodies: 2 Caetano. 1 Jonckheere. 8
Plaxton. 8 Van Hool. 1 Ikarus.
Ops incl: school contracts, excursions &
tours, private hire, express.
Livery: Cream/Blue/Orange.

EDINBURGH, CITY OF

AAA COACHES
UNIT 7, RAW CAMPS INDUSTRIAL
ESTATE, KIRKNEWTON EH27 8DF
Tel: 01506 883000
Fax: 01506 884000
E-mail: info@aaacoaches.co.uk
Web site: www.aaacoaches.co.uk
Man Dir: Mr J T Renton
Fleet: 17 - 3 single-deck bus, 3 midibus, 1
minibus.
Chassis: 1 Bova. 1 Dennis. 1 LDV. 4 MAN.
3 Mercedes.. 7 Volvo.
Bodies: 4 Jonckheere. 2 Leyland. 4
Marcopolo. 2 Plaxton. 2 Sunsundegui.

CITYCIRCLE UK LTD
BUTLERFIELD INDUSTRIAL ESTATE,
BONNYRIGG EH19 3JQ
Tel: 01875 822862
Fax: 01875 822762
Web site: www.citycircleuk.com
Dir: Neil Pegg
Fleet: 5 coach.
Chassis/Bodies: 4 Setra. 1 Volvo.
Ops incl: private hire
(Subsidiary of City Circle, London)

CITY SIGHTSEEING EDINBURGH LTD
ANNANDALE STREET,
EDINBURGH EH7 4AZ
Tel: 0131 220 0770
E-mail: info@edinburghtour.com
Web site: www.edinburghtour.com
Fleet name: City Sightseeing
Ch Exec: Neil Renilson **Fin Dir**: Norman
Strachan **Ops Dir**: William Campbell **Eng
Dir**: William Devlin **Mktg Dir**: Iain Coupar
Fleet: 12 open-top bus
Chassis: 7 Dennis. 5 Leyland.
Bodies: 8 Alexander. 4 Plaxton.
Ops incl: excursions & tours
Livery: Red
Ticket system: Casio

EDINBURGH BUS TOURS
ANNANDALE STREET,
EDINBURGH EH7 4AZ
Tel: 0131 220 0770
E-mail: info@edinburghtour.com
Web site: www.edinburghtour.com
Ch Exec: Neil Renilson **Fin Dir**: Norman
Strachan **Ops Dir**: William Campbell **Eng
Dir**: William Devlin **Mktg Dir**: Iain Coupar
Fleet: 15 open-top bus
Chassis: 15 Leyland
Bodies: 12 Alexander. 3 Roe.
Livery: Cream/Green
Ticket system: Casio

EDINBURGH COACH LINES LTD
81 SALAMANDER STREET, LEITH,
EDINBURGH EH6 7JZ
Tel: 0131 554 5413
Fax: 0131 553 3721
E-mail:
enquiries@edinburghcoachlines.com.
Web site: www.edinburghcoachlines.com.
Dirs: Patric & Thomas Kavanagh **Gen Man**:
Peter Fyvie **Traff Man**: John Blair
Bookings Cnsltnt: Jacqueline Bauld
Fleet: 25 - 20 coach, 4 midicoach, 1 minibus.
Chassis: 1 BMC. 1 MAN. 8 Mercedes. 14
Scania. 1 Volvo.
Bodies: 1 BMC. 1 Caetano. 1 Indcar. 8
Irizar. 4 Setra. 7 Van Hool.
Ops incl: excursions & tours, private hire,
continental tours, school contracts.
subsidiary of Bernard Kavanagh & Sons Rep
of Ireland

FAIRWAY TRAVEL
6 BRIARBANK TERRACE,
EDINBURGH EH11 1ST.
Tel: 0131 467 6717.
Fax: 0131 467 6717.
E-mail: davy@fairwaytravel.freeserve
Web site: www.fairwaytravel.co.uk
Prop: D. Innes.
Fleet: 4 - 1 coach, 2 midicoach, 1 minibus.
Chassis: 1 DAF. 1 Setra. 2 Toyota.
Bodies: 2 Caetano. 1 Leyland. 1 Setra.
Ops incl: school contracts, excursions &
tours, private hire, continental tours.
Livery: Blue and Red on White.

FIRST EDINBURGH LTD
SEE STIRLING

LIBERTON TRAVEL
17-29 ENGINE ROAD,
LOANHEAD EH20 9RF
Tel: 0131 440 4400
Fax: 0131 448 0008
E-mail: sales@libertontravel.co.uk
Dirs: Iain Smith, Alan Boyd
Fleet: 10 - 7 coach, 2 minibus, 1 minicoach.
Chassis: 1 Dennis. 1 Ford Transit. 1 Freight
Rover. 1 Mercedes. 6 Volvo.
Bodies: 1 Caetano. 1 Marcopolo. 4 Plaxton.
Ops incl: school contracts, excursions &
tours, private hire.
Livery: White

Scottish Operators

193

LOTHIAN BUSES PLC

ANNANDALE STREET,
EDINBURGH EH7 4AZ
Tel: 0131 554 4494
Fax: 0131 554 3942
E-mail: mail@lothianbuses.co.uk
Web site: www.lothianbuses.co.uk
Ch Exec: Neil Renilson **Man Dir**: Ian Craig **Fin Dir**: Norman Strachan **Ops Dir**: William Campbell **Eng Dir**: William Devlin **Mktg Dir**: Iain Coupar **Employee Dir**: Jim Dixon **Chmn**: Pilmar Smith **Non Exec Dirs**: William Gallagher, Irene Kitson, A Ross, J Saren, A Guest, B Cox
Fleet: 680 - 545 double-deck bus, 135 single-deck bus.
Chassis: 280 Dennis. 96 Leyland. 5 Scania. 399 Volvo.
Bodies: 221 Alexander. 285 Plaxton. 169 Wright. 5 other.
Ops incl: local bus services.
Livery: Maroon/Red/White/Gold
Ticket system: Wayfarer 3

MAC TOURS LTD

ANNANDALE STREET,
EDINBURGH EH7 4AZ
Tel: 0131 556 2244
E-mail: info@edinburghtour.com
Web site: www.edinburghtour.com
Ch Exec: Neil Renilson **Fin Dir**: Norman Strachan **Ops Dir**: William Campbell **Eng Dir**: William Devlin **Mktg Dir**: Iain Coupar
Fleet: 25 - 1 double-deck bus, 1 single-deck bus, 16 open-top bus, 6 midibus, 1 minibus.
Chassis: 14 AEC. 6 Dennis. 4 Leyland. 1 Mercedes.
Bodies: 8 Alexander. 14 Park Royal. 3 other.
Livery: Red/Cream
Ticket system: Wayfarer/Casio

MAJESTIC TOURS EDINBURGH LTD

ANNANDALE STREET,
EDINBURGH EH7 4AZ
Tel: 0131 220 0770
E-mail: info@edinburghtour.com
Web site: www.edinburghtour.com
Ch Exec: Neil Renilson **Fin Dir**: Norman Strachan **Ops Dir**: William Campbell **Eng Dir**: William Devlin **Mktg Dir**: Iain Coupar
Fleet: 15 - 3 double-deck bus, 12 open-top bus.
Chassis: 6 AEC. 8 Leyland. 1 Volvo.
Bodies: 9 Alexander. 6 Park Royal.
Ops Incl: excursions & tours
Livery: Yellow/Blue
Ticket system: Casio

FALKIRK

FIRST EDINBURGH LTD
SEE STIRLING

P. WOODS MINICOACHES
20 CALDER PLACE, HALLGLEN FK1 2QQ.
Tel: 01324 613085.
Fax: 01324 717976.

FIFE

FIFE SCOTTISH OMNIBUSES LTD

GUTHRIE HOUSE, GLENFIELD INDUSTRIAL ESTATE, COWDENBEATH KY4 9HT
Tel: 01383 511911
Fax: 01383 516450
Recovery: 01383 511911
E-mail: eastscotland@stagecoachbus.com
Web site: www.stagecoachbus.com
Fleetname: Stagecoach in Fife
Man Dir: Doug Fleming **Ops Dir**: Steve Walker **Chief Eng**: Mike Williams
Fleet: 330 - 132 double-deck bus, 114 single-deck bus, 6 single-deck coach, 44 midibus, 34 minibus.
Chassis: 45 Dennis. 14 Leyland. 37 MAN. 19 Mercedes-Benz. 15 Optare. 10 Scania. 190 Volvo.
Bodies: 177 Alexander Dennis. 2 Jonckheere. 88 Northern Counties. 15 Optare. 48 Plaxton.
Ops incl: local bus services, tram services, school contracts, excursions & tours, private hire, express.
Livery: Stagecoach/Citylink
Ticket System: ERG

KINGDOM COACHES
DEN WALK, METHIL KY8 3JH.
Tel: 01333 26109
Fleet: 3 coach.
Chassis: 2 DAF. 1 Ford.
Bodies: 2 Plaxton. 1 Van Hool.
Ops incl: private hire.
Livery: Yellow/White.

MOFFAT & WILLIAMSON LTD

OLD RAILWAY YARD, ST FORT,
NEWPORT-ON-TAY DD6 8RG
Tel: 01382 541159
Fax: 01382 541169
E-mail: enquiries@moffat-williamson.co.uk
Web site: www.moffat-williamson.co.uk
Dirs: John Williamson, Iain Williamson
Fleet: 58 - 24 single-deck bus, 19 single-deck coach, 10 midibus, 3 midicoach, 2 minicoach.
Chassis: 1 DAF. 15 Dennis.1LDV. 5 MAN. 10 Mercedes-Benz. 5 Optare. 21 Volvo.
Bodies: 1 Alexander Dennis. 1 Ikarus 1 Marshall/MCV. 1 Mercedes-Benz. 10 Optare. 32 Plaxton. 3 UVG. 8 Wadham Stringer. 1 Other.
Ops incl: local bus services, school contracts, excursions & tours, private hire, express.
Livery: Brown/Cream/Orange

RENNIES OF DUNFERMLINE LTD

WELLWOOD, DUNFERMLINE KY12 0PY
Tel: 01383 620600
Fax: 01383 620624
E-mail: gordon@rennies.co.uk
Web site: www.rennies.co.uk
Chmn: John Rennie **Gen Man**: Gordon Menzies **Tran Man**: Iain Robertson **Ch Eng**: George Clark
Fleet: 52 - 20 double-deck bus, 25 coach, 3 midicoach, 4 minibus.
Chassis: 3 BMC. 10 Dennis. 1 Iveco. 1 LDV. 20 Leyland. 5 Mercedes. 12 Volvo
Bodies: 1 Beulas. 3 BMC. 4 Caetano. 7 Jonckheere. 1 Mellor. 4 Mercedes. 4 Plaxton. 1 Sunsundegui. 4 Van Hool. 6 Wadham Stringer. 17 other.
Ops incl: local bus services, school contracts, excursions & tours, private hire, continental tours.
Livery: Blue/White.
Ticket system: Almex
Subsidiary of Stagecoach Group

ST ANDREWS EXECUTIVE TRAVEL

UNIT 2, TOM STEWART LANE,
ST ANDREWS KY16 8YB
Tel: 01334 470080
Fax: 01334 470081
E-mail: orders@saxtravel.co.uk
Web Site: www.saxtravel.co.uk
Dir: Gordon Donaldson
Fleet: 8 - 2 minicoach, 6 midicoach.
Chassis: 8 Mercedes-Benz
Bodies: 8 Esker
Ops incl: excursions & tours, private hire.
Livery: Green/White

GLASGOW, CITY OF

ALLANDER COACHES LTD

19 CLOBERFIELD INDUSTRIAL ESTATE,
MILNGAVIE G62 7LN
Tel: 0141 956 5678
Fax: 0141 956 6669
E-mail: enquiries@allandertravel.co.uk
Web site: www.allandertravel.co.uk
Man Dir: J F Wilson **Dir**: E E Wilson **Ch Eng**: G S Wilson **Co Sec**: M Brown **Ops Man**: G F Wilson
Fleet: 25 - 3 double-deck bus, 3 single-deck bus, 19 single-deck coach, 1 midicoach, 1 minibus.
Chassis: 3 Alexander Dennis. 15 Bova. 3 Dennis. 2 Mercedes-Benz. 2 Volvo.
Bodies: 3 Alexander Dennis. 15 Bova. 1 Esker. 2 Jonckheere. 1 Leicester. 3 Wadham Stringer.
Ops incl: excursions & tours, private hire, school contracts, private hire.
Livery: Black/Gold/Orange.

CITY SIGHTSEEING GLASGOW LTD

153 QUEEN STREET, GLASGOW G1 3BJ
Tel: 0141 204 0444
Fax: 0141 248 6582
Web site: www.scotguide.com
E-mial: info@scotguide.com
Dirs: Alex Pringle,
Fleet: 9 double-deck bus.
Chassis: 2 Leyland. 1 MCW. 6 Volvo.
Bodies: 6 Alexander Dennis. 1 Mellor. 2 Northern counties.
Ops incl: excursions & tours.
Livery: Red
Ticket system: Almex

DOIGS OF GLASGOW LTD

TRANSPORT HOUSE, SUMMER STREET,
GLASGOW G40 3TB
Tel: 0141 554 5555
Fax: 0141 551 9000
E-mail: andy@doigs.com
Web site: www.doigs.com
Chmn/Man Dir: Andrew Forsyth **Co Sec**: Iain Forsyth
Fleet: 15 - 1 double-deck bus, 1 single-deck bus, 1 articulated bus, 8 coach, 1 midicoach, 3 minicoach.
Chassis: incl: DAF. Dennis. LDV. Mercedes. Scania. 3 Volvo.
Bodies: 1 Caetano. 1 East Lancs. 7 Irizar. 1 Marcopolo. 2 Mercedes. 1 Optare. 3 Sunsundegui. 1 Wright.
Ops incl: school contracts, excursions & tours, private hire, continental tours.
Livery: Silver/Red lettering

FIRST GLASGOW

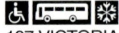

197 VICTORIA ROAD,
GLASGOW G42 7AD.

Tel: 0141 423 6600
Fax: 0141 636 3228
Web Site: www.firstgroup.com.
Man Dir: Mark Savelli
Fleet: 953 - incl: double-deck bus, single-deck bus, minibus.
Chassis: 126 Dennis. 103 Leyland. 36 MCW. 85 Mercedes. 15 Optare. 130 Scania. 497 Volvo.
Bodies: Alexander. East Lancs. MCW. Optare. Plaxton. Wright.
Ops incl: local bus services.

GLASGOW CITYBUS
729 SOUTH STREET,
GLASGOW G14 0BX
Tel: 0141 954 2255
Email: mail@glasgowcitybus.co.uk
Subsidiary of West Coast Motors-see Argyll and Bute

JOHN MORROW COACHES
18 ALBION INDUSTRIAL ESTATE, HALLEY STREET, YOKER, GLASGOW G13 4DJ
Tel: 0141 951 8888
Fax: 0141 952 6445
Prop: John Morrow.
Fleet: 15 - 12 single-deck bus, 1 coach, 1 midibus, 1 minicoach.
Chassis: 9 Mercedes-Benz. 2 Optare. 1 Toyota. 1 Volvo
Bodies: incl- Duple. Leyland
Ops incl: local bus services, private hire, school contracts.
Livery: Brown/Cream
Ticket system: Wayfarer 3

SCOTTISH CITYLINK COACHES LTD
BUCHANAN BUS STATION, KILLERMONT STREET, GLASGOW G2 3NP
Tel: 0141 352 4454
E-mail: info@citylink.co.uk.
Web site: www.citylink.co.uk.
Ops incl: private hire, express.
Livery: Blue/yellow
Ticket system: Wayfarer

SELVEY'S COACHES
HILLCREST HOUSE, 33 HOWIESHILL ROAD, CAMBUSLANG G72 8PW.
Tel: 0141 641 1080.
Fax: 0141 641 2065.
Owner: A. G. Selvey.
Fleet: 8 - 5 coach, 2 midicoach, 1 minicoach.
Chassis: 3 Bedford. 2 Leyland. 1 Mercedes. 2 Volvo.
Bodies: 1 Duple. 1 Jonckheere. 1 Mercedes. 3 Plaxton.
Ops incl: excursions & tours, private hire, school contracts.
Livery: Maroon/Red/Yellow

HIGHLAND

STAGECOACH HIGHLAND
6 BURNETT ROAD, LONGMAN INDUSTRIAL ESATE, INVERNESS IV1 1TF
Tel: 01463 239292
Fax: 01463 712338
Recovery: 01463 239292
E-mail: eastscotland@stagecoachbus.com
Web site: www.stagecoachbus.com
Fleetname: Stagecoach Highland
Man Dir: Charlie Mullen **Ops Dir**: Bob Hall
Eng Dir: John MacPherson **Traffic Man**: Scott Pearson **Eng Man**: Callum MacGregor
Comm Man: William Mainus **Ops Man**: Ali Mac Donald
Fleet: 245 - 26 double-deck bus, 34 single-deck bus, 108 single-deck coach, 64 midibus, 13 minibus.
Chassis: 8 Bedford. 4 DAF. 66 Dennis. 15 Leyland. 23 Mercedes-Benz. 16 Optare. 2 Scania. 1 Setra. 1 Toyota. 1 VW. 107 Volvo.
Bodies: 68 Alexander Dennis. 8 East Lancs. 14 Jonckheere.10 Leyland. 1 Marshall/MCV. 18 Optare. 92 Plaxton. 1 Setra. 24 Van Hool. 7 Wright. 2 Other.
Ops incl: local bus services, school contracts, excursions & tours, private hire, express.
Livery: Stagecoach/Citylink/Megabus
Ticket System: Wayfarer/ERG

D&E COACHES LTD
39 HENDERSON DRIVE,
INVERNESS IV1 1TR
Tel: 01463 222444
Fax: 01463 226700
Recovery: 07770 222612
E-mail: decoaches@aol.com
Web site: www.decoaches.co.uk
Man Dirs Donald Mathieson **Dir**: Elizabeth Mathieson **Ops Man**: Willie Bell **Off Man**: Gayle Peples **Eng Man**: Bryan Fiddey
Fleet: 19 - 2 single-deck bus, 8 single-deck coach, 2 midibus, 4 midicoach, 1 minibus, 2 minicoach.
Chassis: 6 Bova. 1 DAF. 2 Dennis. 6 Mercedes-Benz. 1 Toyota. 2 VW. 1 Volvo.
Bodies: 2 Berkhof. 6 Bova. 1 Caetano. 3 Esker. 1 Mercedes-Benz. 2 Plaxton. 2 Van Hool. 1Wright. 1 Other
Ops incl: local bus services, school contracts, excursions & tours, private hire.
Livery: White
Ticket system: Almex

DUNCAN MACLENNAN
HILL-SIDE, SHIELDAIG,
STRATHCARRON IV54 8XN
Tel/Fax: 01520 755239
Prop: Duncan MacLennan
Fleet: 2 - 1 midicoach, 1 minibus.
Chassis/bodies: 1 Ford. 1 Mercedes.
Ops incl: local bus services, school contracts.

SHIEL BUSES
BLAIN GARAGE, ACHARACLE PH36 4JY.
Tel/Fax: 01967 431272.
E-mail: shiel.buses@virgin.net
Dir: Donnie MacGillivray.
Fleet: 10 - 4 single-deck coach, 6 midibus.
Chassis: 1 Ford Transit. 4 Mercedes. 4 Volvo.
Bodies: 2 Mercedes. 2 Plaxton. 2 Van Hool. 2 Onyx.
Ops incl: local bus services, school contracts, private hire.
Livery: Red/White
Ticket system: Amex

SPA COACHES
KINETTAS, STRATHPEFFER IV14 9BH.
Tel: 01997 421311.
Fax: 01997 421983.
Web site: www.spacoaches.com
Prop: N. MacArthur.
Fleet: 28 - 6 double-deck bus, 13 coach, 5 midibus, 2 minibus.
Chassis: 1 DAF. 2 Ford Transit. 5 Mercedes. 14 Volvo.
Bodies: 1 Duple. 7 Alexander. 2 Caetano. 3 Jonckheere. 5 Plaxton. 6 Van Hool. 4 other.
Ops incl: local bus services,school contracts, excursions & tours, private hire, continental tours.
Livery: Orange/White.
Ticket System: Punch Tickets.

TIM DEARMAN COACHES
INCHNAVIE LOWER, NEWBRIDGE, ARDROSS, ROSS-SHIRE IV17 0XL
Tel: 01348 883585
Fax: 01348 884193
E-mail: tim.dearman@timdearmancoaches.co.uk.
Web site: www.timdearmancoaches.co.uk
Owner: Tim Dearman.
Fleet: 6 - 3 single-deck bus, 2 single-deckcoach, 1 midibus.
Chassis: 1 Cannon. 1 Iveco. 3 Mercedes-Benz. 1 Optare
Bodies: 1 Beulas. 1 Esker. 1 Leicester. 1 Optare. 2 Plaxton
Ops incl: local bus services, school contracts, private hire.
Livery: Maroon/Red
Ticket System: almex

Scottish Operators

GRAHAM URQUHART TRAVEL LTD
28 MIDMILLS ROAD, INVERNESS IV2 3NY
Tel: 01463 222292
Fax: 01463 238880
E-mail: graham@urquharttravel.fsnet.co.uk
Web site: www.grahamurquharttravel.co.uk
Dir: John G Urquhart **Sec**: John G Prant
Fleet: 8 - 4 coach, 2 midicoach, 2 minicoach.
Chassis: 4 Mercedes. 4 Scania.
Bodies: 4 Irizar. 4 Esker.
Ops incl: excursions & tours, private hire.

WHITE HEATHER TOURS
6 RIVERSIDE GROVE, LOCHY SIDE, BANAVIE PH33 7RD
Tel/Fax: 01397 704704
E-mail: enquiries@whiteheathertravel.co.uk
Web site: www.whiteheathertravel.com
Prop: Adam A MacIntyre
Fleet: 5 midicoach.
Chassis/bodies: 2 Caetano. 3 Mercedes.
Ops incl: local bus service, school contracts, excursions & tours, private hire.
Livery: Gold/Green/Red

INVERCLYDE

GILLEN'S COACHES LTD
UNIT 3, KINGSTON BUSINESS PARK, PORT GLASGOW PA14 5DP
Tel/Fax: 01475 744618
Recovery: 07785 873299
Dir: Michael Gillen
Fleet: 14 - single-deck bus, midicoach, minibus, minicoach
Ops incl: local bus services, excursions & tours, private hire.
Livery: White
Ticket system: Wayfarer

GLEN COACHES LTD
6 MACDOUGALL STREET, GREENOCK PA15 2TG.
Tel: 01475 783399.
Fax: 01475 888446.
Owners: W. Wilson, Ms C. Wilson.
Fleet: 10 - 6 coach, 2 midibus, 1 midicoach, 1 minibus.
Chassis: 1 Iveco. 2 Mercedes. 6 Volvo.
Bodies: 1 Beulas. 1 Jonckheere. 2 Plaxton. 5 Van Hool.
Ops incl: local bus services, school contracts, excursions & tours, private hire.
Livery: Blue/White.

McGILLS BUS SERVICE LTD
99, EARNHILL RD, LARKFIELD INDUSTRIAL ESTATE, GREENOCK, RENFREWSHIRE PA16 0EQ
Tel: 01475 711122
Fax: 01475 711133
Web Site: www.mcgillsbuses.co.uk
Gen Man: B Hendry
Ops incl: local bus services
Livery: Blue/White

MIDLOTHIAN

ALLAN'S GROUP
NEWTONLOAN GARAGE, GOREBRIDGE EH23 4LZ
Tel: 01875 820777.
Fax: 01875 822468
Recovery: 01875 820377
E-mail: allanscoaches@aol.com

Web Site: www.allansgroup.com
Dir: D W Allan **Ch Eng**: Neil Mitchell **Office Man**: Mrs D Allan
Fleet: 14 - 9 single-deck bus, 5 midicoach.
Chassis: 5 Mercedes. 9 Scania.
Bodies: 5 Sitcar. 9 Van Hool.
Ops incl: school contracts, private hire.
Livery: Blue/Silver.

FIRST EDINBURGH LTD
SEE STIRLING

WILLIAM HUNTER
OAKFIELD GARAGE, LOANHEAD EH20 9AE
Tel: 0131 440 0704
Fax: 0131 448 2184
E-mail: sales@hunterscoaches.co.uk
Web Site: www.hunterscoaches.co.uk
Props: G I Hunter, W R Hunter.
Fleet: 14 - 12 coach, 2 minibus.
Chassis: 3 Toyota. 11 Volvo.
Bodies: 3 Caetano. 11 Van Hool.
Ops incl: school contracts, private hire.
Livery: Brown/Cream

LIBERTON TRAVEL
See Edinburgh, City of

McKENDRY TRAVEL
100 STRAITON ROAD, LOANHEAD EH20 9NP
Tel: 0131 440 1013
Fax: 0131 448 2160
E-mail: dmckendry@btconnect.com
Web site: www.mckendrycoaches.co.uk
Dir: Ann McKendry **Tran Man**: Stuart McCaw
Fleet: 15 - 1 double-deck bus, 12 coach, 2 minibus.
Chassis: 1 Dennis. 1 Ford Transit. 1 Freight Rover. 1 Leyland National. 4 Scania. 5 Volvo.
Bodies: 1 Caetano. 2 Jonckheere. 2 Plaxton. 5 Van Hool.
Ops incl: excursions & tours, private hire, school contracts.
Livery: White/Blue/Purple/Red vinyls

MORAY

CENTRAL COACHES
CENTRAL GARAGE, CHURCH ROAD, KEITH AB55 5BR
Tel: 01542 882113
Fax: 01542 886945
E-mail: watson@centralcoaches.co.uk
Web site: www.centralcoaches.co.uk
Ptnrs: William Watson Smith, Veronica A Smith, William Andrew Smith
Fleet: 12 - 1 single-deck bus, 9 double-deck coach, 2 minbus.
Chassis: 1 Bova. 2 DAF. 2 Mercedes-Benz. 1 Optare. 6 Volvo.
Bodies: 1 Bova. 1 Caetano. 1 Jonckheere. 1 Leicester. 1 Mercedes.1 Optare/Excel. 4 Plaxton. 2 Van Hool.
Ops incl: local bus services, school contracts, private hire.
Livery: White/Red

MAYNES COACHES LTD
LINKWOOD WAY, ELGIN IV30 1XS
Tel: 01343 555227
Fax: 0142 833572
Recovery: 017836 322200
E-mail: info@maynes.co.uk
Web site: www.maynes.co.uk

Man Dir: David Mayne **Dirs**: Kevin Mayne, Gordon Mayne
Fleet: 11 - 7 single-deck bus, 4 minibus.
Chassis: 1 Dennis. 4 MAN. 2 Mercedes-Benz. 1 Optare. 1 Plaxton.
Bodies: 1 Duple. 3 Marcopolo. 1 Mercedes-Benz. 1 Noge. 1 Optare. 1 Plaxton. 2 Van Hool. 1 Other.
Ops incl: local bus services, school contracts, excursions & tours, private hire, continental tours.
Livery: Blue/White/Gold
Ticket System: Setright

NORTH AYRSHIRE

CLYDE COAST COACHES LTD
55 MONTGOMERIE STREET, ARDROSSAN KA22 8HR
Tel: 01294 605454
Fax: 01294 605460
E-mail: enquiries@clydecoast.com
Web site: www.clydecoast.com
Dirs: Kenneth G McGregor, David H Frazer.
Fleet: 20 - 8 double-deck bus, 10 coach, 2 midibus.
Chassis: 1 Ford Transit. 8 Leyland. 1 VW. 10 Volvo.
Bodies: 3 Alexander. 5 ECW. 2 Sunsundegui. 8 Van Hool. 2 other.
Ops incl: excursions & tours, private hire, school contracts.
Livery: Silver Blue metallic

T & E DOCHERTY
40 BANK STREET, IRVINE KA12 0LP
Tel/Recovery: 01294 278440
Fax: 01294 272510
E-mail: info@coach-hires.co.uk
Web Site: www.coach-hires.co.uk
Owner: Hugh Tait **Gen Man**: Tom Hamilton
Fleet: 31 - 2 double-deck bus, 6 single-deck bus, 10 coach, 4 minicoach, 8 minibus.
Chassis: 7 Bova. 1 Dodge. 2 LDV. 2 Leyland. 10 Mercedes. 2 Optare. 8 Volvo.
Bodies: 2 Alexander. 1 Autobus. 7 Bova. 1 Caetano. 1 East Lancs. 2 LDV. 2 Optare. 6 Plaxton. 1 Reeve Burgess. 2 Van Hool. 6 Wright. 1 Sitcar.
Ops incl: school contracts, excursions & tours, private hire, express, continental tours.
Livery: Buses: Blue/Cream. Coaches: Cream/Beige
Ticket System: Wayfarer 3.

MARBILL TRAVEL
HIGH MAINS GARAGE, MAINS ROAD, BEITH KA15 2AP
Tel: 01505 503367
Fax: 01505 504736
E-mail: marbill@btclick.com
Web site: www.marbillcoaches.com
Man Dir: Margaret Whiteman **Eng Dir**: David Barr **Ops Dir**: Connie Barr
Fleet: 66 - 26 double-deck bus, 20 single-deck bus, 18 coach, 2 minicoach.
Chassis: 2 Bova. 34 Leyland. 2 Mercedes. 28 Volvo
Bodies: 26 Alexander. 2 Bova. 25 Plaxton. 12 Van Hool. 1 Beluga.
Ops incl: school contracts, excursions & tours, private hire.

MILLPORT MOTORS LTD
16 BUTE TERRACE, MILLPORT KA28 0BA.
Tel: 01475 530555.
Fleet: 4 single-deck bus.
Chassis: 3 Leyland. 1 Volvo.
Ops incl: local bus services, private hire.
Livery: Blue/Cream.
Ticket System: Almex.

SHUTTLE BUSES LTD
CALEDONIA HOUSE, LONGFORD AVENUE, KILWINNING KA13 6EX
Tel: 01294 550757
Fax: 01294 558822
Web site: www.shuttlebuses.co.uk
Man Dir: David Granger
Fleet: 24 - 1 single-deck bus, 5 single-deck coach, 10 midibus, 3 midicoach, 5 minibus.
Chassis: 1 AEC. 3 Dennis. 3 Ford Transit. 1 Leyland. 6 Mercedes-Benz. 8 Optare. 1 Scania. 1 Volvo.
Bodies: 2 Alexander-Dennis. 3 Caetano. 3 Mercedes-Benz. 9 Optare. 2 Plaxton. 5 other.
Ops incl: local bus services, school contracts, private hire.
Livery: Yellow/White.
Ticket System: Wayfarer.

NORTH LANARKSHIRE

A&C LUXURY COACHES
4 HILLHEAD AVENUE, MOTHERWELL ML1 4AQ
Tel: 01698 252652
Fax: 01698 433677
E-mail: enquiries@acluxurycoaches.co.uk
Web site: www.acluxurycoaches.co.uk
Prop: Alex Grenfell
Fleet: 6 - 3 coach, 2 midicoach, 1 minicoach.
Chassis: 3 Mercedes. 1 Neoplan. 2 Volvo.
Bodies: 1 Neoplan. 1 Plaxton. 1 Van Hool
Ops incl: school contracts, private hire, excursions & tours.

CANAVAN'S COACHES
CEDAR LODGE, COACH ROAD, KILSYTH G65 0DB.
Tel: 01236 822414.
Prop: M., G., H., & J. Canavan.
Ops incl: local bus services.

DUNN'S COACHES
560 STIRLING ROAD, AIRDRIE ML6 7SS
Tel: 01236 722385
Fax: 01236 722385
E-mail: cdunn53@aol.com
Dirs: Fraser Dunn, Craig Dunn.
Fleet: 14 - double-deck bus, single-deck bus, coach, midibus.
Chassis: 3 Dennis. 1 Leyland. 1 Marshall. 2 Mercedes. 7 Volvo.
Bodies: 1 Marshall. 11 Plaxton. 1 Reeve Burgess.
Ops incl: local bus services, school contracts, private hire, express, continental tours.
Livery: White

ESSBEE COACHES (HIGHLANDS & ISLANDS)
7 HOLLANDHURST ROAD, GARTSHERRIE ML5 2EG
Tel: 01236 423621
Fax: 01236 433677
Man Dir: B. Smith. **Gen Man**: J. Kinnaird.
Ops Man: S. Stewart.
Fleet: 56 - 10 single-deck bus, 19 coach, 2 double-deck coach, 6 midicoach, 19 minibus.
Chassis: 2 DAF. 3 Ford Transit. 13 Leyland. 6 Leyland National. 21 Mercedes. 2 Neoplan. 10 Volvo.
Bodies: 7 Duple. 1 ECW. 1 Jonckheere. 6 Leyland National. 2 Neoplan. 15 Plaxton. 3 Autobus. 2 Crystals.
Ops incl: School contracts, excursions & tours, private hire.
Livery: Red/Silver.
Ticket System: Wayfarer.

GOLDEN EAGLE COACHES
MUIRHALL GARAGE, 197 MAIN STREET, SALSBURGH, BY SHOTTS ML7 4LS
Tel: 01698 870207
Fax: 01698 870217
E-mail: info@goldeneaglecoaches.com
Web site: www.goldeneaglecoaches.com
Dirs: Peter Irvine, Robert Irvine, Ishbel Irvine
Ops Man: Lain Peacock
Fleet: 21 - 8 double-deck bus, 13 single-deck coach.
Chassis: 1 Bova. 4 Dennis. 4 Leyland. 3 MCW. 9 Volvo.
Bodies: 2 Jonckheere. 4 Leyalnd. 3 MCW. 7 Van Hool. 5 Other
Ops incl: school contracts, private hire.
Livery: White/Red & Gold

IRVINE'S OF LAW
LAWMUIR ROAD, LAW ML8 5JB.
Tel: 01698 372452
Fax: 01698 376200
Web site: www.irvinescoaches.co.uk
Prop: Peter Irvine **Man**: Gordon Graham
Ch Eng: Scott Fisher
Fleet: 40 - 14 double-deck bus, 13coach, 13 midibus.
Chassis: DAF. Dennis. Optare. Scania. Volvo.
Bodies: Van Hool
Ops incl: local bus services, excursions & tours, school contracts, private hire, express, continental tours.
Livery: Red/Cream.
Ticket System: Wayfarer.

KELVIN VALLEY COACHES
149 WHITELEES ROAD, CUMBERNAULD G67 3JS
Tel: 01236 614696/734883
Recovery: not 24 hours
E-mail: -kvc@blueyonder.co.uk
Web site: www.kelvinvalleycoaches.com
Proporietors: Robert B Mackenzie, Kirstine Mackenzie
Fleet: 2
Chassis: 2 Leyland
Bodies: 2 Plaxton
Ops incl: excursions & tours, private hire, contracts, event planner available
Livery: Red/Cream/Gold

LONG'S COACHES LTD
157 MAIN STREET, SALSBURGH BY SHOTTS ML7 4LR.
Tel: 01698 870768.
Fax: 01698 870826.
E-mail: info@longscoaches.co.uk
Web site: www.longscoaches.co.uk
Dir: Peter I. Long **Co Sec**: Susan Long.
Fleet: 14 - 13 coach, 1 midicoach.
Chassis: 2 Bova. 12 Volvo.
Bodies: 2 Bova. 12 Van Hool.
Ops incl: excursions & tours, private hire, express, continental tours, school contracts.
Livery: Silver/Maroon.
Ticket System: Wayfarer.

MACPHAILS COACHES
409 HIGH STREET, NEWARTHILL, MOTHERWELL ML1 5SP
Tel: 01698 860249
Fax: 01698 861963
E-mail: macphailscoaches@hotmail.com
Web site: www.macphailscoaches.com
Dirs: Martin MacPhail, Henry MacPhail.
Fleet: 8 coach.
Chassis: 8 Volvo.
Bodies: 1 Plaxton. 7 Van Hool.
Ops incl: excursions & tours, private hire, continental tours.

MCKINDLESS EXPRESS
101 MAIN STREET, NEWMAINS, WISHAW ML2 9PP.
Tel: 01698 356990
Fax: 01698 356991
Web site: wwwmckindlessgroup.co.uk
Prop: M. McKindless.
Ops Incl: local bus services, express, school contracts, private hire.
Livery: Cream/Green
Ops incl: local bus sevices

M.C.T. GROUP TRAVEL LTD
NETHAN STREET DEPOT, NETHAN STREET, MOTHERWELL ML1 3TF
Tel: 01698 253091
Fax: 01698 259208
Recovery: 01698 269301
E-mail: mctgrouptravel@hotmail.com
Web site: www.mctgrouptravel.com
Man Dir: Desmond Heenan **Dir**: Oswald Heenan **Fleet Eng**: Alan Bruce.
Fleet: 14 - 4 coach, 6 midicoach, 4 minicoach.
Chassis: 2 Mercedes. 8 Toyota. 4 Volvo.
Bodies: 6 Caetano. 1 Esker. 4 Jonckheere. 3 Mercedes.
Ops incl: excursions & tours, private hire, continental tours.
Livery: Turquoise/Silver

MILLER'S COACHES
22 WOODSIDE DRIVE, CALDERBANK, AIRDRIE ML6 9TN.
Tel: 01236 763671.
Owner: W. Miller. **Tran Man**: T. Miller.
Fleet: 12 - 8 coach, 4 minicoach.
Chassis: 8 Leyland. 4 Mercedes.
Bodies: 2 Alexander. 1 Mellor. 8 Plaxton. 1 Reeve Burgess.
Ops incl: local bus services, school contracts, private hire.
Livery: Black/White/Grey.

STEPEND COACHES
92 WADDELL AVENUE, GLENMAVIS, AIRDRIE ML6 ONZ.
Tel: 01236 760500.
Prop: S. Chapman.
Ops incl: local bus services.

TRAMONTANA
CHAPELKNOWE ROAD, CARFIN, MOTHERWELL ML1 5LE
Tel: 01698 861790
Fax: 01698 860778
E-mail: wdt@tiscali.uk
Web: www.tramontanancoach.com
Prop: W D Telfer
Fleet: 6 single-deck coach
Chassis: 6 Volvo.
Bodies: 2 Caetano. 1 Irizar. 3 Plaxton.
Ops incl: private hire
Livery: White

WILLIAM STOKES & SONS LTD
22 CARSTAIRS ROAD, CARSTAIRS ML11 8QD
Tel: 01555 870344
Fax: 01555 870601
E-mail: enquires@stokescoaches.co.uk
Web site: www.stokescoaches.co.uk
Dirs: John Stokes, Alex Stokes, William

Stokes **Com Sec:** Walter Stokes
Fleet: 21 - 7 single-deck bus, 8 single-deck coach, 3 midnbus, 1 midibus. 2 minibus.
Chassis: 2 Alexander D.ennis. 4 DAF. 4 Dennis. 3 Mercedes-Benz. 2 Optare. 6 Volvo.
Bodies: 2 Alexander Dennis. 3 Berkof. 1 Caetano. 1 Esker. 5 Ikarus. 2 Jonckheere. 1 Marshall/MCV. 2 Optare
Ops incl: local bus services, schools contracts, excursions & tours, private hire.
Livery: Red/Cream
Ticket System: Almex

ORKNEY

MAYNES COACHES LTD
INDUSTRIAL ESTATE, ST MARGARETS, ORKNEY KW17 2TG
Tel: 01856 831333
Fax: 01542 833572
Recovery: 07836 322200
E-mail: inof@maynes.co.uk
Web site: www.maynes.co.uk
Prop: David Mayne, Kevin Mayne, Gordon Mayne
Fleet: 7 - 6 single-deck coach,1 midibus.
Chassis: 4 Dennis. 1 Mercedes-Benz. 2 Volvo.
Bodies: 6 Plaxton. 1 Van Hool.
Ops incl: school contracts, excursions & tours, private hire
Livery: Blue/White/Gold

STAGECOACH IN ORKNEY
SCOTTS ROAD, HATSTON INDUSTRIAL ESTATE, KIRKWALL KW15 1JY.
Tel: 01856 870555
Gen Man: Monty Smillie
Fleet: 42 - coach, midibus, midicoach, minibus.
Chassis: Bedford. Dennis. Ford. Mercedes. Optare. Toyota. Volvo.
Ops incl: local bus services, school contracts, excursions & tours, private hire.

PERTH & KINROSS

ABERFELDY MOTOR SERVICES
BURNSIDE GARAGE, ABERFELDY PH15 2DD
Tel: 01887 820433
Fax: 01887 829534
E-mail: aberfeldymotors@btconnect.com
Web site: www.aberfeldycoaches.co.uk
Prop: John Stewart **Co Sec:** Lynda Stewart
Ch Eng: David Matthew
Fleet: 8 - 6 coach, 1 midicoach, 1 minicoach.
Chassis: 2 Bova. 2 Mercedes. 4 Volvo.
Bodies: 2 Bova. 1 Esker. 4 Van Hool. 1 other.
Ops incl: excursions & tours, private hire, continental tours, school contracts.
Livery: Blue

BANKFOOT BUSES
ARRAN HOUSE, ARRAN ROAD, PERTH PH1 3DZ
Tel: 01783 459268
Fax: 01783 622055
E-mail: www.bankfootbuses.com
Web site: info@bankfootbuses.com
Prop: Stuart Newing-Davis **Fin Dir:** Sarah Newing-Davis
Fleet: 6 double-deck bus, 15 single-deck bus, 1 single-deck coach, 1 open-top bus, 2 minibus, 1 minicoach.
Ops incl: local bus service, school contracts, excursions & tours, private hire
Livery: Red/White
Ticket system: Wayfarer

CABER COACHES LTD
CHAPEL STREET GARAGE, ABERFELDY PH15 2AS
Tel: 01887 870090
Fax: 01887 829352
E-mail: cabercoaches@btinternet.com
Man Dir: Kenneth Carey **Sec:** Alexandre Carey
Fleet: 8 - 2 coach, 2 midicoach, 4 minibus.
Chassis: 2 Ford Transit. 2 LDV. 2 Mercedes.
Ops incl: local bus services, school contracts, private hire.
Livery: White
Ticket system: Almex

DOCHERTY'S MIDLAND COACHES
PRIORY PARK, AUCHTERARDER PH3 1GB
Tel: 01764 662218
Fax: 01764 664228
E-mail: docherty.midland@virgin.net.
Web site: www.dochertysmidlandcoaches.co.uk
Props: Jim & Edith Docherty, Colin Docherty, Neil Docherty, William Docherty
Fleet: 22 - 2 single-deck bus, 11 single-deck coach, 2 midibus, 4 midicoach, 2 minicoach, 1 vintage.
Chassis: 1 Leyland. 7 Mercedes-Benz. 1 Optare. 4 Scania. 9 Volvo.
Bodies: 2 Irizar. 1 Optare. 3 Plaxton. 1 UVG. 9 Van Hool. 2 Wright. 4 other.
Ops incl: local bus services, school contracts, private hire
Livery: White/Black/Grey
Ticket System: Almex

EARNSIDE COACHES
GREENBANK ROAD, GLENFARG, PERTH PH2 9NW
Tel: 01577 830360
Fax: 01577 830599
E-mail: info@earnside.com.
Web site: www.earnside.com
Ptnrs: David Rutherford, Fiona Rutherford, Gary Rutherford
Fleet: 9 - 8 single-deck coach, 1 midibus.
Chassis: 1 Ford Transit. 1 Leyland. 1 MAN. 1 Neoplan 1 Scania. 5 Volvo.
Bodies: 2 Berkhof. 1 Irizar. 1Neoplan.4 Plaxton.
Ops incl: local bus services, school contracts, excursions & tours, private hire, continental tours.
Livery: White/Yellow
Ticket system: Almex

HIGHWAYMAN COACHES
STATION ROAD, ERROL PH2 7QB
Tel: 01821 642739
Fax: 01821 642683
Web site: www.highwaymancoaches.com
Fleet: 12 - double-deck bus, coach, double-deck coach, midicoach, minicoach.
Chassis: 1 Bova. 2 Dennis. 3 Leyland. 1 Mercedes. 3 Neoplan. 1 Scania. 1 Toyota.
Bodies: 3 Alexander. 1 Bova. 1 Caetano. 1 Irizar. 1 Mercedes. 3 Neoplan. 1 Plaxton. 1 Van Hool.
Ops incl: school contracts, excursions & tours, private hire.
Livery: hite/Blue lines

MEGABUS
10 DUNKELD ROAD,PERTH PH1 5TW
Tel: 01738 522456
Web site: www.megabus.com
Fleet: 60 - incl: 25 double-deck coach

Chassis: incl: 25 MAN
Bodies: incl: 25 MAN.
Ops incl: express.
Livery: Stagecoach (White/Blue/Orange/Red)/Megabus

PEGASUS TRAVEL LTD
28 INVERALMOND ROAD, PERTH PH1 3TW
Tel/Fax: 01738 444070
E-mail: enquiries@pegasus-travel.co.uk, info@pegasus-travel.co.uk
Web site: www.pegasus-travel.co.uk
Man Dir: Duncan Graham **Co Sec:** Mairi Graham **Ops Man:** Trevor White **Ch Eng:** Guy Batchelor
Fleet: 9 - 6 single-deck bus, 3 midicoach.
Chassis: 1 DAF. 1 Iveco. 3 Mercedes. 4 Volvo.
Bodies: 1 Autobus. 8 Plaxton.
Ops incl: local bus services, excursions & tours, private hire, school contracts
Livery: White

SMITH & SONS COACHES
THE COACH DEPOT, WOODSIDE, COUPAR ANGUS, BLAIRGOWRIE PH13 9LW
Tel: 01828 627310
Fax: 01828 628518
E-mail: info@smithandsonscoaches.co.uk
Web: www.smithandsonscoaches.com
Fleet: 21 - 7 Bova. 1 DAF. 6 Mercedes-Benz. 6 Volvo
Ops incl: school contracts, private hire.
Livery: White

STAGECOACH SCOTLAND LTD
RUTHENFIELD ROAD, INVERALMOND, PERTH PH1 3EE
Tel: 01738 629339
Fax: 01738 643264
Recovery: 01738 629339
E-mail: eastscotland@stagecoachbus.com
Web site: www.stagecoachbus.com
Fleetname: Stagecoach in Perth
Man Dir: Doug Fleming **Ops Dir:** Steve Walker **Chief Eng:** Jim Penrose. **Ops Man:** Gus Beveridge **Depot Eng:** John Dick
Fleet: 77 - 16 double-deck bus, 25 single-deck bus, 6 single-deck coach, 10 midibus, 20 minibus.
Chassis: 10 Dennis. 16 Leyland. 16 MAN. 5 Mercedes-Benz. 15 Optare. 15 Volvo.
Bodies: 53 Alexander Dennis. 3 Jonckheere. 3 Neoplan. 15 Optare. 1 Plaxton. 2 Wright.
Ops incl: local bus services, tram services, school contracts, excursions & tours, private hire, express.
Livery: Stagecoach/Megabus
Ticket System: ERG

ELIZABETH YULE
STATION GARAGE, STATION ROAD, PITLOCHRY PH16 5AN
Tel: 01796 472290
Fax: 01796 474214
E-mail: info.elizabeth-yule@virgin.net
Web site: www.perthshirecoaches.co.uk
Dirs: Elizabeth Yule, Alexandra M Bridges (Sandra)
Fleet: 9 - 5 coach, 3 midicoach, 1 minibus.
Chassis: 1 LDV. 3 Mercedes. 5 Volvo.
Ops incl: local bus services, school contracts, private hire.
Livery: White
Ticket System: Almex

RENFREWSHIRE

ALAN ARNOTT
16 TURNHILL CRESCENT, WEST FREELANDS, ERSKINE PA8 7AX
Fleetname: S & A Coaches, City Sprinter

ARRIVA SCOTLAND WEST
INCHINNAN, PAISLEY PA3
Web site: www.arrivabus.co.uk
Fleetnames: Arriva, SPT
Ops Man: Murray Rogers
Fleet: 170 - incl double-deck bus, single-deck bus, midibus
Chassis: incl: Dennis, Leyland. Optare. Scania. Volvo.
Bodies: incl: Alexander, Northern Counties, Plaxton, Wright.
Ops incl: local bus services
Livery: Stone/Aquamarine

JAMES BURNS
24 GLENDOWER WAY, FOX BAR, PAISLEY PA2 0TH.
Fleetname: Green Line Coaches.

VIOLET GRAHAM COACHES
93 IVANHOE ROAD, FOX BAR, PAISLEY PA2 0LF.
Tel: 01505 349758.
Fax: 01505 349758.
Owner: V. Rosike.
Fleet: 2 midicoach.
Chassis: 1 Ford Transit. 1 Freight Rover.
Ops incl: school contracts, private hire.

SHETLAND

ANDREW'S
THE DYKES, WORMADALE, WHITENESS ZE2 9LJ
Tel: 01595 840292
Fax: 01595 840252
E-mail: andrews.adventures@virgin.net
Web: www.andrewscoachhire.com
Prop: Andrew Morrison
Ops Man: Morris Morrison
Fleet: 8 - 4 single-deck bus, 2 midibus, 1 midicoach, 1 minicoach.
Chassis: 2 Mercedes-Benz. 1 Optare. 5 Volvo..
Bodies: 1 Alexander Dennis. 2 Mercedes-Benz. 1 Optare. 3 Plaxton. 1 Volvo.
Ops incl: local bus services, school contracts, excursions & tours, private hire, continental tours.
Livery: White/Red
Ticket system: ERG

R G JAMIESON & SON
MOARFIELD GARAGE, CULLIVOE, YELL ZE2 9DD
Tel: 01957 744214
Fax: 01957 744270
E-mail: rhjamieson@hotmail.com
Ptnr: Robert H Jamieson
Fleet: 5 - 1 single-deck bus, 2 coach, 2 minibus, 1 midicoach.
Chassis: 1 Dennis. 2 Ford Transit. 1 MAN. 2 Mercedes.
Bodies: incl: 1 Berkhof. 3 Plaxton
Ops incl: local bus services, school contracts, excursions & tours, private hire, continental tours.
Livery: White/Blue (three shades)

JOHN LEASK & SON
ESPLANADE, LERWICK ZE1 0LL
Tel: 01595 693162
Fax: 01595 693171
E-mail: info@leaskstravel.co.uk
Web site: www.leaskstravel.co.uk
Ptnrs: Peter R Leask, Andrew J N Leask
Fleet: 19 - 7 single-deck bus, 7 coach, 1 midibus, 1 midicoach, 2 minibus, 2 minicoach.
Chassis: 12 DAF. 2 Dennis. 1 LDV. 3 Mercedes. 1 Optare.
Bodies: 1 Alexander. 5 Ikarus. 1 Optare. 4 Plaxton. 2 Van Hool. 3 Wright. 3 other.
Ops incl: local bus services, school contracts, excursions & tours, private hire.
Livery: Ivory/Blue.
Ticket system: ERG

WHITES COACHES
ENGAMOOR, WEST BURRAFIRTH, BRIDGE OF WALLS, SHETLAND, ZE2 9NT
Tel: 01595 809433
E-mail: john@engamoo-shetland.co.uk
Ptnr: John White
Fleet: 7 - 3 single-deck bus, 1 single-deck coach, 3 minibus.
Chassis: 3 Ford Transit. 3 Mercedes, 1 Volvo.
Bodies: incl: 3 Plaxton. 1 Wright
Ops incl: local bus services, school contracts, private hire.
Livery: White/Yellow/Black

SOUTH AYRSHIRE

DODDS OF TROON LTD
4 EAST ROAD, AYR KA8 9BA
Tel: 01292 288100
Fax: 01292 287700
E-mail: info@doddsoftroon.com
Web site: www.doddsoftroon.com
Man Dir: James Dodds **Dirs:** Douglas Dodds, Norma Dodds
Fleet: 22 - 2 single-deck bus, 17 single-deck coach, 3 midicoach.
Chassis: 4 Leyland. 3 Toyota. 15 Volvo.
Bodies: 4 Alexander-Dennis. 3 Caetano. 8 Jonckheere. 2 Plaxton. 5 Van Hool.
Ops incl: school contracts, excursions & tours, private hire.
Livery: Green/Cream

IBT TRAVEL GROUP
CAIRN HOUSE, 15 SKYE ROAD, PRESTWICK KA9 2TA
Tel: 01292 477771
Fax: 01292 471770.
E-mail: briant@ibtravel.com
Partner: Ian Black
Fleet: 3 coaches
Chassis: Volvo
Bodies: Van Hool
Ops incl: continental tours, private hire
Livery: Blue/Gold flash

KEENAN OF AYR COACH TRAVEL
DARWIN GARAGE, COALHALL BY AYR KA6 6ND
Tel: 01292 591252
Fax: 01292 590980
Web site: www.keenancoaches.co.uk
Dirs: Tony Keenan, Jamie Keenan
Fleet: 20 - 2 double-deck bus, 6 single-deck bus, 10 coach, 1 midibus, 1 midicoach.
Chassis: incl: 8 Leyland. 8 Volvo.
Bodies: 8 Alexander. 4 Duple. 2 Plaxton. 6 Van Hool.
Ops incl: school contracts, excursions & tours, private hire.
Livery: Red/Yellow/Orange/White

MILLIGANS COACH TRAVEL LTD
LOAN GARAGE, MAUCHLINE KA5 6AN
Tel: 01290 550365
Fax: 01290 553291
E-mail: enquiries@milliganscoachtravel.co.uk
Web Site: www.milliganscoachtravel.co.uk
Dir: William Milligan **Ops Man:** Morag Milligan
Fleet: 20 coaches & midicoaches.
Chassis: 8 Bova. 8 Leyland. 4 Scania.
Bodies: 8 Bova. 3 Irizar. 9 Plaxton.
Ops incl: excursions & tours, private hire, school contracts, express.
Livery: Black/Red/Silver

STAGECOACH WEST SCOTLAND
SANDGATE, AYR KA7 1DD
Tel: 01292 613700
Fax: 01292 613501
Web site: www.stagecoachbus.com
Man Dir: Sam Greer **Eng Dir:** Sam Greer
Ops Dir: Sarah Longair
Fleet: 449 - incl 2 open-top bus, 93 double-deck bus, 130 single-deck bus, 16 articulated bus, 54 coach, 92 midibus, 72 minibus.
Chassis: 3 AEC. 92 Dennis. 30 Leyland. 2 Leyland National. 44 MAN. 47 Mercedes. 25 Optare. 7 Scania. 209 Volvo.
Bodies: 276 Alexander. 1 Berkhof. 2 ECW. 11 East Lancs. 22 Jonckheere. 16 Leyland. 5 Neoplan. 2 Northern Counties. 25 Optare. 3 Park Royal. 91 Plaxton. 5 Wright.
Ops incl: local bus services, school contracts, private hire, express.
Livery: Stagecoach
Ticket System: Wayfarer

SOUTH LANARKSHIRE

ALFRA COACH HIRE
26 MACHAN ROAD, LARKHALL ML9 1HG.
Tel: 01698 887581.
Prop: F. Russell.
Fleet: 4 minibus.
Chassis: 2 Ford Transit. 1 Freight Rover. 1 Leyland.
Ops incl: private hire.
Livery: White.

R. & C. S. CRAIG
TOWNFOOT, ROBERTON, BY BIGGAR ML12 6RS.
Tel: 01899 850655.
Dirs: R. Craig, C. S. Craig.
Traf Man/Ch Eng: J. Harvie.
Gen Man: R. Craig.
Fleet: 3 - 2 minibus, 1 minicoach.
Chassis: Freight Rover.
Ops incl: school contracts, private hire.
Livery: White.

PARK'S OF HAMILTON LTD
14 BOTHWELL ROAD, HAMILTON ML3 0AY
Tel: 01698 281222
Fax: 01698 303731
Web site: www.parksofhamilton.co.uk
Chmn: Douglas Park **Ch Eng:** Malcolm Fisher.
Co Sec/Dir: Gerry Donnachie. **Ops Man:** Michael Andrews. **Dir:** Hugh McAteer.
Fleet: 100 - incl: coach, double-deck coach.
Chassis: incl: Neoplan. 30 Volvo. Iveco.
Bodies: incl: 30 Jonckheere. Neoplan. Plaxton. Van Hool. Beulas.
Ops incl: local bus services, school contracts, excursions & tours, private hire, express, continental tours.
Livery: Black
Ticket System: Wayfarer

SILVER CHOICE TRAVEL LTD
1 MILTON ROAD,
EAST KILBRIDE G74 5BU
Tel: 01355 230403
Fax: 01355 265111
E-mail: enquiries@silverchoicetravel.co.uk
Web site: www.silverchoice.co.uk
Dirs: David W Gardiner **Ch Eng**: David Hunter
Fleet: 17 - 10 coach, 5 double-deck coach, 2 minicoach.
Chassis: 3 Bova. 1 Iveco. 2 Mercedes. 2 Neoplan. 3 Scania. 6 Volvo.
Ops incl: school contracts, excursions & tours, private hire, express, continental tours.
Livery: Silver

THE RURAL DEVELOPMENT TRUST
1 POWELL STREET,
DOUGLAS WATER ML11 9PP
Tel: 01555 880551
E-mail: mail@ruraldevtrust.co.uk.
Web site: www.ruraldevtrust.co.uk
Man Dir: Gordon Muir.
Fleet: 10 - 1 midibus, 3 midicoach, 6 minicoach.
Chassis: 7 Mercedes-Benz. 1 Optare. 1 Toyota. 1 Other
Body: 1 Caetano. 6 Mercedes-Benz. 1 Optare. 1 Plaxton. 1 Other.
Ops incl: local bus services, school contracts, private hire

WILLIAM STOKES & SONS LTD
22 CARSTAIRS ROAD,
CARSTAIRS ML11 8QD
Tel: 01555 870344
Fax: 01555 870601
E-mail: enquiries@stokescoaches.co.uk
Web site: www.stokescoaches.co.uk
Dirs: William Stokes, Alexander Stokes, John Stokes **Co Sec**: Walter Stokes,
Fleet: 21 - 8 single-deck bus, 7 coach, 3 midibus, 3 midicoach
Chassis: 3 DAF. 6 Dennis. 2 Leyland. 3 Mercedes. 7 Volvo.
Bodies: 2 Alexander. 3 Berkhof. 1 Caetano. 1 Carlyle. 1 Esker. 4 Ikarus. 1 Jonckheere. 6 Plaxton. 2 Van Hool.
Ops incl: local bus services, school contracts, excursions & tours, private hire.
Livery: Red/Cream
Ticket System: Almex A90

STONEHOUSE COACHES
48 NEW STREET,
STONEHOUSE ML9 3LT.
Tel: 01698 792145.
Prop: N. Collison.
Livery: White/Pink/Navy.

STUART'S OF CARLUKE
CASTLEHILL GARAGE, AIRDRIE ROAD,
CARLUKE ML8 4UF
Tel: 01555 773533
Fax: 01555 752220
Dir: Stuart Shevill **Ops**: John Hane
Fleet: 49 - 10 double-deck bus, 20 single-deck bus, 15 coach, 2 minibus, 2 minicoach
Chassis: 15 Dennis. 1 Ford Transit. 10 Leyland. 3 Mercedes. 1 Optare. 15 Volvo.
Bodies: Alexander. Caetano. ECW. Jonckheere. Northern Counties. Optare. Plaxton. Reeve Burgess. Van Hool.
Ops incl: local bus services, school contracts, excursions and tours, private hire, express, continental tours.
Livery: Silver/Blue
Ticket system: Wayfarer

WHITELAWS COACHES
LOCHPARK INDUSTRIAL ESTATE,
STONEHOUSE ML9 3LR
Tel: 01698 792800
Fax: 01698 793506
E-mail: enquiries@whitelaws.co.uk
Web site: www.whitelaws.co.uk
Gen Man: Sandra Whitelaw **Coach Man**: William Whitelaw
Ops Man: Willie McLean **Office Man**: Janet Whitelaw
Fleet: 37 - 23 single-deck bus, 11 coach, 2 midicoach, 1 minibus.
Chassis: incl: 1 Iveco. 3 Mercedes.
Bodies: incl: 1 Marshall/MCV. 1 Plaxton. 3 Sunsundegui. 2 Van Hool. 1 Volvo.
Ops incl: local bus services, school contracts, excursions & tours, private hire.
Livery: Silver with Red/White/Blue.
Ticket System: Wayfarer 3

STIRLING

BILLY DAVIES EXECUTIVE COACHES
TRANSPORT HOUSE, PLEAN INDUSTRIAL ESTATE, PLEAN,
STIRLING FK7 8BJ
Tel: 01786 816627
Fax: 01786 811433
Recovery: 01786 816627
Web site: www.daviescoaches.co.uk
E-mail: enquiries@daviescoaches.com
Prop: Davies Coaches
Fleet: 10 - 5 double-deck bus, 3 single-deckcoach, 1 midicoach, 1 minicoach.
Chassis: incl - Ayats. Iveco. Leyland. MAN. MCW. Mercedes-Benz.
Bodies: incl - Alexander Dennis. Ayats. Leyland. MCW. Mercedes-Benz. Plaxton. Van Hool.
Ops incl: Local bus service, school contracts, private hire.
Livery: Blue/Yellow
Ticket system: Wayfarer

FIRST EDINBURGH LTD
CARMUIRS HOUSE, STIRLING ROAD,
LARBERT FK5 3NJ
Tel: 01324 602200
Fax: 01324 611287
Customer Service Centre: 08708 727271
Web: www.firstgroup.com
Man Dir: Jane Desmond **Ops Dir**: Juliette Turner **Eng Dir**: Steve Myers **Fin Dir**: David Stewart

FITZCHARLES COACHES LTD
87 NEWHOUSE ROAD,
GRANGEMOUTH FK3 8NJ
Tel: 01324 482093
Fax: 01324 665411
E-mail: info@fitzcharles.co.uk
Web site: www.fitzcharles.co.uk
Man Dir: George R Fitzcharles **Dir/Sec**: Olive King **Ops Man**: Alan Dick
Fleet: 16 - 15 single-deck coach, 1 midibus.
Chassis: 2 DAF. 1 Mercedes-Benz. 13 Volvo.
Bodies: 2 Ayats. 3 Caetano. 7 Plaxton. 4 Sunsundegui.
Ops incl: excursions & tours, private hire, continental tours, school contracts, express.
Livery: Red/Cream.

HARLEQUIN COACHES LTD
8 LEEWOOD PARK,
DUNBLANE FK15 0NX
Tel/Fax: 01786 822547
E-mail: harlequin@adam8.fsneet.co.uk
Web: www.harlequincoaches-dunblare.co.uk
Dir: Robert Adam
Fleet: 9 - 2 single-deck bus, 2 single-deck coach, 1 midicoach, 3 minbus, 1 minicoach.
Chassis: 1 Bedford. 1 Dennis. 3 Iveco. 2 Optare. 1 Toyota. 1 Volvo.
Bodies: 2 Caetano. 2 Mellor. 2 Plaxton. 1 UVG
Ops incl: local bus services, school contracts, private hire.

MITCHELL'S COACHES
PRESIDENT KENNEDY DRIVE, PLEAN FK7 8AY
Tel: 01786 814319
Fax: 01786 814165
Ops incl: local bus services
Livery: White

WEST DUNBARTONSHIRE

D. P. BISHOP
14 LENNOX ROAD, MILTON, DUMBARTON G82 2TL.
Fleetname: DB Travel.

LOCHS AND GLENS HOLIDAYS
SCHOOL ROAD, GARTORCHARN G83 8RW
Tel: 01389 713 713
E-mail: enquiries@lochsandglens.com
Website: www.lochsandglens.com
Tran Man: Brian Nichols
Fleet: 15 coach
Chassis: 15 Volvo.
Bodies: 15 Jonckheere.
Ops incl: excursions & tours
Livery: White with blue letters

McCOLL'S COACHES LTD
BALLAGAN DEPOT, STIRLING ROAD, BALLOCH G83 8LY
Tel: 01389 754321
Fax: 01389 755354
E-mail: mccolls@btconnect.com
Web site: www.mccolls.org.uk
Man: William McColl **Man Dirs:** Thomas McColl, Janet McColl **Co Sec:** Ann McKinlay **Ops Man:** Liam McColl **Head mechanic:** Eddie McKinley
Fleet: double-deck bus, single-deck bus, coach, minibus.
Chassis: DAF. Dennis. Ford. Ford Transit. Leyland. leyland National. MCW. Mercedes. Volvo. other.
Bodies: Leyland National. MCW. Mercedes. other.
Ops incl: local bus services, school contracts, excursions & tours, private hire.

WEST LOTHIAN

DAVIDSON BUSES LTD
UNIT C, WESTWOOD WORKS, WEST CALDER EH55 8PN
Tel: 01506 870226
Web Site: www.davidson-buses.com
Mad Dir: Iain Davidson **Dir:** Francis Gartland
Ops incl: local bus services

FIRST EDINBURGH LTD
SEE STIRLING

LES BROWN TRAVEL
9 HARDHILL ROAD, BATHGATE EH48 2BW
Tel: 01506 656129
Fax: 01506 656129
E-mail: les-brown@btconnect.com
Web Site: www.lesbrowntravel.com
Props: Les Brown, Colin Brown
Fleet: 8 - 2 midicoach, 6 minicoach.
Chassis: 5 Ford Transit. 3 Mercedes.
Ops incl: school contracts, excursions & tours, private hire.

BROWNINGS (WHITBURN) LTD
22 LONGRIDGE ROAD, WHITBURN EH47 0DE
Tel: 01501 740234
Fax: 01501 741265
E-mail: george@browningscoaches.fsnet.co.uk
Web site: www.browningscoaches.co.uk
Dirs: George Browning, Eric Browning, Gary Knox
Fleet: 15 - 3 double-deck bus, 12 single-deck coach
Chassis: 3 Alexander Dennis. 3 Leyland. 9 Volvo.
Bodies: 2 Berkhof. 1 ECW. 2 Plaxton. 5 Van Hool. 3 Waldham Stringer
Ops incl: private hire, school contracts.
Livery: Red/White/Blue.

E & M HORSBURGH
180 UPHALL STATION ROAD, PUMPHERSTON EH53 0PD
Tel: 01506 432251
Fax: 01506 438066
E-mail: horsburgh@btconnect.com
Web site: www.horsburghcoaches.com
Dirs: Eric Horsburgh, Mark Horsburgh
Fleet: 66 - 11 double-deck bus, 23 single-deck bus, 2 coach, 6 midibus, 4 minicoach, 22 minibus.
Chassis: 5 Dennis. 10 Ford Transit. 4 LDV. 14 Leyland. 18 Mercedes. 9 Optare.
Bodies: 4 LDV. 10 Ford. 14 Leyland. 8 Leyland National. 14 Mercedes. 9 Optare. 9 Plaxton.
Ops incl: local bus services, school contracts, private hire.
Livery: Golden Yellow/White
Ticket System: Almex

HOUSTOUN TRAVEL
110 PUMPHERSTON ROAD, UPHALL STATION, LIVINGSTON EH54 5PJ
Tel: 01506 437773.
Fax: 01506 437206.
Prop: Ian Horsburgh.
Fleet: 9 - 1 minibus, 8 minicoach.
Chassis: 1 DAF. 5 Ford Transit. 1 Freight Rover. 2 Mercedes.
Bodies: 1 Carlyle. 1 Leyland. 1 Mercedes. 1 Plaxton. 5 other.
Ops incl: local bus services, school contracts, private hire.

McKECHNIE OF BATHGATE LTD
2 EASTON ROAD, BATHGATE EH48 2QG
Tel: 01506 654337
Fax: 01506 654337
E-mail: pmkcoach@aol.com
Dir: Peter McKechnie **Co Sec:** Catherine McKechnie
Fleet: 8 - 4 coach, 2 midicoach, 2 minicoach
Chassis: 1 Leyland. 3 Volvo. 4 Mercedes
Ops incl: school contracts, private hire.

MARTIN'S COACH TRAVEL
1 SUMMERVILLE COURT, UPHALL STATION, LIVINGSTON EH54 5QG.
Tel: 01506 435968.
Fax: 01506 435968.
E-mail: martcoach@aol.com
Prop: Tony Martin
Fleet: 5 - 4 single-deck coach, 1 midicoach
Chassis: 1 Bova. 1 Iveco. 1 MAN. 2 Volvo.
Bodies: 1 Berkhof. 1 Bova. 2 Caetano. 1 Other.
Ops incl: excursions & tours, private hire, school contracts.
Livery: White/Green/Orange/Blue

PRENTICE WESTWOOD
WESTWOOD, WEST CALDER EH55 8PW
Tel: 01506 871231
Fax: 01506 871734
E-mail: sales@prenticewestwoodcoaches.co.uk
Web site: www.prenticewestwoodcoaches.co.uk
Dirs: Robbie Prentice, David Cowen **Ops Man:** Jock Johnston
Fleet: 61 - 12 double-deck bus, 36 single-deck coach, 7 double-deck coach, 4 midibus, 2 midicoach.
Chassis: 1 Alexander Dennis. 7 Bova. 1 DAF. 1 Enterprise. 10 Leyland. 2 MAN. 2 Mercedes-Benz. 3 Neoplan. 2 Optare. 1 Scania. 31 Volvo.
Bodies: 2 Alexander Dennis. 2 Berkhof. 7 Bova. 5 Caetano. 10 ECW1 Est Lancs. 1 Ikarus. 8 Jonckheere. 3 Neoplan. 2 Optare. 12 Plaxton. 6 Van Hool. 2 other.
Ops incl: local bus services, school contracts, private hire.
Livery: White/Blue/Red.
Ticket System: Almex

WESTERN ISLES

COMHAIRLE NAN EILEAN SIAR
BUS COMHAIRLE, SANDWICK ROAD STORNOWAY, ISLE OF LEWIS HS1 2BW
Tel: 01851 709728
Fax: 01851 709750.
Head of Service: Donald Stuart **Fleet Man:** Donald Stewart. **Fleet Eng:** Neil McLeod
E-mail: bus@cne-siar.gov.uk
Web: www.cne-siar.gov.uk
Fleet Name: bus na comhairle
Fleet: 13 - 7 single-deck coach, 6 midibus.
Chassis: incl: 6 Mercedes-Benz
Bodies: inlc: 7 Plaxton.
Ops incl: local bus services, school contracts, private hire.
Livery: White/Yellow stripe

GALSON-STORNOWAY MOTOR SERVICES LTD
1 LOWER BARVAS, ISLE OF LEWIS HS2 0QZ
Tel: 01851 840269
Fax: 01851 840445
E-mail: galson@sol.co.uk
Web site: www.galsonmotorsltd.co.uk
Dir: I Morrison. **Ops Man:** I Morrison
Fleet: 17 - 1 single-deck bus, 12 coach, 1 midicoach, 3 minibus.
Chassis: 3 Ford Transit. 1 Leyland. 2 Mercedes. 11 Volvo.
Bodies: 1 Autobus. 2 Mercedes. 12 Plaxton. 2 other
Ops incl: local bus services, school contracts, excursions & tours, private hire.
Livery: Yellow/Cream.
Ticket System: Wayfarer

HEBRIDEAN COACHES
HOWMORE, SOUTH UIST HS8 5SH
Tel: 01870 620345
Fax: 01870 620301
Recovery: 01870 620345
Props: D A MacDonald, S MacDonald
Fleet: 11 - 4 single-deck coach, 5 midibus, 2 midicoach
Chassis: 2 Bedford. 3 DAF. 2 Ford Transit. 2 Mercedes-Benz.
Bodies: 4 Duple. 1 Mellor. 2 Plaxton. 1 UVG
Ops incl: local bus services, school contracts, private hire.
Livery: Cream/Green
Ticket System: Almex.

LOCHS MOTOR TRANSPORT LTD
CAMERON TERRACE, LEURBOST, LOCHS, ISLE OF LEWIS HS2 9PE
Tel: 01851 860288.
Fax: 01851 705857.
Dirs: C. MacDonald, R. MacDonald, S. MacDonald, A. MacDonald.
Ch Eng: I. MacKinnon.
Fleet: 20 - 4 single-deck bus, 12 coach, 3 midibus, 1 midicoach.
Chassis: 12 Ford. 1 Freight Rover. 3 Leyland. 4 Mercedes.
Bodies: 5 Alexander. 1 Carlyle. 8 Duple. 2 Marshall. 2 M2M. 3 Plaxton.
Ops incl: local bus services, school contracts, private hire.
Livery: Blue/Cream.

Scottish Operators

201

WELSH OPERATORS

ANGLESEY

CARREGLEFN COACHES
CARREGLEFN GARAGE, AMLWCH LL68 0PR
Tel: 01407 710139
Fax: 01407 710217
Prop: Alun Lewis
Fleet: 10 - 1 single-deck bus, 8 coach, 1 minicoach.
Chassis: 2 Bedford. 1 Toyota. 7 Volvo.
Bodies: 4 Caetano. 1 Duple. 5 Plaxton.
Ops incl: local bus services, school contracts, excursions & tours, private hire.
Livery: Blue/Cream

W C GOODSIR
THE GARAGE CROSS STREET, HOLYHEAD LL65 1EG
Tel: 01407 764340
Livery: White/Black/Yellow/Orange.

GWYNFOR COACHES
ANEYLFA, 1 GREENFIELD AVENUE, LLANGEFNI LL77 7NU
Tel: 01248 722694
Prop: H. Hughes.

O R JONES & SONS
THE BUS & COACH DEPOT, LLANFAETHLU, HOLYHEAD LL65 4NW
Tel: 01407 730204
Fax: 01407 730083
Recovery: 01407 730759
E-Mail: orjonescoaches@hotmail.co.uk
Ops Man: Iolo O Jones   **Tran Man**: Maldwyn O Jones
Fleet: 20 - 4 double-deck bus, 5 single-deck bus, 6 single-deck coach, 1 midicoach, 3 minibus, 1 minicoach, 1 vintage.
Chassis: 3 Bova. 2 Bristol. 3 DAF. 1 Layland. 1 MAN. 3 Mercedes-Benz. 3 Optare. 1 Scania. 2 Other
Bodies: 3 Bova. 1 Caetano. 2 Ikarus. 1 Irizar. 3 Mercedes-Benz. 3 Optare. 2 Plaxton. 5 Other.
Ops incl: local bus services, school contracts, excursions & tours, private hire, express, continental tours.
Livery: Silver
Ticket system: Wayfarer

W E JONES & SON
THE GARAGE, LLANERCHYMEDD LL71 8EB
Tel: 01248 470228
Fax: 01248 852893
Prop: G E Jones
Fleet: 11 - 5 double-deck bus, 2 single-deck bus, 3 coach, 1 minibus.
Chassis: 1 Bedford. 1 Bristol. 1 DAF. 1 Daimler. 1 Dodge. 3 MCW. 1 Mercedes. 1 Volvo.
Bodies: 2 Alexander. 3 MCW. 1

Mercedes. 2 Northern Counties. 1 Plaxton.
Ops incl: school contracts, private hire.
Livery: Red/White

LEWIS-Y-LLAN
MADYN INDUSTRIAL ESTATE, AMLWCH LL68 9DL
Tel: 01407 832181
Fax: 01407 830112
Props: A. H. Lewis, R. M. Lewis.
Fleet: 10 - 2 double-deck bus, 4 coach, 4 midibus.
Chassis: 1 Bedford. 3 Leyland. 3 Mercedes. 2 Volvo. 1 Volkswagen.
Bodies: 1 Alexander. 1 East Lancs. 1 Jonckheere. 1 Leyland. 3 Optare. 3 Plaxton.
Livery: White/Blue.

BLAENAU GWENT

GARY'S COACHES OF TREDEGAR
R24
42 COMMERCIAL STREET, TREDEGAR NP22 3DJ
Tel: 01495 726400
Fax: 01495 726500
Recovery: 01495 723264
E-mail: sales@garys-coaches.co.uk
Web site: www.garys-coaches.co.uk
Props: Mr & Mrs G A Lane   **Ops Man**: D Williams   **Ch Eng**: G Cresswell
Fleet: 14 - 12 coach, 1 midicoach, 1 midibus.
Chassis: 2 DAF. 1 Dennis. 1 Leyland. 2 Mercedes. 8 Volvo.
Bodies: 1 Bova. 4 Duple. 2 Mercedes. 5 Plaxton. 2 Van Hool.
Ops incl: excursions & tours, private hire, school contracts, continental tours.
Livery: White/Blue

HENLEYS BUS SERVICES LTD
HENLEYS COACH GARAGE, VICTOR ROAD, CWMTILLERY NP13 1HU
Tel: 01495 212288
Fax: 01495 320720
Dir: Martin Henley   **Head Eng**: Michael Henley   **Sec**: Daphne Henley
Fleet: 11 - 6 coach, 4 midibus, 1 minicoach.
Chassis: 4 Leyland. 4 Mercedes. 1 Setra. 2 Volvo.
Bodies: 1 Alexander. 1 Duple. 2 East Lancs. 1 Jonckheere. 1 Leicester. 5 Plaxton. 1 Setra.
Ops incl: local bus services, school contracts, excursions & tours, private hire.
Ticket system: Wayfarer

STAGECOACH IN SOUTH WALES
See Torfaen

BRIDGEND

R & D BURROWS LTD
21 CEMETERY ROAD, OGMORE VALE CF32 7HR

Tel: 01656 840259/840345
Fax: 01656 841866
E-mail: burrowscoaches@yahoo.co.uk
Web site: www.burrowscoaches.co.uk
Dirs: J G Jones, S A Jones, P J Jones
Fleet: 7 - 1 double-deck bus, 6 single-deck coach
Chassis: 1 DAF. 1 Ford. 2 Scania. 1 Setra. 2 Volvo.
Bodies: 1 Duple. 1 Irizar. 2 Plaxton. 1 Setra. 2 Van Hool.
Ops incl: private hire, school contracts.
Livery: Blue

G M COACHES LTD
R24 T
MOUNTAIN VIEW GARAGE, TY-FRY ROAD, CEFN CRIBWR CF32 0BB
Tel: 01656 740262
Fax: 01656 746040
E-mail: info@gmcoaches.com
Web site: www.gmcoaches.com
Man Dir: Carl Hookings   **Dirs**: Katherine Hookings, Andrea Lockwood
Ops Man: Idris Hall
Fleet: 32 - 10 double-deck bus, 2 single-deck bus, 14 coach, 2 double-deck coach, 1 open-top bus, 1 midicoach, 1 minicoach, 1 minibus.
Chassis: incl: 3 DAF. 1 Dennis. 2 MAN. 1 Mercedes. 2 Neoplan.
Bodies: 3 Alexander. 4 Berkhof. 2 ECW. 3 East Lancs. 1 Ikarus. 2 Jonckheere. 1 Marshall/MCV. 1 Mercedes. 2 Neoplan. 1 Plaxton. 10 Van Hool.
Ops incl: local bus services, school contracts, excursions & tours, private hire, continental tours.
(Associated with EST Bus, Vale of Glamorgan)

GWYN JONES & SON LTD
WHITE CROFT GARAGE, BRYNCETHIN CF32 9YR
Tel: 01656 720300
Fax: 01656 725632
Recovery: 01656 720182
Chair: John Gwyn Jones   **Dir**: Miriam J. Jones
Fleet: coach.
Chassis: Leyland. Mercedes. Scania. Volvo.
Bodies: Berkhof. Jonckheere. Mercedes. Plaxton. Van Hool.
Ops incl: excursions & tours, private hire, continental tours, school contracts.
Livery: White/Gold/Maroon

PENCOED TRAVEL LTD
18 CAER BERLLAN, PENCOED CF35 6RR
Tel: 01656 860200
Fax: 01656 864793
E-mail: info@pencoedtravel.co.uk
Web site: www.pencoedtravel.co.uk
Man Dir: Denise Cook   **Ch Eng**: Neil Cook
Co Sec: Andrea Talbot   **Ops**: David Morris
Fleet: 10 - 2 double-deck bus, 8 single-deck coach.
Chassis: 2 Bova. 5 DAF. 3 Leyland.
Bodies: 1 Berkhof. 2 Bova. 2 Leyland. 1 Plaxton. 4 Van Hool.
Ops incl: private hire, school contracts
Livery: White/Blue

STAGECOACH IN SOUTH WALES
See Torfaen

CAERPHILLY

CASTELL COACHES LTD
UNITS 3 & 4 EUROPEAN TERMINAL BUILDING, PANTGLAS INDUSTRIAL ESTATE, BEDWAS CF83 8DR
Tel: 029 2086 1863.
Fax: 029 2086 1864
Recovery: 07967 636659
E-mail: sales@castellcoaches.co.uk
Web site: www.castellcoaches.co.uk
Co Sec: Mrs S Kerslake (**Tel**: 07801 515119) **Dir**: C Kerslake. **Ops Man**: B Kerslake (**Tel**: 07801 515117)
Fleet: 21 - 5 double-deck bus, 12 coach, 3 midicoach, 1 minibus.
Chassis: 2 Bova. 4 DAF. 6 Leyland. 4 Mercedes. 7 Volvo.
Bodies: 2 Bova. 1 Duple. 2 Jonckheere. 4 Leyland. 4 Mercedes. 6 Plaxton. 2 Van Hool.
Ops incl: excursions & tours, private hire, continental tours, school contracts.
Livery: White with multicolour

HARRIS COACHES
BRYN GWYN STREET, FLEUR-DE-LIS NP2 1RZ
Tel: 01443 832290
Man Dir: John Harris
Fleetname: Shuttle
Ops incl: local bus services
Livery: Cream/Maroon/Red

ISLWYN BOROUGH TRANSPORT LTD
PENMAEN ROAD DEPOT, PONTLLANFRAITH, BLACKWOOD NP12 2DY
Tel: 01495 235736
Fax: 01495 220871
E-mail: simsr@caerphilly.gov.uk
Web: www.kingfishertravel.com
Web site: www.kingfishertravel.com
Chairmn: David Poole **Dirs**: J Evans, R Gough, R Davies, J Criddle, R Barnett
Man Dir/Co Sec: Roger Sims **Comm Dir**: P Diaper
Ops Man: D Jones
Fleet: 46 - 45 single-deck bus, 1 minibus.
Chassis: 2 Bova. 2 DAF. 2 Dennis. 1 Ford. 1 Leyland. 16 MAN. 4 Mercedes-Benz. 1 Neoplan. 3 Optae. 14 Volvo.
Bodies: 1 Berkhof. 2 Bova. 1 Caetano. 5 East Lancs. 8 Jonckheere. 4 Marshall/MCV. 1 Neoplan. 15 Optare. 5 Plaxton. 1 Setra. 1 Van Hool. 2 other.
Ops incl: local bus services, school contracts, excursions & tours, private hire, continental tours.
Livery: Blue/White
Ticket System: Wayfarer

CARDIFF

CARDIFF CITY TRANSPORT SERVICES LTD
SLOPER ROAD, LECKWITH, CARDIFF CF11 8TB
Tel: 029 2078 7710
Fax: 029 2078 7742
E-mail: headoffice@cardiffbus.com
Web site: www.cardiffbus.com
Chmn: Cllr Steve Pantak **Man Dir**: David Brown **Fin Dir/Co Sec**: Cynthia Ogbonna **Eng Dir**: Andrew Hoseason
Comm Man: Peter Heath **OpsMan**: Gareth Mole
Fleet: 231 - 18 double-deck bus, 194 single-deck bus, 19 articulated bus
Chassis: 166 Dennis. 6 Leyland. 10 MCW. 19 Scania. 12 Transbus. 18 Volvo.
Bodies: 10 Alexander. 6 Leyland. 10 MCW. 15 Northern Counties. 138 Plaxton. 19 Scania. 12 Transbus.
Ops incl: local bus services
Livery: Burgess Blue/Cream
Ticket System: Wayfarer TGX

CROESO TOURS
13 WATERLOO ROAD, PENYLAN, CARDIFF CF23 5AD
Tel: 029 2047 2313
E-mail: jmforster13@hotmail.com
Owner: John M. Forster
Fleet: 3 - 1 midicoach, 1 minibus, 1 minicoach
Chassis: 1 Iveco. 1 LDV. 1 Renault
Ops incl: private hire, school contracts.

GREYHOUND COACHES CO
COACH DEPOT, STATION TERRACE, ELY BRIDGE, CARDIFF CF5 4AA
Tel: 029 2056 1467, 2055 2767
Ptnrs: T. James, Florence James.
Fleet: 14 - 13 coach, 1 minibus.
Chassis: 10 Bedford. 1 Ford Transit. 3 Volvo.
Ops incl: local bus services, excursions & tours, private hire.
Livery: White/Blue.

STAGECOACH IN SOUTH WALES
See Torfaen

WALTONS COACHES
31 AVONDALE ROAD, GRANGETOWN CF1 7DT.
Tel: 029 2039 9511.
Dirs: B. J. Walton, Mrs S. F. Walton, R. J. Walton, D. McCarthy.
Fleet: 6 - 4 coach, 2 midicoach.
Chassis: Bedford. Ford. Mercedes.
Ops incl: private hire, school contracts.
Livery: Blue/White/Red.

WATTS COACHES
OLD POST GARAGE, BONVILSTON CF5 6TQ.
Tel/Fax: 01446 781277.
E-mail: carol.watts@eurotelonline.com
Web site: www.wattscoaches.co.uk
Prop: C. P. Watts. **Tran Man**: J. B. Watts.
Fleet: 23 - 3 double-deck bus, 16 coach, 4 midicoach.
Chassis: 2 Bristol. 2 DAF. 5 Ford. 4 Leyland. 2 MAN. 4 Mercedes. 4 Volvo.
Bodies: 3 Alexander. 3 Caetano. 5 Duple. 1 Optare. 8 Plaxton. 1 Reeve Burgess. 1 Made-to-Measure. 1 Robin Hood.
Ops incl: school contracts, private hire.
Livery: Cream/Red/Gold.

WHEADONS GROUP TRAVEL LTD
STATION TERRACE, ELY BRIDGE, CARDIFF CF5 4AA
Tel: 029 2057 5333
Fax: 029 2057 5384
E-mail: admin@wheadons-group.co.uk
Web site: www.wheadons-group.co.uk
Prop: Ernest Wheadon **Ch Eng**: Steve Osling
Fleet: 34 - 20 coach, 10 midicoach, 4 midibus.
Chassis: Ford Transit. Scania. Toyota. Volvo.
Bodies: Autobus. Caetano. Mercedes. Plaxton. Van Hool.
Ops incl: private hire, school contracts, excursions & tours, continental tours.

CARMARTHENSHIRE

BYSIAU CWM TAF/TAF VALLEY COACHES
PENRHEOL, WHITLAND SA34 0NH
Tel: 01994 240908
Fax: 01994 241264
E-mail: mail@tafvalleycoaches.co.uk
Web site: www.tafvalleycoaches.co.uk
Dirs: Clive Edwards, Heather Edwards
Fleet Name: Taf Valley coaches
Fleet: 14 - 10 coach, 2 midibus, 1 midicoach, minicoach.
Chassis: Dennis. Iveco. LDV. Leyland. Mercedes. Optare. Volvo.
Bodies: Jonckheere. Mercedes. Optare. Plaxton. Reeve Burgess. Transbus. Van Hool
Ops incl: local bus services, excursions & tours, school contracts, private hire, continental tours.
Livery: White/Silver/Blue

CASTLE GARAGE LTD
BROAD STREET, LLANDOVERY SA20 0AA
Tel: 01550 720335
Man Dir: Derek Jones
Fleet: 12 - 4 midibus, 4 midicoach, 4 minibus.
Chassis: 2 Ford Transit. 2 Freight Rover. 8 Mercedes.
Bodies: Mellor. Mercedes. Optare. Plaxton. Reeve Burgess. Wadham Stringer.
Ops incl: local bus services, school contracts, private hire.

FFOSHELIG COACHES
MAES Y PRIOR, ST PETERS, CARMARTHEN SA33 5OS
Tel: 01267 237584
FAX: 01267 236054
E-mail: ffushelig-coaches@btconnect.com
Web site: www.ffushelig.co.uk
Prop: Rhodri Evans
Ops incl: Private hire, excursions and tours

WELSH OPERATORS

203

GARETH EVANS COACHES
80 GLYN ROAD, BRYNAMMAN
SA18 1SS
Tel: 01269 823127
Fax: 01269 824533
Props: K. Davies, Mrs S. Davies.

GWYN WILLIAMS & SONS LTD
DERLWYN GARAGE, LOWER TUMBLE
SA14 6HS
Tel: 01269 841312
Fax: 01269 842256
E-mail: info@gwynwilliamscoaches.com
Web site: www.gwynwilliamscoaches.com
Fleet: 27 - 3 double-deck bus, 8 single-deck bus, 17 coach, 7 minibus
Livery: Two tone Blue/Red.

JONES INTERNATIONAL
STATION ROAD, LLANDEILO SA19 6NG
Tel: 01558 822985
Fax: 01558 822984
Props: Meirion Jones, Myrddin Jones, Neil Jones **Office Man**: Carole Thompson **Ch Eng**: Andrew Vale
Fleet: 7 - 2 single-deck bus, 5 coach.
Chassis: 3 DAF. 3 Leyland. 1 Volvo.
Bodies: 6 Van Hool. 1 Crossley.
Ops incl: excursions & tours, private hire, express, continental tours, school contracts.
Livery: Yellow/Blue

JONES MOTORS (LOGIN) LTD
LOGIN, WHITLAND SA34 0UX
Tel: 01437 563277
Fax: 01437 563393
E-mail: info@joneslogin.co.uk
Web Site: www.joneslogin.co.uk
Man Dirs: E A Jones, A T Jones, E H Jones
Fleet: 17 - 11 coach, 1 midicoach, 4 minibus, 1 single deck bus
Chassis: 8 Dennis. 2 LDV. 11 Mercedes. 1 Scania. 5 Volvo.
Bodies: 1 East Lancs. 1 Irizar. 2 Leyland. 1 Mercedes. 12 Plaxton.
Ops incl: local bus services, school contracts, excursions & tours, private hire, continental tours.

LEWIS COACHES WHITLAND
THE GARAGE, WHITLAND SA34 0AA
Tel: 01944 240274
E-mail: enquiries@lewiscoacheswhitland.co.uk
Web Site: www.lewiscoacheswhitland.co.uk
Dirs: E Lewis
Fleet: 11 - 8 coach, 1 minibus, 2 minicoach.
Chassis: 1 Bedford. 3 Dennis. 2 LDV. 3 Leyland. 2 Volvo.
Bodies: 1 Berkhof. 1 Duple. 2 Leyland. 1 Optare. 6 Plaxton.
Livery: White with Green/Mink stripes.

Ops incl: local bus services, school contracts, private hire
Livery: White/Green with mink stripes
Ticket System: Wayfarer

MORRIS TRAVEL
ALLTYCNAP ROAD, JOHNSTOWN SA31 3QY
Tel: 01267 235090.
Fax: 01267 238183.
E-mail: sales@morristravel.co.uk
Web site: www.morristravel.co.uk
Man Dir/Chmn: T J Freeman **Ops Dir**: C J Freeman. **Dir/Co Sec**: C M Freeman
Ch Eng: A Jones. **Traf Man**: V Shambrook
Traff Controller: P Davies.
Fleet: 29 - 1 single-deck bus, 19 coach, 1 midibus, 6 minibus, 1 minicoach, 1 midicoach.
Chassis: 4 Bedford. 3 DAF. 1 Ford. 1 Freight Rover. 14 LDV. 2 Mercedes. 1 Optare. 4 Volvo.
Bodies: 1 Berkhof. 1 Duple. 14 Leyland. 1 Ford Transit. 2 Mercedes. 1 Optare. 9 Plaxton.
Ops incl: local bus services, school contracts, private hire.
Livery: Blue/Navy/White.
Ticket System: Wayfarer

THOMAS BROS
TOWY GARAGE, LLANGADOG
SA19 9LU.
Tel: 01550 777438
Fax: 01550 777807.
Prop: Gareth Thomas
Fleet: 19 - minibus, coach
Chassis/bodies: incl: 1 Mercedes/Optare Sorocco
Ops incl: local bus services, school contracts, excursions & tours, private hire.
Livery: Cream/Green.
Ticket System: Setright.

CEREDIGION

BRODYR JAMES
GLANYRAFON, LLANGEITHO, TREGARON SY25 6TT
Tel: 01974 821255
Fax: 01974 251618
Dirs: D E James, T M G James
Fleet: 15 - 10 single-deck coach, 3 midibus, 2 midicoach.
Chassis: 4 Dennis. 4 Mercedes-Benz. 1 Toyota. 6 Volvo.
Bodies: 2 Alexander Dennis. 2 Caetano. 1 Jonckheere. 2 Mercedes-Benz. 8 Plaxton.
Ops incl: school contracts, private hire
Livery: White/Red/Gold

LEWIS COACHES
BRYNEITHIN YARD, LLANRHYSTUD SY23 5DN
Tel/Fax: 01974 202495
E-mail: lewisgarage@btconnect.com

Prop: Gwyn R Lewis
Fleet: 18 - 2 single-deck bus, 10 single-deck coach, 1 midicoach, 2 minibus, 3 minicoach.
Chassis: 1 Bedford. 3 DAF. 1 Dennis. 1 Ford Transit. 1 Frieght Rover. 3 Leyland. 2 Mercedes-Benz. 2 Optare. 3 Volvo.
Bodies: 1 Berkhof. 1 Caetano. 1 Duple. 2 Mercedes-Benz. 3 Plaxton. 3 Van Hool.
Ops incl: local bus services, private hire, excursions & tours.
Livery: White/Blue
Ticket System: Wayfarer

LEWIS-RHYDLEWIS CYF
PENRHIW-PAL GARAGE, RHYDLEWIS, LLANDYSUL SA44 5QG
Tel: 01239 851 386
E-mail: lewis_Rhydlewis@hotmail.com
Web site: www.lewis-Rhydlewis.co.uk
Comp sec: Maldwyn Lewis
Fleet: 22 - 16 single-deck coach, 3 midicoach, 3 minibus.
Chassis: 6 Bedfrd. 1 BMC. 2 Dennis. 1 Iveco. 4 Leyland. 2 Setra. 3 Volvo.
Bodies: 1 BMC. 1 Duple. 15 Plaxton. 2 Setra. 3 Other.
Ops incl: school contracts, private hire, excursions & tours.
Livery: Cream/Red/Orange/Maroon.

MID WALES TRAVEL
BRYNHYFRYD GARAGE, PENRHYNCOCH, ABERYSTWYTH SY23 3EH
Tel: 01970 828288
Fax: 01970 828940
Web: www.midwalestravel.co.uk
E-mail: enquires@midwalestravel.co.uk
Dir: J M Evans **Comp Sec**: J H Morgan
Fleet: 19 - 4 single-deck bus, 14 single-deck coach, 1 midicoach.
Chassis: incl - Alexander Dennis. DAF. Dennis. Mercedes-Benz. Volvo
Bodies: incl - Alexander Dennis. Mercedes-Benz. Plaxton. Van Hool.
Ops incl: local bus services, school contracts, excursrions & tours, private hire.

RED KITE COACHES
UNIT 1, GLANDINAS, PENPARCIAU, ABERYSTWYTH SY23 1RR
Tel: 01970 627427
Fax: 01970 624412
E-mail: enquiries@redkitecoaches.co.uk
Web site: www.redkitecoaches.co.uk
Prop: P Bryan
Fleet: 4 - 2 single-deck bus, 1 double-deck coach, 1 midicoach.
Chassis: 1 DAF. 1 Leyland. 1 Scania. 1 Volvo.
Bodies: 2 Plaxton. 1 Wadham Stringer. 1 other
Ops incl: private hire, excursions & tours, express, continental tours.
Livery: White/Blue
Livery: Wayfarer

WELSH OPERATORS

RICHARDS BROS
MOYLGROVE GARAGE, PENTOOD INDUSTRIAL ESTATE, CARDIGAN SA43 3AG
Tel: 01239 613756
Fax: 01239 615193
E-mail: enquiries@richardsbros.co.uk
Web site: www.richardsbros.co.uk
Gen Man: W J M Richards **Ch Eng**: D N Richards **Traf Man**: R M Richards
Ops Man: S M Richards
Fleet: 67 - 23 single-deck bus, 22 coach, 4 midicoach, 4 minibus, 14 midibus.
Chassis: 8 Bedford. 23 DAF. 11 Dennis. 3 LDV. 1 MAN. 12 Mercedes. 2 Volvo.
Bodies: 5 Alexander. 1 Autobus. 1 Caetano. 3 Carlyle. 7 Duple. 2 Ikarus. 2 Marshall. 2 Northern Counties. 9 Optare. 15 Plaxton. 2 Reeve Burgess. 3 Transbus. 8 Van Hool. 3 Wright. 3 other.
Ops incl: local bus services, school contracts, excursions & tours, private hire, continental tours.
Livery: Blue/White/Maroon
Ticket System: Wayfarer

ROBERTS COACHES
UNIT 4, GLANYRAFON INDUSTRIAL ESTATE, ABERYSTWYTH SY23 3JQ
Tel: 01970 611085
Fax: 01970 626855
Prop: G Roberts
Fleet: 5 coach.
Chassis: 2 DAF. 3 Leyland.
Bodies: Plaxton. Duple.
Ops incl: school contracts, private hire, tours & excursions.
Livery: White or Blue

CONWY

ALPINE TRAVEL
CENTRAL COACH GARAGE, BUILDER STREET WEST, LLANDUDNO LL30 1HH
Tel: 01492 879133
Fax: 01492 876055
E-mail: chris@alpine-travel.co.uk
Web site: www.alpine-travel.co.uk
Dirs: Bryan Owens, Patricia Owens, Christopher Owens, Christopher Bryan Owens.
Fleet: 66 - 30 double-deck bus, 10 single-deck bus, 25 coach, 3 minicoach.
Chassis: Alexander Dennis, Autosan, Bedford, Bristol, Irisbus, Leyland, Mercedes, Volvo
Bodies: Bova. Duple. ECW. Plaxton. Marcopolo, Mercedes
Ops incl: local bus services, school contracts, excursions & tours, private hire, continental tours.
Livery: Red/white/Green
Ticket System: Setright.

ARRIVA CYMRU LTD
IMPERIAL BUILDINGS, GLAN-Y-MOR ROAD, LLANDUDNO JUNCTION LL31 9RU
Tel: 01492 592111.
Fax: 01492 592968.
Man Dir: S. Green. **Eng Dir**: M. Evans.
Fin Dir: B. Pegg.
Fleet: 265 - 39 double-deck bus, 129 single-deck bus, 3 coach, 94 midibus.
Chassis: DAF. Dennis. Leyland. Mercedes. Scania. Volvo.
Bodies: Alexander. ECW. Northern Counties. Plaxton. Wright.
Ops incl: local bus services, school contracts, private hire, express.
Livery: Turquoise/Cotswold Stone
Ticket System: Wayfarer III.

GRWP ABERCONWY
MAESDU, LLANDUDNO LL30 1HF.
Tel: 01492 870870.
Fax: 01492 860821.
Fleetname: Great Orme Tours.
Dir: I. Trevette.
Tramway & Coach Man: Rosemary Sutton.
Fleet: 4 midicoach.
Chassis: 3 Bedford. 1 Guy.
Ops incl: local bus services, excursions & tours.
Livery: Blue/Cream.
Ticket System: Almex.

LLEW JONES INTERNATIONAL
STATION YARD, LLANRWST LL26 0EH
Tel: 01492 640320
Fax: 01492 642040
E-mail: sales@llewjones.com
Web site: www.llewjones.com
ManDir: Stephen Jones **Ops Man**: Kevin Williams **Fin Dir**: Eirlys Jones **Dir**: Buddug Jones **Wkshp Man**: Erfyl Roberts
HR & Recruitment: John Grove
Fleet: 30 - 19 single-deck coach, 8 midibus, 3 midicoach.
Chassis: 6 DAF. 3 Dennis. 1 EOS. 1 MAN. 16 Mercedes-Benz. 1 Optare. 3 Volvo.
Bodies: 3 Ayats. 1 Caentano. 3 Duple. 1 Esker. 5 Mercedes-Benz. 1 Noge. 1 Optare. 9 Plaxton. 1 Van Hool. 1 Wadham Stringer. 3 Other.
Ops incl: local bus services, school contracts, excursions & tours, private hire, continental tours.
Livery: White/Silver/Magenta/Blue
Ticket system: Wayfarer TGX 150

ROBERTS MINI COACHES
RHANDIR GARAGE, RHANDIR LL22 8BW.
Tel: 01492 650449.
Fleet: 4 - 3 midicoach, 1 minibus.
Chassis: 1 LDV, 3 Mercedes-Benz.
Bodies: 2 Esker. 1 Plaxton. 1 Other

DENBIGHSHIRE

GHA COACHES
MILL GARAGE, BETWS GWERFIL GOCH, CORWEN LL21 9PU
Tel: See Wrexham for full details

M & H COACHES
UNIT 2 BRICKWORK GARAGE, TREFNANT DENBIGH LL16 4UH.
Tel: 01745 730700.
Prop: Mrs M. Owen.
Livery: Blue/White.
Ops Inc: local bus services

VOEL COACHES LTD
PENISA FILLING STATION, FFORD TALARGOCH, DYSERTH LL18 6BP
Tel: 01745 570154.
Fax: 01745 570307
Email: sales@voelcoaches.com
Web site: www.voelcoaches.com
Man Dir: W M Kerfoot-Davies **Com Man**: Michelle Kerfoot Higginson.
Fleet: 25 - 7 double-deck bus, 4 single-deck bus, 12 coach, 1 minibus, 1 midicoach.
Chassis: Dennis. Mercedes. Scania. Volvo
Bodies: Berkhof. Van Hool.
Ops incl: local bus services, school contracts, excursions & tours, private hire, continental tours.
Livery: Orange

205

FLINTSHIRE

EAGLES AND CRAWFORD
53 NEW STREET, MOLD CH7 1NY
Tel: 01352 700217/8
Fax: 01352 750211
E-mail: eaglesandcrawford@supanet.com
Ptnrs: J. F. J. K. & W. P. Eagles.
Fleet: 15 - 6 double-deck bus, 7 coach, 2 minibus.
Chassis: 6 Bristol. 2 Dennis. 1 Freight Rover. 4 Leyland. 1 Mercedes. 1 Toyota. 1 Van Hool.
Bodies: 1 Caetano. 1 Carlyle. 3 Duple. 6 ECW. 1 Mercedes. 1 Optare. 3 Plaxton. 1 Van Hool.
Ops incl: local bus services, excursions & tours, private hire, continental tours.
Livery: White/Blue/Orange.
Ticket System: Almex.

FOUR GIRLS COACHES
THE OLD POST OFFICE YARD, CORWEN ROAD, PONTYBODKIN, MOLD CH7 4TG
Tel: 01352 770438
Fax: 01352 770253
Ptnrs: Carolyn Thomas, Elaine Williams
Fleet: 9 - 7 coach, 1 minibus, 1 midicoach.
Chassis: 1 DAF. 1 LDV. 6 Volvo.
Bodies: incl: 1 Caetano
Ops incl: school contracts, private hire.
Livery: Turquoise/Red/Yellow

JONES MOTOR SERVICES
CHESTER ROAD, FLINT CH6 5DZ.
Tel: 01352 733292.
Fax: 01352 763353.
E-mail: tours@jonescoaches.co.uk
Web site: www.jonesholidays.co.uk
Ptnr: A. Jones.
Fleet: 10 - 9 coach, 1 midicoach.
Chassis: DAF, Iveco, Leyland.
Bodies: Caetano, Duple, Plaxton, Van Hool.
Ops incl: excursions & tours, private hire, express, continental tours, school contracts.
Livery: Blue.

OARE'S COACHES
TY DRAW. BRYNFORD, HOLYWELL CH8 8LP.
Tel: 01352 713339.
Fax: 01352 714871.
Prop: G. A. Oare.
Livery: White/Red/Silver.
Ops incl: local bus services

P. & O. LLOYD
RHYDWEN GARAGE, BAGILLT CH6 6JJ.
Tel: 01352 710682.
Man Dir: David Lloyd.
Fleet: 36 - 17 double-deck bus, 4 single-deck bus. 6 coach, 7 minibus.
Chassis: incl: Optare. Leyland. Volvo.
Bodies: incl: MCW. East Lancs. MCW. Optare. Plaxton. Van Hool.
Ops incl: local bus services, private hire, school contracts.

Livery: Cream/Red or Cream/Maroon/Gold.
Ticket System: Almex.

PIED BULL COACHES
53 WOODLANDS CLOSE, MOLD CH7 1UU.
Tel/Fax: 01352 754237.
Prop: R. Williams.
Livery: Blue/White.

TOWNLYNX
CAETIA LLWYD, NORTHOP ROAD, HOLYWELL CH8 8AE.
Tel: 01352 710489.
Prop: S. A. Lee.

GWYNEDD

ARVONIA COACHES
THE SQUARE, LLANRUG LL55 4AA.
Tel: 01286 675175.
Fax: 01286 671126.
E-mail: info@arvoniacoaches.co.uk
Web site: www.arvonia.co.uk
Prop: R. Morris.
Fleet: 9 - 6 coach, 2 midibus, 1 minibus.
Chassis: 1 Ford Transit. 1 MAN. 1 Mercedes. 1 Volvo. 3 EOS. 2 Van Hool.
Bodies: 2 Alexander. 1 Carlyle. 2 Van Hool. 3 EOS. 1 Noge.
Ops incl: Excursions & tours, private hire, continental tours.
Livery: White/Orange/Red.
Ticket System: Almex.

CERBYDAU BERWYN COACHES
BERWYN, TREFOR LL54 5LY
Tel: 01286 660315.
Fax: 01286 660110.
Prop: B. Japheth.
Livery: White/Yellow/Brown.

CAELLOI MOTORS
(T. H. JONES & SON)
UNIT 17, GLAN Y DON INDUSTRIAL ESTATE, PWLLHELI LL53 5YT
Tel: 01758 612719

Fax: 01758 612335
Fleet: 6 - 2 single-deck bus, 4 coach
Chassis: 1 DAF. 1 Marshall. 4 Volvo.
Bodies: 1 Berkhof. 1 Marshall. 3 Van Hool. 1 Wright.
Ops incl: local bus services, excursions & tours, private hire, continental tours
Livery: Multi
Ticket System: Almex

CLYNNOG & TREFOR
R24
TREFOR, CAERNARFON LL54 5HP
Tel: 01286 660208
Fax: 01286 660538
Dirs: D C Jones, E Griffiths **Com Sec**: I Williams
Fleet: 34 - 10 double-deck bus, 1 single-deck bus, 12 single-deck coach, 1 midicoach, 10 minibus.
Chassis: 1 Dennis. 11 Leyland. 12 Mercedes-Benz. 11 Vovo.
Bodies: 11 Alexander Dennis. 1 Berkof. 5 ECW. 5 Jonckheere. 1 Mercedes-Benz. 5 Northern Counties. 5 Plaxton
Ops incl: local bus services, school contracts, private hire.
Livery: White
Ticket system: Wayfarer TGX

EMMAS COACHES
BAKER STREET GARAGE, MARIAN ROAD, DOLGELLAU LL40 1EL
Tel: 01341 423934
Fax: 01341 423321
E-mail: info@emmascoaches.co.uk
Web site: www.emmascoaches.co.uk
Dir/Prop: Barry Thomas, **Sec**: Anita Thomas **Tran Man**: Brett Thomas
Fleet: 11 - 1 single-deck bus, 5 coach, 1 double-deck coach, 1 midicoach, 2 minibus, 1 people carrier.
Chassis: 1 Bedford. 1 DAF. 1 Ford. 2 Leyland. 1 Leyland National. 2 Mercedes. 2 Scania. 1 Toyota.
Bodies: 1 Caetano. 2 Mercedes. 1 Optare. 23 Plaxton. 3 Van Hool. 1 other
Ops incl: local bus services, school contracts, excursions & tours, continental tours.
Livery: Green

EXPRESS MOTORS
R24
GERRALT, BONTNEWYDD,
CAERNARFON LL54 UN
Tel: 01286 881108
Fax: 01286 882331
Recovery: 01286 880218
Web site: www.expressmotors.co.uk
E-mail: jones14@btconnect.com
Ptnrs: Eric Wyn Jones
Fleet: 40 - 2 double-deck bus, 8 single-deck bus, 9 single-deck coach, 2 double-deck coach, 1 open-top bus, 12 midibus, 1 midicoach, 2minibus, 3 minicoach.
Chassis: 1 Bedford. 2 Bova. 16 MAN. 3 Neoplan.
Bodies: 10 Mercedes-Benz. 3 Van Hool. 5 Other.
Ops incl: local bus services, excursions & tours, private hire.
Livery: White with transfer
Ticket System: Wayfarer 3

GRIFFITHS COACHES
3 ELIM COTTAGES, SILOH,
PORTDINORWIC LL56 4JR
Tel: 01248 670530
Fax: 01248 671111
Prop: Hefin Griffiths
Fleet: 11 - 5 double-deck bus, 1 single-deck bus, 5 coach.
Chassis: 5 Bristol. 1 Leyland. 5 Volvo.
Bodies: 1 Berkhof. 5 ECW. 3 Jonckheere. 1 Plaxton. 1 Van Hool.
Ops incl: private hire, school contracts.
Livery: Red/Grey/White

JOHN'S COACHES
NORTH WESTERN ROAD, GLAN-Y-PWLL, BLAENEAU FFESTINIOG LL41 3NN
Tel: 01766 831781
Mobile: 0777 167735
Fax: 01766 831781
Prop: J R Edwards
Fleet: 6
Chassis: 1 Berkhof. 3 DAF. 2 Mercedes.
Bodies: Berkhof. Mercedes. Plaxton.
Ops incl: local bus service, school contracts, private hire.
Livery: White/Red
Ticket System: Wayfarer

NEFYN COACHES
WEST END GARAGE, ST DAVIDS ROAD, NEFYN LL53 6HE.
Tel: 01758 720904.
Fax: 01758 720331.
Props: B. G. Owen, M. A. Owen, A. G. Owen.
Fleet: 9 - 1 single-deck bus, 4 coach, 4 minicoach.
Chassis: 1 Freight Rover. 1 Leyland. 3 Mercedes. 3 Volvo. 1 Optare.
Bodies: Reeve Burgess, Plaxton.
Ops incl: local bus services, excursions & tours, private hire.
Livery: Multi-colour.

PADARN BUS
PADARN VIEW, HIGH STREET,
LLANBERIS, LL55 4EN.
Tel: 01286 871347.
Fax: 01286 872121.
E-mail: info@padarnbus.co.uk
Web site: www.padarnbus.co.uk
Props: D & D Price
Ops incl: local bus services, school contracts, excursions & tours, private hire.
Livery: Red.

SILVER STAR COACH HOLIDAYS LTD
13 CASTLE SQUARE, CAERNARFON LL55 2NF
Tel: 01286 672333
Fax: 01286 678118
E-mail: enquiries@silverstarholidays.com
Web site: www.silverstarholidays.com
Man Dir: Elfyn William Thomas **Co Sec**: Helen Jones **Ch Eng**: Barry Thomas **Ops Man**: Eric Wyn Thomas
Fleet: 18 - 5 single-deck bus, 9 coach, 4 midibus. 1 vintage.
Chassis: 1 AEC. 1 Bedford, 3 Bristol. 3 Dennis. 1 Leyland. 8 Mercedes. 3 Neoplan. 1 Optare. 2 Setra. 2 Volvo.
Bodies: 1 Alexander. 3 ECW. 3 Neoplan. 1 Optare. 25 Plaxton. 2 Setra. 2 Van Hool. 1 Burlingham.
Ops incl: local bus services, school contracts, excursions & tours, private hire, continental tours.
Livery: Green coaches/Blue buses.
Ticket System: Wayfarer 3

MERTHYR TYDFIL

SIXTY SIXTY COACHES
THE COACH DEPOT, MERTHYR INDUSTRIAL PARK, PENTREBACH CF48 4DR
Tel: 01443 692060.
Fax: 01443 699061.
E-mail: enquiries@sixsixty.co.uk
Web site: www.sixtysixty.co.uk
Prop: G Handy, C T Handy.
Fleet: 18 - 3 single-deck bus, 9 coach, 2 double-deck coach, 3 midibus, 1 midicoach
Chassis: 6 DAF. 3 Dennis. 1 Leyland. 3 Mercedes. 2 Scania. 3 Volvo.
Bodies: 3 Alexander. 2 Caetano. 1 Duple. 3 Plaxton. 3 Reeve Burgess. 5 Van Hool. 1 LAG.
Ops incl: local bus services, school contracts, excursions & tours, private hire.
Livery: Silver
Ticket system: Wayfarer

STAGECOACH IN SOUTH WALES
See Torfaen

MONMOUTHSHIRE

REES COACH TRAVEL
WAUNLAPRA, LLANELLY HILL,
ABERGAVENNY NP7 0PW
Tel: 01873 830210
Fax: 01873 832167
Recovery: 01873 830210
Snr Prtnr: N A Rees **Ptnrs**: N A Rees, Mrs M E Rees
Fleet: 10 - 9 single-deck coach, 1 minicoach.
Chassis: 3 DAF. 2 Dennis. 10 Ford Transit. 1MAN. 2 Mercedes-Benz. 2 Neoplan. 1 Setra. 1 Toyota
Bodies: 2 Alexander Dennis. 1 Caetano. 2 Jonckheere. 2 Neoplan. 1 Setra. 3 Van Hool.
Ops incl: local bus services, school contracts, excursions & tours, private hire.
Livery: Green/White

STAGECOACH IN SOUTH WALES
See Torfaen

NEATH & PORT TALBOT

BLUEBIRD OF NEATH/ PONTARDAWE
9-10 LONDON ROAD, NEATH SA11 1HB.
Tel/Fax: 01639 643849.
Fleetname: Bluebird Coaches (Neath).
Prop: Ian S. Warren. **Ch Eng**: George Warren. **Sec**: Ms Melanie Evans.
Fleet: 21 - 2 double-deck bus, 18 coach, 1 midibus.
Chassis: 2 Bristol. 1 DAF. 1 Mercedes. 17 Volvo.
Bodies: 4 Jonckheere. 1 Mercedes. Leyland. 10 Plaxton. 6 Van Hool.
Ops incl: local bus services, excursions & tours, private hire, continental tours, school contracts.
Livery: White/Blue/Red.

NELSON & SON (GLYNNEATH) LTD
74A HIGH STREET, GLYNNEATH SA11 5AW.
Tel: 01639 720308.
Fax: 01639 721949.
E-Mail: nelsoncoaches@aol.com
Fleetname: Nelson's Coaches.
Man Dir: J. L. R. Nelson **Comp Sec**: Mrs J Nelson **Fleet Eng**: P Watkins **TSP Man**: G Powell
Fleet: 15 - 12 single-deck coach, 3 midicoach.
Chassis: 4 Bova. 4 DAF. 3 Dennis. 1 Irisbus. 2 Mercedes-Benz.
Bodies: 1 Autobus. 4 Bova. 1 Mashall/MCV. 6 Plaxton. 3 Van Hool.
Ops incl: school contracts, excursions & tours, private hire, continental tours.
Livery: White/Red/Orange.

D J THOMAS COACHES LTD
MILLAND ROAD INDUSTRIAL ESTATE, NEATH SA11 1NJ
Tel/Fax: 01639 635502
E-mail: mail@djthomascoaches.co.uk
Web site: www.djthomascoaches.co.uk
Man Dir/Co Sec: Mrs Andrea Gibson
Man Dir: Richard Thomas **Ch Eng**: Lee Gibson
Fleet: 18 - 1 single-deck bus, 9 coach, 3 minicoach, 3 midicoach, 2 minibus.
Chassis: Ford. Ford Transit Tourneo. Mercedes. Renault. Volvo.
Bodies: Berkhof. Mercedes. Plaxton. Van Hool.
Ops incl: local bus services, excursions & tours, private hire, school contracts.
Ticket system: Wayfarer

WELSH OPERATORS

207

TONNA LUXURY COACHES LTD
TENNIS VIEW GARAGE, HEOL-Y-GLO, TONNA SA11 3NJ
Tel: 01639 642727
Fax: 01639 646052
Dirs: K M Hopkins, A Hopkins
Fleet: 16 coach.
Chassis: 1 DAF. 1 Dennis. 3 Mercedes. 11 Volvo.
Bodies: incl: 1 Alexander. Plaxton. Van Hool.
Ops incl: school contracts, private hire.
Livery: White/Blue

NEWPORT

NEWPORT TRANSPORT LTD
160 CORPORATION ROAD, NEWPORT NP19 0WF
Tel: 01633 670563
Fax: 01633 242589
Web site: www.newporttransport.co.uk
E-mail: enquiries@newporttransport.co.uk
Fleetname: Newport Bus
Chmn: J G J Dally **Man Dir**: T G Roberts
Dir of Delivery: C D Blyth **Fin Dir**: D Jenkins
Fleet: 76 - 6 double-deck bus, 51 single-deck bus, 7 coach, 1 open-top bus, 11 midibus.
Chassis: 17 Dennis. 59 Scania.
Bodies: 42 Alexander. 7 Irizar. 9 Wright. 18 Scania.
Ops incl: local bus services, school contracts, excursions & tours, private hire.
Livery: Green/Cream.
Ticket System: Wayfarer TGX150

STAGECOACH IN SOUTH WALES
See Torfaen

WELSH DRAGON TRAVEL
21 BEAUFORT ROAD, NEWPORT NP19 7ND.
Tel: 01633 761397
E-mail: alan.smith5@ntworld.com
Prop: Alan Barrington Smith.
Fleet: 4 - 1 double-deck bus, 2 coach, 1 open-top bus.
Chassis: 1 Bedford. 1 Bristol. 2 Leyland.
Ops incl: local bus services, school contracts, private hire.
Livery: Red/Cream
Ticket System: Almex

PEMBROKESHIRE

W. H. COLLINS
CUFFERN GARAGE, ROCH, HAVERFORDWEST SA62 6HB.
Tel: 01437 710337.
Fleetname: Collins Coaches.
Prop: P. N. & M. Collins.
Fleet: 18 - 16 minibus, 2 minicoach.
Ops incl: school contracts, private hire.
Livery: Blue/Grey/White.

EDWARDS BROS
THE GARAGE, BROAD HAVEN ROAD, TIERS CROSS, HAVERFORDWEST SA62 3BZ
Tel: 01437 890230
Fax: 01437 890337
Prop: Robert Edwards
Fleet: 18 - 8 coach, 3 midibus, 4 midicoach, 3 minibus.
Chassis: 1 Bova. 1 DAF. 1 Dennis. 2 LDV. 7 Mercedes. 6 Volvo.
Bodies: 1 Bova. 1 Marshall/MCV. 3 Mercedes. 7 Plaxton. 1 Reeve Burgess. 3 Van Hool. 2 other.
Ops incl: local bus services, school contracts, private hire.
Livery: Gold or White.
Ticket System: Wayfarer

MIDWAY MOTORS
MIDWAY GARAGE, CRYMYCH SA41 3QU
Tel: 01239 831267
Fax: 01239 831279
E-mail: reesmidway@hotmail.com
Fleetname: W S Rees & Son
Props: Wyndham Rees, Elan Rees
Fleet: 14 - 2 single-deck bus, 8 single-deck coach, 2 midicoach, 1 minibus, 1 minicoach.
Chassis: 4 Dennis. 1 Ford. 1 LDV. 2 Mercedes-Benz. 1 Renault. 1 Toyota. 4 Volvo.
Bodies: 2 Alexander Dennis. 1 Berkof. 3 Caetano. 1 Mellor. 5 Plaxton. 1 Willowbrook. 1 Other.
Ops incl: local bus services, school contracts, excursions & tours, private hire, continental tours.
Livery: Silver/Blue
Ticket system: Wayfarer

SILCOX MOTOR COACH CO LTD
WATERLOO GARAGE, PEMBROKE DOCK SA72 4RR.
Tel: 01646 683143.
Fax: 01646 621787.
Web: www.silcoxcoaches.co.uk
E-mail: travel@silcoxcoaches.co.uk
Man Dir: K. W. Silcox **Dir**: J Silcox **Traffic Man**: H J Dix **Coach Hire Man**: P Daley
Fleet: 80 - 44 single-deck bus, 19 single-deck coach, 12 midibus, 5 minibus.
Chassis: 1 Aexander Dennis. 1 Bova. 18 Dennis. 2 LDV. 31 Leyland. 1 MAN. 17 Mercedes-Benz. 4 Optare. 1 Renault. 1 Transbus. 6 Volvo.
Bodies: 1 Alexander Dennis. 3 Berkhof. 5 Caetano. 2 Marco Polo. 1 MCW. 4 Optare. 31 Plaxton. 2 UVG.
Ops incl: local bus services, school contracts, excursions & tours, private hire, continental tours.
Livery: Red/Cream.
Ticket System: Wayfarer

SUMMERDALE COACHES
SUMMERDALE GARAGE, LETTERSTON SA62 5UB.
Tel: 01348 840270.
Props: D. G. Davies, B. J. L. Davies, G. R. Jones.
Livery: Yellow/Blue

POWYS

A. & E. HIRE
PENYBRYN, LLANGYNIEW, WELSHPOOL SY21 0JS
Tel: 01938 810518
Dir: Arwyn P Davies
Fleet: 5 minibus
Chassis/bodies: 4 Ford. 1 Freight Rover.
Ops incl: school contracts, private hire

ROY BROWNS COACHES
15 HIGH STREET, BUILTH WELLS LD2 3DN
Tel: 01982 552597
Tel: 01982 552286
E-mail: neil@rbci.fsnet.co.uk
Web site: www.roybrownscoaches.co.uk
Prop: N W Brown **Ops Man**: P H Davies
Fleet: 28 - 6 single-deck bus, 12 coach, 10 minibus.
Chassis: 4 Bedford. 5 DAF. 2 Dennis. 7 Leyland. 3 Optare. 1 Volvo.
Bodies: 4 Caetano. 4 MCW. 10 Plaxton. 1 Wright. 1 other.
Ops incl: local bus services, school contracts, excursions & tours, private hire.
Ticket System: Setright.

CELTIC TRAVEL
NEW STREET, LLANIDLOES SY18 6EH
Tel/Fax: 01686 412231
E-mail: info@celtictravel.net
Web site: www.celtictravel.net
Props: W P L Davies, Mrs J Davies **Ops Man**: P Davies
Fleet: 22 - 15 coach, 7 minibus.
Chassis: 2 Dennis. 7 Ford Transit. 3 Leyland. 10 Volvo
Bodies: 2 Duple. 1 Jonckheere. 7 Plaxton. 3 Van Hool. 2 Wadham Stringer.
Ops incl: school contracts, excursions & tours, private hire.
Livery: Grey with green/red lettering

CENTRAL TRAVEL
OLD BULK YARD, STATION YARD, NEWTOWN SY16 1BA
Tel: 07710 432832
Tel/Fax: 01686 610224
Props: Richard W Bowen
Fleet: 4 - 1 coach, 1 midicoach, 1 minicoach, 1 minibus.
Chassis: 1 Ford Transit. 1 Mercedes. 1 Scania. 1 Volvo
Bodies: 1 Mercedes. 1 Plaxton. 1 Van Hool.
Ops incl: school contracts, private hire.

COACHING CONNECTION
14 GREAT OAK STREET, LLANIDLOES SY18 6BN
Tel: 01686 413714
Fax: 01686 411065
Props: David Corfield, Miss Betty Tonks
Fleet: 1 coach
Chassis/Body: Setra
Ops incl: excursions & tours.
Livery: Cream with orange/brown flashes.

D G DAVIES
AFON MARTEG GARAGE, PANT-Y-DWR LD6 5NA
Tel: 05978 8232
Prop: D G Davies
Fleet: 2
Chassis: Ford.
Bodies: Duple, Plaxton
Ops incl: school contracts, private hire.
Livery: White with red/blue flashing

R G GITTINS - COACHES
THE GARAGE, DOLANOG, WELSHPOOL SY21 0LQ
Tel/fax: 01938 810439
Prop: R G Gittins
Fleet: 3 - 1 coach, 1 midibus, 1 midicoach
Chassis: 1 Bova. 1 MAN. 1 Mercedes.
Ops incl: school contracts, excursions & tours, private hire.

GWYN JONES (MEIFORD)
THE GARAGE, MEIFOD SY22 6DB
Tel: 01938 500249
E-mail: gwynmeifod@talk21.com
Ptnrs: Gwyn Jones, Jean Jones, Martin Jones
Fleet: 3 - 2 single-deck bus, 1 midicoach.
Chassis/Bodies: 1 DAF. 1 Caetano. 1 Mercedes.
Ops incl: school contracts, excursions & tours, private hire, continental tours.
Livery: Green/White

LAKELINE COACHES
EBRAN-DDU, FELINDRE, KNIGHTON LD7 1YN
Tel: 01547 7662
Dir: J E A Lakelin
Fleet: 4 - 3 coach, 1 minibus.
Chassis: 1 Bedford. 1 DAF. 1 Dennis. 1 Ford.
Bodies: 1 Duple. 1 LDV. 2 Plaxton.
Ops incl: school contracts, private hire
Livery: Pale Blue/Dark Blue

LLOYDS COACHES
R24
OLD CROSVILLE GARAGE, DOLL STREET, MACHYNLLETH SY20 8BH
Tel: 01654 702100
Fax: 01654 703900
E-mail: info@llyodscoaches.com
Web: www.llyodscoaches.com
Proprietor: D W LLoyd
Fleet: 23 - 2 single-deck bus, 8 single-deck coach, 5 midibus. 3 midicoach, 5 minibus
Chassis: 3 Ford. 9 Mercedes-Benz. 2 Optare. 9 Volvo.
Bodies: 2 Alexander Dennis. 2 Mercedes-Benz. 2 Optare. 14 Plaxton. 3 Other.
Ops incl: local bus services, school contracts, private hire.
Livery: Silver
Ticket system: Wayfarer

OWEN'S MOTORS LTD
TEMESIDE HOUSE, STATION ROAD, KNIGHTON LD7 1DT
Tel: 01547 528303
Fax: 01547 520512
Web site: www.owensmotors.co.uk
Ops Man: D. Owen. **Ch Eng**: T Owen.
Sec/Dir: J Owen
Fleet: 14 - 11 coach, 3 minibus.
Chassis: 3 Dennis. 1 Ford. 2 LDV. 7 Volvo.
Bodies: 2 Duple. 1 Ford Transit. 2 LDV. 8 Plaxton. 1 Van Hool.
Ops incl: local bus services, school contracts, excursions & tours, private hire, continental tours.
Livery: Blue/Grey

STAGECOACH IN SOUTH WALES
See Torfaen

STOCKHAMS COACH, MINIBUS & TAXIS
19 PLASDERWEN, LLANGATTOCK, CRICKHOWELL NP8 1HY
Tel: 01873 810559
Fax: 01873 810343
Dirs: Mrs Nancy Stockham, Melvyn Stockham, Derek Stockham
Fleet: 6 - 3 single-deck bus, 2 minibus, 1 minicoach.
Chassis: 2 Ford Transit. 1 Iveco. 1 Leyland. 2 Volvo
Ops incl: excursions & tours, private hire.
Livery: Green/Cream

STRATOS TRAVEL
2 SHORTBRIDGE STREET, NEWTOWN SY16 2LW
Tel: 01686 629021
Fax: 01686 626092
E-mail: info@stratostravel.co.uk
Web site: www.stratostravel.co.uk
Prop: M Owen
Fleet: 5 - 1 single-deck bus, 3 coach, 1 midicoach.
Chassis: 1 Ayats. 1 Bova. 1 Dennis. 1 Iveco.1 Toyota.
Bodies: 1 Ayats. 1 Beulas. 1 Bova. 1 Caetano. 1 Plaxton.
Ops incl: local bus services, excursions & tours, private hire, continental tours.
Livery: Silver/Blue
Subsidiary of Owens Coaches Ltd, Shropshire

TANAT VALLEY COACHES
THE GARAGE, LLANRHAEDR YM MOCHNANT, OSWESTRY SY10 0AD
Tel: 01691 780212
Fax: 01691 780634
E-mail: info@tanat.co.uk
Web site: www.tanat.co.uk
Dirs: Michael Morris, Peter Morris, **Ops Man**: Nick Culliford **Ops Foreman**: Phil Jones.
Fleet: 47 - 4 double-deck bus, 17 single-deck bus, 14 single-deck coach, 6 midibus, 3 midicoach, 3 minibus.
Chassis: 2 Alexander Dennis. 3 Dennis. 4 LDV. 15 Leyland. 7 Mercedes-Benz. 4 Optare. 13 Volvo.
Bodies: 4 Alexander. 1 Beulas. 1 Berkhof. 1 Caetano. 2 Carlyle. 2 Duple. 4 East Lancs. 3 Jonckheere. 6 Leyland. 4 Northern Counties. 4 Optare. 6 Plaxton. 2 UVG. 2 Wadham Stringer. 4 Other.
Ops incl: local bus services, school contracts, excursions & tours, private hire, express, continental tours.
Livery: Maroon/Beige
Ticket System: Almex

WILLIAMS COACHES
R24 T
CAMBRIAN WAY, BRECON LD3 7BE
Tel: 01874 622223
Fax: 01874 625218
Recovery: 01874 611534
E-mail: office@williams-coaches.co.uk
Web site: www.williams-coaches.co.uk
Fleet: 26 - 17 single-deck coach, 4 midicoach, 5 minibus.
Chassis: 2 Autosan. 1 Bova. 2 DAF. 1 Dennis. 4 Ford Transit. 1 Irisbus.1 Iveco. 3 MAN. 7 Mercedes-Benz. 1 Neoplan. 1 Optare. 1 Renault. 3 Scania. 7 Setra. 1 Volkswagen.
Bodies: 1 Bova. 1 Caetano. 1 Indcar. 3 Irizar. 1 Jonckheere. 1 Mercedes-Benz. 1 Neoplan. 2 Optare. 1 Plaxton. 7 Setra. 1 Van Hool. 6 Other
Ops incl: school contracts, private hire, excursions & tours, continental tours.
Livery: Cream/Brown- Orange Reliefs

RHONDDA, CYNON, TAFF

BEBB TRAVEL PLC
THE COACH STATION, LLANTWIT FARDRE CF38 2HB
Tel: 01443 215100
Fax: 01443 215134
Web site: www.veolia-transport.co.uk
Chmn: John O'Brien **Man Dir**: Charles Lewis **Fleet Eng**: Dave Witte
Fleet: 44 - 26 single-deck bus, 18 coach.
Chassis: 26 Optare. 18 Volvo.
Bodies: 26 Optare. 18 Plaxton.
Ops incl: local bus services, school contracts, express
Livery: White/Blue/Red/Green
Ticket system: ERG
(Part of Veolia Transport Cymru)

EDWARDS COACHES
R T
NEWTOWN INDUSTRIAL ESTATE, LLANTWIT FARDRE CF38 2EE
Tel: 01443 202048
Fax: 01443 217583
E-mail: admin@edwardscoaches.co.uk
Web site: www.edwardscoaches.co.uk
Owner: Mike Edwards **Dirs**: Shaun Edwards, Jason Edwards, Kelly Edwards, Jessica Edwards
Fleet: 84 - 28 double-deck bus, 47 coach, 5 midicoach, 4 minibus.
Chassis: 14 MCW. 14 Volkswagen.
Bodies: 13 Bova. 7 Irizar. 2 Jonckheere. 5 Marcopolo. 14 MCW. 1 Mellor. 5 Plaxton. 6 Setra.
Ops incl: school contracts, excursions & tours, private hire, continental tours.
Livery: White/Blue

WELSH OPERATORS

209

WELSH OPERATORS

GLOBE COACHES
BROOKLANDS, FFORCHNEOL ROW, GODREAMAN, ABERDARE CF44 6HD.
Tel: 01685 873622.
Fax: 01685 876526
E-mail: wayne@globecoaches.entadsl.com
Web site: www.globecoaches.co.uk
Prop: Wayne Jarvis
Fleet: 18 - 16 coach, 2 midicoach.
Chassis: 2 DAF. 1 Leyland. 1 MAN. 2 Mercedes. 12 Volvo.
Bodies: 2 Berkhof. 2 Caetano. 2 Duple. 6 Jonckheere. 4 Plaxton.
Ops incl: excursions & tours, private hire, school contracts, continental tours.
Livery: White/Blue.

MAISEY
GELYNOG YARD, CASTELLAU ROAD, BEDDAU CF38 1ND
Tel/Fax: 01443 205462
E-mail: info@maiseybus.co.uk
Web site: www.maiseybus.co.uk
Ptnrs: Brian Evans, Graham Evans, Colin Evans.
Fleet: 10 minicoach.
Chassis: 2 Ford. 1 LDV. 7 Renault.
Bodies: 10 other
Ops incl: school contracts, private hire.
Livery: White/Red

STAGECOACH IN SOUTH WALES
See Torfaen

THOMAS OF RHONDDA
BUS DEPOT, PORTH CF39 0AG.
Tel: 01443 433714
Fax: 01443 436542
Proprietors: W A Thomas, I G Thomas, J E Thomas, T D Thomas, K D Thomas. A A Thomas.
Fleet: 57 - 20 double-deck bus, 2 single-deck bus, 20 single-deck coach, 3 double-deck coach, 6 midibus, 1 midicoach, 5 minibus.
Chassis: 4 Bova. 4 DAF. 5 Dennis. 3 Ford. 20 Leyland. 5 Mercedes-Benz. 8 Volvo.
Ops incl: local bus services, excursions & tours, school contracts, private hire, continental tours.
Ticket System: Almex

CITY & COUNTY OF SWANSEA

DIAMOND HOLIDAYS
COACH HOLIDAY CENTRE, 22 FERRYBOAT CLOSE, SWANSEA ENTERPRISE PARK, SWANSEA SA6 8QN
Tel: 01792 791918
Fax: 01792 764829
E-mail: reservations@diamondholidays.co.uk
Web site: www.diamondholidays.co.uk
Man Dir: Chris Roberts. **Ops Dir**: Ryan

Jones **Trans Man**: Stewart Isaac
Fleet: 14 - 13 single-deck coach, 1 minibus.
Chassis: 14 DAF.
Bodies: 14 Bova.
Ops incl: excursions & tours, private hire, express, continental tours.
Livery: Gold/Silver/Black.

FIRST CYMRU BUSES LIMITED
HEOL GWYROSYDD, PENLAN SA5 7BN
Tel: 01792 582233
Fax: 01792 561356
Web Site: www.firstgroup.com
Man Dir: Tony McNiff **Interim Ops Dir**: Mrs C Morgan **Fin Dir**: T McNiff **Ops Dir**: P F Collier **Eng Dir**: P J Davies
Fleet: 360 - 3 double-deck bus, 25 single-deck bus, 45 coach, 270 midcoach, 17 minibus.
Chassis: 6 BMC. 296 Dennis. 3 Iveco. 3 Leyland. 14 Mercedes. 3 Optare. 4 Scania. 31 Volvo.
Bodies: 16 Alexander. 6 BMC. 4 Caetano. 1 Carlyle. 3 Ikarus. 42 Marshall/MCV. 1 Northern Counties. 3 Optare. 279 Plaxton. 4 Reeve Burgess. 1 Willowbrook.
Ops incl: local bus services, school contracts, excursions & tours, private hire, express.
Livery: FirstGroup.
Ticket System: Wayfarer III

PULLMAN COACHES LTD
UNIT 41, PENCLAWDD INDUSTRIAL ESTATE, CROFTY SA4 3RT.
Tel: 01792 851430
Web site: www.veolia-transport.co.uk
Man Dir: Charles Lewis
Dirs: C. W. Lewis, H. S. Rees.
Fleet: 34 - 8 single-deck bus, 25 coach, 1 minicoach.
Livery: Cream/White/Red/Fawn
(Part of Veolia Transport Cymru)

TORFAEN

B'S TRAVEL
13 EAST VIEW, GRIFFITHSTOWN NP4 5DW.
Tel/Fax: 01495 756889.
E-mail: kay@bstravel.fsnet.co.uk
Ptnrs: James Benning, Kay Benning.
Fleet: 4 - 1 coach, 1 midicoach, 1 minibus, 1 minicoach.
Chassis: 1 LDV. 1 MAN. 2 Mercedes.
Bodies: 1 Autobus. 1 Jonckheere. 1 Gem. 1 LDV.
Ops incl: private hire, school contracts.
Livery: White

JENSON TRAVEL
UNIT 10, PONTNEWYNDD INDUSTRIAL ESTATE, PONTNEWYNDD,

PONTYPOOL NP4 6YW
Tel/Fax: 01495 760539
E-mail: jenson01@btconnect.com
Tran Man: Nicola Jenkins **Props**: Gwyn & Nicola Jenkins **Ch Eng**: Peter Ryan
Fleet: 19
Chassis: 6 Dennis. 3 LDV. 1 MAN. 5 Mercedes. 1 Peugeot. 3 Volvo.
Bodies: 2 Jonckheere. 1 EOS. 3 LDV. 1 Optare. 1 Plaxton. 1 Renault. 4 Reeve Burgess. 1 Wadham Stringer.
Ops incl: school contracts, excursions & tours, private hire.
Livery: White with Blue logo

SABRE COACHES
12 ST HILDA'S ROAD, GRIFFITHSTOWN, PONTYPOOL NP4 5HN
Tel: 01495 753051.
E-mail: enquiries@sabrecoaches.com
Web: www.sabrecoaches.com
Prop: L Murphy
Ops incl: Private hire.

STAGECOACH IN SOUTH WALES
1 ST DAVID'S ROAD, CWMBRAN NP44 1PD
Tel: 01633 838856
Fax: 01633 865299
Web site: www.stagecoachbus.com
Man Dir: John Gould **Comm Dir**: Richard Davies **Eng Dir**: David Howe
Fleet: 346 - 4 double-deck bus, 52 single-deck bus, 39 single-deck coach, 156 midibus, 95 minibus.
Chassis: 3 BMC. 128 Dennis. 34 Mercedes-Benz. 80 Optare. 14 Transbus. 87 Volvo.
Bodies: 137 Alexander. 3 BMC. 6 Caetano. 1 Jonckheere. 8 Marshall/MCV. 16 Northern Counties. 82 Optare. 72 Plaxton. 14 Transbus. 6 UVG. 1 Wright.
Ops incl: local bus services, school contracts, express.
Livery: Stagecoach

VALE OF GLAMORGAN

EST BUS LTD
UNIT 2, CROSSWAYS IND ESTATE, LLANTWIT MAJOR ROAD, COWBRIDGE CF71 7LJ
Tel: 01446 773333
Web site: estcoachbus.com
Dir: C Hookings
Ops incl: local bus services, school contracts
Livery: Maroon/Cream

HAYWARD TRAVEL (CARDIFF)
2 MURCH CRESCENT, DINAS POWYS CF64 4RF
Tel. 029 2051 5551
Fax: 029 2051 5113
E-mail: info@haywardtravel.co.uk
Web site: www.haywardtravel.co.uk
Ops incl: private hire

♿	Vehicle suitable for disabled	Seat belt-fitted Vehicle	R24	24 hour recovery service
T	Toilet-drop facilities available	Coach(es) with galley facilities	Replacement vehicle available
R	Recovery service available	Air-conditioned vehicle(s)	Vintage Coach(es) available
	Open top vehicle(s)v	Coaches with toilet facilities	

THOMAS OF BARRY
12 PARK CRESCENT, BARRY CF62 6HD
Tel/Recovery: 01446 722800
Fax: 01446 722766
Web site: www.veolia-transport.co.uk
Man Dir: Charles Lewis
Fleet: 71 - 5 double-deck bus, 15 single-deck bus, 30 coach, 2 double-deck coach, 4 open-top bus, 5 midibus, 3 midicoach, 2 minibus, 5 minicoach.
Chassis: 20 Dennis. 2 Irisbus. 2 MAN. 20 Mercedes. 5 Optare. 20 Scania. 2 Volvo.
Bodies: 4 Beulas. 3 Caetano. 5 Duple. 12 Irizar. 6 Leyland. 5 MCW. 9 Mercedes. 15 Plaxton. 2 Sunsundegui. 3 UVG. 6 Van Hool.
Ops incl: local bus services, school contracts, excursions & tours, private hire, express, continental tours.
Livery: White/Maroon.
Ticket System: Wayfarer 3
(part of Veolia Transport Cymru)

WREXHAM

ACTON COACHES
109 HERBERT JENNING AVENUE, ACTON PARK LL12 7YA
Tel/Fax: 01978 352470
Prop: D B Evans.
Fleet: 4 - 3 coach, 1 midibus
Chassis: 1 DAF. 2 Volvo. 1 Mercedes.
Bodies: 1 Plaxton. 1 Caetano. 1 Van Hool. 1 Optare.
Livery: Blue/White
Ops incl: school contracts, private hire

GEORGE EDWARDS & SON
BERWYN, BWLCHGWYN LL11 5UE.
Tel/Fax: 01978 757281
Props: G F & G Edwards.
Fleet: 7 - coaches
Chassis: 1 DAF
Bodies: 2 Duple. 1 Optare. 4 Van Hool
Ops incl: School contracts, private hire.
Livery: Red/Ivory/Maroon

GHA COACHES
UNIT 11, VAUXHALL INDUSTRIAL ESTATE, RUABON,
WREXHAM LL14 6UY.
Tel: 01978 820820
E-mail: enquiries@ghacoaches.co.uk
Web site: www.ghacoaches.co.uk
Props: E G & A Lloyd Davies.
Fleet: 128-15 double deck bus, 58 single deck bus, 17 coach,
8 midibus, 30 minibus
Chassis: include DAF, Dennis, Leyland, Mercedes, Optare, Scenic & Volvo
Bodies: Include Alexander, Autobus, Berkhof, Duple, ECW, East Lancs, Irizar, Jonckheere, Marshall,, Optare, Plaxton, Transbus, Van Hool, Wadham, Stringer, Wright.
Ops incl: Local bus services, Private hire, School contracts.
Livery: Grey/Red/Maroon
Includes Bryn Melyn Motor Services, Chaloner's, Hanmer's Coaches.

HAYDN'S TOURS & TRAVEL
BEVERLEY, FIELD HEAD, CHIRK LL14 5PU.
Tel/Fax: 01691 773267
E-mail: christopherwilliams@virgin.net
Ptnrs: M Williams, Chris Williams.
Fleet: 2 coach
Chassis: 1 DAF. 1 Volvo.
Bodies: 1 Duple. 1 Plaxton.
Ops incl: excursions & tours, private hire, school contracts.
Livery: Red/White/Yellow/Orange

JOHN'S TRAVEL WREXHAM
1 BRYN MAELOR, SOUTHSEA LL11 6RD.
Tel: 01978 753364
Prop: John F H Ithell
Fleet: 4 - 2 midibus, 2 minibus
Chassis: 4 Mercedes
Bodies: 1 Carlyle.2 Plaxton. 1 Reeve Burgess.
Ops incl: local bus services, private hire
Livery: White with red lettering
Ticket system: Wayfarer

D. JONES & SON
CENTRAL GARAGE, KING STREET, ACREFAIR LU4 3RH.
Tel: 01978 842540
Mobile: 07739 206623
Props: D. & G. Jones.
Fleet: 7 - 1 coach, 6 single-deck bus
Fleet: 1 DAF. 4 Dennis. 2 Mercedes.
Bodies: 3 Caetano. 1 Mercedes. 3Plaxton.
Ops incl: local bus services, school contracts, private hire.
Ops incl: local bus services, private hire
Livery: Blue/Cream.
Ticket system: Wayfarer

E JONES & SONS
MOUNTAIN VIEW, BANK STREET, PONCIAU LL14 1EN.
Tel: 01978 841613.
Props: J B & G Jones.
Fleet: 7
Livery: Blue/White/Orange.

PAT'S COACHES LTD
DERWEN HOUSE, SOUTHSEA ROAD, SOUTHSEA, WREXHAM, LL11 6PP
Tel: 01978 720171
Fax: 01978 758459
E-mail: enquiries@patscoaches.co.uk.fsnet.co.uk
Web site: www.patscoaches.co.uk
Ptnr: P C Davies, J M Davies, D K Davies
Chassis: 1 DAF. 1 LDV. 2 Mercedes. 2 Neoplan. 2 Scania. 8 Volvo.
Bodies: 1 Autobus. 4 Berkhof. 1 Jonckheere. 1 Marcopolo. 1 Marshall/MCV. 2 Mercedes. 2 Neoplan. 2 Plaxton. 1 Van Hool. 1 Wright. 1 other.
Livery: White/Red/Yellow

PRICES COACHES
THE HAVEN, BERSHAM ROAD, SOUTHSEA LL11 6TF
Tel/Fax: 01978 756834
Prop: Tecwyn Price
Fleet: 7 - 2 double-deck bus, 4 coach, 1 midibus
Chassis: 2 Leyland. 1 Mercedes. 1 Setra. 3 Volvo.
Bodies: 2 Leyland. 1 Kassbohrer. 1 Mercedes. 2 Plaxton. 1 Van Hool.
Ops incl: school contracts, private hire
Livery: Primrose/Green/Orange

STRAFFORDS COACHES
UNITS 7/8, FIVE CROSSES INDUSTRIAL ESTATE, MINERA LL11 3RD.
Tel: 01978 756106
Fax: 01978 722705
Proprietors: Mr & Mrs G A Strafford
Fleet: 11 - 8 single-deckcoach, 2 minicoach.
Chassis: . Scania.
Ops incl: school contracts, private hire, excursions & tours, continental tours. .
Livery: White

WELSH OPERATORS

NORTHERN IRELAND

A1 COACH TRAVEL
35 NORBURGH PARK, FOYLE SPRINGS, DERRY/LONDONDERRY BT48 0RG
Tel/Fax: 028 7130 9323
Prop: J. Bradshaw
Fleet: 2 midicoach
Chassis: 1 Mercedes. 1 Renault.
Ops incl: private hire, continental tours, school contracts.

CHAMBERS COACH HIRE LTD
11 CIRCULAR ROAD, MONEYMORE BT45 7PY
Tel: 028 8674 8152
Fax: 028 8674 8152
Web site: www.coachireland.com
Non-Exec Chmn: Ted Hesketh **Dirs**: Des Chambers, Mary Chambers, Paul Chambers, Philip Harkness **Ops Man**: Mary McIver
Fleet: 48 - 16 coach, 2 double-deck coach, 4 midibus, 8 midicoach, 6 minicoach, 12 minibus.
Chassis: 2 Ford Transit. 1 Mercedes. 16 Scania.
Bodies: 2 Berkhof. 15 Irizar. 18 Mercedes. 12 Plaxton.
Ops incl: school contracts, excursions & tours, private hire

CROSS COUNTRY COACHES LTD
31 BALLYLINTAGH ROAD, COLERAINE BT51 3SP
Tel: 028 7086 8989
Fax: 028 7086 9191
E-mail: sales@crosscountrycoaches.com
Dirs: J R Telford, B Telford
Fleet: 5 - 4 coach, 1 vintage.
Chassis: 1 Bedford. 4 DAF.
Bodies: 1 Duple. 4 Van Hool.
Ops incl: excursions & tours, private hire, continental tours.
Livery: White

DARRAGHS COACHES
22 LISHEEGHAN ROAD, BALLYMONEY BT53 7JY
Tel: 028 2954 0684
Fax: 028 2954 0785
E-mail: kdarragh@aol.com
Man: Robert Darragh
GILES TOURS S W A
63 ABBEYDALE AVENUE, NEWTOWNARDS BT23 8RT
Tel/Fax: 028 9181 1099
E-mail: enquiries@gilestours.co.uk
Web site: www.gilestours.co.uk

Dirs: Neil Giles, Patricia Giles
Fleet: 4 - 3 coach, 1 midicoach.
Chassis: 1 Mercedes. 3 Van Hool.
Ops incl: excursions & tours, private hire, continental tours.

LAKELAND TOURS
47 MAIN STREET, TEMPO. Co FERMANAGH BT94 3LU
Tel: 028 8954 1646
Fax: 028 8954 1424
Recovery: 07779 026597
E-mail: lakelandtours@btconnect.com
Web site: www.lakelandtours.co.uk
Prop: Ian McCutcheon
Fleet: 5 - incl: single-deck coach, midicoach, minicoach.
Chassis: incl: Leyland. MAN. Mercedes-Benz. Setra
Bodies: Esker. Mercedes-Benz. Plaxton. Setra.
Ops incl: excursions & tours, private hire, school contracts.

LOGANS EXECUTIVE TRAVEL
58 GALDANAGH ROAD, DUNLOY, BALLYMENA BT44 9DB
Tel: 028 2765 7203
Fax: 028 2765 7559
E-mail: coaches@loganstravel.com
Web site: www.loganstravel.com
Prop: Sean Logan
Fleet: 60 - single-deck coach, midicoach, minibus.
Chassis: 6 Iveco. 6 LDV. 12 Mercedes-Benz. 5 VW. 31 Volvo.
Ops incl: local bus services, school contracts, private hire.

LONDONDERRY & LOUGH SWILLY BUS COMPANY LTD
STRAND ROAD, DERRY/LONDONDERRY BT48 7PY
Tel: 00 353 74 22863
Fleet: 88 - single-deck bus, coach.
Ops incl: local bus services.

POOTS COACH HIRE LTD
118A PORTADOWN ROAD, TANDRAGEE BT62 2JX
Tel: 028 3884 1504
Fax: 028 3884 1724
Dirs: Jim T Poots, Samuel Poots
Fleet: 6 - 3 coach, 3 midicoach.
Chassis: 1 DAF. 3 Mercedes. 2 Leyalnd.
Bodies: 3 Plaxton. 3 Reeve Burgess
Ops incl: excursions & tours, private hire, express, school contracts.
Livery: White
Ticket system: Wayfarer

O. ROONEY COACH HIRE LTD
4 DANA PLACE, HILLTOWN, NEWRY BT34 5UE
Tel: 028 4063 0825
Fax: 028 4063 8028
Recovery: 077721 510955
E-mail: oliver@orcoachireland.com
Web site: www.orcoachireland.com
Man Dir: Oliver Rooney **Ops Man**: Aaron Rooney
Fleet: 12 - 2 single-deck bus, 3 coach, 2 midibus, 5 minibus.
Chassis: 2 Dennis. 1 Leyland. 6 Mercedes. 1 Renault. 2 Volvo.
Bodies: 3 Alexander. 3 Plaxton. 6 Reeve Burgess.
Ops incl: local bus services, excursions & tours, school contracts, private hire.
Livery: White/Yellow

SLOAN TRAVEL
51 KILLOWEN OLD ROAD, ROSTREVOR, NEWRY BT34 3AE.
Tel: 028 4173 8459
Fax: 028 4173 9459
Dir/Ch Eng: B. M. Sloan. **Sec**: Ms M. Sloan.
Fleet: 7 - 6 coach, 1 minibus.
Chassis: 4 Bedford. 3 Ford.
Bodies: 2 Duple. 4 Plaxton.
Ops incl: local bus services, school contracts, excursions & tours, private hire, express, continental tours.
Livery: Mixed.

TRANSLINK
CENTRAL STATION, EAST BRIDGE STREET, BELFAST BT1 3PB
Tel: 028 9089 9400
E-mail: feedback@translink.co.uk
Web site: www.translink.co.uk
Fleetnames: Ulsterbus, Citybus
Chmn: Dr Joan Smyth **Group Chief Exec**: Catherine Mason **Dir of HR**: Alan Mercer **Dir of Ops**: Philip O'Neil **Fin Dir**: Stephen Armstrong **Mktg Exec**: Ciaran Rogan **Head of Projects**: David Laird **Infrastructure Exec**: Clive Bradberry
Fleet: 1,469 – 20 double-deck bus, 1,274 single-deck bus, 40 coach, 2 double-deck coach, 8 articulated bus, 4 open-top bus, 98 minibus, 23 minicoach.
Chassis: 1 Ayats. 84 Bristol. 10 DAF. 43 Dennis. 819 Leyland. 97 Mercedes. 23 Optare. 5 Renault. 43 Scania. 346 Volvo.
Bodies: 1,023 Alexander. 1 Ayats. 7 Caetano. 4 Duple. 3 ECW. 4 Irizar. 10 Mercedes. 23 Optare. 135 Plaxton. 2 Reeve Burgess. 6 Van Hool. 247 Wright, 6 Other makes.

♿	Vehicle suitable for disabled	🪑	Seat belt-fitted Vehicle	R24	24 hour recovery service
T	Toilet-drop facilities available	🍴	Coach(es) with galley facilities		Replacement vehicle available
R	Recovery service available	❄	Air-conditioned vehicle(s)		Vintage Coach(es) available
	Open top vehicle(s)v		Coaches with toilet facilities		

212

REPUBLIC OF IRELAND

AIRCOACH
DUBLIN
Tel: 00 353 1 844 7118
Email: info@aircoach.ie
Web site: www.aircoach.ie
Chassis: incl Setra
Ops incl: express
Livery: Blue
Subsidiary of First Group Plc

ALLIED COACHES
113 GRANGE WAY, BALDOYLE INDUSTRIAL ESTATE, BALDOYLE, DUBLIN D13
Tel: 00 353 1 832 8300
Fax: 00 353 1 832 8299
E-mail: info@alliedcoaches.ie
Web site: www.alliedcoaches.ie
Man Dir: Jim Nolan **Man**: Seamus Nolan
Fleet: 7 - 3 coach, 2 minicoach, 2 minibus.
Chassis: incl: 1 DAF. 2 Mercedes.
Bodies: incl: 1 BMC. 2 Marcopolo
Ops incl: excursions & tours, private hire
Livery: Silver

ARAN TOURS LTD
14 LOWER ALBERT ROAD, SANDYCOVE, Co DUBLIN
Tel: 00 353 1 280 1899
Fax: 00 353 1 280 1799

BARRY'S COACHES LTD
THE GLEN, MAYFIELD, CORK CITY
Tel: 00 353 21 450 5390, 450 1669 (emergencies only)
Fax: 00 353 21 450 9628
Fleet: 15 - 12 coach, 2 minibus, 1 minicoach.
Chassis: 1 AEC. 3 Bedford. 6 Leyland. 2 Mercedes. 2 Volvo.
Bodies: 7 Duple. 1 Jonckheere. 2 Mercedes. 3 Plaxton. 2 Van Hool.
Livery: Blue/White

BARTON TRANSPORT
STRAFFAN ROAD, MAYNOOTH, CO KILDARE.
Tel: 00 353 1 628 6026
Fax: 00 353 1 628 6026
E-mail: info@barton-transport.ie
Web site: www.bartons-transport.ie
Man Dir: Patrick Barton **Man**: Fergal Barton
Fleet: 35 - 1 double-deck bus, 10 single-deck bus, 20 coach, 4 minicoach.
Chassis: 2 BMC. 26 DAF. 3 Irisbus. 3 MAN. 1 Mercedes.
Bodies: 2 Beulas. 13 Berkhof. 2 BMC. 5 Ikarus. 2 Marcopolo. 2 Optare. 5 Plaxton. 4 Temsa.
Ops incl: local bus services, private hire, excursions & tours, school contracts.

RONNIE BRUEN T/A BLUEBIRD COACHES
72 KILBARRON DRIVE, COOLOCK, DUBLIN 5.
Tel/Fax: 00 353 1 847 7896.
Dirs: Ronnie Bruen, Keith Bruen.
Fleet: 7 - 3 coach, 2 midicoach, 2 minibus.
Chassis: Ford Transit. Leyland. Mercedes. Volvo.
Bodies: Mercedes. Duple.
Ops incl: private hire, express, school contracts.
Livery: Cream/Red.

BUCKLEY'S TOURS
KILLARNEY, Co KERRY
Tel: 00 353 64 31945
E-mail: buckleys@iol.ie

BURKE BROS (COACHES) LTD
CLARETUAM, TUAM, Co GALWAY
Tel: 00 353 93 55416
Fax: 00 353 93 55356
Dirs: P .Burke, Ms M. Burke.
Ops Man: P. Steede.
Fleet: 12 - 10 coach, 2 midicoach.
Chassis: Mercedes-Benz, Toyota, Volvo.
Bodies: Caetano, Jonckheere, Plaxton.
Ops incl: local bus services, private hire, continental tours.
Livery: White with Blue/Orange stripes.

BUS EIREANN/IRISH BUS
BROADSTONE, PHIBSBOROUGH, DUBLIN 7
Tel: 00 353 1 830 2222
Fax: 00 353 1 830 9377
E-mail: info@buseireann.ie
Web site: www.buseireann.ie
Chmn: Dr John Lynch **Ch Exec**: Tim Hayes **Co Sec**: Martin Nolan **Ch Mech Eng**: Joe Neiland **Man HR**: Des Tallon
Man Sales&Mktg: Barry Doyle
Fleet: 1,396 - 23 double-deck bus, 567 single-deck bus, 640 coach, 2 open-top bus, 87 midibus, 27 minibus.
Chassis: 201 DAF. 43 Dennis. 2 Ford. 155 GAC. 278 Leyland. 76 Mercedes. 20 Optare. 156 Scania. 415 Volvo.
Bodies: 86 Alexander. 176 Caetano. 24 East Lancs. 31 Hispano. 156 Irizar. 184 Leyland. 20 Mercedes. 1 Northern Counties. 20 Optare. 322 Plaxton. 20 Sunsundegui. 18 Van Hool. 106 Wright. 182 other.
Ops incl: local bus services, school contracts, excursions & tours, private hire, express.
Livery: White/Red.
Ticket System: Wayfarer.

BUTLERS BUSES
17 BROOKVALE, COBH, Co CORK
Tel/Fax: 00 353 21 811660
E-mail: butlersb@gofree.indigo.ie
Prop: Ian Butler

CAHALANE COACHES
UNIT 6, KILBARRY ENTERPRISE CENTRE, DUBLIN HILL, CORK
Tel: 00 353 21 430 4606
Fax: 00 353 21 430 1200
Fleet: includes 14, 24, 29 and 35-seat coaches

CALLINAN COACHES LTD
KINISKA, GLAREGALWAY, Co GALWAY
Tel: 00 353 91 798324
Fax: 00 353 91 798962
Recovery: 00 353 8724 13691
E-mail: info@callinancoaches.ie
Web site: www.callinancoaches.ie
Fleet: 22 single-deck bus
Chassis: 22 Volvo.
Ops incl: excursions & tours, continental tours, private hire

GERRY CARROLL COACH HIRE
BALLYMAKENNY ROAD, DROGHEDA, CO LOUTH
Tel: 00 353 41 98 36074
Prop: Gerry Carroll **Dir**: Patrick Caroll
Sec: Betty Carroll
Fleet: 3 coach.
Chassis: Bedford.
Bodies: Plaxton
Ops incl: local bus services, excursions & tours, private hire.
Livery: White/Blue

CIRCLE LINE BUS CO LTD
STRAFFAN ROAD, MAYNOOTH, CO KILDARE
Tel: 00 353 1 628 6250
E-mail: info@circlelinebus.ie
Web site: www.circlelinebus.ie
Dirs: Paul Morton, Patrick Barton **Man**: Nigel O'Connor
Fleet: 23 - 16 double-deck bus, 7 single-deck bus
Chassis: 6 MAN. 17 Volvo.
Bodies: 14 East Lancs. 3 Ikarus. 4 Marcopolo.
Ops incl: local bus services

COLLIN'S COACHES
CARRICKAMOSS, Co MONAGHAN
Tel: 00 353 42 9661 631
Fax: 00 353 42 9663 462
E-mail: colcoach@iol.ie

CONWAY COACH AND CHAUFFEUR DRIVE
WILLOW GROVE, REDGATE, LIMERICK
Tel: 00 353 61 53366
Prop: R. Conway (Gen Man), Val Conway.
Prop/Ch Eng: Patrick Conway. **Prop/Sec**: Audrey Hurley. **Traf Man**: R. Hurley.
Fleet: 11 midicoach.
Livery: White/Red.

CORCORANS EXECUTIVE TOURS
10 COLLEGE STREET, KILLARNEY, CO KERRY
Tel: 00 353 64 36666
Fax: 00 353 64 35666
Fleet: coach, midicoach
Chassis: incl: Mercedes
Ops incl: private hire

COYLES COACHES
GWEEDORE, Co DONEGAL
Tel: 00 353 75 31208.
E-mail: coylescoaches@eircom.net

CREMIN COACHES
BANTRY, Co CORK
Tel/Fax: 00 353 2 766 906
E-mail: info@cremincoaches.com
Web site: www.cremincoaches.com
Fleet: incl: minicoach
Chassis: incl: Mercedes
Livery: White
Ops incl: private hire

CRONIN'S COACHES LTD
SHANNON BUILDINGS, MALLOW ROAD, CORK
Tel: 00 353 21 430 9090
Fax: 00 353 21 430 5508
Email: cork@croninscoaches.com.
Web Site: www.croninscoaches.com.
Dirs: D. & Joan Cronin. **Ch Eng**: Niall Cronin. **Gen Man**: Nora Cronin.
Fleet: 50 - 47 coach, 3 midicoach.
Chassis: DAF. Leyland. Volvo.
Bodies: Van Hool
Ops incl: private hire
Livery: White with red flash.

CROSSON MOTOR GROUP
UNIT 10/12 NEWTOWN INDUSTRIAL ESTATE, COOLOCK, DUBLIN 17
Tel: 00 353 1 848 5811
Fax: 00 353 1 848 5721
Fleetname: Crosson Coaches.
Chmn: S. Crosson. **Man Dir**: A. Kennedy.
Dirs: J. O'Reilly, B. Cullen, S. Crosson.
Fleet: 1 midicoach.
Chassis: Mercedes. **Body**: Euro Coach.
Ops incl: private hire, continental tours.
Livery: White

MARTIN CROWLEY
CLANCOOL BEG, BANDON, Co CORK
Tel/Fax: 00 353 23 42150
Fleet: incl: minicoach, midicoach
Ops incl: private hire

DERO'S COACH TOURS
R24
22 MAIN STREET, KILLARNEY, Co KERRY
Tel: 00 353 64 31251
Fax: 00 353 64 34077
Email: deroscoachtours@eircom.net.
Web site: www.derostours.com
Prop: Ms E. O'Sullivan Quille. **Sales Dir**: Ms C. O'Sullivan, D O'Sullivan.
Fleet: 18 - 12 coach, 4 midicoach, 2 minicoach.
Chassis: 10 DAF. 6 Mercedes. 2 Volvo.
Livery: White with multi red/Silver/Red/Orange.
Relief drivers and guiding agency also.

JIMMY DONNELLY & SON
46 IRISH STREET, ENNISCORTHY, Co WEXFORD.
Tel: 00 353 54 33956
Ptnrs: James Donnelly, Mary Donnelly, Keith Donnelly
Fleet: 6- 3 midicoach 3 minibus

DONOVAN'S COACH HIRE
HEADFORD, KILLARNEY, Co KERRY
Tel: 00 353 64 54041.
Fax: 00 353 64 54041
Props: Joe & Maureen Donovan.
Fleet: 8 - 5 coach, 2 midicoach, 1 minibus.
Chassis: 1 Ford Transit. 3 LDV. 2 Mercedes. 2 Volvo.
Bodies: 2 Jonckheere. 1 Duple. 2 Mercedes. 1 Plaxton.
Ops incl: school contracts, excursions & tours, private hire.

P. DOYLE LTD
ROUNDWOOD, Co WICKLOW
Tel: 00 353 1 281 8119
Fleetname: St Kevins Bus Service.
Prop/Traf Man: P. Doyle.
Gen Man/Ch Eng: J. Doyle.
Sec: John Doyle.
Fleet: 5 single-deck bus.
Chassis: 5 Leyland.
Bodies: 1 Plaxton. 4 others.
Livery: Blue/Cream.
Ticket System: Setright.

TONY DOYLE COACHES LTD
BALLYORNEY, ENNISKERRY, Co WICKLOW
Tel: 00 353 1 286 7427
Fax: 00 353 1 286 7427
Email: info@tonydoyle.com
Web site: www.tonydoyle.com
Fleet: 17 - 11 coach, 5 midicoach, 1 minicoach.
Chassis: 7 Iveco. 5 MAN. 2 Mercedes. 2 Scania. 1 Volvo.
Bodies: 6 Beulas. 1 Esker. 4 Indcar. 2 Irizar. 1 Noge. 1 Sunsundegui 2 Marcopolo.
Ops incl: excursions & tours, school contracts, private hire.

THE DUALWAY GROUP
KEATINGS PARK, RATHCOOLE, Co DUBLIN
Tel: 00 353 1 458 0054
Fax: 00 353 1 458 0808
E-mail: info@dualwaycoaches.com
Web site: www.dualwaycoaches.com
Fleetnames: Dualway, City Sightseeing, Grayline
Man Dir: Anthony McConn **Gen Man**: David McConn **Fin Controller**: Trish McConn **Admin Man**: Dawn Nolan
Fleet: 56 - 11 double-deck bus, 6 coach, 31 open-top bus, 2 midicoach 3 Minibus
Ops incl: local bus services, excursions & tours, school contracts, private hire.

DUBLIN BUS (BUS ATHA CLIATH)
59 UPPER O'CONNELL STREET, DUBLIN 1.
Tel: 00 353 1 872 0000
Fax: 00 353 1 873 1195
Email: info@dublinbus.ie
Web site: www.dublinbus.ie
Chmn: John Lynch **Ch Exec**: Joe Meagher **Dirs**: David Egan, Arnold O'Byrne, Tom Coffey, Peter Webster
Head of Finance: Paul O'Neill **Ch Eng**: Shane Doyle **Business Dev Man**: Paddy Doherty **Human Resources Man**: Gerry Maguire **Ops Man**: Mick Matthews
Fleet: 1,076 - 966 double-deck bus, 39 single-deck bus, 51 midibus, 20 articulated bus
Chassis: includes DAF. Dennis. Leyland. Volvo.
Bodies: includes: Alexander. ECW. Wright.
Ops incl: local bus services.
Livery: Blue/Yellow with Dublin Blue/White/Darker Blue swoosh

DUBLIN MINI COACHES & CHAUFEUR HIRE
THE TRAVEL BANK LTD, WASDALE HOUSE, 14 CAMAC PARK, OLD NAAS ROAD, DUBLIN 12
Tel: 00 353 861 780049
Fax: 00 353 1 6961001
Email: info.dmc@o2.ie
Web site: www.dublinminicoaches.com
Man Dir: Stephen Millar
Fleet: 12 - 8 midicoach, 4 minicoach.
Chassis/Bodies: 12 Mercedes.
Ops incl: excursions & tours, private hire.

EIREBUS LTD
CORDUFF ROAD, BLANCHARDSTOWN, DUBLIN 15
Tel: 00 353 1 824 2626
Fax: 00 353 1 824 2627
E-mail: eirebus@iol.ie
Web site: www.eirebus.ie
Man Dir: Patrick Kavanagh **Tran Man**: Derek Graham **Gen Man**: Paul Curtis
Fleet: 43 - 10 single-deck bus, 25 single-deck coach, 3 midicoach, 5 minibus.
Chassis: 4 Iveco. 2 MAN. 12 Mercedes. 2 Scania. 2 Toyota. 2 Volvo.
Bodies: 4 Beulas. 2 Caetano. 2 Indcar. 12 Irizar. 1 Plaxton. 10 Van Hool. 2 other.
Ops incl: local bus service, excursions & tours, express.
Livery: White

ENFIELD COACHES LTD
RATHCORE, ENFIELD, Co MEATH
Tel: 00 353 1 824 2626
Fleet: 3 - 1 coach, 3 minibus

FAHERTY'S COACH HIRE
DRUMONEY, MOYCULLEN, Co GALWAY
Tel: 00 353 91 85228
Fleet: 5 - 4 coach, 1 minicoach

FINEGAN COACH HIRE
29 MAIN STREET, CARRICKMACROSS, Co MONAGHAN
Tel: 00 353 42 61313
Fleet: 7 - 5 coach, 1 minicoach, 1 minibus

FINNEGAN - BRAY
OLD COURT INDUSTRIAL ESTATE, BOGHALL ROAD, BRAY, Co WICKLOW
Tel: 00 353 1 286 0061
Fax: 00 353 1 286 8121
E-mail: finnegan-bray@oceanfree.net
Dir: Eugene Finnegan
Fleet: 15 - 2 double-deck bus, 3 single-deck bus, 3 coach, 2 midicoach, 4 midibus, 1 minibus.
Chassis: 4 DAF. 1 Dennis. 6 Mercedes. 1 Optare. 3 Volvo.
Bodies: 1 Alexander. 2 Ikarus. 1 Leyland. 6 Mercedes. 1 Northern Counties. 1 Optare. 2 Plaxton. 1 Van Hool.
Ops incl: local bus services, excursions & tours, school contracts, private hire.
Livery: Red

DECLAN FINNEGAN
THE COACH & CAB CAFE, 10 MAIN STREET, KENMARE, CO KERRY
Tel: 00 353 64 41491
Fax: 00 353 64 42636
Fleet: coach, minicoach
Ops incl: private hire.

TOM FOX
MONAGHAN ROAD, ROCKCORRY, Co MONAGHAN
Tel: 00 353 42 42284
Fleet: 2 coach

MARTIN FUREY COACHES LTD
MILLTOWN, DRUMCLIFFE, Co SLIGO
Tel: 00 353 71 63092
Fleet: 5 - 3 coach, 2 minibus

GALVINS COACHES
MAIN STREET, DUNMANWAY, Co CORK
Tel: 00 353 23 45125
Fax: 00 353 23 45407
Dir: R. E. Galvin
Chassis: Ford. Ford Transit. Leyland National. Scania. Volvo.
Bodies: Leyland National. Mercedes. Plaxton. Van Hool. Willowbrook. Duple.
Fleet: single-deck bus, coach, double-deck coach, midibus, midicoach.

GLYNNS COACH HIRE (ENNIS) LTD
KNOCKADERRY, TULLA ROAD, ENNIS, Co CLARE
Tel: 00 353 65 682 8234
Fax: 00 353 65 684 0678
Recovery: 00 353 8625 97037
Email: info@glynnscoaches.com
Web site: www.glynnscoaches.com
Fleetname: Glynns of Ennis
Chmn: Jackie Cronin. **Sec**: Niamh Cronin.
Fleet: 14 - 5 coach, 4 midicoach, 2 minibus, 3 minicoach, 2 Irsbus.
Chassis: 2 Beulas. 1 DAF. 1 Iveco. 3 MAN. 5 Mercedes. 1 Setra. 3 Volvo.
Bodies: 1 Ikarus. 3 Indcar. 5 Mercedes . 1 Noge. 2 Plaxton. 1 Setra. 1 Euro.

JAMES GLYNN
GRAIGUE NA SPIDOGUE (POST GRAIGUECULLEN), NURNEY
Tel: 00 353 503 46616
Prop/Gen Man/Traf Man: J. Glynn
Prop/Ch Eng: A. Glynn **Prop/Sec**: Mrs J. Glynn.
Fleet: 4 - 3 single-deck bus, 1 coach.
Livery: Cream/Blue.

HALPENNY TRANSPORT
ASHVILLE, THE SQUARE, BLACKROCK, DUNDALK
Tel: 00 353 42 21608
Fleetname: Halpenny Transport
Man Dir: John Halpenny
Fleet: 14 - includes 2 double-deck bus, 2 single-deck bus, 8 coach
Chassis: mainly Volvo.
Bodies: include 1 Sunsundegui
Ops incl: local bus services, private hire, continental tours
Livery: White with Red/Blue/Green, Blue/Cream

HEALY COACHES
CASTLEGAR, GALWAY
Tel: 00 353 91 770066
Fax: 00 353 91 753335
Web site: www.healybus.com
Email: healybus@iol.ie.
Prop: Michael Healy, Paul Healy
Fleet: 13 - 4 single-deck bus, 6 coach, 1 open-top bus, 1 midicoach 1 Midibus
Chassis: 1 Leyland. 5 MAN. 3 Volvo 1DAF 1 Dennis 1 Scania.
Bodies: 1 Alexander. 2 Ikarus. 2 Noge. 4 Plaxton 3 Indcar.

M. HOGAN
LIBERTY STREET, THURLES, Co TIPPERARY
Tel: 00 353 50 421622
Fleetname: Shamrock Bus Service.
Prop/Gen Man: M. Hogan.
Ch Eng: T. Maher. **Sec**: J. Maher.
Fleet: 2 coach.
Livery: Cream/Orange.
Ticket System: Setright.

IRELAND COACHES
COOLQUAY, THE WARD, Co DUBLIN
Tel: 00 353 1 835 2714
Fax: 00 353 1 835 2715
E-mail: irelandcoaches@eircom.net
Fleet: 30 coaches, midicoaches, minicoaches

IRISH COACHES
ULSTER BANK CHAMBERS, 2-4 LOWER O'CONNELL STREET, DUBLIN
Tel: 00 353 1 878 8894/8898
Fax: 00 353 1 878 8916
E-mail: dch@irishcoaches.ie
Web site: www.irishcoaches.ie
Chmn: Patric Barton **Dir**: Dermot Cronin
Man Dir: D C Hughes
Fleet: 4 - 3 coach, 1 midicoach
Chassis: 4 DAF
Bodies: 1 Ayats. 1 Berkhof. 2 Marcopolo.
Livery: yellow

DONAL JOYCE MINIBUS HIRE
GENTIAN HILL HOUSE, KNOCKNACARRA, Co GALWAY
Tel: 00 353 91 521427
Fax: 00 353 91 52 4284
Fleet: 8 -2 minicoaches,8 midibus
Ops incl: excursions & tours, private hire

BERNARD KAVANAGH & SONS LTD
BRIDGE GARAGE, URLINGFORD, Co KILKENNY
Tel: 00 353 56 31189
Fax: 00 353 56 31314
Email: info@bkavcoaches.com.
Web Site: www.bkavcoaches.com.
Fleet: 54 - 50 coach, 4 midicoach.
Chassis: incl: 3 Bova. 7 MAN. 2 Setra. 4 Volvo.
Bodies: 5 Beulas. 2 Indcar. 10 Irizar. 2 Jonckheere. 3 Plaxton. 2 Setra. 30 Van Hool.
Ops incl: excursions & tours, private hire, express, continental tours.
Livery: White/Multi

J J KAVANAGH & SONS
MAIN STREET, URLINGFORD, Co KILKENNY
Tel: 00 353 56 31106
Fax: 00 353 56 31106
E-mail: info@jjkavanagh.ie
Web site: www.jjkavanagh.ie
Joint Man Dir/Fin Cont: J. J. Kavanagh
Joint Man Dir/Ops Man: Paul Kavanagh
Maintenance Man: Edward Scully
Fleet: 38 - 1 double-deck bus, 36 coach, 1 open-top bus
Chassis: 6 MAN. 25 Setra. 45 Volvo.
Bodies: 15 Caetano. 2 Leyland. 4 Mercedes. 2 Northern Counties. 20 Plaxton. 25 Setra. 7 Van Hool. 1 Wright.
Ops incl: local bus services

M. KAVANAGH
LIMERICK ROAD, TIPPERARY
Tel: 00 353 62 51563
Fax: 00 353 62 51593
E-mail: mattkavanagh3@aol.net
Fleet: 19 - 12 coaches, 5 single-deck bus, 2 minibus.

PIERCE KAVANAGH COACHES
CHURCH VIEW, URLINGFORD, COKILKENNY
Tel: 00 353 56 31213
Fax: 00 353 56 31599
E-mail: info@kavanaghscoaches.com
Web site: www.kavanaghscoaches.com
Dirs: Pierce Kavanagh, John Kavanagh **Ch Eng**: John Kenny **Co Sec**: Jim Bannon
Fleet: 20 - 1 single-deck bus, 18 coach, 1 midicoach.
Chassis: 1 Bova. 1 DAF. 2 Ford. 5 Ford Transit. 4 Leyland. 5 MAN. 1 Mercedes. 3 Scania. 2 Volvo

KEENAN COMMERCIALS LTD
BELLURGAN, DUNDALK, Co LOUTH
Tel: 00 353 42 937 1405
Fax: 00 353 42 937 1893
Fleetname: Anchor Coaches
Man Dir: Seamus Keenan
Fleet: 17 - 8 single-deck bus, 7 coach, 2 minibus.

KENNEALLY'S BUS SERVICE LTD
BLENHEIM, WATERFORD
Tel: 00 353 51 872777
Fax: 00 353 51 872770
Joint Man Dirs: J J Kavanagh, Paul Kavanagh **Tran Man**: Tony Crean
Ops Man: Michael Ryan
Fleet: 27 - 6 double-deck bus, 3 single-deck bus, 18 coach
Chassis: 1 AEC. 2 Leyland. 5 MAN. 15 Setra. 30 Volvo.
Bodies: 4 Alexander. 5 Caetano. 4 Northern Counties. 15 Setra. 10 Van Hool. 1 Wright.
Ops incl: local bus services, excursions & tours, private hire, express, continental tours.
Livery: Green/Blue/Red on White
Subsidiary of J J Kavanagh, Urlingford

REPUBLIC OF IRELAND

215

KENNEDY COACHES
ANNASCAUL, TRALEE, Co KERRY
Tel: 00 353 66 91 57106
Fax: 00 353 66 91 57427
Fleet: 5 - 3 double-deck bus, 3 minibus

K. M. KEOGH
39A WEXFORD ROAD, ARKLOW
Tel: 00 353 40 22560
Fleet: 4 coach

KERRY COACHES LTD
INISFALLEN, 15 MAIN STREET, KILLARNEY, Co KERRY
Tel: 00 353 64 31945
Fax: 00 353 64 31903
Email: buckleys@iol.ie
Web site: www.kerrycoaches.com
Ops Man: Alan O'Connor
Fleetnames: Buckley Tours, Kerry Tours
Man Dir: M Buckley
Fleet: 19 - 14 coach, 2 midicoach, 3 minibus.
Chassis: incl: 2 Setra

DAVE LONG COACH TRAVEL
CURRAGH, SKIBBEREEN
Tel: 00 353 28 21138
Fleet: 1 coach

LESCLACHA LTD
28 AVONDALE, NEWMARKET-ON-FERGUS
Tel: 00 353 61 71233
Fleetname: Lovetts Coaches
Fleet: 9 - 1 single-deck bus, 6 coach, 1 midibus, 1 minibus.
Chassis: Leyland.

LUAS
LUAS DEPOT, RED COW ROUNDABOUT, CLONDALKIN, DUBLIN
Tel: 00 353 1 461 4910
Web site: www.luas.ie
Man Dir: Richard Dujardin
Gen Man: Brian Brennan
Fleet: 40 tram
Chassis/bodies: Alstom Citadis
Ops: tram service

P. J. McCONNON
GREENLEE, CLONES ROAD, MONAGHAN
Tel: 00 353 47 82020
Fleet: 4 coaches
Chassis: Volvo
Bodies: Plaxton

JAMES McGEE (BUSES)
BALLINA MAIN ROAD, FALCARRAGH, LETTERKENNY
Tel: 00 353 74 35174
Fleet: 8 minibus.
Chassis: 1 Ford. 3 Toyota.
Ops incl: private hire.
Livery: White

JOHN McGINLEY COACH TRAVEL
MAGHEERCARTY, GORTAHEEK, Co DONEGAL
Tel: 00 353 7491 35201
Fax: 00 353 7491 35960
E-mail: info@jchhmcginley.com
Web site: www.jchhmcginley.com
Prop: James McGinley
Fleet: 16 - 8 coach, 8 minibus.
Chassis: Ford Transit. Mercedes. Volvo.
Bodies: Plaxton. Van Hool.
Ops incl: local bus services, excursions & tours, continental tours, school contracts, private hire, express, continental tours.

GERALD MANNING
CASTLE ROAD, CROOM, LIMERICK
Tel: 00 353 61 88311
E-mail: gmanning@indigo.ie
Fleet: 13 - 10 coach, 2 minibus, 1 midibus.

ALAN MARTIN COACHES
1 KIRKFIELD COTTAGE, CLONSILLA, DUBLIN 15
Tel: 00 353 1 835 1560
Fax: 00 353 1 835 1816
Dirs: A. Martin, B. C. Martin. **Ch Eng**: M. Reilly. **Traf Man**: M. Clarke.
Fleet: 8 - 6 single-deck bus, 1 double-deck bus, 1 minibus.
Chassis: 6 Ford. 2 Leyland. 4 MAN. 2 Mercedes. 3 Scania. 2 Toyota. 5 Volvo.
Ops incl: local bus services, school contracts, excursions & tours, private hire, express.
Livery: White with two Blue stripes.

MARTIN'S COACHES (CAVAN) LTD
CORRATILLION, CORLOUGH, BELTURBET, Co CAVAN
Tel: 00 353 49 26222
Fax: 00 353 49 23116
E-mail: jimmartin@eircom.net
Dirs: James G Martin Snr; James G Martin Jnr: Derek Martin Alan Martin;
Fleet: 16 - 5 coach, 5 midicoach, 6 minibus.
Chassis: 5 DAF. 6 Ford Transit. 5 Mercedes.
Bodies Inc: Caetaro, Marcopolo, Plaxton.

MD COACH HIRE
25 TARA LAWN, THE DONAHIES, RAHENY, DUBLIN 13
Tel/Fax: 00 353 1 847 9591
Prop: Michael Dunne.

MICHAEL MEERE COACH HIRE
33 CHURCH DRIVE, CLARECASTLE, ENNIS, Co CLARE
Tel: 00 353 65 682 4833
Fax: 00 353 65 684 4544
E-mail: michaelmeere@clarelive.com

MIDLAND BUS CO LTD
LOUGHNASKIN, ATHLONE
Tel: 00 353 90 22427
Dir/Gen Man: N. Henry
Fleet: 14 coach
Chassis: Leyland, Volvo, Mercedes.
Ops incl: local bus services, excursions & tours.

JOE MORONEY
HERMITAGE, ENNIS, Co CLARE.
Tel: 00 353 66 824146
Fax: 00 353 65 686 9480
E-mail: mcoachesennis@eire.com
Fleet: 7 - 1 double-deck coach, 1 coach

MORTON'S COACHES DUBLIN
TAYLORS LANE, BALLYBODEN, DUBLIN 16
Tel: 00 353 1 494 4927
E-mail: mortonscoaches@clubi.ie, info@circlelinebus.com
Fleet: Circle Line Bus Co
Prop: Paul Morton
Fleet: 13 - 1 double-deck bus, 3 single-deck bus, 6 coach, 3 double-deck coach
Chassis: Ayats. DAF. MAN. Mercedes. Volvo.
Bodies: Ayats. East Lancs. Marcopolo. Wright.
Ops incl: local bus services, school contracts, excursions & tours, private hire, continental tours.
Livery: White

THOMAS MURPHY & SONS
KILBRIDE HOUSE, KILBRIDE LANE, BRAY, Co WICKLOW
Tel: 00 353 1 286 2471
Fleet: 11 - 8 coach, 1 minibus, 2 minicoach.
Chassis: Volvo, Mercedes, Scania.

NAUGHTON COACH TOURS
SHANAGURRANE, SPIDDAL, Co GALWAY
Tel: 00 353 91 553188
Fax: 00 353 91 553302
E-mail: naugtour@iol.i.e
Web site: www.wombat.ie/pages/oneachtain-tours
Dir: Steve Naughton **Dir/Sec**: Maureen Naughton
Fleet: 8 - 5 coach, 1 double-deck bus, 2 midicoach.
Chassis: 1 Daimler. 1 MAN. 3 Mercedes. 1 Toyota. 2 Volvo
Bodies: 1 Caetano. 1 Jonckheere. 1 Leyland. 2 Plaxton.
Ops incl: excursions & tours, private hire

NESTORBUS LTD, GALWAY & DUBLIN
TURLOUGHMORE, ATHENRY, Co GALWAY
Tel: 00 353 91 797144, 00 353 1 832 0094
Fax: 00 353 91 797244
E-mail: busnestor@eircom.net
Web Site: www.busnestor.galway.net
Prop: P. Nestor
Fleet: 9 - 8 coach, 1 double-deck coach.
Chassis: 8 Mercedes. 1 Setra.
Ops incl: excursions & tours, private hire, express, continental tours.
Livery: Red/Cream

NOLAN COACHES
19 CLONSHAUGH LAWN, COOLOCK, DUBLIN 17
Tel: 00 353 1 847 3487
Mobile: 0862 592000
Prop: David Nolan
Fleet: 1 coach
Ops incl: school contracts, private hire.

O'CONNELL COACHES
PORTUMNA ROAD, BALLINASLOE
Tel: 00 353 905 43339
Prop: J. O'Connell
Fleet: 5 coach

REPUBLIC OF IRELAND

Chassis: Ford. **Bodies**: Plaxton
Ops incl: private hire.

O'CONNOR AUTOTOURS LTD
ROSS ROAD, KILLARNEY
Tel: 00 353 64 31052
Fax: 00 353 64 31703
Dir/Gen Man: B. O'Connor.
Ch Eng: R. Downing. **Sec**: C. Enright.
Traf Man: D. Fenton
Fleet: 5 - 1 midibus, 4 minicoach.
Chassis: Leyland. Mercedes. Volvo.
Bodies: Reeve Burgess. Van Hool. Euro.
Ops incl: excursions & tours, private hire.
Livery: Maroon/Yellow.

TOM O'CONNOR
CLOGHANE, TRALEE, Co KERRY
Tel: 00 353 66 713 8140

FEDA O'DONNELL COACHES
RANAFAST, Co DONEGAL
Tel/Fax: 00 353 75 48114
E-mail: busfeda@eircom.net
Web site: fedaodonnell.com
Prop: Pat O'Flaherty.
Fleet: 13 - 9 coach, 2 minibus, 2 minicoach.
Ops incl: express

O'FLAHERTY TRANSPORT LTD
LISDOONVARNA, Co CLARE
Tel/Fax: 00 353 65 74117.
Fleet: 1 midicoach.
Prop: Pat O'Flaherty

LARRY O'HARA MINI COACHES
13 SKIBBEREEN LAWN, WATERFORD CITY
Tel: 00 353 51 372232
Fax: 00 353 51 357566
E-mail: larryohara@eircom.net
Fleetname: O'Hara Autotours
Props: Larry O'Hara, Helen O'Hara
Fleet: 4 - 2 midicoach, 2 minibus,
Chassis/Bodies: 4 Mercedes.

O'MALLEY COACHES
FOILDARRIG, NEWPORT,
Co TIPPERARY
Tel: 00 353 61 378119
Fax: 00 353 61 378002
Owner: E. O'Malley
Fleet: 16 - 2 single-deck bus, 9 coach, 2 midibus, 2 midicoach, 1 minibus.
Ops incl: local bus services, school contracts, excursions & tours, private hire, express.
Livery: Blue/White.

O'S COACHES
HOSPITAL, Co LIMERICK
Tel: 00 353 61 383 222
Fax: 00 353 61 383 222
E-mail: oscoaches@eircom.net
Prop: Sean F. O'Sullivan **Ch Eng**: Patrick Leahy.
Fleet: double-deck bus
Chassis: Leyland,Leyland National, Mercedes
Bodies: Leyland, Leyland National, Mercedes
Ops incl: school contracts
Livery: Blue/Cream

O'SULLIVANS COACHES
FARRAHY ROAD, KILDORRERY, MALLOW, Co CORK
Tel: 00 353 22 25185
Fax: 00 353 22 25731
Prop: C O'Sullivan
Fleet: 12 - 9 coach, 3 midicoach.
Chassis: 2 Bedford. 1 Ford Transit. 1 Leyland. 2 Mercedes. 4 Volvo.
Bodies: 1 Duple. 3 Plaxton. 3 Van Hool. 3 Van Conversions.

GEORGE PLANT
AREDNAGEEHA, BANTRY, Co CORK
Tel/Fax: 00 353 27 5064
Fleet: incl: minicoach, minibus
Ops incl: private hire, excursions & tours

JACKY POWER TOURS
2 LOWER ROCK STREET, TRALEE, Co KERRY
Tel: 00 353 66 713 6300
Fax: 00 353 66 712 9444
Fleet: 7 - 5 midicoach, 2 midibus.

JOHN ROSS
97 SLIAGH BREAGH, PEPPERSTOWN, ARDEE,
Co LOUTH
Tel: 00 353 41 53158
Fleet: 8 - 3 coach, 2 midicoach, 2 minibus, 1 midibus

O'BRIEN COACHES LTD T/A ROVER COACHES
LYNN ROAD, MULLINGAR,
Co WESTMEATH
Tel: 00 353 44 934 4429
Fax: 00 353 44 938 5020
Recovery: 086 2571 645
E-mail: info@rovercoaches.ie
Fleet Name: Rover
Dirs: Patrick O'Brien, John Farrell
Fleet: 16 - 9 coach, 4 midibus, 2 midicoach, 1 minibus.
Chassis: 1 DAF. 2 Ford Transit. 1 Iveco. MAN. 3 Mercedes. 2 Renault. 1 Toyota. 8 Volvo.
Bodies: 3 Caetano. 1 Esker. 2 Jonckheere. 4 Plaxton. 1 Setra. 3 other.
Ops incl: excursions & tours, school contracts, private hire, express, continental tours.

SEALANDAIR COACHING (IRELAND) LTD/PAB TOURS
51 MIDDLE ABBEY STREET, DUBLIN 1
Tel: 00 353 1 873 3411
Fax: 00 353 1 873 2639
E-mail: info@pabtours.com
Web site: www.pabtours.com
Fleetname: PAB Tours
Man Dir: Anthony Kelly
Fleet: 5 coach
Chassis: Leyland
Bodies: Duple

MATT SHANAHAN COACHES
ST MARTINS, LACKEN ROAD,
KILBARRY, WATERFORD
Tel: 00 353 51 74192
Fleet: 2 - single-deck bus

ST KEVINS BUS SERVICE
See P Doyle, above

SUIRWAY BUS & COACH SERVICES LTD
PASSAGE EAST, Co WATERFORD
Tel: 00 353 51 382209
Fax: 00 353 51 382676
E-mail: suirway@eircom.net
Web site: www.suirway.com
Fleetname: Suirway
Dir: Brian Lynch
Fleet: 10 - 6 coach, 2 single-deck bus, 2 midicoach.
Chassis: 2 Mercedes. 8 Volvo.
Bodies: 2 Esker. 2 Jonckheere. 4 Van Hool. 2 Wright.
Ops incl: local bus services, excursions & tours, private hire.
Livery: White

SWILLY BUS SERVICE
LETTERKENNY, Co DONEGAL
Tel: 00 353 74 22863
Ops incl: local bus service

TREACY COACHES
ERRIGAL, KILLALA ROAD, BALLINA, Co MAYO
Tel: 00 353 96 22563
Fax: 00 353 96 70968
E-mail: treacycoaches@eipcom.net
Dirs:
A. Treacy (**Gen Man**). Sec: M. Treacy.
Fleet: 8 - 1 minibus, 7 coach.
Ops incl: excursions & tours, private hire, express.
Livery: White/Blue

	Vehicle suitable for disabled		24 hour recovery service
	Toilet-drop facilities available		Replacement vehicle available
	Recovery service available		Vintage Coach(es) available
	Open top vehicle(s)v		
	Seat belt-fitted Vehicle		
	Coach(es) with galley facilities		
	Air-conditioned vehicle(s)		
	Coaches with toilet facilities		

REPUBLIC OF IRELAND

Whatever your interests, historic or modern, we have possibly the most extensive range for the bus enthusiast.

Birmingham
47 Stephenson Street
Birmingham | B2 4DH
Tel: 0121 643 2496 | Fax: 0121 643 6855
Email: bcc@ianallanpublishing.co.uk

Cardiff
31 Royal Arcade
Cardiff | CF10 1AE
Tel: 029 2039 0615 | Fax: 029 2039 0621
Email: cardiff@ianallanpublishing.co.uk

London
45/46 Lower Marsh | Waterloo
London | SE1 7RG
Tel: 020 7401 2100 | Fax: 020 7401 2887
Email: waterloo@ianallanpublishing.co.uk

Manchester
5 Piccadilly Station Approach
Manchester | M1 2GH
Tel: 0161 237 9840 | Fax: 0161 237 9921
Email: manchester@ianallanpublishing.co.uk

Ian Allan PUBLISHING

IAN ALLAN BOOKSHOPS

- Books
- Magazines
- Diecast Models
- DVDs
- CD-ROMs

& much more...

Visit our website:
www.ianallanpublishing.co.uk

Section 5

Indices

TRADE INDEX

Several of the traders listed in this index will have more than one entry; only the first is shown here in each case.

A

ABACUS TUBULAR PRODUCTS LTD	35
ACIS	52
ACT	45
ACTIA UK Ltd	28
ACTION TOURS LTD	60
AD COACH SALES	16
ADGROUP	50
ADG TRANSPORT CONSULTANCY	50
ADVANCED VEHICLE BUILDERS	14
AFTERMARKET COACH SUPPLIES	14
AIRCONCO	14
AIR DOOR SERVICES	26
AJP COMMERCIALS	16
ALBATROSS TRAVEL GROUP	60
ALBION AUTOMOTIVE LTD	26
ALCOA	49
ALEXANDER DENNIS LTD	12
ALLEN & DOUGLAS CORPORATE CLOTHING LTD	48
ALLIED VEHICLES	16
ALLISON TRANSMISSION	34
ALMEX INFORMATION SYSTEMS	45
ALSTOM TRANSPORT	13
ALTRO	33
AMA LTD	19
ANTAL INTERNATIONAL NETWORK	52
AP BORG & BECK / AP LOCKHEED	
- see Capoco AP Braking	
ARDEE COACH TRIM LTD	41
ARRIVA BUS AND COACH	12
ARVIN MERITOR	22
ASHLEY BANKS LTD	23
ASHTREE GLASS LTD	37
ATLANTIS INTERNATIONAL	49
ATLAS LIGHTING COMPONENTS	37
ATOS ORIGIN	45
AUSTIN ANALYTICS	50
AUTOGLASS	50
AUTOLIFT LTD	37
AUTOMATE WHEEL COVERS	33
AUTOMOTIVE TEXTILE INDUSTRIES LTD	41
AUTOPRO SOFTWARE UK	52
AUTOSAN	12
AUTOSOUND LTD	19
AVID VEHICLES LTD	14
AVONDALE INTERNATIONAL LTD	16
AVS STEPS	20
AVT SYSTEMS	19
AYATS (GB) LTD	12

B

BALFOUR BEATTY RAIL PLANT LTD	40
BARNWELL SERVICES	38
BARRONS CHARTERED ACCOUNTANTS	50
BARTONS TRANSPORT	12
B A S E	13
BBA FRICTION LTD	22
BELMONT INTERNATIONAL LTD	56
BELVOIR CASTLE	60
BEMROSEBOOTH LTD	47
BERNSTEIN ENGINEERING LTD	42
BESTCHART LTD	53
BEST IMPRESSIONS	51
BETA RESEARCH (ZEBRA)	20
BEULAS	13
M. BISSELL DISPLAY	32
BLACKPOOL COACH SERVICES	20
BLACKPOOL TRIM SHOPS LTD	49
BLUEBIRD VEHICLES LTD	15
BLYTHSWOOD MOTORS LTD	16
BMC UK	12
BOB VALE COACH SALES LTD	16
BOMBARDIER TRANSPORTATION	13
BORLAND, WINDER-DIXON LLP	50
BOTEL LTD	60
BRADTECH LTD	26
BRECKNELL WILLIS & CO LTD	40
BRIAN NOONE	12
BRIDGE OF WEIR LEATHER CO LTD	49
BRIGADE ELECTRONICS PLC	41
BRIGHT-TECH DEVELOPMENTS LTD	25
BRISTOL BUS & COACH SALES	16
BRISTOL ELECTRIC RAILBUS LTD	40
BRITAX PMG LTD	27
BRITISH BUS PUBLISHING	58
BRITISH BUS SALES	16
BRITTANY FERRIES	55
BROADWATER MOULDINGS LTD	47
DAVID BROWN VEHICLE TRANSMISSIONS LTD	34
BRT BEARINGS LTD	14
COLIN BUCHANAN & PARTNERS	50
BULWARK BUS & COACH ENGINEERING LTD	20
BURNT TREE VEHICLE SOLUTIONS	15
BUS & COACH BUYER	59
BUS AND COACH PROFESSIONAL	59
BUSES	59
BUS USER	59
BUS SHELTERS LTD	43
BUSES WORLDWIDE	59
BUSS BIZZ	23
BUTTS OF BAWTRY GARGE EQUIPMENT	34
BUZZLINES LTD	54

C

SALVADOR CAETANO (UK) LTD	13
CALEDONIAN MACBRAYNE LTD	55
CALOTELS HOTELS	56
CAMIRA FABRICS LTD	42
CANN PRINT	47
CAPARO AP BRAKING LTD	22
CAPOCO DESIGN	54
CAREYBROOK LTD	50
CARLYLE BUS & COACH LTD	20
CARMANAH TECHNOLOGIES	43
CARRIER SUTRAK	19
CASH PROCESSING SOLUTIONS LTD	22

CHADWELL ASSOCIATES LTD	51
CHANNEL COMMERCIALS PLC	20
CHAPMAN DRIVERS SEATING	42
CHASSIS DEVELOPMENTS LTD	15
CI COACHLINES	32
CIE TOURS	56
CLAN TOOLS & PLANT LTD	41
CLAYTON HEATERS LTD	14
COACH-AID	23
COACH & BUS	55
COACH & BUS WEEK	55
COACH CARPETS	33
COACH DISPLAYS LTD	55
COACH DIRECT	50
COACHFINDER LIMITED	52
COGENT PASSENGER SEATING LTD	42
COLIN BUCHANAN & PARTNERS	50
COMPAK RAMPS LTD	37
CONCEPT COACHCRAFT LTD	15
CONDOR FERRIES	55
CONSERVE UK LTD	14
COURTSIDE CONVERSIONS LTD	15
CRAIG TILSLEY & SON LTD	30
CREATIVE MANAGEMENT DEVELOPMENT	53
CRESCENT FACILITIES LTD	26
CREST COACH CONVERSIONS	20
CREWE ENGINES LTD	30
CRONER CCH GROUP LTD	53
CROWN COACHBUILDERS LTD	15
CSM LIGHTING	37
CUBIC TRANSPORTATION SYSTEMS LTD	32
CUMMINS UK	20
CUMMINS-ALLISON LTD	22
CVI	15
CYBERLYNE COMMUNICATIONS LTD	44

D

DAF COMPONENTS LTD	30
DATS (DAVE'S ACCIDENT & TRAINING SERVICES)	54
DAVID BROWN VEHICLE TRANSMISSIONS LTD	34
R. L. DAVISON & CO LTD	56
DAWSONRENTALS BUS & COACH	16
DAYCO — TRANSPORT & TRADE DISTRIBUTION LTD	30
DCA DESIGN INTERNATIONAL	53
DE LA RUE	47
DEANS SYSTEMS (UK) LTD	26
DECKER MEDIA LTD	50
DFDS SEAWAYS	55
DIESEL DYE LTD	34
DIESEL POWER ENGINEERING	30
DINEX EXHAUSTS LTD	28
DIRECT PARTS LTD	19
DISTINCTIVE SYSTEMS LTD	53
T & E DOCHERTY	52
DRINKMASTER LTD	26
DRIVER HIRE	52
DRURY & DRURY	19
DUNLOP TYRES LTD	48
DUOFLEX LTD	36

E

EAST LANCASHIRE COACHBUILDERS LTD	13
EASTGATE COACH TRIMMERS	21
EATON LTD	23
EBERSPACHER (UK) LTD	19
KEITH EDMONSON	47
ELECTRONIC TICKET MACHINE SOFTWARE SERVICES (UK)	22
ELITE SERVICES LTD	41
ELLIS TRANSPORT SERVICES	53
ELSAN LTD	26
EMINOX LTD	32
ENECO	20
ENSIGN BUS COMPANY LTD	16
ERENTEK LTD	22
ERF MEDWAY LTD	45
ERRINGTONS OF EVINGTON LTD	16
ESKER BUS & COACH SALES, IRELAND	13
ESKER BUS & COACH, UK	15
E T M SOFTWARE SERVICES	22
EURO COACH BUILDERS LTD	15
EUROTUNNEL	55
EVOBUS (UK) LTD	12
EXCEL CONVERSIONS	15
EXPO MANAGEMENT LTD	55
EXPRESS COACH REPAIRS LTD	13

F

R. W. FAULKS FCIT	53
FCAV & CO	19
FINANCIAL INSPECTION SERVICES LTD	53
FIREMASTER EXTINGUISHER LTD	32
FIRTH FURNISHINGS LTD	33
FIRST CHOICE NAMEPLATES	37
DAVID FISHWICK COACH SALES	16
FJORD LINE	60
FLEET AUCTION GROUP	14
FORD MOTOR COMPANY	14
4 FARTHINGS INTERNATIONAL RECRUITMENT	53
FRASER EAGLE MANAGEMENT SERVICES	52
FTA VEHICLE INSPECTION SERVICE	29
FUMOTO ENGINEERING OF EUROPE LTD	31
FURROWS COMMERCIAL VEHICLES	16
FWT	51

G

GABRIEL & COMPANY LTD	35
GARDNER PARTS LTD	35
GEMCO EQUIPMENT LTD	34
GHE	21
GLIDE RITE	43
GM COACHWORK LTD	15
IAN GORDON COMMERCIALS	16
GOSKILLS	58
GRASSHOPPER INN	56
GREATDAYS TRAVEL GROUP, MANCHESTER	60
GREATDAYS TRAVEL GROUP, LONDON	60
TONY GREAVES GRAPHICS	51
LEONARD GREEN ASSOCIATES	53
JOHN GROVES TICKET SYSTEMS	22
GSM-ABBOT BROWN	20

H

HANDLEY COACH UNIFORMS	48
HANOVER DISPLAYS LTD	25
HANSAR FINANCE LTD	55
HANTS & DORSET TRIM LTD	21
HAPPICH V&I COMPONENTS LTD	32
THOMAS HARDIE - WIGAN	16

HART BROTHERS (ENGINEERING) LTD	22
HATCHER COMPONENTS LTD	49
HATTS GARAGE & SERVICES	56
P J HAYMAN	56
HAYWARD TRAVEL (CARDIFF)	52
HB PUBLICATIONS LTD	58
HENRY BOOTH GROUP (see BEMROSE BOOTH)	
B HEPWORTH & CO	50
HILTECH DEVELOPMENTS LTD	29
J. HIPWELL & SON	49
HISPACOLD	19
HL SMITH TRANSMISSIONS	27
JOHN HOLDSWORTH & CO LTD	49
HOLLOWAY COMMERCIALS	16
B D HOLT	16
HWP (H W PICKRELL)	17

I

IAN ALLAN PRINTING LTD	58
IAN GORDON COMMERCIALS	16
IBPTS	45
IMAGE & PRINT GROUP	56
IMAGE FIRST CORPORATE CLOTHING LTD	48
IMEXPART LTD	22
IMPERIAL ENGINEERING	22
INDEPENDENT COACH TRAVEL	60
INDCAR SA	15
INDICATORS INTERNATIONAL LTD	25
INDUSTRIAL & COMMERCIAL WINDOW CO LTD	50
INIT	47
INTELLITEC LTD	27
INTERLUBE SYSTEMS LTD	34
INVERTEC LTD	21
IRISBUS (UK) LTD	12
IRISH COMMERCIALS	16
IRISH FERRIES	55
IRIZAR	13
ISLE OF MAN STEAM PACKET COMPANY	55
IVECO	30
ANDY IZATT	50

J

J W GLASS LTD	50
JACOBS BABTIE GROUP LTD	53
THE JANE AUSTEN CENTRE	60
JANES URBAN TRANSPORT SYSTEMS	59
JAYCAS	16
JBF SERVICES LTD	29
JDC-JOHN DENNIS COACHBUILDERS	15
JES BUSCYCLE	22
JMW	34
JOHN GROVES TICKET SYSTEMS	22
JOHN BRADSHAW LTD	14
JONCKHEERE	13
JOURNEYPLAN LTD	40
JUBILEE AUTOMOTIVE GROUP	15

K

KAB SEATING LTD	43
KARIVE LTD	26
KEITH EDMONDSON	43
KELLETT (UK) LTD	23
KERNOW ASSOCIATES	50
KING LONG PLC	12
KNORR-BREMSE SYSTEMS	22

THOMAS KNOWLES - TRANSPORT CONSULTANT	54
KVC MANUFACTURING LTD	14

L

LANCES MOBILE PAINTING	38
LANTERN RECOVERY SPECIALISTS	52
THE LAWTON MOTOR BODY BUILDING CO LTD	19
LDV LTD	14
LEICESTER CARRIAGE BUILDERS	13
LEINSTER VEHICLE DISTRIBUTORS/LVD	16
LEISUREWEAR DIRECT	48
LEONARD GREEN ASSOCIATES	53
LEXCEL POWER SYSTEMS PLC	20
LEYLAND PRODUCT DEVELOPMENTS LTD	29
LH GROUP SERVICES LTD	27
LHE FINANCE LTD	55
LONDON BUS EXPORT	16
LOOK CCTV LTD	44
LOUGHSHORE AUTOS LTD	16
LRTA PUBLICATIONS see TRAMWAYS & URBAN TRANSIT	
LUNAR SEATING LTD	43

M

M A C LTD	19
MACEMAIN + AMSTAD	43
MAJORLIFT HYDRAULIC EQUIPMENT LTD	34
MAJORLINE ENGINEERING LTD	17
MAN TRUCK & BUS UK LTD	12
MARCOPOLO	13
MARK TERRILL PSV BADGES	20
MARK TERRILL TICKET MACHINERY	22
MARKET ENGINEERING	58
MARTYN INDUSTRIALS LTD	21
MASS SPECIAL ENGINEERING LTD	17
MAUN INTERNATIONAL	54
MARSHALLS COMMERCIAL ENGINEERING LTD	29
MCI EXHIBITIONS LTD	55
MCV BUS & COACH LTD	13
McKENNA BROTHERS LTD	25
MELLOR COACHCRAFT	15
MERCEDES-BENZ	12
MID WEST BUS & COACH SALES LTD	17
MIDLAND COUNTIES PUBLICATIONS	58
MINIBUS OPTIONS LTD	15
MINIMISE YOUR RISK	51
MINITRAM SYSTEMS LTD	13
MIRROR IMAGE MODELS	36
MISTRAL GROUP (UK) PLC	14
MOCAP LIMITED	39
MONOWASH (BRUSH REPLACEMENT SERVICE)	49
STEPHEN C MORRIS	51
MOSELEY DISTRIBUTORS	13
MOSELEY (PCV) LTD	12
MOSELEY IN THE SOUTH LTD	12
MOTIONAL MEDIA LTD	40
MOTT MACDONALD	54
MTB EQUIPMENT LTD	41
MVA	51
MYSTERY TRAVELLERS	51

N

NATIONWIDE CLEANING & SUPPORT	49
NEALINE WINDSCREEN WIPER PRODUCTS	27
NEERMAN & PARTNERS	51

NEOMAN BUS UK	12
NEOPLAN	12
NEXT BUS LTD	17
NOGE	13
NORBURY BLINDS	25
NORFOLKLINE	55
NORTON FOLGATE FQ PLC	56
NU-TRACK	14

O
OLYMPUS COACHCRAFT LTD	15
OMNI WHITTINGTON	56
OMNIBUS	53
OMNIBUS TRAINING LTD	55
OPTARE COACH SALES	12
OPTARE GROUP	12
ORVEC INTERNATIONAL	36
OWENS OF OSWESTRY BMC	17

P
P&O FERRIES	55
PACEL ELECTRONICS	22
PACET MANUFACTURING	25
PARTLINE LTD	20
PARRY PEOPLE MOVERS	13
PASSENGER LIFT SERVICES LTD	37
PAYPOINT	47
PERCY LANE PRODUCTS LTD	25
PENINSULA GROUP	52
PERKINS GROUP LTD	30
PETERS DOOR SYSTEMS LTD	26
PHOENIX SEATING	42
H W PICKRELL	17
PINDAR	58
PIONEER WESTON	36
PJA LTD	54
PLAXTON LTD, *SCARBOROUGH*	12
PLAXTON COACH SALES CENTRE	14
PLUM DIGITAL PRINT	51
PNEUMAX LTD	26
POLYBUSH	43
POWER BATTERIES (GB) LTD	20
POWERTRAIN PRODUCTS LTD	19
PRE METRO OPERATIONS LTD	40
PRESTOLITE ELCTRIC	28
PROFESSIONAL TRANSPORT SERVICES	51
PSS - STEERING & HYDRAULICS DIVISION	44
PSV GLASS	47
PSV PRODUCTS	19
PVS MANUFACTURING LTD	15

Q
Q'STRAINT	39
QUEENSBRIDGE (PSV) LTD	29
QUEENSBURY SHELTERS	43
QUICK CHANGE (UK) LTD	23

R
RAINBOW CORPORATEWEAR	48
RATCLIFF TAIL LIFTS LTD	37
RED FUNNEL	55
RENAULT UK LTD	14
RESCROFT LTD	42
RH BODYWORKS	21
RICON UK LTD	37
RIGTON INSURANCE SERVICES	56
ROADLEASE	56
ROADLINK INTERNATIONAL LTD	22
ROBERTSON TRANSPORT CONSULTING	54
ROEVILLE COMPUTER SYSTEMS	55
ROUTE ONE	59

S
SAFEGUARD	33
SAFETEX LTD	42
SALTIRE COMMUNICATIONS	51
SALVADOR CAETANO (UK) LTD	13
SAMMYS GARAGE	58
SC COACHBUILDERS	13
SCAN COIN LTD	23
SCANDUS UK	42
SCANIA (GB) LTD	12
SCHADES LTD	47
SEAFRANCE	55
SECURON (AMERSHAM) LTD	42
SERGEANT (B&A) LTD	22
SETRA	12
SHADES-TECHNICS LTD	26
SHAWSON SUPPLY LTD	25
SIEMENS TRAFFIC CONTROLS LTD	40
SIEMENS VDO TRADING LTD	45
SILFLEX LTD	25
SKILLPLACE TRAINING	55
SMART CENTRAL COACH SYSTEMS	49
SMITH BROS & WEBB	49
H L SMITH	25
SNOWCHAINS EUROPRODUCTS	48
SOMERS TOTALKARE LTD	34
SOUTHDOWN PSV	16
SPECIALIST TRAINING & CONSULTANCY SERVICES	54
SSL SIMULATIONS SYSTEMS LTD	40
STAFFORD BUS CENTRE	17
STAGE HOTEL — LEICESTER	56
STANFORD COACHWORKS	15
STENA LINE	58
STERTIL UK LTD	34
STEPHEN C MORRIS	51
STEPHENSONS OF ESSEX	17
JOHN STEWART & CO (WISHAW) LTD	15
PHIL STOCKFORD GARAGE EQUIPMENT LTD	34
STOKE TRUCK & BUS CENTRE	17
STUART MANUFACTURING CO LTD	47
SUPERFAST FERRIES	55
SUSTRACO LTD	40
SUTRAK: See CARRIER SUTRAK	

T
TAGTRONICS LTD	53
TALISMAN	48
TARA SUPPORT SERVICES	52
TAS PARTNERSHIP	54
TAWE COACHBUILDERS	15
TAYLORS COACH SALES	17
TELMA RETARDER LTD	41
TERENCE BARKER TANKS	34
MARK TERRILL PSV BADGES	19
MARK TERRILL TICKET MACHINERY	22

THOMAS AUTOMATICS CO LTD	23
THOMAS HARDIE - WIGAN	19
THOMAS KNOWLES	54
TIFLEX LTD	34
TIME TRAVEL (UK)	51
TITAN BUS UK LTD	51
TONY GREAVES GRAPHICS	51
TOP GEARS DESTINATIONS	25
TOWERGATE CHAPMAN STEVENS	56
TOYOTA	14
TRAMONTANA COACH DISTRIBUTORS	13
TRAM POWER LTD	13
TRAMWAYS & URBAN TRANSIT	59
TRANMAN SOLUTIONS	53
TRANSIT MAGAZINE	59
TRANSMANCHE FERRIES	55
TRANSPORT DESIGN INTERNATIONAL	29
TRANSPORT STATIONERY SERVICES	59
TRANSPORT TICKET SERVICES	23
TRANSPORT & TRAINING SERVICES LTD	51
TRANSPORTATION MANAGEMENT SOLUTIONS	20
TRAPEZE GROUP (UK) LTD	
TRAVEL INFORMATION SYSTEMS	53
TRAVELGREEN	52
TRAVELPATH 3000	60
TREVOR WIGLEY & SON BUS LTD	17
TRIMPLEX SAFETY TREAD LTD	34
TRISCAN SYSTEMS LTD	34
TRUCK ALIGN CO LTD	21
TRUEFORM ENGINEERING LTD	43
TUBE PRODUCTS LTD	43
TVAC	15

U

UK BUS DISMANTLERS LTD	17
UNITEC PARTS & SERVICE LTD	19
UNITEC LONDON	19
UNITEC ROTHERHAM	19
UNITEC SCOTLAND	19
UNWIN SAFETY SYSTEMS	35
USED COACH SALES	17
UVMODULAR	16

V

BOB VALE COACH SALES	16
VAN HOOL	12
VAPOR STONE	26
VARLEY & GULLIVER LTD	34
VARTA AUTOMOTIVE BATTERIES LTD	26
VAUXHALL	14
VCA	54
VDL BOVA	12
VDL BUS INTERNATIONAL	12
VDO KIENZLE UK LTD	28
VENTURA BUS & COACH SALES	17
VETRO DESIGN	51
VICTORIA COACH STATION LTD	52
V L TEST SYSTEMS LTD	34
VOITH TURBO LTD	35
VOLKSWAGEN COMMERCIAL VEHICLES	14
VOLVO BUS LTD	12
VOLVO BUS & COACH CENTRE	17
VOLVO FINANCIAL SERVICES	56
VOR TRANSMISSIONS LTD	35
VOSA	55
VULTRON INTERNATIONAL LTD	25

W

WABCO AUTOMOTIVE UK LTD	22
WACTON COACH SALES & SERVICES	17
WALLMINSTER LTD	31
WALSH'S ENGINEERING LTD	31
WARD INTERNATIONAL CONSULTING LTD	45
WAYFARER TRANSIT SYSTEMS LTD	47
WEALDEN PSV LTD	17
WEALDSTONE ENGINEERING	31
WEBASTO PRODUCT LTD	19
WEBB'S	54
WEDLAKE SAINT	54
WEST END TRAVEL & RUTLAND TRAVEL	54
WIDNEY UK LTD	41
ALAN WHITE COACH SALES	17
WHITELEY ELECTRONICS	43
WIGHTLINK ISLE OF WIGHT FERRIES	55
WIGLEY TREVOR	17
WILKER GROUP	16
WILKINSON VEHICLE SOLUTIONS	22
WILLIS LTD	56
WILSURE INSURANCE BROKERS	56
WINCHESTER MARINE LTD	17
WINDOW CLEAN SERVICES	49
WOODBRIDGE FOAM UK LTD	43
WRIGHT GROUP	13
WRIGHTSURE INSURANCE SERVICES	56
WS ATKINS see ATKINS	

Y

YORKSHIRE BUS & COACH SALES	17

Z

ZF POWERTRAIN	27

OPERATOR INDEX

Operator	Page
1ST CHOICE SCORPIO TRAVEL, SLOUGH	88
2ND 4TH LTD, FERNDOWN	110

A

Operator	Page
AAA COACHES, KIRKNEWTON	193
A1 COACH TRAVEL, LONDONDERRY	212
A1 TRAVEL, YEOVIL	164
A1A LTD, BIRKENHEAD	148
A.2.B TRAVEL UK LTD, PRENTON	148
AtoB TRAVEL LTD, LUTON	87
A & C LUXURY COACHES, MOTHERWELL	197
A & E HIRE, WELSHPOOL	208
A & J COACHES OF WASHINGTON CO LTD, WASHINGTON, TYNE & WEAR	175
AA, KNIGHTS OF THE ROAD, GREATER LONDON	142
A B COACHES LTD, TOTNES	105
A M K, LIPHOOK	126
A R TRAVEL, HEMEL HEMPSTEAD	130
ABBEY COACHWAYS LTD, CARLTON, Nr GOOLE	115
ABBEY TRAVEL LTD, HITCHIN	130
ABBEY TRAVEL, LEICESTER	159
G. ABBOTT & SONS, LEEMING	154
ABERFELDY MOTOR SERVICES,	198
ABUS, BRISTOL	90
ACE TRAVEL, BURNTWOOD	169
ACKLAMS COACHES, BEVERLEY	115
ACTON COACHES, WREXHAM	211
ADAMS TOURS, BLOXWICH	177
ADAMSON'S COACHES, CRAMLINGTON	158
ADLINGTON TAXIS AND MINICOACHES, HORWICH	123
ADRAINS OF BRINKWORTH	185
AINTREE COACHLINE, BOOTLE	148
AIRCOACH, DUBLIN	213
AIRLYNX LTD, SOUTHAMPTON	126
AIRPARKS SERVICES LTD, BIRMINGHAM	177
ALAN ARNOTT, ERSKINE	199
ALDERMASTON COACHES, BLENHAM	88
ALEXCARS LTD, CIRENCESTER	120
ALFA COACHES LTD, STOCKTON-ON-TEES	111
ALFA TRAVEL, CHORLEY	136
ALFRA COACH HIRE, LARKHALL	199
A LINE COACHES, GATESHEAD	175
ALLAN'S GROUP, GOREBRIDGE	196
ALLANDER COACHES LTD, MILNGAVIE	194
ALLIED COACHES, BALDOYLE, DUBLIN	213
ALLIED COACHLINES LTD, HAYES	149
ALPHA BUS & COACH CO, HULL	115
ALPHA PERSONALISED TRAVEL LTD, WATFORD	130
ALPINE TRAVEL, LLANDUDNO	205
ALS COACHES LTD, BIRKENHEAD	148
ALTONA COACH SERVICES & TRAVEL CONSULTANT, GATESHEAD	175
ALTONIAN COACHES, ALTON	126
AMBASSADOR TRAVEL (ANGLIA) LTD, GREAT YARMOUTH	151
AMBER TRAVEL, TURRIFF	189
AMK CHAUFFUER DRIVE, LIPHOOK	126
GEOFF AMOS COACHES, DAVENTRY	157
AMPORT & DISTRICT COACHES LTD, ANDOVER	126
ANDERSON COACHES LTD, SHEFFIELD	166
ANDERSON TRAVEL LTD, LONDON SE1	142
ANDERSON'S COACHES, FERRYBRIDGE	182
ANDERSON'S COACHES, LANGHOLM	191
ANDREW JAMES QUALITY TRAVEL, MALMESBURY	185
ANDREW'S, SHETLAND	199
ANDREW'S OF TIDESWELL LTD	102
ANDREWS COACHES, FOXTON, CAMBRIDGE	93
ANDYBUS AND COACH LTD, MALMESBURY	185
ANGEL MOTORS (EDMONTON) LTD, TOTTENHAM	42
ANGEL TRAVEL, WARRINGTON	96
ANGELA COACHES LTD, BURSLEDON	126
ANGLIAN COACHES LTD, BECCLES	171
ANITAS BRITISH & CONTINENTAL TOURS LTD, STANSTED AIRPORT	116
ANTHONYS TRAVEL, RUNCORN	96
APL TRAVEL, CRUDWELL	153
APPLEBYS COACHES, LOUTH	153
APT COACHES LTD, RAYLEIGH	116
ARAN TOURS, SANDYCOVE, Co DUBLIN	213
ARLEEN COACH HIRE & SERVICES LTD, PEASEDOWN ST JOHN	164
R. K. ARMSTRONG COACHES, CASTLE DOUGLAS	191
ALAN ARNOTT, ERSKINE	199
ARON COACHLINES LTD, HAYES	149
ARRIVA CYMRU LTD, LLANDUDNO JUNCTION	205
ARRIVA DERBY LTD	102
ARRIVA LONDON	143
ARRIVA MIDLANDS, LEICESTER	139
ARRIVA MIDLANDS, CANNOCK	169
ARRIVA NORTH EAST LTD, SUNDERLAND	175
ARRIVA NORTH WEST & WALES, AINTREE	148
ARRIVA PLC	80
ARRIVA SCOTLAND WEST, PAISLEY	199
ARRIVA SOUTHEND	116
ARRIVA SOUTHERN COUNTIES, MAIDSTONE	133
ARRIVA SURREY & WEST SUSSEX, GUILDFORD	173
ARRIVA THE SHIRES & ESSEX, LUTON	87
ARRIVA YORKSHIRE, WAKEFIELD	182
ARROWEBROOK COACHES, CHESTER	96
ARUN COACHES/FAWLTY TOURS, HORSHAM	181
ARVONIA COACHES, CAERNARFON	206
ASHALL'S COACHES, MANCHESTER	123
ASHFORD LUXURY COACHES, FELTHAM	149
ASHLEY COACHES, NEWCASTLE	175
ASHLEY TRAVEL LTD t/a GRANT & McALLIN, SHEFFIELD	166
G. ASHTON COACHES, ST HELENS	148
ASM COACHES, WHITSTABLE	133
ASMAL COACHES, LEICESTER	139
J. & F. ASPDEN (BLACKBURN) LTD	136
ASTONS COACHES, WORCESTER	187
ASTONS OF NEWPORT, SHROPSHIRE	162
ATBUS LTD, FELTHAM	175
H. ATKINSON & SONS (INGLEBY), NORTHALLERTON	154
AUSDEN CLARK LTD, LEICESTER	134
AUSTIN TRAVEL, EARLSTON	191
AUTOCAR BUS & COACH, TONBRIDGE	133

225

Operator	Page
AUTODOUBLE LTD, MILTON KEYNES	92
AVENSIS COACH TRAVEL, ROMSEY	126
AVON COACH & BUS COMPANY, BIRKENHEAD	148
AWAY DAYS, SHANKLIN	132
AXE VALE COACHES, AXBRIDGE	164
AXE VALLEY MINI TRAVEL, SEATON	105
AYREVILLE COACHES, PLYMOUTH	105
AZTEC COACH TRAVEL, BRISTOL	90

B

Operator	Page
B & J TRAVEL, MIDDLESTOWN	182
B B COACHES LTD, HALESOWEN	177
B'S TRAVEL, PONTYPOOL	210
BACK ROADS TOURING CO LTD, LONDON W5	143
BAGNALLS COACHES, SWADLINCOTE	102
BAILEY'S COACHES LTD, WATNALL	159
BAKERS COACHES, BIDDULPH	169
BAKERS COACHES, MORETON-IN-MARSH	120
BAKERS COACHES, YEOVIL	164
BAKERS COMMERCIAL SERVICES, ENSTONE	161
BAKERS DOLPHIN COACH TRAVEL, WESTON-SUPER-MARE	164
BAKEWELL COACHES, BAKEWELL	102
BALDRY'S COACHES, YORK	154
BANBURYSHIRE ETA LTD, BANBURY	161
BANKFOOT BUSES, PERTH	198
BANSTEAD COACHES LTD, banstead	173
BARCROFT TOURS & EVENTS, HASTINGS	113
BARFORDIAN COACHES LTD, BEDFORD	87
BARNES COACHES LTD, SWINDON	185
BARRATT'S COACHES, SANDBACH	96
BARRY'S COACHES LTD, CORK	213
BARRY'S COACHES LTD, WEYMOUTH	109
BARTON TRANSPORT, MAYNOOTH	213
BATH BUS COMPANY	164
BATTERSBY SILVER GREY, MORECAMBE	136
BATTERSBY'S COACHES, WALKDEN	123
BEACON COACHES, CHELMSLEY WOOD	177
BEAVIS HOLIDAYS, BUSSAGE	121
BEBB TRAVEL, LLANTWIT FARDRE	209
BEECHES TRAVEL, TWICKENHAM	149
BEECROFT COACHES, FEWSTON, NR HARROGATE	154
BEELINE (R&R) COACHES LTD, WARMINSTER	185
BEESTONS COACHES LTD, HADLEIGH	171
BELLS LUXURY COACHES, SALISBURY	185
BEN GEORGE TRAVEL, BROUGHTON	153
BENNETT'S COACHES, GLOUCESTER	121
BENNETT'S TRAVEL, WARRINGTON	96
BENNETTS TRAVEL (CRANBERRY) LTD, HEATH	169
BERKELEY COACH AND TRAVEL LTD, PAULTON, BRISTOL	90
BERRY'S COACHES (TAUNTON) LTD	164
BESSWAY TRAVEL, WEST HARROW	149
BETTER MOTORING SERVICES, STRATTON-ST MARGARET	185
JAMES BEVAN LTD, LYDNEY	121
BIBBY'S OF INGLETON	154
BIG BUS COMPANY, LONDON SW1H	143
BIRMINGHAM INTERNATIONAL COACHES LTD, TILE CROSS	177
D. P. BISHOP, DUMBARTON	201
B J S TRAVEL, GREAT WAKERING	116
BL TRAVEL, HEMSWORTH	182
BLACKPOOL TRANSPORT LTD	136
BLACK VELVET TRAVEL, EASTLEIGH	126
BLAGDON LIONESS COACHES LTD, BRISTOL	164
BLAKES COACHES LTD, TIVERTON	105
BLUE DIAMOND COACHES, HARLOW	116
BLUE IRIS COACHES, NAILSEA	90
BLUEBIRD BUS & COACH, MIDDLETON	123
BLUEBIRD BUSES, ABERDEEN	189
BLUEBIRD COACHES (WEYMOUTH) LTD	109
BLUEBIRD OF NEATH/PONTARDAWE	207
BLUELINE COACHES, MAGHULL	148
BLUESTAR, EASTLEIGH	126
BLUE TRIANGLE BUSES, RAINHAM	116
BLUEWAYS GUIDELINE COACHES LTD, LONDON	143
BLUNSDON'S COACH TRAVEL, BLADON	161
C. BODMAN & SONS, DEVIZES	185
A. S. BONE & SONS, HOOK	126
A & H BOOTH LTD, HYDE	123
BORDACOACH, RAYLEIGH	116
BOSTOCK'S COACHES LTD, CONGLETON	96
BOTTERILLS, THORNTON DALE	154
BOULTONS OF SHROPSHIRE, CHURCH STRETTON	162
BOURNEMOUTH TRANSPORT LTD	109
L F BOWEN LTD, TAMWORTH	169
BOWERS COACHES LTD, CHAPEL-EN-LE-FRITH	102
D K & N BOWMAN, WREAY, CARLISLE	100
BOWMAN'S COACHES (MULL) LTD, CRAIGNURE	190
BOWYER'S COACHES, HEREFORD	129
BRADSHAWS TRAVEL, KNOTT END ON SEA	136
BRAZIERS MINI COACHES, BUCKINGHAM	92
BRENTONS OF BLACKHEATH, LONDON SE3	143
BRENTWOOD COACHES	116
BRIGHTON & HOVE BUS & COACH CO LTD	113
BRIGHTONIAN COACHES, BRIGHTON	113
BRIJAN TOURS, CULDRIDGE	126
BRITANNIA COACHES, DOVER	133
BRITANNIA TRAVEL, OTLEY	182
BRITTAINS COACHES LTD, NORTHAMPTON	157
BRODYR JAMES, TREGARON	204
BROMYARD OMNIBUS COMPANY, BROMYARD	129
A T BROWN, TELFORD	162
EDDIE BROWN TOURS LTD, YORK	154
H E BROWN, CONGLETON	96
LES BROWN TRAVEL, BATHGATE	201
BROWNINGS (WHITBURN) LTD	201
S H BROWNRIGG LTD, EGREMONT	100
WILLIAM BROWNRIGG, THORNHILL	192
BROWNS COACHES LTD, PONTEFRACT	182
BROWNS COACHES, ASHFORD	133
BROWNS OF DURHAM, DURHAM	111
ROY BROWNS COACHES, BUILTH WELLS	208
RONNIE BRUEN, COOLOCK, DUBLIN	213
BRYANS OF ENFIELD	143
BRYLAINE TRAVEL, BOSTON	141
BUCKBY'S COACHES, ROTHWELL	157
BUCKLEYS, DONCASTER	166
BUCKLEY'S TOURS, KILLARNEY	213
BUDDENS COACHES LTD, See AVENSIS	
BUGLERS COACHES LTD, BRISTOL	164
R. BULLOCK & CO (TRANSPORT) LTD, CHEADLE	123
BURDETTS COACHES LTD, MOSBOROUGH	166
BURGHFIELD MINI COACHES LTD, READING	88

Operator	Page
BURKE BROS (COACHES) LTD, TUAM, Co GALWAY	213
JAMES BURNS, PAISLEY	194
BURRELLS (BARNARD CASTLE COACHES), RICHMOND	154
R & D BURROWS LTD, OGMORE VALE, BRIDGEND	202
BURTONS COACHES LTD, HAVERHILL	171
BUS EIREANN/IRISH BUS, DUBLIN	213
TERRY BUSHELL TRAVEL, BURTON-ON-TRENT	169
BUSES4U, TANDRIDGE	173
BUTLER BROTHERS, KIRKBY IN ASHFIELD	159
BUTLERS BUSES, COBH, Co CORK	213
BUTTERS COACHES, MARKET DRAYTON	162
BU-VAL, LITTLEBOROUGH	123
BUZZLINES, HYTHE	133
BYNGS INTERNATIONAL COACHES, PORTSMOUTH	126
BYRAN COACHES LTD, SHEFFIELD	166
BYSIAU CWM TAF/TAF VALLEY COACHES, WHITLAND	203
LES BYWATER & SONS LTD, ROCHDALE	123

C

Operator	Page
C & G COACHES SERVICES, CHATTERIS	93
C & S COACHES, HEATHFIELD	115
C I COACHLINES, CHELMSFORD	116
C. L. COACHES, LANCING	181
C N ENTERPRISES, ROMFORD	116
CABER COACHES, ABERFELDY	198
CABIN COACHES, HAYES	150
CAELLOI MOTORS, PWLLHELI	206
CAHALANE COACHES, CORK	213
CALDEW COACHES, CARLISLE	100
CALL-A-COACH, WALTON-ON-THAMES	173
CALLINAN COACHES, GLAREGALWAY	213
CANAVAN'S COACHES, KILSYTH	197
DEN CANEY COACHES LTD, BIRMINGHAM	178
CANTABRICA COACHES, WATFORD	130
CARADOC COACHES, CHURCH STRETTON	162
CARADON RIVIERA TOURS, LISKEARD	98
CARAVELLE COACHES, EDGWARE	150
CARDIFF BUS, CARDIFF	203
CARMEL COACHES, OKEHAMPTON	105
J. W. CARNELL LTD, SUTTON BRIDGE	141
PETER CAROL PRESTIGE COACHING, WHITCHURCH, BRISTOL	90
CARR'S COACHES, SILLOTH	100
CARREGLEFN COACHES, AMLWCH	202
CAROUSEL BUSES, HIGH WYCOMBE	92
GERRY CARROLL COACH HIRE, DROGHEDA	213
CARSVILLE COACHES, URMSTON	123
CASTELL COACHES LTD, BEDWAS	203
CASTLE GARAGE LTD, LLANDOVERY	203
CASTLEWAYS LTD, WINCHCOMBE	121
CATHEDRAL COACHES LTD, GLOUCESTER	121
CATTERALLS OF SOUTHAM, SOUTHAM	177
CAVALIER TRAVEL SERVICES, HESTON	143
CEDAR COACHES, BEDFORD	87
CEDRIC COACHES, WIVENHOE	116
CELTIC TRAVEL, LLANIDLOES	208
CENTAUR TRAVEL MINICOACHES, SIDCUP	143
CENTRAL BUSES BIRMINGHAM	177
CENTRAL CONNECT, BIRMINGHAM	178
CENTRAL GARAGE, TODMORDEN	183
CENTRAL COACHES, KEITH	196
CENTRAL MINI COACHES, DOVER	133
CENTRAL TRAVEL, NEWTOWN	208
CENTREBUS, LEICESTER	139
CENTREBUS, LUTON	87
CENTURION TRAVEL, MIDSOMER NORTON	164
CERBYDAU BERWYN COACHES, TREFOR, PWLLHELI	206
CHADWELL HEATH COACHES, ROMFORD	116
CHALFONT COACHES OF HARROW LTD, SOUTHALL	150
CHALFONT LINE LTD, WEST DRAYTON	150
CHALKWELL COACH HIRE & TOURS, SITTINGBOURNE	133
CHAMBERS COACH HIRE LTD, MONEYMORE	212
CHAMBERS COACHES (STEVENAGE) LTD	130
H. C. CHAMBERS & SON LTD, BURES	171
CHANDLERS COACH TRAVEL, WESTBURY	185
CHAPEL END COACHES, NUNEATON	177
CHARIOTS OF ESSEX LTD, STANFORD-LE-HOPE	116
CHARLTON-ON-OTMOOR SERVICES, OXFORD	161
CHARTER COACH LTD, YORK	154
CHAUFFEURS OF BIRMINGHAM, EDGBASTON	178
CHEAM COACHES, CHEAM, SUTTON	173
CHENERY TRAVEL, DISS	151
CHENEY COACHES LTD, BANBURY	161
CHEYNE'S COACHES, INVERURIE	189
CHILTERN TRAVEL, HENLOW	87
CHIVERS COACHES LTD, WALLINGTON	173
CIRCLE LINE, MAYNOOTH, IRELAND	213
CITYCIRCLE UK, BONNYRIGG	193
CITY SIGHTSEEING EDINBURGH LTD, EDINBURGH	193
CITY SIGHTSEEING GLASGOW LTD, GLASGOW	194
CITY TRAVEL, BRADFORD	183
CLAPTON COACHES LTD, RADSTOCK	164
CLARIBEL COACHES, TILE CROSS	178
CLARKES OF LONDON, LONDON SE26	143
CLARKSON COACHWAYS, BARROW IN FURNESS	100
CLARKSONS HOLIDAYS, SOUTH ELMSALL	183
CLASSIC COACHES LTD, ANNFIELD PLAIN	111
CLEGG & BROOKING COACHES, STOCKBRIDGE	127
CLINTONA MINICOACHES, BRENTWOOD	117
CLOWES COACHES, LONGNOR	102
CLYDE COAST COACHES LTD, ARDROSSAN	196
CLYNNOG & TREFOR MOTORS, CAERNARFON	206
COACH COMPANIONS LTD, LEOMINSTER	129
COACH HOUSE TRAVEL, DORCHESTER	109
COACHLINERS, SOUTH SHIELDS	176
COACH OPTIONS, rochdale	123
COACH SERVICES LTD, THETFORD	151
COACHING CONNECTION, LLANIDLOES	208
COACHSTYLE LTD, CHIPPENHAM	186
COAST TO COAST PACKHORSE, KIRKBY STEPHEN	100
COASTAL & COUNTRY COACHES LTD, WHITBY	154
COASTAL COACHES, NEWICK, LEWES	113
COCHRANE'S, PETERLEE	111
COLISEUM COACHES LTD, WEST END, SOUTHAMPTON	127
COLLIN PHILLIPSON, GOOLE	115, 168

Operator	Page
COLLIN'S COACHES, CARRICKAMOSS, Co MONAGHAN	213
COLLINS COACHES LTD, LONDON W7	143
COLLINS COACHES, CAMBRIDGE	93
COLLINS COACHES, SELBY	154
W. H. COLLINS, ROCH	208
COLRAY COACH HIRE, BLACKPOOL	136
COMFI-LUX COACHES, HILLINGDON	150
COMFORT DELGRO	84
COMPASS ROYSTON COACHES, DURHAM	111
COMPASS TRAVEL, WORTHING	181
CONFIDENCE BUS/COACH HIRE, LEICESTER	139
CONISTON COACHES LTD, BROMLEY	143
CONNEX LTD, St HELIER, JERSEY	188
CONWAY COACH AND CHAUFFEUR DRIVE, LIMERICK	213
COOKS COACHES, WELLINGTON, SOMERSET	165
COOKS COACHES, WESTCLIFF-ON-SEA	117
COOMBS TRAVEL, WESTON-SUPER-MARE	165
HENRY COOPER, ANNITSFORD	176
COOPERS COACHES, WOOLSTON	127
COOPERS TOURS LTD, KILLAMARSH	166
COPELAND TOURS (STOKE-ON-TRENT) LTD, MEIR	169
DAVID CORBEL OF LONDON LTD, EDGWARE	143
CORCORANS EXECUTIVE TOURS, KILLARNEY, Co KERRY	213
CORPORATE COACHING, LUTON	87
COUNTRY HOPPER, IBSTOCK	139
COUNTRY BUS, NEWTON ABBOT	105
COUNTRY LION (NORTHAMPTON) LTD	157
COUNTRYLINER COACH HIRE LTD, GUILDFORD	173
COUNTRYWIDE TRAVEL, FARNHAM	105
COUNTRYWIDE TRAVEL SERVICES, SHEERNESSS	134
COUNTRYSIDE BUS SERVICES, SCARBOROUGH	154
COUNTY COACHES, BRENTWOOD	117
COUNTY MINI COACHES, LEICESTER	139
L. S. COURT LTD, FILLONGLEY	177
COURTESY TRAVEL, SHREWSBURY	162 178
COURTNEY COACHES, BRACKNELL	88
COX'S OF BELPER	102
COYLES COACHES, GWEEDORE, Co DONEGAL	213
R. & C. S. CRAIG, ROBERTON	199
CRAIG OF CAMPBELTOWN, CAMPBELTOWN	190
CRAIGGS TRAVEL EUROPEAN, AMBLE	158
HENRY CRAWFORD COACHES LTD, NEILSTON	193
CRAWLEY LUXURY, THREE BRIDGES	180
CREMIN COACHES, BANTRY, WEST CORK	214
CRESSWELLS COACHES (GRESLEY) LTD, SWADLINCOTE	102
N N CRESSWELL, EVESHAM	187
CRISTAL HIRE COACHES OF SWANWICK	102
CROESO TOURS, PENYLAN	203
CRONIN'S COACHES LTD, CORK	214
CROPLEY, FOSDYKE	141
CROPPER COACHES, TOTTINGTON	123
CROSS COUNTRY COACHES, COLERAINE	212
CROSSKEYS COACHES, FOLKESTONE	154
CROSSON MOTOR GROUP, COOLOCK, DUBLIN	214
MARTIN CROWLEY, BANDON Co CORK	214
CROWN COACHES, BICKLEY	143
CROYDON TRAMLINK	144
CRUISERS LTD, REDHILL	125
CRUSADE TRAVEL, PENKRIDGE	169
CRUSADER HOLIDAYS, CLACTON-ON-SEA	117
CRYSTALS COACHES LTD, LONDON SW10	144
CUCKMERE COMMUNITY BUS, POLEGATE	113
CUMBRIA COACHES, CARLISLE	100
CUMFI-LUX COACHES, HILLINGDON	145
CUMFYBUS LTD, SOUTHPORT	148
CUNNINGHAM CARRIAGE CO, CORRINGHAM	117

D

Operator	Page
D & E COACHES, INVERNESS	195
D & G COACH & BUS LTD, STOKE ON TRENT	170
D & H TRAVEL, KENDAL	100
D A C COACHES, GUNNISLAKE	98
D H CARS OF DENSTONE LTD, UTTOXETER	170
D R M BUS & CONTRAC SERVICES, BROMYARD	129
D. R. P. MINIBUS TRAVEL, NEWPORT PAGNELL	92
D-WAY TRAVEL, BUNGAY	172
DAGLISH COACHES, FRIZINGTON	100
DAIMLER, BIRMINGHAM	178
DAISHS TRAVEL, TORQUAY	105
DALESMAN, GUISELEY	183
DAM EXPRESS, ARDWICK GREEN	123
DAMORY COACHES, BLANDFORD FORUM	109
DANS LUXURY TRAVEL LTD, LONDON E18	144
DARLEY FORD TRAVEL, LISKEARD	98
DARRAGHS COACHES, BALLYMONEY	212
DART PLEASURE CRAFT, DARTMOIUTH	105
DARTLINE COACHES, EXETER	105
DAVIAN COACHES, LONDON	144
DAVID PALMER COACHES LTD, NORMANTON	184
DAVIDSON BUSES, WEST CALDER	201
BILLY DAVIES EXECUTIVE COACHES, STIRLING	200
D G DAVIES, RHAYADER	209
DAWLISH COACHES LTD	105
DAWSON'S MINICOACHES, ALFRETON	103
TIM DEARMAN, ARDROSS	195
MIKE DE COURCEY TRAVEL LTD, COVENTRY	178
DELAINE BUSES LTD, BOURNE	141
DEN CANEY COACHES LTD, BIRMINGHAM	177
DERBY COMMUNITY TRANSPORT	103
DEREK HIRCOCKS COACHES, UPWELL, Nr WISBECH	93
DEROS COACH TOURS, KILLARNEY	214
DERWENT COACHES LTD, STANLEY, CO DURHAM	176
DEWHIRST COACHES, BRADFORD	183
DEWS COACHES, SOMERSHAM	93
D'COACHES (DIAMOND HOLIDAYS), MORRISTON	210
DIAMOND BUS LTD, BIRMINGHAM	178
DIRECT COACH TOURS, BIRMINGHAM	178
DOBSON'S BUSES LTD, NORTHWICH	196
T. & E. DOCHERTY, IRVINE	198
DOCHERTY'S MIDLAND COACHES, AUCHTERARDER	298
DOCKLANDS BUSES LTD, SILVERTOWN E16	144
DODDS OF TROON LTD, AYR	199
J. DODSWORTH (COACHES) LTD, BOROUGHBRIDGE	154
DOIGS OF GLASGOW LTD	194
JIMMY DONNELLY & SON, ENNISCORTHY, Co WEXFORD	214
DONOVAN'S COACH HIRE, KILLARNEY	214

Operator	Page
DONS COACHES DUNMOW LTD, GREAT DUNMOW	117
DORSET COUNTY COUNCIL, PASSENGER TRANSPORT SECTION	109
DOUGLAS CORPORATION TRAMWAY	188
DOWN MOTORS, OTERY ST MARY	105
C J DOWN, TAVISTOCK	105
P. DOYLE LTD, ROUNDWOOD, Co WICKLOW	214
TONY DOYLE COACHES, ENNISKERRY, Co WICKLOW	214
K&H DOYLE, ALFRETON	103
TIM DRAPER HOLIDAYS, ALFRETON	103
DRP TRAVEL, MILTON KEYNES	92
DRURY COACHES, GOOLE	115
DUALWAY COACHES, RATHCOOLE, Co DUBLIN	214
DUBLIN BUS	214
DUBLIN MINI COACHES, DUBLIN	214
DUDLEY'S COACHES LTD, WORCESTER	187
DUNCAN MACLENNAN, STRATH-CARRON	195
DUNN'S COACHES, AIRDRIE	197
DUNN-LINE, NOTTINGHAM	157
DURHAM CITY COACHES LTD	111
DURHAM TRAVEL, SEAHAM	111

E

Operator	Page
'E' COACHES OF ALFRETON	103
EAGLE COACHES, BRISTOL	90
EAGLE LINE TRAVEL, CHELTENHAM	121
EAGLE TRAVEL, STAFFORD	170
EAGLES & CRAWFORD, MOLD	206
EAGRE, MORTON	141
EALING COMMUNITY TRANSPORT, LONDON W3	144
EARNSIDE COACHES, GLENFARG	198
EASSONS COACHES LTD, ITCHEN	127
EAST LONDON BUS GROUP, ILFORD	84 144
EAST YORKSHIRE MOTOR SERVICES LTD, HULL	115
EASTBOURNE BUSES LTD	113
A. W. EASTON'S COACHES LTD, STRATTON STRAWLESS, NORWICH	151
EASTONWAYS LTD, RAMSGATE	134
EASTVILLE COACHES LTD, BRISTOL	90
EASTWARD COACHES, IVYBRIDGE	106
EAVESWAY TRAVEL LTD, ASHTON-IN-MAKERFIELD	136
EBLEY COACH SERVICES, NAILSWORTH	121
EDS MINIBUS & COACH HIRE, EAST TILBURY	117
EDINBURGH BUS TOURS, EDINBURGH	193
EDINBURGH COACH LINES, EDINBURGH	193
EDWARDS BROS, TIERS CROSS	208
EDWARDS COACHES, LLANTWIT FARDRE	209
GEORGE EDWARDS & SON, BWLCHGWYN	211
L J EDWARDS COACH HIRE, HAILSHAM	113
EIREBUS LTD, DUBLIN	214
ELCOCK REISEN LTD, MADELEY	162
ELITE SERVICES LTD, STOCKPORT	123
ELIZABETH YULE, PITLOCHRY	198
ELLEN SMITH (TOURS) LTD, ROCHDALE	123
ELLENDERS COACHES, SHEFFIELD	166
ELLIE ROSE TRAVEL, HULL	115
P & J ELLIS LTD, LONDON NW10	144
ELLISON'S COACHES, ASHTON KEYNES	186
ELTHAM EXECUTIVE CHARTER, LONDON SE9	144
EMBLINGS COACHES, GUYHIRN	93
EMMERSON COACHES, IMMINGHAM	153
EMMAS COACHES, DOLGELLAU	206
EMPRESS COACHES LTD, ST LEONARDS-ON-SEA	113
EMPRESS MOTORS LTD, LONDON E2	144
EMSWORTH & DISTRICT, SOUTHBOURNE	127
ENDEAVOUR COACHES, BIRMINGHAM	178
ENFIELD COACHES, ENFIELD, Co MEATH	214
ENSIGNBUS COMPANY, PURFLEET	117
ENTERPRISE TRAVEL, DARLINGTON	111
EPSOM COACHES GROUP, EPSOM	173
ERB SERVICES, BYKER	176
ESSBEE COACHES, COATBRIDGE	197
E.S.T. BUS Ltd, LLANDow	210
EUROLINK FOLKESTONE	134
EUROSUN COACHES, CROMER	151
EUROTAXIS, BRISTOL	90
EUROLINERS, REDNAL, BIRMINGHAM	178
GARETH EVANS COACHES, BRYNAMMAN	204
EVE CARS & COACHES, DUNBAR	193
EXCALIBUR COACHES, LONDON SE15	144
EXCALIBUR COACH TRAVEL, SOUTHMINSTER	117
EXCEL PASSENGER LOGISTICS LTD, STANSTED AIRPORT	117
EXCELSIOR COACHES LTD, BOURNEMOUTH	109
EXPERT COACH SERVICES LTD, GRIMSBY	153
EXPRESS MOTORS, PENYGROES CAERNARFON	207
EXPRESSLINES LTD, BEDFORD	87
EXPRESSWAY COACHES, ROTHERHAM	167
EYMS GROUP LTD	84

F

Operator	Page
FAHERTY'S COACH HIRE, MOYCULLEN, Co GALWAY	214
FAIRWAY TRAVEL, EDINBURGH	193
FALCON TRAVEL, SHEPPERTON	150
FARELINE BUS & COACH SERVICES, EYE	172
FARESAVER BUSES, CHIPPENHAM	186
FARGO COACHLINES, BRAINTREE	117
FARLEIGH COACHES, ROCHESTER	134
FARNHAM COACHES, FARNHAM	174
FELIX BUS SERVICES LTD, STANLEY, DERBYS	103
FENN HOLIDAYS LTD, MARCH	93
FERNHILL TRAVEL LTD, BRACKNELL	88
FERRERS COACHES LTD, SOUTH WOODHAM FERRERS	117
FERRYMAN TRAVEL, LEYBOURNE	134
FFOSHELIG COACHES, CARMARTHEN	203
DAVID FIELD, NEWENT	121
FIFE SCOTTISH OMNIBUSES LTD, COWDENBEATH	194
FILERS TRAVEL, ILFRACOMBE	106
FINEGAN COACH HIRE, CARRICKMACROSS, Co MONAGHAN	214
FINGLANDS COACHWAYS, RUSHOLME	123
DECLAN FINNEGAN, KENMARE, Co KERRY	215
EUGENE FINNEGAN (TRANSPORT), BRAY, Co WICKLOW	214
FIRST IN ABERDEEN	189
FIRST BERKSHIRE, BRACKNELL	88
FIRST BRADFORD	183
FIRST BRISTOL, BRISTOL	90
FIRST CALDERDALE & HUDDERSFIELD	183
FIRST CYMRU, SWANSEA	210
FIRST IN CHESTER & THE WIRRAL	96, 148

Operator	Page
FIRST DEVON & CORNWALL	106
FIRST EASTERN COUNTIES, NORWICH	151
FIRST EDINBURGH	200
FIRST ESSEX BUSES, CHELMSFORD	117
FIRST GLASGOW	195
FIRST HAMPSHIRE & DORSET LTD, SOUTHAMPTON	127
FIRST IN LEEDS	183
FIRST LEICESTER	139
FIRST LONDON	144
FIRST IN MANCHESTER, OLDHAM	124
FIRST NORTHAMPTON	157
FIRST POTTERIES (NORTH STAFFS)	170
FIRST SOMERSET & AVON, WESTON-SUPER-MARE	165
FIRST SOUTH YORKS, ROTHERHAM	167
FIRST IN WYVERN, WORCESTER	187
FIRST YORK	154
FIRSTGROUP PLC	81
FISHERS TOURS, DUNDEE	192
JOHN FISHWICK & SONS, LEYLAND	137
FITZCHARLES COACHES LTD, GRANGEMOUTH	200
FIVE STAR GROUP TRAVEL, PRESCOTT	148
JOHN FLANAGAN COACH TRAVEL, GRAPPENHALL, WARRINGTON	96
FLIGHTS HALLMARK LTD, BIRMINGHAM	178
FLYGHT TRAVEL, COSHAM	127
FORDS COACHES, ALTHORNE	118
FOREST COACHES, LONDON E6	144
FORESTDALE COACHES LTD, CROYDON	144
FORGET-ME-NOT (TRAVEL) LTD, IPSWICH	172
FORMBY COACHWAYS LTD, FORMBY	149
FOUNTAIN EXECUTIVE, ABERDEEN	189
FOUR GIRLS COACHES, PONTYBODKIN	206
FOWLERS TRAVEL, HOLBEACH DROVE	141
TOM FOX, ROCKCORRY, Co MONAGHAN	215
FRASER EAGLE LTD, PADIHAM	137
FREEBIRD, BURY	124
FREESTONES COACHES, BEETLEY, DEREHAM	152
JAMES FRENCH & SON, EYEMOUTH	191
MARTIN FUREY COACHES LTD, DRUMCLIFFE, Co SLIGO	215
L. FURNESS & SONS, HIGH GREEN	167

G

Operator	Page
G & S TRAVEL, RAMSGATE	134
G. J. TRAVEL LTD, CHERTSEY	174
G. M. COACHES, CEFN CRIBWR	202
G. P. D. TRAVEL, HEYWOOD	124 137
GAIN TRAVEL EXPERIENCE LTD, BRADFORD	183
GALLEON TRAVEL LTD, HARLOW	118
GALLOWAY EUROPEAN, MENDLESHAM	172
GALSON-STORNOWAY, ISLE OF LEWIS	201
GALVINS COACHES, DUNMANWAY, Co CORK	215
GANGE'S COACHES, COWES	132
GARDINERS TRAVEL, SPENNYMOOR	111
GARELOCHEAD COACHES	190
GARETH EVANS COACHES, BRYNAMMAN	204
GARNETT'S COACHES, BISHOP AUCKLAND	111
GARRETT COACHES LTD, NEWTON ABBOT	106
GARY'S COACHES OF TREDEGAR	202
STANLEY GATH (COACHES) LTD, DEWSBURY	183
GATWICK FLYER, ROMFORD	118
GEE-VEE TRAVEL, BARNSLEY	167
GEMINI TRAVEL, IPSWICH	172
GEMINI TRAVEL, MARCHWOOD	127
GENIAL TRAVEL, STANWAY	118
BEN GEORGE TRAVEL, BRIGG	153
GHA COACHES, CORWEN	205 211
GILLEN COACHES, PORT GLASGOW	196
R G GITTINS, WELSHPOOL	209
G-LINE, St ANNES	137
G-LINE MINICOACHES, SWINDON	186
GLASGOW CITYBUS	195
GLEN COACHES LTD, GREENOCK	196
GLENVIC OF BRISTOL LTD	90
GLOBE COACHES, ABERDARE	210
GLOVERS COACHES LTD, ASHBOURNE	103
JAMES GLYNN, NURNEY	215
GLYNNS COACH HIRE (ENNIS) LTD	215
GO NORTH EAST, GATESHEAD	176
GO-AHEAD GROUP PLC	82
GO-GOODWINS, ECCLES	124
J D GODSON, CROSSGATES	183
PETER GODWARD COACHES, SOUTH WOODHAM FERRERS	118
GOLD STANDARD, THE, GREENFORD	145
GOLD STAR COACHES, TORQUAY	106
GOLD STAR TRAVEL, BROMSGROVE	187
GOLDEN BOY COACHES LTD, HODDESDON	130
GOLDEN EAGLE COACHES, SALSBURGH	197
GOLDEN GREEN LUXURY TOURS, LONGNOR BUXTON	103
GOLDEN PIONEER TRAVEL, HEREFORD	129
GOLDENSTAND SOUTHERN LTD, LONDON, NW10	144
GOODE COACHES, NORTHAMPTON	157
GOODE'S COACHWAYS, WEDNESBURY	179
W. C. GOODSIR, HOLYHEAD	202
GOODWIN'S COACHES, BRAINTREE	118
W. GORDON & SONS, ROTHERHAM	167
GOSPEL'S COACHES, HUCKNALL	159
G. W. GOULDING, KNOTTINGLEY	183
GRAHAM URQUHART TRAVEL, INVERNESS	196
VIOLET GRAHAM COACHES, PAISLEY	199
GRAHAM'S COACHES, BRISTOL	90
GRAHAM'S, KELVEDON	118
GRAND HOTEL TOURS, SANDOWN	132
GRAMPIAN COACHES, ABERDEEN	189
GRAND PRIX COACHES, BROUGH	100
GRANT PALMER PASSENGER SERVICES, DUNSTABLE	87
GRAVES COACHES, BROXBOURNE	130
GRAY'S TRAVEL OF COVENTRY	177
GRAYLINE COACHES, BICESTER	161
GRAYS LUXURY TRAVEL, HOYLAND COMMON	167
GRAYWAY COACHES, WIGAN	124
GRAYSCROFT BUS SERVICES LTD, MABLETHORPE	141
A. GREEN COACHES LTD, WALTHAMSTOW	145
GREEN BUS SERVICE (WARSTONE MOTORS), GREAT WYRLEY	171
GRETTON'S COACHES, PETERBOROUGH	93
GREYHOUND COACHES CO, CARDIFF	203
GREY CARS, TORBAY	106
GREYS OF ELY	93
GRIERSONS COACHES, STOCKTON-ON-TEES	111
GRIFFIN BUS, SEVENOAKS	134
GRIFFITHS COACHES, PORTDINORWIC	207

Operator	Page
JEFF GRIFFITHS COACHES, ST ANNES	137
GRINDLES COACHES LTD, CINDERFORD	121
GROUP TRAVEL, BODMIN	98
GROVE COACHES, HERTFORD	130
GRWP ABERCONWY, LLANDUDNO	205
GUSCOTT'S COACHES LTD, BEAWORTHY	106
GWYN JONES & SON LTD, BRYNCETHIN	202
GWYN JONES (MEIFORD), MEIFOD	209
GWYN WILLIAMS & SONS LTD, LOWER TUMBLE	204
GWYNFOR COACHES, LLANGEFNI	202

H

Operator	Page
HCT GROUP, LONDON E8	145
HAGUES COACHES, ROTHERHAM	167
HAILSTONE TRAVEL, LITTLE BURSTEAD	118
PHIL HAINES COACHES, BOSTON	141
MIKE HALFORD, BRIDPORT	109
A. HALPENNY, BLACKROCK, DUNDALK	215
HALTON BOROUGH TRANSPORT LTD, WIDNES	97
HAMILTON OF UXBRIDGE	150
HAMS TRAVEL, FLIOMWELL	114
R. HANDLEY & SONS LTD, MIDDLEHAM	155
HAPPY DAYS COACHES, STAFFORD	170
HARDINGS COACHES, BETCHWORTH	174
HARDINGS INTERNATIONAL, REDDITCH	187
HARDINGS TOURS LTD, HUYTON	149
HARDY MILES COACHES LTD, SOUTHEND	118
HARDYS, ILFRACOMBE	100
HARGREAVES COACHES, HEBDEN, Nr SKIPTON	155
HARLEQUIN COACHES, DUNBLANE	200
HARLEQUIN TRAVEL, IPSWICH	172
HARPUR'S COACHES, DERBY	103
HARRIS COACHES, BLACKWOOD	203
HARRIS EXECUTIVE TRAVEL, BROMSGROVE	187
HARRISON'S TRAVEL, ALFRETON	103
D & H HARROD (COACHES) LTD, KING'S LYNN	152
HARROGATE & DISTRICT TRAVEL LTD	155
HARROGATE COACH TRAVEL LTD	155
HARWOOD COACHES, WEYBRIDGE	174
HATTS COACHES, CHIPPENHAM	186
HAYDN'S TOURS & TRAVEL, CHIRK	211
HAYTON'S COACHES, BURNAGE	124
HAYWARD TRAVEL (CARDIFF)	210
HAYWARDS COACHES, NEWBURY	88
HEALINGS INTERNATIONAL COACHES, OLDHAM	124
HEALY COACHES, GALWAY	215
HEARD'S COACHES, BIDEFORD	106
HEARNS COACHES, HARROW WEALD	145
HEATON'S OF SHEFFIELD	167
HEBRIDEAN COACHES, HOWMORE, SOUTH UIST	201
HEDINGHAM & DISTRICT OMNIBUSES LTD, SIBLE HEDINGHAM	118
HEMMINGS COACHES, HOLSWORTHY	106
HENLEYS BUS SERVICES, ABERTILLERY	202
HENRY CRAWFORD COACHES LTD, NEILSTON	193
HENSHAWS COACHES, JACKSDALE	159
HERBERTS TRAVEL, SHEFFORD	87
HERITAGE TOURS, ST MARY'S, ISLES OF SCILLY	188
HERRINGTON COACHES LTD, FORDINGBRIDGE	127
HEYFORDIAN TRAVEL LTD, BICESTER	161
HIGHLAND HERITAGE, DALLMALLY	190
HIGHLAND ROVER COACHES, TAYNUILT	190
HIGHWAYMAN COACHES, PERTH	198
HILLS OF HERSHAM, HERSHAM	174
HILLS SERVICES, TORRINGTON	106
HILLARYS COACHES, PRUDHOE	158
DEREK HIRCOCKS COACHES, UPWELL, Nr WISBECH	93
JOHN HOBAN TRAVEL LTD, WORKINGTON	100
HODDER MOTOR SERVICES LTD, CLITHEROE	137
HODGE'S COACHES (SANDHURST) LTD, SANDHURST	88
HODGSONS COACHES, BARNARD CASTLE	111
HODSON COACHES LTD, NAVENBY	141
M. HOGAN, THURLES, Co TIPPERARY	215
HOLLINSHEAD COACHES LTD, BIDDULPH	170
HOLLOWAY COACHES LTD, SCUNTHORPE	153
J. R. HOLLYHEAD INTERNATIONAL, WILLENHALL	179
G & J HOLMES, CLAY CROSS	103
HOLMES GROUP TRAVEL, NEWPORT	162
HOLMESWOOD COACHES LTD, ORMSKIRK	137
HOMEWARD BOUND TRAVEL, WIMBORNE	109
HOOKWAYS CLASSIC TOURS, PAIGNTON	106
HOOKWAYS GREENSLADES, EXETER	107
HOOKWAYS JENNINGS, BUDE	98
HOOKWAYS PLEASUREWAYS, OKEHAMPTON	107
HOPLEYS BUS & COACH, TRURO	98
HOPWOOD COACHES, ASKHAM BRYAN, YORK	155
HORNSBY TRAVEL, SCUNTHORPE	153
HORROCKS, LYDBURY NORTH	162
E & M HORSBURGH, PUMPHERSTON	201
HORSEMAN COACHES LTD, READING	88
JOHN HOUGHTON, LONDON W5	145
HOUNSLOW MINI COACHES, FELTHAM	150
HOUSTON'S OF LONDON, LONDON N15	145
HOUSTOUN TRAVEL, LIVINGSTON	201
HOWLETTS COACHES, WINSLOW	92
JIM HUGHES COACHES, SUNDERLAND	176
VIC HUGHES & SON LTD, FELTHAM	150
HULLEYS OF BASLOW, BAKEWELL	103
HULME HALL COACHES LTD, CHEADLE HULME	97
HUMBLES COACHES, SHILDON	112
HUNTS TRAVEL, ALFORD	141
WILLIAM HUNTER, LOANHEAD	196
HUTTON COACH HIRE, WESTON-SUPER-MARE	165
HYTHE & WATERSIDE COACHES, HYTHE	127

I

Operator	Page
IBT TRAVEL GROUP, PRESTWICK	199
IMPACT OF LONDON, GREENFORD	145
IMPERIAL BUS CO LTD, RAINHAM	118
INDEPENDENT COACHWAYS LTD, HORSFORTH	183
INGLEBY'S LUXURY COACHES LTD, YORK	155
INTERNATIONAL COACH LINES LTD, THORNTON HEATH	145
IPSWICH BUSES LTD	172
IRELAND COACHES, Co DUBLIN	215
IRISH COACHES, DUBLIN	215
IRVINE'S OF LAW, LAW	197
IRVINGS COACH HIRE LTD, CARLISLE	100
ISLAND COACH SERVICES, LAKE, IoW	132
ISLAND COACHWAYS, ST PETER PORT	188
ISLAND ROVER, SCILLYISLES	188
ISLE COACHES, OWSTON FERRY	167
ISLE OF MAN TRANSPORT, DOUGLAS	188
ISLE OF WIGHT COUNCIL, NEWPORT	132
ISLWYN BOROUGH TRANSPORT LTD,	

Operator	Page
BLACKWOOD	203
IVYBRIDGE & DISTRICT, IVYBRIDGE	107

J

Operator	Page
J & C COACHES, NEWTON AYCLIFFE	112
J & D EURO TRAVEL, HARROW	150
J B C MALVERNIAN TOURS, MALVERN	187
J C S COACHES, CORBY	157
J R J COACHES, CORBY	157
J R TRAVEL, YORK	155
J W COACHES LTD, BANCHORY	189
JACKSON'S COACHES, BLACKPOOL	137
ANDREW JAMES QUALITY TRAVEL, CHIPPENHAM	185
BRODYR JAMES, TREGARON	204
JAMES KING COACHES, NEWTON STEWART	192
PAUL JAMES COACHES, COALVILLE	139
R. G. JAMIESON & SON, YELL	199
JANS COACHES, SOHAM, ELY	94
JAYLINE BAND SERVICES, HORDEN,	112
JEFFS COACHES LTD, HELMDON	157
JEMS TRAVEL, STANNINGTON	167
JENSON TRAVEL, PONTYPOOL	210
JOHN MORROW COACHES, GLASGOW	195
JOHN'S COACHES, BLANEAU-FFESTINIOG	207
JOHN'S TRAVEL, WREXHAM	211
JOHNSON'S TOURS, HODTHORPE	159
JOHNSONS COACH & BUS TRAVEL, HENLEY-IN-ARDEN	179
D JONES & SON, RHOSLLANERCRUGOG	211
E JONES & SONS, PONCIAU	211
JONES EXECUTIVE COACHES LTD, WALKDEN	124
JONES INTERNATIONAL, LLANDEILO	204
JONES MOTOR SERVICES, FLINT	206
JONES MOTORS (LOGIN) LTD, WHITLAND	204
O R JONES & SONS LTD, LLANFAETHLU	202
P W JONES COACHES, HEREFORD	129
W E JONES & SON, LLANERCHYMEDD	202
JOSEPHS MINI COACHES, NEWCASTLE-UNDER-LYME	170
DONAL JOYCE MINIBUS HIRE, GALWAY	215

K

Operator	Page
K & B TRAVEL, CLIBURN	101
K & S COACHES, MANSFIELD	159
K. M. MOTORS LTD, BARNSLEY	167
KARDAN TRAVEL, COWES, IoW	132
BERNARD KAVANAGH & SONS LTD, URLINGFORD	215
J. J. KAVANAGH & SONS, URLINGFORD	215
M. KAVANAGH, TIPPERARY	215
PIERCE KAVANAGH COACHES, URLINGFORD	215
KEENAN OF AYR COACH TRAVEL, COALHALL	199
KEENAN COMMERCIALS, DUNDALK, CO LOUTH	215
KELVIN VALLEY COACHES, CUMBERNAULD	197
KENNEALLY'S BUS SERVICE LTD, WATERFORD	215
KENNEDY COACHES, TRALEE	206
KENT COACH TOURS LTD, ASHFORD	134
KENT COUNTY COUNCIL, AYLESFORD	134
KENZIES COACHES LTD, ROYSTON	130
K. M. KEOGH, ARKLOW	216
KERRY COACHES, KILLARNEY, Co KERRy	216
KESTREL COACHES, STOURPORT ON SEVERN	187
KETTLEWELL (RETFORD) LTD	159
R. KIME & CO LTD, FOLKINGHAM	141
KINCH BUS LTD, HEANOR	103
KINEIL COACHES, FRASERBURGH	190
JAMES KING COACHES, NEWTON STEWART	192
KINGDOM COACHES, LEVEN	194
KINGDOM'S TOURS LTD, TIVERTON	107
KINGFISHER MINICOACHES, READING	89
KINGS COACHES, STANWAY	118
THE KINGS FERRY, GILLINGHAM	134
KINGS LUXURY COACHES, MIDDLESBROUGH	155
KINGSNORTON COACHES, BIRMINGHAM	179
KINGSLEY COACHES, BIRTLEY	176
KINGSMAN INTERNATIONAL TRAVEL, FAVERSHAM	134
KINGSTON COACHES, SALISBURY	186
KINGSWINFORD COACHWAYS, BRIERLY HILL	179
KIRBYS COACHES, RAYLEIGH	119
KIRKBY LONSDALE COACH HIRE, CARNFORTH	137
KIWI LUXURY TRAVEL, NEWTON STEWART	192
KONECTBUS, DEREHAM	152

L

Operator	Page
LADYBIRD TRAVEL, WORKINGTON	101
LADYLINE, RAWMARSH	167
LAKELAND TOURS, TEMPO, Co FERMANAGH	212
LAKELINE COACHES, KNIGHTON	209
LAKES SUPERTOURS, WINDERMERE	101
LAKESIDE COACHES, ELLESMERE (SHROPSHIRE)	163
LAMBS COACHES, STOCKPORT	124
LAMBERT'S COACHES (BECCLES) LTD	172
LANGSON VIP, CLEVEDON	165
LANGSTON & TASKER, BUCKINGHAM	92
LEANDER COACH TRAVEL, SWADLINCOTE	103
JOHN LEASK & SON, LERWICK	199
LEE'S COACHES, LANGLEY MOOR	112
LENDOR, MOSSLEY	124
LEOLINE TRAVEL, HAMPTON	150
LEONS COACH TRAVEL, STAFFORD	170
LE-RAD COACHES & LIMOUSINES WOODLEY Nr STOCKPORT	97
LESCLACHA LTD, NEWMARKET-ON-FERGUS	216
LEVERS COACHES LTD, SALISBURY	186
LEWIS-RHYDLEWIS, RHYDLEWIS	204
LEWIS COACHES, LLANDRHYSTUD	204
LEWIS TRAVEL UK, LONDON SE1	145
LEWIS'S COACHES, whitland	204
LEWIS-Y-LLAN, AMLWCH	202
LIBERTON TRAVEL, EDINBURGH	193
ARNOLD LIDDELL COACHES, BRISTOL	90
LIDDELL'S COACHES, AUCHINLECK	193
LINK LINE COACHES LTD, LONDON	145
LINKFAST LTD T/A S&M COACHES, BENFLEET	119
LITTLE BUS COMPANY, THE, ELSTREE	146
LITTLE JIM'S BUSES, BERKHAMSTED	120
LITTLE TRANSPORT LTD, ILKESTON	103
LIVERPOOL CITY COACHES	149
LLEW JONES INTERNATIONAL, LLANWRST	205
P&O LLOYD, BAGILLT	206
LLOYDS COACHES, MACHYNLLETH	209
LOCHS MOTOR TRANSPORT LTD, LEWIS	201
LOCHS & GLENS HOLIDAYS, GARTOCHAN	201
LODGE COACHES, HIGH EASTER	119
LOGANS EXECUTIVE TRAVEL, DUNLOY	212
LOGANS TOURS, NORTHFLEET GREEN	135

Operator	Page
LONDON BUSES, LONDON E8	146
LONDON CENTRAL, MITCHAM	146
LONDON GENERAL, MITCHAM	146
LONDONDERRY & LOUGH SWILLY, LONDONDERRY	212
LONDON sovereign, TWICKENHAM	150
LONDON united bus co, TWICKENHAM	150
DAVE LONG COACH TRAVEL, SKIBBEREEN	216
LONG'S COACHES LTD, SALSBURGH	197
LONGMYND TRAVEL, SHREWSBURY	163
J. J. LONGSTAFF & SONS LTD, DEWSBURY	183
LONGSTAFF'S COACHES, MORPETH	159
LOTHIAN BUSES, EDINBURGH	194
LUAS, DUBLIN	216
LUCKETTS TRAVEL, FAREHAM	127
LUDLOWS OF HALESOWEN	179
LUGG VALLEY PRIMROSE TRAVEL, LEOMINSTER	129
A. LYLES & SON, BATLEY	185

M

Operator	Page
M. LINE INTERNATIONAL COACHES, ALLOA	191
M & E COACHES, HERSHAM	174
M & H COACHES, DENBIGH	205
M & J TRAVEL, CRAVEN ARMS	163
M & M COACH LINES, HARROW WEALD	150
M & S COACHES, LEOMINSTER	129
M.C.T. GROUP TRAVEL LTD, MOTHERWELL	197
M D COACH HIRE, DUBLIN	216
M P MINICOACHES, TELFORD	163
M T P CHARTER COACHES, LONDON E11	146
MAC TOURS LTD, EDINBURGH	194
MacEWAN'S COACH SERVICES, AMISFIELD	192
MACKIE'S COACHES OF ALLOA, ALLOA	191
DUNCAN MacLENAN, STRATH-CARRON	195
MacPHAILS COACHES, MOTHERWELL	197
MacPHERSON COACHES LTD, SWADLINCOTE	104
MAGPIE TRAVEL, HIGH WYCOMBE	92
MAIRS COACHES, ABERDEEN	189
MAISEY, PONTYPRIDD	210
MAJESTIC TOURS EDINBURGH LTD	194
MALCYS, SHEFFIELD	167
GERALD MANNING, CROOM, LIMERICK	216
MANOR TRAVEL, BEEFORD	115
MANSFIELD'S COACHES, SWINDON	186
MARBILL COACH SERVICES LTD, BEITH	196
MARCHANTS COACHES LTD, CHELTENHAM	121
MARCHWOOD MOTORWAYS LTD,TOTTON	128
MARPLE MINI COACHES	97 124
MARSHALLS COACHES, LEIGHTON BUZZARD	87 130 146
MARSHALLS OF SUTTON-ON-TRENT, NEWARK	159
ALAN MARTIN COACHES, DUBLIN	216
WALTER MARTIN COACHES, SHEFFIELD	168
MARTIN'S OF TYSOE	177
MARTIN'S COACH TRAVEL, LIVINGSTON	201
MARTINS COACHES, LONDON	146
MARTINS COACHES, CHAPELTOWN	168
MARTINS COACHES, KETTERING	157
MARTINS SELF DRIVE, REDFIELD	91
MARTIN'S COACHES, CAVAN	216
MASS TRANSIT, ANSTON	168
MASTER TRAVEL, WELWYN GARDEN CITY	130
MATTHEWS COACHES, KINGS LYNN	152
MAUDES COACHES, BARNARD CASTLE	112
MAUN CRUSADER TOURS, SUTTON-IN-ASHFIELD	159
MAYDAY TRAVEL, CROYDON	174
MAYFIELD COACHES	168
MAYNE COACHES LTD, WARRINGTON	97
MAYNE OF MANCHESTER, MANCHESTER	124
MAYNES COACHES, BUCKIE	190 196
MAYNES COACHES, ORKNEY	198
MAYPOLE COACHES, MELLING	149
ROY McCARTHY COACHES, MACCLESFIELD	97
McCOLLS OF ARGYLL, DUNOON	191
McCOLLS COACHES, ALEXANDRIA	201
P. J. McCONNON, MONAGHAN	216
McCULLOCH AND SON, STRANRAER	192
JAMES McGEE (BUSES), LETTERKENNY	216
JOHN McGINLEY COACHES, LETTERKENNY, Co DONEGAL	216
McGILLS BUS SERVICE LTD, GREENOCK	296
McKECHNIE OF BATHGATE LTD	201
McKENDRY TRAVEL, LOANHEAD	196
McKINDLESS EXPRESS, WISHAW	197
McLAUGHLIN'S TOURS, PENWORTHAM	138
McLEANS COACHES, WITNEY	161
MEADWAY PRIVATE HIRE, BIRMINGHAM	173
MICHAEL MEERE COACH HIRE, ENNIS	216
megabus, perth	198
MEMORY LANE COACHES, OLD BOLINGBROKE	142
MEMORY LANE VINTAGE OMNIBUS SERVICES MAIDENHEAD	89
MEREDITHS COACHES, MALPAS	97
merton community transport, mitcham	174
MERVYN'S COACHES, MICHELDEVER	128
MESSENGER COACHES, WIGTON	101
METRO COACHES, STOCKTON-ON-TEES	155
METROBUS LTD, CRAWLEY	181
METROLINE TRAVEL LTD, HARROW	151
METROLINK, MANCHESTER	125
MID DEVON COACHES, CREDITON	107
MIDLAND BUS CO LTD, ATHLONE	216
MIDLAND RIDER, OLDBURY	179
MID WALES TRAVEL, PENRHYNCOCH	204
MIDWAY MOTORS, CRYMYCH	208
MIKES COACHES, BASILDON	119
MIL-KEN TRAVEL LTD, LITTLEPORT	94
MIL-KEN TRAVEL LTD, NEWMARKET	172
KEN MILLER TRAVEL, SHENSTONE	179
MILLER'S COACHES, AIRDRIE	197
MILLIGANS COACH TRAVEL, MAUCHLINE	193 199
MILLMAN COACHES, GRIMSBY	153
MILLMAN'S OF WARRINGTON	97
MILLPORT MOTORS LTD	196
ALEX MILNE, NEW BYTH	190
MINIBUS & COACH HIRE, EARL STONHAM	172
MINIBUS SERVICES, WATFORD	130
MINSTERLEY MOTORS, SHREWSBURY	163
MITCHELL'S COACHES, PLEAN	200
MK METRO LTD, MILTON KEYNES	92
MOFFAT & WILLIAMSON LTD, GAULDRY	194
MOOR TO SEA, NEWTON ABBOT	107
MOORE'S COACHES LTD, HOLMES CHAPEL	97
JOE MORONEY, ENNIS	216
MORRIS TRAVEL, CARMARTHEN	204
JOHN MORROW COACHES, GLASGOW	195
MORTON'S COACH, maynooth, ireland	216

Operator	Page
MOSLEYS TOURS, DEWSBURY	168
MOTTS COACHES (AYLESBURY) LTD, AYLESBURY	92
MOUNTAIN GOAT LTD, WINDERMERE	101
MOUNTS BAY COACHES, PENZANCE	98
C. W. MOXON LTD, OLDCOTES	159
MULLEYS MOTORWAYS LTD, IXWORTH	172
MUNRO'S OF JEDBURGH	191
THOMAS MURPHY & SONS, BRAY, Co WICKLOW	216
GAVIN MURRAY & ELLISONS COACHES, ST HELENS	149
MYKANN COACH HIRE, SWADLINCOTE	104

N

Operator	Page
NASHS COACHES LTD, SMETHWICK	180
NATIONAL EXPRESS GROUP PLC	82
NATIONAL EXPRESS LTD, EDGBASTON	180
NATIONAL HOLIDAYS, HULL	115
NAUGHTON COACH TOURS, SPIDDAL	216
NBM HIRE LTS, PENRITH	101
N.C.B. MOTORS LTD, WEM	163
NCP CHALLENGER, TWICKENHAM	151
NEAL'S TRAVEL LTD, ISLEHAM, ELY	94
NEFYN COACHES, NEFYN, PWLLHELI	207
NELSON & SON (GLYNNEATH) LTD, NEATH	207
W. H. NELSON (COACHES) LTD, WICKFORD	119
NESBIT BROS LTD, MELTON MOWBRAY	140
NESTORBUS LTD, GALWAY & DUBLIN	216
NETWORK COLCHESTER	119
NEW BHARAT COACHES LTD, SOUTHALL	146
NEW ENTERPRISE COACHES, TONBRIDGE	135
NEWBOURNE COACHES, LEIGHTON BUZZARD	146
NEWBURY COACHES, LEDBURY	129
NEWBURY & DISTRICT, NEWBURY	89
NEWBURY TRAVEL, OLDBURY	180
NEWPORT TRANSPORT LTD	208
M. W. NICOLL'S COACH HIRE, LAUREiNCEKIRK	190
NIDDRIE COACHES, MIDDLEWICH	99
NIELSEN TRAVEL SERVICES, SHEFFIELD	168
NIGEL JACKSON TRAVEL, QUENIBOROUGH	140
NOLAN COACHES, COOLOCK, DUBLIN	216
NORFOLK GREEN, KINGS LYNN	152
NORTH SOMERSET COACHES, NAILSEA	91
NORTH WEST COACHES & LIMOS THORNTON CLEVELEYS	138
NORTON MINI TRAVEL, STOCKTON-ON-TEES	112
NOTTINGHAM CITY TRANSPORT LTD	160
NOTTINGHAM EXPRESS TRANSIT	160
NOTTS & DERBY TRACTION CO LTD, HEANOR	104
NU-VENTURE COACHES LTD, AYLESFORD	135

O

Operator	Page
OFJ CONNECTIONS LTD, HEATHROW	146
OTS MINIBUS & COACH HIRE, CONSTANTINE	98
O'CONNELL COACHES, BALLINASLOE	216
O'CONNOR AUTOTOURS LTD, KILLARNEY	217
TOM O'CONNOR, TRALEE	217
FEDA O'DONNELL, DONEGAL	217
O'FLAHERTY TRANSPORT, LISDOONVARNA	217
LARRY O'HARA, WATERFORD	217
O'MALLEY COACHES, NEWPORT, Co TIPPERARY	217
O'S COACHES, HOSPITAL, Co LIMERICK	217
O'SULLIVANS COACHES, MALLOW, Co CORK	217
OARE'S COACHES, HOLYWELL	206
OBAN & DISTRICT BUSES LTD	191
OCEAN COACHES, PORTSLADE	114
DAVID OGDEN COACHES, ST HELENS	149
OLYMPIA TRAVEL, HINDLEY	138
OLYMPIAN COACHES LTD, HARLOW	119
ON A MISSION COACHES, SOULBURY	87
THE ORIGINAL LONDON TOUR, WANDSWORTH	146
OTTER COACHES, OTTERY ST MARY	105
OWEN'S MOTORS LTD, KNIGHTON	209
OWENS COACHES, OSWESTRY	163
OXFORD BUS COMPANY	161

P

Operator	Page
P&M COACHES, WICKFORD	119
PADARN BUS, LLANBERIS	207
DAVID PALMER COACHES LTD, NORMANTON	184
PARAGON TRAVEL, UTTOXETER	170
PARAMOUNT MINI-COACHES, PLYMOUTH	107
PARK'S OF HAMILTON	199
PARKSIDE TRAVEL, BROXBOURNE	131
PARRYS INTERNATIONAL TOURS LTD, CHESLYN HAY	170
PAT'S COACHES, NEW BROUGHTON	211
PATRON TRAVEL, FLINTHAM	160
PAVILION COACHES, HOVE	114
D. A. PAYNE COACH HIRE, ST NEOTS	94
PAYNES COACHES & CAR HIRE LTD, BUCKINGHAM	92
PC COACHES OF LINCOLN	142
J D PEACE & CO, ABERDEEN	189
PEARCES PRIVATE HIRE, WALLINGFORD	161
PEARSON COACHES, HULL	115
PEELINGS COACHES, KING'S LYNN	152
PEGASUS TRAVEL, PERTH	198
PENCOED TRAVEL LTD, BRIDGEND	202
PENMERE MINIBUS SERVICES, FALMOUTH	98
PERRY'S COACHES, MALTON	155
PERRYMAN BUSES, BERWICK UPON TWEED	158 191
PETER CAROL PRESTIGE COACHING, WHITCHURCH, BRISTOL	90
PETERBOROUGH TRAVEL CONSULTANTS PETERBOROUGH	94
PETE'S TRAVEL - see PEOPLES EXPRESS	
PEWSEY VALE COACHES, PEWSEY	186
PHILLIPS COACHES, SOUTH WOODHAM FERRERS	119
COLLIN PHILLIPSON MINICOACHES, OUSEFLEET	115, 168
PICKERING COACHES, SOUTH GODSTONE	174
PIED BULL COACHES, MOLD	206
JOHN PIKE COACHES, ANDOVER	128
PLANET TRAVEL, EARITH	94
GEORGE PLANT, BANTRY, Co CORK	217
PLANTS LUXURY TRAVEL, CHEADLE, STAFFS	170
PLASTOWS COACHES, WHEATLEY	161
DAVID PLATT COACHES & MINITRAVEL OF LEES OLDHAM	125
PLYMOUTH CITYBUS LTD	107
POOTS COACH HIRE, TANDRAGEE	212
JOHN POWELL TRAVEL, HELLABY	167
POWELLS COACHES, CREDITON	107
POWELLS COACHES, SHERBORNE	109
JACKY POWER TOURS, TRALEE	219
POYNTERS COACHES, ASHFORD, KENT	135

Operator	Page
PREMIER CONNECTIONS, LUTON	87
PREMIER TRAVEL, BRISTOL	91
PREMIER TRAVEL, NOTTINGHAM	160
PRENTICE WESTWOOD, WEST CALDER	201
PRESTON BUS LTD	138
PRICES COACHES, SOUTHSEA, WALES	211
PRINCESS COACHES, WEST END, SOUTHAMPTON	128
PRIORY MOTOR COACH CO LTD, NORTH SHIELDS	176
F PROCTER & SON LTD, FENTON	170
PROCTERS COACHES (NORTH YORKSHIRE), LEEMING BAR	155
PROSPECT COACHES (WEST) LTD, STOURBRIDGE	180
PROTOURS (ISLE OF MAN), DOUGLAS	188
PROTOURS, SWADLINCOTE	104
PROVENCE PRIVATE HIRE, ST ALBANS	131
PULFREYS COACHES, GRANTHAM	142
PULHAM & SON, BURTON ON THE WATER	121
PULLMAN COACHES LTD, SWANSEA	210
PULLMAN DINER, KNOTTINGLEY	184

Q
QUANTOCK MOTOR SERVICES, TAUNTON	165

R
R & B COACHES, LUDLOW	163
R. & R. COACHES LTD (BEELINE), WARMINSTER	185
R. K. F. TRAVEL, STROOD	135
RADLEY COACH TRAVEL, BRIGG	142 153
RADMORES COACHES, PLYMPTON	107
RAINHAM COACH CO, THE, GILLINGHAM	135
RAMBLER COACHES, HASTINGS	114
RAMON TRAVEL, BOSCOMBE	110
RAYS COACHES, PLYMOUTH	107
RB TRAVEL, PYTCHLEY	157
READING & WOKINGHAM COACHES, WOKINGHAM	89
READING HERITAGE TRAVEL, READING	89
READING TRANSPORT LTD	89
REAYS COACHES LTD, WIGTON	101
RED ARROW COACHES LTD, HUDDERSFIELD	184
RED KITE COMMERCIAL SERVICES LEIGHTON BUZZARD	88
REDLINE BUSES, AYLESBURY	92
RED ROSE TRAVEL LTD, AYLESBURY	92
REDROUTE BUSES, NORTHFLEET	135
REDFERN COACHES (MANSFIELD) LTD	160
RED KITECOMMERCIAL SERVICES, TILSWORTH	88
RED KITE COACHES, ABERYSTWYTH	204
REDLINE COACHES, LEYLAND	138
REDWING COACHES, LONDON SE24	146
REDWOODS TRAVEL, CULLOMPTON	107
REES MOTOR (TRAVEL), LLANELLY HILL, ABERGAVENNY	207
REEVES COACH HOLIDAYS, CHORLEY	138
REG'S COACHES LTD, HERTFORD	131
REGAL BUSWAYS, CHELMSFORD	119
REGENT COACHES, WHITSTABLE	135
REIDS OF RHYNIE, RHYNIE, BY HUNTLY	190
RELIANCE, BENFLEET,	119
RELIANCE MOTOR SERVICES, SUTTON-ON-FOREST	155
RENNIES OF DUNFERMLINE LTD	194
RENOWN COACHES, BEXHILL	114
REYNOLDS COACHES OF CAISTER, GREAT YARMOUTH	152
REYNOLDS DIPLOMAT COACHES, WATFORD	131
RICHARDS BROS, CARDIGAN	205
RICHARDSON COACHES, HARTLEPOOL	112
RICHARDSON TRAVEL LTD, MIDHURST	181
RICHMOND'S COACHES, BARLEY	131
RIDDLER'S COACHES, ARBROATH	190
RIDLERS, DULVERTON	165
RIDUNA BUSES, ALDERNEY	188
JOHN RIGBY TRANSPORT & TRAVEL, BATLEY	184
RIGBY'S EXECUTIVE COACHES, ALTHAM	137
RINGWOOD COACHES, STAVELEY	104
RIVERSIDE COACHES, TELFORD	163
ROADLINER PASSENGER TRANSPORT, POOLE	110
ROADMARK TRAVEL LTD, ASHINGTON	181
ROBERTS COACHES, ABERYSTWYTH	205
ROBERTS COACHES, HUGGLESCOTE	140
ROBERTS MINI COACHES, RHANDIR	205
ROBERTS TOURS, WINGATE	112
ROBIN HOOD TRAVEL LTD, LEEK	170
ROBINSON KIMBOLTON, KIMBOLTON	94
ROBINSONS HOLIDAYS, GREAT HARWOOD	138
ROBINSONS COACHES, APPLEBY	101
RODGER'S COACHES, CORBY	157
ROWLANDS GILL TAXIS & COACHES, ROWLANDS GILL	175
ROLLINSON SAFEWAY LTD, LEEDS	184
RONDO TRAVEL, HARROGATE	155
O. ROONEY, HILLTOWN	212
ELLIE ROSE TRAVEL, HULL	115
ROSELYN COACHES, PAR	94
JOHN ROSS, ARDEE, Co LOUTH	217
ROSS TRAVEL, FEATHERSTONE	184
ROSSENDALE TRANSPORT LTD, HASLINGDEN	138
ROTALA PLC	84
ROUNDABOUT BUSES, BEXLEYHEATH	147
ROUTESPEK COACH HIRE LTD, BUNGAY	172
ROVER COACHES, MULLINGAR, IRELAND	217
ROVER EUROPEAN TRAVEL, HORSLEY, STROUD	121
ROWE & TUDHOPE, KILMARNOCK	193
ROWELL COACHES, LOW PRUDHOE	158
ROY BROWNS COACHES, BUILTH WELLS	208
ROYLES TRAVEL, SHEFFIELD	168
ROY PHILLIPS, SLEAFORD	142
RURAL DEVELOPMENT TRUST, DOUGLAS WATER	200
RUTHERFORDS TRAVEL, EASTERGATE	181

S
SABRE COACHES, PONTYPOOL	210
SAFEGUARD COACHES, GUILDFORD	174
SAFFORDS COACHES LTD, SANDY	94
SANDERS COACHES, HOLT	152
SANDGROUNDER, SOUTHPORT	138
SARGEANTS BROS LTD, KINGTON	129
SCARBOROUGH & DISTRICT	156
SCARLET BAND, WEST CORNFORTH	112
SCHOFIELD TRAVEL LTD, LOUGHBOROUGH	140
SCOTLAND & BATES, APPLEDORE	135
SCOTTISH CITYLINK COACHES LTD, GLASGOW	195
SEAVIEW SERVICES, SANDOWN	133
SEA VIEW COACHES (POOLE) LTD	110
SEAGER'S COACHES LTD, CHIPPENHAM	186

Operator	Page
SEALANDAIR COACHING (IRELAnd) DUBLIN	217
SEATH COACHES, EAST STUDDAL, Nr DOVER	135
SELVEY'S COACHES, CAMBUSLANG	195
SELWYNS TRAVEL, MANCHESTER AIRPORT	97, 125
H. SEMMENCE & CO LTD, WYMONDHAM	152
SERENE TRAVEL, BEDLINGTON	158
SEWARDS COACHES, AXMINSTER	108
SHAFTESBURY & DISTRICT MOTOR SERVICES	110
MATT SHANAHAN COACHES, WATERFORD	217
SHARPE & SONS (NOTTINGHAM), NOTTINGHAM	160
HARRY SHAW, COVENTRY	180
SHAWS OF MAXEY, PETERBOROUGH	94
SHEARER OF HUNTLY LTD, HUNTLEY	190
SHEARINGS see W.A. SHEARINGS	
SHERBURN VILLAGE COACHES	112
SHERWOOD TRAVEL, IMMINGHAM	153
SHIEL BUSES, ACHARACLE	195
SHIRE COACHES, ST ALBANS	131
SHIRE TRAVEL INTERNATIONAL, HEDNESFORD	170
SHOREY'S TRAVEL, MAULDEN	88
B. R. SHREEVE & SONS LTD, LOWESTOFT	173
SHROPSHIRE COUNTY COUNCIL, SHREWSBURY	163
SHUTTLE BUSES LTD, KILWINNING	197
SIDLAW EXECUTIVE TRAVEL, AUCHTERHOUSE	190 192
SIESTA INTERNATIONAL, MIDDLESBROUGH	156
SILCOX COACHES, PEMBROKE DOCK	208
SILVER CHOICE TRAVEL LTD, EAST KILBRIDE	200
SILVER STAR COACH HOLIDAYS LTD, CAERNARFON	207
SILVERDALE LONDON LTD, LONDON NW10	147
SILVERDALE TOURS (NOTTINGHAM) LTD, NOTTINGHAM	160
SILVERLINE LANDFLIGHT, SOLIHULL	180
SIMS TRAVEL, BOOT	101
SIMONDS COACH & TRAVEL, DISS	152
SIMPSON'S COACHES, ROSEHEARTY	190
SIXTY SIXTY COACHES, PENTREBACH	207
D. W. SKELTON, BRIDGWATER	165
SKILLS MOTOR COACHES, BULWELL	160
SKINNERS OF OXTED	174
SKYLINERS LTD, NUNEATON	177
SLACKS TRAVEL, MATLOCK	164
SLEAFORDIAN COACHES. SLEAFORD	142
SLEIGHTS COACHES, SWINTON	168
SLOAN TRAVEL, ROSTREVOR	212
SMITH & SONS COACHES, COUPAR ANGUS	198
JOHN SMITH & SONS, THIRSK	156
SMITH'S COACHES (BE & GW SMITH), SHEPTON MALLET	165
SMITH BUNTINGFORD	131
SMITHS COACHES MARPLE	124
SMITHS COACHES, CORBY GLEN, Nr GRANTHAM	142
G. A. SMITHS COACHES LTD, TRING	131
SMITHS MOTORS (LEDBURY) LTD	129
SNOWDON COACHES, EASINGTON	112
SOLENT COACHES, RINGWOOD	128
SOLID ENTERTAINMENTS, GRIMSBY	153
SOLUS COACH TRAVEL, TAMWORTH	171
SOMERBUS, BRISTOL	165
SOULS COACHES LTD, OLNEY	93
SOUTH GLOUCESTERSHIRE BUS & COACH COMPANY, PATCHWAY, BRISTOL	91
SOUTH LANCS TRAVEL, ATHERTON	125
SOUTH MIMMS TRAVEL LTD	131
SOUTH WEST COACHES LTD, WINCANTON	166
SOUTHDOWN PSV, COPTHORNE	181
SOUTHERN COACHES (NM) LTD, BARRHEAD	193
SOUTHERN VECTIS, NEWPORT, IoW	133
SOUTHGATE & FINCHLEY COACHES LTD, LONDON N11	147
SOVEREIGN COACHES, LYME REGIS	110
SPA COACHES, STRATHPEFFER	195
SPOT HIRE TRAVEL , BEARSTED	135
SPRATTS COACHES LTD, WRENINGHAM	152
SQUIRRELL'S COACHES, HITCHAM	173
ST ANDREWS EXECUTIVE TRAVEL	194
ST KEVINS BUS SERVICE (P. DOYLE), ROUNDWOOD, Co WICKLOW	217
STAGECOACH IN CAMBRIDGESHIRE, CAMBRIDGE	94
STAGECOACH EAST, NORTHAMPTON	158
STAGECOACH IN EAST KENT & HASTINGS	135
STAGECOACH IN HASTINGS, ST LEONARDS ON SEA	114
STAGECOACH EAST MIDLANDS, CHESTERFIELD	104
STAGECOACH IN FIFE	194
STAGECOACH GROUP	83
STAGECOACH IN HAMPSHIRE, BASINGSTOKE	128
STAGECOACH HANTS & SURREY,ALDERSHOT	128
STAGECOACH HIGHLAND	195
STAGECOACH IN HULL	115
STAGECOACH LINCOLNSHIRE,	142
STAGECOACH MANCHESTER, ARDWICK	125
STAGECOACH MERSEYSIDE, LIVERPOOL	149
STAGECOACH NORTH EAST, SUNDERLAND	176
STAGECOACH NORTH WEST, CARLISLE	101
STAGECOACH IN ORKNEY	198
STAGECOACH IN OXFORDSHIRE	161
STAGECOACHIN PETERBOROUGH	198
STAGECOACH SCOTLAND, PERTH	198
STAGECOACH SHEFFIELD	168
STAGECOACH (SOUTH), CHICHESTER	181
STAGECOACH IN SOUTH WALES, CWMBRAN	210
STAGECOACH SOUTH WEST, EXETER	109
STAGECOACH YORKSHIRE, BARNSLEY	168
STAGECOACH SUPERTRAM, SHEFFIELD	168
STAGECOACH TRANSIT, STOCKTON	112
STAGECOACH IN WArwickshire, RUGBY	177
STAGECOACH WEST, GLOUCESTER	122
STAGECOACH WEST SCOTLAND, AYR	199
F. W. STAINTON & SON LTD, KENDAL	101
STALLION COACHES, CHELMSFORD	119
STAN'S COACHES, MALDON	119
STANLEY TAXIS & MINICOACHES	112
STANSTED TRANSIT, BRAINTREE	119
STANWAYS COACHES, KIDSGROVE	171
STEELS LUXURY COACHES, ADDINGHAM	184
STEPEND COACHES, GLENMAVIS	197
STEPHENSONS OF EASINGWOLD	156
STEPHENSONS OF ESSEX LTD, ROCHFORD	119
STEVE'S OF AMBLESIDE LTD	101
L. F. STEWART & SON LTD, DALAYICH, BY TAYNUILT	191
STEVE STOCKDALE COACHES, SELBY	156
STEWARTS OF MORTIMER, READING	89
STODDARDS LTD, CHEADLE, STAFFS	171

Operator	Page
STOCKHAMS COACHES, CRICKHOWELL	209
WILLIAM STOKES & SONS LTD, CARSTAIRS	197 200
STONEHOUSE COACHES	200
JIM STONES COACHES	97
STONES COACHES OF BATH	166
E STOTT & SONS, MILNSBRIDGE	184
STOTT'S TOURS (OLDHAM) LTD	125
STRAFFORD'S COACHES, MINERA	211
STRATHTAY SCOTLAND OMNIBUSES LTD, DUNDEE	192
STRATOS TRAVEL LTD, NEWTOWN, POWYS	209
STREAMLINE, MAIDSTONE	135
STREETS COACHWAYS LTD, BARNSTAPLE	108
STRINGERS PONTEFRACT MOTORWAYS	184
STUARTS OF CARLUKE	200
SUIRWAY BUS & COACH SERVICES LTD PASSAGE EAST, Co WATERFORD, IRELAND	217
SULLIVAN BUSES, POTTERS BAR	131
SUMMERCOURT TRAVEL, SUMMERCOURT	99
SUMMERDALE COACHES, LETTERSTON	208
SUMMERFIELD COACHES LTD, SOUTHAMPTON	108
SUNBEAM COACHES LTD, NORWICH	152
SUNBURY COACHES, SHEPPERTON	151
SUNRAY TRAVEL, EPSOM	174
SUPERTRAVEL OMNIBUS LTD, SPEKE	149
SUPREME COACHES, SOUTHEND	120
SURELINE, PORTLAND	110
SURELINE COACHES, WOKING	175
SURREY CONNECT, CRAWLEY	175
SUSSEX COUNTRY COACH HIRE, SHOREHAM	114 182
SUTTON COMMUNITY TRANSPORT	175
SWALLOW COACH CO LTD, RAINHAM, ESSEX	120
SWANBROOK TRANSPORT LTD, CHELTENHAM	122
SWANS TRAVEL, OLDHAM	125
SWEYNE COACHES, GOOLE	115
SWIFTS HAPPY DAYS TRAVEL, DONCASTER	168
SWIFTSURE TRAVEL (BURTON UPON TRENT) LTD	171
SWILLY BUS, LETTERKENNY, Co DONEGAL	217

T

Operator	Page
T & S TRAVEL, PONTEFRACT	184
TF MINI COACHES, BARKING	120
T M TRAVEL, STAVELEY	168
T N C COACHES, CASTLE BROMWICH	180
TALLY HO! COACHES, KINGSBRIDGE	108
TANAT VALLEY COACHES, LLANRHAEDR YM, OSWESTRY	209
TANTIVY BLUE COACH TOURS, ST HELIER, JERSEY	188
TAPPINS COACHES, DIDCOT	162
TATES COACHES, MARKYATE	132
TAVISTOCK COMMUNITY TRANSPORT, GREENLANDS	99
TAW & TORRIDGE COACHES LTD, OKEHAMPTON	108
TAYLORS COACH TRAVEL, YEOVIL	166
TELFORD'S COACHES, NEWCASTLETON	191
TELLINGS GOLDEN MILLER COACHES LTD, HEATHROW AIRPORT	147
TERRYS COACH HIRE, COVENTRY	180
TERRY'S COACHES, HEMEL HEMPSTEAD	132
TEST VALLEY TRAVEL, WHITEPARISH	186
TETLEYS MOTOR SERVICES, LEEDS	184
THAMESDOWN TRANSPORT LTD, SWINDON	186
THAMES TRAVEL, WALLINGFORD	162
THOMAS BROS, LLANGADOG	204
D J THOMAS COACHES OF NEATH	207
EDWARD THOMAS & SON, WEST EWELL	175
THOMAS OF BARRY	211
THOMAS OF RHONDDA, PORTH	210
THOMPSON'S, FRAMLINGHAM	173
THOMSETT'S COACHES, DEAL	135
THORNES INDEPENDENT LTD, HEMINGBROUGH	156
THREE STAR COACHES, LUTON	88
TIGER EUROPEAN, WOTTINGHAM	160
TILLEY'S COACHES, BUDE	99
TIMEBUS TRAVEL, ST ALBANS	147
TITTERINGTON COACHES LTD, BLENCOW	101
TOMORROWS TRANSPORT, ENFIELD	107
TONNA LUXURY COACHES LTD, NEATH	208
TOP TRAVEL, BASINGSTOKE	128
TOTNES & DARTMOUTH RING & RIDE, TOTNES	108
TOURIST COACHES LTD, SALISBURY	186
TOWER COACHES, WIGTON	102
TOWLERS COACHES, WISBECH	94
TOWN & COUNTRY COACHES, NEWTON ABBOT	108
TOWN & COUNTRY MOTOR SERVICES LTD HURWORTH MOOR, Nr DARLINGTON	112
TOWNLYNX, HOLYWELL	206
TRACKS VEHICLE SERVICES, ROMNEY MARSH	136
TRAMONTANA, MOTHERWELL	197
TRANSDEV PLC	82
TRANSDEV BURNLEY & PENDLE	138
TRANSDEV KEIGHLEY & DISTRICT	184
TRANSDEV LANCASHIRE UNITED	138
TRANSDEV NORTHERN BLUE	139
TRANSDEV YORK	156
TRANSIT EXPRESS TRAVEL, LENTON	160
TRANSLINC LTD, LINCOLN	142
TRANSLINK, BELFAST	212
TRATHENS TRAVEL SERVICES, PLYMOUTH	108
TRAVEL DUNDEE	192
TRAVEL EXPRESS, WOLVERHAMPTON	180
TRAVEL LONDON, LONDON SE5	147
travelmasters, sheerness	136
TRAVEL MIDLANDS METRO	180
TRAVEL SURREY, LONDON SE5	175
TRAVEL WEST MIDLANDS, BIRMINGHAM	180
TRAVEL WRIGHT, NEWARK-ON-TRENT	160
TRAVELGREEN COACHES, DONCASTER	168
TRAVELINE, MINEHEAD	166
TRAVELLERS CHOICE, THE, CARNFORTH,	139
TRAVELSPEED - see NORTHERN BLUE	
TRAVELSURE, SEAHOUSES	158
TRAVEL-WRIGHT, MOUNTSORREL	140
TREACY COACHES, BALLINA, Co MAYO	217
TRELEY MOTORS, PENZANCE	99
TRENT BARTON, HEANOR	104
TRUEMANS COACHES, FLEET	128
TRURONIAN LTD, TRURO	99
TUERS MOTORS LTD, PENRITH	102
TURNERS TOURS, CHULMLEIGH	108
TURNERS COACHWAYS (BRISTOL) LTD, BRISTOL	91
T W COACHES LTD, SOUTH MOLTON	108
TWIN VALLEY COACHES, SOWERBY BRIDGE	185
TYNE VALLEY COACHES LTD, HEXHAM	158
TYNEDALE GROUP TRAVEL, HALTWISTLE	158
TYRER TOURS LTD, PADIHAM	139

U

UNICORN COACHES LTD, HATFIELD	132
UNITY COACHES, RETFORD	160
UNO LTD, HATFIELD	132
GRAHAM URQUHART TRAVEL, INVERNESS	196

V

VALE TRAVEL, AYLESBURY	93
VENTURE TRANSPORT (HENDON) (1965) LTD, HARROW	151
VEOLIA TRANSPORT,	84
VICEROY OF ESSEX LTD, SAFFRON WALDEN	120
VICTORY TOURS, POOLE	110
VIKING COACHES, HEYWOOD	125
VIKING MINICOACHES, BROADSTAIRS	136
VIKING TOURS & TRAVEL, SWADLINCOTE	98
VILLAGER MINIBUS, SHARNBROOK	88
VINCE COACHES, BURGHCLERE, Nr NEWBURY	89
VINTAGE TOURS, RYDE, IOW	133
VISION TRAVEL INTERNATIONAL LTD, WATERLOOVILLE	128
VOEL COACHES LTD, DYSERTH	205

W

W+H MOTORS, CRAWLEY	182
H+M TRAVEL, WISBECH	95
WA SHEARINGS LTD, EXHALL	180
WA SHEARINGS LTD, NORMANTON	185
WA SHEARINGS LTD, TORQUAY	108
WA SHEARINGS LTD, WARRINGTON	97
WA SHEARINGS LTD, WIGAN	125
WALDEN TRAVEL LTD, SAFFRON WALDEN	120
WALLIS COACHWAYS, BILSTHORPE, Nr NEWARK	160
WALTONS COACHES, GRANGETOWN, CARDIFF	203
WARRINGTON BOROUGH TRANSPORT LTD	98
WARRINGTON COACHES, ILAM	104
WARSTONE MOTORS LTD, GREAT WYRLEY	171
WATERSIDE TOURS - see HYTHE & WATERSIDE	
PAUL WATSON TRAVEL, DARLINGTON	113
WATTS COACHES, BONVILSTON, Nr CARDIFF	203
WAVERLEY COACHES LTD, ST HELIER, JERSEY	188
WEARDALE MOTOR SERVICES LTD, STANHOPE	113
WEAVAWAY TRAVEL, NEWBURY	89
WEBB'S PETERBOROUGH	95
WEBBER BUS, BRIDGWATER	166
WELLGLADE LTD	84
WELSH DRAGON TRAVEL NEWPORT, MONMOUTHSHIRE	208
WELSH'S COACHES, PONTEFRACT	185
WESSEX TRAVEL, BRISTOL	91
WEST END/RUTLAND TRAVEL, MELTON MOWBRAY	140
WEST KENT BUSES	136
WEST MIDLANDS SPECIAL NEEDS TRANSPORT BIRMINGHAM	180
WESTBUS COACH SERVICES LTD, HOUNSLOW	147
WESTERHAM COACHES, OXTED	175
WESTERN GREYHOUND, NEWQUAY	99
WESTRINGS COACHES, EAST WITTERING	182
WEST'S COACHES LTD, WOODFORD GREEN	147
WESTWAY COACH SERVICES, LONDON SW20	148
WHEADONS GROUP TRAVEL, CARDIFF	203
WHEELERS TRAVEL, SOUTHAMPTON	128
WHEAL BRITON COACHES, TRURO	99
WHIPPET COACHES LTD, FENSTANTON	95
WHITE BUS SERVICES, WINDSOR	89
WHITE HEATHER TOURS, FORT WILLIAM	196
WHITEGATE TRAVEL, NORTHWICH	98
WHITELAWS COACHES, STONEHOUSE	200
WHITES COACHES, SHETLAND	199
WHITTLE COACH & BUS, KIDDERMINSTER	187
WHYTES COACH TOURS, NEWMACHAR	189
WICKSONS TRAVEL, BROWNHILLS	181
WIDE HORIZON LUXURY TRAVEL, HINCKLEY	140
WIGHTROLLERS, SANDOWN, ISLE OF WIGHT	133
ALBERT WILDE COACHES, HEAGE	104
WILFREDA BEEHIVE, ADWICK-LE-STREET	169
WILKINSONS TRAVEL, ROTHERHAM	169
F R WILLETTS & CO, PILLOWELL Nr LYDNEY	122
A C WILLIAMS, ANCASTER	142
WILLIAMS COACHES, BRECON	209
F. T. WILLIAMS TRAVEL, CAMBORNE	99
GWYN WILLIAMS & SONS LTD, LOWER TUMBLE	204
WILLIAMSONS OF ROTHERHAM	169
WILLS MINI COACHES, KINGSBRIDGE	108
WILSON'S COACHES, ROSSINGTON	169
WILTS & DORSET BUS COMPANY LTD, POOLE	110
WINDSOR-GRAY TRAVEL, WOLVERHAMPTON	181
WINDSORIAN COACHES LTD, WINDSOR	89
WINGS LUXURY TRAVEL LTD, HAYES	148
WINN BROS, NORTHALLERTON	156
PAUL S. WINSON COACHES LTD, LOUGHBOROUGH	140
WINTS COACHES, BUTTERTON, Nr LEEK	171
WISE COACHES LTD, HAILSHAM	114
WISTONIAN COACHES, SELBY	156
MAL WITTS EXECUTIVE TRAVEL, GLOUCESTER	122
WOOD BROTHERS TRAVEL LTD, BUCKFASTLEIGH	108
WOODS COACHES LTD, LEICESTER	140
WOODS COACHES, TILLICOULTRY	191
P. WOODS MINICOACHES, HALLGLEN	194
WOODS TRAVEL LTD, BOGNOR REGIS	182
WOODSTONES COACHES LTD, KIDDERMINSTER	187
WOODWARD'S COACHES LTD, GLOSSOP	104
WOOTTENS, CHESHAM	93
J.P.A. WORTH, BUXTON	171
WORTHEN TRAVEL, LITTLE MINSTERLEY	163
WORTHING COACHES	182
WORTHS MOTOR SERVICES LTD, ENSTONE	162
WRIGHT BROS (COACHES) LTD, NENTHEAD	102
LEN WRIGHT BAND SERVICES LTD, WATFORD	132
WRIGLEY'S COACHES, IRLAM	125

Y

YARDLEY TRAVEL LTD, BIRMINGHAM	181
YARRANTON BROS LTD, TENBURY WELLS	187
YELLOW ROSE COACHES, CARNFORTH	137
YEOMANS CANYON TRAVEL LTD, HEREFORD	129
YESTERYEAR MOTOR SERVICES, DISEWORTH, DERBY	104
YORK PULLMAN BUS CO LTD	156
YORKS COACHES, COGENHOE	157
YORKSHIRE COASTLINER LTD, MALTON	156
YOUNGS OF ROMSLEY, HALESOWEN	181
YULE, PITLOCHRY	198

Operator index